W9-CCX-426

VBA and Macros

for Microsoft® Office

Excel® 2007

Bill "MrExcel" Jelen

Tracy Syrstad

800 E. 96th Street
Indianapolis, Indiana 46240

VBA and Macros for Microsoft® Office Excel® 2007

ISBN-13: 978-0-7897-3682-6
ISBN-10: 0-7897-3682-9

Jelen, Bill.
   VBA and macros for Microsoft Office Excel 2007 / Bill Jelen.
      p. cm.
   ISBN 0-7897-3682-9
   1. Microsoft Excel (Computer file) 2. Microsoft Visual Basic for applications. 3. Business—Computer programs. 4. Electronic spreadsheets. I. Title. II. Title: Visual Basic for applications and macros for Microsoft Office Excel 2007.
   HF5548.4.M523J457 2008
   005.54—dc22

                                        2007024410

Printed in the United States of America

Third Printing: October 2008

Trademarks

All terms mentioned in this book that are known to be trademarks or service marks have been appropriately capitalized. Que Publishing cannot attest to the accuracy of this information. Use of a term in this book should not be regarded as affecting the validity of any trademark or service mark.

Warning and Disclaimer

Every effort has been made to make this book as complete and as accurate as possible, but no warranty or fitness is implied. The information provided is on an "as is" basis. The authors and the publisher shall have neither liability nor responsibility to any person or entity with respect to any loss or damages arising from the information contained in this book.

Bulk Sales

Que Publishing offers excellent discounts on this book when ordered in quantity for bulk purchases or special sales. For more information, please contact

   U.S. Corporate and Government Sales
   1-800-382-3419
   corpsales@pearsontechgroup.com

For sales outside of the U.S., please contact

   International Sales
   international@pearsoned.com

 This Book Is Safari Enabled

The Safari® Enabled icon on the cover of your favorite technology book means the book is available through Safari Bookshelf. When you buy this book, you get free access to the online edition for 45 days. Safari Bookshelf is an electronic reference library that lets you easily search thousands of technical books, find code samples, download chapters, and access technical information whenever and wherever you need it.

To gain 45-day Safari Enabled access to this book:

- Go to www.quepublishing.com/safarienabled
- Complete the brief registration form
- Enter the coupon code NYJQ-ZEZK-UXZR-DGKI-JEDP

If you have difficulty registering on Safari Bookshelf or accessing the online edition, please email customer-service@safaribooksonline.com.

Associate Publisher
Greg Wiegand

Acquisitions Editor
Loretta Yates

Development Editor
Laura Norman

Managing Editor
Gina Kanouse

Project Editor
Betsy Harris

Copy Editor
Keith Cline

Senior Indexer
Cheryl Lenser

Proofreader
Paula Lowell

Technical Editor
Christian Kenyeres

Publishing Coordinator
Cindy Teeters

Book Designer
Anne Jones

Compositor
Nonie Ratcliff

Contents

About the Authors

Bill Jelen, Excel MVP and MrExcel, has been using spreadsheets since 1985, and he launched the MrExcel.com website in 1998. Bill has made more than 50 guest appearances on Call for Help with Leo Laporte and has produced more than 250 episodes of his daily video podcast, Learn Excel from MrExcel. He is the host of Total Training's Excel 2007 Advanced DVD. He also enjoys taking his show on the road, doing a one- to four-hour power Excel seminar anywhere that a room full of accountants or Excellers will show up. Before founding MrExcel.com, Jelen spent 12 years in the trenches—working as a financial analyst for finance, marketing, accounting, and operations departments of a $500 million public company. He lives near Akron, Ohio, with his wife, Mary Ellen, and sons, Josh and Zeke.

Tracy Syrstad remembers the painful trek up the VBA learning curve while developing applications for herself and co-workers at a former job. Now, as the project manager for the MrExcel consulting team, she enjoys helping clients develop custom solutions for their unique situations, observing the myriad ways people use Excel and other Microsoft Office applications.

Dedications

Dedicated to Josh Jelen
—Bill

Dedicated to my parents, Russ and Marcelle
—Tracy

Acknowledgments

Thanks to Tracy Syrstad for being a great co-author and for doing a great job of managing all the consulting projects at MrExcel. Mala Singh is the smartest charting wizard I know and vetted the chapter on charting with VBA. Jerry Kohl provided inspiration for many of the ideas in this book.

Thanks to everyone who ever asked a question at the Power Macros class at the University of Akron. You helped improve this second edition. Thanks to all the MrExcel.com readers and MVPs and clients. Thanks to Chad Rothschiller at Microsoft for teaching me everything there is to know about Excel XML. Thanks to Dave Gainer, Steve Zaske, Eric Patterson, and Joe Chirilov at Microsoft. Thanks to Pam Gensel for macro lesson number 1 and to Robert F. Jelen for being my first programming fan. Robert K. Jelen, Emil T. Hoffman, and Khalil F. Matta were early influences who shaped my decision to start programming.

Thanks to Leo Laporte, everyone at The Lab with Leo, and Craig Crossman for being great tech journalists.

Thanks to Dan Bricklin and Bob Frankston for inventing the computer spreadsheet. Thanks to Mitch Kapor for Lotus 1-2-3. Like everyone else who uses computers to make a living, I owe a debt of gratitude to these three pioneers.

Thanks to Barb Jelen for keeping MrExcel running while I wrote. Lora White is our office manager and was forced into riding shotgun and shooting screen shots for this book on long car trips. As always, thanks to the hundreds of people answering 30,000 Excel questions a year at the MrExcel message board. Thanks to Duane Aubin, Wei Jiang, Suat Ozgur, Nate Oliver, and Jake Hildebrand for their programming expertise.

At Pearson, Loretta Yates is an awesome acquisitions editor. Thanks to Judi Taylor, Greg Wiegand, Betsy Harris, Laura Norman, Christian A. Kenyeres, and Keith Cline. Thanks to William Brown and Waterside.

Thanks to Lavan Alexander, Steve Aronson, Oliver Berghaus, Von Brinkley, Wendy Cooke, Chris Crockett, Christy Dare, Joe Degraauw, Todd Feltner, Sylvia Gomez, Louis Grajeda, Jennie Heskin, Michael Himes, Mary Hulshouser, Steve Hunt, Edward Hyden, Richard Irwin, Therese Klassen, Shirley Miller, George Moore, Michael Moreno, Ali Mozaffari, Kiesha Neil, Jay Nelapudi, Ky Nguyen, Victor Omiyale, Andrea Patzkowsky, Earl Pearce, Courtney Robinson, Juan Rubio, Kim Sabatini, Chris Simmons, Michael Snowden, Marlin Snyder, Laree Snyder, Todd Thornbrough, Derek Truman, and Yan Yang for suggestions on the content of Chapter 6 during the first Data Analyst Boot Camp in Frisco, TX.

Finally, thanks to Josh Jelen, Zeke Jelen, and Mary Ellen Jelen.

—Bill

Thanks to Juan Pablo González Ruiz for offering his expertise, especially with the functions found in Chapter 4. Thanks to Daniel Klann, Dennis Wallentin, Ivan F. Moala, Juan Pablo González Ruiz, Masaru Kaji, Nathan P. Oliver, Richie Sills, Russell Hauf, Suat Mehmet Ozgur, Tom Urtis, Tommy Miles, and Wei Jiang for their contributions to Chapter 14.

Thanks to the MrExcel.com MVPs for helping me understand the intricacies of the Excel world we share. Thanks to Jacob Hilderbrand for his expertise on automating Word.

Thanks to the developers of DOOM 3—it kept John occupied as I worked late into the night. Thanks to Dani Jaacks for forcing me to take a break when I needed one.

And last, but not least, thanks to Bill Jelen. His site, MrExcel.com, is a place where thousands come for help. It's also a place where I, and others like me, have an opportunity to assist others.

—Tracy

We Want to Hear from You!

As the reader of this book, *you* are our most important critic and commentator. We value your opinion and want to know what we're doing right, what we could do better, what areas you'd like to see us publish in, and any other words of wisdom you're willing to pass our way.

As an associate publisher for Que, I welcome your comments. You can email or write me directly to let me know what you did or didn't like about this book—as well as what we can do to make our books better.

Please note that I cannot help you with technical problems related to the topic of this book. We do have a User Services group, however, where I will forward specific technical questions related to the book.

When you write, please be sure to include this book's title and author as well as your name, email address, and phone number. I will carefully review your comments and share them with the authors and editors who worked on the book.

Email: feedback@quepublishing.com

Mail: Greg Wiegand
         Associate Publisher
         Que Publishing
         800 East 96th Street
         Indianapolis, IN 46240 USA

For more information about this book or another Que title, visit our website at www.quepublishing.com. Type the ISBN or the title of a book in the Search field to find the page you're looking for.

Introduction

Getting Results with VBA

As corporate IT departments have found themselves with long backlogs of requests, Excel users have found that they can produce the reports needed to run their business themselves using the macro language *Visual Basic for Applications* (VBA). VBA enables you to achieve tremendous efficiencies in your day-to-day use of Excel. This is both a good and bad thing. On the good side, without waiting for resources from IT, you've probably been able to figure out how to import data and produce reports in Excel. On the bad side, you are now stuck importing data and producing reports in Excel.

What Is in This Book

You've taken the right step by purchasing this book. I can help you get up the learning curve so that you can write your own VBA macros and put an end to the burden of generating reports manually.

Getting Up the Learning Curve

This introduction provides a brief history of spreadsheets. Chapter 1 introduces the tools and confirms what you probably already know: The macro recorder does not work. Chapter 2 helps you understand the crazy syntax of VBA. Chapter 3 breaks the code on how to efficiently work with ranges and cells.

By the time you get to Chapter 4, you will know enough to put to immediate use the 25 sample user-defined functions in that chapter.

Chapter 5 covers the power of looping using VBA. In Valerie's case study, after we wrote the program to produce the first department report, it took only another minute to wrap that report routine in a loop that produced all 46 reports.

Chapter 6 covers R1C1-style formulas. Chapter 7 takes a look at what changed in Excel VBA from Excel 2003 to Excel 2007. In the past, it was fairly easy to create VBA code that would run on any of the recent versions of Excel. Unfortunately, with the sweeping changes in Excel 2007, this will become significantly more difficult. Chapter 8 covers names. Chapter 9 has some great tricks that use event programming. Chapter 10 introduces custom dialog boxes that you can use to collect information from the human using Excel.

Excel VBA Power

Chapters 11 through 13 provide an in-depth look at charting, Advanced Filter, and pivot tables. Any report automation tool is going to rely heavily on these concepts.

Chapter 14 includes another 25 code samples designed to exhibit the power of Excel VBA.

Chapters 15 through 18 handle data visualizations, Web queries, XML, and automating another Office program such as Word.

The Techie Stuff Needed to Produce Applications for Others

Chapter 19 shows you how to use arrays to build fast applications. Chapters 20 and 21 handle reading and writing to text files and Access databases. The techniques for using Access databases enable you to build an application with the multi-user features of Access yet keep the friendly front end of Excel.

Chapter 22 covers VBA from the point of view of a Visual Basic programmer. It teaches you about classes and collections. Chapter 23 discusses advanced userform topics. Chapter 24 teaches you some tricky ways to achieve tasks using the Windows application programming interface. Chapters 25 through 27 deal with error handling, custom menus, and add-ins.

Does This Book Teach Excel?

Microsoft believes the average Office user touches only 10 percent of the features in Office. I realize everyone reading this book is above average. I think that I have a pretty smart audience at MrExcel.com. A poll of 8,000 MrExcel.com readers shows that only 42 percent of smarter-than-average users are using any one of the top 10 power features in Excel. I regularly do a Power Excel seminar for accountants. These are hard-core Excelers who use Excel 30 to 40 hours every week. Again, two things come out in every seminar. First, half the audience gasps when they see how quickly you can do tasks with a particular feature (such as automatic subtotals or pivot tables). Second, I am routinely trumped by someone in the audience. Someone will ask a question, I will answer, and someone in the second row will raise a hand and give a better answer. The point? You and I both really know a lot about Excel. However, I will assume that in any given chapter, maybe 58 percent of the people haven't used pivot tables before and maybe even less have used the "Top 10 Filter" feature of pivot tables. Before I show you how to automate something in VBA, I briefly cover how to do the same task in the Excel interface. This book does not teach you how to do pivot tables, but it does alert you that you might want to go explore something and learn it elsewhere.

Monthly Accounting Reports

This is a true story. Valerie is a business analyst in the accounting department of a medium-size corporation. Her company recently installed an overbudget $16 million ERP system. As the project ground to a close, there were no resources left in the IT budget to produce the monthly report that this corporation used to summarize each department.

Valerie, however, had been close enough to the implementation process to think of a way to produce the report herself. She understood that she could export General Ledger data from the ERP system to a text file with comma-separated values. Using Excel, Valerie was able to import the G/L data from the ERP system into Excel.

Creating the report was not easy. Like many companies, there were exceptions in the data. Valerie knew that certain accounts in one particular cost center needed to be reclassed as an expense. She knew that other accounts needed to be excluded from the report entirely. Working carefully in Excel, Valerie made these adjustments. She created one pivot table to produce the first summary section of the report. She cut the pivot table results and pasted them into a blank worksheet. Then she created a new pivot table report for the second section of the summary. After about three hours, she had imported the data, produced five pivot tables, arranged them in a summary, and had neatly formatted the report in color.

Becoming the Hero

Valerie handed this report to her manager. The manager had just heard from the IT department that it would be months before they could get around to producing "that convoluted report." Valerie walked in, handed the Excel report over, and became the instant hero of the day. In three hours, Valerie had managed to do the impossible. Valerie was on cloud nine after a well-deserved "atta-girl."

More Cheers

The next day, this manager attended the monthly department meeting. When the department managers started complaining that they couldn't get the report from the ERP system, this manager pulled out his department report and placed it on the table. The other managers were amazed. How was he able to produce this report? Everyone was greatly relieved to hear that someone had cracked the code. The company president asked Valerie's manager if he could have the report produced for each department.

The Cheers Turn to Dread

You can certainly see this coming. This particular company had 46 departments. That means 46 one-page summaries had to be produced once a month. Each required importing data from the ERP system, backing out certain accounts, producing five pivot tables, and then formatting in color. It had taken Valerie three hours to produce the first report. She found that after she got into the swing of things, she was able to produce the 46 reports in 40 hours. This is horrible. Valerie had a job to do before she won the responsibility of spending 40 hours a month producing these reports in Excel.

VBA to the Rescue

Valerie found my company, MrExcel Consulting, and explained her situation. In the course of about a week, I was able to produce a series of macros in Visual Basic that did all the mundane tasks. It imported the data. It backed out certain accounts. It did five pivot tables and applied the color formatting. From start to finish, the entire 40-hour manual process was reduced to two button clicks and about 4 minutes.

Right now, either you or someone in your company is probably stuck doing manual tasks in Excel that can be automated with VBA. I am confident that I can walk into any company with 20 or more Excel users and find a case as amazing as Valerie's.

The Future of VBA and Windows Versions of Excel

Four years ago, there were a lot of rumblings that Microsoft might stop supporting VBA. There is now a lot of evidence that VBA will be around in Windows versions of Excel through 2015. (The future is not so certain for the Macintosh version of Excel.) Microsoft Office Excel 2007 was released on January 30, 2007. Microsoft is saying that in the next version of Excel (Excel 14), it will stop providing support for XLM macros. These macros were replaced by VBA 14 years ago, but they are still being supported. At the 2005 MVP Summit, members of the Office development team predicted support for VBA for another 10 to 15 years. There is even talk of an improvement to the Visual Basic Editor in Excel 14.

Still, you can see Microsoft's lack of commitment to VBA. Office 2003 offered a few features, such as the Research Pane and SmartTags, which could only be automated with Visual Basic .Net. In Excel 2007, the macro recorder works for about 50 percent of charting commands but fails to record a significant amount of charting.

The tools that you learn today will be good for the next 10 years. If Microsoft decides to scrap VBA in favor of Visual Studio Tools for Office (VSTO) or some other tool, you will likely be able to transfer your coding skills to the new platform.

Versions

This second edition of *VBA and Macros for Microsoft Office Excel 2007* is designed to work with Excel 2007. Our previous edition covered code for Excel 97 through Excel 2003. In 80 percent of the chapters, the code for Excel 2007 will be identical to code in previous versions. There are exceptions. Microsoft offers new sorting logic. Charts have changed completely. The conditional formatting and data visualization tools in Chapter 15 are brand new. Pivot tables have changed slightly. The XML examples in Chapter 17 will only work with Excel 2003 or newer. Although Excel for Windows and Excel for the Mac are similar in their user interface, there are a number of differences when you compare the VBA environment. Certainly, nothing in Chapter 24 that uses the Windows API will work on the Mac. The overall concepts discussed in the book apply to the Mac, but differences will exist. You can find a general list of differences as they apply to the Mac at www.mrexcel.com/macvba.html.

Special Elements and Typographical Conventions

The following typographical conventions are used in this book:

- *Italic*—Indicates new terms when they are defined, special emphasis, non-English words or phrases, and letters or words used as words
- `Monospace`—Indicates parts of VBA code, such as object or method names, and file-names
- `Italic monospace`—Indicates placeholder text in code syntax
- **`Bold monospace`**—Indicates user input

In addition to these text conventions, there are also several special elements. Each chapter has at least one case study, which shows you real-world solutions to common problems and practical applications of topics discussed in the text. In addition to these case studies, you will also see New icons, Notes, Tips, and Cautions.

 Features which are new or significantly different in Excel 2007 are marked with this icon.

> **NOTE**
> Notes provide additional information outside the main thread of the chapter discussion that might still be useful for you to know.

> **TIP**
> Tips provide you with quick workarounds and time-saving techniques to help you do your work more efficiently.

> **CAUTION**
> Cautions warn you about potential pitfalls you might encounter. Pay attention to these, because they could alert you to problems that otherwise could cause you hours of frustration.

Code Files

As a thank-you for buying this book, the authors have put together a set of 50 Excel work-books demonstrating the concepts in this book. This set of files includes all of the code from the book, sample data, additional notes from the authors, plus 25 bonus macros. To download the code files, visit this book's page at www.quepublishing.com or www.mrexcel.com/getcode2007.html.

Next Steps

Chapter 1 introduces the editing tools of the Visual Basic environment and shows you why using the macro recorder is not an effective way to write VBA macro code.

Unleash the Power of Excel with VBA

The Power of Excel

Visual Basic for Applications (VBA) combined with Microsoft Excel is probably the most powerful tool available to you. This tool is sitting on the desktops of 500 million users of Microsoft Office, and most have never figured out how to harness the power of VBA in Excel. Using VBA, you can speed the production of any task in Excel. If you regularly use Excel to produce a series of monthly charts, you can have VBA do the same task for you in a matter of seconds.

Barriers to Entry

There are two barriers to learning successful VBA programming. First, Excel's macro recorder is flawed and does not produce workable code for you to use as a model. Second, for many who learned a programming language such as BASIC, the syntax of VBA is horribly frustrating.

The Macro Recorder Doesn't Work!

Microsoft began to dominate the spreadsheet market in the mid-1990s. Although it was wildly successful in building a powerful spreadsheet program toward which any Lotus 1-2-3 user could easily transition, the macro language was just too different. Anyone proficient in recording Lotus 1-2-3 macros who tried recording a few macros in Excel most likely failed. Although the Microsoft VBA programming language is far more powerful than the Lotus 1-2-3 macro language, the one fundamental flaw is that the macro recorder does not work.

With Lotus 1-2-3, you could record a macro today, play it back tomorrow, and it would faithfully work. When you attempt the same feat in Microsoft Excel, the macro might work today but not tomorrow. I was horribly frustrated in 1995 when I tried to record my first Excel macro.

Visual Basic Is Not Like BASIC

The code generated by the macro was unlike anything that I had ever seen. It said this was "Visual Basic." I had the pleasure of learning half a dozen programming languages at various times; this bizarre-looking language was horribly unintuitive and did not at all resemble the BASIC language that I had learned in high school.

To make matters worse, even in 1995, I was the spreadsheet wizard in my office. My company had just forced everyone to convert from Lotus 1-2-3 to Excel. I was now faced with a macro recorder that didn't work and a language that I couldn't understand. This was not a good combination of events.

My assumption in writing this book is that you are pretty talented with a spreadsheet. You probably know more than 90 percent of the people in your office. I will assume that you are not a programmer, but that you might have taken a class in BASIC in high school. This isn't a requirement—it actually is a barrier to entry into the ranks of being a successful VBA programmer. There is a pretty good chance that you've recorded a macro in Excel and a similar chance that you were not happy with the results.

The Good News—It Is Easy to Climb the Learning Curve

Even if you've been frustrated with the macro recorder before, it is really just a small speed bump on your road to writing powerful programs in Excel. This book will teach you why the macro recorder fails, but also will show how to easily change the recorded code into something useful. For all the former BASIC programmers in the audience, I will decode this bizarre-looking language so that you can easily pick through recorded macro code and understand what is going on.

The Great News—Excel with VBA Is Worth the Effort

Although you've probably been frustrated with Microsoft over your inability to record macros in Excel, the great news is that Excel VBA is powerful. Absolutely anything that you can do in the Excel interface can be duplicated with stunning speed in Excel VBA. If you find yourself routinely creating the same reports manually day after day or week after week, Excel VBA will greatly streamline those tasks.

The authors work for MrExcel Consulting. In this role, we get to help automate reports for hundreds of clients. The stories are often similar: The MIS department has a several-month backlog of requests. Someone in accounting or engineering discovers that he or she can import some data into Excel and get the reports necessary to run the business. This is a liberating event—you no longer need to wait months for the IT department to write a program. However, the problem is that after you import the data into Excel and win accolades from your manager for producing the report, you then find yourself producing the same report every month or every week. This becomes very tedious.

Again, the great news is that with a few hours of VBA programming, you can automate the reporting process and turn it into a few button clicks. The reward is great. Hang with me as we cover a few of the basics.

This chapter is going to expose why the macro recorder does not work. I will walk through a simple example of recorded code and demonstrate why it will work today but fail tomorrow. You will be seeing code here, and I realize that this code might not be familiar to you yet. That's okay. The point of this chapter is to demonstrate the fundamental problem with the macro recorder. We also cover the fundamentals of the Visual Basic environment.

Knowing Your Tools—The Developer Ribbon

 We'll start with a basic overview of the tools needed to get around with VBA. By default, Microsoft hides the VBA tools. You have to change a setting in Excel options to access the Developer ribbon.

From the Office icon, select Excel Options. The third setting in the Popular category is Show Developer Tab in the Ribbon. Choose this option and click OK. Excel displays the Developer ribbon shown in Figure 1.1.

Figure 1.1
The Developer ribbon provides an interface for running and recording macros.

The Code group of the Developer ribbon contains icons used for recording and playing back VBA macros.

- **Visual Basic icon**—Opens the Visual Basic Editor.
- **Macros icon**—Displays the Macro dialog, where you can choose to run or edit a macro from the list of macros.
- **Record Macro icon**—Begins the process of recording a macro.
- **Use Relative Reference icon**—Toggles between using relative or absolute recording. With relative recording, Excel will record that you move down three cells. With absolute recording, Excel will record that you selected cell A4.
- **Macro Security icon**—Accesses the Trust Center, where you can choose to allow or disallow macros to run on this computer.

The Controls group of the Developer ribbon contains an Insert menu where you can access a variety of programming controls that you can place on the worksheet. See "Assigning a Macro to a Form Control, a Text Box, or a Shape" later in this chapter.

Other icons in this group allow you to work with the on-sheet controls. The Run Dialog button enables you to display a custom dialog box or userform that you have designed in VBA. For more on userforms, see Chapter 10, "Userforms—An Introduction."

> **NOTE** The XML group of the Developer ribbon contains tools for importing and exporting XML documents. See Chapter 17, "XML in Excel 2007."

Macro Security

After VBA macros were used as the delivery method for some high-profile viruses, Microsoft changed the default security settings to prevent macros from running. Therefore, before we can begin discussing the recording of a macro, we need to show you how to adjust the default settings.

 In Excel 2007, you can either globally adjust the security settings or control macro settings for certain workbooks by saving the workbooks in a trusted location. Any workbooks stored in a folder that is marked as a trusted location will automatically have its macros enabled.

You can find the macro security settings under the Macro Security icon on the Developer ribbon. When you click this icon, you see the Macro Settings category of the Trust Center. You can use the left navigation bar in the dialog to access the Trusted Locations list.

Adding a Trusted Location

 You can choose to store your macro workbooks in a folder that is marked as a trusted location. Any workbook stored in a trusted folder will have its macros enabled. Microsoft suggests that a trusted location should be on your hard drive. The default setting is that you cannot trust a location on a network drive.

To specify a trusted location, follow these steps:

1. Click Macro Security in the Developer ribbon.
2. Click Trusted Locations in the left navigation pane of the Trust Center.
3. If you want to trust a location on a network drive, choose Allow Trusted Locations on My Network.
4. Click the Add New Location button. Excel displays the Microsoft Office Trusted Locations dialog (see Figure 1.2).
5. Click the Browse button. Excel displays the Browse dialog.
6. Browse to the parent folder of the folder you want to be a trusted location. Click the trusted folder. Although the folder name does not appear in the Folder Name box, you can click OK. The correct folder name will appear in the Browse dialog.

7. If you want to trust subfolders of the selected folder, choose Subfolders of This Location Will Be Trusted.

8. Click OK to add the folder to the Trusted Locations list.

Figure 1.2
Manage trusted folders on the Trusted Locations category of the Trust Center.

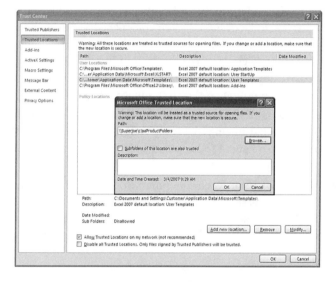

CAUTION

Use care when selecting a trusted location. When you double-click an Excel attachment in an email, Outlook will temporarily store the file in a temp folder on your C: drive. You would not want to globally add C:\ and all subfolders to the Trusted Locations list.

Although trusted locations are not new in Excel 2007, Microsoft has made the process of adding trusted locations more discoverable in Excel 2007.

Using Macro Settings to Enable Macros in Workbooks Outside of Trusted Locations

 For all macros not stored in a trusted location, Excel relies on the macro settings. The Low, Medium, High, and Very High settings that have been used for the past eight years have been renamed.

To access the macro settings, click Macro Security in the Developer ribbon. Excel displays the Macro Settings category of the Trust Center dialog. Choose the second option, Disable All Macros with Notification. A description of each option follows:

- **Disable All Macros without Notification**—This setting prevents all macros from running. This setting is for people who never intend to run macros. Because you are currently holding a book that teaches you how to use macros, I will assume that this is not you. This setting is roughly equivalent to the old Very High Security setting in Excel 2003. With this setting, only macros in the trusted locations folders can run.

- **Disable All Macros with Notification**—This setting is similar to Medium security in Excel 2003 and is the setting that I recommend. In Excel 2003, a Medium setting would cause a box to be displayed when you opened a file containing macros. This box would force the person to choose either Enable or Disable. I think a lot of novice Excel users would randomly choose from this box. In Excel 2007, the message is displayed in the Message Area that macros have been disabled. You can choose to enable the content by clicking that option, as shown in Figure 1.3.

- **Disable All Macros Except Digitally Signed Macros**—This setting would require you to obtain a digital signing tool from VeriSign or another provider. This might be appropriate if you are going to be selling add-ins to others, but a bit of a hassle if you just want to write your own macros for your own use.

- **Enable All Macros (Not Recommended: Potentially Dangerous Code Can Run)**—This setting is similar to Low macro security in Excel 2003. Although it requires the least amount of hassle, it also opens your computer up to attacks from malicious Melissa-like viruses. Microsoft suggests that you do not use this setting.

Figure 1.3
Open a macro workbook using the Disable All Macros with Notification setting and you can easily enable the macros.

Using Disable All Macros with Notification

My recommendation is that you set your macro settings to Disable All Content with Notification. If you use this setting and open a workbook that contains macros, you will see a Security Warning in the area just above the formula bar. Follow these steps to enable the macros:

1. Click the Options button next to the Security Warning. Excel displays the Microsoft Office Security Options.

2. Assuming you were expecting macros in this workbook, choose Enable This Content.

3. Click OK. Macros are now enabled in that workbook.

If you do not want to enable macros for the current workbook, dismiss the Security Warning by clicking the X at the far right of the message bar.

If you forget to enable the macros and you attempt to run a macro, Excel indicates that you cannot run the macro because all macros have been disabled. If you need to reopen the message bar, you can use the Message Bar check box in the Show/Hide group of the View ribbon.

Overview of Recording, Storing, and Running a Macro

Recording a macro is very useful when you do not have enough experience in writing lines of code in a macro. As you gain more knowledge and experience, you will begin to record lines of code less and less frequently.

To begin recording a macro, select Record Macro from the Developer ribbon. Before recording begins, Excel displays the Record Macro dialog box, as shown in Figure 1.4.

Filling Out the Record Macro Dialog

In the Macro Name field, type a name for the macro. Be sure to type continuous characters; for example, type `Macro1` and not Macro 1 (with a space). Assuming you will soon be creating many macros, use a meaningful name for the macro. A name such as FormatReport is more useful than Macro1.

Figure 1.4
Use the Record Macro dialog box to assign a name and a shortcut key to the soon-to-be-recorded macro.

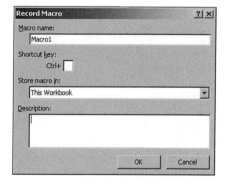

The second field in the Record Macro dialog box is a shortcut key. If you type **J** in this field, and then press Ctrl+J, this macro runs.

In the Record Macro dialog box, you can choose where you want to save a macro when you record it: Personal Macro Workbook, New Workbook, This Workbook. I recommend storing macros related to a particular workbook in This Workbook.

The Personal Macro Workbook (Personal.xlsm) is not an open workbook; it is created if you choose to save the recording in the Personal Macro Workbook. This workbook is used to save a macro in a workbook that will open automatically when you start Excel, thereby enabling you to use the macro. After Excel is started, the workbook is hidden. If you want to display it, select Unhide from the Window menu.

It is not recommended you use the personal workbook for every macro you save. Save only those macros that will assist you in general tasks—not in tasks that are performed in a specific sheet or workbook.

The fourth box in the Record Macro dialog is for a description. This description will be added as a comment to the beginning of your macro. Note that previous versions of Excel automatically noted the date and user name of the person recording the macro. Excel 2007 no longer automatically inserts this information in the Description field.

After you select the location where you want to store the macro, click OK. Record your macro. When you are finished recording the macro, click the Stop Recording icon in the Developer ribbon.

> **TIP**   You can also access a Stop Recording icon in the lower-left corner of the Excel window. Look for a small blue square to the right of the word *Ready* in the status bar. Using this Stop button might be more convenient than returning to the Developer ribbon. When you are not recording a macro, this icon changes to a small red dot on an Excel worksheet. That icon is a shortcut to begin recording a new macro.

Running a Macro

If you assigned a shortcut key to your macro, you can play it by pressing the key combination. Macros can also be assigned to toolbar buttons, forms controls, drawing objects, or you can run them from the Visual Basic toolbar.

Creating a Macro Button

You can add an icon to the Quick Access toolbar to run your macro. If your macro is stored in the Personal Macro Workbook, you can have the button permanently displayed in the Quick Access toolbar. If the macro is stored in the current workbook, you can specify that the icon should only appear when the workbook is open. Follow these steps to add a macro button to the Quick Access toolbar:

1. Click the Office button and choose Excel Options to open the Excel Options dialog.

2. In the Excel Options dialog, choose the Customize category from the left-side navigation. (Note that a shortcut to replace steps 1 and 2 is to right-click the Quick Access toolbar and choose Customize Quick Access Toolbar.)

3. If your macro should be available only when the current workbook is open, open the upper-right drop-down and change For All Documents (Default) to For <FileName.xlsm>. Any icons associated with the current workbook are displayed at the end of the Quick Access toolbar.

4. Open the upper-left drop-down and choose Macros from the list. The Macros category is fourth in the list. Excel displays a list of available macros in the left list box.

5. Choose a macro from the left list box. Click the Add button in the center of the dialog. Excel moves the macro to the right list box. Excel uses a generic VBA icon for all macros. You can change the icon by following steps 6 through 8.

6. Click the macro in the right list box. Click the Modify button at the bottom of the right list box. Excel displays a list of 181 possible icons (see Figure 1.5). Considering that Excel 2003 offered 4,096 possible icons, plus an icon editor, the list of 181 is a major disappointment.

Figure 1.5
Attach a macro to a button on the Quick Access toolbar.

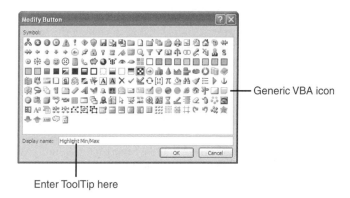

Generic VBA icon

Enter ToolTip here

7. Choose an icon from the list. In the Display Name box, replace the macro name with a short name that will appear in the ToolTip for the icon.

8. Click OK to close the Modify Button dialog.

9. Click OK to close Excel options. The new button appears on the Quick Access toolbar.

Assigning a Macro to a Form Control, a Text Box, or a Shape

If you want to create a macro specific to a workbook, store the macro to the workbook and attach it to a form control or any object on the sheet.

Follow these steps to attach a macro to a form control on the sheet:

1. On the Developer ribbon, click the Insert button to open its drop-down list. Excel offers 12 form controls and 12 ActiveX controls. Many icons look similar in this drop-down. Click the Button Form Control icon at the upper-left icon in the drop-down.

2. Move your cursor over the worksheet; the cursor changes to a plus sign.

3. Draw a button on the sheet by clicking and holding the left mouse button while drawing a box shape. Release the button when you have finished.

4. Select a macro from the Assign Macro dialog box and click OK. The button is created with generic text such as Button 1. To customize the text or the button appearance, follow steps 5 through 7.

5. Ctrl+click the button to select it. Drag the cursor over the text on the button to select the text. Type a new label for the button. Note that while you are typing, the selection border around the button changes from dots to diagonal lines to indicate that you are in Text Edit mode. You cannot change the button color while in Text Edit mode. To exit Text Edit mode, either click the diagonal lines to change them to dots or Ctrl+click the button again.

6. Right-click the dots surrounding the button and choose Format Control. Excel displays the Format Control dialog with seven tabs across the top. If your Format Control dialog has only a Font tab, you failed to exit Text Edit mode. Close the dialog, Ctrl+click the button, and repeat this step.

7. Use the settings in the Format Control dialog to change the font size, font color, margins, and similar settings for the control. Click OK to close the Format Control dialog when you have finished.

8. Click the button to run the macro.

Macros can be assigned to any worksheet object such as clip art, a shape, SmartArt graphics, or a text box. In Figure 1.6, the top button is a traditional button form control. The other images are clip art, a shape with WordArt and a SmartArt graphic. To assign a macro to any object, right-click the object, and choose Assign Macro.

Figure 1.6
Assigning a macro to a form control or an object appropriate for macros stored in the same workbook as the control. You can assign a macro to any of these objects.

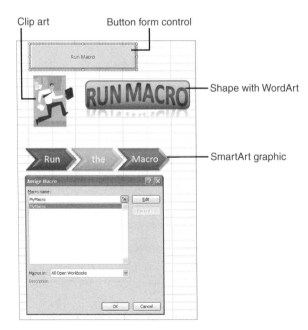

Clip art   Button form control

Shape with WordArt

SmartArt graphic

Using New File Types in Excel 2007

Excel 2007 offers support for four file types. Macros are not allowed to be stored in the default file type. You either have to use the Save As setting for all of your macro workbooks, or you can change the default file type used by Excel 2007.

The available files types are as follows:

- **Excel Workbook (.xlsx)**—Files are stored as a series of XML objects and then zipped into a single file. This new file-saving paradigm in Excel 2007 allows for significantly smaller file sizes. It also allows other applications (even Notepad!) to edit or create Excel workbooks. Unfortunately, macros cannot be stored in files with an .xlsx extension.

- **Excel Macro-Enabled Workbook (.xlsm)**—This is similar to the default .xlsx format, except macros are allowed. The basic concept is that if someone has an .xlsx file, they don't need to worry about malicious macros, but if they see an .xlsm file, they need to be concerned that there might be macros attached.

- **Excel Binary Workbook (.xlsb)**—This is a binary format designed to handle the larger 1.1-million-row grid size in Excel 2007. All previous versions of Excel stored their files in a proprietary binary format. Although binary formats might load quicker, they are more prone to corruption; a few lost bits can destroy the whole file. Macros are allowed in this format.

- **Excel 97-2003 Workbook (.xls)**—This format produces files that can be read by anyone using legacy versions of Excel. It is a binary format, and macros are allowed. However, when you save in this format, you lose access to any cells outside of A1:IV65536. You lose access to all new features in Excel.

To avoid having to choose a macro-enabled workbook in the Save As dialog, you can customize your copy of Excel to always save new files in the .xlsm format. Follow these steps:

1. Click the Office button and choose Excel Options.

2. In the Excel Options dialog, choose the Save category from the left navigation pane.

3. The first drop-down is Save Files in This Format. Open the drop-down and choose Excel Macro-Enabled Workbook (*.xlsm). Click OK.

> **NOTE**
>
> Although you and I are not afraid of using macros, I've run into some people who seem to completely freak out when they see the .xlsm file type. They actually seem angry that I sent them an .xlsm file that didn't have any macros. Their reaction seemed reminiscent of King Arthur's "You got me all worked up!" line in *Monty Python and the Holy Grail*.
>
> If you encounter someone who seems to have an irrational fear of the .xlsm file type, remind them of these points:

continues

continued

- Every workbook created in the past 20 years could have had macros, and most did not.
- If someone is trying to avoid macros, they should use the security settings to prevent macros from running anyway (turn back to page Figure 1.3). They can still open the .xlsm file to get the data in the spreadsheet.

With these arguments, you can hopefully overcome any irrational fears of the .xlsm file type and make it be your default file type.

Understanding the Visual Basic Editor

Figure 1.7 shows an example of the typical VB Editor screen. You can see three windows: Project Explorer, the Properties window, and the Programming window. Don't worry if your window doesn't look exactly like this; as we review the editor, I show you how to display the windows you'll need.

Figure 1.7
The VB Editor window.

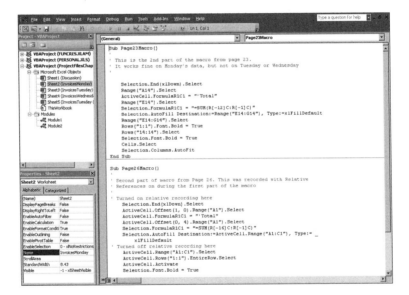

VB Editor Settings

Several settings in the VB Editor enable you to customize it as you want. I'm going to go over only the ones that will help you with your programming.

Customizing VB Editor Options Settings

Under Tools, Options, Editor, you'll find several useful settings. All settings except for one are set correctly by default. The remaining setting requires some consideration on your part. This setting is Require Variable Declaration. By default, Excel doesn't require you to declare variables. I prefer this setting. It can save you time in creating a program.

My co-author, Tracy, prefers changing this setting to require variable declaration. This forces the compiler to stop if it finds a variable that it does not recognize. This cuts down on misspelled variable names. It is a matter of your personal preference if you turn this on or keep it off.

Enabling Digital Signatures

If you're like me, you write a lot of personal macros. After a while, it gets tiresome having to approve the enabling of macros you wrote. That's where digital signatures come in. You can buy a digital signature from one of a number of third-party vendors. Microsoft provides a list of approved vendors at http://msdn2.microsoft.com/en-us/library/ms995347.aspx. Once you have purchased a digital signature, use Tools, Digital Signature to attach the signature to your VBA project.

The Project Explorer

The Project Explorer lists any open workbooks and add-ins that are loaded. If you click the + icon next to the VBA Project, you will see that there is a folder with Microsoft Excel objects. There can also be folders for forms, class modules, and (standard) modules. Each folder includes one or more individual components.

Right-clicking a component and selecting View Code, or just double-clicking the components, brings up any code in the Programming window (except for userforms, where double-clicking displays the userform in Design view).

To display this window, select View, Project Explorer from the menu, press Ctrl+R, or click the Project Explorer icon on the toolbar.

Figure 1.8 shows the Project Explorer pane. This pane can show Microsoft Excel objects, userforms, modules, and class modules.

Figure 1.8
The Project Explorer, displaying different types of modules.

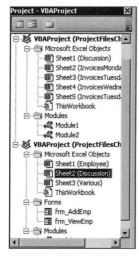

To insert a module, right-click your project, select Insert, and then select the type of module you want. The available modules are as follows:

- **Microsoft Excel objects**—By default, a project consists of sheet modules for each sheet in the workbook and a single ThisWorkbook module. Code specific to a sheet, such as controls or sheet events, is placed on the corresponding sheet. Workbook events are placed in the ThisWorkbook module. You'll learn more about events in Chapter 9, "Event Programming."

- **Forms**—Excel allows you to design your own forms to interact with the user. You'll learn more about these forms in Chapter 10, "Userforms—An Introduction."

- **Modules**—When you record a macro, Excel automatically creates a module to place the code. It is in these types of modules that most of your code will reside.

- **Class modules**—Class modules are Excel's way of letting you create your own objects. Also, class modules allow pieces of code to be shared among programmers without the programmer needing to understand how it works. You'll learn more about class modules in Chapter 22, "Creating Classes, Records, and Collections."

The Properties Window

The Properties window enables you to edit the properties of various components—sheets, workbooks, modules, and form controls. Its Property list varies according to what component is selected.

To display this window, select View, Properties Window from the menu, press F4, or click the Project Properties icon on the toolbar.

Understanding Shortcomings of the Macro Recorder

Suppose you work in an accounting department. Each day you receive a text file from the company system showing all the invoices produced the prior day. This text file has commas separating each field. The columns in the file are InvoiceDate, InvoiceNumber, SalesRepNumber, CustomerNumber, ProductRevenue, ServiceRevenue, and ProductCost (see Figure 1.9).

Figure 1.9
Invoice.txt file.

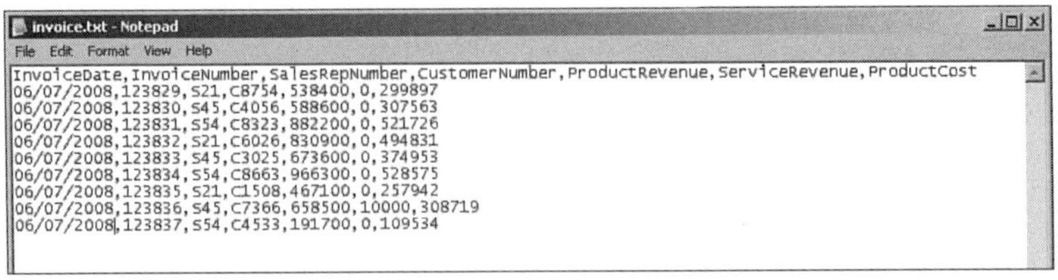

As you arrive at work each morning, you manually import this file into Excel. You add a total row to the data, bold the headings, and then print the report for distribution to a few managers.

This seems like a fairly simple process that would be ideally suited to using the macro recorder. However, due to some problems with the macro recorder, your first few attempts might not be successful.

CASE STUDY

Preparing to Record the Macro

This is a task that is perfect for a macro. Before you record any macro, think about the steps that you will use before you begin. In our case, these steps are as follows:

1. Click the Office button and select Open.
2. Navigate to the folder where invoice.txt is stored.
3. Choose All Files(*.*) from the Files of Type drop-down list.
4. Select Invoice.txt.
5. Click Open.
6. In the Text Import Wizard—Step 1 of 3, select Delimited from the Original Data Type section.
7. Click Next.
8. In the Text Import Wizard—Step 2 of 3, uncheck the Tab key and check Comma in the Delimiters section.
9. Click Next.
10. In the Text Import Wizard—Step 3 of 3, select General in the Column Data Format section and change it to `Date: MDY`.
11. Click Finish to import the file.
12. Press the End key followed by the down arrow to move to the last row of data.
13. Press the down arrow one more time to move to the total row.
14. Type the word `Total`.
15. Press the right-arrow key four times to move to Column E of the total row.
16. Click the Autosum button and press Ctrl+Enter to add a total to the Product Revenue column while remaining in that cell.
17. Grab the AutoFill handle and drag it from Column E over to Column G to copy the total formula over to Columns F and G.
18. Highlight Row 1 and click the Bold icon on the Home ribbon to set the headings in bold.
19. Highlight the Total row and click the Bold icon on the Home ribbon to set the totals in bold.
20. Press Ctrl+A to select all cells.
21. From the Home ribbon, select Format, AutoFit Column Width.

After you've rehearsed these steps in your head, you are ready to record your first macro. Open a blank workbook and save it with a name like MacroToImportInvoices.xlsm. Click the Record Macro button on the Developer ribbon.

In the Record Macro dialog, the default macro name is Macro1. Change this to something descriptive like ImportInvoice. Make sure that the macros will be stored in This Workbook. You might want an easy way to run this macro later, so enter the letter *i* in the Shortcut Key field. In the Description field, add a little descriptive text to tell what the macro is doing (see Figure 1.10). When you are ready, click OK.

Figure 1.10
Before recording your macro, complete the Record Macro dialog box.

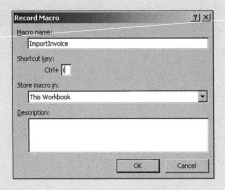

Recording the Macro

Don't be nervous, but the Macro Recorder is now recording your every move. You want to try to perform your steps in exact order without extraneous actions. If you accidentally move to Column F and then back to E to enter the first total, the recorded macro blindly makes that same mistake day after day after day. Recorded macros move fast, but this is nothing like having to watch your same mistakes played out by the macro recorder again and again.

Carefully, execute all the actions necessary to produce the report. After you have performed the final step, click the Stop button in the lower-left corner of the Excel window or click Stop Recording in the Developer ribbon .

It is time to take a look at your code. Switch to the VB Editor by choosing Visual Basic from the Developer ribbon or pressing Alt+F11.

Examining Code in the Programming Window

Let's take a look at the code you just recorded from the case study; don't worry if it doesn't make sense yet.

To open the VB Editor, press Alt+F11. In your VBA Project (MacroToImportInvoices.xls), find the component Module1, right-click it, and select View Code. Notice that some lines start with an apostrophe—these are comments and are ignored by the program. The macro recorder starts your macros with a few comments, using the description that you entered in the Record Macro dialog. The comment for the Keyboard Shortcut is there to remind you of the shortcut.

> **NOTE** The comment does *not* assign the shortcut. If you change the comment to be Ctrl+J, it does not change the shortcut. You must change the setting in the Macro dialog box in Excel or run this line of code:
>
> ```
> Application.MacroOptions Macro:="ImportInvoice", _
>     Description:="", ShortcutKey:="j"
>     ActiveCell.FormulaR1C1 = "Hello World!"
>     Range("A3").Select
> ```

Recorded macro code is usually pretty neat (see Figure 1.11). Each noncomment line of code is indented four characters. If a line is longer than 100 characters, the recorder breaks it into multiple lines and indents the lines an additional 4 characters. To continue a line of code, you type a space and an underscore at the end of the line. Note that the physical limitations of this book do not allow 100 characters on a single line. I will break the lines at 80 characters so that they fit on this page. Your recorded macro might look slightly different from the ones that appear here.

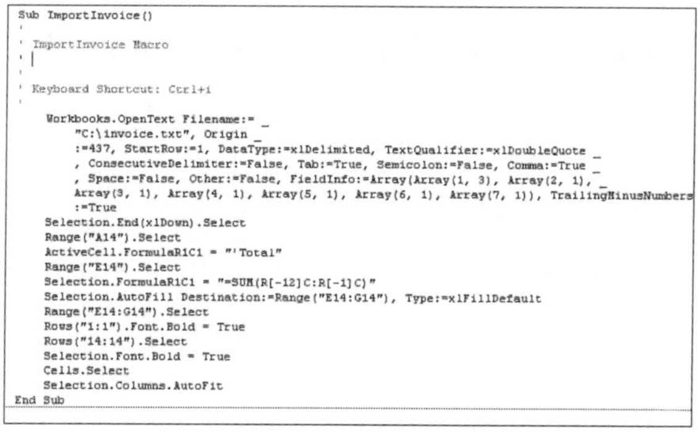

Figure 1.11

The recorded macro is neat looking and nicely indented.

```
Sub ImportInvoice()
'
' ImportInvoice Macro
' |
'
' Keyboard Shortcut: Ctrl+i
'
    Workbooks.OpenText Filename:= _
        "C:\invoice.txt", Origin _
        :=437, StartRow:=1, DataType:=xlDelimited, TextQualifier:=xlDoubleQuote _
        , ConsecutiveDelimiter:=False, Tab:=True, Semicolon:=False, Comma:=True _
        , Space:=False, Other:=False, FieldInfo:=Array(Array(1, 3), Array(2, 1), _
        Array(3, 1), Array(4, 1), Array(5, 1), Array(6, 1), Array(7, 1)), TrailingMinusNumbers _
        :=True
    Selection.End(xlDown).Select
    Range("A14").Select
    ActiveCell.FormulaR1C1 = "'Total"
    Range("E14").Select
    Selection.FormulaR1C1 = "=SUM(R[-12]C:R[-1]C)"
    Selection.AutoFill Destination:=Range("E14:G14"), Type:=xlFillDefault
    Range("E14:G14").Select
    Rows("1:1").Font.Bold = True
    Rows("14:14").Select
    Selection.Font.Bold = True
    Cells.Select
    Selection.Columns.AutoFit
End Sub
```

Consider that the following seven lines of recorded code is actually only one line of code that has been broken down into seven lines for readability:

```
Workbooks.OpenText Filename:= _
    "C:\invoice.txt", Origin:=437, StartRow:=1, DataType:=xlDelimited, _
    TextQualifier:=xlDoubleQuote, ConsecutiveDelimiter:=False, _
    Tab:=True, Semicolon:=False, Comma:=True, Space:=False, _
    Other:=False, FieldInfo:=Array(Array(1, 3), Array(2, 1), Array(3, 1), _
    Array(4, 1), Array(5, 1), Array(6, 1), Array(7, 1)), _
    TrailingMinusNumbers:=True
```

Counting the above as one line, the macro recorder was able to record our 21-step process in 14 lines of code, which is pretty impressive.

> **NOTE** Each action that you perform in the Excel user interface might equate to one or more lines of recorded code. Some actions might generate a dozen lines of code.

It is always a good idea to test out your macro. Return to the regular Excel interface by pressing Alt+F11. Close Invoice.txt without saving any changes. You still have MacroToImportInvoices.xls open.

Press Ctrl+I to run the recorded macro. It works beautifully! The data is imported, totals are added, bold formatting is applied, and the columns are made wider. This seems like a perfect solution (see Figure 1.12).

Figure 1.12
The macro formats the data in the sheet beautifully.

	A	B	C	D	E	F	G
1	InvoiceDate	InvoiceNumber	SalesRepNumber	CustomerNumber	ProductRevenue	ServiceRevenue	ProductCost
2	6/7/2008	123801	S82	C8754	639600	12000	325438
3	6/7/2008	123802	S93	C7874	964600	0	435587
4	6/7/2008	123803	S43	C4844	988900	0	587630
5	6/7/2008	123804	S54	C4940	673800	15000	346164
6	6/7/2008	123805	S43	C7969	513500	0	233842
7	6/7/2008	123806	S93	C8468	760600	0	355305
8	6/7/2008	123807	S82	C1620	894100	0	457577
9	6/7/2008	123808	S17	C3238	316200	45000	161877
10	6/7/2008	123809	S32	C5214	111500	0	62956
11	6/7/2008	123810	S45	C3717	747600	0	444162
12	6/7/2008	123811	S87	C7492	857400	0	410493
13	6/7/2008	123812	S43	C7780	200700	0	97937
14	Total				7668500	72000	3918968
15							

Running the Same Macro on Another Day Produces Undesired Results

So, you would have saved your macro file. The next day, you come to work and you have a new invoice.txt file from the system. You open the macro, press Ctrl+I to run it, and disaster strikes. The data for June 7 happened to have 12 invoices. The data for the June 8 had 16 invoices. However, the recorded macro blindly added the totals in Row 14 because this was where we put the totals when the macro was recorded (see Figure 1.13).

Figure 1.13
On another day, the macro fails horribly. The intent of the recorded macro was to add a total at the end of the data, but the recorder made a macro to always add totals at Row 14.

	A	B	C	D	E	F	G
1	InvoiceDate	InvoiceNumber	SalesRepNumber	CustomerNumber	ProductRevenue	ServiceRevenue	ProductCost
2	6/8/2008	123813	S82	C8754	716100	12000	423986
3	6/8/2008	123814		C4894	224200	0	131243
4	6/8/2008	123815	S43	C7278	277000	0	139208
5	6/8/2008	123816	S54	C6425	746100	15000	350683
6	6/8/2008	123817	S43	C6291	928300	0	488988
7	6/8/2008	123818	S43	C1000	723200	0	383069
8	6/8/2008	123819	S82	C6025	982600	0	544025
9	6/8/2008	123820	S17	C8026	490100	45000	243808
10	6/8/2008	123821	S43	C4244	615800	0	300579
11	6/8/2008	123822	S45	C1007	271300	0	153253
12	6/8/2008	123823	S87	C1878	338100	0	165666
13	6/8/2008	123824	S43	C3068	567900	0	265775
14	Total	123825	S87	C4913	6880700	72000	3590283
15	6/8/2008	123826	S55	C7181	37900	0	19811
16	6/8/2008	123827	S43	C7570	582700	0	292000
17	6/8/2008	123828	S87	C5302	495000	0	241504
18							

This first problem arises because the macro recorder is recording all your actions in absolute mode by default. Instead of using the default state of the macro recorder, the next section discusses relative recording and how this might get you closer to the final solution.

A Possible Solution: Using Relative References When Recording

By default, the macro recorder records all actions as *absolute* actions. If you navigate to Row 14 when you record the macro on Monday, the macro will always go to Row 14 when the macro is run. When dealing with variable numbers of rows of data, this is rarely appropriate.

There is an option to use relative references when recording.

Macros recorded with absolute references note that actual address of the cell pointer (for example, A14). Macros recorded with relative references note that the cell pointer should move a certain number of rows and columns from its current position. For example, if the cell pointer starts in cell A1, the code `ActiveCell.Offset(16, 1).Select` would move the cell pointer to B17 (the cell 16 rows down and one column to the right).

Let's try the same case study again, this time using relative references. The solution will be much closer to working.

CASE STUDY

Let's try to record the macro again, using relative references. Close Invoice.txt without saving changes. In the workbook MacroToImportInvoices.xls, record a new macro by choosing Record Macro from the Developer ribbon. Give the new macro a name of `ImportInvoicesRelative` and assign it a different shortcut key, such as Ctrl+J (see Figure 1.14).

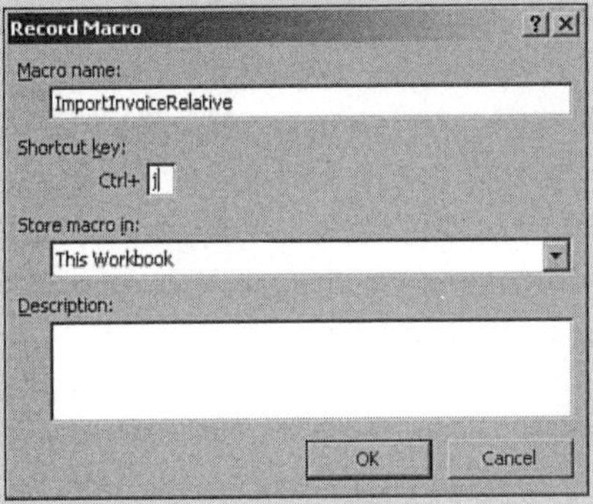

Figure 1.14
Getting ready to record a second try.

As you start to record the macro, go through the process of opening the invoice.txt file. Before navigating to the last row of data (press the End key + down-arrow key), click the Use Relative Reference button on the Developer ribbon (refer to Figure 1.2).

Continue through the actions in the script from the case study:

1. Press the End key followed by the down-arrow key to move to the last row of data.
2. Press the down arrow one more time to move to the total row.
3. Type the word `Total`.
4. Press the right-arrow key four times to move to Column E of the Total row.

5. Press the Autosum button, and then press Ctrl+Enter to add a total to the Product Revenue column while remaining in that cell.

6. Grab the AutoFill handle and drag from Column E over to Column G to copy the total formula over to Columns F and G.

7. Press Shift+spacebar to select the entire row and apply bold formatting to it.

At this point, you need to move to Cell A1 to apply bold to the headings. You do not want the macro recorder to record the movement from Row 18 to Row 1—it would record this as moving 17 rows up, which might not be correct tomorrow. Before moving to A1, toggle the Use Relative Recording button off, and then continue recording the rest of the macro.

8. Highlight Row 1 and click the Bold icon to set the headings in bold.

9. Press Ctrl+A to select all cells.

10. From the Home ribbon, select Format, AutoFit Column Width.

11. Stop recording.

Press Alt+F11 to go to the VB Editor to review your code. The new macro appears in Module1 below the previous macro.

> **CAUTION**
>
> If you close Excel between recording the first and second macro, Excel inserts a new module, called Module2, for the newly recorded macro.

I've edited the following code with two comments to show where I remember turning the relative recording on and then off.

```
Sub ImportInvoicesRelative
'
' This was recorded with Relative
' References on during the first part of the macro
'
' Turned on relative recording here
    Selection.End(xlDown).Select
    ActiveCell.Offset(1, 0).Range("A1").Select
    ActiveCell.FormulaR1C1 = "'Total"
    ActiveCell.Offset(0, 4).Range("A1").Select
    Selection.FormulaR1C1 = "=SUM(R[-16]C:R[-1]C)"
    Selection.AutoFill Destination:=ActiveCell.Range("A1:C1"), Type:= _
        xlFillDefault
' Turned off relative recording here
    ActiveCell.Range("A1:C1").Select
    ActiveCell.Rows("1:1").EntireRow.Select
    ActiveCell.Activate
    Selection.Font.Bold = True
    Rows("1:1").Select
    Selection.Font.Bold = True
    Cells.Select
    Selection.Columns.AutoFit
End Sub
```

To test the macro, close Invoice.txt without saving, and then run the macro with Ctrl+J. Everything looks good—I get the same results.

The next test is to see whether the program works on the next day when you might have more rows. Figure 1.15 shows the data for June 9.

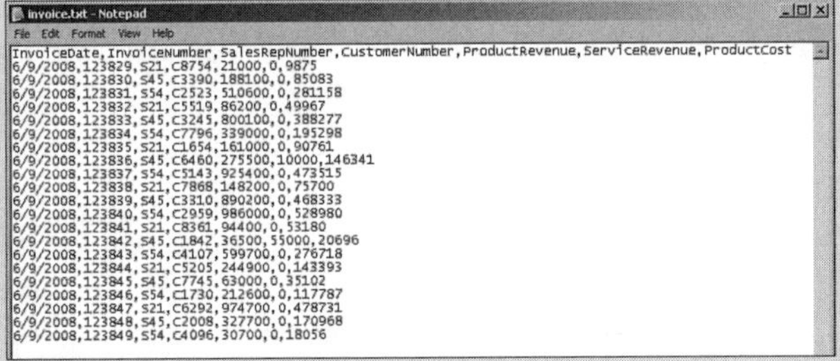

Invoice.txt - Notepad

File Edit Format View Help

```
InvoiceDate,InvoiceNumber,SalesRepNumber,CustomerNumber,ProductRevenue,ServiceRevenue,ProductCost
6/9/2008,123829,S21,C8754,21000,0,9875
6/9/2008,123830,S45,C3390,188100,0,85083
6/9/2008,123831,S54,C2523,510600,0,281158
6/9/2008,123832,S21,C5519,86200,0,49967
6/9/2008,123833,S45,C3245,800100,0,388277
6/9/2008,123834,S54,C7796,339000,0,195298
6/9/2008,123835,S21,C1654,161000,0,90761
6/9/2008,123836,S45,C6460,275500,10000,146341
6/9/2008,123837,S54,C5143,925400,0,473515
6/9/2008,123838,S21,C7868,148200,0,75700
6/9/2008,123839,S45,C3310,890200,0,468333
6/9/2008,123840,S54,C2959,986000,0,528980
6/9/2008,123841,S21,C8361,94400,0,53180
6/9/2008,123842,S45,C1842,36500,55000,20696
6/9/2008,123843,S54,C4107,599700,0,276718
6/9/2008,123844,S21,C5205,244900,0,143393
6/9/2008,123845,S45,C7745,63000,0,35102
6/9/2008,123846,S54,C1730,212600,0,117787
6/9/2008,123847,S21,C6292,974700,0,478731
6/9/2008,123848,S45,C2008,327700,0,170968
6/9/2008,123849,S54,C4096,30700,0,18056
```

Figure 1.15
Will the macro with relative references work with this data?

I open MacroToImportInvoices.xls and run the new macro with Ctrl+J. This time, everything looks pretty good. The totals are where they are supposed to be. Look at Figure 1.16—see anything out of the ordinary?

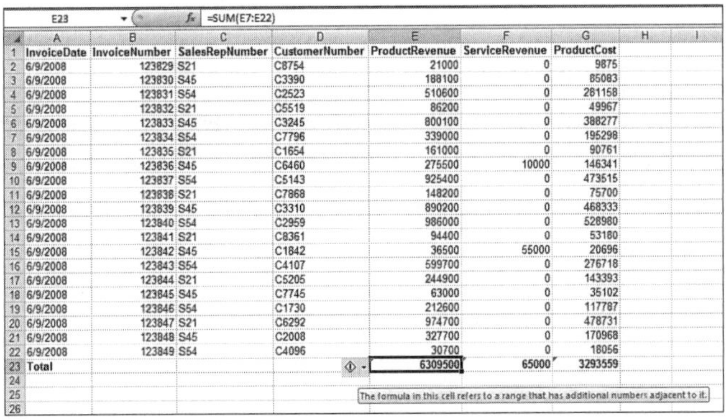

E23 =SUM(E7:E22)

	A	B	C	D	E	F	G	H	I
1	InvoiceDate	InvoiceNumber	SalesRepNumber	CustomerNumber	ProductRevenue	ServiceRevenue	ProductCost		
2	6/9/2008	123829	S21	C8754	21000	0	9875		
3	6/9/2008	123830	S45	C3390	188100	0	85083		
4	6/9/2008	123831	S54	C2523	510600	0	281158		
5	6/9/2008	123832	S21	C5519	86200	0	49967		
6	6/9/2008	123833	S45	C3245	800100	0	388277		
7	6/9/2008	123834	S54	C7796	339000	0	195298		
8	6/9/2008	123835	S21	C1654	161000	0	90761		
9	6/9/2008	123836	S45	C6460	275500	10000	146341		
10	6/9/2008	123837	S54	C5143	925400	0	473515		
11	6/9/2008	123838	S21	C7868	148200	0	75700		
12	6/9/2008	123839	S45	C3310	890200	0	468333		
13	6/9/2008	123840	S54	C2959	986000	0	528980		
14	6/9/2008	123841	S21	C8361	94400	0	53180		
15	6/9/2008	123842	S45	C1842	36500	55000	20696		
16	6/9/2008	123843	S54	C4107	599700	0	276718		
17	6/9/2008	123844	S21	C5205	244900	0	143393		
18	6/9/2008	123845	S45	C7745	63000	0	35102		
19	6/9/2008	123846	S54	C1730	212600	0	117787		
20	6/9/2008	123847	S21	C6292	974700	0	478731		
21	6/9/2008	123848	S45	C2008	327700	0	170968		
22	6/9/2008	123849	S54	C4096	30700	0	18056		
23	Total				6309500	65000	3293559		
24									
25									
26									

Figure 1.16
The result of running the Relative macro.

If you aren't careful, you might just print these off for your manager. You would be in trouble. Look in Cell E23. Luckily, Excel has a green triangle there telling you to look at the cell. If you would have happened to try this back in Excel 95 or Excel 97 before we had smart tags, there would have been no indicator that anything was wrong.

Move the cell pointer to E23. An alert indicator pops up near the cell. The indicator tells you that the formula fails to include adjacent cells. If you look in the formula bar, you can see that the macro totaled only from Row 7 to Row 22. Neither the relative recording nor the nonrelative recording is smart enough to replicate the logic of the AutoSum button.

At this point, any sane person would give up. But imagine that you might have had fewer invoice records on this particular day. Excel would have rewarded you with the illogical formula of =SUM(E10:E1048571) and a circular reference, as shown in Figure 1.17.

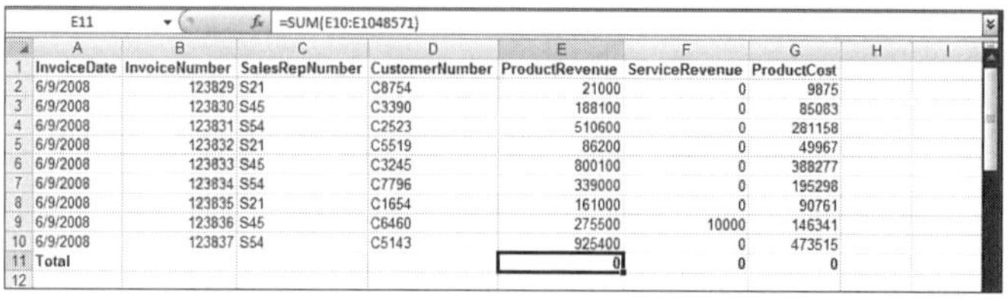

Figure 1.17
The result of running the Relative macro with fewer invoice records.

My guess is that if you have tried using the macro recorder that you have run into similar problems as the ones produced in the last two case studies. While this is frustrating, you should be happy to know that the macro recorder actually gets you 95% of the way to a useful macro.

Your job is to recognize where the macro recorder is likely to fail and then to be able to dive into the VBA code to fix the one or two lines that require adjusting in order to have a perfect macro.

You need to dive in and figure out Visual Basic. With some added human intelligence, you can produce awesome macros to speed up your daily work.

If you are like me, you are cursing Microsoft. We've wasted a good deal of time over a couple of days, and neither macro will work. What makes it worse is that this sort of procedure would have been handled perfectly by the old Lotus 1-2-3 macro recorder introduced in 1983. Mitch Kapor solved this problem 21 years ago, and Microsoft still can't get it right.

Did you know that up through Excel 97, Microsoft Excel secretly would run Lotus command-line macros? I didn't either, but I found out right after Microsoft quit supporting Excel 97. A number of companies then upgraded to Excel XP, which no longer supported the Lotus 1-2-3 macros. Many of these companies hired us to convert the old Lotus 1-2-3 macros to Excel VBA. It is interesting that from Excel 5, Excel 95, and Excel 97, Microsoft offered an interpreter that could handle the Lotus macros that solved this problem correctly, yet their own macro recorder couldn't (and still can't!) solve the problem.

Next Steps: Learning VBA Is the Solution

In Chapter 2, "This Sounds Like BASIC, So Why Doesn't It Look Familiar?" we take a look at these two macros we recorded in an effort to make some sense out of them. After you know how to decode the VBA code, it will feel natural to either correct the recorded code or simply write code from scratch. Hang on through one more chapter and you will be writing useful code that works consistently.

This Sounds Like BASIC, So Why Doesn't It Look Familiar?

2

I Can't Understand This Code

As I mentioned before, if you've taken a class in a procedural language such as BASIC or COBOL, you might be really confused when you look at VBA code. Yes, VBA stands for Visual Basic for Applications, but it is an *object-oriented* version of BASIC. Here is a bit of VBA code:

```
Selection.End(xlDown).Select
Range("A14").Select
ActiveCell.FormulaR1C1 = "'Total"
Range("E14").Select
Selection.FormulaR1C1 = "=SUM(R[-12]C:R[-1]C)"
Selection.AutoFill _
    Destination:=Range("E14:G14"), _
    Type:=xlFillDefault
```

This code will likely make no sense to anyone who knows only procedural languages, and unfortunately, your first introduction to programming in school (assuming you are over 25 years old) would have been a procedural language.

Here is a section of code written in the BASIC language:

```
For x = 1 to 10
    Print Rpt$(" ",x);
    Print "*"
Next x
```

If you run this code, you get a pyramid of asterisks on your screen:

```
*
 *
  *
   *
    *
     *
      *
       *
        *
         *
```

If you've ever been in a procedural programming class, you can probably look at the code and figure out what is going on. I think that a procedural language is more English-like than object-oriented languages. The statement `Print "Hello World"` follows the verb-object format and is how you would generally talk. Let's step away from programming for a second and think about a concrete example.

Understanding the Parts of VBA "Speech"

If you were going to play soccer using BASIC, the instruction to kick a ball would look something like

"Kick the Ball"

Hey—this is how we talk! It makes sense. You have a verb (kick) and then a noun (the ball). In the BASIC code in the preceding section, you have a verb (print) and a noun (an asterisk). Life is good.

Here is the problem. VBA doesn't work like this. No object-oriented language works like this. In an object-oriented language, the objects (the nouns) are most important (hence, the name: object oriented). If you are going to play soccer with VBA, the basic structure would be:

Ball.Kick

You have a noun—the ball. It comes first. In VBA, this is an *object*. Then you have the verb—to kick. It comes next. In VBA, this is a *method*.

The basic structure of VBA is a bunch of lines of code where you have

Object.Method

Sorry, this is not English. If you took a romance language in high school, you will remember that they used a "noun adjective" construct, but I don't know anyone who speaks in "noun verb" when telling someone to do something. Do you talk like this?

```
Water.Drink
Food.Eat
Girl.Kiss
```

Of course not. That is why VBA is so confusing to someone who previously stepped foot in a procedural programming class.

Let's carry the analogy on a bit. Imagine you walk onto a grassy field and there are five balls in front of you. There is a soccer ball, a basketball, a baseball, a bowling ball, and a tennis ball. You want to instruct the kid on your soccer team to

Kick the soccer ball

If you tell him kick the ball (or `ball.kick`), you really aren't sure which one he will kick. Maybe he will kick the one closest to him. This could be a real problem if he is standing in front of the bowling ball.

For almost any noun, or object, in VBA, there is a collection of that object. Think about Excel. If you can have a row, you can have a bunch of rows. If you can have a cell, you can have a bunch of cells. If you can have a worksheet, you can have a bunch of worksheets. The only difference between an object and a collection is that you will add an *s* to the name of the object:

> Row becomes Rows
>
> Cell becomes Cells
>
> Ball becomes Balls

When you refer to something that is a collection, you have to tell the programming language to which item you are referring. There are a couple of ways to do this. You can refer to an item by using a number:

```
Balls(2).Kick
```

This will work fine, but it seems a dangerous way to program. It might work on Tuesday; but if you get to the field on Wednesday and someone has rearranged the balls, `Balls(2).Kick` might be a painful exercise.

The other way is to use a name for the object. To me, this is a far safer way to go. You can say:

```
Balls("Soccer").Kick
```

With this method, you always know that it will be the soccer ball that it being kicked.

So far, so good. You know you can kick a ball, and you know that it will be the soccer ball. For most of the verbs, or methods, in Excel VBA, there are parameters that tell *how* to do the action. These act as adverbs. You might want the soccer ball to be kicked to the left and with a hard force. Most methods have a number of parameters that tell how the program should perform the method:

```
Balls("Soccer").Kick Direction:=Left, Force:=Hard
```

As you are looking at VBA code, when you see the colon-equals combination, you know that you are looking at parameters of how the verb should be performed.

Sometimes, a method will have a list of ten parameters. Some may be optional. Perhaps the `Kick` method has an `Elevation` parameter. You might have this line of code:

```
Balls("Soccer").Kick Direction:=Left, Force:=Hard, Elevation:=High
```

Here is the radically confusing part. Every method has a default order for its parameters. If you are not a conscientious programmer and you happen to know the order of the parameters, you can leave off the parameter names. The following code is equivalent to the previous line of code.

```
Balls("Soccer").Kick Left, Hard, High
```

This throws a monkey wrench into our understanding. Without the colon-equals, it is not obvious that we have parameters. Unless you know the parameter order, you might not understand what is being said. It is pretty easy with `Left`, `Hard`, and `High`, but when you have parameters like the following:

```
WordArt.Add Left:=10, Top:=20, Width:=100, Height:=200
```

it gets really confusing to see:

```
WordArt.Add 10, 20, 100, 200
```

The preceding is valid code, but unless you know that the default order of the parameters for this `Add` method is `Left`, `Top`, `Width`, `Height`, this code will not make sense. The default order for any particular method is the order of the parameters as shown in the help topic for that method.

To make life more confusing, you are allowed to start specifying parameters in their default order without naming them, and then all of a sudden switch to naming parameters when you hit one that does not match the default order. If you want to kick the ball to the left and high, but do not care about the force (you are willing to accept the default force), the following two statements are equivalent:

```
Balls("Soccer").Kick Direction:=Left, Elevation:=High
Balls("Soccer").Kick Left, Elevation:=High
```

As soon as you start naming parameters, they have to be named for the remainder of that line of code.

Some methods simply act on their own. To simulate pressing the F9 key, you use this code:

```
Application.Calculate
```

Other methods perform an action and create something. For example, you can add a worksheet with

```
Worksheets.Add Before:=Worksheets(1)
```

However, because `Worksheets.Add` actually creates a new object, you can assign the results of this method to a variable. In this case, you must surround the parameters with parentheses:

```
Set MyWorksheet = Worksheets.Add(Before:=Worksheets(1))
```

One final bit of grammar is necessary. Adjectives. Adjectives describe a noun. Properties describe an object. We are all Excel fans here, so I am going to switch from the soccer analogy to an Excel analogy midstream. There is an object to describe the active cell. Luckily for us, it has the very intuitive name of

```
ActiveCell
```

Let's suppose that we want to change the color of the active cell to yellow. There is a property called `InteriorColor` for a cell. It uses a complex series of codes, but you can turn a cell to yellow by using this code:

```
ActiveCell.Interior.ColorIndex = 6
```

Did I lose you? Can you see how this is so confusing? Again there's the Noun-dot-Something construct, but this time it is `Object.Property` rather than `Object.Method`.

How do you tell them apart? Well, it is really subtle. There is no colon before the equals sign. A property is almost always being set equal to something, or perhaps the value of a property is being assigned to something else.

To make this cell color the same as cell A1, you might say

```
ActiveCell.Interior.ColorIndex = Range("A1").Interior.ColorIndex
```

`Interior.ColorIndex` is a property. By changing the value of a property, you can make things look different. It is kind of bizarre—change an adjective and you are actually doing something to the cell. Humans would say, "Color the cell yellow." VBA would say

```
ActiveCell.Interior.ColorIndex = 30
```

Table 2.1 summarizes the VBA "parts of speech."

Table 2.1   The Parts of the VBA Programming Language

VBA Component	Analogous To	Notes
Object	Noun	
Collection	Plural noun	Usually specifies which object: Worksheets(1).
Method	Verb	`Object.Method.`
Parameter	Adverb	Lists parameters after the method. Separate the parameter name from its value with :=.
Property	Adjective	You can set a property `activecell.height = 10` or query the value of a property `x = activecell.height`.

Is VBA Really This Hard? No!

Knowing whether you are dealing with properties or methods will help you to set up the correct syntax for your code. Don't worry if it all seems confusing right now. When you are writing VBA code from scratch, it is tough to know whether the process of changing a cell to yellow requires a verb or just an adjective. Is it a method or a property?

This is where the beauty of the macro recorder comes in. When you don't know how to code something, you record a short little macro, look at the recorded code, and figure out what is going on.

VBA Help Files—Using F1 to Find Anything

This is a radically cool feature, but I might make you jump through hoops first. If you are going to write VBA macros, you absolutely *must* have the VBA help topics installed. The problem: The VBA help topics are not installed in the default Office install. Here is how to see whether you have it.

1. Open Excel and switch to the VB Editor by pressing Alt+F11. From the Insert menu, select Module (see Figure 2.1).

Figure 2.1
Insert a new module in the blank workbook.

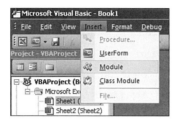

2. Type the three lines of code shown in Figure 2.2. Click inside the word *MsgBox*.

Figure 2.2
Click inside the word *MsgBox* and press F1.

3. With the cursor in the word *MsgBox*, press the F1 key on the keyboard. If the VBA help topics are installed, you will see the help topic shown in Figure 2.3.

Figure 2.3
If the VBA help topics have been installed, you will get this screen.

If instead you get a message saying that help is not available on this topic, you have to find the original CDs (or get your network administrator to grant rights to the installation folder) so that you can install the VBA help topics. Go through the process of doing a reinstall. During reinstall, select the custom install and be sure to select the VBA help files.

Using Help Topics

If you request help on a function or method, the help walks you through the various arguments available to you. If you browse to the bottom of most help topics, the help provides code samples under the Example heading. This section of each help topic is a great resource (see Figure 2.4).

Figure 2.4
Most help topics have an example.

It is possible to select the code, copy it to the clipboard by pressing Ctrl+C (see Figure 2.5), and then paste it into your module by pressing Ctrl+V.

After you record a macro, undoubtedly there will be objects or methods that you are not sure of. Insert the cursor in any keyword and press F1 to get help on that topic.

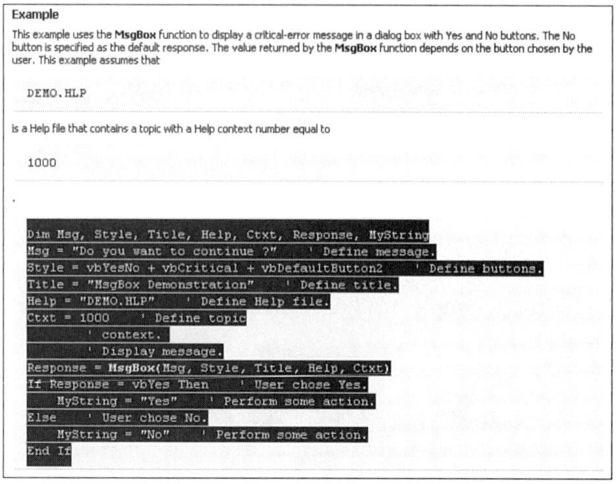

Figure 2.5
Highlight code in
the help file and
copy with Ctrl+C.

> **Example**
> This example uses the **MsgBox** function to display a critical-error message in a dialog box with Yes and No buttons. The No button is specified as the default response. The value returned by the **MsgBox** function depends on the button chosen by the user. This example assumes that
>
>   DEMO.HLP
>
> is a Help file that contains a topic with a Help context number equal to
>
>   1000
>
> ```
> Dim Msg, Style, Title, Help, Ctxt, Response, MyString
> Msg = "Do you want to continue ?"    ' Define message.
> Style = vbYesNo + vbCritical + vbDefaultButton2    ' Define buttons.
> Title = "MsgBox Demonstration"    ' Define title.
> Help = "DEMO.HLP"    ' Define Help file.
> Ctxt = 1000    ' Define topic
>     ' context.
>     ' Display message.
> Response = MsgBox(Msg, Style, Title, Help, Ctxt)
> If Response = vbYes Then    ' User chose Yes.
>     MyString = "Yes"    ' Perform some action.
> Else    ' User chose No.
>     MyString = "No"    ' Perform some action.
> End If
> ```

Examining Recorded Macro Code—Using the VB Editor and Help

Let's take a look at the code that was recorded when you followed along in the example in Chapter 1, to see whether it makes more sense now in the context of objects, properties, and methods. You can also see whether it's possible to correct the errors brought about by the macro recorder.

Here is the first code that Excel recorded in the example in Chapter 1 (see Figure 2.6).

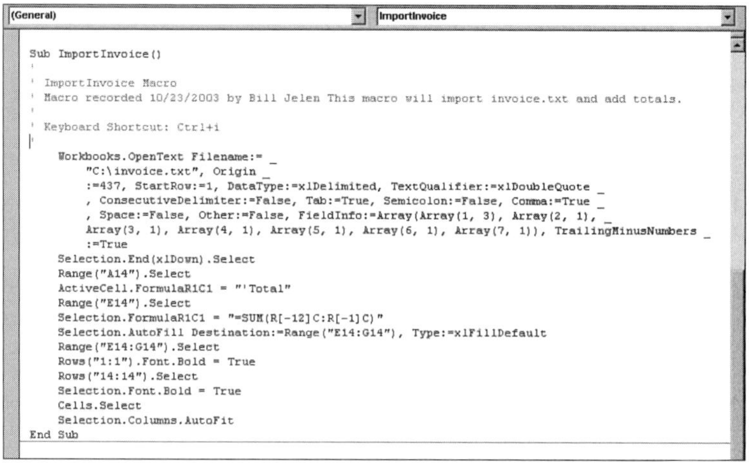

Figure 2.6
Recorded code from
example in Chapter 1.

```
Sub ImportInvoice()
'
' ImportInvoice Macro
' Macro recorded 10/23/2003 by Bill Jelen This macro will import invoice.txt and add totals.
'
' Keyboard Shortcut: Ctrl+i
'
    Workbooks.OpenText Filename:= _
        "C:\invoice.txt", Origin _
        :=437, StartRow:=1, DataType:=xlDelimited, TextQualifier:=xlDoubleQuote _
        , ConsecutiveDelimiter:=False, Tab:=True, Semicolon:=False, Comma:=True _
        , Space:=False, Other:=False, FieldInfo:=Array(Array(1, 3), Array(2, 1), _
        Array(3, 1), Array(4, 1), Array(5, 1), Array(6, 1), Array(7, 1)), TrailingMinusNumbers _
        :=True
    Selection.End(xlDown).Select
    Range("A14").Select
    ActiveCell.FormulaR1C1 = "'Total"
    Range("E14").Select
    Selection.FormulaR1C1 = "=SUM(R[-12]C:R[-1]C)"
    Selection.AutoFill Destination:=Range("E14:G14"), Type:=xlFillDefault
    Range("E14:G14").Select
    Rows("1:1").Font.Bold = True
    Rows("14:14").Select
    Selection.Font.Bold = True
    Cells.Select
    Selection.Columns.AutoFit
End Sub
```

Now that you understand the concept of Noun.Verb or Object.Method, look at the first line of code. It says, Workbooks.OpenText. In this case, Workbooks is an object. OpenText is a method. Click your cursor inside the word *OpenText* and press F1 for an explanation of the OpenText method (see Figure 2.7).

Figure 2.7
Help topic for the OpenText method.

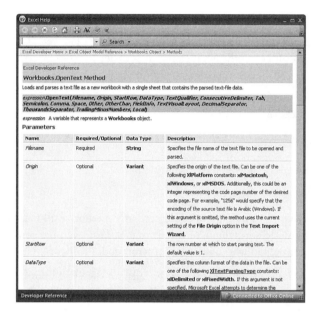

The help file confirms that OpenText is a method or an action word. In the gray box is the default order for all the arguments that can be used with OpenText. Notice that only one argument is required: FileName. All the other arguments are listed as optional.

Optional Parameters

What happens if you skip an optional parameter? The help file can tell you. For StartRow, the help file indicates that the default value is 1. If you leave out the StartRow parameter, Excel starts importing at row 1. This is fairly safe. Look at the help file note about Origin. If this argument is omitted, you inherit whatever value was used for Origin the last time someone used this feature in Excel on this computer. That is certainly a recipe for disaster—your code may work 98 percent of the time, but immediately after someone imports an Arabic file, Excel will remember the setting for Arabic and assume this is what your macro wants if you don't explicitly code this parameter.

Defined Constants

Look at the help file entry for DataType in Figure 2.7. The help file says that it can be one of these constants: xlDelimited or xlFixedWidth. The help file says that these are the valid xlTextParsingType constants. These constants are predefined in Excel VBA. In the VB

Editor, press Ctrl+G to bring up the Immediate window. In the Immediate window, type this line and press Enter:

```
Print xlFixedWidth
```

The answer appears in the Immediate window. `xlFixedWidth` is the equivalent of saying "2" (see Figure 2.8). Ask the Immediate window to `Print xlDelimited`. This is really the same as typing 1. Microsoft correctly assumes that it is easier for someone to read code that uses the somewhat English-like term `xlDelimited` rather than 1.

Figure 2.8
In the Immediate window of the VB Editor, query to see the true value of constants such as `xlFixedWidth`.

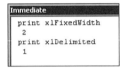

If you were an evil programmer, you could certainly memorize all these constants and write code using the numeric equivalents of the constants. However, the programming gods (as well as the next person who has to look at your code) will curse you for this.

In most cases, the help file either specifically calls out the valid values of the constants, or offers a blue hyperlink that causes the help file to expand and show you the valid values for the constants (see Figure 2.9).

Figure 2.9
Click the blue hyperlink to see all the possible constant values. Here, the ten possible `xlColumnDataType` constants are revealed in a new help topic.

My one complaint with this excellent help system is that it does not identify which parameters may be new to a given version. In this particular case, TrailingMinusNumbers was introduced in Excel 2002. If you attempt to give this program to someone who is still using Excel 2000, the code doesn't run because it does not understand the TrailingMinusNumbers parameter. This is a frustrating problem, and the only way to learn to handle it is through trial and error.

If you read the help topic on OpenText, you can surmise that it is basically the equivalent of opening a file using the Text Import Wizard. In the first step of the wizard, you normally choose either Delimited or Fixed Width. You also specify the File Origin and at which row to start (see Figure 2.10). This first step of the wizard is handled by these parameters of the OpenText method:

```
Origin:=437
StartRow:=1
DataType:=xlDelimited
```

Figure 2.10
The first step of the Text Import Wizard in Excel is covered by three parameters of the OpenText method.

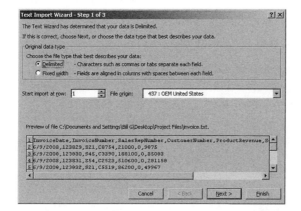

Step 2 of the Text to Columns Wizard enables you to specify that your fields are delimited by a comma. We don't want to treat two commas as a single comma, so Treat Consecutive Delimiters as One is unchecked. Sometimes, a field may contain a comma—for example "XYZ, Inc." In this case, the field should have quotes around the value. This is specified in the Text Qualifier box (see Figure 2.11). This second step of the wizard is handled by these parameters of the OpenText method:

```
TextQualifier:=xlDoubleQuote
ConsecutiveDelimiter:=False
Tab:=False
Semicolon:=False
Comma:=True
Space:=False
Other:=False
```

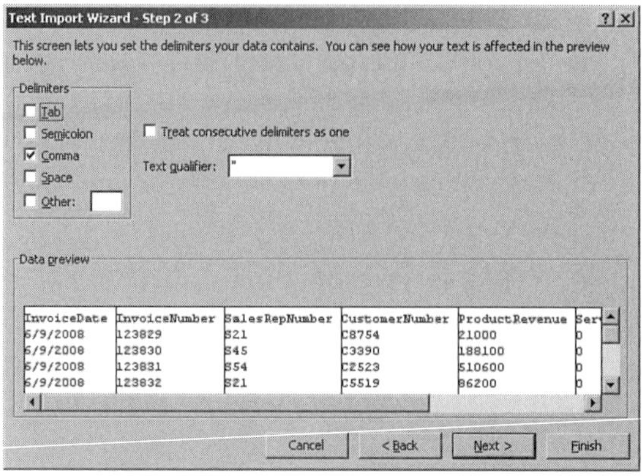

Figure 2.11
Step 2 of the Text Import Wizard is handled by the seven parameters of the `OpenText` method.

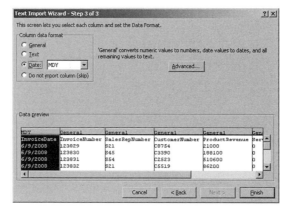

Step 3 of the wizard is where you actually identify the field types. In our case, we left all fields as General except for the first field, which was marked as a date in MDY (Month, Day, Year) format (see Figure 2.12). This is represented in code by the `FieldInfo` parameter.

Figure 2.12
The third step of the Text Import Wizard is fairly complex. The entire `FieldInfo` parameter of the `OpenText` method duplicates the choices made on this step of the wizard.

If you would happen to click the Advanced button on step 3 of the wizard, you have an opportunity to specify something other than the default Decimal and Thousands separator, plus the setting for Trailing Minus for negative numbers (see Figure 2.13). Note that the macro recorder does not write code for `DecimalSeparator` or `ThousandsSeparator` unless you change these from the defaults. The macro recorder does always record the `TrailingMinusNumbers` parameter.

At this point, you can more or less see how just about every option that you do in Excel while the macro recorder is running corresponds to a bit of code in the recorded macro.

Here is another example. The next line of code in the macro is

```
Selection.End(xlDown).Select
```

Figure 2.13
The `TrailingMinus Numbers` parameter comes from this Advanced Text Import Settings. If you had changed either of the separator fields, new parameters would have been recorded by the macro recorder.

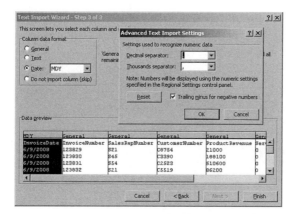

You can click and get help for three topics in this line of code: `Selection`, `End`, and `Select`. Assuming that `Selection` and `Select` are somewhat self-explanatory, click in the word *End* and press F1 for help. A Context Help dialog box pops up, saying that there are two possible help topics for `End`. There is one in the Excel library and one in the VBA library (see Figure 2.14).

Figure 2.14
Sometimes when you click in a VBA keyword and press F1, you must guess which help library to use.

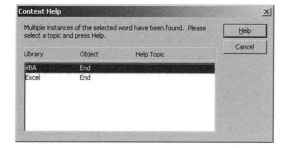

If you are new to VBA, it can be frustrating to know which one to select. Take your best guess and click Help. In this case, the End help topic in the VBA library is talking about the End statement (see Figure 2.15), which is not what we have here.

Figure 2.15
If you guess wrong, you are taken to a help topic that is completely off-topic. It is easy enough to try again.

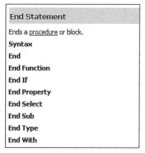

Close Help, press F1 again, and choose the `End` object in the Excel library. This help topic says that `End` is a property. It returns a `Range` object that is equivalent to pressing End+Up or End+Down in the Excel interface (see Figure 2.16). If you click the blue hyperlink for `xlDirection`, you will see the valid parameters that can be passed to the `End` function.

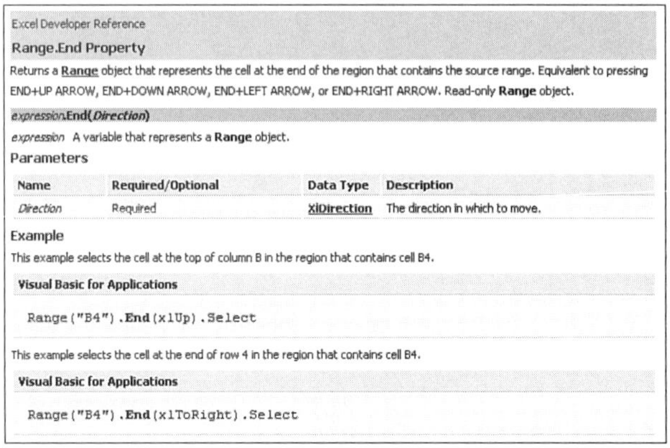

Excel Developer Reference

Range.End Property

Returns a Range object that represents the cell at the end of the region that contains the source range. Equivalent to pressing END+UP ARROW, END+DOWN ARROW, END+LEFT ARROW, or END+RIGHT ARROW. Read-only **Range** object.

expression.**End**(***Direction***)

expression A variable that represents a **Range** object.

Parameters

Name	Required/Optional	Data Type	Description
Direction	Required	XlDirection	The direction in which to move.

Example

This example selects the cell at the top of column B in the region that contains cell B4.

Visual Basic for Applications

```
Range("B4").End(xlUp).Select
```

This example selects the cell at the end of row 4 in the region that contains cell B4.

Visual Basic for Applications

```
Range("B4").End(xlToRight).Select
```

Figure 2.16
The correct help topic for the `End` property.

Properties Can Return Objects

In the discussion at the start of this chapter, I said that the basic syntax of VBA is `Object.Method`. In this particular line of code, the method is `Select`. The `End` keyword is a property, but from the help file, you see that it returns a Range object. Because the `Select` method can apply to a Range object, the method is actually appended to a property.

You might then assume that `Selection` is the object in this line of code. If you click the mouse in the word *`Selection`* and press F1, you will see that according to the help topic, `Selection` is actually a property and not an object. In reality, the proper code would be to say `Application.Selection`; however, when you are running within Excel, VBA assumes you are referring to the Excel object model, so you can leave off the Application object. If you were to write a program in Word VBA to automate Excel, you would be required to include an object variable before the `Selection` property to qualify to which application you are referring.

In this case, the `Application.Selection` can return several different types of objects. If a cell is selected, it returns the Range object.

Using Debugging Tools to Figure Out Recorded Code

The Visual Basic Editor features some awesome debugging tools. These are excellent for helping you see what a recorded macro code is doing.

Stepping Through Code

Generally, a macro runs really fast. You start it, and less than a second later, it is done. If something goes wrong, you have no opportunity to figure out what it is doing. Using Excel's Step Into feature, it is possible to run one line of code at a time.

Make sure the cursor is in the `ImportInvoice` procedure and from the menu select Debug, Step Into, as shown in Figure 2.17 (or press F8).

Figure 2.17
Stepping into code allows you to run a single line at a time.

The VB Editor is now in Step mode. The line about to be executed is highlighted in yellow with a yellow arrow in the margin before the code (see Figure 2.18).

Figure 2.18
The first line of the macro is about to run.

```
Sub ImportInvoice()
'
' ImportInvoice Macro
'
' Keyboard Shortcut: Ctrl+i
'
    Workbooks.OpenText Filename:= _
        "C:\invoice.txt", Origin _
        :=437, StartRow:=1, DataType:=xlDelimit
        , ConsecutiveDelimiter:=False, Tab:=Tru
        , Space:=False, Other:=False, FieldInfo
        Array(3, 1), Array(4, 1), Array(5, 1),
        :=True
    Selection.End(xlDown).Select
    Range("A14").Select
    ActiveCell.FormulaR1C1 = "'Total"
    Range("E14").Select
    Selection.FormulaR1C1 = "=SUM(R[-12]C:R[-1]
    Selection.AutoFill Destination:=Range("E14:
    Range("E14:G14").Select
    Rows("1:1").Font.Bold = True
    Rows("14:14").Select
    Selection.Font.Bold = True
    Cells.Select
    Selection.Columns.AutoFit
End Sub
```

In this case, the next line to be executed is the `Sub ImportInvoice()` line. This basically says, "We are about to start running this procedure." Press the F8 key to execute the line in yellow and move to the next line of code. The long code for `OpenText` is then highlighted. Press F8 to run this line of code. When you see that `Selection.End(xlDown).Select` is highlighted, you know that Visual Basic has finished running the `OpenText` command. Indeed, you can press Alt+Tab to switch to Excel and see the `Invoice.txt` file has been parsed into Excel. Note that A1 is selected (see Figure 2.19).

Figure 2.19
Switching to Excel shows that the `Invoice.txt` file has indeed been imported.

▲	A	B	C	D	E	F	G	H
1	InvoiceDa	InvoiceNu	SalesRepl	Customer	ProductRe	ServiceRe	ProductCost	
2	6/7/2008	123829	S21	C8754	538400	0	299897	
3	6/7/2008	123830	S45	C4056	588600	0	307563	
4	6/7/2008	123831	S54	C8323	882200	0	521726	
5	6/7/2008	123832	S21	C6026	830900	0	494831	
6	6/7/2008	123833	S45	C3025	673600	0	374953	
7	6/7/2008	123834	S54	C8663	966300	0	528575	
8	6/7/2008	123835	S21	C1508	467100	0	257942	
9	6/7/2008	123836	S45	C7366	658500	10000	308719	
10	6/7/2008	123837	S54	C4533	191700	0	109534	
11								

Switch back to the VB Editor by pressing Alt+Tab. The next line about to be executed is `Selection.End(xlDown).Select`. Press F8 to run this code. Switch to Excel to see the results. Now A10 is selected (see Figure 2.20).

Figure 2.20
Verify that the `End(xlDown).Select` command worked as expected. This is equivalent to pressing the End key and then the down arrow.

▲	A	B	C	D	E	F	G	H
1	InvoiceDa	InvoiceNu	SalesRepl	Customer	ProductRe	ServiceRe	ProductCost	
2	6/7/2008	123829	S21	C8754	538400	0	299897	
3	6/7/2008	123830	S45	C4056	588600	0	307563	
4	6/7/2008	123831	S54	C8323	882200	0	521726	
5	6/7/2008	123832	S21	C6026	830900	0	494831	
6	6/7/2008	123833	S45	C3025	673600	0	374953	
7	6/7/2008	123834	S54	C8663	966300	0	528575	
8	6/7/2008	123835	S21	C1508	467100	0	257942	
9	6/7/2008	123836	S45	C7366	658500	10000	308719	
10	6/7/2008	123837	S54	C4533	191700	0	109534	
11								

Press F8 again to run the `Range("A14").Select` line. If you switch to Excel by pressing Alt+Tab, you will see that this is where the macro starts to have problems. Instead of moving to the first blank row, the program moved to the wrong row (see Figure 2.21).

Figure 2.21
The recorded macro code blindly moves to Row 14 for the Total row.

▲	A	B	C	D	E	F	G	H
1	InvoiceDa	InvoiceNu	SalesRepl	Customer	ProductRe	ServiceRe	ProductCost	
2	6/7/2008	123829	S21	C8754	538400	0	299897	
3	6/7/2008	123830	S45	C4056	588600	0	307563	
4	6/7/2008	123831	S54	C8323	882200	0	521726	
5	6/7/2008	123832	S21	C6026	830900	0	494831	
6	6/7/2008	123833	S45	C3025	673600	0	374953	
7	6/7/2008	123834	S54	C8663	966300	0	528575	
8	6/7/2008	123835	S21	C1508	467100	0	257942	
9	6/7/2008	123836	S45	C7366	658500	10000	308719	
10	6/7/2008	123837	S54	C4533	191700	0	109534	
11								
12								
13								
14								
15								

Now that you have identified the problem area, you can either stop the code execution by using the Reset command (either by selecting Run, Reset or by clicking the Reset button on the toolbar; see Figure 2.22). After clicking Reset, you should return to Excel and undo anything done by the partially completed macro. In this case, close the Invoice.txt file without saving.

Figure 2.22
The Reset button in the toolbar stops a macro that is in Break mode.

More Debugging Options—Breakpoints

If you have hundreds of lines of code, you might not want to step through each line one by one. You might have a general knowledge that the problem is happening in one particular section of the program. In this case, you can set a breakpoint. You can then have the code start to run, but the macro breaks just before it executes the breakpoint line of code.

To set a breakpoint, click in the gray margin area to the left of the line of code on which you want to break. A large brown dot appears next to this code, and the line of code is highlighted in brown (see Figure 2.23).

Figure 2.23
The large brown dot signifies a breakpoint.

```
Sub ImportInvoice()
'
'  ImportInvoice Macro
'
'  Keyboard Shortcut: Ctrl+i
'
    Workbooks.OpenText Filename:= _
        "C:\invoice.txt", Origin _
        :=437, StartRow:=1, DataType:=xlDelimited, TextQualifier:=xlDoubleQuote _
        , ConsecutiveDelimiter:=False, Tab:=True, Semicolon:=False, Comma:=True _
        , Space:=False, Other:=False, FieldInfo:=Array(Array(1, 3), Array(2, 1), _
        Array(3, 1), Array(4, 1), Array(5, 1), Array(6, 1), Array(7, 1)), TrailingMinusNumbers _
        :=True
    Selection.End(xlDown).Select
    Range("A14").Select
    ActiveCell.FormulaR1C1 = "'Total"
    Range("E14").Select
    Selection.FormulaR1C1 = "=SUM(R[-12]C:R[-1]C)"
    Selection.AutoFill Destination:=Range("E14:G14"), Type:=xlFillDefault
    Range("E14:G14").Select
    Rows("1:1").Font.Bold = True
    Rows("14:14").Select
    Selection.Font.Bold = True
    Cells.Select
    Selection.Columns.AutoFit
End Sub
```

Now, from the menu select Run, Run Sub or press F5. The program quickly executes but stops just before the breakpoint. The VB Editor shows the breakpoint line highlighted in yellow. You can now press F8 to begin stepping through the code (see Figure 2.24).

After you have finished debugging your code, remove the breakpoints. You can do this by clicking the dark brown dot in the margin to toggle off the breakpoint. You can also select Debug, Clear All Breakpoints or press Ctrl+Shift+F9 to clear all breakpoints that you've set in the project.

Figure 2.24
The yellow line signifies that the breakpoint line is about to be run next.

```
Sub ImportInvoice()
'
' ImportInvoice Macro
'
' Keyboard Shortcut: Ctrl+i
'
    Workbooks.OpenText Filename:= _
        "C:\invoice.txt", Origin _
        :=437, StartRow:=1, DataType:=xlDelimited, TextQualifier:=xlDoubleQuote _
        , ConsecutiveDelimiter:=False, Tab:=True, Semicolon:=False, Comma:=True _
        , Space:=False, Other:=False, FieldInfo:=Array(Array(1, 3), Array(2, 1), _
        Array(3, 1), Array(4, 1), Array(5, 1), Array(6, 1), Array(7, 1)), TrailingMinusNumbers _
        :=True
    Selection.End(xlDown).Select
    Range("A14").Select
    ActiveCell.FormulaR1C1 = "'Total"
    Range("E14").Select
    Selection.FormulaR1C1 = "=SUM(R[-12]C:R[-1]C)"
    Selection.AutoFill Destination:=Range("E14:G14"), Type:=xlFillDefault
    Range("E14:G14").Select
    Rows("1:1").Font.Bold = True
    Rows("14:14").Select
    Selection.Font.Bold = True
    Cells.Select
    Selection.Columns.AutoFit
End Sub
```

Backing Up or Moving Forward in Code

When you are stepping through code, you might want to jump over some lines of code. Or, perhaps you've corrected some lines of code and you want to run them again. In Step mode, it is easy to do this. My favorite method is to use the mouse to grab the yellow arrow. The cursor changes to an icon, meaning that you can move the next line up or down. Drag the yellow line to whichever line you want to execute next (see Figure 2.25). The other option is to click the cursor in the line to which you want to jump and then choose Debug, Set Next Statement.

Figure 2.25
The cursor as it appears when dragging the yellow line to a different line of code to be executed next.

```
    Selection.FormulaR1C1 = "=SUM(R[-12]C:R[-1]C)"
    Selection.AutoFill Destination:=Range("E14:G14"), Type:=xlFillDefault
    Range("E14:G14").Select
    Rows("1:1").Font.Bold = True
```

Not Stepping Through Each Line of Code

When you are stepping through code, you might want to run a section of code without stepping through each line. This is common when you get to a loop. You might want VBA to run through the loop 100 times so that you can step through the lines after the loop. It is particularly monotonous to press the F8 key hundreds of times to step through a loop. Click the cursor on the line you want to step to and press Ctrl+F8 or select Debug, Run to Cursor.

Querying Anything While Stepping Through Code

We haven't talked about variables yet (the macro recorder never records a variable), but you can query the value of anything while in Step mode.

Using the Immediate Window

Press Ctrl+G to display the Immediate window in the VB Editor. While the macro is in Break mode, you can ask the VB Editor to tell you the currently selected cell, the name of the active sheet, or the value of any variable. Figure 2.26 shows several examples of queries typed into the Immediate window.

Figure 2.26
Queries (and their answers), which can be typed into the Immediate window while a macro is in Break mode.

```
Immediate
    Print Selection.Address
    $E$14
    Print Selection.Value
    5797300
    Print ActiveSheet.Name
    invoice
```

When invoked with Ctrl+G, the Immediate Window usually appears at the bottom of the Code window. You can use the resize handle (above the blue Immediate title bar) to make the Immediate window larger or smaller (see Figure 2.27).

Figure 2.27
Resizing the Immediate window.

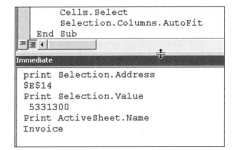

```
            Cells.Select
            Selection.Columns.AutoFit
        End Sub

Immediate
    print Selection.Address
    $E$14
    Print Selection.Value
    5331300
    Print ActiveSheet.Name
    Invoice
```

There is a scrollbar on the side of the Immediate window. You can use this to scroll backward or forward through past entries in the Immediate window.

It is not necessary to run queries only at the bottom of the Immediate window. Here is an example. In this case, I've just run one line of code. In the Immediate window, I ask for the Selection.Address to ensure that this line of code worked (see Figure 2.28).

Figure 2.28
The Immediate window shows the results before the current line is executed.

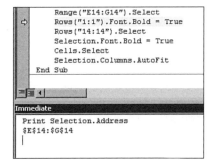

```
        Range("E14:G14").Select
        Rows("1:1").Font.Bold = True
        Rows("14:14").Select
        Selection.Font.Bold = True
        Cells.Select
        Selection.Columns.AutoFit
    End Sub


Immediate
    Print Selection.Address
    $E$14:$G$14
```

Press the F8 key to run the next line of code. Instead of retyping the same query, I can click in the Immediate window at the end of the line containing the last query (see Figure 2.29).

Figure 2.29

There is no need to type the same commands over in the Immediate window. Place the cursor at the end of the previous command and press Enter.

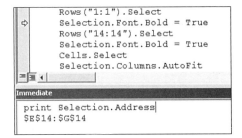

```
        Rows("1:1").Select
⇨       Selection.Font.Bold = True
        Rows("14:14").Select
        Selection.Font.Bold = True
        Cells.Select
        Selection.Columns.AutoFit
=■■ ◄
Immediate
   print Selection.Address|
   $E$14:$G$14
```

Press Enter, and the Immediate window runs this query again, displaying the results on the next line and pushing the old results farther down the window. In this case, the selected address is $1:$1. The previous answer, $E$14:$G$14, is pushed down the window (see Figure 2.30).

Figure 2.30

The prior answer ($E$14:$G$14) is shifted down, and the current answer ($1:$1) appears below the query.

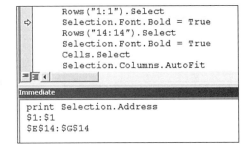

```
        Rows("1:1").Select
⇨       Selection.Font.Bold = True
        Rows("14:14").Select
        Selection.Font.Bold = True
        Cells.Select
        Selection.Columns.AutoFit
=■■ ◄
Immediate
   print Selection.Address
   $1:$1
   $E$14:$G$14
```

Press F8 four more times to run through the line of code with `Cells.Select`. Again, position the cursor in the Immediate window just after `Print Selection.Address` and press Enter. The query is run again, and the most recent address is shown with the prior answers moved down in the Immediate window (see Figure 2.31).

Figure 2.31

After selecting all cells with `Cells.Select`, place the cursor after the query in the Immediate window and press Enter. The new answer is that the selected range is all rows from 1 to 1,084,576.

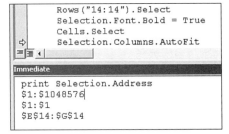

```
        Rows("14:14").Select
        Selection.Font.Bold = True
        Cells.Select
⇨       Selection.Columns.AutoFit
=■■ ◄
Immediate
   print Selection.Address
   $1:$1048576|
   $1:$1
   $E$14:$G$14
```

You can also use this method to change the query. Click to the right of the word *Address* in the Immediate window. Press the Backspace key to erase the word *Address* and instead type **Rows.Count**. Press Enter, and the Immediate window shows you the number of rows in the selection (see Figure 2.32).

Figure 2.32
Delete part of a query, type something new, and press Enter. The previous answers are pushed down, and the current answer is displayed.

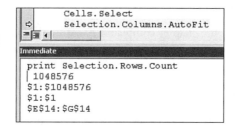

```
              Cells.Select
              Selection.Columns.AutoFit

Immediate
print Selection.Rows.Count
 1048576
$1:$1048576
$1:$1
$E$14:$G$14
```

This technique is excellent when you are trying to figure out a sticky bit of code. I might find myself querying the name of the active sheet (Print Activesheet.Name), the selection (Print Selection.Address), the active cell (Print ActiveCell.Address), the formula (Print ActiveCell.Formula) in the active cell, the value of the active cell (Print ActiveCell.Value, or Print ActiveCell because Value is the default property of a cell), and so on.

To dismiss the Immediate window, click the X in the upper-right corner of the Immediate window. (Ctrl+G does not toggle the window on and off.)

Querying by Hovering

In many instances, you can hover your cursor over an expression in the code. Wait a second, and a ToolTip pops up showing you the current value of the expression. This is invaluable for you to understand when you get to looping in Chapter 5, "Looping and Flow Control." And, it still will come in handy with recorded code. Note that the expression that you hover over does not have to be in the line of code just executed. In Figure 2.33, Visual Basic just selected Row 1 (making A1 the ActiveCell). If I hover the cursor over ActiveCell.Formula, I get a ToolTip showing me that the formula in the ActiveCell is the word *InvoiceDate*.

Figure 2.33
Hover the mouse cursor over any expression for a few seconds, and a ToolTip shows the current value of the expression.

```
        Selection.End(xlDown).Select
        Range("A14").Select
        ActiveCell.FormulaR1C1 = "'Total"
  ActiveCell.FormulaR1C1 = "InvoiceDate"
        Selection.FormulaR1C1 = "=SUM(R[-12]C:R[-1]C)"
        Selection.AutoFill Destination:=Range("E14:G14"), Type:=xlFillDefault
        Range("E14:G14").Select
        Rows("1:1").Font.Bold = True
        Rows("14:14").Select
        Selection.Font.Bold = True
        Cells.Select
        Selection.Columns.AutoFit
  End Sub
```

Sometimes the VBA window seems to not respond to hovering. Because some expressions are not supposed to show a value, it is difficult to tell whether VBA is not displaying the value on purpose or whether you are in the buggy "not responding" mode. Try hovering over something that you know should respond (such as a variable). If you get no response, hover, click into the variable, and continue to hover. This tends to wake Excel up from the stupor, and hovering will work again.

Are you impressed yet? I started the chapter complaining that this didn't seem much like BASIC, but you have to admit that the Visual Basic environment is great to work in. These debugging tools are excellent.

Querying by Using a Watch Window

In Visual Basic, a watch is not something you wear on your wrist. It allows you to watch the value of any expression while you step through code. Let's say that in the current example, I want to watch to see what is selected as the code runs. I would set up a watch for `Selection.Address`.

From the VB Editor Debut menu, select Add Watch.

In the Add Watch dialog, enter **Selection.Address** in the Expression text box and click OK (see Figure 2.34).

Figure 2.34
Setting up a watch to see the address of the current selection.

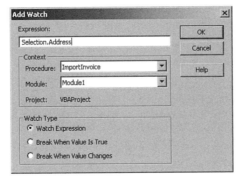

A Watches window is added to the busy Visual Basic window. It is usually added at the bottom of the code window. I started running the macro, importing the file and pressing End+Down to move to the last row with data. Right after the `Cells.Select` code is executed, the Watches window shows me that `Selection.Address` is `$A$10` (see Figure 2.35).

Figure 2.35
Without having to hover or type in the Immediate window, you can always see the value of watched expressions.

Press the F8 key to run the code `Range("A14").Select`. The Watches window is updated to show the current address of the `Selection` is now `$A$14` (see Figure 2.36).

Figure 2.36
After running another line of code, the value in the Watches window updates to indicate the address of the new selection.

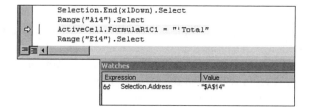

```
    Selection.End(xlDown).Select
    Range("A14").Select
⇨ | ActiveCell.FormulaR1C1 = "'Total"
    Range("E14").Select
```

Watches		
Expression		Value
6d Selection.Address		"$A$14"

Using a Watch to Set a Breakpoint

Right-click the glasses icon in the Watches window and choose Edit Watch. In the Watch Type section of the Edit Watch dialog, select Break When Value Changes (see Figure 2.37). Click OK.

Figure 2.37
Select Break When Value Changes in the bottom of the Edit Watch dialog.

The glasses icon has changed to a hand with triangle icon. You can now press F5 to run the code. The macro starts running lines of code until something new is selected. This is very powerful. Instead of having to step through each line of code, you can now conveniently have the macro stop only when something important has happened. A watch can also be set up to stop when the value of a particular variable changes.

Using a Watch on an Object

In the preceding example, we watched a specific property: `Selection.Address`. It is also possible to watch an object, such as Selection. In Figure 2.38, you have set up a watch on Selection. You get the glasses icon and a + icon.

Figure 2.38
Setting a watch on an object gives you a + icon next to the glasses.

By clicking the + icon, you can see all the properties associated with Selection. Look at Figure 2.39! You can now see more than you ever wanted to know about Selection. There are properties that you probably never realized were available. You can see that the AddIndent property is set to False, and the AllowEdit property is set to True. There are useful properties in the list—you can see the Formula of the selection.

Figure 2.39
Clicking the + icon shows a plethora of properties and their current values.

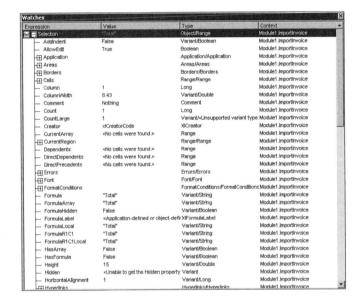

In this Watches window, some entries can be expanded. The Borders collection has a plus next to it. Click any + icon to see even more details.

The Ultimate Reference to All Objects, Methods, Properties

In the VB Editor, press F2 to open the Object Browser (see Figure 2.40). The Object Browser lets you browse and search the entire Excel object library. I own a thick book that is a reprint of this entire object model from the Object Browser. It took up 409 pages of text. I've never used those 409 pages because the built-in Object Browser is far more powerful and always available at the touch of F2. I'll take a few pages to teach you how to use the Object Browser.

Figure 2.40
Press F2 to display the
Object Browser.

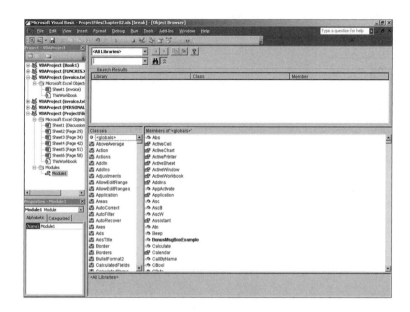

Press F2 and the Object Browser appears where the code window normally appears. The topmost drop-down currently shows <All Libraries>. There is an entry in this drop-down for Excel, Office, VBA, each workbook that you have open, plus additional entries for anything that you check in Tools, References. Go to the drop-down and select only Excel for now.

In the left window of the Object Browser is a list of all classes available for Excel. Click the Application class in the left window. The right window adjusts to show all properties and methods that apply to the Application object (see Figure 2.41). Click something in the right window like ActiveCell. The bottom window of the Object Browser tells you that ActiveCell is a property that returns a range. It tells you that ActiveCell is read-only—an alert that you cannot assign an address to ActiveCell to move the cell pointer.

We have learned from the Object Browser that ActiveCell returns a range. Click the green hyperlink for Range in the bottom window and you will see all the properties and methods that apply to Range objects and hence to the ActiveCell property. Click any property or method and click the yellow question mark near the top of the Object Browser to go to the help topic for that property or method.

Type any term in the text box next to the binoculars and click the binoculars to find all matching members of the Excel library.

The search capabilities and hyperlinks available in the Object Browser make it far more valuable than an alphabetic printed listing of all of the information. Learn to make use of the Object Browser in the VBA window by pressing F2. To close the Object Browser and return to your code window, click the lower X in the upper-right corner (see Figure 2.42).

Figure 2.41
Select a class, and then a member. The bottom window tells you the basics about the particular member. Methods appear as green books with speed lines. Properties appear as index cards with a hand pointing to them.

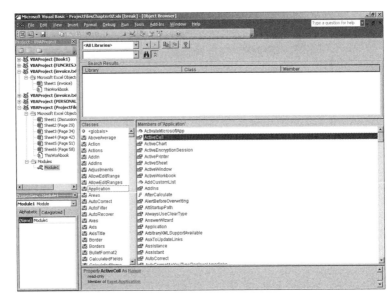

Figure 2.42
Close the Object Browser and return to your code window by clicking this X.

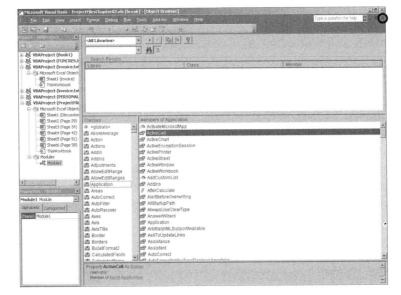

Five Easy Tips for Cleaning Up Recorded Code

I apologize. We are nearly to the end of Chapter 2, and the crazy macro we recorded in Chapter 1 still doesn't work. I am sure you want to get to the heart of the matter and find out how to make the recorded macro work. Here are five easy rules that will quickly have your code running fast and working well.

Tip 1: Don't Select Anything

Nothing screams "recorded code" more than having code that selects things before acting upon them. This makes sense—in the Excel interface, you have to select Row 1 before you can make it bold.

However, in VBA we rarely have to do this. (There are a couple buggy features in charts where you do have to select the chart object to make the method work, but that's an exception.) It is possible to directly turn on bold font to Row 1 without selecting it. The following two lines of code turn into one line.

Macro recorder code before being streamlined:

```
Rows("1:1").Select
Selection.Font.Bold = True
```

After streamlining the recorded code:

```
Rows("1:1").Font.Bold = True
```

There are several advantages to this method. First, there will be half as many lines of code in your program. Second, the program will run faster.

After recording code, I literally highlight from before the word *Select* at the end of one line all the way to the dot after the word *Selection* on the next line and press Delete (see Figures 2.43 and 2.44).

Figure 2.43
Select from here to here...

```
Range("A14").Select
ActiveCell.FormulaR1C1 = "'Total"
Range("E14").Select
Selection.FormulaR1C1 = "=SUM(R[-12]C:R[-1]C)"
Selection.AutoFill Destination:=Range("E14:G14"), Type:=xlFillDefault
Range("E14:G14").Select
```

Figure 2.44
...and press the Delete key. This is basic "101" of cleaning up recorded macros.

```
ActiveCell.FormulaR1C1 = "'Total"
Range("E14").FormulaR1C1 = "=SUM(R[-12]C:R[-1]C)"
Selection.AutoFill Destination:=Range("E14:G14"), Type:=xlFillDefault
```

Tip 2: Ride the Range from the Bottom to Find Last Row

It is difficult to trust data from just anywhere. If you are analyzing data in Excel, remember that the data is often coming from who-knows-what system written who-knows-how-long ago. The universal truth is that sooner or later, some clerk somewhere will find a way to break the source system and will manage to enter a record without an invoice number. Maybe it takes a power failure to do it, but invariably, we cannot count on having every cell filled in.

This is a problem when using the End+Down shortcut. This key combination does not take you to the last row with data in the worksheet. It takes you to the last row with data in the current range. In Figure 2.45, pressing End+Down would move the cursor to cell A6 rather than cell A10.

Figure 2.45
End+Down fails in the user interface if a record is missing a value. Similarly, End(xlDown) fails in Excel VBA.

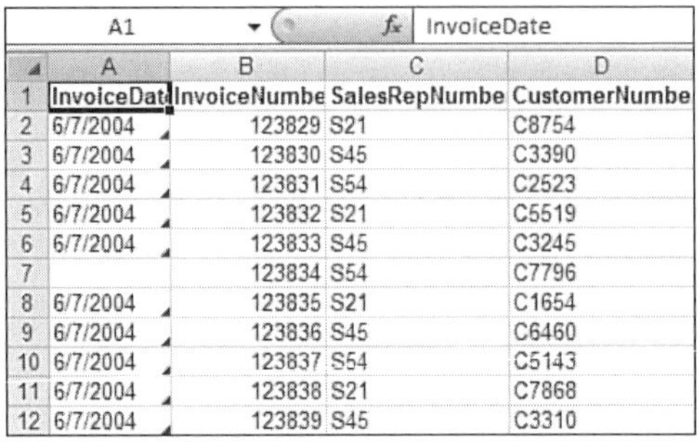

	A1	▼	fx	InvoiceDate	
▲	A	B	C	D	
1	InvoiceDate	InvoiceNumbe	SalesRepNumbe	CustomerNumbe	
2	6/7/2004	123829	S21	C8754	
3	6/7/2004	123830	S45	C3390	
4	6/7/2004	123831	S54	C2523	
5	6/7/2004	123832	S21	C5519	
6	6/7/2004	123833	S45	C3245	
7		123834	S54	C7796	
8	6/7/2004	123835	S21	C1654	
9	6/7/2004	123836	S45	C6460	
10	6/7/2004	123837	S54	C5143	
11	6/7/2004	123838	S21	C7868	
12	6/7/2004	123839	S45	C3310	

The better solution is to start at the bottom of the Excel worksheet and press End+Up. Now, this seems silly in the Excel interface because you can easily see whether you are really at the end of the data. But, because it is easy in Excel VBA to start at the last row, get in the habit of using this code to find the true last row:

```
Cells(Rows.Count, 1).End(xlUp)
```

> **NOTE**
>
> From 1995 through 2006, Excel worksheets featured 65,536 rows. In the prior edition of this book, the coding style was to use `Range("A65536").End(xlUp)` to find the last row. With the expansion to 1,048,576 rows, you might be tempted to use `Range("A1048576").End(xlUp)` in Excel 2007.
>
> However, `Rows.Count` will return the number of rows in the active workbook. This covers the possibility that the workbook is in compatibility mode, or even the possibility that someone is running the code in Excel 2003.

Tip 3: Use Variables to Avoid Hard-Coding Rows and Formulas

The macro recorder never records a variable. They are very easy to use. They are discussed in more detail later; but just as in BASIC, a variable can remember a value.

My recommendation is to set the last row with data to a variable. I like to use meaningful variable names, so my favorite for this is FinalRow:

```
FinalRow = Cells(Rows.Count, 1).End(xlUp).Row
```

Now that you know the row number of the last record, it is easy to put the word Total in Column A of the next row:

```
Range("A" & FinalRow + 1).Value = "Total"
```

→ For simpler methods of referring to this range, **see** "Using the `Offset` Property to Refer to a Range," **p. 65**, in Chapter 3, "Referring to Ranges."

You can even use the variable when building the formula. This formula totals everything from E2 to the `FinalRow` of E:

```
Range("E" & FinalRow + 1).Formula = "=SUM(E2:E" & FinalRow & ")"
```

Tip 4: Learn to Copy and Paste in a Single Statement

Recorded code is notorious for copying a range, selecting another range, and then doing an `ActiveSheet.Paste`. The `Copy` method as it applies to a range is actually much more powerful. You can specify what to copy and specify the destination in one statement.

Recorded code:

```
Range("E14").Select
Selection.Copy
Range("F14:G14").Select
ActiveSheet.Paste
```

Better code:

```
Range("E14").Copy Destination:=Range("F14:G14")
```

Tip 5: Use `With...End With` If You Are Performing Multiple Actions to the Same Cell or Range of Cells

If you were going to make the total row bold, double underline, with a larger font and a special color, you might get recorded code like this:

```
Range("A14:G14").Select
Selection.Font.Bold = True
Selection.Font.Size = 12
Selection.Font.ColorIndex = 5
Selection.Font.Underline = xlUnderlineStyleDoubleAccounting
```

For four of those lines of code, VBA must resolve the expression `Selection.Font`. Because you have four lines that all refer to the same object, you can name the object once at the top of a `With` block. Inside the `With...End With` block, everything that starts with a period is assumed to refer to the `With` object:

```
With Range("A14:G14").Font
    .Bold = True
    .Size = 12
    .ColorIndex = 5
    .Underline = xlUnderlineStyleDoubleAccounting
End With
```

Putting It All Together—Fixing the Recorded Code

Changing the Recorded Code

Using the five tips given in this chapter, you can convert the recorded code into efficient, professional-looking code. Here is the code as recorded by the macro recorder:

```
' ImportInvoice Macro
'
' Keyboard Shortcut: Ctrl+i
'

    Workbooks.OpenText Filename:= _
        "C:\invoice.txt", Origin _
        :=437, StartRow:=1, DataType:=xlDelimited, TextQualifier:=xlDoubleQuote _
        , ConsecutiveDelimiter:=False, Tab:=True, Semicolon:=False, Comma:=True _
        , Space:=False, Other:=False, FieldInfo:=Array(Array(1, 3), Array(2, 1), _
        Array(3, 1), Array(4, 1), Array(5, 1), Array(6, 1), Array(7, 1)), _
        TrailingMinusNumbers:=True
    Selection.End(xlDown).Select
    Range("A14").Select
    ActiveCell.FormulaR1C1 = "'Total"
    Range("E14").Select
    Selection.FormulaR1C1 = "=SUM(R[-12]C:R[-1]C)"
    Selection.AutoFill Destination:=Range("E14:G14"), Type:=xlFillDefault
    Range("E14:G14").Select
    Rows("1:1").Select
    Selection.Font.Bold = True
    Rows("14:14").Select
    Selection.Font.Bold = True
    Cells.Select
    Selection.Columns.AutoFit
End Sub
```

Follow these steps to clean up the macro:

1. The Workbook.OpenText lines are fine as recorded.

2. The following lines of code attempt to locate the final row of data so that the program knows where to enter the total row:

```
    Selection.End(xlDown).Select
```

You don't need to select anything to find the last row. Also, it helps to assign the row number of the final row and the total row to a variable so that they can be used later. To handle the unexpected case where a single cell in Column A is blank, start at the bottom of the worksheet and go up to find the last used row:

```
    ' Find the last row with data. This might change every day
    FinalRow = Cells(Rows.Count, 1).End(xlUp).Row
    TotalRow = FinalRow + 1
```

3. These lines of code enter the word *Total* in Column A of the Total row:

```
Range("A14").Select
ActiveCell.FormulaR1C1 = "'Total"
```

The better code will use the `TotalRow` variable to locate where to enter the word *Total*. Again, there is no need to select the cell before entering the label:

```
' Build a Total row below this
Range("A" & TotalRow).Value = "Total"
```

4. These lines of code enter the `Total` formula in Column E and copy it over to the next two columns:

```
Range("E14").Select
Selection.FormulaR1C1 = "=SUM(R[-12]C:R[-1]C)"
Selection.AutoFill Destination:=Range("E14:G14"), Type:=xlFillDefault
Range("E14:G14").Select
```

There is no reason to do all this selecting. The following line enters the formula in three cells. The R1C1 style of formulas is discussed completely in Chapter 6, "R1C1-Style Formulas":

```
Range("E" & TotalRow).Resize(1, 3).FormulaR1C1 = "=SUM(R2C:R[-1]C)"
```

5. The macro recorder selects a range and then applies formatting:

```
Rows("1:1").Select
Selection.Font.Bold = True
Rows("14:14").Select
Selection.Font.Bold = True
```

There is no reason to select before applying the formatting. These two lines perform the same action and do it much quicker:

```
Rows("1:1").Font.Bold = True
Rows(TotalRow & ":" & TotalRow).Font.Bold = True
```

6. The macro recorder selects all cells before doing the `AutoFit` command:

```
Cells.Select
Selection.Columns.AutoFit
```

There is no need to select the cells before doing the `AutoFit`:

```
Cells.Columns.AutoFit
```

7. The macro recorder adds a short description to the top of each macro:

```
' ImportInvoice Macro
```

Now that you have changed the recorded macro code into something that will actually work, feel free to add your name as author to the description and mention what the macro will do:

```
' ImportInvoice Macro
' Written by Bill Jelen This macro will import invoice.txt and add totals.
```

Here is the final macro with the changes:

```
Sub ImportInvoiceFixed()
'
' ImportInvoice Macro
' Written by Bill Jelen This macro will import invoice.txt and add totals.
'
```

```
' Keyboard Shortcut: Ctrl+i
'
    Workbooks.OpenText Filename:= _
        "C:\invoice.txt", Origin _
        :=437, StartRow:=1, DataType:=xlDelimited, TextQualifier:=xlDoubleQuote _
        , ConsecutiveDelimiter:=False, Tab:=True, Semicolon:=False, Comma:=True _
        , Space:=False, Other:=False, FieldInfo:=Array(Array(1, 3), Array(2, 1), _
        Array(3, 1), Array(4, 1), Array(5, 1), Array(6, 1), Array(7, 1)), _
        TrailingMinusNumbers:=True
    ' Find the last row with data. This might change every day
    FinalRow = Cells(Rows.Count, 1).End(xlUp).Row
    TotalRow = FinalRow + 1
    ' Build a Total row below this
    Range("A" & TotalRow).Value = "Total"
    Range("E" & TotalRow).Resize(1, 3).FormulaR1C1 = "=SUM(R2C:R[-1]C)"
    Rows("1:1").Font.Bold = True
    Rows(TotalRow & ":" & TotalRow).Font.Bold = True
    Cells.Columns.AutoFit
End Sub
```

Next Steps

Our goal by now is that you know how to record a macro. You can use help and debugging to figure out how the code works. You also have five tools for making the recorded code look like professional code.

The next chapters go into more detail about referring to ranges, looping, and the crazy (but useful) R1C1 style of formulas that the macro recorder loves to use. We also introduce you to 30 useful code samples that you can use.

Referring to Ranges

3

A *range* can be a cell, row, column, or a grouping of any of these. The RANGE object is probably the most frequently used object in Excel VBA—after all, you're manipulating data on a sheet. Although a range can refer to any grouping of cells on a sheet, it can refer to only one sheet at a time; if you want to refer to ranges on multiple sheets, you have to refer to each sheet separately.

This chapter shows you different ways of referring to ranges, such as specifying a row or column. You'll also learn how to manipulate cells based on the active cell and how to create a new range from overlapping ranges.

The Range Object

The following is the Excel object hierarchy:

Application ➡ Workbook ➡ Worksheet ➡ Range

The Range object is a property of the Worksheet object. This means it requires that either a sheet be active or it must reference a worksheet. Both of the following lines mean the same thing if Worksheets(1) is the active sheet:

```
Range("A1")
Worksheets(1).Range("A1")
```

There are several ways to refer to a Range object. Range("A1") is the most identifiable because that is how the macro recorder does it. But each of the following is equivalent:

```
Range("D5")
[D5]
Range("B3").Range("C3")
Cells(5,4)
Range("A1").Offset(4,3)
Range("MyRange") 'assuming that D5 has a Name
'of MyRange
```

Which format you use depends on your needs. Keep reading—it will all make sense soon!

Using the Upper-Left and Lower-Right Corners of a Selection to Specify a Range

The Range property has two acceptable syntaxes. To specify a rectangular range in the first syntax, you specify the complete range reference just as you would in a formula in Excel:

```
Range("A1:B5").Select
```

In the alternative syntax, you specify the upper-left corner and lower-right corner of the desired rectangular range. In this syntax, the equivalent statement might be this:

```
Range("A1", "B5").Select
```

For either corner, you can substitute a named range, the Cells property, or the ActiveCell property. This line of code selects the rectangular range from A1 to the active cell:

```
Range("A1", ActiveCell).Select
```

The following statement selects from the active cell to five rows below the active cell and two columns to the right:

```
Range(ActiveCell, ActiveCell.Offset(5, 2)).Select
```

Named Ranges

You've probably already used named ranges on your sheets and in formulas. You can also use them in VBA.

To refer to the range "MyRange" in Sheet1, do this:

```
Worksheets("Sheet1").Range("MyRange")
```

Notice that the name of the range is in quotes—unlike the use of named ranges in formulas on the sheet itself. If you forget to put the name in quotes, Excel thinks you are referring to a variable in the program, unless you are using the shortcut syntax discussed in the previous section, in which case, quotes are not used.

Shortcut for Referencing Ranges

A shortcut is available when referencing ranges. It uses square brackets, as shown in Table 3.1.

Table 3.1   Shortcuts for Referring to Ranges

Standard Method	Shortcut
Range("D5")	[D5]
Range("A1:D5")	[A1:D5]
Range ("A1:D5," "G6:I17")	[A1:D5, G6:I17]
Range("MyRange")	[MyRange]

Referencing Ranges in Other Sheets

Switching between sheets by activating the needed sheet can drastically slow down your code. To avoid this slowdown, you can refer to a sheet that is not active by referencing the Worksheet object first:

```
Worksheets("Sheet1").Range("A1")
```

This line of code references Sheet1 of the active workbook even if Sheet2 is the active sheet.

If you need to reference a range in another workbook, include the Workbook object, the Worksheet object, and then the Range object:

```
Workbooks("InvoiceData.xls").Worksheets("Sheet1").Range("A1")
```

Be careful if you use the `Range` property as an argument within another `Range` property. You must identify the range fully each time. Suppose, for example, that Sheet1 is your active sheet and you need to total data from Sheet2:

```
WorksheetFunction.Sum(Worksheets("Sheet2").Range(Range("A1"), Range("A7")))
```

This line does not work. Why? Because `Range(Range("A1"), Range("A7"))` refers to an extra range at the beginning of the code line. Excel does not assume that you want to carry the Worksheet object reference over to the other Range objects. So, what do you do? Well, you could write this:

```
WorksheetFunction.Sum(Worksheets("Sheet2").Range(Worksheets("Sheet2"). _
    Range("A1"), Worksheets("Sheet2").Range("A7")))
```

But this is not only a long line of code, it is difficult to read! Thankfully, there is a simpler way, `With...End With`:

```
With Worksheets("Sheet2")
    WorksheetFunction.Sum(.Range(.Range("A1"), .Range("A7")))
End With
```

Notice now that there is a `.Range` in your code, but without the preceding object reference. That's because `With Worksheets("Sheet2")` implies that the object of the range is the worksheet.

Referencing a Range Relative to Another Range

Typically, the `RANGE` object is a property of a worksheet. It is also possible to have `RANGE` be the property of another range. In this case, the `Range` property is relative to the original range! This makes for code that is very unintuitive. Consider this example:

```
Range("B5").Range("C3").Select
```

This actually selects cell D7. Think about cell C3. It is located two rows below and two columns to the right of cell A1. The preceding line of code starts at cell B5. If we assume that B5 is in the A1 position, VBA finds the cell that would be in the C3 position relative to

B5. In other words, VBA finds the cell that is two rows below and two columns to the right of B5, and this is D7.

Again, I consider this coding style to be very unintuitive. This line of code mentions two addresses, and the actual cell being selected is neither of these addresses! It seems misleading when you are trying to read this code.

You might consider using this syntax to refer to a cell relative to the active cell. For example, this line activates the cell three rows down and four columns to the right of the currently active cell:

```
Selection.Range("E4").Select
```

This syntax is mentioned only because the macro recorder uses it. Remember that back in Chapter 1, "Unleash the Power of Excel with VBA!" when we were recording a macro with Relative References on, the following line was recorded:

```
ActiveCell.Offset(0, 4).Range("A2").Select
```

It found the cell four columns to the right of the active cell, and from there selected the cell that would correspond to A2. This is not the easiest way to write code, but that's the macro recorder.

Although a worksheet is usually the object of the `Range` property, on occasion, such as during recording, a range may be the property of a range.

Using the `Cells` Property to Select a Range

The `Cells` property refers to all the cells of the specified range object, which can be a worksheet or a range of cells. For example, this line selects all the cells of the active sheet:

```
Cells.Select
```

Using the `Cells` property with the Range object might seem redundant:

```
Range("A1:D5").Cells
```

The line refers to the original Range object. However, the `Cells` property has a property, `Item`, which makes the `Cells` property very useful. The `Item` property enables you to refer to a specific cell relative to the Range object.

The syntax for using the `Item` property with the `Cells` property is as follows:

```
Cells.Item(Row,Column)
```

You must use a numeric value for `Row`, but you may use the numeric value or string value for `Column`. Both the following lines refer to cell C5:

```
Cells.Item(5,"C")
Cells.Item(5,3)
```

Because the `Item` property is the default property of the `RANGE` object, you can shorten these lines:

```
Cells(5,"C")
Cells(5,3)
```

The ability to use numeric values for parameters proves especially useful if you need to loop through rows or columns. The macro recorder usually uses something like `Range("A1")`. `Select` for a single cell and `Range("A1:C5").Select` for a range of cells. If you are learning to code simply from the recorder, you might be tempted to write code like this:

```
FinalRow = Cells(Rows.Count, 1).End(xlUp).Row
For i = 1 to FinalRow
    Range("A" & i & ":E" & i).Font.Bold = True
Next i
```

This little piece of code, which loops through rows and bolds the cells in Columns A through E, is awkward to read and write. But, how else can you do it?

```
FinalRow = Cells(Rows.Count, 1).End(xlUp).Row
For i = 1 to FinalRow
    Cells(i,"A").Resize(,5).Font.Bold = True
Next i
```

Instead of trying to type out the range address, the new code uses the `Cells` and `Resize` properties to find the required cell, based on the active cell.

Using the `Cells` Property in the `Range` Property

You can use `Cells` properties as parameters in the `Range` property. The following refers to the range A1:E5:

```
Range(Cells(1,1),Cells(5,5))
```

This proves especially useful when you need to specify your variables with a parameter, as in the previous looping example.

Using the `Offset` Property to Refer to a Range

You've already seen a reference to `Offset`; the macro recorder used it when we were recording a relative reference. It enables you to manipulate a cell based off the location of the active cell. In this way, you don't have to know the address of a cell.

The syntax for the `Offset` property is this:

```
Range.Offset(RowOffset, ColumnOffset)
```

To affect cell F5 from cell A1, write this:

```
Range("A1").Offset(RowOffset:=4, ColumnOffset:=5)
```

Or, shorter yet, write this:

```
Range("A1").Offset(4,5)
```

The count starts at A1 but does not include A1.

But what if you need to go over only a row or a column, but not both? You don't have to enter both the row and column parameter. If you need to refer to a cell one column over, use one of these:

```
Range("A1").Offset(ColumnOffset:=1)
Range("A1").Offset(,1)
```

Both lines mean the same. The choice is yours. Referring to a cell one row up is similar:

```
Range("B2").Offset(RowOffset:=-1)
Range("B2").Offset(-1)
```

Once again, the choice is yours. It is a matter of readability of the code.

Let's suppose you have a list of produce with totals next to them, and you want to find any total equal to zero and place LOW in the cell next to it. You could do it this way:

```
Set Rng = Range("B1:B16").Find(What:="0", LookAt:=xlWhole, LookIn:=xlValues)
Rng.Offset(, 1).Value = "LOW"

Sub MyOffset()
With Range("B1:B16")
    Set Rng = .Find(What:="0", LookAt:=xlWhole, LookIn:=xlValues)
    If Not Rng Is Nothing Then
        firstAddress = Rng.Address
        Do
            Rng.Offset(, 1).Value = "LOW"
            Set Rng = .FindNext(Rng)
        Loop While Not Rng Is Nothing And Rng.Address <> firstAddress
    End If
End With
End Sub
```

The LOW totals are quickly noted by the program, as shown in Figure 3.1.

Offsetting isn't only for single cells—it can be used with ranges. You can shift the focus of a range over in the same way you can shift the active cell. The following line refers to B2:D4 (see Figure 3.2):

```
Range("A1:C3").Offset(1,1)
```

Figure 3.1
Find the produce with the 0 total.

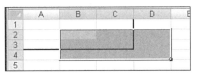

Figure 3.2
Offsetting a range—
`Range("A1:C3").`
`Offset(1,1).`
`Select.`

Using the Resize **Property to Change the Size of a Range**

The Resize property enables you to change the size of a range based on the location of the active cell. You can create a new range as you need it.

The syntax for the Resize property is this:

```
Range.Resize(RowSize, ColumnSize)
```

To create a range B3:D13, use this:

```
Range("B3").Resize(RowSize:=11, ColumnSize:=3)
```

Or, simpler, use this:

```
Range("B3").Resize(11, 3)
```

But what if you need to resize by only a row or a column, not both? You don't have to enter both the row and column parameters. If you need to expand by two columns, use one of these:

```
Range("B3").Resize(ColumnSize:=2)
```

or

```
Range("B3").ReSize(,2)
```

Both lines mean the same. The choice is yours. Resizing just the rows is similar:

```
Range("B3").Resize(RowSize:=2)
```

or

```
Range("B3").Resize(2)
```

Once again, the choice is yours. It is a matter of readability of the code.

From the list of produce, find the zero total and color the cells of the total and corresponding produce (see Figure 3.3):

```
Set Rng = Range("B1:B16").Find(What:="0", LookAt:=xlWhole, LookIn:=xlValues)
Rng.Offset(, -1).Resize(, 2).Interior.ColorIndex = 15
```

Notice that the Offset property was used first to move the active cell over; when you are resizing, the upper-left corner cell must remain the same.

Resizing isn't only for single cells—it can be used to resize an existing range. For example, if you have a named range but need it and the two columns next to it, use this:

```
Range("Produce").Resize(,2)
```

Remember, the number you resize by is the total number of rows/columns you want to include.

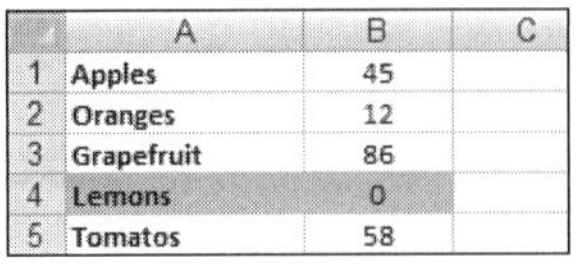

	A	B	C
1	Apples	45	
2	Oranges	12	
3	Grapefruit	86	
4	Lemons	0	
5	Tomatos	58	

Figure 3.3
Resizing a range to extend the selection.

Using the `Columns` and `Rows` Properties to Specify a Range

`Columns` and `Rows` refer to the columns and rows of a specified Range object, which can be a worksheet or a range of cells. They return a Range object referencing the rows or columns of the specified object.

You've seen the following line used, but what is it doing?

```
FinalRow = Cells(Rows.Count, 1).End(xlUp).Row
```

This line of code finds the last row in a sheet in which Column A has a value and places the row number of that Range object into `FinalRow`. This can be very useful when you need to loop through a sheet row by row—you'll know exactly how many rows you need to go through.

> **CAUTION**
>
> Some properties of columns and rows require contiguous rows and columns to work properly. For example, if you were to use the following line of code, 9 would be the answer because only the first range would be evaluated:
>
> ```
> Range("A1:B9, C10:D19").Rows.Count
> ```
>
> But if the ranges are grouped separately,
>
> ```
> Range("A1:B9", "C10:D19").Rows.Count
> ```
>
> the answer would be 19.

Using the `Union` Method to Join Multiple Ranges

The `Union` method enables you to join two or more noncontiguous ranges. It creates a temporary object of the multiple ranges, allowing you to affect them together:

```
Application.Union(argument1, argument2, etc.)
```

The following code joins two named ranges on the sheet, inserts the `=RAND()` formula, and bolds them:

```
Set UnionRange = Union(Range("Range1"), Range("Range2"))
With UnionRange
    .Formula = "=RAND()"
    .Font.Bold = True
End With
```

Using the `Intersect` Method to Create a New Range from Overlapping Ranges

The `Intersect` method returns the cells that overlap between two or more ranges:

```
Application.Intersect(argument1, argument2, etc.)
```

The following code colors the overlapping cells of the two ranges.

```
Set IntersectRange = Intersect(Range("Range1"), Range("Range2"))
IntersectRange.Interior.ColorIndex = 6
```

Using the `ISEMPTY` Function to Check Whether a Cell Is Empty

The `ISEMPTY` function returns a Boolean value of whether a single cell is empty or not; `True` if empty, `False` if not. The cell must truly be empty. Even if it has a space in it, which you cannot see, Excel does not consider it empty:

```
IsEmpty(Cell)
```

Look at Figure 3.4. You have several groups of data separated by a blank row. You want to make the separations a little more obvious.

Figure 3.4
Blank empty rows
separating data.

	A	B	C	D
1	**Apples**	**Oranges**	**Grapefruit**	**Lemons**
2	45	12	86	15
3	61%	99%	54%	17%
4				
5	**Tomatos**	**Cabbage**	**Lettuce**	**Green Peppers**
6	58	24	31	0
7	42%	96%	74%	2%
8				
9	**Potatos**	**Yams**	**Onions**	**Garlic**
10	10	61	26	29
11	19%	31%	57%	88%

The following code goes down the data in Column A; where it finds an empty cell, it colors in the first four cells for that row (see Figure 3.5):

```
LastRow = Cells(Rows.Count, 1).End(xlUp).Row
For i = 1 To LastRow
    If IsEmpty(Cells(i, 1)) Then
        Cells(i, 1).Resize(1, 4).Interior.ColorIndex = 1
    End If
Next i
```

Figure 3.5
Colored rows
separating data.

	A	B	C	D
1	Apples	Oranges	Grapefruit	Lemons
2	45	12	86	15
3	61%	99%	54%	17%
4				
5	Tomatos	Cabbage	Lettuce	Green Peppers
6	58	24	31	0
7	42%	96%	74%	2%
8				
9	Potatos	Yams	Onions	Garlic
10	10	61	26	29
11	19%	31%	57%	88%

Using the `CurrentRegion` Property to Quickly Select a Data Range

`CurrentRegion` returns a Range object representing a set of contiguous data. As long as the data is surrounded by one empty row and one empty column, you can select the table with `CurrentRegion`:

```
RangeObject.CurrentRegion
```

Look at Figure 3.6. The following line selects A1:D3 because this is the contiguous range of cells around cell A1:

```
Range("A1").CurrentRegion.Select
```

This is useful if you have a table whose size is in constant flux.

Figure 3.6
Use `CurrentRegion`
to quickly select a range
of contiguous data
around the active cell.

	A	B	C	D
1	Apples	Oranges	Grapefruit	Lemons
2	82	80	46	59
3	17%	78%	2%	46%
4				

CASE STUDY

Using the `SpecialCells` Method to Select Specific Cells

Even Excel power users may never have encountered the Go To Special dialog box. If you press the F5 key in an Excel worksheet, you get the normal Go To dialog box (see Figure 3.7). In the lower-left corner of this dialog is a button labeled Special. Click that button to get to the super-powerful Go To Special dialog (see Figure 3.8).

In the Excel interface, the Go To Special dialog enables you to select only cells with formulas, or only blank cells, or only the visible cells. Selecting visible cells only is excellent for grabbing the visible results of AutoFiltered data.

To simulate the Go To Special dialog in VBA, use the `SpecialCells` method. This enables you to act on cells that meet a certain criteria:

```
RangeObject.SpecialCells(Type, Value)
```

Figure 3.7
Although the Go To dialog doesn't seem very useful, click the Special button in the lower-left corner.

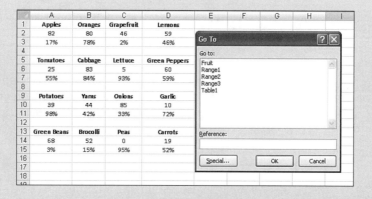

Figure 3.8
The Go To Special dialog has many incredibly useful selection tools.

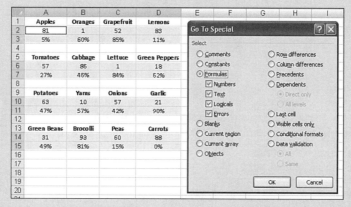

This method has two parameters: `Type` and `Value`. `Type` is one of the `xlCellType` constants:

xlCellTypeAllFormatConditions	xlCellTypeFormulas
xlCellTypeAllValidation	xlCellTypeLastCell
xlCellTypeBlanks	xlCellTypeSameFormatConditions
xlCellTypeComments	xlCellTypeSameValidation
xlCellTypeConstants	xlCellTypeVisible

`Value` is optional and can be one of the following:

xlErrors	xlNumbers
xlLogical	xlTextValues

The following code returns all the ranges that have conditional formatting set up. It produces an error if there are no conditional formats. It puts a border around each contiguous section it finds:

```
Set rngCond = ActiveSheet.Cells.SpecialCells(xlCellTypeAllFormatConditions)
If Not rngCond Is Nothing Then
    rngCond.BorderAround xlContinuous
End If
```

Have you ever had someone send you a worksheet without all the labels filled in? Some people consider that the data shown in Figure 3.9 looks neat. They enter the Region field only once for each region. This might look aesthetically pleasing, but it is impossible to sort. Even Excel's pivot table routinely returns data in this annoying format.

Figure 3.9
The blank cells in the region column make data tables such as this very difficult to sort.

	A	B	C
1	Region	Product	Sales
2	Central	ABC	766,469
3		DEF	776,996
4		XYZ	832,414
5	East	ABC	703,255
6		DEF	891,799
7		XYZ	897,949
8	West	ABC	631,646
9		DEF	494,919
10		XYZ	712,365
11			

Using the `SpecialCells` method to select all the blanks in this range is one way to quickly fill in all the blank region cells with the region found above them:

```
Sub FillIn()
    On Error Resume Next 'Need this because if there aren't any blank cells,
    'the code will error
    Range("A1").CurrentRegion.SpecialCells(xlCellTypeBlanks).FormulaR1C1 _
    = "=R[-1]C"
    Range("A1").CurrentRegion.Value = Range("A1").CurrentRegion.Value
End Sub
```

In this code, `Range("A1").CurrentRegion` refers to the contiguous range of data in the report. The `SpecialCells` method returns just the blank cells in that range. Although you can read more about R1C1 style formulas in Chapter 6, "R1C1-Style Formulas," this particular formula fills in all the blank cells with a formula that points to the cell above the blank cell. The second line of code is a fast way to simulate doing a Copy and then Paste Special Values. Figure 3.10 shows the results.

Figure 3.10
After the macro runs, the blank cells in the Region column have been filled in with data.

	A	B	C
1	Region	Product	Sales
2	Central	ABC	766,469
3	Central	DEF	776,996
4	Central	XYZ	832,414
5	East	ABC	703,255
6	East	DEF	891,799
7	East	XYZ	897,949
8	West	ABC	631,646
9	West	DEF	494,919
10	West	XYZ	712,365
11			

Using the Areas Collection to Return a Noncontiguous Range

The Areas collection is a collection on noncontiguous ranges within a selection. It consists of individual Range objects representing contiguous ranges of cells within the selection. If the selection contains only one area, the Areas collection contains a single Range object corresponding to that selection.

You might be tempted to loop through the sheet, copy a row, and paste it to another section. But there's an easier way (see Figure 3.11):

```
Range("A:D").SpecialCells(xlCellTypeConstants, 1).Copy Range("I1")
```

Figure 3.11
The Areas collection makes it easy to manipulate noncontiguous ranges.

	A	B	C	D	E	F	G	H	I	J	K	L
1	Apples	Oranges	Grapefruit	Lemons					45	12	86	15
2	45	12	86	15					58	24	31	0
3	54%	24%	3%	40%					10	61	26	29
4									46	64	79	95
5	Tomatos	Cabbage	Lettuce	Green Peppers								
6	58	24	31	0								
7	2%	74%	82%	65%								
8												
9	Potatos	Yams	Onions	Garlic								
10	10	61	26	29								
11	99%	55%	89%	39%								
12												
13	Green Beans	Brocolli	Peas	Carrots								
14	46	64	79	95								
15	81%	22%	6%	72%								
16												

3

Referencing Tables

 With Excel 2007, we're introduced to a new way of interacting with ranges of data: tables. These special ranges offer the convenience of referencing named ranges, but are not created in the same manner. For more information on how to create a named table, see Chapter 8, "Create and Manipulate Names in VBA."

The table itself is referenced using the standard method of referring to a ranged name. To refer to the data in table Table1 in Sheet1, do this:

```
Worksheets(1).Range("Table1")
```

This references just the data part of the table; it does not include the header or total row. To include the header and total row, do this:

```
Worksheets(1).Range("Table1[#All]")
```

What I really like about this new feature is the ease of referencing specific columns of a table. You don't have to know how many columns in from a starting position or the letter/number of the column, and you don't have to use a FIND function. You can just use the header name of the column. To reference the Qty column of the table, for example, do this:

```
Worksheets(1).Range("Table1[Qty]")
```

Next Steps

Now that you're getting an idea of how Excel works, it's time to apply it to useful situations. The next chapter looks at user-defined functions, uses the skills you've learned so far, and introduces other programming methods that you will learn more about throughout this book.

3

User-Defined Functions

4

Creating User-Defined Functions

Excel provides many built-in formulas, but sometimes you need a complex custom formula not offered—for example, a formula that sums a range of cells based on their interior color.

So, what do you do? You could go down your list and copy the colored cells to another section. Or, perhaps you have a calculator next to you as you work your way down your list—beware you don't enter the same number twice! Both methods are time-consuming and prone to accidents. What to do? You could write a procedure—after all, that's what this book is about. But, you have another option: user-defined functions (UDFs).

You can create functions in VBA that can be used just like Excel's built-in functions, such as SUM. After the custom function is created, a user needs to know only the function name and its arguments.

> **NOTE**
> UDFs can be entered only into standard modules. Sheet and ThisWorkbook modules are a special type of module; if you enter the function there, Excel won't recognize that you are creating a UDF.

CASE STUDY

Custom Functions—Example and Explanation

Let's build a custom function used to add two values. After we've created it, we'll use it on a worksheet.

Insert a new module in the VB Editor. Type the following function into the module. It is a function called ADD that will total two numbers in different cells. The function has two arguments:

```
Add(Number1,Number2)
```

Number1 is the first number to add; Number2 is the second number to add:

```
Function Add(Number1 As Integer, Number2 As Integer) As Integer
Add = Number1 + Number2
End Function
```

Let's break this down:

- Function name: ADD.
- Arguments are placed in parentheses after the name of the function. This example has two arguments: Number1 and Number2.
- As Integer defines the variable type of the result as a whole number.
- ADD =Number1 + Number2: The result of the function is returned.

Here is how to use the function on a worksheet:

1. Type numbers into cells A1 and A2.
2. Select cell A3.
3. Press Shift+F3 to open the Paste Function dialog box (or from the Formulas ribbon, choose Insert Function).
4. Select the User Defined category (see Figure 4.1).

Figure 4.1
You can find your UDFs under the User Defined category of the Insert Function dialog box.

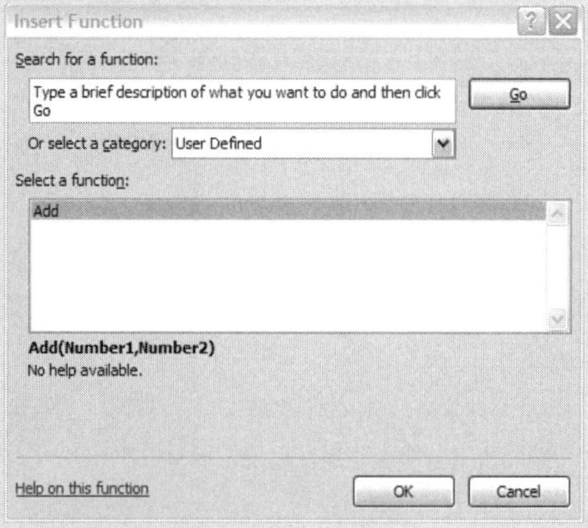

5. Select the ADD function.

6. In the first argument box, select cell A1 (see Figure 4.2).

Figure 4.2
Use the Function
Arguments dialog to
enter your arguments.

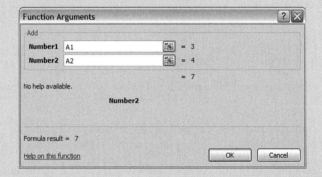

7. In the second argument box, select cell A2.

8. Click OK.

Congratulations! You have created your first custom function.

> **NOTE**
> You can easily share custom functions because the users are not required to know how the function works. See the section "Sharing UDFs" later in this chapter for more information.

Most of the same functions used on sheets can also be used in VBA and vice versa. In VBA, however, you call the UDF (ADD) from a procedure (Addition):

```
Sub Addition ()
Dim Total as Integer
Total = Add (1,10) 'we use a user-defined function Add
MsgBox "The answer is: " & Total
End Sub
```

Sharing UDFs

Where you store a UDF affects how you can share it:

- **Personal.xlsb**—If the UDF is just for your use and won't be used in a workbook opened on another computer, you can store the UDF in the Personal.xlsb.

- **Workbook**—If the UDF needs to be distributed to many people, you can store it in the workbook in which it is being used.

- **Add-in**—If the workbook is to be shared among a select group of people, you can distribute it via an add-in (see Chapter 27, "Creating Add-Ins" for information on how to create an add-in).
- **Template**—If several workbooks need to be created using the UDF and the workbooks are distributed to many people, you can store it in a template.

Useful Custom Excel Functions

The sections that follow include a sampling of functions that can be useful in the everyday Excel world.

This chapter contains functions donated by several Excel programmers. These are functions that they have found useful and that they hope will be of help to you, too.

Different programmers have different programming styles and we did not rewrite the submissions. As you review the lines of code, you might notice different ways of doing the same task, such as referring to ranges.

Set the Current Workbook's Name in a Cell

The following function is to set the name of the active workbook in a cell, as shown in Figure 4.3:

```
MyName()
```

Figure 4.3
Use a UDF to show the filename or the filename with directory path.

	A	B
1	ProjectFilesChapter04.xlsm	=MyName()
2	C:\Excel VBA 2007 by Jelen & Syrstad\Chapter 4 - UDFs\ProjectFilesChapter04.xlsm	=MyFullName()

No arguments are used with this function:

```
Function MyName() As String
    MyName = ThisWorkbook.Name
End Function
```

Set the Current Workbook's Name and File Path in a Cell

A variation of the previous function, this one sets the file path and name of the active workbook in a cell, as shown previously in Figure 4.3:

```
MyFullName()
```

No arguments are used with this function:

```
Function MyFullName() As String
    MyFullName = ThisWorkbook.FullName
End Function
```

Check Whether a Workbook Is Open

There might be times when you need to check whether a workbook is open. The following function returns `True` if the workbook is open and `False` if it is not:

```
BookOpen(Bk)
```

The argument is `Bk`, the name of the workbook being checked:

```
Function BookOpen(Bk As String) As Boolean
Dim T As Excel.Workbook
Err.Clear 'clears any errors
On Error Resume Next 'if the code runs into an error, it skips it and continues
Set T = Application.Workbooks(Bk)
BookOpen = Not T Is Nothing
'If the workbook is open, then T will hold the workbook object and therefore
'will NOT be Nothing
Err.Clear
On Error GoTo 0
End Function
```

Here is an example of using the function:

```
Sub OpenAWorkbook()
Dim IsOpen As Boolean
Dim BookName As String
BookName = "ProjectFilesChapter04.xlsm"
IsOpen = BookOpen(BookName) 'calling our function - don't forget the parameter
If IsOpen Then
    MsgBox BookName & " is already open!"
Else
    Workbooks.Open (BookName)
End If
End Sub
```

Check Whether a Sheet in an Open Workbook Exists

This function requires that the workbook(s) it checks be open. It returns `True` if the sheet is found and `False` if it is not:

```
SheetExists(SName, WBName)
```

The arguments are as follows:

> SName—The name of the sheet being searched
> WBName—(Optional) The name of the workbook containing the sheet

```
Function SheetExists(SName As String, Optional WB As Workbook) As Boolean
    Dim WS As Worksheet
    ' Use active workbook by default
    If WB Is Nothing Then
        Set WB = ActiveWorkbook
    End If

    On Error Resume Next
        SheetExists = CBool(Not WB.Sheets(SName) Is Nothing)
    On Error GoTo 0

End Function
```

Here is an example of using this function:

```
Sub CheckForSheet()
Dim ShtExists As Boolean
ShtExists = SheetExists("Sheet9")
'notice that only one parameter was passed; the workbook name is optional
If ShtExists Then
    MsgBox "The worksheet exists!"
Else
    MsgBox "The worksheet does NOT exist!"
End If
End Sub
```

Count the Number of Workbooks in a Directory

This function searches the current directory, and its subfolders if you want, counting all Excel macro workbook files (XLSM) or just the ones starting with a string of letters:

```
NumFilesInCurDir (LikeText, Subfolders)
```

The arguments are as follows:

LikeText—(Optional) A string value to search for, must include an asterisk (*); for example: `Mr*`

Subfolders—(Optional) `True` to search subfolders, `False` (default) not to

> **NOTE**
>
> `FileSystemObject` requires the Microsoft Scripting Runtime reference library. To enable this setting, go to Tools, References and check Microsoft Scripting Runtime.

```
Function NumFilesInCurDir(Optional strInclude As String = "", _
        Optional blnSubDirs As Boolean = False)
Dim fso As FileSystemObject
Dim fld As Folder
Dim fil As File
Dim subfld As Folder
Dim intFileCount As Integer
Dim strExtension As String
  strExtension = "XLSM"
  Set fso = New FileSystemObject
  Set fld = fso.GetFolder(ThisWorkbook.Path)
  For Each fil In fld.Files
    If UCase(fil.Name) Like "*" & UCase(strInclude) & "*." & _
        UCase(strExtension) Then
      intFileCount = intFileCount + 1
    End If
  Next fil
  If blnSubDirs Then
    For Each subfld In fld.Subfolders
      intFileCount = intFileCount + NumFilesInCurDir(strInclude, True)
    Next subfld
  End If
```

```
  NumFilesInCurDir = intFileCount
  Set fso = Nothing
End Function
```

Here is an example of using this function:

```
Sub CountMyWkbks()
Dim MyFiles As Integer
MyFiles = NumFilesInCurDir("MrE*", True)
MsgBox MyFiles & " file(s) found"
End Sub
```

Retrieve USERID

Ever need to keep a record of who saves changes to a workbook? With the USERID function, you can retrieve the name of the user logged in to a computer. Combine it with function discussed in the "Retrieve Permanent Date and Time" section and you'll have a nice log file. You can also use it to set up user rights to a workbook:

```
WinUserName ()
```

No arguments are used with this function.

> **NOTE**
> This function is an advanced function that uses the application programming interface (API), which we will review in Chapter 24, "Windows Application Programming Interface (API)."

This first section (Private declarations) must be at the top of the module:

```
Private Declare Function WNetGetUser Lib "mpr.dll" Alias "WNetGetUserA" _
    (ByVal lpName As String, ByVal lpUserName As String, _
        lpnLength As Long) As Long
Private Const NO_ERROR = 0
Private Const ERROR_NOT_CONNECTED = 2250&
Private Const ERROR_MORE_DATA = 234
Private Const ERROR_NO_NETWORK = 1222&
Private Const ERROR_EXTENDED_ERROR = 1208&
Private Const ERROR_NO_NET_OR_BAD_PATH = 1203&
```

You can place the following section of code anywhere in the module as long as it is below the previous section:

```
Function WinUsername() As String
    'variables
    Dim strBuf As String, lngUser As Long, strUn As String
    'clear buffer for user name from api func
    strBuf = Space$(255)
    'use api func WNetGetUser to assign user value to lngUser
    'will have lots of blank space
    lngUser = WNetGetUser("", strBuf, 255)
    'if no error from function call
    If lngUser = NO_ERROR Then
        'clear out blank space in strBuf and assign val to function
```

```
        strUn = Left(strBuf, InStr(strBuf, vbNullChar) - 1)
        WinUsername = strUn
    Else
    'error, give up
        WinUsername = "Error :" & lngUser
    End If
End Function
```

Function example:

```
Sub CheckUserRights()
Dim UserName As String
UserName = WinUsername
Select Case UserName
    Case "Administrator"
        MsgBox "Full Rights"
    Case "Guest"
        MsgBox "You cannot make changes"
    Case Else
        MsgBox "Limited Rights"
End Select
End Sub
```

Retrieve Date and Time of Last Save

This function retrieves the saved date and time of any workbook, including the current one, as shown in Figure 4.4.

Figure 4.4
Retrieve date and time of last save.

> **NOTE**
> The cell must be formatted properly to display the date/time.

```
LastSaved(FullPath)
```

The argument is `FullPath`, a string showing the full path and filename of the file in question:

```
Function LastSaved(FullPath As String) As Date
LastSaved = FileDateTime(FullPath)
End Function
```

Retrieve Permanent Date and Time

Because of the volatility of the NOW function, it isn't very useful for stamping a worksheet with the creation or editing date—every time the workbook is opened or recalculated, the result of the NOW function gets updated. The following function uses the NOW function; but because you need to reenter the cell to update the function, it is much less volatile, as shown in Figure 4.5:

```
DateTime()
```

Figure 4.5
Retrieve permanent date and time.

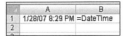

	A	B
1	1/28/07 8:29 PM	=DateTime
2		

No arguments are used with this function:

```
DateTime()
```

> **NOTE**
> The cell must be formatted properly to display the date/time.

Function example:

```
Function DateTime()
    DateTime = Now
End Function
```

Validate an Email Address

If you manage an email subscription list, you may receive invalid email addresses, such as addresses with a space before the "at" symbol (@). The ISEMAILVALID function can check addresses and confirm that they are proper email addresses (see Figure 4.6):

Figure 4.6
Validating email addresses.

	A	B	C	D
1	Tracy@ MrExcel.com	FALSE	<-a space after the @	
2	Bill@MrExcel.com	TRUE		
3	consult?@MrExcel/com	FALSE	<-invalid characters	
4				

> **CAUTION**
> This function cannot verify that an email address is an existing one. It only checks the syntax to verify that the address may be legitimate.

```
IsEmailValid (StrEmail)
```

The argument is StrEmail, an email address:

```
Function IsEmailValid(strEmail As String) As Boolean
Dim strArray As Variant
Dim strItem As Variant
Dim i As Long
Dim c As String
```

```
Dim blnIsItValid As Boolean
blnIsItValid = True
'count the @ in the string
i = Len(strEmail) - Len(Application.Substitute(strEmail, "@", ""))
'if there is more than one @, invalid email
If i <> 1 Then IsEmailValid = False: Exit Function
ReDim strArray(1 To 2)
'the following two lines place the text to the left and right
'of the @ in their own variables
strArray(1) = Left(strEmail, InStr(1, strEmail, "@", 1) - 1)
strArray(2) = Application.Substitute(Right(strEmail, Len(strEmail) - _
    Len(strArray(1))), "@", "")

For Each strItem In strArray
    'verify there is something in the variable.
'If there isn't, then part of the email is missing
    If Len(strItem) <= 0 Then
        blnIsItValid = False
        IsEmailValid = blnIsItValid
        Exit Function
    End If
    'verify only valid characters in the email
    For i = 1 To Len(strItem)
'lowercases all letters for easier checking
        c = LCase(Mid(strItem, i, 1))
        If InStr("abcdefghijklmnopqrstuvwxyz_-.", c) <= 0 _
        And Not IsNumeric(c) Then
            blnIsItValid = False
            IsEmailValid = blnIsItValid
            Exit Function
        End If
    Next i
'verify that the first character of the left and right aren't periods
    If Left(strItem, 1) = "." Or Right(strItem, 1) = "." Then
        blnIsItValid = False
        IsEmailValid = blnIsItValid
        Exit Function
    End If
Next strItem
'verify there is a period in the right half of the address
If InStr(strArray(2), ".") <= 0 Then
    blnIsItValid = False
    IsEmailValid = blnIsItValid
    Exit Function
End If
i = Len(strArray(2)) - InStrRev(strArray(2), ".") 'locate the period
'verify that the number of letters corresponds to a valid domain extension
If i <> 2 And i <> 3 And i <> 4 Then
    blnIsItValid = False
    IsEmailValid = blnIsItValid
    Exit Function
End If
'verify that there aren't two periods together in the email
If InStr(strEmail, "..") > 0 Then
    blnIsItValid = False
    IsEmailValid = blnIsItValid
```

```
        Exit Function
    End If
    IsEmailValid = blnIsItValid
    End Function
```

Sum Cells Based on the Interior Color

You have a list of clients and how much each owes you. You've colored in the amounts of the clients that are 30 days past due and want to sum up just those cells.

> **NOTE** Cells colored by conditional formatting will not work; the cells must have an interior color.

```
SumColor(CellColor, SumRange)
```

The arguments are as follows:

CellColor—The address of a cell with the target color

SumRange—The range of cells to be searched

```
Function SumByColor(CellColor As Range, SumRange As Range)
Dim myCell As Range
Dim iCol As Integer
Dim myTotal
iCol = CellColor.Interior.ColorIndex 'get the target color
For Each myCell In SumRange 'look at each cell in the designated range
'if the cell color matches the target color
If myCell.Interior.ColorIndex = iCol Then
'add the value in the cell to the total
myTotal = WorksheetFunction.Sum(myCell) + myTotal
    End If
Next myCell
SumByColor = myTotal
End Function
```

Figure 4.7 shows an example worksheet using this function.

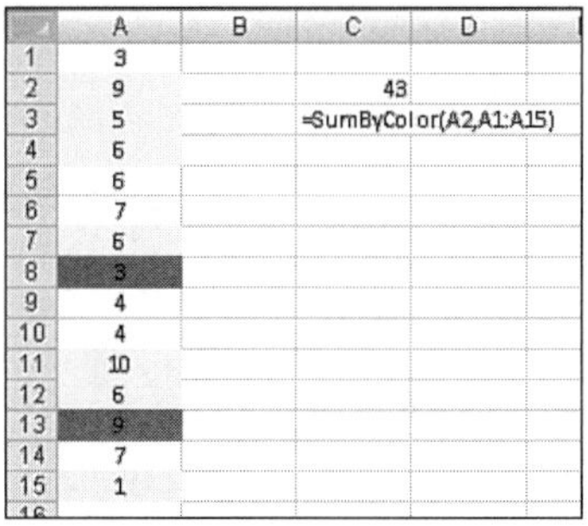

Figure 4.7
Sum cells based on interior color.

Count Unique Values

How many times have you had a long list of values and needed to know how many were unique values? This function goes through a range and tells you just that, as shown in Figure 4.8:

```
NumUniqueValues(Rng)
```

Figure 4.8
Count the number of unique values in a range.

	A	B	C	D	E
1	A		11	=NumUniqueValues(A1:A16)	
2	R				
3	T				
4	A				
5	V				
6	F				
7	EE				
8	1				
9	19				
10	V				
11	Q				
12	V				
13	GE				
14	V				
15	123				
16	1				

The argument is Rng, the range to search unique values.

Function example:

```
Function NumUniqueValues(Rng As Range) As Long
Dim myCell As Range
Dim UniqueVals As New Collection
Application.Volatile 'forces the function to recalculate when the range changes
On Error Resume Next
'the following places each value from the range into a collection
'because a collection, with a key parameter, can contain only unique values,
'there will be no duplicates the error statements force the program to
'continue when the error messages appear for duplicate items in the collection
For Each myCell In Rng
    UniqueVals.Add myCell.Value, CStr(myCell.Value)
Next myCell
On Error GoTo 0
'returns the number of items in the collection
NumUniqueValues = UniqueVals.Count
End Function
```

Remove Duplicates from a Range

How often have you had a list of items and needed to list only the unique values? The following function goes through a range and stores only the unique values:

```
UniqueValues (OrigArray)
```

The argument is OrigArray, an array from which to remove duplicates.

This first section (Const declarations) must be at the top of the module:

```
Const ERR_BAD_PARAMETER = "Array parameter required"
Const ERR_BAD_TYPE = "Invalid Type"
Const ERR_BP_NUMBER = 20000
Const ERR_BT_NUMBER = 20001
```

You can place the following section of code anywhere in the module as long as it is below the previous section:

```
Public Function UniqueValues(ByVal OrigArray As Variant) As Variant
    Dim vAns() As Variant
    Dim lStartPoint As Long
    Dim lEndPoint As Long
    Dim lCtr As Long, lCount As Long
    Dim iCtr As Integer
    Dim col As New Collection
    Dim sIndex As String
    Dim vTest As Variant, vItem As Variant
    Dim iBadVarTypes(4) As Integer
    'Function does not work if array element is one of the
    'following types
    iBadVarTypes(0) = vbObject
    iBadVarTypes(1) = vbError
    iBadVarTypes(2) = vbDataObject
    iBadVarTypes(3) = vbUserDefinedType
    iBadVarTypes(4) = vbArray
    'Check to see whether the parameter is an array
    If Not IsArray(OrigArray) Then
        Err.Raise ERR_BP_NUMBER, , ERR_BAD_PARAMETER
        Exit Function
    End If
    lStartPoint = LBound(OrigArray)
    lEndPoint = UBound(OrigArray)
    For lCtr = lStartPoint To lEndPoint
        vItem = OrigArray(lCtr)
        'First check to see whether variable type is acceptable
        For iCtr = 0 To UBound(iBadVarTypes)
            If VarType(vItem) = iBadVarTypes(iCtr) Or _
               VarType(vItem) = iBadVarTypes(iCtr) + vbVariant Then
                Err.Raise ERR_BT_NUMBER, , ERR_BAD_TYPE
                Exit Function
            End If
        Next iCtr
        'Add element to a collection, using it as the index
        'if an error occurs, the element already exists
        sIndex = CStr(vItem)
        'first element, add automatically
        If lCtr = lStartPoint Then
            col.Add vItem, sIndex
            ReDim vAns(lStartPoint To lStartPoint) As Variant
            vAns(lStartPoint) = vItem
        Else
            On Error Resume Next
            col.Add vItem, sIndex
            If Err.Number = 0 Then
                lCount = UBound(vAns) + 1
                ReDim Preserve vAns(lStartPoint To lCount)
                vAns(lCount) = vItem
            End If
```

4

```
            End If
            Err.Clear
      Next lCtr
      UniqueValues = vAns
End Function
```

Here is an example of using this function. See Figure 4.9 for the result on a worksheet:

```
Function nodupsArray(rng As Range) As Variant
    Dim arr1() As Variant
    If rng.Columns.Count > 1 Then Exit Function
    arr1 = Application.Transpose(rng)
    arr1 = UniqueValues(arr1)
    nodupsArray = Application.Transpose(arr1)
End Function
```

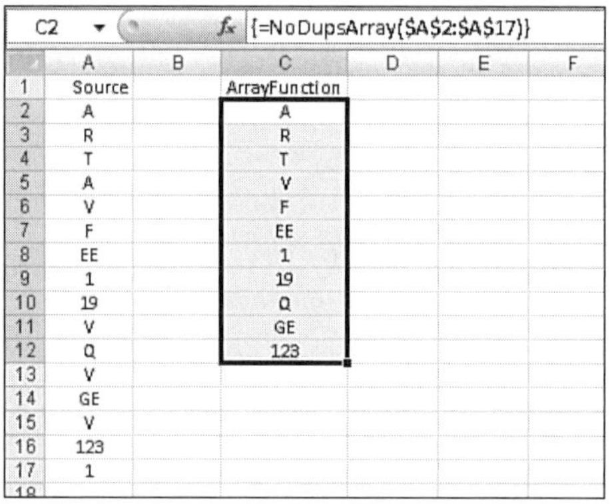

Figure 4.9
List unique values from a range.

Find the First Non-Zero-Length Cell in a Range

You import a large list of data with a lot of empty cells. Here is a function that evaluates a range of cells and returns the value of the first non-zero-length cell:

```
FirstNonZeroLength(Rng)
```

The argument is Rng, the range to search.

Function example:

```
Function FirstNonZeroLength(Rng As Range)
Dim myCell As Range
FirstNonZeroLength = 0#
For Each myCell In Rng
    If Not IsNull(myCell) And myCell <> "" Then
        FirstNonZeroLength = myCell.Value
        Exit Function
    End If
Next myCell
FirstNonZeroLength = myCell.Value
End Function
```

Figure 4.10 shows the function on an example worksheet.

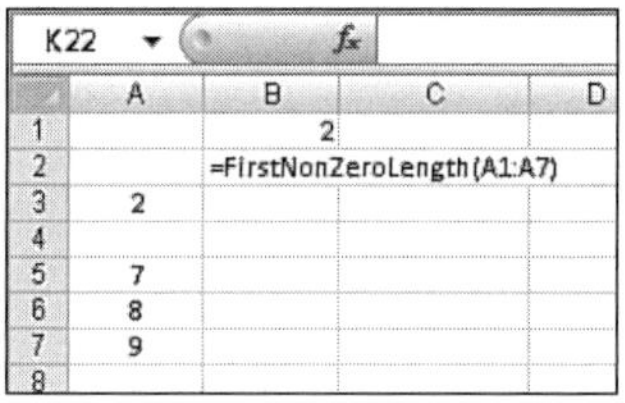

Figure 4.10
Find the value of the
first non-zero-length
cell in a range.

	A	B	C	D
1		2		
2		=FirstNonZeroLength(A1:A7)		
3	2			
4				
5	7			
6	8			
7	9			
8				

K22

Substitute Multiple Characters

Excel has a substitute function, but it is a value-for-value substitution. What if you have several characters you need to substitute? Figure 4.11 shows several examples of how this function works:

```
MSubstitute(trStr, frStr, toStr)
```

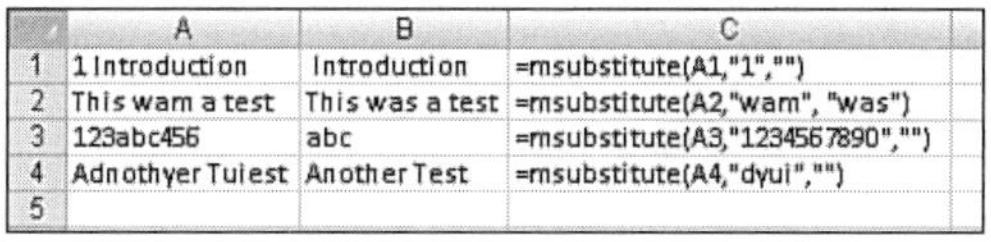

Figure 4.11
Substitute multiple
characters in a cell.

	A	B	C
1	1 Introduction	Introduction	=msubstitute(A1,"1","")
2	This wam a test	This was a test	=msubstitute(A2,"wam", "was")
3	123abc456	abc	=msubstitute(A3,"1234567890","")
4	Adnothyer Tuiest	Another Test	=msubstitute(A4,"dyui","")
5			

The arguments are as follows:

trStr—The string to be searched

frStr—The text being searched for

toStr—The replacement text

> **CAUTION**
>
> toStr is assumed to be the same length as frStr. If not, the remaining characters are considered null (" "). The function is case sensitive. To replace all instances of a, use a and A. You can't replace one character with two characters. This
>
> ```
> =MSUBSTITUTE("This is a test","i","$@")
> ```
>
> results in this:
>
> ```
> "Th$s $s a test"
> ```

Function example:

```
Function MSUBSTITUTE(ByVal trStr As Variant, frStr As String, _
        toStr As String) As Variant
Dim iCol As Integer
Dim j As Integer
```

4

```
Dim Ar As Variant
Dim vfr() As String
Dim vto() As String
ReDim vfr(1 To Len(frStr))
ReDim vto(1 To Len(frStr))
'place the strings into an array
For j = 1 To Len(frStr)
    vfr(j) = Mid(frStr, j, 1)
    If Mid(toStr, j, 1) <> "" Then
        vto(j) = Mid(toStr, j, 1)
    Else
        vto(j) = ""
    End If
Next j
'compare each character and substitute if needed
If IsArray(trStr) Then
    Ar = trStr
    For iRow = LBound(Ar, 1) To UBound(Ar, 1)
        For iCol = LBound(Ar, 2) To UBound(Ar, 2)
            For j = 1 To Len(frStr)
                Ar(iRow, iCol) = Application.Substitute(Ar(iRow, iCol), _
            vfr(j), vto(j))
            Next j
        Next iCol
    Next iRow
Else
    Ar = trStr
    For j = 1 To Len(frStr)
        Ar = Application.Substitute(Ar, vfr(j), vto(j))
    Next j
End If
MSUBSTITUTE = Ar
End Function
```


Retrieve Numbers from Mixed Text

This function extracts and returns numbers from text that is a mix of numbers and letters, as shown in Figure 4.12:

```
RetrieveNumbers (myString)
```

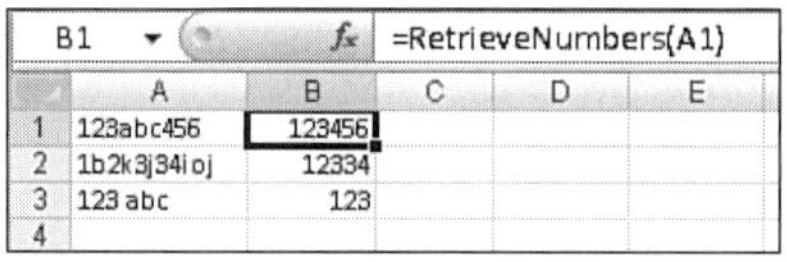

B1 =RetrieveNumbers(A1)

	A	B	C	D	E
1	123abc456	123456			
2	1b2k3j34ioj	12334			
3	123 abc	123			
4					

Figure 4.12
Extract numbers from mixed text.

The argument is `myString`, the text containing the numbers to be extracted.

Function example:

```
Function RetrieveNumbers(myString As String)
Dim i As Integer, j As Integer
Dim OnlyNums As String
'starting at the END of the string and moving backwards (Step -1)
For i = Len(myString) To 1 Step -1
```

```
'IsNumeric is a VBA function that returns True if a variable is a number
'When a number is found, it is added to the OnlyNums string
    If IsNumeric(Mid(myString, i, 1)) Then
        j = j + 1
        OnlyNums = Mid(myString, i, 1) & OnlyNums
    End If
    If j = 1 Then OnlyNums = CInt(Mid(OnlyNums, 1, 1))
Next i
RetrieveNumbers = CLng(OnlyNums)
End Function
```

Convert Week Number into Date

Ever receive a spreadsheet report and all the headers showed the week number? I don't know about you, but I don't know what Week 15 actually is. I would have to get out my calendar and count the weeks. And what if you need to look at a past year? What we need is a nice little function that will convert Week ## Year into the date of the Monday for that week, as shown in Figure 4.13:

```
Weekday(Str)
```

Figure 4.13
Convert a week number into a date more easily referenced.

	A	B	C
1	Week 15 2007	April 9, 2007	
2		=convertWEEKDAY(A1)	
3			

The argument is `Str`, the week to be converted in `"Week ##, YYYY"` format.

> **NOTE** The result must be formatted as a date.

Function example:

```
Function ConvertWeekDay(Str As String) As Date
Dim Week As Long
Dim FirstMon As Date
Dim TStr As String
FirstMon = DateSerial(Right(Str, 4), 1, 1)
FirstMon = FirstMon - FirstMon Mod 7 + 2
TStr = Right(Str, Len(Str) - 5)
Week = Left(TStr, InStr(1, TStr, " ", 1)) + 0
ConvertWeekDay = FirstMon + (Week - 1) * 7
End Function
```

Separate Delimited String

In this example, you need to paste a column of delimited data. You could use Excel's Text to Columns, but you need only an element or two from each cell. Text to Columns parses the entire thing. What you need is a function that lets you specify the number of the element in a string that you need, as shown in Figure 4.14:

```
StringElement(str,chr,ind)
```

Figure 4.14
Extracting a single element from delimited text.

	A	B	C	D	E	F	G	H
1					ind			
2	str	chr	1	2	3	4	5	6
3	A|B|C|D|E|F	|	A	B	C	D	E	F
4			=StringElement($A$3,$B$3,C2)					
5								

The arguments are as follows:

str—The string to be parsed

chr—The delimiter

ind—The position of the element to be returned

Function example:

```
Function StringElement(str As String, chr As String, ind As Integer)
Dim arr_str As Variant
arr_str = Split(str, chr) 'Not compatible with XL97
StringElement = arr_str(ind - 1)
End Function
```

Sort and Concatenate

What about taking a column of data, sorting it, and concatenating it, using a comma (,) as the delimiter (see Figure 4.15)?

```
SortConcat(Rng)
```

Figure 4.15
Sort and concatenate a range of variables.

	A	B
1	Unsorted List	Sorted String
2	q	1,14,50,9,a,f,gg,q,r,rrrr
3	r	=sortConcat(A2:A11)
4	f	
5	a	
6	gg	
7	1	
8	9	
9	50	
10	14	
11	rrrrr	
12		

The argument is Rng, the range of data to be sorted and concatenated. SortConcat calls another procedure, BubbleSort, that must be included.

Function example:

```
Function SortConcat(Rng As Range) As Variant
Dim MySum As String, arr1() As String
Dim j As Integer, i As Integer
```

```
Dim cl As Range
Dim concat As Variant
On Error GoTo FuncFail:
'initialize output
SortConcat = 0#
'avoid user issues
If Rng.Count = 0 Then Exit Function
'get range into variant variable holding array
ReDim arr1(1 To Rng.Count)
'fill array
i = 1
For Each cl In Rng
    arr1(i) = cl.Value
    i = i + 1
Next
'sort array elements
Call BubbleSort(arr1)
'create string from array elements
For j = UBound(arr1) To 1 Step -1
    If Not IsEmpty(arr1(j)) Then
        MySum = arr1(j) & ", " & MySum
    End If
Next j
'assign value to function
SortConcat = Left(MySum, Len(MySum) - 2)
'exit point
concat_exit:
Exit Function
'display error in cell
FuncFail:
SortConcat = Err.Number & " - " & Err.Description
Resume concat_exit
End Function
```

The following function is the ever-popular `BubbleSort`, a program used by many to do a simple sort of data:

```
Sub BubbleSort(List() As String)
'   Sorts the List array in ascending order
Dim First As Integer, Last As Integer
Dim i As Integer, j As Integer
Dim Temp
First = LBound(List)
Last = UBound(List)
For i = First To Last - 1
    For j = i + 1 To Last
        If UCase(List(i)) > UCase(List(j)) Then
            Temp = List(j)
            List(j) = List(i)
            List(i) = Temp
        End If
    Next j
Next i
End Sub
```

Sort Numeric and Alpha Characters

This function takes a mixed range of numeric and alpha characters and sorts them—numerically first and then alphabetically. The result is placed in an array that can be displayed on a worksheet through the use of an array formula, as shown in Figure 4.16:

```
sorter(Rng)
```

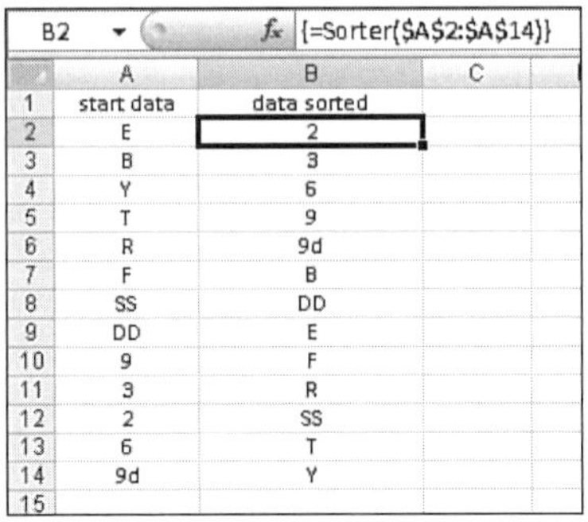

B2 {=Sorter($A$2:$A$14)}

	A	B	C
1	start data	data sorted	
2	E	2	
3	B	3	
4	Y	6	
5	T	9	
6	R	9d	
7	F	B	
8	SS	DD	
9	DD	E	
10	9	F	
11	3	R	
12	2	SS	
13	6	T	
14	9d	Y	
15			

Figure 4.16 Sort a mixed alphanumeric list.

The argument is `Rng`, the range to be sorted.

Function example:

```
Function sorter(Rng As Range) As Variant
'returns an array
Dim arr1() As Variant
If Rng.Columns.Count > 1 Then Exit Function
arr1 = Application.Transpose(Rng)
QuickSort arr1
sorter = Application.Transpose(arr1)
End Function
```

The function uses the following two procedures to sort the data in the range:

```
Public Sub QuickSort(ByRef vntArr As Variant,
    Optional ByVal lngLeft As Long = -2, _
    Optional ByVal lngRight As Long = -2)
Dim i, j, lngMid As Long
Dim vntTestVal As Variant
If lngLeft = -2 Then lngLeft = LBound(vntArr)
If lngRight = -2 Then lngRight = UBound(vntArr)
If lngLeft < lngRight Then
    lngMid = (lngLeft + lngRight) \ 2
    vntTestVal = vntArr(lngMid)
    i = lngLeft
    j = lngRight
    Do
        Do While vntArr(i) < vntTestVal
            i = i + 1
        Loop
        Do While vntArr(j) > vntTestVal
            j = j - 1
```

```
            Loop
            If i <= j Then
                Call SwapElements(vntArr, i, j)
                i = i + 1
                j = j - 1
            End If
        Loop Until i > j
        If j <= lngMid Then
            Call QuickSort(vntArr, lngLeft, j)
            Call QuickSort(vntArr, i, lngRight)
        Else
            Call QuickSort(vntArr, i, lngRight)
            Call QuickSort(vntArr, lngLeft, j)
        End If
    End If
End Sub

Private Sub SwapElements(ByRef vntItems As Variant,
    ByVal lngItem1 As Long, _
    ByVal lngItem2 As Long)
Dim vntTemp As Variant
vntTemp = vntItems(lngItem2)
vntItems(lngItem2) = vntItems(lngItem1)
vntItems(lngItem1) = vntTemp
End Sub
```

Search for a String within Text

Ever needed to find out which cells contain a specific string of text? This function can search strings in a range, looking for specified text. It returns a result identifying which cells contain the text, as shown in Figure 4.17:

```
ContainsText(Rng,Text)
```

Figure 4.17
Return a result identifying which cell(s) contain(s) a specified string.

	A	B	C	D	E
1	This is an apple	A3	=ContainsText(A1:A3,"banana")		
2	This is an orange	A1,A2	=ContainsText(A1:A3,"This is")		
3	Here is a banana				
4					

The arguments are as follows:

Rng—The range in which to search

Text—The text for which to search

Function example:

```
Function ContainsText(Rng As Range, Text As String) As String
Dim T As String
Dim myCell As Range
For Each myCell In Rng 'look in each cell
    If InStr(myCell.Text, Text) > 0 Then 'look in the string for the text
        If Len(T) = 0 Then 'if the text is found, add the address to my result
```

```
            T = myCell.Address(False, False)
        Else
            T = T & "," & myCell.Address(False, False)
        End If
    End If
Next myCell
ContainsText = T
End Function
```

Reverse the Contents of a Cell

This function is mostly fun, but you might find it useful—it reverses the contents of a cell:

```
ReverseContents(myCell, IsText)
```

The arguments are as follows:

> myCell—The specified cell
>
> IsText—(Optional) Whether the cell value should be treated as text (default) or a number

Function example:

```
Function ReverseContents(myCell As Range, Optional IsText As Boolean = True)
Dim i As Integer
Dim OrigString As String, NewString As String
OrigString = Trim(myCell) 'remove leading and trailing spaces
For i = 1 To Len(OrigString)
'by adding the variable NewString to the character,
'instead of adding the character to NewStringthe string is reversed
    NewString = Mid(OrigString, i, 1) & NewString
Next i
If IsText = False Then
    ReverseContents = CLng(NewString)
Else
    ReverseContents = NewString
End If
End Function
```

Multiple Max

MAX finds and returns the maximum value in a range, but it doesn't tell you whether there is more than one maximum value. This function returns the address(es) of the maximum value(s) in a range, as shown in Figure 4.18:

```
ReturnMaxs(Rng)
```

The argument is Rng, the range to search for the maximum value(s).

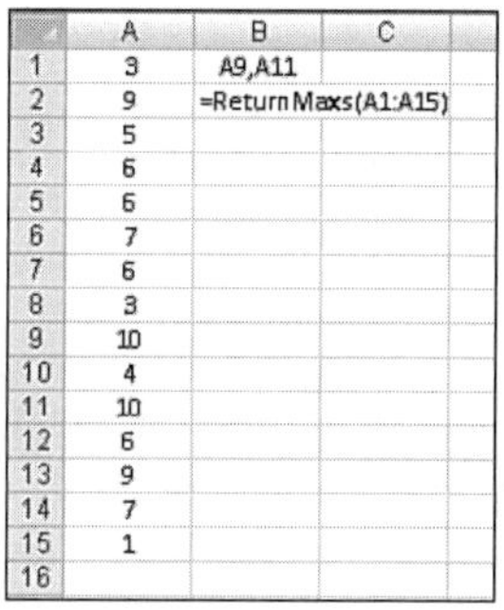

Figure 4.18

Return the addresses of all maximum values in a range.

	A	B	C
1	3	A9,A11	
2	9	=ReturnMaxs(A1:A15)	
3	5		
4	6		
5	6		
6	7		
7	6		
8	3		
9	10		
10	4		
11	10		
12	6		
13	9		
14	7		
15	1		
16			

Function example:

```
Function ReturnMaxs(Rng As Range) As String
Dim Mx As Double
Dim myCell As Range
'if there is only one cell in the range, then exit
If Rng.Count = 1 Then ReturnMaxs = Rng.Address(False, False): Exit Function
Mx = Application.Max(Rng) 'uses Excel's Max to find the max in the range
'Because you now know what the max value is,
'search the ranging finding matches and return the address
For Each myCell In Rng
    If myCell = Mx Then
        If Len(ReturnMaxs) = 0 Then
            ReturnMaxs = myCell.Address(False, False)
        Else
            ReturnMaxs = ReturnMaxs & ", " & myCell.Address(False, False)
        End If
    End If
Next myCell
End Function
```

Return Hyperlink Address

You've received a spreadsheet with a list of hyperlinked information. You want to see the actual links, not the descriptive text. You could just right-click it and choose Edit Hyperlink, but you want something more permanent. This function extracts the hyperlink address, as shown in Figure 4.19:

```
GetAddress(Hyperlink)
```

Figure 4.19

Extract the hyperlink address from behind a hyperlink.

	A	B	C	D
1	Tracy Syrstad	Tracy@MrExcel.com	=GetAddress(A1)	
2	The Best Site for Excel Answers	http://www.mrexcel.com/		
3				

The argument is Hyperlink, the hyperlinked cell from which you want the address extracted.

Function example:

```
Function GetAddress(HyperlinkCell As Range)
    GetAddress = Replace(HyperlinkCell.Hyperlinks(1).Address, "mailto:", "")
End Function
```

Return the Column Letter of a Cell Address

You can use CELL("Col") to return a column number; but what if you need the column letter? This function extracts the column letter from a cell address, as shown in Figure 4.20:

```
ColName(Rng)
```

Figure 4.20
Return the column letter of a cell address.

	A	B
1	A	=ColName(A1)
2	XFD	=ColName(XFD1048576)
3		

The argument is Rng, the cell for which you want the column letter.

Function example:

```
Function ColName(Rng As Range) As String
ColName = Left(Rng.Range("A1").Address(True, False), _
    InStr(1, Rng.Range("A1").Address(True, False), "$", 1) - 1)
End Function
```

Static Random

The function =RAND() can prove very useful for creating random numbers, but it constantly recalculates. What if you need random numbers, but don't want them to change constantly? The following function places a random number, but the number changes only if you force the cell to recalculate, as shown in Figure 4.21:

```
StaticRAND()
```

Figure 4.21
Produce random numbers not quite so volatile.

	A	B
1	0.129781902	=StaticRAND()
2	41.21850133	=StaticRAND()*100
3	34.82	=StaticRAND()*100
4		

There are no arguments for this function.

Function example:

```
Function StaticRAND() As Double
Randomize
STATICRAND = Rnd
End Function
```

Using Select Case **on a Worksheet**

Have you ever nested an If...Then...Else on a worksheet to return a value? The Select...Case statement available in VBA case makes this a lot easier, but you can't use Select...Case statements in a worksheet formula. Instead, you can create a UDF (see Figure 4.22).

Figure 4.22
An example of using a Select...Case structure in a UDF rather than nested If...Then statements.

	A	B	C	D
1	mth	yr		
2	4	2007		
3				
4	period:			
5	October 1, 2006 through October 31, 2006			
6	=State_Period(A2,B2)			
7				
8				

The following function shows how you can use Select statements to produce the results of a nested If...Then statement:

```
Function state_period(mth As Integer, yr As Integer)
Select Case mth
  Case 1
    state_period = "July 1, " & yr - 1 & " through July 31, " & yr - 1
  Case 2
    state_period = "August 1, " & yr - 1 & " through August 31, " & yr - 1
  Case 3
    state_period = "September 1, " & yr - 1 & " through September 30, " & yr - 1
  Case 4
    state_period = "October 1, " & yr - 1 & " through October 31, " & yr - 1
  Case 5
    state_period = "November 1, " & yr - 1 & " through November 30, " & yr - 1
  Case 6
    state_period = "December 1, " & yr - 1 & " through December 31, " & yr - 1
  Case 7
    state_period = "January 1, " & yr & " through January 31, " & yr
  Case 8
    state_period = "February 1, " & yr & " through February 28, " & yr
  Case 9
    state_period = "March 1, " & yr & " through March 31, " & yr
  Case 10
    state_period = "April 1, " & yr & " through April 30, " & yr
  Case 11
    state_period = "May 1, " & yr & " through May 31, " & yr
  Case 12
    state_period = "June 1, " & yr & " through June 30, " & yr
  Case 13
    state_period = "Pre-Final"
  Case 14
    state_period = "Closeout"
End Select
End Function
```

4

Next Steps

The next chapter describes a fundamental component of any programming language: loops. You will be familiar with basic loop structures if you've taken any programming classes, and VBA supports all the usual loops. You will also learn about a special loop, For Each...Next, which is unique to object-oriented programming, such as VBA.

4

Looping and Flow Control

5

Loops are a fundamental component of any programming language. If you've taken any programming classes, even BASIC, you've likely encountered a `For...Next` loop. Luckily, VBA supports all the usual loops, plus a special loop that is excellent to use with VBA.

This chapter covers the basic loop constructs:

- `For...Next`
- `Do...While`
- `Do...Until`
- `While...Loop`
- `Until...Loop`

We also discuss the cool loop construct unique to object-oriented languages:

- `For Each...Next`

For...Next **Loops**

`For` and `Next` are common loop constructs. Everything between `For` and `Next` is run multiple times. Each time that the code runs, a certain counter variable (specified in the `For` statement) has a different value.

Consider this code:

```
For I = 1 to 10
    Cells(I, I).Value = I
Next I
```

As this program starts to run, we've given the counter variable a name of `I`. The first time through the code, the variable `I` is set to 1. The first time that the loop is executed, `I` is equal to 1, so the cell in Row 1, Column 1 will be set to 1 (see Figure 5.1).

Figure 5.1

After the first iteration through the loop, the cell in Row 1, Column 1 has the value of 1.

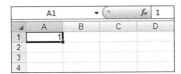

Let's take a close look at what happens as VBA gets to the line that says `Next I`. Before running this line, the variable `I` is equal to 1. During the execution of `Next I`, VBA must make a decision. VBA adds 1 to the variable `I` and compares it to the maximum value in the `To` clause of the `For` statement. If it is within the limits specified in the `To` clause, the loop is not finished. In this case, the value of `I` will be incremented to 2. Code execution then moves back to the first line of code after the `For` statement. Figure 5.2 shows the state of the program before running the `Next` line. Figure 5.3 shows what happens after executing the `Next` line.

Figure 5.2

Before running the `Next I` statement, `I` is equal to 1. VBA can safely add 1 to `I` and it will be less than the 10 specified in the `To` clause of the `For` statement.

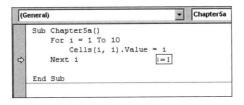

Figure 5.3

After running the `Next I` statement, `I` is incremented to 2. Code execution continues with the line of code immediately following the `For` statement.

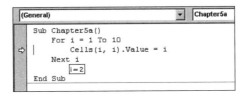

The second time through the loop, the value of `I` is 2. The cell in Row 2, Column 2 (that is, cell B2) gets a value of 2 (see Figure 5.4).

Figure 5.4

After the second time through the loop, cells A1 and B2 are filled in.

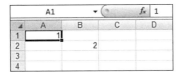

As the process continues, the `Next I` statement advances `I` up to 3, 4, and so on. On the tenth pass through the loop, the cell in Row 10, Column 10 is assigned a value of 10.

It is interesting to watch what happens to the variable I on the last pass through Next I. In Figure 5.5, you can see that before executing Next I the tenth time, the variable I is equal to 10.

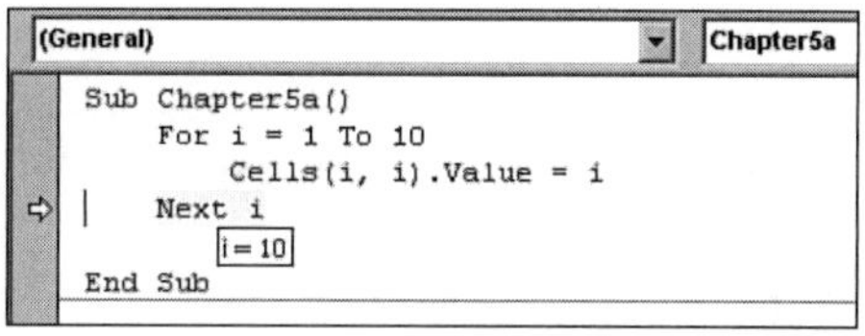

Figure 5.5
Before running Next I for the tenth time, the variable I is equal to 10.

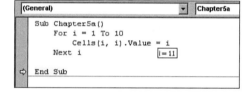

VBA is now at a decision point. It adds 1 to the variable I. I is now equal to 11, which is greater than the limit in the For...Next loop. VBA then moves execution to the next line in the macro after the Next statement (see Figure 5.6). In case you are tempted to use the variable I later in the macro, it is important to realize that it might be incremented beyond the limit specified in the To clause of the For statement.

Figure 5.6
After incrementing I to 11, code execution moves to the line after the Next statement.

At the end of the loop, you get the result shown in Figure 5.7.

Figure 5.7
After the loop completes all ten iterations, this is the result.

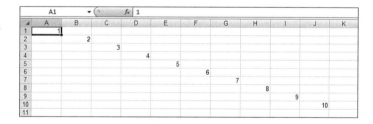

The common use for such a loop is to walk through all the rows in a dataset and decide to perform some action on the basis of some criteria. For example, if you want to mark all the rows with positive service revenue in Column F, you could use this loop:

```
For I = 2 to 10
    If Cells(I, 6).Value > 0 Then
        Cells(I, 8).Value = "Service Revenue"
        Cells(I, 1).Resize(1, 8).Interior.ColorIndex = 4
    End If
Next i
```

This loop checks each item of data from Row 2 through Row 10. If there is a positive number in Column F, Column H of that row will have a new label, and the cells in Columns A:H of the row will be colored green. After running this macro, the results look like Figure 15.8.

Figure 5.8
After the loop completes all nine iterations, any rows with positive values in Column F are colored green and have the label "Service Revenue" added to Column H.

	A	B	C	D	E	F	G	H	I
1	InvoiceDate	InvoiceNumber	SalesRepNumber	CustomerNumber	ProductRevenue	ServiceRevenue	ProductCost		
2	6/9/2008	123829	S21	C8754	21000	0	9875		
3	6/9/2008	123834	S54	C7796	339000	0	195298		
4	6/9/2008	123835	S21	C1654	161000	0	90761		
5	6/9/2008	123836	S45	C6460	275500	10000	146341	Service Revenue	
6	6/9/2008	123837	S54	C5143	925400	0	473515		
7	6/9/2008	123841	S21	C8361	94400	0	53180		
8	6/9/2008	123842	S45	C1842	36500	55000	20696	Service Revenue	
9	6/9/2008	123843	S54	C4107	599700	0	276718		
10	6/9/2008	123844	S21	C5205	244900	0	143393		

Using Variables in the For **Statement**

The previous example is not very useful in that it works only when there are exactly ten rows of data. It is possible to use a variable to specify the upper/lower limit of the For statement. This code sample identifies FinalRow with data, and then loops from Row 2 to that row:

```
FinalRow = Cells(Rows.Count, 1).End(xlUp).Row
For I = 2 to FinalRow
    If Cells(I, 6).Value > 0 Then
        Cells(I, 8).Value = "Service Revenue"
        Cells(I, 1).Resize(1, 8).Interior.ColorIndex = 4
    End If
Next I
```

Exercise caution when using variables. What if the imported file today is empty and has only a heading row? In this case, the FinalRow variable is equal to 1. This makes the first statement of the loop essentially say, "For I = 2 to 1." Because the start number is higher than the end number, the loop does not execute at all. The variable I is equal to 2, and code execution jumps to the line after Next.

Variations on the For...Next **Loop**

In a For...Next loop, it is possible to have the loop variable jump up by something other than 1. You might use it to apply green-bar formatting to every other row in a dataset, for example. In this case, you would want to have the counter variable I examine every other row in the dataset. Indicate this by adding the Step clause to the end of the For statement:

```
FinalRow = Cells(Rows.Count, 1).End(xlUp).Row
For i = 2 to FinalRow Step 2
    Cells(i, 1).Resize(1, 8).Interior.ColorIndex = 35
Next i
```

While running this code, VBA adds a light green shading to Rows 2, 4, 6, and so on (see Figure 5.9).

The Step clause can easily be any number. You might want to check every tenth row of a dataset to extract a random sample. In this case, you would use Step 10:

```
FinalRow = Cells(Rows.Count, 1).End(xlUp).Row
NextRow = FinalRow + 5
Cells(NextRow-1, 1).Value = "Random Sample of Above Data"
For I = 2 to FinalRow Step 10
    Cells(I, 1).Resize(1, 8).Copy Destination:=Cells(NextRow, 1)
    NextRow = NextRow + 1
Next i
```

Figure 5.9

The Step clause in the For statement of the loop causes the action to occur on every other row.

	A	B	C	D	E	F	G	H
1	InvoiceDate	InvoiceNumber	SalesRepNumber	CustomerNumber	ProductRevenue	ServiceRevenue	ProductCost	
2	6/7/2004	123829	S21	C8754	21000	0	9875	
3	6/7/2004	123830	S45	C3390	188100	0	85083	
4	6/7/2004	123831	S54	C2523	510600	0	281158	
5	6/7/2004	123832	S21	C5519	86200	0	49967	
6	6/7/2004	123833	S45	C3245	800100	0	388277	
7	6/7/2004	123834	S54	C7796	339000	0	195298	
8	6/7/2004	123835	S21	C1654	161000	0	90761	
9	6/7/2004	123836	S45	C6460	275500	10000	146341	
10	6/7/2004	123837	S54	C5143	925400	0	473515	
11	6/7/2004	123838	S21	C7868	148200	0	75700	
12	6/7/2004	123839	S45	C3310	890200	0	468333	
13	6/7/2004	123840	S54	C2959	986000	0	528980	
14	6/7/2004	123841	S21	C8361	94400	0	53180	
15	6/7/2004	123842	S45	C1842	36500	55000	20696	
16	6/7/2004	123843	S54	C4107	599700	0	276718	
17	6/7/2004	123844	S21	C5205	244900	0	143393	
18	6/7/2004	123845	S45	C7745	63000	0	35102	
19	6/7/2004	123846	S54	C1730	212600	0	117787	
20	6/7/2004	123847	S21	C6292	974700	0	478731	
21	6/7/2004	123848	S45	C2008	327700	0	170968	
22	6/7/2004	123849	S54	C4096	30700	0	18056	
23								

You can also have a For...Next loop run backward from high to low. This is particularly useful if you are selectively deleting rows. To do this, reverse the order of the For statement and have the Step clause specify a negative number:

```
' Delete all rows where column C is the Internal rep - S54
FinalRow = Cells(Rows.Count, 1).End(xlUp).Row
For I = FinalRow to 2 Step -1
    If Cells(I, 3).Value = "S54" Then
        Cells(I, 1).EntireRow.Delete
    End If
Next i
```

Exiting a Loop Early after a Condition Is Met

Sometimes you don't need to execute the whole loop. Perhaps you just need to read through the dataset until you find one record that meets a certain criteria. In this case, you want to find the first record and then stop the loop. A statement called Exit For does this.

The following sample macro looks for a row in the dataset where service revenue in Column F is positive and product revenue in Column E is 0. If such a row is found, you might indicate a message that the file needs manual processing today and move the cell pointer to that row:

5

```
' Are there any special processing situations in the data?
FinalRow = Cells(Rows.Count, 1).End(xlUp).Row
ProblemFound = False
For I = 2 to FinalRow
    If Cells(I, 6).Value > 0 Then
        If cells(I, 5).Value = 0 Then
            Cells(I, 6).Select
            ProblemFound = True
            Exit For
        End If
    End If
Next I
If ProblemFound Then
    MsgBox "There is a problem at row " & I
    Exit Sub
End If
```

Nesting One Loop Inside Another Loop

It is okay to run a loop inside another loop. Perhaps the first loop is running through all the rows in your recordset. The second loop then might run through all the columns in your recordset. Consider the dataset shown in Figure 5.10.

Figure 5.10
By nesting one loop inside the other, VBA can loop through each row and then each column.

	A	B	C	D	E	F	G	H	I	J	K	L	M
1	Item	January	February	March	April	May	June	July	August	September	October	November	December
2	Hardware Revenue	1,972,637	1,655,321	1,755,234	1,531,060	1,345,699	1,172,668	1,644,299	1,538,936	1,975,409	1,197,156	1,144,025	1,533,728
3	Software Revenue	236,716	198,639	210,628	183,727	161,484	140,720	197,316	184,672	237,049	143,659	137,283	184,047
4	Service Revenue	473,433	397,277	421,256	367,454	322,968	281,440	394,632	369,345	474,098	287,317	274,566	368,095
5	Cost of Good Sold	1,084,951	910,427	965,379	842,083	740,135	644,967	904,364	846,415	1,086,475	658,436	629,214	843,550
6	Selling Expense	394,527	331,064	351,047	306,212	269,140	234,534	328,860	307,787	395,082	239,431	228,805	306,746
7	G&A Expense	150,000	150,000	150,000	150,000	150,000	150,000	150,000	150,000	150,000	150,000	150,000	150,000
8	R&D	125,000	125,000	125,000	125,000	125,000	125,000	125,000	125,000	125,000	125,000	125,000	125,000

```
' Loop through each row and column
' Add a checkerboard format
FinalRow = Cells(Rows.Count, 1).End(xlUp).Row
FinalCol = Cells(1, 255).End(xlToLeft).Column
For I = 2 to FinalRow
    ' For even numbered rows, start in column 1
    ' For odd numbered rows, start in column 2
    If I Mod 2 = 1 Then
        StartCol = 1
    Else
        StartCol = 2
    End If
    For J = StartCol to FinalCol Step 2
        Cells(I, J).Interior.ColorIndex = 35
    Next J
Next I
```

In this code, the outer loop is using the I counter variable to loop through all the rows in the dataset. The inner loop is using the J counter variable to loop through all the columns in that row. Because Figure 5.10 has seven data rows, the code runs through the I loop seven times. Each time through the I loop, the code runs through the J loop six or seven times. This means that the line of code that is inside the J loop ends up being executed several times for each pass through the I loop. Figure 5.11 shows the result.

Figure 5.11

The result of nesting one loop inside the other; VBA can loop through each row and then each column.

Do **Loops**

There are several variations of the Do loop. The most basic Do loop is great for doing a bunch of some mundane task. I once had someone send me a list of addresses going down a column, as shown in Figure 5.12.

Figure 5.12

Someone sent addresses typed in this format, but it is more useful to have them in a database format so that they can later be used in a mail merge.

◢	A
1	
2	John Smith
3	123 Main Street
4	Akron OH 44308
5	
6	Jane Doe
7	245 State Street
8	Chicago IL 60011
9	
10	Ralph Emerson
11	345 2nd Ave
12	New York NY 10011
13	
14	George Washington
15	456 3rd St
16	Philadelphia PA 12345
17	
18	John Adams
19	543 4th Ave
20	Baltimore MD 12345
21	
22	Thomas Jefferson
23	654 5th Ave
24	Roanoke VA 12345
25	
26	James Madison
27	987 6th St
28	Hollywood CA 12345
29	

I needed to rearrange these addresses into a database with name in Column B, street in Column C, city and state in Column D. By setting Relative Recording (see Chapter 1, "Unleash the Power of Excel with VBA") and using a hot key of Ctrl+A, I recorded this little bit of useful code. The code is designed to copy one single address into database format. It also navigates the cell pointer to the name of the next address in the list. This allowed me to sit at my desk, and each time that I pressed Ctrl+A, it would reformat one address for me.

→ For a discussion of Relative Recording, **see** "A Possible Solution: Using Relative References When Recording," **p. 25**, in Chapter 1.

```
Sub Macro3()
'
' Macro3 Macro
' Macro recorded 10/29/2003 by Bill Jelen
```

```
' Move one address into database format.
' Then move the cell pointer to the start of the next address.
'
' Keyboard Shortcut: Ctrl+Shift+A
'
    Selection.Copy
    ActiveCell.Offset(0, 1).Range("A1").Select
    ActiveSheet.Paste
    ActiveCell.Offset(1, -1).Range("A1").Select
    Application.CutCopyMode = False
    Selection.Copy
    ActiveCell.Offset(-1, 2).Range("A1").Select
    ActiveSheet.Paste
    ActiveCell.Offset(2, -2).Range("A1").Select
    Application.CutCopyMode = False
    Selection.Copy
    ActiveCell.Offset(-2, 3).Range("A1").Select
    ActiveSheet.Paste
    ActiveCell.Offset(4, -3).Range("A1").Select
End Sub
```

> **NOTE**
>
> I am not suggesting that the preceding code is suitable for a professional application. However, sometimes we are writing macros just to automate a one-time mundane task.

Without a macro, I would have done a lot of copying and pasting manually. Now, with the preceding recorded macro, I could place the cell pointer on a name in Column A and press Ctrl+Shift+A. That one address would be copied into three columns, and the cell pointer would move to the start of the next address (see Figure 5.13).

Figure 5.13
After running the macro once, one address is moved into the proper format and the cell pointer is positioned to run the macro again.

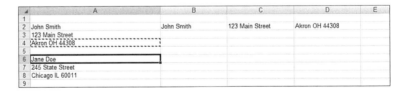

I was pretty happy with this macro because it allowed me to process an address every second using the hot key. I soon realized that I had 5,000 addresses and I didn't want to keep running the same macro over and over.

Using a Do...Loop, I could set up the macro to run continuously. If I were to just enclose the recorded code with Do at the top and Loop at the end, VBA would continuously run my code over and over. This would allow me to sit back and watch the code do the work. This insanely boring task was now done in minutes rather than hours.

Note that this particular Do...Loop will run forever. There is no mechanism to stop it. That worked for the task at hand—I could watch the progress on the screen and after the program had advanced past the end of this database, I just pressed Ctrl+Break to stop execution:

```
Sub Macro3()
'
' Macro3 Macro
' Macro recorded 10/29/2003 by Bill Jelen
' Move one address into database format.
' Then move the cell pointer to the start of the next address.
'
' Keyboard Shortcut: Ctrl+Shift+A
'
Do
    Selection.Copy
    ActiveCell.Offset(0, 1).Range("A1").Select
    ActiveSheet.Paste
    ActiveCell.Offset(1, -1).Range("A1").Select
    Application.CutCopyMode = False
    Selection.Copy
    ActiveCell.Offset(-1, 2).Range("A1").Select
    ActiveSheet.Paste
    ActiveCell.Offset(2, -2).Range("A1").Select
    Application.CutCopyMode = False
    Selection.Copy
    ActiveCell.Offset(-2, 3).Range("A1").Select
    ActiveSheet.Paste
    ActiveCell.Offset(4, -3).Range("A1").Select
Loop
End Sub
```

All of these examples are "quick and dirty" loops. They are great for when you need to accomplish a task quickly. The Do...Loop provides a number of options to allow you to automatically have the program stop when it accomplishes the end of the task.

The first option is to have a line in the Do...Loop that detects the end of the dataset and exits the loop. In the current example, this could be accomplished by using the Exit Do command in an If statement. If the current cell is on a cell that is empty, you can assume that you've reached the end of the data and stopped processing the loop:

```
Do
    If Not Selection.Value > "" Then Exit Do
    Selection.Copy
    ActiveCell.Offset(0, 1).Range("A1").Select
    ActiveSheet.Paste
    ActiveCell.Offset(1, -1).Range("A1").Select
    Application.CutCopyMode = False
    Selection.Copy
    ActiveCell.Offset(-1, 2).Range("A1").Select
    ActiveSheet.Paste
    ActiveCell.Offset(2, -2).Range("A1").Select
    Application.CutCopyMode = False
    Selection.Copy
    ActiveCell.Offset(-2, 3).Range("A1").Select
    ActiveSheet.Paste
    ActiveCell.Offset(4, -3).Range("A1").Select
Loop
End Sub
```

5

Using the While or Until **Clause in** Do **Loops**

There are four variations of using While or Until. These clauses can be added to either the Do statement or the Loop statement. In every case, the While or Until clause includes some test that evaluates to True or False.

With a Do While <test expression>...Loop construct, the loop is never executed if <test expression> is false. If you are reading records from a text file, you cannot assume that the file has one or more records, so you need to test to see whether you are already at the end of file with the EOF function before you enter the loop:

```
' Read a text file, skipping the Total lines
    Open "C:\Invoice.txt" For Input As #1
    R = 1
    Do While Not EOF(1)
        Line Input #FileNumber, Data
        If Not Left (Data, 5) = "TOTAL" Then
            ' Import this row
            r = r + 1
            Cells(r, 1).Value = Data
        End If
    Loop
    Close #1
```

In this example, I used the NOT keyword. EOF(1) evaluates to True after there are no more records to be read from invoice.txt. Some programmers believe it is hard to read a program that contains a lot of NOTs. To avoid the use of NOT, use the Do Until <test expression> ...Loop construct:

```
' Read a text file, skipping the Total lines
    Open "C:\Invoice.txt" For Input As #1
    R = 1
    Do Until EOF(1)
        Line Input #1, Data
        If Not (Data, 5) = "TOTAL" Then
            ' Import this row
            r = r + 1
            Cells(r, 1).Value = Data
        End If
    Loop
    Close #1
```

In other examples, you always want the loop to be executed the first time. In these cases, you move the While or Until instruction to the end of the loop. This code sample asks the user to enter sales amounts made that day. It continually asks them for sales amounts until they enter a zero:

```
TotalSales = 0
Do
    x = InputBox(Prompt:="Enter Amount of Next Invoice. Enter 0 when done.")
    TotalSales = TotalSales + x
Loop Until x = 0
MsgBox "The total for today is $" & TotalSales
```

In the following loop, a check amount is entered, and then it looks for open invoices to which to apply the check. It is often the case that a single check is received, and it covers many invoices. This program sequentially applies the check to the oldest invoices until 100 percent of the check has been applied:

```
' Ask for the amount of check received
AmtToApply = InputBox("Enter Amount of Check") + 0
' Loop through the list of open invoices.
' Apply the check to the oldest open invoices and Decrement AmtToApply
NextRow = 2
Do While AmtToApply > 0
    OpenAmt = Cells(NextRow, 3)
    If OpenAmt > AmtToApply Then
        ' Apply total check to this invoice
        Cells(NextRow, 4).Value = AmtToApply
        AmtToApply = 0
    Else
        Cells(NextRow, 4).Value = OpenAmt
        AmtToApply = AmtToApply - OpenAmt
    End If
    NextRow = NextRow + 1
Loop
```

Because you can construct the `Do...Loop` with the `While` or `Until` qualifiers at the beginning or end, you have a lot of subtle control over whether the loop is always executed once, even if the condition is `True` at the beginning.

`While...Wend` **Loops**

`While...Wend` loops are included in VBA for backward compatibility. In the VBA help file, Microsoft suggests that `Do...Loops` are more flexible. However, because you might encounter `While...Wend` loops in code written by others, here is a quick example. In this loop, the first line is always `While` condition. The last line of the loop is always `Wend`. Note that there is no `Exit While` statement. In general, these loops are okay, but the `Do...Loop` construct is more robust and flexible. Because the `Do` loop offers either the `While` or `Until` qualifier, this qualifier can be at the beginning or end of the loop, and there is the possibility to exit a `Do` loop early:

```
' Read a text file, adding the amounts
    Open "C:\Invoice.txt" For Input As #1
    TotalSales = 0
    While Not EOF(1)
        Line Input #1, Data
        TotalSales = TotalSales + Data
    Wend
    MsgBox "Total Sales=" & TotalSales
    Close #1
```

The VBA Loop: `For Each`

This is an excellent loop, and the macro recorder never records this type of loop. VBA is an object-oriented language. It's common to have a collection of objects in Excel, such as a

5

collection of worksheets in a workbook, cells in a range, pivot tables on a worksheet, or data series on a chart.

This special type of loop is great for looping through all the items in the collection. Before discussing this loop in detail, you need to understand a special kind of variable called *object variables.*

Object Variables

At this point, you've seen a variable that contains a single value. When you have a variable such as TotalSales = 0, TotalSales is a normal variable and generally contains only a single value. It is also possible to have a more powerful variable called an *object variable.* An object variable holds many values; basically, any property that is associated with the object is associated with the object variable.

I generally do not take the time to declare my variables. Many books implore you to use the DIM statement to identify all your variables at the top of the procedure. This allows you to specify that a certain variable is of a certain type, such as Integer or Double. Although this saves a tiny bit of memory, it requires you to know up front which variables you plan on using. I tend to invent variables as I go, whipping up a new variable on-the-fly as the need arises. However, there are great benefits to declaring object variables. The VBA AutoComplete feature turns on if you declare an object variable at the top of your procedure. The following lines of code declare three object variables, one as a worksheet, one as a range, and one as a pivot table:

```
Sub Test()
    Dim WSD as Worksheet
    Dim MyCell as Range
    Dim PT as PivotTable
    Set WSD = ThisWorkbook.Worksheets("Data")
    Set MyCell = WSD.Cells(Rows.Count, 1).End(xlUp).Offset(1, 0)
    Set PT = WSD.PivotTables(1)
    …
```

In the preceding example, you can see that just an equals statement is not used to assign object variables. You need to use the Set statement to assign a specific object to the object variable.

There are many great reasons for using object variables, not the least of which is the fact that it can be a great shorthand notation. It is a lot easier to have a lot of lines of code referring to WSD rather than ThisWorkbook.Worksheets("Data").

Also, as mentioned earlier, the object variable inherits all the properties of the object to which it refers.

The For Each...Loop employs an object variable rather than a Counter variable. The following code loops through all the cells in Column A. The code uses the .CurrentRegion property to define the current region and then uses the .Resize property to limit the selected range to a single column. The object variable is called Cell. I could have used any name for the object variable, but `Cell` seems more appropriate than something arbitrary like Fred:

```
For Each cell in Range("A1").CurrentRegion.Resize(, 1)
    If cell.Value = "Total" Then
        cell.resize(1,8).Font.Bold = True
    End If
Next cell
```

This code sample searches all open workbooks, looking for one with a particular sheet name:

```
For Each wb in Workbooks
    If wb.Worksheets(1).Name = "Menu" Then
    WBFound = True
    WBName = wb.Name
    Exit For
End If
Next wb
```

In this code sample, all shapes on the current worksheet are deleted:

```
For Each Sh in ActiveSheet.Shapes
    Sh.Delete
Next Sh
```

This code sample deletes all pivot tables on the current sheet:

```
For Each pt in ActiveSheet.PivotTables
    pt.TableRange2.Clear
Next pt
```

CASE STUDY

Looping Through All Files in a Directory

Here are some useful procedures that make extensive use of loops.

> **NOTE** Creating a list of all files in a directory used to be fairly simple using the `FileSearch` object. For inexplicable reasons, Microsoft stopped supporting `FileSearch` in Excel 2007.

The first procedure uses VBA's `FileSearch` object to find all JPG picture files in a certain directory. Each file is listed down a column in Excel.

The outer `For i` loop iterates through each image file found in a particular folder and all its subfolders. Each pass through the outer loop will return a new path and filename in the variable `ThisEntry`. To separate the path from the filename, the inner `For j` loop will search the path and filename from the end to the beginning, looking for the final path separator:

```
Sub FindJPGFilesInAFolder()
    Dim fso As Object
    Dim strName As String
    Dim strArr(1 To 1048576, 1 To 1) As String, i As Long

    ' Enter the folder name here
    Const strDir As String = "C:\Artwork\"

    Let strName = Dir$(strDir & "*.jpg")
    Do While strName <> vbNullString
        Let i = i + 1
        Let strArr(i, 1) = strDir & strName
        Let strName = Dir$()
    Loop
    Set fso = CreateObject("Scripting.FileSystemObject")
    Call recurseSubFolders(fso.GetFolder(strDir), strArr(), i)
    Set fso = Nothing
    If i > 0 Then
        Range("A1").Resize(i).Value = strArr
    End If

    ' Next, loop through all found files
    ' and break into path and filename
    FinalRow = Cells(Rows.Count, 1).End(xlUp).Row
    For i = 1 To FinalRow
        ThisEntry = Cells(i, 1)
        For j = Len(ThisEntry) To 1 Step -1
            If Mid(ThisEntry, j, 1) = Application.PathSeparator Then
                Cells(i, 2) = Left(ThisEntry, j)
                Cells(i, 3) = Mid(ThisEntry, j + 1)
                Exit For
            End If
        Next j
    Next i

End Sub

Private Sub recurseSubFolders(ByRef Folder As Object, _
    ByRef strArr() As String, _
    ByRef i As Long)
Dim SubFolder As Object
Dim strName As String
For Each SubFolder In Folder.SubFolders
    Let strName = Dir$(SubFolder.Path & "*.jpg")
    Do While strName <> vbNullString
        Let i = i + 1
        Let strArr(i, 1) = SubFolder.Path & strName
        Let strName = Dir$()
    Loop
    Call recurseSubFolders(SubFolder, strArr(), i)
Next
End Sub
```

My idea in this case is that I want to organize the photos into new folders. In Column D, if I want to move a picture to a new folder, I type the path of that folder. The following For Each loop takes care of copying the pictures. Each time through the loop, the object variable named Cell will contain a reference to a cell in Column A. You can use Cell.Offset(0, 3) to return the value from the cell three columns to the right of the range represented by the variable Cell:

```
Sub CopyToNewFolder()
    FinalRow = Cells(Rows.Count, 1).End(xlUp).Row
    For Each Cell In Range("A2:A" & FinalRow)
        OrigFile = Cell.Value
        NewFile = Cell.Offset(0, 3) & Application.PathSeparator & _
            Cell.Offset(0, 2)
        FileCopy OrigFile, NewFile
    Next Cell
End Sub
```

Flow Control: Using If...Then...Else and Select Case

Another aspect of programming that will never be recorded by the macro recorder is the concept of flow control. Sometimes, you do not want every line of your program to be executed every time you run the macro. VBA offers two excellent choices for flow control: the If...Then...Else construct, and the Select Case construct.

Basic Flow Control: If...Then...Else

The most common device for program flow control is the If statement. Suppose, for instance, that you have a list of products as shown in Figure 5.14. You want to loop through each product in the list and copy it to either a Fruits list or a Vegetables list. As a beginning programmer, I was tempted to loop through the rows twice; I wanted to loop through once looking for fruit, and a second time looking for vegetables. However, there is no need to loop through twice. On a single loop, you can use an If...Then...Else construct to copy each row to the correct place.

Figure 5.14

A single loop can look for fruits or vegetables.

▲	A	B	C	D
1	Class	Product	Quantity	
2	Fruit	Apples	1	
3	Fruit	Apricots	3	
4	Vegetable	Apsaragus	62	
5	Fruit	Bananas	55	
6	Fruit	Blueberry	17	
7	Vegetable	Broccoli	56	
8	Vegetable	Cabbage	35	
9	Fruit	Cherries	59	
10	Herbs	Dill	91	
11	Vegetable	Eggplant	94	
12	Fruit	Kiwi	86	

5

Conditions

Any If statement needs a condition that is being tested. The condition should always evaluate to TRUE or FALSE. Here are some examples of simple and complex conditions:

- If Range("A1").Value = "Title" Then

- If Not Range("A1").Value = "Title" Then

- If Range("A1").Value = "Title" And Range("B1").Value = "Fruit" Then

- If Range("A1").Value = "Title" Or Range("B1").Value = "Fruit" Then

If...Then...End If

After the If statement, you may include one or more program lines that will be executed only if the condition is met. You should then close the If block with an End If line. Here is a simple example of an If statement:

```
Sub ColorFruitRedBold()
    FinalRow = Cells(Rows.Count, 1).End(xlUp).Row

    For i = 2 To FinalRow
        If Cells(i, 1).Value = "Fruit" Then
            Cells(i, 1).Resize(1, 3).Font.Bold = True
            Cells(i, 1).Resize(1, 3).Font.ColorIndex = 3
        End If
    Next i

    MsgBox "Fruit is now bold and red"
End Sub
```

Either/Or Decisions: If...Then...Else...End If

Sometimes you will want to do one set of statements if the condition is true, and another set of statements if the condition is not true. To do this with VBA, the second set of conditions would be coded after the Else statement. There is still only one End If statement associated with this construct. Suppose, for example, that you want to color the fruit red and the vegetables green:

```
Sub FruitRedVegGreen()
    FinalRow = Cells(Rows.Count, 1).End(xlUp).Row

    For i = 2 To FinalRow
        If Cells(i, 1).Value = "Fruit" Then
            Cells(i, 1).Resize(1, 3).Font.ColorIndex = 3
        Else
            Cells(i, 1).Resize(1, 3).Font.ColorIndex = 50
        End If
    Next i

    MsgBox "Fruit is red / Veggies are green"
End Sub
```

Using If…Else If…End If **for Multiple Conditions**

Notice that our product list includes one item that is classified as an herb. We really have three conditions for which to test. It is possible to build an If…End If structure with multiple conditions. First, test to see whether the record is a fruit. Next, use an Else If to test whether the record is a vegetable. Then, test to see whether the record is an herb. Finally, if the record is none of those, highlight the record as an error:

```
Sub MultipleIf()
    FinalRow = Cells(Rows.Count, 1).End(xlUp).Row

    For i = 2 To FinalRow
        If Cells(i, 1).Value = "Fruit" Then
            Cells(i, 1).Resize(1, 3).Font.ColorIndex = 3
        ElseIf Cells(i, 1).Value = "Vegetable" Then
            Cells(i, 1).Resize(1, 3).Font.ColorIndex = 50
        ElseIf Cells(i, 1).Value = "Herbs" Then
            Cells(i, 1).Resize(1, 3).Font.ColorIndex = 5
        Else
            ' This must be a record in error
            Cells(i, 1).Resize(1, 3).Interior.ColorIndex = 6
        End If
    Next i

    MsgBox "Fruit is red / Veggies are green / Herbs are blue"
End Sub
```

Using Select Case…End Select **for Multiple Conditions**

When you have many different conditions, it becomes unwieldy to use many Else If statements. VBA offers another construct known as the Select Case construct. In our running example, we always want to check the value of the Class in column A. This value is called the *test expression*. The basic syntax of this construct starts with the words Select Case followed by the test expression:

```
Select Case Cells(i, 1).Value
```

Thinking about our problem in English, you might say, "In cases where the record is fruit, color the record with red." VBA uses a shorthand version of this. You write the word Case followed by the literal "Fruit". Any statements that follow Case "Fruit" will be executed whenever the test expression is a fruit. After these statements, you would have the next Case statement: Case "Vegetables". You would continue in this fashion, writing a Case statement followed by the program lines that will be executed if that case is true.

After you've listed all the possible conditions you can think of, you may optionally include a Case Else section at the end. This section includes what the program should do if the test expression matches none of your cases. Finally, close the entire construct with the End Select statement.

5

The following program does the same operation as the previous macro, but uses a `Select Case` statement:

```
Sub SelectCase()
    FinalRow = Cells(Rows.Count, 1).End(xlUp).Row

    For i = 2 To FinalRow
        Select Case Cells(i, 1).Value
            Case "Fruit"
                Cells(i, 1).Resize(1, 3).Font.ColorIndex = 3
            Case "Vegetable"
                Cells(i, 1).Resize(1, 3).Font.ColorIndex = 50
            Case "Herbs"
                Cells(i, 1).Resize(1, 3).Font.ColorIndex = 5
            Case Else
        End Select
    Next i

    MsgBox "Fruit is red / Veggies are green / Herbs are blue"
End Sub
```

Complex Expressions in Case Statements

It is possible to have fairly complex expressions in `Case` statements. You might want to perform the same actions for all berry records:

```
Case "Strawberry", "Blueberry", "Raspberry"
    AdCode = 1
```

If it makes sense, you might code a range of values in the `Case` statement:

```
Case 1 to 20
    Discount = 0.05
Case 21 to 100
    Discount = 0.1
```

You can include the keyword `Is` and a comparison operator, such as > or <:

```
Case Is < 10
    Discount = 0
Case Is > 100
    Discount = 0.2
Case Else
    Discount = 0.10
```

Nesting If Statements

It is possible and common to nest an `If` statement inside another `If` statement. In this situation, it is very important to use proper indenting. You will find that you often have several `End If` lines at the end of the construct. By having proper indenting, it is easier to tell which `End If` is associated with a particular `If`.

The final macro has a lot of logic. Our discount rules are as follows:

- For Fruit, quantities under 5 cases get no discount.
- Quantities from 5 to 20 cases get a 10 percent discount.
- Quantities above 20 cases get a 15 percent discount.
- For Herbs, quantities under 10 cases get no discount.
- Quantities from 10 cases to 15 cases get a 3 percent discount.
- Quantities above 15 cases get a 6 percent discount.
- For Vegetables except Asparagus, 5 cases and above earn a 12 percent discount.
- Asparagus requires 20 cases for a discount of 12 percent.
- None of the discounts apply if the product is on sale this week. The sale price is 25 percent off the normal price. This week's sale items are Strawberry, Lettuce, and Tomatoes.

The code to execute this logic follows:

```
Sub ComplexIf()
    FinalRow = Cells(Rows.Count, 1).End(xlUp).Row

    For i = 2 To FinalRow
        ThisClass = Cells(i, 1).Value
        ThisProduct = Cells(i, 2).Value
        ThisQty = Cells(i, 3).Value

        ' First, figure out if the item is on sale
        Select Case ThisProduct
            Case "Strawberry", "Lettuce", "Tomatoes"
                Sale = True
            Case Else
                Sale = False
        End Select

        ' Figure out the discount
        If Sale Then
            Discount = 0.25
        Else
            If ThisClass = "Fruit" Then
                Select Case ThisQty
                    Case Is < 5
                        Discount = 0
                    Case 5 To 20
                        Discount = 0.1
                    Case Is > 20
                        Discount = 0.15
                End Select
            ElseIf ThisClass = "Herbs" Then
                Select Case ThisQty
                    Case Is < 10
                        Discount = 0
```

5

```
                    Case 10 To 15
                        Discount = 0.03
                    Case Is > 15
                        Discount = 0.05
                End Select
            ElseIf ThisClass = "Vegetables" Then
                ' There is a special condition for asparagus
                If ThisProduct = "Asparagus" Then
                    If ThisQty < 20 Then
                        Discount = 0
                    Else
                        Discount = 0.12
                    End If
                Else
                    If ThisQty < 5 Then
                        Discount = 0
                    Else
                        Discount = 0.12
                    End If
                End If ' Is the product asparagus or not?
            End If ' Is the product a vegetable?
        End If ' Is the product on sale?

        Cells(i, 4).Value = Discount

        If Sale Then
            Cells(i, 4).Font.Bold = True
        End If

    Next i

    Range("D1").Value = "Discount"

    MsgBox "Discounts have been applied"

End Sub
```

Next Steps

Loops add a tremendous amount of power to your recorded macros. Any time that you need to repeat a process over all worksheets or all rows in a worksheet, a loop is the way to go. Excel VBA supports the traditional programming loops of For...Next and Do...Loop, as well as the object-oriented loop of For Each...Next. Next, Chapter 6, "R1C1-Style Formulas," discusses the seemingly arcane R1C1 style of formulas and shows you why it is important in Excel VBA.

R1C1-Style Formulas

6

Referring to Cells: A1 Versus R1C1 References

We can trace the A1 style of referencing back to VisiCalc. Dan Bricklin and Bob Frankston used A1 to refer to the cell in the upper-left corner of the spreadsheet. Mitch Kapor used this same addressing scheme in Lotus 1-2-3. Upstart Multiplan from Microsoft attempted to buck the trend and used something called R1C1-style addressing. In R1C1 addressing, the cell known as A1 is referred to as R1C1 because it is in Row 1, Column 1.

With the dominance of Lotus 1-2-3 in the 1980s and early 1990s, the A1 style became the standard. Microsoft realized it was fighting a losing battle and eventually offered either R1C1-style addressing or A1-style addressing in Excel. When you open Excel today, the A1 style is used by default. Officially, however, Microsoft supports both styles of addressing.

You would think that this chapter would be a nonissue. Anyone who uses the Excel interface would agree that the R1C1 style is dead. However, we have what on the face of it would seem to be an annoying problem: The macro recorder records formulas in the R1C1 style. So, you might be thinking that you just need to learn R1C1 addressing so that you can read the recorded code and switch it back to the familiar A1 style.

I have to give Microsoft credit. After you understand R1C1-style formulas, they are actually more efficient, especially when you are dealing with writing formulas in VBA. Using R1C1-style addressing allows you to write more efficient code. Plus, there are some features, such as setting up array formulas or conditional formatting with the Formula Is option, where you are required to enter the formula in R1C1 style.

I can hear the collective groan from Excel users everywhere. I would be all for skipping 14 pages of this old-fashioned addressing style if it were only an annoyance or an efficiency issue. However, because it is necessary to understand R1C1 addressing to effectively use important features such as array formulas or conditional formatting, we have to dive in and learn this style.

Switching Excel to Display R1C1 Style References

To switch to R1C1-style addressing, select Excel Options from the Office icon menu. In the Formulas category, check the box for R1C1 reference style (see Figure 6.1).

R1C1 reference style

Figure 6.1
Checking R1C1 reference style on the General tab of the Options box causes Excel to revert to R1C1 style in the Excel user interface.

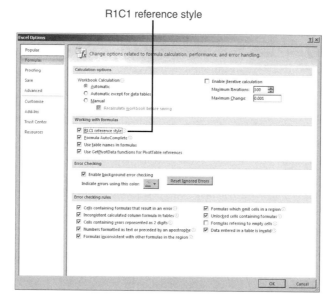

After you switch to R1C1 style, the column letters A, B, C across the top of the worksheet are replaced by numbers 1, 2, 3 (see Figure 6.2).

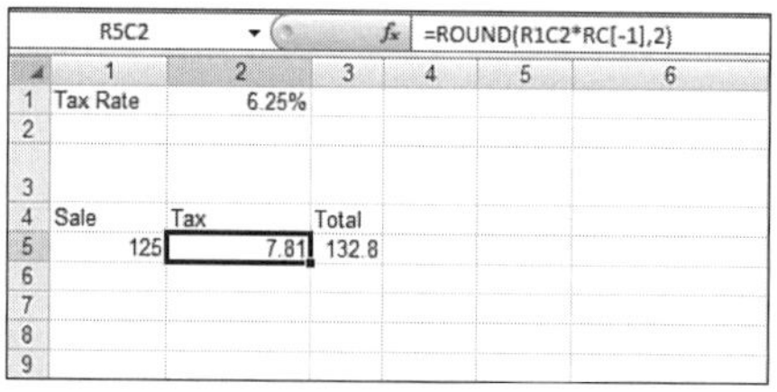

Figure 6.2
In R1C1 style, the column letters are replaced by numbers.

In this format, the cell that you know as B5 is called R5C2 because it is in Row 5, Column 2.

Every couple of weeks, someone manages to accidentally turn this option on, and we get an urgent support request at MrExcel; the style is very foreign to 99 percent of spreadsheet users.

The Miracle of Excel Formulas

Automatically recalculating thousands of cells is the main benefit of electronic spreadsheets over the green ledger paper used up until 1979. However, I would say a close second prize award would be that you can enter one formula and copy that formula to thousands of cells.

Enter a Formula Once and Copy 1,000 Times

Consider this simple worksheet in Figure 6.3. Enter a simple formula like =C4*B4 in Cell D4, double-click the AutoFill handle, and the formula intelligently changes as at is copied down the range.

Figure 6.3
Double-click the AutoFill handle and Excel intelligently copies this relative-reference formula down the column.

	A	B	C	D	E	F	G
1	Tax	6.25%					
2							
3	SKU	Quantity	Unit Price	Total Price	Taxable?	Tax	Total
4	217	12	12.45	149.4	TRUE	9.34	
5	123	144	1.87		TRUE		
6	329	18	19.95		TRUE		
7	616	1	642		FALSE		
8	909	64	17.5		TRUE		
9	527	822	0.12		TRUE		
10	Total						
11							
12							

The formula in F4 includes both relative and absolute formulas: =IF(E4,ROUND(D4*$B$1,2),0). Thanks to the dollar signs inserted in B1, you can copy this formula down, and it always multiplies the Total Price in this row by the tax rate in Cell B1.

The numeric results in Figure 6.4 are achieved by the formulas shown in Figure 6.5. (Ctrl+~ in Excel switches between Normal view and Formula view.) Considering that I had to enter formulas only in Rows 4 and 10, I think it is amazing that Excel was able to intelligently copy the formulas down the column.

As Excel users, we take this behavior for granted, but people in my beginning Excel class are fairly amazed that the formula =F4+D4 in Cell G4 automatically changed to =F5+D5 when it was copied to Cell G5.

6

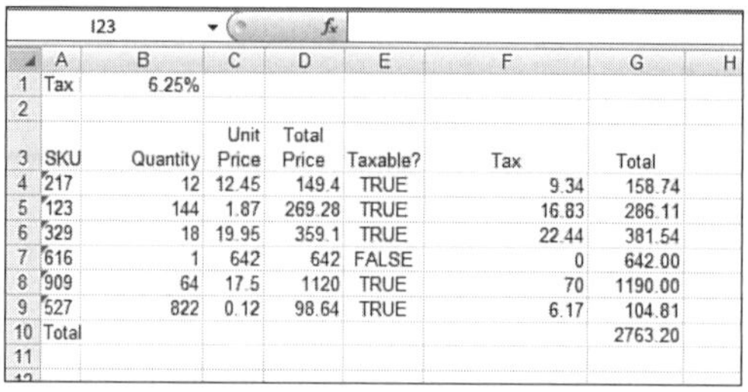

	A	B	C	D	E	F	G	H
1	Tax	6.25%						
2								
3	SKU	Quantity	Unit Price	Total Price	Taxable?	Tax	Total	
4	217	12	12.45	149.4	TRUE	9.34	158.74	
5	123	144	1.87	269.28	TRUE	16.83	286.11	
6	329	18	19.95	359.1	TRUE	22.44	381.54	
7	616	1	642	642	FALSE	0	642.00	
8	909	64	17.5	1120	TRUE	70	1190.00	
9	527	822	0.12	98.64	TRUE	6.17	104.81	
10	Total						2763.20	
11								

Figure 6.4
These results in Columns D, F, and G are achieved by the formulas shown in Figure 6.5.

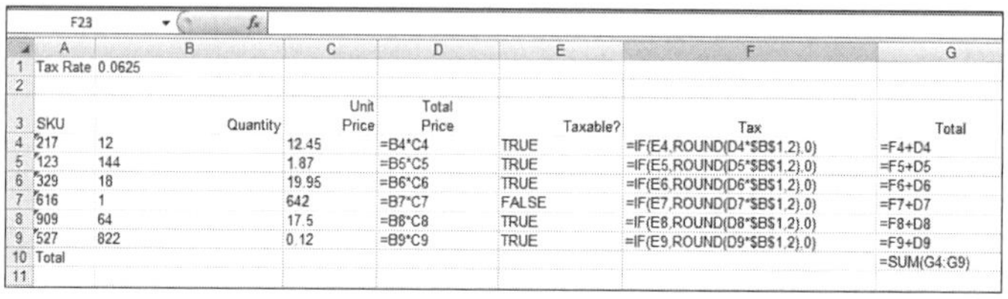

	A	B	C	D	E	F	G
1	Tax Rate	0.0625					
2							
3	SKU	Quantity	Unit Price	Total Price	Taxable?	Tax	Total
4	217	12	12.45	=B4*C4	TRUE	=IF(E4,ROUND(D4*$B$1,2),0)	=F4+D4
5	123	144	1.87	=B5*C5	TRUE	=IF(E5,ROUND(D5*$B$1,2),0)	=F5+D5
6	329	18	19.95	=B6*C6	TRUE	=IF(E6,ROUND(D6*$B$1,2),0)	=F6+D6
7	616	1	642	=B7*C7	FALSE	=IF(E7,ROUND(D7*$B$1,2),0)	=F7+D7
8	909	64	17.5	=B8*C8	TRUE	=IF(E8,ROUND(D8*$B$1,2),0)	=F8+D8
9	527	822	0.12	=B9*C9	TRUE	=IF(E9,ROUND(D9*$B$1,2),0)	=F9+D9
10	Total						=SUM(G4:G9)
11							

Figure 6.5
Press Ctrl+~ to switch to showing formulas rather than their results. It is amazing that Excel adjusts the cell references in each formula as you copy down the column.

The Secret—It Is Not That Amazing

Remember that Excel does everything in R1C1-style formulas. Excel shows addresses and formulas in A1 style merely because it needs to adhere to the standard made popular by VisiCalc and Lotus.

If you switch the worksheet in Figure 6.5 to use R1C1 notation, you will notice that the "different" formulas in D4:D9 are all actually identical formulas in R1C1 notation. The same is true of F4:F9 and G4:G9. Use the Options dialog to change the sample worksheet to R1C1-style addresses. If you examine the formulas in Figure 6.6, you will see that in R1C1 language, every formula in Column D is exactly identical. Given that Excel is storing the formulas in R1C1 style, copying them, and then merely translating to A1 style for us to understand, it is no longer that amazing that Excel can easily manipulate A1-style formulas as it does.

6

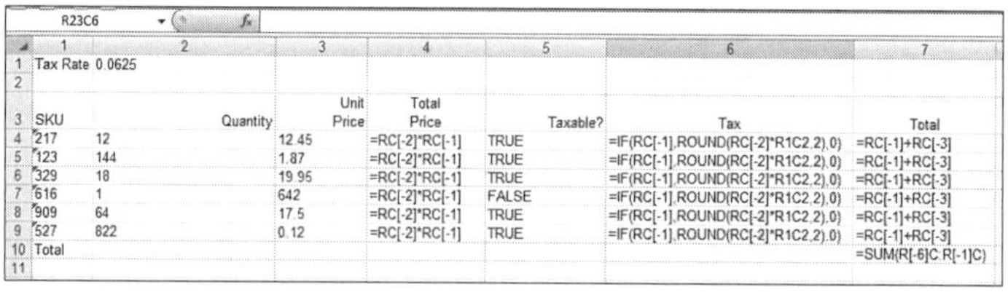

	1	2	3	4	5	6	7
1	Tax Rate	0.0625					
2							
3	SKU	Quantity	Unit Price	Total Price	Taxable?	Tax	Total
4	217	12	12.45	=RC[-2]*RC[-1]	TRUE	=IF(RC[-1],ROUND(RC[-2]*R1C2,2),0)	=RC[-1]+RC[-3]
5	123	144	1.87	=RC[-2]*RC[-1]	TRUE	=IF(RC[-1],ROUND(RC[-2]*R1C2,2),0)	=RC[-1]+RC[-3]
6	329	18	19.95	=RC[-2]*RC[-1]	TRUE	=IF(RC[-1],ROUND(RC[-2]*R1C2,2),0)	=RC[-1]+RC[-3]
7	616	1	642	=RC[-2]*RC[-1]	FALSE	=IF(RC[-1],ROUND(RC[-2]*R1C2,2),0)	=RC[-1]+RC[-3]
8	909	64	17.5	=RC[-2]*RC[-1]	TRUE	=IF(RC[-1],ROUND(RC[-2]*R1C2,2),0)	=RC[-1]+RC[-3]
9	527	822	0.12	=RC[-2]*RC[-1]	TRUE	=IF(RC[-1],ROUND(RC[-2]*R1C2,2),0)	=RC[-1]+RC[-3]
10	Total						=SUM(R[-6]C:R[-1]C)
11							

Figure 6.6
The same formulas in R1C1 style. Note that every formula in Column 4 or Column 6 is the same as all other formulas in that column.

This is one of the reasons that R1C1-style formulas are more efficient in VBA. You can enter the same formula in an entire range of data in a single statement.

CASE STUDY

Entering A1 Versus R1C1 in VBA

Think about how you would set this spreadsheet up in the Excel interface. First, you enter a formula in Cells D4, F4, G4. Next, you copy these cells, and then paste them the rest of the way down the column. The code might look something like this:

```
Sub A1Style()
    ' Locate the FinalRow
    FinalRow = Cells(Rows.Count, 2).End(xlUp).Row
    ' Enter the first formula
    Range("D4").Formula = "=B4*C4"
    Range("F4").Formula = "=IF(E4,ROUND(D4*$B$1,2),0)"
    Range("G4").Formula = "=F4+D4"
    ' Copy the formulas from Row 4 down to the other cells
    Range("D4").Copy Destination:=Range("D5:D" & FinalRow)
    Range("F4:G4").Copy Destination:=Range("F5:G" & FinalRow)
    ' Enter the Total Row
    Cells(FinalRow + 1, 1).Value = "Total"
    Cells(FinalRow + 1, 6).Formula = "=SUM(G4:G" & FinalRow & ")"
End Sub
```

In this code, it takes three lines to enter the formulas at the top of the row, and then another two lines to copy the formulas down the column.

The equivalent code in R1C1 style allows the formulas to be entered for the entire column in a single statement. Remember, the advantage of R1C1 style formulas is that all the formulas in Columns D, F, and most of G are identical:

```
Sub R1C1Style()
    ' Locate the FinalRow
    FinalRow = Cells(Rows.Count, 2).End(xlUp).Row
    ' Enter the first formula
    Range("D4:D" & FinalRow).FormulaR1C1 = "=RC[-1]*RC[-2]"
    Range("F4:F" & FinalRow).FormulaR1C1 = "=IF(RC[-1],ROUND(RC[-2]*R1C2,2),0)"
    Range("G4:G" & FinalRow).FormulaR1C1 = "=+RC[-1]+RC[-3]"
    ' Enter the Total Row
    Cells(FinalRow + 1, 1).Value = "Total"
    Cells(FinalRow + 1, 6).Formula = "=SUM(G4:G" & FinalRow & ")"
End Sub
```

6

Explanation of R1C1 Reference Style

An R1C1-style reference includes the letter R to refer to row and the letter C to refer to column. Because the most common reference in a formula is a relative reference, let's look at relative references in R1C1 style first.

Using R1C1 with Relative References

Imagine you are entering a formula in a cell. To point to a cell in a formula, you use the letters **R** and **C**. After each letter, enter the number of rows or columns in square brackets.

The following list explains the "rules" for using R1C1 relative references:

- For columns, a positive number means to move to the right a certain number of columns, and a negative number means to move to the left a certain number of columns. From cell E5, use RC[1] to refer to F5 and RC[-1] to refer to D5.

- For rows, a positive number means to move down the spreadsheet a certain number of rows. A negative number means to move toward the top of the spreadsheet a certain number of rows. From cell E5, use R[1]C to refer to E6 and use cell R[-1]C to refer to E4.

- If you leave off the square brackets for either the R or the C, it means that you are pointing to a cell in the same row or column as the cell with the formula.

- If you enter =R[-1]C[-1] in cell E5, you are referring to a cell one row up and one column to the left. This would be cell D4.

- If you enter =RC[-1] in cell E5, you are referring to a cell in the same row, but one column to the left. This would be cell D5.

- If you enter =RC[1] in cell E5, you are referring to a cell in the same row, but one column to the right. This would be cell F5.

- If you enter =RC in cell E5, you are referring to a cell in the same row and column, which is cell E5 itself. You would generally never do this because it would create a circular reference.

Figure 6.7 shows how you would enter a reference in cell E5 to point to various cells around E5.

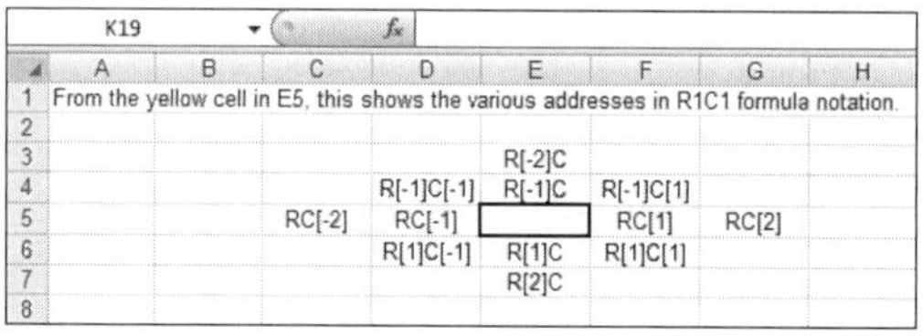

Figure 6.7
Here are various relative references. These would be entered in cell E5 to describe each cell around E5.

You can use R1C1 style to refer to a range of cells. If you want to add up the 12 cells to the left of the current cell, the formula is this:

=SUM(RC[-12]:RC[-1])

Using R1C1 with Absolute References

An absolute reference is one where the row and column remain fixed when the formula is copied to a new location. In A1-style notation, Excel uses a $ before the row number or column letter to keep that row or column absolute as the formula is copied.

To always refer to an absolute row or column number, just leave off the square brackets. This reference refers to cell $B$2 no matter where it is entered:

```
=R2C2
```

Using R1C1 with Mixed References

A mixed reference is one where the row is fixed and the column is allowed to be relative, or where the column is fixed and the row is allowed to be relative. In many situations, this will be useful.

Imagine you've written a macro to import Invoice.txt into Excel. Using .End(xlUp), you find where the total row should go. As you are entering totals, you know that you want to sum from the row above the formula up to Row 2. The following code would handle that:

```
Sub MixedReference()
    TotalRow = Cells(Rows.Count, 1).End(xlUp).Row + 1
    Cells(TotalRow, 1).Value = "Total"
    Cells(TotalRow, 5).Resize(1, 3).FormulaR1C1 = "=SUM(R2C:R[-1]C)"
End Sub
```

In this code, the reference R2C:R[1]C indicates that the formula should add from Row 2 in the same column to the row just above the formula in the current column. Do you see the advantage to R1C1 formulas in this case? A single R1C1 formula with a mixed reference can be used to easily enter a formula to handle an indeterminate number of rows of data (see Figure 6.8).

Figure 6.8
After running the macro, the formulas in Columns E:G of the total row will have a reference to a range that is locked to Row 2, but all other aspects are relative.

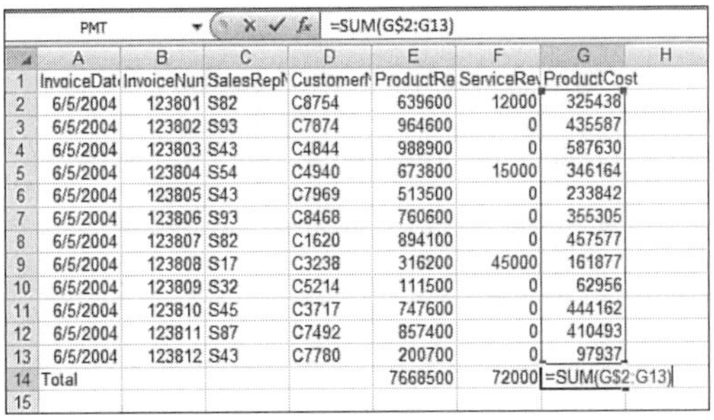

	A	B	C	D	E	F	G	H
					=SUM(G$2:G13)			
1	InvoiceDat	InvoiceNun	SalesRepl	Customer	ProductRe	ServiceRe	ProductCost	
2	6/5/2004	123801	S82	C8754	639600	12000	325438	
3	6/5/2004	123802	S93	C7874	964600	0	435587	
4	6/5/2004	123803	S43	C4844	988900	0	587630	
5	6/5/2004	123804	S54	C4940	673800	15000	346164	
6	6/5/2004	123805	S43	C7969	513500	0	233842	
7	6/5/2004	123806	S93	C8468	760600	0	355305	
8	6/5/2004	123807	S82	C1620	894100	0	457577	
9	6/5/2004	123808	S17	C3238	316200	45000	161877	
10	6/5/2004	123809	S32	C5214	111500	0	62956	
11	6/5/2004	123810	S45	C3717	747600	0	444162	
12	6/5/2004	123811	S87	C7492	857400	0	410493	
13	6/5/2004	123812	S43	C7780	200700	0	97937	
14	Total				7668500	72000	=SUM(G$2:G13)	
15								

Referring to Entire Columns or Rows with R1C1 Style

You will occasionally write a formula that refers to an entire column. For example, you might want to know the maximum value in Column G. If you don't know how many rows you will have in G, you can write =MAX($G:$G) in A1 style or =MAX(C7) in R1C1 style. To find the minimum value in Row 1, use =MIN($1:$1) in A1 style or =MIN(R1) in R1C1 style. You can use relative reference for either rows or columns. To find the average of the row above the current cell, use =AVERAGE(R[-1]).

Replacing Many A1 Formulas with a Single R1C1 Formula

After you get used to R1C1-style formulas, they actually seem a lot more intuitive to build. One classic example to illustrate R1C1-style formulas is building a multiplication table. It is easy to build a multiplication table in Excel using a single mixed-reference formula.

Building the Table

Enter the numbers `1` through `12` going across B1:M1. Copy and transpose these so the same numbers are going down A2:A13. Now the challenge is to build a single formula that works in all cells of B2:M13 and that shows the multiplication of the number in Row 1 times the number in Column 1. Using A1-style formulas, you must press the F4 key five times to get the dollar signs in the proper locations. The following is a far simpler formula in R1C1 style:

```
Sub MultiplicationTable()
    ' Build a multiplication table using a single formula
    Range("B1:M1").Value = Array(1, 2, 3, 4, 5, 6, 7, 8, 9, 10, 11, 12)
    Range("B1:M1").Font.Bold = True
    Range("B1:M1").Copy
    Range("A2:A13").PasteSpecial Transpose:=True
    Range("B2:M13").FormulaR1C1 = "=RC1*R1C"
    Cells.EntireColumn.AutoFit
End Sub
```

The R1C1-style reference `=RC1*R1C` couldn't be simpler. In English, it is saying, "Take this row's Column 1 and multiply it by Row 1 of this column." It works perfectly to build the multiplication table shown in Figure 6.9.

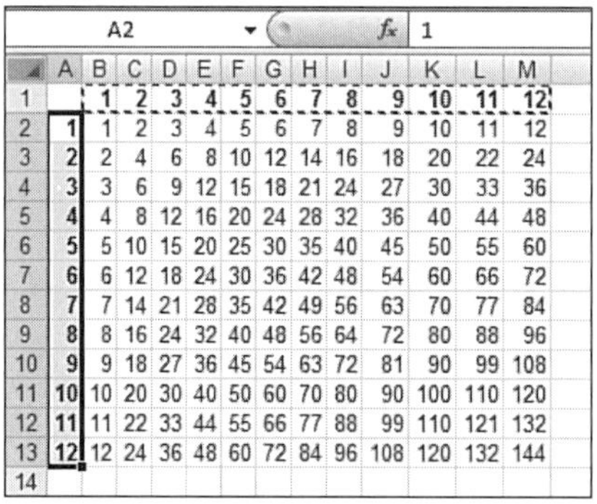

	A	B	C	D	E	F	G	H	I	J	K	L	M
1		1	2	3	4	5	6	7	8	9	10	11	12
2	1	1	2	3	4	5	6	7	8	9	10	11	12
3	2	2	4	6	8	10	12	14	16	18	20	22	24
4	3	3	6	9	12	15	18	21	24	27	30	33	36
5	4	4	8	12	16	20	24	28	32	36	40	44	48
6	5	5	10	15	20	25	30	35	40	45	50	55	60
7	6	6	12	18	24	30	36	42	48	54	60	66	72
8	7	7	14	21	28	35	42	49	56	63	70	77	84
9	8	8	16	24	32	40	48	56	64	72	80	88	96
10	9	9	18	27	36	45	54	63	72	81	90	99	108
11	10	10	20	30	40	50	60	70	80	90	100	110	120
12	11	11	22	33	44	55	66	77	88	99	110	121	132
13	12	12	24	36	48	60	72	84	96	108	120	132	144
14													

Figure 6.9
The macro creates a multiplication table. The formula in B2 uses two mixed references: `=$A2*B$1`.

> **NOTE** After running the macro and producing the multiplication table in Figure 6.9, note that Excel still has the copied range from line 2 of the macro as the active clipboard item. If the user of this macro would select a cell and press Enter, the contents of those cells would copy to the new location. This is generally not desirable. To get Excel out of Cut/Copy mode, add this line of code before your programs ends:
>
> ```
> Application.CutCopyMode = False
> ```

An Interesting Twist

Try this experiment. Move the cell pointer to F6. Turn on macro recording using the Record Macro button on the Developer ribbon. Click the Use Relative Reference button on the Developer ribbon. Enter the formula =**A1** and press Ctrl+Enter to stay in F6. Click the Stop Recording button on the floating toolbar.

You get this single-line macro, which enters a formula that points to a cell five rows up and five columns to the left:

```
Sub Macro1()
    ActiveCell.FormulaR1C1 = "=R[-5]C[-5]"
End Sub
```

Now, move the cell pointer to cell A1 and run the macro that you just recorded. You might think that pointing to a cell five rows above A1 would lead to the ubiquitous Run Time Error 1004. But it doesn't! When you run the macro, the formula in cell A1 is pointing to =XFA1048572, meaning that R1C1-style formulas actually wrap from the left side of the workbook to the right side. I cannot think of any instance where this would be actually useful, but for those of you who rely on Excel to error out when you ask for something that doesn't make sense, be aware that your macro will happily provide a result, and probably not the one that you expected!

Remembering Column Numbers Associated with Column Letters

I like these formulas enough to use them regularly in VBA. I don't like them enough to change my Excel interface over to R1C1-style numbers. So, I routinely have to know that the cell known as U21 is really R21C21.

Knowing that U is the twenty-first letter of the alphabet is not something that comes naturally. We have 26 letters, so A is 1 and Z is 26. M is the halfway point of the alphabet and is Column 13. The rest of the letters are pretty nonintuitive. I found that by playing this little game for a few minutes each day, I soon had memorized the column numbers:

```
Sub QuizColumnNumbers()
    Do
        i = Int(Rnd() * 26) + 1
        Ans = InputBox("What column number is the letter " & Chr(64 + i) & "?")
        If Ans = "" Then Exit Do
        If Not (Ans + 0) = i Then
            MsgBox "Letter " & Chr(64 + i) & " is column # " & i
        End If
    Loop
End Sub
```

If you don't think that memorizing column numbers sounds like fun, or even if you have to figure out the column number of Column DG someday, there is a fairly easy way to do so using the Excel interface. Move the cell pointer to cell A1. Hold down the Shift key and start pressing the right-arrow key. For the first screen of columns, the column number appears in the name box to the left of the formula bar (see Figure 6.10).

Figure 6.10
While you select cells
with the keyboard, the
Name box displays how
many columns are
selected for the first
screen full of columns.

As you keep pressing the right-arrow key beyond the first screen, a tool tip box to the right of the current cell tells you how many columns are selected. When you get to Column CS, it informs you that you are at Column 97 (see Figure 6.11).

Figure 6.11
After the first screen
of columns, a tool tip
bar keeps track of the
column number.

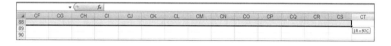

Conditional Formatting—R1C1 Required

When you set up conditional formatting, it is important to use R1C1-style formulas. This is not a well-documented statement. The problem is intermittent, but I find that 1 out of every 50 cells set up with conditional formatting will exhibit strange behavior if you use A1-style formulas. When Excel is presented with a conditional formatting rule that looks like it might contain an R1C1 style formula, Excel assumes it is using R1C1 style references. The problem is that some A1 style references, such as R2 to mean a single cell, can be ambiguously interpreted as an R1C1 style reference to all of Row 2.

Setting Up Conditional Formatting in the User Interface

The Excel user interface emphasizes conditional formatting in which the format of the cell is based on the value in that cell. For most of the conditional formatting options shown in Figure 6.12, Excel simply has to look at the value in the current cell.

In Excel 2007, Microsoft introduced several conditional formatting options in which the format of the cell is based on the comparison between the cell and other cells in the selected range. For example, Duplicate Values or Above Average are new conditional formats in which Excel has to compare each cell to others in a range. All the new visualizations, such as data bars, color scales, and icon sets, compare each cell to the other cells in the range.

However, there is another powerful type of conditional formatting where the format is based on a formula and that formula can point outside of the range. In Excel 97-2003, you would change the first dropdown in the Conditional Format dialog from Cell Value Is to Formula Is. Many people never noticed this dropdown and never found the powerful conditional formatting. In Excel 2007, the option is equally well hidden. You have to select Conditional Formatting, Highlight Cells Rules, More Rules. In the New Formatting Rule dialog, choose the last option in the list, Use a Formula to Determine Which Cells to Format (see Figure 6.13). The formula syntax allows you to build any formula or function that evaluates to True or False. This formula may point to cells other than the current cell, or it may combine multiple conditions with the OR or AND function.

Figure 6.12
Conditional formatting traditionally sets the format of the cell based on only the value in one cell.

Figure 6.13
You have to access More Rules, and then choose Use a Formula to reach the most powerful conditional format.

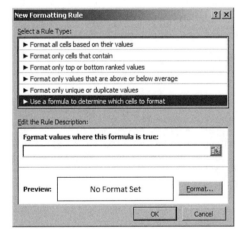

Here is a fairly advanced example. We want to hide any error cells and then color negative numbers in red. The basic idea is to set up a conditional format that checks to see whether the cell contains an error or NA. If either is true, we set the font color up to match the background. This first condition relies on the Formula Is syntax. The second condition is straightforward and relies on the Cell Value Is syntax. Figure 6.14 shows how this would be set up in the Excel user interface.

Figure 6.14
This cell contains a pair of conditional formats. The first is designed to hide any error value and uses the powerful `Formula Is` syntax. The second condition uses the more common `Cell Value Is` syntax.

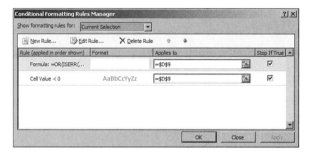

Setting Up Conditional Formats in VBA

Say you have a workbook with liberal use of cell fill colors. You need a way to turn the font to light blue when an error occurred in a light blue cell, and to turn the font to light yellow when an error occurred in a yellow cell. A quick macro in VBA was the perfect way to do this.

The `FormatConditions` object is used to set up conditional formats. Because each cell can have three `FormatConditions`, the following code first deletes all the existing conditional formats on the sheet. The code then loops through all nonblank cells in the worksheet and applies two conditional formats. In the first conditional format, the type is `xlExpression`, which means we are using the `Formula` syntax. Note that the formula specified for `Formula1` is in R1C1-style notation. The second conditional format uses the `xlCellValue` type, which requires both specifying an operator and a value. After we've added the condition, we set the `ColorIndex` for the font for conditions 1 and 2:

```
Sub ApplySpecialFormattingAll()
    For Each ws In ThisWorkbook.Worksheets
        ws.UsedRange.FormatConditions.Delete
        For Each cell In ws.UsedRange.Cells
            If Not IsEmpty(cell) Then
                cell.FormatConditions.Add Type:=xlExpression, _
                    Formula1:="=or(ISERR(RC),isna(RC))"
                cell.FormatConditions(1).Font.Color = cell.Interior.Color
                cell.FormatConditions.Add Type:=xlCellValue, Operator:=xlLess, _
                    Formula1:="0"
                cell.FormatConditions(2).Font.ColorIndex = 3
            End If
        Next cell
    Next ws
End Sub
```

> **CAUTION**
>
> Do not use A1-style formulas for Formula1 in conditional formats. The code appears to work on one cell or a few cells. However, if you apply this to 50 or more cells, you will find some cells where the formula starts pointing to a totally different cell. If you use R1C1-style formulas for Formula1, you do not have this problem. See the following case study for more specifics.

Identifying Row with Largest Value in G

One of the classic examples to illustrate conditional formatting is this example to highlight the row with the minimum and maximum value. Figure 6.15 shows how to set this up in the Excel interface.

Figure 6.15
This classic conditional formatting example points out an interesting problem in VBA code.

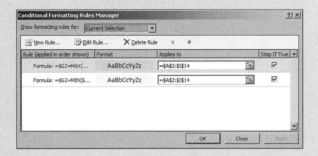

Look at the code to create this conditional format. The formula to find the highest value in Column G, expressed in R1C1 style, is MAX(C7). This can be resolved two ways: either as an A1-style formula or as an R1C1-style formula. Remember, Microsoft started with the R1C1 style and offered the A1 style only to be compatible with Lotus 1-2-3. This is undocumented, but clearly Excel first tries to resolve the formula using R1C1-style formatting and the following code works perfectly.

```
Sub FindMinMax()
    ' Highlight row with highest revenue in Green
    ' Highlight row with lowest revenue in Yellow
    FinalRow = Cells(Application.Rows.Count, 1).End(xlUp).Row
    With Range("A2:I" & FinalRow)
        .FormatConditions.Delete
        .FormatConditions.Add Type:=xlExpression, Formula1:="=RC7=MAX(C7)"
        .FormatConditions(1).Interior.ColorIndex = 4
        .FormatConditions.Add Type:=xlExpression, Formula1:="=RC7=MIN(C7)"
        .FormatConditions(2).Interior.ColorIndex = 6
    End With
End Sub
```

Now, imagine what happens if you try to set up a conditional format pointing to cell C7 or R22. Any of these formats is likely to fail because Excel will interpret the C7 as a reference to Column 7.

With conditional formatting, Excel tries to accommodate either A1 or R1C1 formulas, but there are clearly situations where the formula can be interpreted as either style formula. In this case, Excel always assumes it is R1C1 style, so I recommend using R1C1 style for every conditional format that you set up.

Array Formulas Require R1C1 Formulas

Array formulas are powerful "super-formulas." At MrExcel.com, I call these CSE formulas, because you have to use Ctrl+Shift+Enter to enter them. If you are not familiar with array formulas, they look like they should not work.

6

The array formula in E20, shown in Figure 6.16, is a formula that does 18 multiplications and then sums the result. It looks like this would be an illegal formula, and if you happen to enter it without using Ctrl+Shift+Enter, you get the expected `#VALUE!` error. However, if you enter it with Ctrl+Shift+Enter, the formula miraculously multiplies row by row and then sums the result. (You do not type the curly braces when entering the formula.)

Figure 6.16
The array formula in E20 does 18 multiplications and then sums them. You must use Ctrl+Shift+Enter to enter this formula.

E21 {=SUM(D$2:D20*E$2:E20)}

	A	B	C	D	E	F	G
1	Region	Product	Date	Quantity	Unit Price	Unit Cost	
2	East	XYZ	1/1/2001	1000	22.81	10.22	
3	Central	DEF	1/2/2001	100	22.57	9.84	
4	East	ABC	1/2/2001	500	20.49	8.47	
5	Central	XYZ	1/3/2001	500	22.48	10.22	
6	Central	XYZ	1/4/2001	400	23.01	10.22	
7	East	DEF	1/4/2001	800	23.19	9.84	
8	East	XYZ	1/4/2001	400	22.88	10.22	
9	Central	ABC	1/5/2001	400	17.15	8.47	
10	East	ABC	1/7/2001	400	21.14	8.47	
11	East	DEF	1/7/2001	1000	21.73	9.84	
12	West	XYZ	1/7/2001	600	23.01	10.22	
13	Central	ABC	1/9/2001	800	20.52	8.47	
14	East	XYZ	1/9/2001	900	23.35	10.22	
15	Central	XYZ	1/10/2001	900	23.82	10.22	
16	East	XYZ	1/10/2001	900	23.85	10.22	
17	Central	ABC	1/12/2001	300	20.89	8.47	
18	West	XYZ	1/12/2001	400	22.86	10.22	
19	Central	ABC	1/14/2001	100	17.4	8.47	
20	East	XYZ	1/14/2001	100	24.01	10.22	
21				Total Revenue	234198		
22							

The array formulas in E22:E24 are also powerful array formulas. The formula for E22 is this:

```
=SUM(IF(A$2:A$19=$A22,D$2:D$19*E$2:E$19,0))
```

The code to enter these formulas follows. Although the formulas appear in the user interface in A1-style notation, you must use R1C1-style notation for entering array formulas:

```
Sub EnterArrayFormulas()
    ' Add a formula to multiply unit price x quantity
    FinalRow = Cells(Rows.Count, 1).End(xlUp).Row
    Cells(FinalRow + 1, 5).FormulaArray = "=SUM(R2C[-1]:R[-1]C[-1]*R2C:R[-1]C)"
End Sub
```

> **TIP** To quickly find the R1C1 formula, use this trick. Enter a regular A1-style formula or an array formula in any cell in Excel. Select that cell. Switch to the VBA editor. Press Ctrl+G to display the Immediate window. Type **`Print ActiveCell.FormulaR1C1`** and press Enter. Excel will convert the formula in the formula bar to an R1C1 style formula.

Next Steps

Conditional formatting is one of the features that changed in Excel 2007 VBA. Read Chapter 7, "What's New in Excel 2007 and What's Changed"), to learn many more features that have changed significantly in Excel 2007.

What's New in Excel 2007 and What's Changed

If It's Changed in the Front End, It's Changed in VBA

Thankfully, not too much of VBA doesn't work anymore, but a few things in the object model have changed. For most items, it's obvious that, because the Excel user interface changed, the VBA has changed.

> **NOTE**
>
> **NEW** The New graphic is used throughout the book to point out those sections discussing items that have changed from previous versions. For example, overall, names (discussed in Chapter 8) have not changed that much, but the Name Manager has changed, so there is a New graphic to bring your attention to this.

The Ribbon

The Ribbon is one of the first changes you'll notice when you open Excel 2007. Although the CommandBars object does still work to a point, if you want to flawlessly integrate your custom controls into the Ribbon, you need to make some major changes.

→ **See** Chapter 26, "Customizing the Ribbon to Run Macros," for more information.

Charts

Charts have many new features that are not backward compatible with earlier versions of Excel. And although the macro recorder does record most of your actions on the Design and Layout ribbons, it won't record action on the Format ribbon in the Format dialog boxes. This doesn't mean the VBA code isn't available; it's just that you can't learn it by recording it.

→ **See** Chapter 11, "Creating Charts," for more information.

Pivot Tables

Pivot tables have a few new features available that aren't backward compatible, such as subtotals at the top and the report layout options. Tables 13.1 and 13.2, in Chapter 13, "Using VBA to Create Pivot Tables," list the new methods and properties in Excel 2007 that you have to watch out for if you need to make a backward-compatible workbook.

Conditional Formatting

Conditional formatting has been completely reinvented. Where we were once limited to three conditions and changing a few cell formatting options, it seems now the sky's the limit. To get an idea of how much this feature has changed, consider this: *Special Edition Using Microsoft Office Excel 2007* (ISBN 0-7897-3611-X) has a 40-page chapter just to review the options available. Compare that to almost any Excel 2003 or earlier book, in which conditional formatting coverage was just a footnote or two scattered throughout the book. This feature has come a long way, which means so has the code. Compare the following two recorded macros. They both are relatively simple. A cell's fill is changed to red if the value in the cell is between 1 and 5. Notice, however, how much more code is involved with the new options that you now need to set in 2007.

Excel 2003 recorded macro:

```
Sub Macro2()
'
' Macro2 Macro
'

'
    Selection.FormatConditions.Delete
    Selection.FormatConditions.Add Type:=xlCellValue, Operator:=xlBetween, _
        Formula1:="1", Formula2:="5"
    Selection.FormatConditions(1).Interior.ColorIndex = 3
    ActiveCell.FormulaR1C1 = "2"
    Range("A2").Select
End Sub
```

Excel 2007 recorded macro:

```
Sub Macro2()
'
' Macro2 Macro
'

'
    Selection.FormatConditions.AddColorScale ColorScaleType:=2
    Selection.FormatConditions(Selection.FormatConditions.Count).SetFirstPriority
    Selection.FormatConditions(1).ColorScaleCriteria(1).Type = _
```

7

```
            xlConditionValueNumber
    Selection.FormatConditions(1).ColorScaleCriteria(1).Value = 1
    With Selection.FormatConditions(1).ColorScaleCriteria(1).FormatColor
        .Color = 255
        .TintAndShade = 0
    End With
    Selection.FormatConditions(1).ColorScaleCriteria(2).Type = _
            xlConditionValueNumber
    Selection.FormatConditions(1).ColorScaleCriteria(2).Value = 5
    With Selection.FormatConditions(1).ColorScaleCriteria(2).FormatColor
        .Color = 255
        .TintAndShade = 0
    End With
    ActiveCell.FormulaR1C1 = "2"
    Range("A2").Select
End Sub
```

Tables

Tables are a convenient way to deal with data that is already set up as tables (multiple records set up beneath a row of column headers). For this new functionality, there are corresponding new objects, properties, and methods.

→ To learn more, **see** "Referencing Tables," **p. 73** in Chapter 3, "Referring to Ranges," and "Tables," **p. 150** in Chapter 8, "Create and Manipulate Names in VBA."

Sorting

Because of the increased sorting options (such as sorting by color), sort code has gone through a few changes. Instead of a single line of code with a few options to set, you need to configure the sort options and then do the sort, as shown here:

```
Sub Macro2()
'
' Macro2 Macro
'

'
    Range("A1:A4").Select
    'clear current sort options
    ActiveWorkbook.Worksheets("Sheet1").Sort.SortFields.Clear
    'set the new sort option - this is just a simple A-Z sort
    ActiveWorkbook.Worksheets("Sheet1").Sort.SortFields.Add Key:=Range("A1"), _
        SortOn:=xlSortOnValues, Order:=xlAscending, DataOption:=xlSortNormal
    'do the actual sort
    With ActiveWorkbook.Worksheets("Sheet1").Sort
        .SetRange Range("A1:A4")
        .Header = xlYes
        .MatchCase = False
        .Orientation = xlTopToBottom
        .SortMethod = xlPinYin
        .Apply
    End With
End Sub
```

SmartArt

SmartArt is the new function that has replaced the Diagram feature of earlier versions of Excel. Although in the past you couldn't record diagram actions, you could write code for them. In Excel 2007, you can't record or code it. The original diagram code won't work either.

The Macro Recorder Won't Record Actions That It Did Record in Earlier Excel Versions

There is one glaring negative change to VBA. Actions that were once recordable aren't. For example, in Excel 2003, you could record the insertion of a text box and some text on a sheet and get the following (slightly modified to fit this page):

```
Sub Macro1()
'
' Macro1 Macro
'


    '
ActiveSheet.Shapes.AddTextbox(msoTextOrientationHorizontal, 268.5, 178.5, _
    116.25, 145.5).Select
Selection.Characters.Text = _
    "This is a test of inserting a text box to a sheet and adding some text." & _
    "This is a test of inserting a text box to a sheet and adding some text." & _
    "This is a test of inserting a text box to a sheet and ad"
Selection.Characters(201).Insert String:="ding some text. "
With Selection.Characters(Start:=1, Length:=216).Font
    .Name = "Arial"
    .FontStyle = "Regular"
    .Size = 10
    .Strikethrough = False
    .Superscript = False
    .Subscript = False
    .OutlineFont = False
    .Shadow = False
    .Underline = xlUnderlineStyleNone
    .ColorIndex = xlAutomatic
End With
Range("I15").Select
End Sub
```

Try the same thing in Excel 2007, and you get this:

```
Sub Macro1()
'
' Macro1 Macro
'
    Selection.Copy
    ActiveSheet.Paste
    ActiveSheet.Paste
    Range("I5").Select
End Sub
```

7

Not very useful at all—the recorder is ignoring the existance of the text box! However, it doesn't mean you can't use VBA to add a text box—it's just a little harder to figure out how to make it do what you want.

To figure out how to make it work, I typed **textbox** in the VB Editor Help and selected AddTextbox Method from the list of articles. From there, I modified the required parts of the Excel 2003 code that I had previously recorded, which consisted of changing how the text box and its text is added, and then came up with the following:

```
Sub AddTextBox()
ActiveSheet.Shapes.AddTextBox(msoTextOrientationHorizontal, 268.5, 178.5, _
    116.25, 145.5).TextFrame.Characters.Text = _
    "This is a test of inserting a text box to a sheet and adding some text." & _
    "This is a test of inserting a text box to a sheet and adding some text." & _
    "This is a test of inserting a text box to a sheet and adding some text."
With Selection.Characters(Start:=1, Length:=216).Font
    .Name = "Arial"
    .FontStyle = "Regular"
    .Size = 10
    .Strikethrough = False
    .Superscript = False
    .Subscript = False
    .OutlineFont = False
    .Shadow = False
    .Underline = xlUnderlineStyleNone
    .ColorIndex = xlAutomatic
End With
Range("I15").Select
End Sub
```

Learning the New Objects and Methods

Excel's VBA Help files have several tables of changes for objects and methods in Excel that you can refer to. They're even broken up by version number, as shown in Figure 7.1. To access these tables, click the Help icon in the VB Editor toolbar and select What's New from the dialog that appears.

Figure 7.1
Excel's VBA Help has several sections to help you find what will and won't work in the new Excel.

7

When you review the "Object Model Changes Since …" sections, you may be wondering what Microsoft means when they say an item's status is Hidden (see Figure 7.2). If you use one of these items in your code, such as `FileSearch`, the program will compile just fine, but it won't run in Excel 2007. Microsoft has allowed you to include the item in your code for legacy usage and will compile it, but when you try to run it, the program won't know what to do with it. Unless you have some kind of compatibility mode check in your code, your program will debug at runtime.

Figure 7.2
Some items appear as Hidden in the Object Model Changes reference tables. This means Excel will compile them for use in legacy versions, but they won't actually work in Excel 2007.

Compatibility Mode

With all the changes in Excel 2007, now more than ever it's important to verify the application's version. Two ways you can do this are `Version` and `Excel8CompatibilityMode`.

Dealing with Compatibility Issues

Creating a compatibility mode workbook can be problematic. Most code will still run in earlier versions, so long as the program doesn't run into an item from the Excel 2007 object model. If you use any items from the Excel 2007 object model, however, the code will not compile in earlier versions. To work around this, comment out the 2007-specific lines of code, compile, and then comment the lines back in.

If your only Excel 2007 issue is the use of constant values, partially treat your code as if you were doing late binding to an external application (see the section "Using Constant Values" in Chapter 18, "Automating Word," for more information). If you only have constant values that are incompatible, treat them like late binding arguments, assigning a variable the numeric value of the constant. The following section shows an example of this.

Version

The `Version` property returns a string containing the active Excel application version. For 2007, this is 12. This can prove useful if you've developed an add-in to use across versions; but some parts of it, such as saving the active workbook, are version specific:

```
Sub wkbkSave()
Dim xlVersion As String
Dim myxlOpenXMLWorkbook As String

myxlOpenXMLWorkbook = "51"

xlVersion = Application.Version

Select Case xlVersion
    Case Is = "9.0", "10.0", "11.0"
        ActiveWorkbook.SaveAs Filename:="LegacyVersionExcel.xls"
    Case Is = "12.0"
        ActiveWorkbook.SaveAs Filename:="Excel2007Version", _
        FileFormat:=myxlOpenXMLWorkbook
End Select
End Sub
```

Note that for the `FileFormat` property of the Excel 2007 case, I had to create my own variable, `myxlOpenXMLWorkbook`, to hold the constant value of `xlOpenXMLWorkbook`. If I were to try to run this in an earlier version of Excel just using the Excel 2007 constant, `xlOpenXMLWorkbook`, the code would not even compile.

NEW Excel8CompatibilityMode

This property returns a Boolean, to let you know whether a workbook is in Compatibility mode—that is, saved as an Excel 97-2003 file. You use this, for example, if you have an add-in using the new conditional formatting, but you wouldn't want the user to try and use it on the workbook. The following function, `CompatibilityCheck`, returns `True` if the active workbook is in Compatibility mode and `False` if it is not. The procedure, `CheckCompatibility`, uses the result to inform the user of an incompatible feature, as shown in Figure 7.3:

```
Function CompatibilityCheck() As Boolean
Dim blMode As Boolean

If Application.Version = "12.0" Then
    blMode = ActiveWorkbook.Excel8CompatibilityMode
    If blMode = True Then
        CompatibilityCheck = True
    ElseIf blMode = False Then
        CompatibilityCheck = False
    End If
End If
End Function

Sub CheckCompatibility()
Dim xlCompatible As Boolean
```

7

```
xlCompatible = CompatibilityCheck

If xlCompatible = True Then
    MsgBox "You are attempting to use an Excel 2007 function " & Chr(10) & _
    "in a 97-2003 Compatibility Mode workbook"
End If
End Sub
```

Figure 7.3
Use Excel8
CompatibilityCheck
to inform a user certain
features in your add-in
won't work in a 97-2003
Excel file opened in Excel
2007.

Next Steps

Now that you have an idea about the differences you might run into, you're ready to move on to the next chapter, which discusses using named ranges to simplify your coding, including one of my favorite new methods, the Table method.

Create and Manipulate Names in VBA

8

Excel Names

You've named ranges in a worksheet by highlighting a range and typing a name in the Name box to the left of the formula field. Perhaps you've also created more complicated names containing formulas—such as for finding the last row in a column. The ability to set a name to a range makes it much easier to write formulas and set tables.

The ability to create and manipulate names is also available in VBA and provides the same benefits as naming ranges in a worksheet: You can store, for example, a new range in a name.

This chapter explains different types of names and the various ways you can use them.

Global Versus Local Names

Names can be *global*—that is, available anywhere in the workbook—or *local*—available only on a specific worksheet. With local names, you can have multiple references in the workbook with the same name. Global names must be unique to the workbook.

 In previous versions of Excel, it was difficult to tell whether you were looking at a global or local name—you had to be on the correct sheet and compare the list of names on different sheets. With Excel 2007, you have the Name Manager dialog box, which lists all the names in a workbook, even a name that has been assigned to both the global and local levels. The Scope column lists the scope of the name, whether it is the workbook or a specific sheet, such as Sheet1.

8

For example, in Figure 8.1, the name Apples is assigned to Sheet1, but also to the workbook.

Figure 8.1
The Name Manager lists all local and global names.

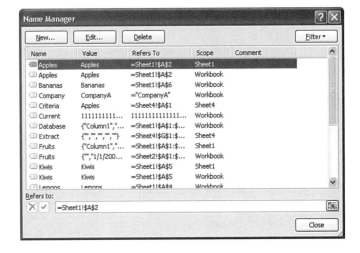

Adding Names

If you record the creation of a named range and then view the code, you see something like this:

```
ActiveWorkbook.Names.Add Name:="Fruits", RefersToR1C1:="=Sheet2!R1C1:R6C6"
```

This creates a global name `"Fruits"`, which includes the range A1:F6 (R1C1:R6C6). The formula is enclosed in quotes, and the equal sign in the formula must be included. Also, the range reference must be absolute (include the $ sign) or in R1C1 notation. If the sheet on which the name is created is the active sheet, the sheet reference does not have to be included; however, it can make the code easier to understand.

> **NOTE**
>
> If the reference is not absolute, the name may be created, but will not point to the correct range. For example, if you run this line of code
>
> ```
> ActiveWorkbook.Names.Add Name:="Citrus", _
>     RefersToR1C1:="=Sheet1!A1"
> ```
>
> the name is created in the workbook. As you can see in Figure 8.2, however, it hasn't actually been assigned to the range.

Figure 8.2
Cell A1 doesn't have the name Citrus assigned to it because the name formula lacks absolute referencing and is not properly recognized by Excel.

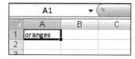

To create a local name, include the sheet name:

```
ActiveWorkbook.Names.Add Name:="Sheet2!Fruits", _
    RefersToR1C1:="=Sheet2!R1C1:R6C6"
```

Or, specify that the Names collection belongs to a worksheet:

```
Worksheets("Sheet1").Names.Add Name:="Fruits", _
    RefersToR1C1:="=Sheet1!R1C1:R6C6"
```

The preceding example is what you would learn from the macro recorder. There is a simpler way:

```
Range("A1:F6").Name = "Fruits"
```

Or, for a local variable only, you can use this:

```
Range("A1:F6").Name = "Sheet1!Fruits"
```

When creating names with this method, absolute referencing is not required.

> **NOTE**
> Table names are a new feature in Excel 2007. You can use them like defined names, but you don't create them the same way. See the "Tables" section later in this chapter for more information about creating table names.

Although this is much easier and quicker than what the macro recorder creates, it is limited in that it works only for ranges. Formulas, strings, numbers, and arrays require the use of the Add method.

The Name property of the name ObjectName is an object but still has a Name property. The following line renames an existing name:

```
Names("Fruits").Name = "Produce"
```

Fruits no longer exists; Produce is now the name of the range.

When you are renaming names in which a local and global reference both carry the same name, the previous line renames the local reference first.

If Range("A1:F6").Name = "Fruits" exists early in the code and then Range("A1:F6").Name = "Produce" is added later, Produce overwrites Fruits, as shown in Figure 8.3. An attempt to access the local name Fruits later in the program creates an error because it no longer exists.

Figure 8.3
It's easy to overwrite an existing name if you aren't careful. The local name Fruits has been overwritten by the local name Produce. The name Fruits you see is the global variable, not the local one.

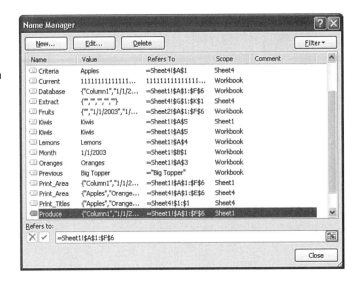

> **TIP**
>
> Data Validation (the Data Validation icon on the Data ribbon) limits you to selecting a range on the active sheet. To get around this, assign a name to the data you want to include in the validation.

Deleting Names

Use the Delete method to delete a name:

```
Names("ProduceNum").Delete
```

An error occurs if you attempt to delete a name that doesn't exist.

> **CAUTION**
>
> If both local and global references with the same name exist, be more specific as to which name is being deleted.

Adding Comments

With Excel 2007, you can now add comments about names. You can add any additional information that you want, such as why the name was created or where it is used. To insert a comment for the local name LocalOffice, do this:

```
ActiveWorkbook.Worksheets("Sheet7").Names("LocalOffice").Comment = _
"Holds the name of the current office"
```

The comments will appear in a column in the Name Manager, as shown in Figure 8.4.

> **CAUTION**
>
> The name must exist before a comment can be added to it.

8

Figure 8.4
You can add comments about names to help you remember their purpose.

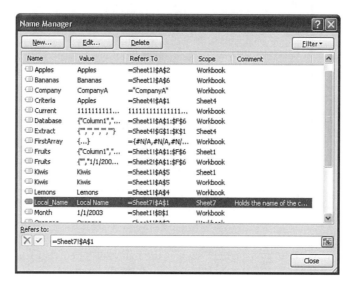

Types of Names

The most common use of names is for storing ranges. But names can store more than that. After all, that's what they're for: Names store information. They make it simple to remember and use potentially complex or large amounts of information. And, unlike variables, names remember what they store beyond the life of the program.

We've already covered creating range names, but we can also assign names to name formulas, strings, numbers, and arrays.

Formulas

The syntax for storing a formula in a name is the same as for a range because the range is, in essence, a formula:

```
Names.Add Name:="ProductList", _
    RefersTo:="=OFFSET(Sheet2!$A$2,0,0,COUNTA(Sheet2!$A:$A))"
```

The preceding code allows for a dynamic named column, which is very useful for creating dynamic tables or for referencing any dynamic listing on which calculations may be performed, as shown in Figure 8.5.

Figure 8.5
Dynamic formulas can be
assigned to names.

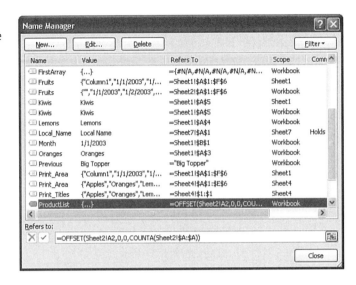

Strings

When using names to hold strings, such as the name of the current fruit producer, enclose the string value in quotes. Because there is no formula involved, an equal sign is not needed:

```
Names.Add Name: = "Company", RefersTo:="CompanyA"
```

Figure 8.6 shows how the coded name would appear in the Name Manager window.

Figure 8.6
A string value can be
assigned to a name.

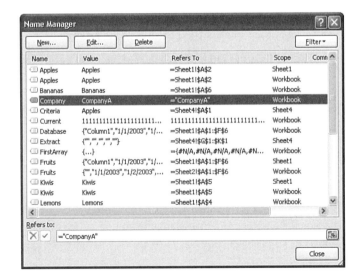

Using Names to Store Values

Because names do not lose their references between sessions, this is a great way to store values as opposed to storing values in cells from which the information would have to be retrieved. For example, to track the leading producer between seasons, create a name Leader. If the new season's leading producer matches the name reference, a special report comparing the seasons could be created. The other option is to create a special sheet to track the values between sessions and then retrieve the values when needed. With names, the values are readily available.

The following procedure shows how cells in a variable sheet are used to retain information between sessions:

```
Sub NoNames(ByRef CurrentTop As String)
TopSeller = Worksheets("Variables").Range("A1").Value
If CurrentTop = TopSeller Then
    MsgBox ("Top Producer is " & TopSeller & " again.")
Else
    MsgBox ("New Top Producer is " & CurrentTop)
End If
End Sub
```

The following procedure shows how names are used to store information between sessions:

```
Sub WithNames()
If Evaluate("Current") = Evaluate("Previous") Then
    MsgBox ("Top Producer is " & Evaluate("Previous") & " again.")
Else
    MsgBox ("New Top Producer is " & Evaluate("Current"))
End If
End Sub
```

If Current and Previous are previously declared names, you access them directly rather than create variables to pass them in. Note the use of the Evaluate method to extract the values in names. The string being stored cannot have more than 255 characters.

Numbers

You can also use names to store numbers between sessions. Use this:

```
NumofSales = 5123
Names.Add Name:="TotalSales", RefersTo:=NumofSales
```

Or use this:

```
Names.Add Name:="TotalSales", RefersTo:=5123
```

Notice the lack of quotes or an equal sign. Using quotes changes the number to a string; and with the addition of an equal sign, the number changes to a formula.

To retrieve the value in the name, you have two options:

```
NumofSales = Names("TotalSales").Value
```

Or the shorter version:

```
NumofSales = [TotalSales]
```

8

Keep in mind that someone reading your code might not be familiar with the use of the `Evaluate` method (square brackets). If you know that someone else will be reading your code, avoid the use of the `Evaluate` method or add a comment explaining it.

Tables

 Excel tables share some of the properties of defined names, but also have their own unique methods. Unlike defined names, which are what we're used to dealing with, tables cannot be created manually—that is, you cannot select a range on a sheet and type a name in the Name field. However, you can manually create them via VBA.

Tables aren't created using the same method as the defined names. Instead of `Range(xx).Add` or `Names.Add`, we use `ListObjects.Add`.

To create a table from cells A1:F6, and assuming the table has column headers, as shown in Figure 8.7, do this:

```
ActiveSheet.ListObjects.Add(xlSrcRange, Range("$A$1:$F$6"), , xlYes).Name = _
"Table1"
```

`xlSrcRange` (the `SourceType`) tells Excel the source of the data is an Excel range. You then need to specify the range (the source) of the table. If you have headers in the table, include the row when indicating the range. The next argument, not used in the preceding example, is the `LinkSource`, a Boolean indicating whether there is an external data source and is not used if the `SourceType` is `xlSrcRange`. The `xlYes` lets Excel know the data table has column headers; otherwise, Excel automatically generates them. The final argument, not shown in the preceding example, is the destination, used when the `SourceType` is `xlSrcExternal`, indicating the upper-left cell where the table will begin.

Figure 8.7
You can assign a special name to a data table.

Table1 ▼		f_x	Apples		
	A	B	C	D	E	F
1	Column1 ▼	1/1/2003 ▼	1/2/2003 ▼	1/3/2003 ▼	1/4/2003 ▼	1/5/2003 ▼
2	Apples	274	412	159	314	837
3	Oranges	228	776	344	245	487
4	Lemons	160	183	502	583	100
5	Kiwis	478	724	755	618	778
6	Bananas	513	438	600	456	51
7	Total					2253
8						

Using Arrays in Names

A name can also store the data stored in an array. The array size is limited by available memory. See Chapter 19, "Arrays," for more information about arrays.

An array reference is stored in a name the same way as a numeric reference:

```
Sub NamedArray()
Dim myArray(10, 5)
Dim i As Integer, j As Integer
```

```
'The following For loops fill the array myArray
For i = 1 To 10
    For j = 1 To 5
        myArray(i, j) = i + j
    Next j
Next i
'The following line takes our array and gives it a name
Names.Add Name:="FirstArray", RefersTo:=myArray
End Sub
```

Because the name is referencing a variable, no quotes or equal signs are required.

Reserved Names

Excel uses local names of its own to keep track of information. These local names are considered reserved, and if you use them for your own references, they might cause problems.

Highlight an area on a sheet. Then from the Page Layout ribbon, select Print Area, Set Print Area.

As shown in Figure 8.8, a Print_Area listing is in the Range Name field. Deselect the area and look again in the Range Name field. The name is still there. Select it, and the print area previously set is now highlighted. If you save, close, and reopen the workbook, Print_Area is still set to the same range. Print_Area is a name reserved by Excel for its own use.

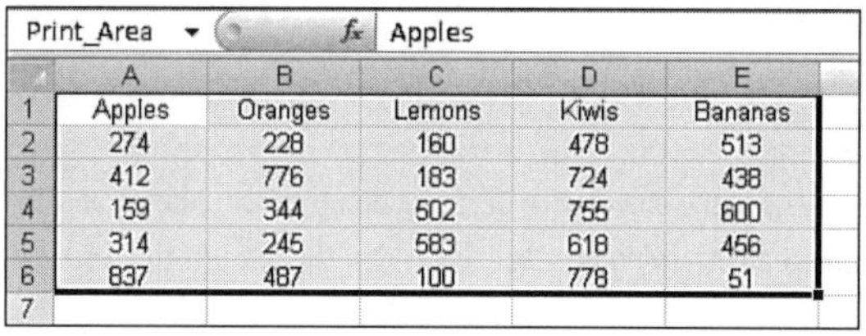

Figure 8.8
Excel creates its own names.

	A	B	C	D	E
1	Apples	Oranges	Lemons	Kiwis	Bananas
2	274	228	160	478	513
3	412	776	183	724	438
4	159	344	502	755	600
5	314	245	583	618	456
6	837	487	100	778	51
7					

Print_Area ▾ f_x Apples

CAUTION

Each sheet has its own print area. Also, setting a new print area on a sheet with an existing print area overwrites the original print area name.

Luckily, Excel does not have a large list of reserved names:

Criteria

Database

Extract

Print_Area

Print_Titles

Criteria and Extract are used when the Advanced Filter (on the Data ribbon, select Advanced Filter) is configured to extract the results of the filter to a new location.

Database is no longer required in Excel, but some features, such as Data Form, do recognize it. Older versions of Excel used it to identify the data you wanted to manipulate in certain functions.

Print_Area is used when a print area is set (from the Page Layout ribbon, select Print Area, Set Print ARea) or when Page Setup options that designate the print area from the Page Layout ribbon, Scale) are changed.

Print_Titles is used when print titles are set (Page Layout, Print Titles).

These names should be avoided and variations used with caution. For example, if you create a name PrintTitles, you might accidentally code this:

```
Worksheets("Sheet4").Names("Print_Titles").Delete
```

You've just deleted the Excel name rather than your custom name.

Hiding Names

Names are incredibly useful, but you don't necessarily want to see all the names you've created. Like many other objects, names have a `Visible` property. To hide a name, set the `Visible` property to `False`. To unhide a name, set the `Visible` property to `True`:

```
Names.Add Name:="ProduceNum", RefersTo:="=$A$1", Visible:=False
```

> **CAUTION**
> If a user creates a Name object with the same name as your hidden one, the hidden name is overwritten without any warning message. To prevent this, protect the worksheet.

Checking for the Existence of a Name

You can use the following function to check for the existence of a user-defined name, even a hidden one, but it does not return the existence of Excel's reserved names. It's a handy addition to your arsenal of "programmer's useful code":

```
Function NameExists(FindName As String) As Boolean
Dim Rng As Range
Dim myName As String
On Error Resume Next
myName = ActiveWorkbook.Names(FindName).Name
If Err.Number = 0 Then
    NameExists = True
Else
    NameExists = False
End If
End Function
```

The preceding code is also an example of how to use errors to your advantage. If the name for which you are searching doesn't exist, an error message is generated. By adding the `On Error Resume Next` line at the beginning, you force the code to continue. Then you use `Err.Number` to tell you whether you ran into an error. If you didn't, `Err.Number` is zero, which means the name exists; otherwise, you had an error, and the name does not exist.

CASE STUDY

Using Named Ranges for VLOOKUP

Every day, you import a file of sales data from a chain of retail stores. The file includes the store number but not the store name. You obviously don't want to have to type store names every day, but you would like to have store names appear on all the reports that you run.

Normally, you would enter a table of store numbers and names in an out-of-the way spot on a back worksheet. You can use VBA to help maintain the list of stores each day and then use the VLOOKUP function to get store names from the list into your dataset.

The basic steps are as follows:

1. Import the data file.
2. Find all the unique store numbers in today's file.
3. See whether any of these store numbers are not in your current table of store names.
4. For any stores that are new, add them to the table and ask the user for a store name.
5. The Store Names table is now larger, so reassign the named range used to describe the store table.
6. Use a VLOOKUP function in the original dataset to add a store name to all records. This VLOOKUP references the named range of the newly expanded Store Names table.

The following code handles these six steps:

```
Sub ImportData()
' This routine imports sales.csv to the data sheet
' Check to see whether any stores in column A are new
' If any are new, then add them to the StoreList table
Dim WSD As Worksheet
Dim WSM As Worksheet
Dim WB As Workbook

Set WB = ThisWorkbook
' Data is stored on the Data worksheet
Set WSD = WB.Worksheets("Data")
' StoreList is stored on a menu worksheet
Set WSM = WB.Worksheets("Menu")

' Open the file..This makes the csv file active
Workbooks.Open Filename:="C:\Sales.csv"
' Copy the data to WSD and close
ActiveWorkbook.Range("A1").CurrentRegion.Copy Destination:=WSD.Range("A1")
ActiveWorkbook.Close SaveChanges:=False
```

```
' Find a list of unique stores from column A
FinalRow = WSD.Cells(WSD.Rows.Count, 1).End(xlUp).Row
WSD.Range("A1").Resize(FinalRow, 1).AdvancedFilter Action:=xlFilterCopy, _
    CopyToRange:=WSD.Range("Z1"), Unique:=True

' For all the unique stores, see whether they are in the
' current store list.
FinalStore = WSD.Range("Z" & WSD.Rows.Count).End(xlUp).Row
WSD.Range("AA1").Value = "There?"
WSD.Range("AA2:AA" & FinalStore).FormulaR1C1 = _
    "=ISNA(VLOOKUP(RC[-1],StoreList,1,False))"

' Find the next row for a new store. Because StoreList starts in A1
' of the Menu sheet, find the next available row
NextRow = WSM.Range("A" & WSM.Rows.Count).End(xlUp).Row + 1

' Loop through the list of today 's stores.If they are shown
' as missing, then add them at the bottom of the StoreList
For i = 2 To FinalStore
    If WSD.Cells(i, 27).Value = True Then
        ThisStore = Cells(i, 26).Value
        WSM.Cells(NextRow, 1).Value = ThisStore
        WSM.Cells(NextRow, 2).Value = _
            InputBox(Prompt:="What is name of store " _
            & ThisStore, Title:="New Store Found")
        NextRow = NextRow + 1
    End If
Next i

' Delete the temporary list of stores in Z &AA
WSD.Range("Z1:AA" & FinalStore).Clear

' In case any stores were added, re-define StoreList name
FinalStore = WSM.Range("A" & WSM.Rows.Count).End(xlUp).Row
WSM.Range("A1:B" & FinalStore).Name = "StoreList"

' Use VLOOKUP to add StoreName to column B of the dataset
WSD.Range("B1").EntireColumn.Insert
WSD.Range("B1").Value = "StoreName"
WSD.Range("B2:B" & FinalRow).FormulaR1C1 = "=VLOOKUP(RC1,StoreList,2,False)"

' Change Formulas to Values
WSD.Range("B2:B" & FinalRow).Value = Range("B2:B" & FinalRow).Value

'Release our variables
Set WB = Nothing
Set WSD = Nothing
Set WSM = Nothing
End Sub
```

Next Steps

In the next chapter, you'll learn how code can be written to run automatically based on users' actions, such as activating a sheet or selecting a cell. This is done with events, which are actions in Excel that can be captured and used to your advantage.

Event Programming

Levels of Events

Earlier in the book, you saw mention of workbook events and have seen examples of worksheet events. Events are Excel's way of letting you execute code based on certain actions that take place in a workbook.

These events can be found at the following levels:

- **Application level**—Control based on application actions, such as `Application_ NewWorkbook`

- **Workbook level**—Control based on workbook actions, such as `Workbook_Open`

- **Worksheet level**—Control based on worksheet actions, such as `Worksheet_ SelectionChange`

- **Chart sheet level**—Control based on chart actions, such as `Chart_Activate`

Workbook events go into the ThisWorkbook module. Worksheet events go into the module of the sheet they affect (such as Sheet1). Chart sheet events go into the module of the chart sheet they affect (such as Chart1). And, embedded charts and application events go into class modules. The events can still make procedure or function calls outside their own modules. So, if you want the same action to take place for two different sheets, you don't have to copy the code twice—instead, place the code in a module and have each sheet event call the procedure.

In this chapter, you'll learn about the different levels of events, where to find them, and how to use them.

NOTE   Userform and control events are discussed in Chapter 10, "UserForms—An Introduction," and Chapter 23, "Advanced Userform Techniques."

Using Events

Each level consists of several types of events, and memorizing the syntax of them all would be a feat. Excel makes it easy to view and insert the available events in their proper modules right from the VB Editor.

When a ThisWorkbook, Sheet, Chart Sheet, or Class module is active, the corresponding events are available through the Object and Procedure drop-downs, as shown in Figure 9.1.

Object drop-down   Procedure drop-down

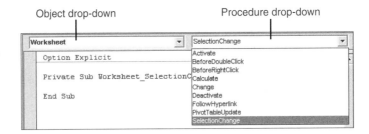

Figure 9.1
The different events are easy to access from the VB Editor Object and Procedure drop-downs.

After the object is selected, the Procedure drop-down updates to list the events available for that object. Selecting a procedure automatically places the procedure header (`Private Sub`) and footer (`End Sub`) in the editor, as shown in Figure 9.2.

Figure 9.2
The procedure header and footer are automatically placed.

Event Parameters

Some events have parameters, such as `Target` or `Cancel`. These parameters allow values to be passed into the procedure. For example, some procedures are triggered before the actual event—such as `BeforeRightClick`. Assigning `True` to the `Cancel` parameter prevents the default action from taking place; in this case, the shortcut menu is prevented from appearing:

```
Private Sub Worksheet_BeforeRightClick(ByVal Target As Range, Cancel As Boolean)
Cancel = True
End Sub
```

Enabling Events

Some events can trigger other events, including themselves. For example, the `Worksheet_Change` event is triggered by a change in a cell. If the event is triggered and the procedure itself changes a cell, the event gets triggered again, which changes a cell, triggering the event, and so on. The procedure gets stuck in an endless loop.

To prevent this, disable the events and then reenable them at the end of the procedure:

```
Private Sub Worksheet_Change(ByVal Target As Range)
Application.EnableEvents = False
Range("A1").Value = Target.Value
Application.EnableEvents = True
End Sub
```

> **TIP** To interrupt a macro, press Esc or Ctrl+Break. To restart it, use Run on the toolbar or press F5.

Workbook Events

The following event procedures are available at the workbook level.

Workbook_Activate()

`Workbook_Activate` occurs when the workbook containing this event becomes the active workbook.

Workbook_Deactivate()

`Workbook_Deactivate` occurs when the active workbook is switched from the workbook containing the event to another workbook.

Workbook_Open()

`Workbook_Open` is the default workbook event. This procedure is activated when a workbook is opened—no user interface is required. It has a variety of uses, such as checking the username and then customizing the user's privileges in the workbook.

The following code checks the `UserName`; if it is not Admin, this code protects each sheet from user changes. (`UserInterfaceOnly` allows macros to make changes, but not the user.)

```
Private Sub Workbook_Open()
Dim sht As Worksheet
If Application.UserName <> "Admin" Then
    For Each sht In Worksheets
```

```
            sht.Protect UserInterfaceOnly:=True
        Next sht
    End If
End Sub
```

You can also use `Workbook_Open` to create custom menus or toolbars. The following code adds the menu MrExcel Programs to the Add-ins ribbon with two options underneath it (see Figure 9.3).

Figure 9.3
You can use the Open event to create custom menus under the Add-ins ribbon.

→   For more information about custom menus, **see** Chapter 26, "Customizing the Ribbon to Run Macros,"
    p. 543.

```
Sub Workbook_Open()
Dim cbWSMenuBar As CommandBar
Dim Ctrl As CommandBarControl, muCustom As CommandBarControl
Dim iHelpIndex As Integer
Set cbWSMenuBar = Application.CommandBars("Worksheet menu bar")
iHelpIndex = cbWSMenuBar.Controls("Help").Index
Set muCustom = cbWSMenuBar.Controls.Add(Type:=msoControlPopup, _
    Before:=iHelpIndex, Temporary:=True)
For Each Ctrl In cbWSMenuBar.Controls
    If Ctrl.Caption = "&MrExcel Programs" Then
        cbWSMenuBar.Controls("MrExcel Programs").Delete
    End If
Next Ctrl
With muCustom
    .Caption = "&MrExcel Programs"
    With .Controls.Add(Type:=msoControlButton)
        .Caption = "&Import and Format"
        .OnAction = "ImportFormat"
    End With
    With .Controls.Add(Type:=msoControlButton)
        .Caption = "&Calculate Year End"
        .OnAction = "CalcYearEnd"
    End With
End With
End Sub
```

Workbook_BeforeSave(ByVal SaveAsUI As Boolean, Cancel As Boolean)

`Workbook_BeforeSave` occurs when the workbook is saved. `SaveAsUI` is set to `True` if the Save As dialog box is to be displayed. `Cancel` set to `True` prevents the workbook from being saved.

Workbook_BeforePrint(Cancel As Boolean)

Workbook_BeforePrint occurs when any print command is used—menu, toolbar, keyboard, or macro. Cancel set to True prevents the workbook from being printed.

The following code tracks each time a sheet is printed. It logs the date, time, username, and the sheet printed in a hidden print log (see Figure 9.4):

```
Private Sub Workbook_BeforePrint(Cancel As Boolean)
Dim LastRow As Long
Dim PrintLog As Worksheet
Set PrintLog = Worksheets("PrintLog")
LastRow = PrintLog.Cells(PrintLog.Rows.Count, 1).End(xlUp).Row + 1
With PrintLog
    .Cells(LastRow, 1).Value = Now()
    .Cells(LastRow, 2).Value = Application.UserName
    .Cells(LastRow, 3).Value = ActiveSheet.Name
End With
End Sub
```

Figure 9.4
You can use the BeforePrint event to keep a hidden print log in a workbook.

	A	B	C
1	Date/Time	Username	Sheet Printed
2	1/27/2007 16:07	Tracy	PrintLog
3			

You can also use the BeforePrint event to add information to a header or footer before the sheet is printed. Although you can now enter the file path into a header or footer through the Page Setup, before Office XP the only way to add the file path was with code. This piece of code was commonly used:

```
Private Sub Workbook_BeforePrint(Cancel As Boolean)
    ActiveSheet.PageSetup.RightFooter = ActiveWorkbook.FullName
End Sub
```

Workbook_BeforeClose(Cancel As Boolean)

Workbook_BeforeClose occurs when a workbook is closed. Cancel set to True prevents the workbook from closing.

If the Open event is used to create a custom menu, the BeforeClose event is used to delete it:

```
Private Sub Workbook_BeforeClose(Cancel As Boolean)
Dim cbWSMenuBar As CommandBar
On Error Resume Next
Set cbWSMenuBar = Application.CommandBars("Worksheet menu bar")
cbWSMenuBar.Controls("MrExcel Programs").Delete
End Sub
```

This is a nice little procedure, but there is one problem: If changes are made to the workbook and it isn't saved, Excel pops up the Do You Want to Save? dialog box. This dialog box pops up after the BeforeClose event has run. So, if the user decides to cancel, the menu is now gone.

The solution is to create your own Save dialog in the event:

```
Private Sub Workbook_BeforeClose(Cancel As Boolean)
Dim Msg As String
Dim Response
Dim cbWSMenuBar As CommandBar
If Not ThisWorkbook.Saved Then
    Msg = "Do you want to save the changes you made to " & Me.Name & "?"
    Response = MsgBox(Msg, vbQuestion + vbYesNoCancel)
    Select Case Response
        Case vbYes
            ThisWorkbook.Save
        Case vbNo
            ThisWorkbook.Saved = True
        Case vbCancel
            Cancel = True
            Exit Sub
        End Select
End If
On Error Resume Next
Set cbWSMenuBar = Application.CommandBars("Worksheet menu bar")
cbWSMenuBar.Controls("MrExcel Programs").Delete
End Sub
```

Workbook_NewSheet(ByVal Sh As Object)

Workbook_NewSheet occurs when a new sheet is added to the active workbook. Sh is the new Worksheet or Chart Sheet object.

Workbook_WindowResize(ByVal Wn As Window)

Workbook_WindowResize occurs when the active workbook is resized. Wn is the window.

> **NOTE**
> Only resizing the active workbook window starts this event. Resizing the application window is an application-level event and is not affected by the workbook-level event.

This code disables the resizing of the active workbook:

```
Private Sub Workbook_WindowResize(ByVal Wn As Window)
Wn.EnableResize = False
End Sub
```

> **CAUTION**
> If you disable the capability to resize, the minimize and maximize buttons are removed, and the workbook cannot be resized. To undo this, type `ActiveWindow.EnableResize = True` in the Immediate window.

Workbook_WindowActivate(ByVal Wn As Window)

Workbook_WindowActivate occurs when any workbook window is activated. Wn is the window. Only activating the workbook window starts this event.

Workbook_WindowDeactivate(ByVal Wn As Window)

Workbook_WindowDeactivate occurs when any workbook window is deactivated. Wn is the window. Only deactivating the workbook window starts this event.

Workbook_AddInInstall()

Workbook_AddInInstall occurs when the workbook is installed as an add-in (by selecting the Microsoft Office button, Excel Options, Add-ins). Double-clicking on an XLAM file (an add-in) to open it does not activate the event.

Workbook_AddInUninstall

Workbook_AddInUninstall occurs when the workbook (add-in) is uninstalled. The add-in is not automatically closed.

Workbook_SheetActivate(ByVal Sh As Object)

Workbook_SheetActivate occurs when any chart sheet or worksheet in the workbook is activated. Sh is the active sheet.

To affect a specific worksheet, refer to Worksheet_Activate; for chart sheets, refer to Chart_Activate.

Workbook_SheetBeforeDoubleClick (ByVal Sh As Object, ByVal Target As Range, Cancel As Boolean)

Workbook_SheetBeforeDoubleClick occurs when the user double-clicks any chart sheet or worksheet in the active workbook. Sh is the active sheet; Target is the object double-clicked; Cancel set to True prevents the default action from taking place.

To affect a specific worksheet, refer to Worksheet_BeforeDoubleClick; for chart sheets, refer to Chart_BeforeDoubleClick.

Workbook_SheetBeforeRightClick(ByVal Sh As Object, ByVal Target As Range, Cancel As Boolean)

Workbook_SheetBeforeRightClick occurs when the user right-clicks any worksheet in the active workbook. Sh is the active worksheet; Target is the object right-clicked; Cancel set to True prevents the default action from taking place.

To affect a specific worksheet, refer to Worksheet_BeforeRightClick; for chart sheets, refer to Chart_BeforeRightClick.

Workbook_SheetCalculate(ByVal Sh As Object)

Workbook_SheetCalculate occurs when any worksheet is recalculated or any updated data is plotted on a chart. Sh is the active sheet.

To affect a specific worksheet, refer to Worksheet_Calculate; for chart sheets, refer to Chart_Calculate.

Workbook_SheetChange (ByVal Sh As Object, ByVal Target As Range)

Workbook_SheetChange occurs when any range in a worksheet is changed. Sh is the worksheet; Target is the changed range.

To affect a specific worksheet, refer to Worksheet_Change.

Workbook_Sync(ByVal SyncEventType As Office.MsoSyncEventType)

Workbook_Sync occurs when the local copy of a sheet in a workbook that is part of a Document Workspace is synchronized with the copy on the server. SyncEventType is the status of the synchronization.

Workbook_SheetDeactivate (ByVal Sh As Object)

Workbook_SheetDeactivate occurs when any chart sheet or worksheet in the workbook is deactivated. Sh is the sheet being switched from.

To affect a specific worksheet, refer to Worksheet_Deactivate; for chart sheets, refer to Chart_Deactivate.

Workbook_SheetFollowHyperlink (ByVal Sh As Object, ByVal Target As Hyperlink)

Workbook_SheetFollowHyperlink occurs when any hyperlink is clicked in Excel. Sh is the active worksheet; Target is the hyperlink.

To affect a specific worksheet, refer to Worksheet_FollowHyperlink.

Workbook_SheetSelectionChange(ByVal Sh As Object, ByVal Target As Range)

Workbook_SheetSelectionChange occurs when a new range is selected on any sheet. Sh is the active sheet; Target is the affected range.

To affect a specific worksheet, refer to Worksheet_SelectionChange.

Workbook_PivotTableCloseConnection(ByVal Target As PivotTable)

Workbook_PivotTableCloseConnection occurs when a pivot table report closes its connection to its data source. Target is the pivot table that has closed the connection.

Workbook_PivotTableOpenConnection(ByVal Target As PivotTable)

Workbook_PivotTableOpenConnection occurs when a pivot table report opens a connection to its data source. Target is pivot table that has opened the connection.

NEW Workbook_RowsetComplete(ByVal Description As String, ByVal Sheet As String, ByVal Success As Boolean)

Workbook_RowsetComplete occurs when the user drills through a recordset or calls upon the rowset action on an OLAP PivotTable. Description is a description of the event; Sheet is the name of the sheet on which the recordset is created; Success indicates success or failure.

Worksheet Events

The following event procedures are available at the worksheet level.

Worksheet_Activate()

Worksheet_Activate occurs when the sheet on which the event is becomes the active sheet.

Worksheet_Deactivate()

Worksheet_Deactivate occurs when another sheet becomes the active sheet.

> **NOTE** If a Deactivate event is on the active sheet and you switch to a sheet with an Activate event, the Deactivate event runs first, followed by the Activate event.

Worksheet_BeforeDoubleClick(ByVal Target As Range, Cancel As Boolean)

Worksheet_BeforeDoubleClick allows control over what happens when the user double-clicks the sheet. Target is the selected range on the sheet; Cancel is set to False by default, but if set to True, it prevents the default action (such as entering a cell) from happening.

The following code prevents the user from entering a cell with a double-click. And if the formula field is also hidden, the user cannot enter information in the traditional way:

```
Private Sub Worksheet_BeforeDoubleClick(ByVal Target As Range, _
    Cancel As Boolean)
Cancel = True
End Sub
```

> **NOTE** The preceding code does not prevent the user from sizing a row or column with a double-click.

Preventing the double-click from entering a cell allows it to be used for something else, such as highlighting a cell. The following code changes a cell's interior color to red when it is double-clicked:

```
Private Sub Worksheet_BeforeDoubleClick(ByVal Target As Range, _
    Cancel As Boolean)
Dim myColor As Integer
Target.Interior.ColorIndex = 3
End Sub
```

Worksheet_BeforeRightClick(ByVal Target As Range, Cancel As Boolean)

Worksheet_BeforeRightClick is triggered when the user right-clicks a range. Target is the object right-clicked; Cancel set to True prevents the default action from taking place.

Worksheet_Calculate()

Worksheet_Calculate occurs after a sheet is recalculated.

The following example compares a month's profits between the previous and the current year. If profit has fallen, a red down arrow appears below the month; if profit has risen, a green up arrow appears (see Figure 9.5):

```
Private Sub Worksheet_Calculate()
Select Case Range("C3").Value
    Case Is < Range("C4").Value
        SetArrow 10, msoShapeDownArrow
    Case Is > Range("C4").Value
        SetArrow 3, msoShapeUpArrow
End Select
End Sub

Private Sub SetArrow(ByVal ArrowColor As Integer, ByVal ArrowDegree)
' The following code is added to remove the prior shapes
For Each sh In ActiveSheet.Shapes
    If sh.Name Like "*Arrow*" Then
        sh.Delete
    End If
Next sh
ActiveSheet.Shapes.AddShape(ArrowDegree, 17.25, 43.5, 5, 10).Select
With Selection.ShapeRange
    With .Fill
        .Visible = msoTrue
        .Solid
        .ForeColor.SchemeColor = ArrowColor
        .Transparency = 0#
    End With
    With .Line
        .Weight = 0.75
        .DashStyle = msoLineSolid
        .Style = msoLineSingle
        .Transparency = 0#
        .Visible = msoTrue
        .ForeColor.SchemeColor = 64
```

```
        .BackColor.RGB = RGB(255, 255, 255)
    End With
End With
Range("A3").Select 'Place the selection back on the dropdown
End Sub
```

Figure 9.5
Use the `Calculate` event to add graphics emphasizing the change in profits.

	A	B	C
1	2005 vs 2006 Profit		
2			
3	June	**Current**	3307
4	⇑	**Previous**	1383
5			
6			
7		**2005**	**2006**
8	January	3018	7258
9	February	9704	3459
10	March	3950	3874
11	April	7518	3907
12	May	4542	9774
13	June	1383	3307
14	July	2888	4741
15	August	8493	8232
16	September	642	9775
17	October	5308	2090
18	November	6040	7490
19	December	6845	6845
20			

Worksheet_Change(ByVal Target As Range)

`Worksheet_Change` is triggered by a change to a cell's value, such as when text is entered, edited, or deleted. `Target` is the cell that has been changed.

> **NOTE**
> The event can also be triggered by pasting values. Recalculation of a value does not trigger the event; use the `Calculation` event instead.

Worksheet_SelectionChange(ByVal Target As Range)

`Worksheet_SelectionChange` occurs when a new range is selected. `Target` is the newly selected range.

The following example helps identify the selected cell by highlighting the row and column:

> **CAUTION**
> This example makes use of conditional formatting and overwrites any existing conditional formatting on the sheet. Also, the code may clear the clipboard, making it difficult to copy and paste on the sheet.

```
Private Sub Worksheet_SelectionChange(ByVal Target As Range)
Dim iColor As Integer
On Error Resume Next
iColor = Target.Interior.ColorIndex
If iColor < 0 Then
    iColor = 36
Else
    iColor = iColor + 1
End If
If iColor = Target.Font.ColorIndex Then iColor = iColor + 1
Cells.FormatConditions.Delete
With Range("A" & Target.Row, Target.Address)
    .FormatConditions.Add Type:=2, Formula1:="TRUE"
    .FormatConditions(1).Interior.ColorIndex = iColor
End With
With Range(Target.Offset(1 - Target.Row, 0).Address & ":" & _
    Target.Offset(-1, 0).Address)
    .FormatConditions.Add Type:=2, Formula1:="TRUE"
    .FormatConditions(1).Interior.ColorIndex = iColor
End With
End Sub
```

Worksheet_FollowHyperlink(ByVal Target As Hyperlink)

Worksheet_FollowHyperlink occurs when a hyperlink is clicked. Target is the hyperlink.

CASE STUDY

Quickly Entering Military Time into a Cell

You're entering arrival and departure times and want the times to be formatted with a 24-hour clock (military time). You've tried formatting the cell, but no matter how you enter the times, they are displayed in the 0:00 hours and minutes format.

The only way to get the time to appear correctly, such as with 23:45, is to have it entered in the cell as such. But typing the colon is time-consuming—it would be much more efficient just to enter the numbers and let Excel format it for you.

The solution? Use a Change event to take what is in the cell and insert the colon for you:

```
Private Sub Worksheet_Change(ByVal Target As Range)
Dim ThisColumn As Integer
Dim UserInput As String, NewInput As String
ThisColumn = Target.Column
If ThisColumn < 3 Then
    UserInput = Target.Value
    If UserInput > 1 Then
        NewInput = Left(UserInput, Len(UserInput) - 2) & ":" & _
        Right(UserInput, 2)
        Application.EnableEvents = False
        Target = NewInput
        Application.EnableEvents = True
    End If
End If
End Sub
```

An entry of 2345 will display as 23:45. Note that the format change is limited to Columns A and B (`If ThisColumn < 3`)—without this, entering numbers anywhere on a sheet, such as in a totals column, would force it to be reformatted.

> **TIP**
> Use `Application.EnableEvents = False` to prevent the procedure from calling itself when the value in the target is updated.

Chart Sheet Events

Chart events occur when a chart is changed or activated. Embedded charts require the use of class modules to access the events.

→ For more information about class modules, **see** Chapter 22, "Creating Classes, Records, and Collections," **p. 477**.

Embedded Charts

Because embedded charts do not create chart sheets, the chart events are not as readily available. You can make them available by adding a class module, as follows:

1. Insert a class module.

2. Rename the module to `cl_ChartEvents`.

3. Enter the following line of code in the class module:

   ```
   Public WithEvents myChartClass As Chart
   ```

   The chart events are now available to the chart, as shown in Figure 9.6. They are accessed in the class module rather than on a chart sheet.

4. Insert a standard module.

5. Enter the following lines of code in a standard module:

   ```
   Dim myClassModule As New cl_ChartEvents
   Sub InitializeChart()
       Set myClassModule.myChartClass = _
           Worksheets(1).ChartObjects(1).Chart
   End Sub
   ```

   These lines initialize the embedded chart to be recognized as a Chart object. The procedure must be run once per session. (Use `Workbook_Open` to automate this.)

Figure 9.6
Embedded chart events are now available in the class module.

Chart_Activate()

Chart_Activate occurs when a chart sheet is activated or changed.

Chart_BeforeDoubleClick(ByVal ElementID As Long, ByVal Arg1 As Long, ByVal Arg2 As Long, Cancel As Boolean)

Chart_BeforeDoubleClick occurs when any part of a chart is double-clicked. ElementID is the part of the chart that is double-clicked, such as the legend; Arg1 and Arg2 are dependent upon the ElementID; Cancel set to True prevents the default double-click action from occurring.

The following sample hides the legend when it is double-clicked; double-clicking either axis brings back the legend:

```
Private Sub MyChartClass_BeforeDoubleClick(ByVal ElementID As Long, _
    ByVal Arg1 As Long, ByVal Arg2 As Long, Cancel As Boolean)
Select Case ElementID
    Case xlLegend
        Me.HasLegend = False
        Cancel = True
    Case xlAxis
        Me.HasLegend = True
        Cancel = True
End Select
End Sub
```

Chart_BeforeRightClick(Cancel As Boolean)

Chart_BeforeRightClick occurs when a chart is right-clicked. Cancel set to True prevents the default right-click action from occurring.

Chart_Calculate()

Chart_Calculate occurs when a chart's data is changed.

Chart_Deactivate()

Chart_Deactivate occurs when another sheet becomes the active sheet.

Chart_MouseDown(ByVal Button As Long, ByVal Shift As Long, ByVal x As Long, ByVal y As Long)

Chart_MouseDown occurs when the cursor is over the chart and any mouse button is pressed. Button is the mouse button that was clicked; Shift is whether a Shift, Ctrl, or Alt key was pressed; x is the X coordinate of the cursor when the button is pressed; y is the Y coordinate of the cursor when the button is pressed.

The following code zooms in on a left mouse click and zooms out on a right mouse click. Use the Cancel argument in the BeforeRightClick event to handle the menus that appear when right-clicking on a chart:

```
Private Sub MyChartClass_MouseDown(ByVal Button As Long, ByVal Shift _
    As Long, ByVal x As Long, ByVal y As Long)
If Button = 1 Then
    ActiveChart.Axes(xlValue).MaximumScale = _
    ActiveChart.Axes(xlValue).MaximumScale - 50
End If
If Button = 2 Then
    ActiveChart.Axes(xlValue).MaximumScale = _
    ActiveChart.Axes(xlValue).MaximumScale + 50
End If
End Sub
```

Chart_MouseMove(ByVal Button As Long, ByVal Shift As Long, ByVal x As Long, ByVal y As Long)

Chart_MouseMove occurs as the cursor is moved over a chart. Button is the mouse button being held down, if any; Shift is whether a Shift, Ctrl, or Alt key was pressed; x is the X coordinate of the cursor on the chart; y is the Y coordinate of the cursor on the chart.

Chart_MouseUp(ByVal Button As Long, ByVal Shift As Long, ByVal x As Long, ByVal y As Long)

Chart_MouseUp occurs when any mouse button is released while the cursor is on the chart. Button is the mouse button that was clicked; Shift is whether a Shift, Ctrl, or Alt key was pressed; x is the X coordinate of the cursor when the button is released; y is the Y coordinate of the cursor when the button is released.

Chart_Resize()

Chart_Resize occurs when a chart is resized using the sizing handles, but not when the size is changed using the size control on the Format ribbon of the chart tools.

Chart_Select(ByVal ElementID As Long, ByVal Arg1 As Long, ByVal Arg2 As Long)

Chart_Select occurs when a chart element is selected. ElementID is the part of the chart selected, such as the legend; Arg1 and Arg2 are dependent upon the ElementID.

The following code highlights the data set when a point on the chart is selected—assuming the series starts in A1 and each row is a point to plot—as shown in Figure 9.7:

```
Private Sub MyChartClass_Select(ByVal ElementID As Long, ByVal Arg1 _
    As Long, ByVal Arg2 As Long)
If Arg1 = 0 Then Exit Sub
Sheets("Sheet1").Cells.Interior.ColorIndex = xlNone
    If ElementID = 3 Then
    If Arg2 = -1 Then
        ' Selected the entire series in Arg1
        Sheets("Sheet1").Range("A2:A22").Offset(0, Arg1).Interior.ColorIndex = 19
    Else
        ' Selected a single point in range Arg1, Point Arg2
        Sheets("Sheet1").Range("A1").Offset(Arg2, Arg1).Interior.ColorIndex = 19
    End If
End If
End Sub
```

Figure 9.7
You can use the
Chart_Select event
to highlight the data
used to create a point on
the chart.

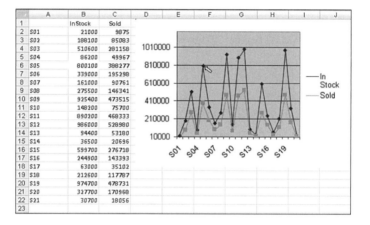

Chart_SeriesChange(ByVal SeriesIndex As Long, ByVal PointIndex As Long)

Chart_SeriesChange occurs when a chart data point is updated. SeriesIndex is the offset in the Series collection of updated series; PointIndex is the offset in the Point collection of updated point.

Chart_DragOver()

Chart_DragOver occurs when a range is dragged over to a chart. This event no longer works in Excel 2007, but a program using it will compile for use in previous versions of Excel.

Chart_DragPlot()

Chart_DragPlot occurs when a range is dragged and dropped on a chart. This event no longer works in Excel 2007, but a program using it will compile for use in previous versions of Excel.

Application-Level Events

Application-level events affect all open workbooks in an Excel session. They require a class module to access them (similar to the class module used to access events for embedded chart events). Follow these steps to create the class module:

1. Insert a class module.

2. Rename the module **cl_AppEvents**.

3. Enter the following line of code in the class module:

   ```
   Public WithEvents AppEvent As Application
   ```

   The application events are now available to the workbook, as shown in Figure 9.8. They are accessed in the class module rather than in a standard module.

4. Insert a standard module.

5. Enter the following lines of code in the standard module:

   ```
   Dim myAppEvent As New cl_AppEvents
   Sub InitializeAppEvent()
       Set myAppEvent.AppEvent = Application
   End Sub
   ```

   These lines initialize the application to recognize application events. The procedure must be run once per session (use Workbook_Open to automate this).

Figure 9.8
Application events are now available through the class module.

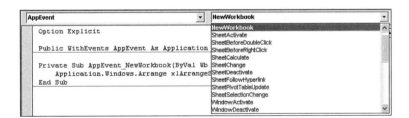

> **NOTE**
> The object in front of the event, such as AppEvent, is dependent on the name given in the class module.

NEW AppEvent_AfterCalculate()

AppEvent_AfterCalculate occurs after all calculations are complete and there aren't any outstanding queries or incomplete calculations.

> **NOTE** This event occurs after all other Calculation, AfterRefresh, and SheetChange events and after Application.CalculationState is set to xlDone.

AppEvent_NewWorkbook(ByVal Wb As Workbook)

AppEvent_NewWorkbook occurs when a new workbook is created. Wb is the new workbook. The following sample arranges the open workbooks in a tiled configuration:

```
Private Sub AppEvent_NewWorkbook(ByVal Wb As Workbook)
    Application.Windows.Arrange xlArrangeStyleTiled
End Sub
```

AppEvent_SheetActivate (ByVal Sh As Object)

AppEvent_SheetActivate occurs when a sheet is activated. Sh is the sheet (worksheet or chart sheet).

AppEvent_SheetBeforeDoubleClick(ByVal Sh As Object, ByVal Target As Range, Cancel As Boolean)

AppEvent_SheetBeforeDoubleClick occurs when the user double-clicks a worksheet. Target is the selected range on the sheet; Cancel is set to False by default, but if set to True, it prevents the default action (such as entering a cell) from happening.

AppEvent_SheetBeforeRightClick(ByVal Sh As Object, ByVal Target As Range, Cancel As Boolean)

AppEvent_SheetBeforeRightClick occurs when the user right-clicks any worksheet. Sh is the active worksheet; Target is the object right-clicked; Cancel set to True prevents the default action from taking place.

AppEvent_SheetCalculate(ByVal Sh As Object)

AppEvent_SheetCalculate occurs when any worksheet is recalculated or any updated data is plotted on a chart. Sh is the active sheet.

AppEvent_SheetChange(ByVal Sh As Object, ByVal Target As Range)

AppEvent_SheetChange occurs when the value of any cell is changed. Sh is the worksheet; Target is the changed range.

AppEvent_SheetDeactivate`(ByVal Sh As Object)`

`AppEvent_SheetDeactivate` occurs when any chart sheet or worksheet in a workbook is deactivated. `Sh` is the sheet being deactivated.

AppEvent_SheetFollowHyperlink`(ByVal Sh As Object,`
`ByVal Target As Hyperlink)`

`AppEvent_SheetFollowHyperlink` occurs when any hyperlink is clicked in Excel. `Sh` is the active worksheet; `Target` is the hyperlink.

AppEvent_SheetSelectionChange`(ByVal Sh As Object,`
`ByVal Target As Range)`

`AppEvent_SheetSelectionChange` occurs when a new range is selected on any sheet. `Sh` is the active sheet; `Target` is the selected range.

AppEvent_WindowActivate`(ByVal Wb As Workbook,`
`ByVal Wn As Window)`

`AppEvent_WindowActivate` occurs when any workbook window is activated. `Wb` is the workbook being deactivated; `Wn` is the window.

AppEvent_WindowDeactivate`(ByVal Wb As Workbook,`
`ByVal Wn As Window)`

`AppEvent_WindowDeactivate` occurs when any workbook window is deactivated. `Wb` is the active workbook; `Wn` is the window.

AppEvent_WindowResize`(ByVal Wb As Workbook, ByVal Wn As Window)`

`AppEvent_WindowResize` occurs when the active workbook is resized. `Wb` is the active workbook; `Wn` is the window.

> **CAUTION**
>
> If you disable the capability to resize (`EnableResize = False`), the minimize and maximize buttons are removed, and the workbook cannot be resized. To undo this, type
> `ActiveWindow.EnableResize = True` in the Immediate window.

AppEvent_WorkbookActivate`(ByVal Wb As Workbook)`

`AppEvent_WorkbookActivate` occurs when any workbook is activated. `Wn` is the window. The following sample maximizes any workbook when it is activated:

```
Private Sub AppEvent_WorkbookActivate(ByVal Wb as Workbook)
    Wb.WindowState = xlMaximized
End Sub
```

AppEvent_WorkbookAddinInstall(ByVal Wb As Workbook)

AppEvent_WorkbookAddinInstall occurs when a workbook is installed as an add-in (Microsoft Office Button, Excel Options, Add-ins). Double-clicking an XLAM file to open it does not activate the event. Wb is the workbook being installed.

AppEvent_WorkbookAddinUninstall(ByVal Wb As Workbook)

AppEvent_WorkbookAddinUninstall occurs when a workbook (add-in) is uninstalled. The add-in is not automatically closed. Wb is the workbook being uninstalled.

AppEvent_WorkbookBeforeClose(ByVal Wb As Workbook, Cancel As Boolean)

AppEvent_WorkbookBeforeClose occurs when a workbook closes. Wb is the workbook; Cancel set to True prevents the workbook from closing.

AppEvent_WorkbookBeforePrint(ByVal Wb As Workbook, Cancel As Boolean)

AppEvent_WorkbookBeforePrint occurs when any print command is used—menu, toolbar, keyboard, or macro. Wb is the workbook; Cancel set to True prevents the workbook from being printed.

The following sample places the username in the footer of each sheet printed:

```
Private Sub AppEvent_WorkbookBeforePrint(ByVal Wb As Workbook, _
    Cancel As Boolean)
Wb.ActiveSheet.PageSetup.LeftFooter = Application.UserName
End Sub
```

AppEvent_WorkbookBeforeSave(ByVal Wb As Workbook, ByVal SaveAsUI As Boolean, Cancel As Boolean)

AppEvent_Workbook_BeforeSave occurs when the workbook is saved. Wb is the workbook; SaveAsUI is set to True if the Save As dialog box is to be displayed; Cancel set to True prevents the workbook from being saved.

AppEvent_WorkbookNewSheet(ByVal Wb As Workbook, ByVal Sh As Object)

AppEvent_WorkbookNewSheet occurs when a new sheet is added to the active workbook. Wb is the workbook; Sh is the new worksheet or chart sheet object.

AppEvent_WorkbookOpen(ByVal Wb As Workbook)

> AppEvent_WorkbookOpen occurs when a workbook is opened. Wb is the workbook that was just opened.

AppEvent_WorkbookPivotTableCloseConnection(ByVal Wb As Workbook, ByVal Target As PivotTable)

> AppEvent_PivotTableCloseConnection occurs when a pivot table report closes its connection to its data source. Wb is the workbook containing the pivot table that triggered the event; Target is pivot table that has closed the connection.

AppEvent_WorkbookPivotTableOpenConnection(ByVal Wb As Workbook, ByVal Target As PivotTable)

> AppEvent_PivotTableOpenConnection occurs when a pivot table report opens a connection to its data source. Wb is the workbook containing the pivot table that triggered the event; Target is the pivot table that has opened the connection.

AppEvent_WorkbookRowsetComplete(ByVal Wb As Workbook, ByVal Description As String, ByVal Sheet As String, ByVal Success As Boolean)

> AppEvent_RowsetComplete occurs when the user drills through a recordset or calls upon the rowset action on an OLAP pivot table. Wb is the workbook that triggered the event; Description is a description of the event; Sheet is the name of the sheet on which the recordset is created; Success indicates success or failure.

AppEvent_WorkbookSync(ByVal Wb As Workbook, ByVal SyncEventType As Office.MsoSyncEventType)

> AppEvent_Workbook_Sync occurs when the local copy of a sheet in a workbook that is part of a Document Workspace is synchronized with the copy on the server. Wb is the workbook that triggered the event; SyncEventType is the status of the synchronization.

Next Steps

In this chapter, you learned more about interfacing with Excel. The next chapter introduces you to tools you can use to interact with the users, prompting them for information to use in your code, warning them of illegal actions, or just providing them with an interface to work with other than the spreadsheet.

Userforms—An Introduction

10

User Interaction Methods

Userforms enable you to display information and allow the user to input information. `InputBox` and `MsgBox` controls are simple ways of doing this. You can use the userform controls in the VB Editor to create more complex forms.

This chapter covers simple user interface using input boxes and message boxes and the basics of creating userforms in the VB Editor. For more advanced programming, see Chapter 23, "Advanced Userform Techniques."

Input Boxes

The `InputBox` function is used to create a basic interface element that requests input from the user before the program can continue. You can configure the prompt, the title for the window, a default value, the window position, and user help files. Only two buttons are provided: OK and Cancel. The returned value is a string.

The following code asks the user for the number of months to be averaged. Figure 10.1 shows the resulting `InputBox`.

```
AveMos = InputBox(Prompt:="Enter the number " & _
" of months to average", Title:="Enter Months", _
Default:="3")
```

Figure 10.1
A simple, but effective
input box.

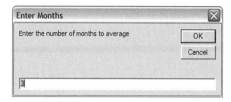

Message Boxes

The MsgBox function creates a message box that displays information and waits for the user to click a button before continuing. Whereas InputBox only has OK and Cancel buttons, MsgBox allows you to choose from several configurations of buttons, including Yes, No, OK, and Cancel. You can also configure the prompt, the window title, and help files. The following code produces a simple prompt to find out whether the user wants to continue. A Select Case statement is then used to continue the program with the appropriate action. Figure 10.2 shows the resulting customized message box.

```
MyMsg = "Do you want to Continue?"
Response = MsgBox(myMsg, vbExclamation + vbYesNoCancel, myTitle)
Select Case Response
    Case Is = vbYes
        ActiveWorkbook.Close SaveChanges:=False
    Case Is = vbNo
        ActiveWorkbook.Close SaveChanges:=True
    Case Is = vbCancel
        Exit Sub
End Select
```

Figure 10.2
The MsgBox function is
used to display informa-
tion and obtain a basic
response from the user.

Creating a Userform

Userforms combine the capabilities of InputBox and MsgBox to create a more efficient way of interacting with the user. For example, rather than have the user fill out personal information on a sheet, you can create a userform that prompts for the required data (see Figure 10.3).

Figure 10.3
You can create a custom
userform to get more
information from
the user.

Insert a userform in the VB Editor by choosing Insert, UserForm from the main menu. A UserForm module is added to the Project Explorer, a blank form appears in the window where your code usually is, and the Controls toolbox appears.

You can resize the form by grabbing and dragging the handles on the right side, bottom edge, or lower-right corner of the userform. To add controls to the form, click the desired control in the toolbox and draw it on the form. Controls can be moved and resized at any time.

> **NOTE**
>
> The toolbox, by default, displays the most common controls. To access more controls, right-click the toolbox and select Additional Controls. But be careful; other users may not have the same additional controls as you do. If you send them a form with a control they don't have installed, the program will generate an error.

After a control is added to a form, its properties can be changed from the Properties window. These properties can be set manually now or set later programmatically. If the Properties window is not visible, you can bring it up by selecting View, Properties Window. Figure 10.4 shows the Properties window for a text box.

10

Figure 10.4
Use the Properties window to change the properties of a control.

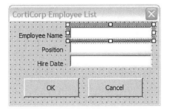
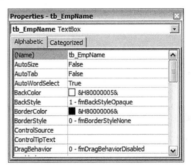

Calling and Hiding a Userform

A userform can be called from any module. `FormName.Show` pops up a form for the user:

```
frm_AddEmp.Show
```

The `Load` method can also be used to call a userform. This allows a form to be loaded, but remain hidden:

```
Load frm_AddEmp
```

To hide a userform, use the `Hide` method. The form is still active but is now hidden from the user. The controls on the form can still be accessed programmatically:

```
Frm_AddEmp.Hide
```

The Unload method unloads the form from memory and removes it from the user's view. The form can no longer be accessed by the user or programmatically:

```
Unload Me
```

Programming the Userform

The code for a control goes in the forms module. Unlike the other modules, double-clicking the Forms module opens up the form in Design view. To view the code, right-click the module or the userform in Design mode and select View Code.

Userform Events

Just like a worksheet, a userform has events triggered by actions. After the userform has been added to the project, the events are available in the Properties drop-down list at the top-right of the code window (see Figure 10.5) by selecting UserForm from the Objects drop-down on the left.

Figure 10.5
Various events for the userform can be selected from the drop-down list at the top of the code window.

The available events for userforms are described in Table 10.1.

Table 10.1   The Events for Userforms

Event	Description
Activate	Occurs when a userform is shown either from being loaded or unhidden. This event is triggered after the Initialize event.
AddControl	Occurs when a control is added to a userform at runtime. Does not run at design time or upon userform initialization.
BeforeDragOver	Occurs while the user does a drag and drop onto the userform.
BeforeDroporPaste	Occurs right before the user is about to drop or paste data into the userform.
Click	Occurs when the user clicks the userform with the mouse.
DblClick	Occurs when the user double-clicks the userform with the mouse.
Deactivate	Occurs when a userform is deactivated.
Error	Occurs when the userform runs into an error and can't return the error information.

Event	Description
Initialize	Occurs when the userform is first loaded, before the Activate event. If you hide then show a form, Initialize won't trigger.
KeyDown	Occurs when the user presses a key on the keyboard.
KeyPress	Occurs when the user presses an ANSI key. An ANSI key is a typeable character, such as the letter *A*. A nontypeable character would be, for example, the Tab key.
KeyUp	Occurs when the user releases a key on the keyboard.
Layout	Occurs when the control changes size.
MouseDown	Occurs when the user presses the mouse button within the borders of the userform.
MouseMove	Occurs when the user moves the mouse within the borders of the userform.
MouseUp	Occurs when the user releases the mouse button within the borders of the userform.
QueryClose	Occurs before a userform closes. It allows you to recognize the method used to close a form and have code respond accordingly.
RemoveControl	Occurs when a control is deleted from within the userform.
Resize	Occurs when the userform is resized.
Scroll	Occurs when the scrollbar box, if visible, is repositioned.
Terminate	Occurs after the userform has been unloaded. It's triggered after QueryClose.
Zoom	Occurs when the zoom value is changed.

Programming Controls

To program a control, highlight it and select View, Code. The footer, header, and default action for the control is automatically entered in the programming field. To see what other actions are available for a control, select the control from the Object drop-down and view the actions in the Properties drop-down, as shown in Figure 10.6.

Figure 10.6
Various actions for a control can be selected from the VB Editor drop-downs.

The controls are objects, like `ActiveWorkbook`. They have properties and methods, dependent on the type of control. Most of the programming for the controls is done behind the form; but if another module needs to refer to a control, the parent, which is the form, needs to be included with the object.

```
Private Sub btn_EmpCancel_Click()
Unload Me
End Sub
```

The preceding code can be broken down into three sections:

- `btn_EmpCancel`—Name given to the control
- `Click`—Action of the control
- `Unload Me`—The code behind the control (in this case, unloading the form)

CASE STUDY

Adding Controls to an Existing Form

If you have a userform that you've been using for some time and later try to add a new control, you might find that Excel seems to get confused about the control. You will see that the control is added to the form, but when you right-click the control and choose View Code, the code module does not seem to acknowledge that the control exists. The control name will not be available in the left drop-down at the top of the code module.

To work around this situation, follow these steps:

1. Add all the controls you need to add to the existing form.
2. In the Project Explorer, right-click the userform and choose Export File. Choose Save to save the file in the default location.
3. In the Project Explorer, right-click the userform and choose Remove. Because you just exported, you can click No to the question about exporting.
4. Right-click anywhere in the Project Explorer and choose Import File. Select the filename that you saved in step 2.

The new controls will now be available in the code pane of the userform.

Using Basic Form Controls

Each control has different events associated with it, allowing you to code what happens based on the user's actions. A table reviewing the control events is available at the end of each of the sections that follow.

Using Labels, Text Boxes, and Command Buttons

Our basic form, as shown in Figure 10.7, consists of labels, text boxes, and command buttons. It is a simple yet effective method of requesting information from the user. After the text boxes have been filled in, the user clicks OK, and the information is added to a sheet (see Figure 10.8).

Figure 10.7
A simple form to collect information from the user.

Figure 10.8
The information gets added to the sheet.

	A	B	C
1	Add	View	
2	**Name**	**Position**	**Hire Date**
3	Tracy Syrstad	Project Consultant	20-Jul-03
4	Cort Chilldon-Hoff	CEO	1-Jan-01
5			

```
Private Sub btn_EmpOK_Click()
Dim LastRow As Long
LastRow = Worksheets("Employee").Cells(Worksheets("Employee").Rows.Count, 1) _
        .End(xlUp).Row + 1
Cells(LastRow, 1).Value = tb_EmpName.Value
Cells(LastRow, 2).Value = tb_EmpPosition.Value
Cells(LastRow, 3).Value = tb_EmpHireDate.Value
End Sub
```

With a change in code as shown in the following sample, the same form design can be used to retrieve information. The following code sample retrieves the position and hire date after the employee name has been entered:

```
Private Sub btn_EmpOK_Click()
Dim EmpFound As Range
With Range("EmpList") 'a named range on a sheet listing the employee names
    Set EmpFound = .Find(tb_EmpName.Value)
    If EmpFound Is Nothing Then
        MsgBox ("Employee not found!")
        tb_EmpName.Value = ""
        Exit Sub
    Else
        With Range(EmpFound.Address)
            tb_EmpPosition = .Offset(0, 1)
            tb_HireDate = .Offset(0, 2)
        End With
    End If
End With
End Sub
```

The available events for `Label`, `TextBox`, and `CommandButton` controls are described in Table 10.2.

Table 10.2   The Events for `Label`**,** `TextBox`**, and** `CommandButton` **Controls**

Event	Description
`AfterUpdate`[2]	Occurs after the control's data has been changed by the user.
`BeforeDragOver`	Occurs while the user drags and drops data onto the control.
`BeforeDropOrPaste`	Occurs right before the user is about to drop or paste data into the control.
`BeforeUpdate`[2]	Occurs before the data in the control is changed.
`Change`[2]	Occurs when the value of the control is changed.
`Click`[1,3]	Occurs when the user clicks the control with the mouse.
`DblClick`	Occurs when the user double-clicks the control with the mouse.
`DropButtonClick`[2]	Occurs when the user presses F4 on the keyboard. This is similar to the drop-down control on the combo box, but there is no drop-down on a text box.
`Enter`[2,3]	Occurs right before the control receives the focus from another control on the same userform.
`Error`	Occurs when the control runs into an error and can't return the error information.
`Exit`[2,3]	Occurs right after the control loses focus to another control on the same userform.
`KeyDown`[2,3]	Occurs when the user presses a key on the keyboard.
`KeyPress`[2,3]	Occurs when the user presses an ANSI key. An ANSI key is a typeable character, such as the letter *A*. A nontypeable character would be, for example, the Tab key.
`KeyUp`[2,3]	Occurs when the user releases a key on the keyboard.
`MouseDown`	Occurs when the user presses the mouse button within the borders of the control.
`MouseMove`	Occurs when the user moves the mouse within the borders of the control.
`MouseUp`	Occurs when the user releases the mouse button within the borders of the control.

[1] `Label` *control only*

[2] `TextBox` *control only*

[3] `CommandButton` *control only*

Deciding Whether to Use List Boxes or Combo Boxes in Forms

You can let users type in an employee name to search for, but what if they misspell the name? You need a way of making sure that the name is entered correctly. Which do you use: a list box or a combo box?

■ A list box displays a list of values from which the user can choose.

 ■ A combo box displays a list of values from which the user can choose and allows the user to enter a new value.

In this case, where we want to limit user options, we use a list box to list the employee names, as shown in Figure 10.9.

Figure 10.9
Use a list box to control user input.

In the `RowSource` property of the list box, enter the range from which the control should draw its data. Use a dynamic named range to keep the list updated if employees are added:

```
Private Sub btn_EmpOK_Click()
Dim EmpFound As Range
With Range("EmpList")
    Set EmpFound = .Find(lb_EmpName.Value)
    If EmpFound Is Nothing Then
        MsgBox ("Employee not found!")
        lb_EmpName.Value = ""
        Exit Sub
    Else
        With Range(EmpFound.Address)
            tb_EmpPosition = .Offset(0, 1)
            tb_HireDate = .Offset(0, 2)
        End With
    End If
End With
End Sub
```

Using the `MultiSelect` Property of a List Box

List boxes have a `MultiSelect` property, which allows the user to select multiple items from the choices in the list box, as shown in Figure 10.10:

■ `fmMultiSelectSingle`—The default setting allows only a single item selection at a time.

■ `fmMultiSelectMulti`—Allows an item to be deselected by clicking it again; multiple items can also be selected.

■ `fmMultiSelectExtended`—Allows the Ctrl and Shift keys to be used to select multiple items.

Figure 10.10
MultiSelect can
allow the user to select
multiple items from a
list box.

If multiple items are selected, the Value property cannot be used to retrieve the items. Instead, check whether the item is selected, and then manipulate it as needed:

```
Private Sub btn_EmpOK_Click()
Dim LastRow As Long, i As Integer
LastRow = Worksheets("Sheet2").Cells(Worksheets("Sheet2").Rows.Count, 1) _
        .End(xlUp).Row + 1
Cells(LastRow, 1).Value = tb_EmpName.Value
'check the selection status of the items in the ListBox
For i = 0 To lb_EmpPosition.ListCount - 1
'if the item is selected, add it to the sheet
    If lb_EmpPosition.Selected(i) = True Then
        Cells(LastRow, 2).Value = Cells(LastRow, 2).Value & _
        lb_EmpPosition.List(i) & ","
    End If
Next i
Cells(LastRow, 3).Value = tb_HireDate.Value
End Sub
```

The items in a list box start counting at zero; so if you use the ListCount property, you must subtract one from the result:

```
For i = 0 To lb_EmpPosition.ListCount - 1
```

The available events for ListBox controls and ComboBox controls are described in Table 10.3.

Table 10.3   Events for ListBox and ComboBox Controls

Event	Description
AfterUpdate	Occurs after the control's data has been changed by the user.
BeforeDragOver	Occurs while the user drags and drops data onto the control.
BeforeDropOrPaste	Occurs right before the user is about to drop or paste data into the control.
BeforeUpdate	Occurs before the data in the control is changed.
Change	Occurs when the value of the control is changed.
Click	Occurs when the user selects a value from the list box or combo box.
DblClick	Occurs when the user double-clicks the control with the mouse.
DropButtonClick[1]	Occurs when the drop-down list appears after the user clicks the drop-down arrow of the combo box or presses F4 on the keyboard.

Event	Description
Enter	Occurs right before the control receives the focus from another control on the same userform.
Error	Occurs when the control runs into an error and can't return the error information.
Exit	Occurs right after the control loses focus to another control on the same userform.
KeyDown	Occurs when the user presses a key on the keyboard.
KeyPress	Occurs when the user presses an ANSI key. An ANSI key is a typeable character, such as the letter *A*. A nontypeable character would be, for example, the Tab key.
KeyUp	Occurs when the user releases a key on the keyboard.
MouseDown	Occurs when the user presses the mouse button within the borders of the control.
MouseMove	Occurs when the user moves the mouse within the borders of the control.
MouseUp	Occurs when the user releases the mouse button within the borders of the control.

[1] ComboBox *control only*

Adding Option Buttons to a Userform

Option buttons are similar to check boxes in that they can be used to make a selection. But, unlike check boxes, option buttons can be easily configured to allow only one selection out of a group.

Using the Frame tool, draw a frame to separate the next set of controls from the other controls on the userform. The frame is used to group option buttons together, as shown in Figure 10.11.

Figure 10.11
Use a frame to group
option buttons together.

Option buttons have a GroupName property. If you assign the same group name, Buildings, to a set of option buttons, you force them to act collectively as a toggle, so that only one button in the set can be selected. Selecting an option button automatically deselects the other buttons in the same group or frame. To prevent this behavior, either leave the GroupName property blank or enter another name.

> **TIP**
>
> For users who prefer to select the option button's label rather than the button itself, add code to the label to trigger the option button.
>
> ```
> Private Sub Lbl_Bldg1_Click()
> Obtn_Bldg1.Value = True
> End Sub
> ```

The available events for OptionButton controls and Frame controls are described in Table 10.4.

Table 10.4   Events for OptionButton and Frame Controls

Event	Description
AfterUpdate[1]	Occurs after the control's data has been changed by the user.
AddControl[2]	Occurs when a control is added to a frame on a form at runtime. Does not run at design time or upon userform initialization.
BeforeDragOver	Occurs while the user does a drag and drop onto the control.
BeforeDropOrPaste	Occurs right before the user is about to drop or paste data into the control.
BeforeUpdate[1]	Occurs before the data in the control is changed.
Change[1]	Occurs when the value of the control is changed.
Click	Occurs when the user clicks the control with the mouse.
DblClick	Occurs when the user double-clicks the control with the mouse.
Enter	Occurs right before the control receives the focus from another control on the same userform.
Error	Occurs when the control runs into an error and can't return the error information.
Exit	Occurs right after the control loses focus to another control on the same userform.
KeyDown	Occurs when the user presses a key on the keyboard.
KeyPress	Occurs when the user presses an ANSI key. An ANSI key is a typeable character, such as the letter *A*. A nontypeable character would be, for example, the Tab key.

Event	Description
KeyUp	Occurs when the user releases a key on the keyboard.
Layout[2]	Occurs when the frame changes size.
MouseDown	Occurs when the user presses the mouse button within the borders of the control.
MouseMove	Occurs when the user moves the mouse within the borders of the control.
MouseUp	Occurs when the user releases the mouse button within the borders of the control.
RemoveControl[2]	Occurs when a control is deleted from within the frame control.
Scroll[2]	Occurs when the scrollbar box, if visible, is repositioned.
Zoom[2]	Occurs when the zoom value is changed.

[1] *OptionButton control only*

[2] *Frame control only*

10

Adding Graphics to a Userform

A listing on a form can be even more helpful if a corresponding graphic is added to the form.

The following code displays the photograph corresponding to the selected employee from the list box:

```
Private Sub lb_EmpName_Change()
Dim EmpFound As Range
With Range("EmpList")
    Set EmpFound = .Find(lb_EmpName.Value)
    If EmpFound Is Nothing Then
        MsgBox ("Employee not found!")
        lb_EmpName.Value = ""
        Exit Sub
    Else
        With Range(EmpFound.Address)
            tb_EmpPosition = .Offset(0, 1)
            tb_HireDate = .Offset(0, 2)
            On Error Resume Next
            Img_Employee.Picture = LoadPicture _
        ("C:\Excel VBA 2007 by Jelen & Syrstad\" & EmpFound & ".bmp")
            On Error GoTo 0
        End With
    End If
End With
```

The available events for `Graphic` controls are described in Table 10.5.

Table 10.5   Events for `Graphic` Controls

Event	Description
BeforeDragOver	Occurs while the user drags and drops data onto the control.
BeforeDropOrPaste	Occurs right before the user is about to drop or paste data into the control.
Click	Occurs when the user clicks the image with the mouse.
DblClick	Occurs when the user double-clicks the image with the mouse.
Error	Occurs when the control runs into an error and can't return the error information.
MouseDown	Occurs when the user presses the mouse button within the borders of the image.
MouseMove	Occurs when the user moves the mouse within the borders of the image.
MouseUp	Occurs when the user releases the mouse button within the borders of the control.

Using a Spin Button on a Userform

As it is, the Hire Date field allows the user to enter the date in any format: 1/1/1 or January 1, 2001. This possible inconsistency can create problems later on if you need to use or search for dates. The solution? Force users to enter dates in a unified manner.

Spin buttons allow the user to increment/decrement through a series of numbers. In this way, the user is forced to enter numbers rather than text.

Draw a spin button for a Month entry on the form. In the Properties, set the Min to 1 (for January) and the Max to 12 (for December). In the Value property, enter 1, the first month. Next, draw a text box next to the spin button. This is the text box that will reflect the value of the spin button. (Labels can also be used.)

```
Private Sub SpBtn_Month_Change()
tb_Month.Value = SpBtn_Month.Value
End Sub
```

Finish building the form. Use a Min of 1 and Max of 31 for days; Min of 1900 and a Max of 2100 for Year:

```
Private Sub btn_EmpOK_Click()
Dim LastRow As Long, i As Integer
LastRow = Worksheets("Sheet2").Cells(Worksheets("Sheet2").Rows.Count, 1) _
        .End(xlUp).Row + 1
Cells(LastRow, 1).Value = tb_EmpName.Value
For i = 0 To lb_EmpPosition.ListCount - 1
```

```
        If lb_EmpPosition.Selected(i) = True Then
            Cells(LastRow, 2).Value = Cells(LastRow, 2).Value & _
            lb_EmpPosition.List(i) & ","
        End If
    Next i
    'Concatenate the values from the textboxes to create the date
    Cells(LastRow, 3).Value = tb_Month.Value & "/" & tb_Day.Value & __
        "/" & tb_Year.Value
    End Sub
```

The available events for `SpinButton` controls are described in Table 10.6.

Table 10.6   Events for `SpinButton` Controls

Event	Description
AfterUpdate	Occurs after the control's data has been changed by the user.
BeforeDragOver	Occurs while the user drags and drops data onto the control.
BeforeDropOrPaste	Occurs right before the user is about to drop or paste data into the control.
BeforeUpdate	Occurs before the data in the control is changed.
Change	Occurs when the value of the control is changed.
DblClick	Occurs when the user double-clicks the control.
Enter	Occurs right before the control receives the focus from another control on the same userform.
Error	Occurs when the control runs into an error and can't return the error information.
Exit	Occurs right after the control loses focus to another control on the same userform.
KeyDown	Occurs when the user presses a key on the keyboard.
KeyPress	Occurs when the user presses an ANSI key. An ANSI key is a typeable character, such as the letter *A*. A nontypeable character would be, for example, the Tab key.
KeyUp	Occurs when the user releases a key on the keyboard.
SpinDown	Occurs when the user clicks the lower or left spin button, decreasing the value.
SpinUp	Occurs when the user clicks the upper or right spin button, increasing the value.

Using the `MultiPage` Control to Combine Forms

The `MultiPage` control provides a neat way of organizing multiple forms. Instead of having a form for personal employee information and one for on-the-job information, combine the information into one multipage form, as shown in Figures 10.12 and 10.13.

Figure 10.12
Use the `MultiPage` control to combine multiple forms. The first page of the form.

Figure 10.13
The second page.

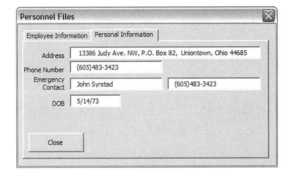

> **TIP**
>
> Multipage forms should be planned from the beginning—adding them after the rest of the form is created is not an easy task. If you decide at a later point you need a multipage form, insert a new form, draw the multipage, and copy/paste the controls from the other forms to the new form.

> **NOTE**
>
> Unlike the other controls, you can't right-click the `MultiPage` control and view code. Instead, select the control and press F7 on the keyboard or go to View, Code.

You can modify a page by right-clicking the page and bringing up a menu of options: Insert a New Page, Delete the Page You Right-Clicked On, Rename a Page, or Move a Page.

Unlike many of the other controls where the `Value` property holds a user-entered or selected value, the `Value` property of the `MultiPage` control holds the number of the active page, starting a zero. For example, if you have a five-page form and want to activate the fourth page, do this:

```
MultiPage1.Value = 4
```

If you have a control you want all the pages to share—such as Save or Cancel buttons—place the control on the main userform rather than on the individual pages, as shown in Figure 10.14.

Figure 10.14
Place common controls on the main userform.

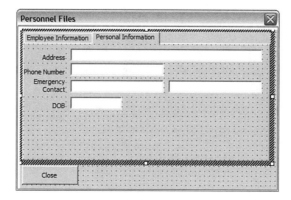

The available events for `MultiPage` controls are described in Table 10.7.

Table 10.7   Events for the `MultiPage` Control

Event	Description
AddControl	Occurs when a control is added to a page of the `MultiPage` control. Does not run at design time or upon userform initialization.
BeforeDragOver	Occurs while the user drags and drops data onto a page of the `MultiPage` control.
BeforeDropOrPaste	Occurs right before the user is about to drop or paste data onto a page of the `MultiPage` control.
Change	Occurs when the user changes pages of a multipage.
Click	Occurs when the user clicks on a page of the `MultiPage` control.
DblClick	Occurs when the user double-clicks a page of the `MultiPage` control with the mouse.
Enter	Occurs right before the multipage receives the focus from another control on the same userform.
Error	Occurs when the `MultiPage` control runs into an error and can't return the error information.
Exit	Occurs right after the multipage loses focus to another control on the same userform.
KeyDown	Occurs when the user presses a key on the keyboard.

continues

Table 10.7   Continued

Event	Description
KeyPress	Occurs when the user presses an ANSI key. An ANSI key is a typeable character, such as the letter *A*. A nontypeable character would be, for example, the Tab key.
KeyUp	Occurs when the user releases a key on the keyboard.
MouseDown	Occurs when the user presses the mouse button within the borders of the control.
MouseMove	Occurs when the user moves the mouse within the borders of the control.
MouseUp	Occurs when the user releases the mouse button within the borders of the control.
RemoveControl	Occurs when a control is removed from a page of the multipage.
Scroll	Occurs when the scrollbar box, if visible, is repositioned.
Zoom	Occurs when the zoom value is changed.

Verifying Field Entry

Even if users are told to fill in all the fields, there is no way to force them to do so—except with an electronic form. As a programmer, you can ensure that all required fields are filled in by not allowing the user to continue until all requirements are met:

```
If tb_EmpName.Value = "" Then
    frm_AddEmp.Hide
    MsgBox ("Please enter an Employee Name")
    frm_AddEmp.Show
    Exit Sub
End If
```

Illegal Window Closing

The userforms created in the VB Editor are not that different from normal windows: They also include the X close button in the upper-right corner. Although using the button is not wrong, it can cause problems, depending on the objective of the userform. In cases like this, you might want to control what happens if the user presses the button. Use the QueryClose event of the userform to find out what method is used to close the form and code an appropriate action:

```
Private Sub UserForm_QueryClose(Cancel As Integer, CloseMode As Integer)
If CloseMode = vbFormControlMenu Then
    MsgBox "Please use the OK or Cancel buttons to close the form", vbCritical
    Cancel = True
End If
End Sub
```

After you know the method the user used to try and close the form, you can create a message box similar to Figure 10.15 to warn the user that the method was illegal.

Figure 10.15
Control what happens when the user clicks the X button.

The `QueryClose` event can be triggered in three other ways:

- `vbFormCode`—The `Unload` statement was used.
- `vbAppWindows`—Windows shuts down.
- `vbAppTaskManager`—The application was shut down by the Task Manager.

Getting a Filename

One of the most common client interactions is when you need the client to specify a path and filename. Excel VBA has a built-in function to display the File Open dialog box, as shown in Figure 10.16. The client browses to and selects a file. When the client chooses the Open button, Excel VBA does not open the file, but instead returns the selected file to you.

Figure 10.16
Use the File Open dialog box to allow the user to select a file.

```
Sub SelectFile()
' Ask which file to copy
x = Application.GetOpenFilename( _
    FileFilter:="Excel Files (*.xls*), *.xls*", _
    Title:="Choose File to Copy", MultiSelect:=False)

' check in case no files were selected
If x = "False" Then Exit Sub

MsgBox "You selected " & x
End Sub
```

The above code will allow the client to select one file. If you want them to specify multiple files, use this code:

```
Sub ManyFiles()
Dim x As Variant

x = Application.GetOpenFilename( _
    FileFilter:="Excel Files (*.xls*), *.xls*", _
    Title:="Choose Files", MultiSelect:=True)

' check in case no files were selected
On Error Resume Next
If x = "False" Then Exit Sub
On Error GoTo 0

For i = 1 To UBound(x)
    MsgBox "You selected " & x(i)
Next i
End Sub
```

In a similar fashion, you can use `Application.GetSaveAsFileName` to find the path and file-name that should be used for saving a file.

Next Steps

Now that you've seen how to work with userforms, the next chapter examines charts. You'll learn how spreadsheet charting has become a highly customizable resource capable of handling large amounts of data.

Creating Charts

11

Charting in Excel 2007

Microsoft took the ambitious leap to attempt to replace the entire charting engine on which they relied for the past 15 years. Although I appreciate their desire to do something completely new, there was not quite enough development time to completely finish the task. This leaves us with three problems:

- Code for all the new features is not backward compatible with previous versions of Excel. There is a nagging subset of features that work in the current version of Excel but do not work in earlier versions of Excel. However, all the good features in charting are new to Excel 2007; consequently, hardly any of the code in this chapter is backward compatible with Excel 97–Excel 2003. If you need to write code to create Excel 2003 charts, you can use the examples from Chapter 10 of our book *VBA and Macros for Microsoft Excel* (ISBN 978-0-7897-3129-0, Que Publishing). The project file from that chapter is available at www.mrexcel.com/vba2007data.html.

- Microsoft was able to finish some work on the macro recorder for the new charting features. The macro recorder can record most actions on the Design and Layout ribbons, but it completely ignores actions on the Format ribbon or in the Format dialog boxes. VBA code is available to micro-format chart elements, but you have to write code to perform actions on the Format ribbon from scratch. You have this book as a reference to help with that endeavor.

You should also review "Using the Watch Window to Discover Object Settings," later in this chapter for a technique to learn VBA code that is not recorded by the macro recorder.

■ There are bugs in the Excel 2007 charting engine. In some cases, editing the SERIES function causes Excel to crash. In other cases, the SERIES function won't even appear. Try creating a chart below row 1100. Page down, page back up, and the chart will render in strange ways. To mitigate this problem, watch for an Office 2007 service release in 2008 and download it as soon as it is available.

Coding for New Charting Features in Excel 2007

Charts have been completely rewritten in Excel 2007. Most code from Excel 2003 will continue to work in Excel 2007. However, if you write code to take advantage of the new charting features, that code will not be backward compatible with Excel 2003.

The following are some of the new methods and features available in Excel 2007:

■ **ApplyLayout**—This method applies one of the chart layouts available on the Design ribbon.

■ **SetElement**—This method chooses any of the built-in element choices from the Layout ribbon.

■ **ChartFormat**—This object enables you to change the fill, glow, line, reflection, shadow, soft edge, or 3D format of most individual chart elements. This is similar to settings on the Format ribbon.

■ **AddChart**—This method enables you to add a chart to an existing worksheet.

Referencing Charts and Chart Objects in VBA Code

If you go back far enough in Excel history, you find that all charts used to be created as their own chart sheets. Then, in the mid-1990s, Excel added the amazing capability to embed a chart right onto an existing worksheet. This allowed a report to be created with tables of numbers and charts all on the same page, something we take for granted today.

These two different ways of dealing with charts have made it necessary for us to deal with two separate object models for charts. When a chart is on its own standalone chart sheet, you are dealing with a Chart object. When a chart is embedded in a worksheet, you are dealing with a ChartObject object. Excel 2007 introduces a third evolutionary branch because objects on a worksheet are also a member of the Shapes collection.

In Excel 2003, to reference the color of the chart area for an embedded chart, you would have to refer to the chart in this manner:

```
Worksheets("Jan").ChartObjects("Chart 1").Chart.ChartArea.Interior.ColorIndex = 4
```

In Excel 2007, you can instead use the Shapes collection:

```
Worksheets("Jan").Shapes("Chart 1").Chart.ChartArea.Interior.ColorIndex = 4
```

In any version of Excel, if a chart is on its own chart sheet, you don't have to specify the container; you can simply refer to the Chart object:

```
Sheets("Chart1").ChartArea.Interior.ColorIndex = 4
```

Creating a Chart

In earlier versions of Excel, you used the `Charts.Add` command to add a new chart. You then specified the source data, the type of chart, and whether the chart should be on a new sheet or embedded on an existing worksheet. The first three lines of the following code create a clustered column chart on a new chart sheet. The fourth line moves the chart back to be an embedded object in `Sheet1`:

```
Charts.Add
ActiveChart.SetSourceData Source:=Worksheets("Sheet1").Range("A1:E4")
ActiveChart.ChartType = xlColumnClustered
ActiveChart.Location Where:=xlLocationAsObject, Name:="Sheet1"
```

If you plan to share your macros with people who still use Excel 2003, you should use the `Charts.Add` method. However, if your application will only be running in Excel 2007, you can use the new `AddChart` method. The code for the `AddChart` method can be as simple as the following:

```
' Create chart on the current sheet
ActiveSheet.Shapes.AddChart.Select
ActiveChart.SetSourceData Source:=Range("A1:E4")
ActiveChart.ChartType = xlColumnClustered
```

Or, you can specify the chart type, size, and location as part of the `AddChart` method, as described in the next section.

Specifying the Size and Location of a Chart

The `AddChart` method has additional parameters you can use to specify the type of chart, the chart's location on the worksheet, and the size of the chart.

The location and size of a chart are specified in points (72 points = 1 inch). For example, the `Top` parameter requires the number of points from the top of row 1 to the top edge of the worksheet.

The following code creates a chart that roughly covers the range C11:J30:

```
Sub SpecifyLocation()
    Dim WS As Worksheet
    Set WS = Worksheets("Sheet1")
    WS.Shapes.AddChart(xlColumnClustered, _
        Left:=100, Top:=150, _
        Width:=400, Height:=300).Select
    ActiveChart.SetSourceData Source:=WS.Range("A1:E4")
End Sub
```

It would require a lot of trial and error to randomly figure out the exact distance in points to cause a chart to line up with a certain cell. Luckily, you can ask VBA to tell you the distance in points to a certain cell. If you ask for the Left property of any cell, you find the distance to the top-left corner of that cell. You can also ask for the width of a range or the height of a range. For example, the following code creates a chart in exactly C11:J30:

```
Sub SpecifyExactLocation()
    Dim WS As Worksheet
    Set WS = Worksheets("Sheet1")
    WS.Shapes.AddChart(xlColumnClustered, _
        Left:=WS.Range("C11").Left, _
        Top:=WS.Range("C11").Top, _
        Width:=WS.Range("C11:J11").Width, _
        Height:=WS.Range("C11:C30").Height).Select
    ActiveChart.SetSourceData Source:=WS.Range("A1:E4")
End Sub
```

In this case, you are not moving the location of the Chart object; rather, you are moving the location of the container that contains the chart. In Excel 2007, it is either the ChartObject or the Shape object. If you try to change the actual location of the chart, you move it within the container. Because you can actually move the chart area a few points in either direction inside the container, the code will run, but you will not get the desired results.

To move a chart that has already been created, you can reference either ChartObject or the Shape and change the Top, Left, Width, and Height properties as shown in the following macro:

```
Sub MoveAfterTheFact()
    Dim WS As Worksheet
    Set WS = Worksheets("Sheet1")
    With WS.ChartObjects("Chart 9")
        .Left = WS.Range("C21").Left
        .Top = WS.Range("C21").Top
        .Width = WS.Range("C1:H1").Width
        .Height = WS.Range("C21:C25").Height
    End With
End Sub
```

Later Referring to a Specific Chart

When a new chart is created, it is given a sequential name, such as Chart 1. If you select a chart and then look in the name box, you see the name of the chart. In Figure 11.1, the name of the chart is Chart 16. This does not mean that there are 16 charts on the worksheet. In this particular case, many individual charts have been created and deleted.

Figure 11.1
You can select a chart and look in the name box to find the name of the chart.

Name Box

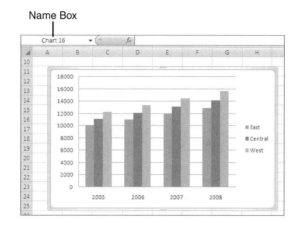

This means that on any given day that your macro runs, the Chart object might have a different name. If you need to reference the chart later in the macro, perhaps after you have selected other cells and the chart is no longer active, you might ask VBA for the name of the chart and store it in a variable for later use, as shown here:

```
Sub RememberTheName()
    Dim WS As Worksheet
    Set WS = Worksheets("Sheet1")
    WS.Shapes.AddChart(xlColumnClustered, _
        Left:=WS.Range("C11").Left, _
        Top:=WS.Range("C11").Top, _
        Width:=WS.Range("C11:J11").Width, _
        Height:=WS.Range("C11:C30").Height _
        ).Select
    ActiveChart.SetSourceData Source:=WS.Range("A1:E4")
    ' Remember the name in a variable
    ThisChartObjectName = ActiveChart.Parent.Name
    ' more lines of code...
    ' then later in the macro, you need to re-assign the chart
    With WS.Shapes(ThisChartObjectName)
        .Chart.SetSourceData Source:=WS.Range("A20:E24"), PlotBy:=xlColumns
        .Top = WS.Range("C26").Top
    End With
End Sub
```

In the preceding macro, the variable ThisChartObjectName contains the name of the Chart object. This method works great if your changes will happen later in the same macro. However, after the macro finishes running, the variable will be out of scope, and you won't be able to access the name later.

If you want to be able to remember a chart name, you could store the name in an out-of-the-way cell on the worksheet. The first macro here stores the name in cell Z1, and the second macro then later modifies the chart using the name stored in cell Z1:

11

```
Sub StoreTheName()
    Dim WS As Worksheet
    Set WS = Worksheets("Sheet1")
    WS.Shapes.AddChart(xlColumnClustered, _
        Left:=WS.Range("C11").Left, _
        Top:=WS.Range("C11").Top, _
        Width:=WS.Range("C11:J11").Width, _
        Height:=WS.Range("C11:C30").Height _
        ).Select
    ActiveChart.SetSourceData Source:=WS.Range("A1:E4")
    Range("Z1").Value = ActiveChart.Parent.Name
End Sub
```

After the previous macro stored the name in cell Z1, the following macro will use the value in Z1 to figure out which macro to change:

```
Sub ChangeTheChartLater()
    Dim WS As Worksheet
    Set WS = Worksheets("Sheet1")
    MyName = WS.Range("Z1").Value
    With WS.Shapes(MyName)
        .Chart.SetSourceData Source:=WS.Range("A20:E24"), PlotBy:=xlColumns
        .Top = WS.Range("C26").Top
    End With

End Sub
```

If you need to modify a preexisting chart—such as a chart that you did not create—and there is only one chart on the worksheet, you can use this line of code:

```
WS.ChartObjects(1).Chart.Interior.ColorIndex = 4
```

If there are many charts and you need to find the one with the upper-left corner located in cell A4, you could loop through all the Chart objects until you find one in the correct location, like this:

```
For each Cht in ActiveSheet.ChartObjects
    If Cht.TopLeftCell.Address = "$A$4" then
        Cht.Interior.ColorIndex = 4
    end if
Next Cht
```

NEW Recording Commands from the Layout or Design Ribbons

With charts in Excel 2007, there are three levels of chart changes. The global chart settings—chart type and style—are on the Design ribbon. Selections from the built-in element settings appear on the Layout ribbon. You make micro-changes by using the Format ribbon.

The macro recorder in Excel 2007 does a great job of recording changes on the Design and Layout ribbon, so if you need to make certain changes, you can quickly record a macro and then copy its code.

Specifying a Built-in Chart Type

There are 73 built-in chart types in Excel 2007. To change a chart to one of the 73 types, you use the `ChartType` property. This property can either be applied to a chart or to a series within a chart. Here's an example that changes the type for the entire chart:

```
ActiveChart.ChartType = xlBubble
```

To change the second series on a chart to a line chart, you use this:

```
ActiveChart.Series(2).ChartType = xlLine
```

Table 11.1 lists the 73 chart type constants that you can use to create various charts. The sequence of Table 11.1 matches the sequence of the charts in the Chart Type dialog.

Table 11.1   Chart Types for Use in VBA

Chart Type	Constant
Clustered Column	`xlColumnClustered`
Stacked Column	`xlColumnStacked`
100% Stacked Column	`xlColumnStacked100`
3-D Clustered Column	`xl3DColumnClustered`
Stacked Column in 3-D	`xl3DColumnStacked`
100% Stacked Column in 3-D	`xl3DColumnStacked100`
3-D Column	`xl3DColumn`
Clustered Cylinder	`xlCylinderColClustered`
Stacked Cylinder	`xlCylinderColStacked`
100% Stacked Cylinder	`xlCylinderColStacked100`
3-D Cylinder	`xlCylinderCol`
Clustered Cone	`xlConeColClustered`
Stacked Cone	`xlConeColStacked`
100% Stacked Cone	`xlConeColStacked100`

continues

Table 11.1   Continued

Chart Type	Constant
3-D Cone	xlConeCol
Clustered Pyramid	xlPyramidColClustered
Stacked Pyramid	xlPyramidColStacked
100% Stacked Pyramid	xlPyramidColStacked100
3-D Pyramid	xlPyramidCol
Line	xlLine
Stacked Line	xlLineStacked
100% Stacked Line	xlLineStacked100
Line with Markers	xlLineMarkers
Stacked Line with Markers	xlLineMarkersStacked
100% Stacked Line with Markers	xlLineMarkersStacked100
3-D Line	xl3DLine
Pie	xlPie
Pie in 3-D	xl3DPie
Pie of Pie	xlPieOfPie
Exploded Pie	xlPieExploded
Exploded Pie in 3-D	xl3DPieExploded
Bar of Pie	xlBarOfPie
Clustered Bar	xlBarClustered
Stacked Bar	xlBarStacked
100% Stacked Bar	xlBarStacked100

Chart Type		**Constant**
	Clustered Bar in 3-D	xl3DBarClustered
	Stacked Bar in 3-D	xl3DBarStacked
	100% Stacked Bar in 3-D	xl3DBarStacked100
	Clustered Horizontal Cylinder	xlCylinderBarClustered
	Stacked Horizontal Cylinder	xlCylinderBarStacked
	100% Stacked Horizontal Cylinder	xlCylinderBarStacked100
	Clustered Horizontal Cone	xlConeBarClustered
	Stacked Horizontal Cone	xlConeBarStacked
	100% Stacked Horizontal Cone	xlConeBarStacked100
	Clustered Horizontal Pyramid	xlPyramidBarClustered
	Stacked Horizontal Pyramid	xlPyramidBarStacked
	100% Stacked Horizontal Pyramid	xlPyramidBarStacked100
	Area	xlArea
	Stacked Area	xlAreaStacked
	100% Stacked Area	xlAreaStacked100
	3-D Area	xl3DArea
	Stacked Area in 3-D	xl3DAreaStacked
	100% Stacked Area in 3-D	xl3DAreaStacked100
	Scatter with only Markers	xlXYScatter
	Scatter with Smooth Lines and Markers	xlXYScatterSmooth
	Scatter with Smooth Lines	xlXYScatterSmoothNoMarkers

continues

11

Table 11.1   Continued

Chart Type		Constant
	Scatter with Straight Lines and Markers	xlXYScatterLines
	Scatter with Straight Lines	xlXYScatterLinesNoMarkers
	High-Low-Close	xlStockHLC
	Open-High-Low-Close	xlStockOHLC
	Volume-High-Low-Close	xlStockVHLC
	Volume-Open-High-Low-Close	xlStockVOHLC
	3-D Surface	xlSurface
	Wireframe 3-D Surface	xlSurfaceWireframe
	Contour	xlSurfaceTopView
	Wireframe Contour	xlSurfaceTopViewWireframe
	Doughnut	xlDoughnut
	Exploded Doughnut	xlDoughnutExploded
	Bubble	xlBubble
	Bubble with a 3-D Effect	xlBubble3DEffect
	Radar	xlRadar
	Radar with Markers	xlRadarMarkers
	Filled Radar	xlRadarFilled

Specifying a Template Chart Type

Excel 2007 allows you to create a custom chart template with all your preferred settings, such as colors and fonts. This is a great technique for saving time when you are creating a chart with a lot of custom formatting.

A VBA macro can make use of a custom chart template, provided that you plan on distributing the custom chart template to each person who will run your macro.

In Excel 2007, you save custom chart types as .crtx files and store them in the %appdata%\Microsoft\Templates\Charts\ folder.

To apply a custom chart type, you use the following:

```
ActiveChart.ApplyChartTemplate ("MyChart.crtx")
```

If the chart template does not exist, VBA returns an error. If you would like Excel to simply continue without displaying a debug error, you can turn off an error handler before the code and turn it back on when you are done. Here's how you do that:

```
On Error Resume Next
ActiveChart.ApplyChartTemplate ("MyChart.crtx")
On Error GoTo 0 ' that final character is a zero
```

Changing a Chart's Layout or Style

Two galleries—the Chart Layout gallery and the Styles gallery—make up the bulk of the Design ribbon.

The Chart Layout gallery offers from 4 to 12 combinations of chart elements. These combinations are different for various chart types. When you look at the gallery shown in Figure 11.2, the ToolTips for the layouts show that the layouts are imaginatively named Layout 1 through Layout 11.

Layout 1

Figure 11.2
The built-in layouts are numbered 1 through 11. For other chart types, you might have from 4 to 12 layouts.

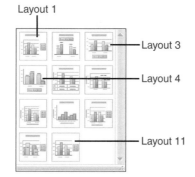

Layout 3

Layout 4

Layout 11

To apply one of the built-in layouts in a macro, you have to use the ApplyLayout method with a number from 1 through 12 to correspond to the built-in layouts. The following code will apply Layout 1 to the active chart:

```
ActiveChart.ApplyLayout 1
```

11

CAUTION

Whereas line charts offer 12 built-in layouts, other types such as radar charts offer as few as 4 built-in layouts. If you attempt to specify apply a layout number that is larger than the layouts available for the current chart type, Excel returns a runtime error 5. Unless you just created the active chart in the same macro, there is always the possibility that the person running the macro changed your line charts to radar charts, so include some error handling before you use the `ApplyLayout` command.

Clearly, to effectively use a built-in layout, you must have actually built a chart by hand and found a layout that you actually like.

As shown in Figure 11.3, the Styles gallery contains 48 styles. These styles are also numbered sequentially, with Styles 1 through 8 in row 1, Styles 9 through 16 in row 2, and so on. These styles actually follow a bit of a pattern:

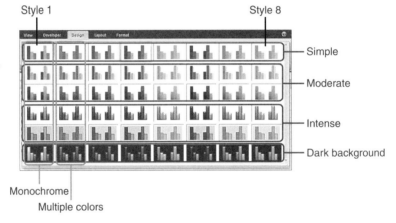

Figure 11.3
The built-in styles are numbered 1 through 48.

- Styles 1, 9, 17, 25, 33, and 41 (that is, the styles in column 1) are monochrome.
- Styles 2, 10, 18, 26, 34, and 42 (that is, the styles in column 2) use different colors for each point.
- All the other styles use hues of a particular theme color.
- Styles 1 through 8 are simple styles.
- Styles 17 through 24 use moderate effects.
- Styles 33 through 40 have intense effects.
- Styles 41 through 48 appear on a dark background.

If you are going to mix styles in a single workbook, consider staying within a single row or a single column of the gallery.

To apply a style to a chart, you use the ChartStyle property, assigning it a value from 1 to 48:

```
ActiveChart.ChartStyle = 1
```

The ChartStyle property changes the colors in the chart. However, a number of formatting changes from the Format ribbon do not get overwritten when you change the ChartStyle property. For example, in Figure 11.4, the second series previously had a glow applied and the third series had a clear glass bevel applied. Running the preceding code did not clear that formatting.

Figure 11.4
Setting the ChartStyle property does not override all settings.

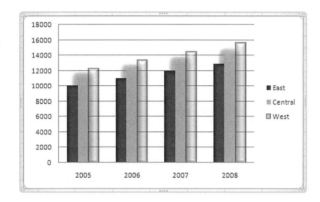

To clear any previous formatting, you use the ClearToMatchStyle method:

```
ActiveChart.ChartStyle = 1
ActiveChart.ClearToMatchStyle
```

⭐ Using SetElement to Emulate Changes on the Layout Ribbon

The Layout ribbon contains a number of built-in settings. Figure 11.5 shows a few of the built-in menu items for the Legend tab. There are similar menus for each of the icons in the figure.

If you use a built-in menu item to change the titles, legend, labels, axes, gridlines, or background, it is probably handled in code that uses the SetElement method, which is new in Excel 2007.

SetElement does not work with the More choices at the bottom of each menu. It also does not work with the 3-D Rotation button. Other than that, you can use SetElement to change everything in the Labels, Axes, Background, and Analysis groups.

11

Figure 11.5
There are built-in menus similar to this one for each icon. If your choice is in the menu, the VBA code uses the SetElement method.

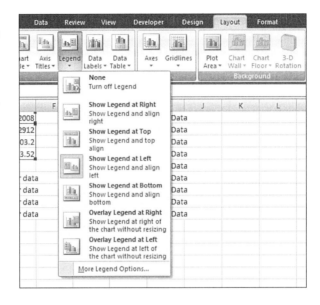

The macro recorder always works for the built-in settings on the Layout ribbon. If you don't feel like looking up the proper constant in this book, you can always quickly record a macro.

The SetElement method is followed by a constant that specifies which menu item to select. For example, if you want to choose Show Legend at Left, you can use this code:

```
ActiveChart.SetElement msoElementLegendLeft
```

Table 11.2 shows all the available constants that you can use with the SetElement method. These are in roughly the same order as they appear on the Layout ribbon.

Table 11.2   Constants Available with SetElement

Layout Ribbon Icon	Chart Element Constant
Chart Title	msoElementChartTitleNone
Chart Title	msoElementChartTitleCenteredOverlay
Chart Title	msoElementChartTitleAboveChart
Axis Titles	msoElementPrimaryCategoryAxisTitleNone
Axis Titles	msoElementPrimaryCategoryAxisTitleBelowAxis
Axis Titles	msoElementPrimaryCategoryAxisTitleAdjacentToAxis
Axis Titles	msoElementPrimaryCategoryAxisTitleHorizontal
Axis Titles	msoElementPrimaryCategoryAxisTitleVertical
Axis Titles	msoElementPrimaryCategoryAxisTitleRotated

Layout Ribbon Icon	Chart Element Constant
Axis Titles	msoElementSecondaryCategoryAxisTitleAdjacentToAxis
Axis Titles	msoElementSecondaryCategoryAxisTitleBelowAxis
Axis Titles	msoElementSecondaryCategoryAxisTitleHorizontal
Axis Titles	msoElementSecondaryCategoryAxisTitleNone
Axis Titles	msoElementSecondaryCategoryAxisTitleRotated
Axis Titles	msoElementSecondaryCategoryAxisTitleVertical
Axis Titles	msoElementPrimaryValueAxisTitleAdjacentToAxis
Axis Titles	msoElementPrimaryValueAxisTitleBelowAxis
Axis Titles	msoElementPrimaryValueAxisTitleHorizontal
Axis Titles	msoElementPrimaryValueAxisTitleNone
Axis Titles	msoElementPrimaryValueAxisTitleRotated
Axis Titles	msoElementPrimaryValueAxisTitleVertical
Axis Titles	msoElementSecondaryValueAxisTitleBelowAxis
Axis Titles	msoElementSecondaryValueAxisTitleHorizontal
Axis Titles	msoElementSecondaryValueAxisTitleNone
Axis Titles	msoElementSecondaryValueAxisTitleRotated
Axis Titles	msoElementSecondaryValueAxisTitleVertical
Axis Titles	msoElementSeriesAxisTitleHorizontal
Axis Titles	msoElementSeriesAxisTitleNone
Axis Titles	msoElementSeriesAxisTitleRotated
Axis Titles	msoElementSeriesAxisTitleVertical
Axis Titles	msoElementSecondaryValueAxisTitleAdjacentToAxis
Legend	msoElementLegendNone
Legend	msoElementLegendRight
Legend	msoElementLegendTop
Legend	msoElementLegendLeft
Legend	msoElementLegendBottom
Legend	msoElementLegendRightOverlay
Legend	msoElementLegendLeftOverlay
Data Labels	msoElementDataLabelCenter
Data Labels	msoElementDataLabelInsideEnd

11

continues

Table 11.2   Continued

Layout Ribbon Icon	Chart Element Constant
Data Labels	msoElementDataLabelNone
Data Labels	msoElementDataLabelInsideBase
Data Labels	msoElementDataLabelOutSideEnd
Data Labels	msoElementDataLabelTop
Data Labels	msoElementDataLabelBottom
Data Labels	msoElementDataLabelRight
Data Labels	msoElementDataLabelLeft
Data Labels	msoElementDataLabelShow
Data Labels	msoElementDataLabelBestFit
Data Table	msoElementDataTableNone
Data Table	msoElementDataTableShow
Data Table	msoElementDataTableWithLegendKeys
Axis	msoElementPrimaryCategoryAxisNone
Axis	msoElementPrimaryCategoryAxisShow
Axis	msoElementPrimaryCategoryAxisWithoutLabels
Axis	msoElementPrimaryCategoryAxisReverse
Axis	msoElementPrimaryCategoryAxisThousands
Axis	msoElementPrimaryCategoryAxisMillions
Axis	msoElementPrimaryCategoryAxisBillions
Axis	msoElementPrimaryCategoryAxisLogScale
Axis	msoElementSecondaryCategoryAxisNone
Axis	msoElementSecondaryCategoryAxisShow
Axis	msoElementSecondaryCategoryAxisWithoutLabels
Axis	msoElementSecondaryCategoryAxisReverse
Axis	msoElementSecondaryCategoryAxisThousands
Axis	msoElementSecondaryCategoryAxisMillions
Axis	msoElementSecondaryCategoryAxisBillions
Axis	msoElementSecondaryCategoryAxisLogScaIe
Axis	msoElementPrimaryValueAxisNone
Axis	msoElementPrimaryValueAxisShow
Axis	msoElementPrimaryValueAxisThousands

11

Layout Ribbon Icon	Chart Element Constant
Axis	msoElementPrimaryValueAxisMillions
Axis	msoElementPrimaryValueAxisBillions
Axis	msoElementPrimaryValueAxisLogScale
Axis	msoElementSecondaryValueAxisNone
Axis	msoElementSecondaryValueAxisShow
Axis	msoElementSecondarWValueAxisThousands
Axis	msoElementSecondaryValueAxisMillions
Axis	msoElementSecondaryValueAxisBillions
Axis	msoElementSecondaryValueAxisLogScale
Axis	msoElementSeriesAxisNone
Axis	msoElementSeriesAxisShow
Axis	msoElementSeriesAxisReverse
Axis	msoElementSeriesAxisWithoutLabeling
GridLines	msoElementPrimaryCategoryGridLinesNone
GridLines	msoElementPrimaryCategoryGridLinesMajor
GridLines	msoElementPrimaryCategoryGridLinesMinor
GridLines	msoElementPrimaryCategoryGridLinesMinorMajor
GridLines	msoElementSecondaryCategoryGridLinesNone
GridLines	msoElementSecondaryCategoryGridLinesMajor
GridLines	msoElementSecondaryCategoryGridLinesMinor
GridLines	msoElementSecondaryCategoryGridLinesMinorMajor
GridLines	msoElementPrimaryValueGridLinesNone
GridLines	msoElementPrimaryValueGridLinesMajor
GridLines	msoElementPrimaryValueGridLinesMinor
GridLines	msoElementPrimaryValueGridLinesMinorMajor
GridLines	msoElementSecondaryValueGridLinesNone
GridLines	msoElementSecondaryValueGridLinesMajor
GridLines	msoElementSecondaryValueGridLinesMinor
GridLines	msoElementSecondaryValueGridLinesMinorMajor
GridLines	msoElementSeriesAxisGridLinesNone
GridLines	msoElementSeriesAxisGridLinesMajor

11

continues

Table 11.2 Continued

Layout Ribbon Icon	Chart Element Constant
GridLines	msoElementSeriesAxisGridLinesMinor
GridLines	msoElementSeriesAxisGridLinesMinorMajor
Plot Area	msoElementPlotAreaNone
Plot Area	msoElementPlotAreaShow
Chart Wall	msoElementChartWallNone
Chart Wall	msoElementChartWallShow
Chart Floor	msoElementChartFloorNone
Chart Floor	msoElementChartFloorShow
Trendline	msoElementTrendlineNone
Trendline	msoElementTrendlineAddLinear
Trendline	msoElementTrendlineAddExponential
Trendline	msoElementTrendlineAddLinearForecast
Trendline	msoElementTrendlineAddTwoPeriodMovingAverage
Lines	msoElementLineNone
Lines	msoElementLineDropLine
Lines	msoElementLineHiLoLine
Lines	msoElementLineDropHiLoLine
Lines	msoElementLineSeriesLine
Up/Down Bars	msoElementUpDownBarsNone
Up/Down Bars	msoElementUpDownBarsShow
Error Bar	msoElementErrorBarNone
Error Bar	msoElementErrorBarStandardError
Error Bar	msoElementErrorBarPercentage
Error Bar	msoElementErrorBarStandardDeviation

CAUTION

If you attempt to format an element that is not present, Excel returns a −2147467259 Method Failed error.

Changing a Chart Title Using VBA

The Layout ribbon's built-in menus enable you to add a title above a chart, but they don't enable you to change the characters in a chart title or axis title.

In the user interface, you can simply double-click the chart title text and type a new title to change the title. Unfortunately, the macro recorder does not record this action.

To specify a chart title, you must type this code:

```
ActiveChart.ChartTitle.Caption = "My Chart"
```

Similarly, you can specify the axis titles by using the `Caption` property. The following code changes the axis title along the category axis:

```
ActiveChart.Axes(xlCategory, xlPrimary).AxisTitle.Caption = "Months"
```

Emulating Changes on the Format Ribbon

In Excel 2007, the macro recorder does not record any actions that happen in the Format ribbon or in the More dialog boxes on the Layout ribbon. This is incredibly frustrating. It is particularly frustrating because Excel 2003 could record these changes with the macro recorder. One solution, if you still have Excel 2003 installed, is to format your chart in Excel 2003 while the macro recorder is on. You can then use that code in Excel 2007, although you then cannot make use of all the new formatting features. For information on discovering charting elements without the assistance of the macro recorder, see the section "Using the Watch Window to Discover Object Settings," later in this chapter.

11

NEW Using the `Format` Method to Access New Formatting Options

Excel 2007 introduces a new object called the ChartFormat object. This object contains the settings for `Fill`, `Glow`, `Line`, `PictureFormat`, `Shadow`, `SoftEdge`, `TextFrame2`, and `ThreeD`. You can access the ChartFormat object by using the `Format` method on many chart elements. Table 11.3 lists a sampling of chart elements that can be formatted using the `Format` method.

Table 11.3   Chart Elements to Which Formatting Applies

Chart Element	VBA to Refer to This Chart Element
Chart Title	`ChartTitle`
Axis Title - Category	`Axes(xlCategory, xlPrimary).AxisTitle`
Axis Title - Value	`Axes(xlValue, xlPrimary).AxisTitle`
Legend	`Legend`
Data Labels for Series 1	`SeriesCollection(1).DataLabels`
Data Labels for Point 2	`SeriesCollection(1).DataLabels(2)` or `SeriesCollection(1).Points(2).DataLabel`

continues

Table 11.3 Continued

Chart Element	VBA to Refer to This Chart Element
Data Table	`DataTable`
Axes – Horizontal	`Axes(xlCategory, xlPrimary)`
Axes – Vertical	`Axes(xlValue, xlPrimary)`
Axis – Series (Surface Charts Only)	`Axes(xlSeries, xlPrimary)`
Major Gridlines	`Axes(xlValue, xlPrimary).MajorGridlines`
Minor Gridlines	`Axes(xlValue, xlPrimary).MinorGridlines`
Plot Area	`PlotArea`
Chart Area	`ChartArea`
Chart Wall	`Walls`
Chart Back Wall	`BackWall`
Chart Side Wall	`SideWall`
Chart Floor	`Floor`
Trendline for Series 1	`SeriesCollection(1).TrendLines(1)`
Droplines	`ChartGroups(1).DropLines`
Up/Down Bars	`ChartGroups(1).UpBars`
Error Bars	`SeriesCollection(1).ErrorBars`
Series(1)	`SeriesCollection(1)`
Series(1) DataPoint	`SeriesCollection(1).Points(3)`

The `Format` method is the gateway to settings for `Fill`, `Glow`, and so on. Each of those objects has different options. The following sections give examples of how to set up each type of format.

Changing an Object's Fill

As shown in Figure 11.6, the Shape Fill drop-down on the Format ribbon allows you to choose a single color, a gradient, a picture, or a texture for the fill.

To apply a specific color, you can use the RGB (red, green, blue) setting. To create a color, you specify a value from 0 to 255 for levels of red, green, and blue. The following code applies a simple blue fill:

```
Dim cht As Chart
Dim upb As UpBars
Set cht = ActiveChart
Set upb = cht.ChartGroups(1).UpBars
upb.Format.Fill.ForeColor.RGB = RGB(0, 0, 255)
```

Figure 11.6
Fill options include a
solid color, a gradient, a
texture, or a picture.

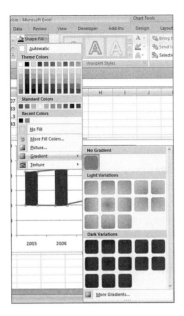

If you would like an object to pick up the color from a specific theme accent color, you use
the `ObjectThemeColor` property. The following code changes the bar color of the first series
to accent color 6 (which is an orange color in the Office theme but might be another color
if the workbook is using a different theme):

```
Sub ApplyThemeColor()
    Dim cht As Chart
    Dim ser As Series
    Set cht = ActiveChart
    Set ser = cht.SeriesCollection(1)
    ser.Format.Fill.ForeColor.ObjectThemeColor = msoThemeColorAccent6
End Sub
```

To apply a built-in texture, you use the `PresetTextured` method. The following code applies
a green marble texture to the second series, but there are 20 different textures that you can
apply:

```
Sub ApplyTexture()
    Dim cht As Chart
    Dim ser As Series
    Set cht = ActiveChart
    Set ser = cht.SeriesCollection(2)
    ser.Format.Fill.PresetTextured (msoTextureGreenMarble)
End Sub
```

> **TIP**
>
> When you type `PresetTextured` followed by an open parenthesis, the VB Editor offers a com-
> plete list of possible texture values.

To fill the bars of a data series with a picture, you use the `UserPicture` method and specify the path and filename of an image on the computer, as in the following example:

```
Sub FormatWithPicture()
    Dim cht As Chart
    Dim ser As Series
    Set cht = ActiveChart
    Set ser = cht.SeriesCollection(1)
    MyPic = "C:\PodCastTitle1.jpg"
    ser.Format.Fill.UserPicture (MyPic)
End Sub
```

Gradients are more difficult to specify than fills. Excel 2007 offers three methods that help you set up the common gradients. The `OneColorGradient` and `TwoColorGradient` methods require that you specify a gradient direction such as `msoGradientFromCorner`. You can then specify one of four styles, numbered 1 through 4, depending on whether you want the gradient to start at the top left, top right, bottom left, or bottom right. After using a gradient method, you need to specify the `ForeColor` and the `BackColor` settings for the object. The following macro sets up a two-color gradient using two theme colors:

```
Sub TwoColorGradient()
    Dim cht As Chart
    Dim ser As Series
    Set cht = ActiveChart
    Set ser = cht.SeriesCollection(1)
    MyPic = "C:\PodCastTitle1.jpg"
    ser.Format.Fill.TwoColorGradient msoGradientFromCorner, 3
    ser.Format.Fill.ForeColor.ObjectThemeColor = msoThemeColorAccent6
    ser.Format.Fill.BackColor.ObjectThemeColor = msoThemeColorAccent2
End Sub
```

When using the `OneColorGradient` method, you specify a direction, a style (1 through 4), and a darkness value between 0 and 1 (0 for darker gradients or 1 for lighter gradients).

When using the `PresetGradient` method, you specify a direction, a style (1 through 4), and the type of gradient (for example, `msoGradientBrass`, `msoGradientLateSunset`, or `msoGradientRainbow`). Again, as you are typing this code in the VB Editor, the AutoComplete tool provides a complete list of the available preset gradient types.

Formatting Line Settings

The LineFormat object formats either a line or the border around an object. You can change numerous properties for a line, such as the color, arrows, dash style, and so on.

The following macro formats the trendline for the first series in a chart:

```
Sub FormatLineOrBorders()
    Dim cht As Chart
    Set cht = ActiveChart
    With cht.SeriesCollection(1).Trendlines(1).Format.Line
        .DashStyle = msoLineLongDashDotDot
        .ForeColor.RGB = RGB(50, 0, 128)
        .BeginArrowheadLength = msoArrowheadShort
        .BeginArrowheadStyle = msoArrowheadOval
```

```
            .BeginArrowheadWidth = msoArrowheadNarrow
            .EndArrowheadLength = msoArrowheadLong
            .EndArrowheadStyle = msoArrowheadTriangle
            .EndArrowheadWidth = msoArrowheadWide
        End With
End Sub
```

When you are formatting a border, the arrow settings are not relevant, so the code is shorter than the code for formatting a line. The following macro formats the border around a chart:

```
Sub FormatBorder()
    Dim cht As Chart
    Set cht = ActiveChart
    With cht.ChartArea.Format.Line
        .DashStyle = msoLineLongDashDotDot
        .ForeColor.RGB = RGB(50, 0, 128)
    End With
End Sub
```

Formatting Glow Settings

To create a glow, you have to specify a color and a radius. The radius value can be from 1 to 20. A radius of 1 is barely visible, and a radius of 20 is often way too thick.

> **NOTE** A glow is actually applied to the shape outline. If you try to add a glow to an object where the outline is set to None, you cannot see the glow.

The following macro adds a line around the title and adds a glow around that line:

```
Sub AddGlowToTitle()
    Dim cht As Chart
    Set cht = ActiveChart
    cht.ChartTitle.Format.Line.ForeColor.RGB = RGB(255, 255, 255)
    cht.ChartTitle.Format.Line.DashStyle = msoLineSolid
    cht.ChartTitle.Format.Glow.Color.ObjectThemeColor = msoThemeColorAccent6
    cht.ChartTitle.Format.Glow.Radius = 8
End Sub
```

Formatting Shadow Settings

A shadow is composed of a color, a transparency, and the number of points by which the shadow should be offset from the object. If you increase the number of points, it appears that the object is farther from the surface of the chart. The horizontal offset is known as OffsetX, and the vertical offset is known as OffsetY.

The following macro adds a light blue shadow to the box surrounding a legend:

```
Sub FormatShadow()
    Dim cht As Chart
    Set cht = ActiveChart
    With cht.Legend.Format.Shadow
```

11

```
        .ForeColor.RGB = RGB(0, 0, 128)
        .OffsetX = 5
        .OffsetY = -3
        .Transparency = 0.5
        .Visible = True
    End With
End Sub
```

Formatting Reflection Settings

No chart elements can have reflections applied. The Reflection settings on the Format ribbon are constantly grayed out when a chart is selected. Similarly, the ChartFormat object does not have a reflection object.

Formatting Soft Edges

There are six levels of soft edge settings. The settings feather the edges by 1, 2.5, 5, 10, 25, or 50 points. The first setting is barely visible. The biggest settings are usually larger than most of the chart elements you are likely to format.

Microsoft says that the following is the proper syntax for SoftEdge:

```
Chart.Seriess(1).Points(i).Format.SoftEdge.Type = msoSoftEdgeType1
```

However, msoSoftEdgeType1 and words like it are really variables defined by Excel. To try a cool trick, go to the VB Editor and open the Immediate window by pressing Ctrl+G. In the Immediate window, type **Print msoSoftEdgeType2** and press Enter. The Immediate window tells you that using this word is equivalent to typing 2. So, you could either use msoSoftEdgeType2 or the value 2.

If you use msoSoftEdgeType2, your code will be slightly easier to understand than if you use simply 2. However, if you hope to format each point of a data series with a different format, you might want to use a loop such as this one, in which case it is far easier to use just the numbers 1 through 6 than msoSoftEdgeType1 through msoSoftEdgeType6, as shown in this macro:

```
Sub FormatSoftEdgesWithLoop()
    Dim cht As Chart
    Dim ser As Series
    Set cht = ActiveChart
    Set ser = cht.SeriesCollection(1)
    For i = 1 To 6
        ser.Points(i).Format.SoftEdge.Type = i
    Next i
End Sub
```

> **CAUTION**
>
> It is a bit strange that the soft edges are defined as a fixed number of points. In a chart that is sized to fit an entire sheet of paper, a 10-point soft edge might work fine. However, if you resize the chart so that you can fit six charts on a page, a 10-point soft edge applied to all sides of a column might make the column completely disappear.

Formatting 3-D Rotation Settings

The 3-D settings handle three different menus on the Format ribbon. In the Shape Effects drop-down, settings under Preset, Bevel, and 3-D are all actually handled by the ThreeD object in the ChartFormat object. This section discusses settings that affect the 3-D rotation. The next section discusses settings that affect the bevel and 3-D format.

The methods and properties that can be set for the ThreeD object are very broad. In fact, the 3-D settings in VBA include more preset options than do the menus on the Format ribbon.

Figure 11.7 shows the presets available in the 3-D Rotation fly-out menu.

Figure 11.7
Whereas the 3-D Rotation menu offers 25 presets, VBA offers 62 presets.

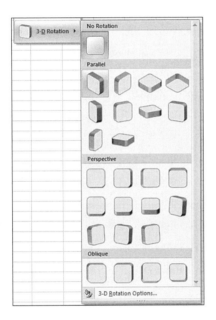

To apply one of the 3-D rotation presets to a chart element, you use the `SetPresetCamera` method, as shown here:

```
Sub Assign3DPreset()
    Dim cht As Chart
    Dim shp As Shape
    Set cht = ActiveChart
    Set shp = cht.Shapes(1)
    shp.ThreeD.SetPresetCamera msoCameraIsometricLeftDown
End Sub
```

Table 11.4 lists all the possible `SetPresetCamera` values. If the first column indicates that it is a bonus or an Excel 2003 style, the value is a preset that is available in VBA but was not chosen by Microsoft to be included in the 3-D Rotation fly-out menu.

Table 11.4   3-D Preset Formats and Their VBA Constant Values

Menu Location	Description	VBA Value
Parallel group, row 1, column 1	Isometric Left Down	`msoCameraIsometricLeftDown`
Parallel group, row 1, column 2	Isometric Right Up	`msoCameraIsometricRightUp`
Parallel group, row 1, column 3	Isometric Top Up	`msoCameraIsometricTopUp`
Parallel group, row 1, column 4	Isometric Bottom Down	`msoCameraIsometricBottomDown`
Parallel group, row 2, column 1	Isometric OffAxis1 Left	`msoCameraIsometricOffAxis1Left`
Parallel group, row 2, column 2	Isometric OffAxis1 Right	`msoCameraIsometricOffAxis1Right`
Parallel group, row 2, column 3	Isometric OffAxis1 Top	`msoCameraIsometricOffAxis1Top`
Parallel group, row 2, column 4	Isometric OffAxis2 Left	`msoCameraIsometricOffAxis2Left`
Parallel group, row 3, column 1	Isometric OffAxis2 Right	`msoCameraIsometricOffAxis2Right`
Parallel group, row 3, column 2	Isometric OffAxis2 Top	`msoCameraIsometricOffAxis2Top`
Parallel group, bonus selection	Isometric Bottom Up	`msoCameraIsometricBottomUp`
Parallel group, bonus selection	Isometric Left Up	`msoCameraIsometricLeftUp`
Parallel group, bonus selection	Isometric OffAxis3 Bottom	`msoCameraIsometricOffAxis3Bottom`
Parallel group, bonus selection	Isometric OffAxis3 Left	`msoCameraIsometricOffAxis3Left`
Parallel group, bonus selection	Isometric OffAxis3 Right	`msoCameraIsometricOffAxis3Right`
Parallel group, bonus selection	Isometric OffAxis4 Bottom	`msoCameraIsometricOffAxis4Bottom`
Parallel group, bonus selection	Isometric OffAxis4 Left	`msoCameraIsometricOffAxis4Left`
Parallel group, bonus selection	Isometric OffAxis4 Right	`msoCameraIsometricOffAxis4Right`
Parallel group, bonus selection	Isometric Right Down	`msoCameraIsometricRightDown`
Parallel group, bonus selection	Isometric Top Down	`msoCameraIsometricTopDown`
Perspective group, row 1, column 1	Perspective Front	`msoCameraPerspectiveFront`
Perspective group, row 1, column 2	Perspective Left	`msoCameraPerspectiveLeft`
Perspective group, row 1, column 3	Perspective Right	`msoCameraPerspectiveRight`
Perspective group, row 1, column 4	Perspective Below	`msoCameraPerspectiveBelow`
Perspective group, row 2, column 1	Perspective Above	`msoCameraPerspectiveAbove`
Perspective group, row 2, column 2	Perspective Relaxed Moderately	`msoCameraPerspectiveRelaxedModerately`
Perspective group, row 2, column 3	Perspective Relaxed	`msoCameraPerspectiveRelaxed`
Perspective group, row 2, column 4	Perspective Contrasting Left Facing	`msoCameraPerspectiveContrastingLeftFacing`

Menu Location	Description	VBA Value
Perspective group, row 3, column 1	Perspective Contrasting Right Facing	`msoCameraPerspectiveContrasting RightFacing`
Perspective group, row 3, column 2	Perspective Heroic Extreme Left Facing	`msoCameraPerspectiveHeroic ExtremeLeftFacing`
Perspective group, row 3, column 3	Perspective Heroic Extreme Right Facing	`msoCameraPerspectiveHeroic ExtremeRightFacing`
Perspective group, bonus selection	Perspective Above Left Facing	`msoCameraPerspectiveAboveLeftFacing`
Perspective group, bonus selection	Perspective Above Right Facing	`msoCameraPerspectiveAboveRightFacing`
Perspective group, bonus selection	Perspective Heroic Left Facing	`msoCameraPerspectiveHeroicLeftFacing`
Perspective group, bonus selection	Perspective Heroic Right Facing	`msoCameraPerspectiveHeroicRightFacing`
Perspective group, Excel 2003 styles	Legacy Perspective Bottom	`msoCameraLegacyPerspectiveBottom`
Perspective group, Excel 2003 styles	Legacy Perspective Lower Left	`msoCameraLegacyPerspectiveBottomLeft`
Perspective group, Excel 2003 styles	Legacy Perspective Lower Right	`msoCameraLegacyPerspectiveBottomRight`
Perspective group, Excel 2003 styles	Legacy Perspective Front	`msoCameraLegacyPerspectiveFront`
Perspective group, Excel 2003 styles	Legacy Perspective Left	`msoCameraLegacyPerspectiveLeft`
Perspective group, Excel 2003 styles	Legacy Perspective Right	`msoCameraLegacyPerspectiveRight`
Perspective group, Excel 2003 styles	Legacy Perspective Top	`msoCameraLegacyPerspectiveTop`
Perspective group, Excel 2003 styles	Legacy Perspective Upper Left	`msoCameraLegacyPerspectiveTopLeft`
Perspective group, Excel 2003 styles	Legacy Perspective Upper Right	`msoCameraLegacyPerspectiveTopRight`
Oblique group, row 1, column 1	Oblique Upper Left	`msoCameraObliqueTopLeft`
Oblique group, row 1, column 2	Oblique Upper Right	`msoCameraObliqueTopRight`

11

continues

Table 11.4   Continued

Menu Location	Description	VBA Value
Oblique group, row 1, column 3	Oblique Lower Left	`msoCameraObliqueBottomLeft`
Oblique group, row 1, column 4	Oblique Lower Right	`msoCameraObliqueBottomRight`
Oblique group, bonus selection	Oblique Bottom	`msoCameraObliqueBottom`
Oblique group, bonus selection	Oblique Left	`msoCameraObliqueLeft`
Oblique group, bonus selection	Oblique Right	`msoCameraObliqueRight`
Oblique group, bonus selection	Oblique Top	`msoCameraObliqueTop`
Oblique group, bonus selection	Orthographic Front	`msoCameraOrthographicFront`
Oblique group, Excel 2003 styles	Legacy Oblique Bottom	`msoCameraLegacyObliqueBottom`
Oblique group, Excel 2003 styles	Legacy Oblique Lower Left	`msoCameraLegacyObliqueBottomLeft`
Oblique group, Excel 2003 styles	Legacy Oblique Lower Right	`msoCameraLegacyObliqueBottomRight`
Oblique group, Excel 2003 styles	Legacy Oblique Front	`msoCameraLegacyObliqueFront`
Oblique group, Excel 2003 styles	Legacy Oblique Left	`msoCameraLegacyObliqueLeft`
Oblique group, Excel 2003 styles	Legacy Oblique Right	`msoCameraLegacyObliqueRight`
Oblique group, Excel 2003 styles	Legacy Oblique Top	`msoCameraLegacyObliqueTop`
Oblique group, Excel 2003 styles	Legacy Oblique Upper Left	`msoCameraLegacyObliqueTopLeft`
Oblique group, Excel 2003 styles	Legacy Oblique Upper Right	`msoCameraLegacyObliqueTopRight`

If you prefer not to use the presets, you can explicitly control the rotation around the x-, y-, or z-axis. You can use the following properties and methods to change the rotation of an object:

- `RotationX`—Returns or sets the rotation of the extruded shape around the x-axis, in degrees. This can be a value from -90 through 90. A positive value indicates upward rotation; a negative value indicates downward rotation.

- `RotationY`—Returns or sets the rotation of the extruded shape around the y-axis, in degrees. Can be a value from -90 through 90. A positive value indicates rotation to the left; a negative value indicates rotation to the right.

- `RotationZ`—Returns or sets the rotation of the extruded shape around the z-axis, in degrees. Can be a value from -90 through 90. A positive value indicates upward rotation; a negative value indicates downward rotation.

- `IncrementRotationX`—Changes the rotation of the specified shape around the x-axis by the specified number of degrees. You specify an increment from `-90` to `90`. Negative degrees tip the object down, and positive degrees tip the object up. (You can use the `RotationX` property to set the absolute rotation of the shape around the x-axis.)

- `IncrementRotationY`—Changes the rotation of the specified shape around the y-axis by the specified number of degrees. A positive value tilts the object left, and a negative value tips the object right. (You can use the `RotationY` property to set the absolute rotation of the shape around the y-axis.)

- `IncrementRotationZ`—Changes the rotation of the specified shape around the z-axis by the specified number of degrees. A positive value tilts the object left, and a negative value tips the object right. (You can use the `RotationZ` property to set the absolute rotation of the shape around the z-axis.)

- `IncrementRotationHorizontal`—Changes the rotation of the specified shape horizontally by the specified number of degrees. You specify an increment from `-90` to `90` to specify how much (in degrees) the rotation of the shape is to be changed horizontally. A positive value moves the shape left; a negative value moves it right.

- `IncrementRotationVertical`—Changes the rotation of the specified shape vertically by the specified number of degrees. You specify an increment from `-90` to `90` to specify how much (in degrees) the rotation of the shape is to be changed horizontally. A positive value moves the shape left; a negative value moves it right.

- `ResetRotation`—Resets the extrusion rotation around the x-axis and the y-axis to `0` so that the front of the extrusion faces forward. This method does not reset the rotation around the z-axis.

Changing the Bevel and 3-D Format

There are 12 presets in the Bevel fly-out menu. These presets affect the bevel on the top face of the object. Usually in charts you see the top face; however, there are some bizarre rotations of a 3-D chart where you see the bottom face of charting elements.

The Format Shape dialog contains the same 12 presets as the Bevel fly-out, but allows you to apply the preset to the top or bottom face. You can also control the width and height of the bevel. The VBA properties and methods correspond to the settings on the 3-D Format category of the Format Shape dialog (see Figure 11.8).

You set the type of bevel by using the `BevelTopType` and `BevelBottomType` properties. You can further modify the bevel type by setting the `BevelTopInset` value to set the width and the `BevelTopDepth` value to set the height. The following macro adds a bevel to the columns of Series 1:

```
Sub AssignBevel()
    Dim cht As Chart
    Dim ser As Series
    Set cht = ActiveChart
```

```
        Set ser = cht.SeriesCollection(1)
        ser.Format.ThreeD.Visible = True
        ser.Format.ThreeD.BevelTopType = msoBevelCircle
        ser.Format.ThreeD.BevelTopInset = 16
        ser.Format.ThreeD.BevelTopDepth = 6
    End Sub
```

Figure 11.8
You can control the 3-D Format settings, such as bevel, surface, and lighting.

The 12 possible settings for the bevel type are shown in Table 11.5; these settings correspond to the thumbnails in the fly-out menu. To turn off the bevel, you use msoBevelNone.

Table 11.5 Bevel Types

Constant	Constant
msoBevelCircle	msoBevelConvex
msoBevelRelaxedInset	msoBevelSlope
msoBevelCross	msoBevelDivot
msoBevelCoolSlant	msoBevelRiblet
msoBevelAngle	msoBevelHardEdge
msoBevelSoftRound	msoBevelArtDeco

Usually, the accent color used in a bevel is based on the color used to fill the object. If you would like control over the extrusion color, however, you first specify that the extrusion color type is custom and then specify either a theme accent color or an RGB color, as in the following example:

```
ser.Format.ThreeD.ExtrusionColorType = msoExtrusionColorCustom
' either use this:
ser.Format.ThreeD.ExtrusionColor.ObjectThemeColor = msoThemeColorAccent1
' or this:
ser.Format.ThreeD.ExtrusionColor.RGB = RGB(255, 0, 0)
```

You use the `Depth` property to control the amount of extrusion in the bevel, and you specify the depth in points. Here's an example:

```
ser.Format.ThreeD.Depth = 5
```

For the contour, you can specify either a color and a size of the contour or both. You can specify the color as an RGB value or a theme color. You specify the size in points, using the `ContourWidth` property. Here's an example:

```
ser.Format.ThreeD.ContourColor.RGB = RGB(0, 255, 0)
ser.Format.ThreeD.ContourWidth = 10
```

The Surface drop-downs are controlled by the following properties:

- **PresetMaterial**—This contains choices from the Material drop-down.
- **PresetLighting**—This contains choices from the Lighting drop-down.
- **LightAngle**—This controls the angle from which the light is shining on the object.

The Material drop-down menu from the 3-D category of the Format dialog box offers 11 settings, although it appears that Microsoft designed a twelfth setting in the object model. It is not clear why Microsoft does not offer the `SoftMetal` style in the dialog box, but you can use it in VBA. There are also three legacy styles in the object model that are not available in the Format dialog box. In theory, the new `Plastic2` material is better than the old `Plastic` material. Table 11.6 shows the settings for each thumbnail.

Table 11.6 VBA Constants for Material Types

	Type	VBA Constant	Value
	Matte	msoMaterialMatte2	5
	Warm Matte	msoMaterialWarmMatte	8
	Plastic	msoMaterialPlastic2	6
	Metal	msoMaterialMetal2	7

continues

Table 11.6 Continued

Type	VBA Constant	Value
Dark Edge	msoMaterialDarkEdge	11
Soft Edge	msoMaterialSoftEdge	12
Flat	msoMaterialFlat	14
Wire Frame	msoMaterialWireFrame	4
Powder	msoMaterialPowder	10
Translucent Powder	msoMaterialTranslucentPowder	9
Clear	msoMaterialClear	13
	msoMaterialMatte	1
	msoMaterialPlastic	2
	msoMaterialMetal	3
Bonus	msoMaterialSoftMetal	15

In Excel 2003, the material property was limited to matte, metal, plastic, and wire frame. Microsoft apparently was not happy with the old matte, metal, and plastic settings. It left those values in place to support legacy charts but created the new Matte2, Plastic2, and Metal2 settings. These settings are actually available in the dialog box. In VBA, you are free to use either the old or the new settings. The columns in Figure 11.9 compare the new and old settings. The final column is for the SoftMetal setting that Microsoft left out of the Format dialog box. This was probably an aesthetic decision instead of an "oh no; this setting crashes the computer" decision. You can feel free to use msoMaterialSoftMetal to create a look that has a subtle difference from charts others create using the settings in the Format dialog box.

The Lighting drop-down menu from the 3-D category of the Format dialog box offers 15 settings. The object model offers these 15 settings, plus 13 legacy settings from the Excel 2003 Lighting toolbar. Table 11.7 shows the settings for each of these thumbnails.

Figure 11.9
Comparison of some new
and old material presets.

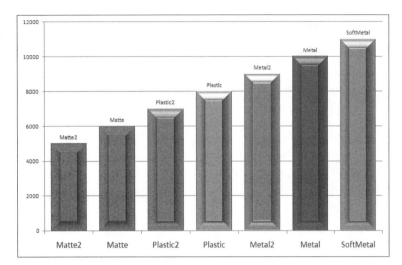

Table 11.7 VBA Constants for Lighting Types

Type	VBA Constant	Value
Neutral Category		
ThreePoint	msoLightRigThreePoint	13
Balanced	msoLightRigBalanced	14
Soft	msoLightRigSoft	15
Harsh	msoLightRigHarsh	16
Flood	msoLightRigFlood	17
Contrasting	msoLightRigContrasting	18
Warm Category		
Morning	msoLightRigMorning	19
Sunrise	msoLightRigSunrise	20
Sunset	msoLightRigSunset	21

continues

Table 11.7 Continued

Type	VBA Constant	Value
Cool Category		
Chilly	msoLightRigChilly	22
Freezing	msoLightRigFreezing	23
Special Category		
Flat	msoLightRigFlat	24
TwoPoint	msoLightRigTwoPoint	25
Glow	msoLightRigGlow	26
BrightRoom	msoLightRigBrightRoom	27
Legacy Category		
Flat 1	msoLightRigLegacyFlat1	1
Flat 2	msoLightRigLegacyFlat2	2
Flat 3	msoLightRigLegacyFlat3	3
Flat 4	msoLightRigLegacyFlat4	4
Harsh 1	msoLightRigLegacyHarsh1	9
Harsh 2	msoLightRigLegacyHarsh2	10
Harsh 3	msoLightRigLegacyHarsh3	11
Harsh 4	msoLightRigLegacyHarsh4	12
Normal 1	msoLightRigLegacyNormal1	5
Normal 2	msoLightRigLegacyNormal2	6
Normal 3	msoLightRigLegacyNormal3	7
Normal 4	msoLightRigLegacyNormal4	8
Mixed	msoLightRigMixed	-2

Using the Watch Window to Discover Object Settings

It is frustrating that the macro recorder does not record certain actions when you're working with charts. Actually, there are two levels of frustration. First, the macro recorder does not record the action of creating SmartArt graphics because Microsoft made a conscious decision not to allow you to create SmartArt using VBA. I do not agree with that decision, but I can understand why the macro recorder doesn't record these steps. Second, when you are using the Format ribbon, the macro recorder does nothing; however, you can control all the actions with the Format ribbon by using VBA.

With earlier versions of Excel, I relied on the macro recorder to teach me which objects, properties, and methods responded to various actions in the Excel interface. Without the macro recorder, it becomes very difficult to learn these aspects.

In case you need to use a property that is not covered in this book, there is a way to be able to explore the properties for certain chart elements. The following is an example in which the macro defines a Chart object variable and a ChartGroup object variable and then stops:

```
Sub ExploreChartElements()
    Dim cht As Chart
    Dim chtg As ChartGroup
    Dim ser As Series
    Set cht = ActiveChart
    Set chtg = cht.ChartGroups(1)
    Set ser = cht.SeriesCollection(1)
    Stop
End Sub
```

The Stop command in the macro is key to the success of this technique. Excel enters Break mode when it encounters the Stop code. This allows you to examine the object variables while they are still in scope.

You follow these steps to discover new chart properties:

1. Enter the preceding macro in your workbook.
2. Create a chart.
3. Select the chart.
4. Run the macro. VBA stops and highlights the Stop line in yellow. You are now in Break mode.
5. Right-click the ser object variable and choose Add Watch. Click OK in the Add Watch dialog box. Excel displays a new Watch window at the bottom of the VB Editor. This window displays a single line with a pair of eyeglasses, a plus sign, and the name of the variable, as shown in Figure 11.10.
6. Click the plus sign next to the watch. A list of many properties for the series opens. One property is the Format property. This is where all of the Format ribbon settings are stored.
7. Click the plus sign next to the Format entry. It expands to show the settings for Fill, Glow, Line, and so on.
8. Click the plus sign next to the Fill entry. You see many settings that define the fill used in Series 1. The GradientDegree setting is highlighted in Figure 11.11. You can see that Gradient Degree is a property of the Fill property, and Fill is a property of the Format property. From this, you can ascertain that the proper code would be this:
   ```
   ser.Format.Fill.GradientDegree = 0.8825
   ```

Figure 11.10
Initially, the watched variable shows a single, useless line.

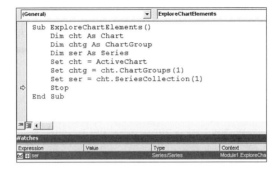

```
(General)                              ExploreChartElements

    Sub ExploreChartElements()
        Dim cht As Chart
        Dim chtg As ChartGroup
        Dim ser As Series
        Set cht = ActiveChart
        Set chtg = cht.ChartGroups(1)
        Set ser = cht.SeriesCollection(1)
⇨       Stop
    End Sub
```

Watches			
Expression	Value	Type	Context
ser		Series/Series	Module1.ExploreCha

Figure 11.11
After browsing through the Watch window, you can locate a property without the macro recorder.

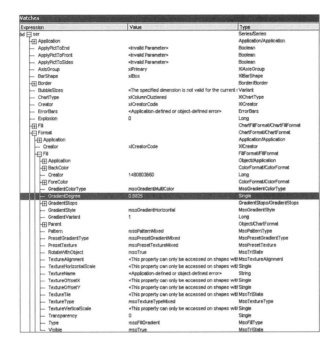

This isn't exactly as easy as using the macro recorder to examine objects, properties, and methods, but it makes it possible to figure out how to write code.

> **NOTE**
> In the ExploreChartElements macro, there are variables for the chart, the series, and the chart group. You might have to add watches for each of these variables and begin exploring to find the actual setting.

The Watch window is "somewhat" live. With a few steps, you can change the chart formatting in the Excel user interface and then return to the VB Editor to discover the new settings:

1. While in Break mode, switch back to Excel using Alt+Tab or by clicking Excel in the taskbar.
2. Make some changes to the active chart in Excel. Make sure not to deactivate the chart.
3. Switch back to the VB Editor.
4. There is a yellow arrow to the left of the Stop line in your code window. Grab this arrow and drag upward to point to the line that set up your watched variable. In the current example, you are watching the ser variable, so you just have to move up one line, to the Set ser line.
5. Press the F8 key to rerun the line highlighted in yellow. The Watch window updates to show the settings you made in step 2.

When you have finished exploring, click the Reset button in the VBA toolbar (the square dot located below the Run menu).

CASE STUDY

Using the Watch Window to Learn Rotation Settings

There is one icon on the Layout ribbon that is not recorded by the macro recorder. If you change the rotation of a 3-D chart, the macro recorder records nothing. To see an example of this, you can follow these steps:

1. Turn on the macro recorder.
2. Select a surface chart.
3. Change the rotation settings.
4. Stop the macro recorder.
5. Switch back to Excel and change the formatting of the columns in the first series. Excel records this macro, which is of little use:

```
Sub RotateChartRecordedMacro()
'
' RotateChartRecordedMacro Macro
'
'
    ActiveSheet.ChartObjects("Chart 1").Activate
End Sub
```

To solve this problem and learn how to programmatically rotate a chart, you can follow these steps:

1. Type this macro in the VB Editor:

```
Sub ExploreChartElements()
    Dim cht As Chart
```

```
        Set cht = ActiveChart
        Stop
    End Sub
```

2. In Excel, select the chart. On the Layout ribbon, choose the 3-D Rotation icon. Note the X, Y, and Perspective settings (for example, 200, 10, and 15).

3. Click Close to close the Format Chart Area dialog.

4. Switch to VBA.

5. Run the ExploreChartElements macro. VBA enters Break mode.

6. Right-click the `cht` variable and choose Add Watch. Click OK in the Add Watch dialog.

7. In the Watch window, click the plus sign to expand the chart.

8. Scan through the properties. You are looking for properties that might have values of 200, 10, and 15. There is an `Elevation` property with a value of 10. There is a `Rotation` property with the value of 200. There is a Perspective setting with a value of 30. This one is maddening because the name is exactly right, but the value is incorrect.

9. Switch back to Excel. Choose 3-D Rotation and change the Perspective setting from 15 to 20 in the Format dialog box.

10. Switch back to VBA and rerun the macro. Look in the Watch window. The Perspective setting has changed to 40. You can theorize that this is the right property but that the Perspective value shown in the Format dialog box needs to be doubled when entered in VBA.

You now have enough information to write the following macro to change the rotation of the chart using VBA:

```
Sub RotateChart()
    Dim cht As Chart
    Set cht = ActiveChart
    cht.Rotation = 100
    cht.Elevation = 30
    cht.Perspective = 60 ' Really means 30%
End Sub
```

Creating Advanced Charts

In *Charts & Graphs for Microsoft Excel 2007*, I showed off some amazing charts that don't look like they are possible to create using Excel. Building these charts usually involves adding a rogue data series that appears in the chart as an XY series to complete some effect. The process of creating these charts manually is very tedious and will ensure that most people would never resort to creating such charts.

However, if you could automate the process of creating the charts using VBA, the creation of the charts starts to become feasible.

███ Creating True Open-High-Low-Close Stock Charts

If you are a fan of stock charts in the *Wall Street Journal* or finance.yahoo.com, you will recognize the chart type known as Open-High-Low-Close (OHLC) chart. Microsoft Excel does not offer such a chart. Its High-Low-Close (HLC) chart is missing the left-facing dash that represents the opening for each period. Now, you might feel that HLC charts are close enough to OHLC chart, but one of my personal pet peeves is that the WSJ can create better-looking charts than Excel can create.

In Figure 11.12, you can see a true OHLC chart in the top of the figure and Excel's HLC chart in the bottom of the figure.

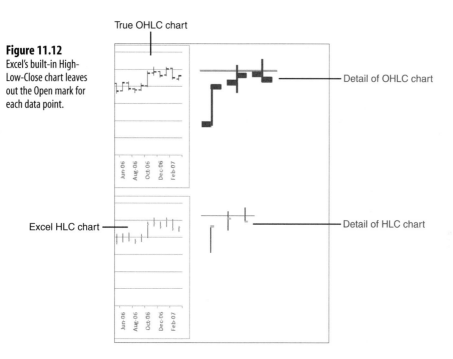

Figure 11.12
Excel's built-in High-Low-Close chart leaves out the Open mark for each data point.

In Excel 2007, you can specify a custom picture to be used as the marker in a chart. I immediately went to Photoshop and created a left-facing dash as a GIF file. This tiny graphic makes up for the fundamental flaw in Excel's chart marker selection: Excel offers a right-facing dash, but not a left-facing dash. You can download LeftDash.gif from www.mrexcel.com/getcode2007.html.

In the Excel user interface, you would indicate that the Open series should have a custom picture and then specify LeftDash.gif as the picture. In VBA code, you use the `UserPicture` method, as shown here:

```
ActiveChart Cht.SeriesCollection(1).Fill.UserPicture ("C:\leftdash.gif")
```

To create a true OHLC chart, follow these steps:

1. Create a line chart from four series; Open, High, Low, Close.

2. Change the line style to none for all four series.

3. Eliminate the marker for the High and Low series.

4. Add a High-Low line to the chart.

5. Change the marker for Close to a right-facing dash (called a dot in VBA) with a size of 9.

6. Change the marker for Open to a custom picture and load LeftDash.gif as the fill for the series.

The following code creates the top chart in Figure 11.12:

```
Sub CreateOHCLChart()
    ' Download leftdash.gif from the sample files for this book
    ' and save it in the same folder as this workbook
    Dim Cht As Chart
    Dim Ser As Series

    ActiveSheet.Shapes.AddChart(xlLineMarkers).Select
    Set Cht = ActiveChart
    Cht.SetSourceData Source:=Range("Sheet1!$A$1:$E$33")
    ' Format the Open Series
    With Cht.SeriesCollection(1)
        .MarkerStyle = xlMarkerStylePicture
        .Fill.UserPicture ("C:\leftdash.gif")
        .Border.LineStyle = xlNone
        .MarkerForegroundColorIndex = xlColorIndexNone
    End With
    ' Format High & Low Series
    With Cht.SeriesCollection(2)
        .MarkerStyle = xlMarkerStyleNone
        .Border.LineStyle = xlNone
    End With
    With Cht.SeriesCollection(3)
        .MarkerStyle = xlMarkerStyleNone
        .Border.LineStyle = xlNone
    End With
    ' Format the Close series
    Set Ser = Cht.SeriesCollection(4)
    With Ser
        .MarkerBackgroundColorIndex = 1
        .MarkerForegroundColorIndex = 1
        .MarkerStyle = xlDot
        .MarkerSize = 9
        .Border.LineStyle = xlNone
    End With
    ' Add High-Low Lines
    Cht.SetElement (msoElementLineHiLoLine)
    Cht.SetElement (msoElementLegendNone)

End Sub
```

Creating Bins for a Frequency Chart

Suppose that you have results from 3,000 scientific trials. There must be a good way to produce a chart of those results. However, if you just select the results and create a chart, you will end up with chaos (see Figure 11.13).

Figure 11.13
Try to chart the results from 3,000 trials and you will have a jumbled mess.

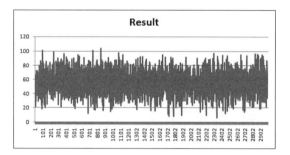

The trick to creating an effective frequency distribution is to define a series of categories, or *bins*. A FREQUENCY array function counts the number of items from the 3,000 results that fall within each bin.

The process of creating bins manually is rather tedious and requires knowledge of array formulas. It is better to use a macro to perform all of the tedious calculations.

The macro in this section requires you to specify a bin size and a starting bin. If you expect results in the 0 to 100 range, you might specify bins of 10 each, starting at 0. This would create bins of 0–10, 11–20, 21–30 and so on. If you specify bin sizes of 15 with a starting bin of 5, the macro will create bins of 5–20, 21–35, 36–50 and so on.

To use the following macro, your trial results should start in row 2 and should be in the rightmost column of a data set. Three variables near the top of the macro define the starting bin, the ending bin, and the bin size:

```
' Define Bins
BinSize = 10
FirstBin = 0
LastBin = 100
```

After that, the macro skips a column and then builds a range of starting bins. In cell D4 in Figure 11.14, the 10 is used to tell Excel that you are looking for the number of values larger than the 0 in D3, but equal to or less than the 10 in D4.

Although the bins extend from D3:D13, the FREQUENCY function entered in column E needs to include one extra cell, in case any results are larger than the last bin. This single formula returns many results. Formulas that return more than one answer are called *array formulas*. In the Excel user interface, you specify an array formula by holding down Ctrl+Shift while pressing Enter to finish the formula. In Excel VBA, you need to use the FormulaArray property. The following lines of the macro set up the array formula in column E:

```
' Enter the Frequency Formula
Form = "=FREQUENCY(R2C" & FinalCol & ":R" & FinalRow & "C" & FinalCol & _
    ",R3C" & NextCol & ":R" & _
    LastRow & "C" & NextCol & ")"
Range(Cells(FirstRow, NextCol + 1), Cells(LastRow, NextCol + 1)). _
    FormulaArray = Form
```

Figure 11.14
The macro summarizes the results into bins and provides a meaningful chart of the data.

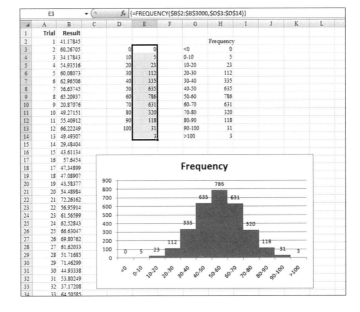

It is not evident to the reader if the bin indicated in column D is the upper or lower limit. The macro builds readable labels in column G and then copies the frequency results over to column H.

After the macro builds a simple column chart, the following line eliminates the gap between columns, creating the traditional histogram view of the data:

```
Cht.ChartGroups(1).GapWidth = 0
```

The macro to create the chart in Figure 11.14 follows:

```
Sub CreateFrequencyChart()
    ' Find the last column
    FinalCol = Cells(1, Columns.Count).End(xlToLeft).Column
    ' Find the FinalRow
    FinalRow = Cells(Rows.Count, FinalCol).End(xlUp).Row

    ' Define Bins
    BinSize = 10
    FirstBin = 0
    LastBin = 100

    'The bins will go in row 3, two columns after FinalCol
    NextCol = FinalCol + 2
```

```
FirstRow = 3
NextRow = FirstRow - 1

' Set up the bins for the Frequency function
For i = FirstBin To LastBin Step BinSize
    NextRow = NextRow + 1
    Cells(NextRow, NextCol).Value = i
Next i

' The Frequency function has to be one row larger than the bins
LastRow = NextRow + 1

' Enter the Frequency Formula
Form = "=FREQUENCY(R2C" & FinalCol & ":R" & FinalRow & "C" & FinalCol & _
    ",R3C" & NextCol & ":R" & _
    LastRow & "C" & NextCol & ")"
Range(Cells(FirstRow, NextCol + 1), Cells(LastRow, NextCol + 1)). _
    FormulaArray = Form

' Build a range suitable a chart source data
LabelCol = NextCol + 3
Form = "=R[-1]C[-3]&""-""&RC[-3]"
Range(Cells(4, LabelCol), Cells(LastRow - 1, LabelCol)).FormulaR1C1 = _
    Form
' Enter the > Last formula
Cells(LastRow, LabelCol).FormulaR1C1 = "="">""&R[-1]C[-3]"
' Enter the < first formula
Cells(3, LabelCol).FormulaR1C1 = "=""<""&RC[-3]"

' Enter the formula to copy the frequency results
Range(Cells(3, LabelCol + 1), Cells(LastRow, LabelCol + 1)).FormulaR1C1 = _
    "=RC[-3]"
' Add a heading
Cells(2, LabelCol + 1).Value = "Frequency"

' Create a column chart
Dim Cht As Chart
ActiveSheet.Shapes.AddChart(xlColumnClustered).Select
Set Cht = ActiveChart
Cht.SetSourceData Source:=Range(Cells(2, LabelCol), _
    Cells(LastRow, LabelCol + 1))
Cht.SetElement (msoElementLegendNone)
Cht.ChartGroups(1).GapWidth = 0
Cht.SetElement (msoElementDataLabelOutSideEnd)

End Sub
```

Creating a Stacked Area Chart

The stacked area chart shown in Figure 11.15 is incredibly difficult to create in the Excel user interface. Although the chart appears to contain four independent charts, this chart actually contains nine series:

- The first series contains the values for the East region.
- The second series contains 1,000 minus the East values. This series is formatted with a transparent fill.

- Series 3, 5, and 7 contain values for Central, Northwest, and Southwest.
- Series 4, 6, and 8 contain 1,000 minus the preceeding series.
- The final series is a XY series used to add labels for the left axis. There is one point for each gridline. The markers are positioned at an X position of 0. Custom data labels are added next to invisible markers to force the labels along the axis to start again at 0 for each region.

Figure 11.15
A single chart appears
to hold four
different charts.

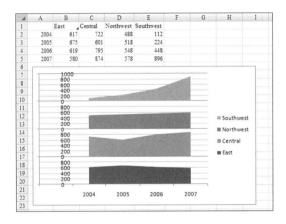

To use the macro provided here, your data should begin in column A and row 1. The macro adds new columns to the right of the data and new rows below the data, so the rest of the worksheet should be blank.

Two variables at the top of the macro define the height of each chart. In the current example, leaving a height of 1000 allows the sales for each region to fit comfortably. The LabSize value should indicate how frequently labels should appear along the left axis. This number must be evenly divisible into the chart height. In this example, values of 500, 250, 200, 125, or 100 would work:

```
' Define the height of each area chart
ChtHeight = 1000
' Define Tick Mark Size
' ChtHeight should be an even multiple of LabSize
LabSize = 200
```

The macro builds a copy of the data to the right of the original data. New "dummy" series are added to the right of each region to calculate 1,000 minus the data point. In Figure 11.16, this series is shown in G1:O5.

The macro then creates a stacked area chart for the first eight series. The legend for this chart indicates values of East, dummy, Central, dummy, and so on. To delete every other legend entry, use this code:

```
' Fill the dummy series with no fill
For i = FinalSeriesCount To 2 Step -2
    Cht.SeriesCollection(i).Interior.ColorIndex = xlNone
Next i
```

Figure 11.16

Extra data to the right and below the original data are created by the macro to create the chart.

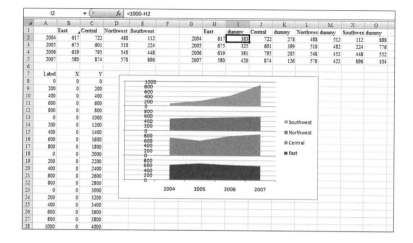

Similarly, the fill for each even numbered series in the chart needs to be set to transparent:

```
' Fill the dummy series with no fill
For i = FinalSeriesCount To 2 Step -2
    Cht.SeriesCollection(i).Interior.ColorIndex = xlNone
Next i
```

The trickiest part of the process is adding a new final series to the chart. This series will have far more data points than the other series. Range B8:C28 contains the X and Y values for the new series. You will see that each point has an X value of 0 to ensure that it appears along the left side of the plot area. The Y values increase steadily by the value indicated in the LabSize variable. In column A next to the X and Y points are the actual labels that will be plotted next to each marker. These labels give the illusion that the chart starts over with a value of 0 for each region.

The process of adding the new series is actually much easier in VBA than in the Excel user interface. The following code identifies each component of the series and specifies that it should be plotted as an XY chart:

```
' Add the new series to the chart
Set Ser = Cht.SeriesCollection.NewSeries
With Ser
    .Name = "Y"
    .Values = Range(Cells(AxisRow + 1, 3), Cells(NewFinal, 3))
    .XValues = Range(Cells(AxisRow + 1, 2), Cells(NewFinal, 2))
    .ChartType = xlXYScatter
    .MarkerStyle = xlMarkerStyleNone
End With
```

11

Finally, code from earlier in this chapter applies a data label from column A to each point in the final series:

```
' Label each point in the series
' This code actually adds fake labels along left axis
For i = 1 To TickMarkCount
    Ser.Points(i).HasDataLabel = True
    Ser.Points(i).DataLabel.Text = Cells(AxisRow + i, 1).Value
Next i
```

The complete code to create the stacked chart in Figure 11.16 is shown here:

```
Sub CreatedStackedChart()
    Dim Cht As Chart
    Dim Ser As Series
    FinalRow = Cells(Rows.Count, 1).End(xlUp).Row
    FinalCol = Cells(1, Columns.Count).End(xlToLeft).Column
    OrigSeriesCount = FinalCol - 1
    FinalSeriesCount = OrigSeriesCount * 2

    ' Define the height of each area chart
    ChtHeight = 1000
    ' Define Tick Mark Size
    ' ChtHeight should be an even multiple of LabSize
    LabSize = 200

    ' Make a copy of the data
    NextCol = FinalCol + 2
    Cells(1, 1).Resize(FinalRow, FinalCol).Copy _
        Destination:=Cells(1, NextCol)
    FinalCol = Cells(1, Columns.Count).End(xlToLeft).Column

    ' Add in new columns to serve as dummy series
    MyFormula = "=" & ChtHeight & "-RC[-1]"
    For i = FinalCol + 1 To NextCol + 2 Step -1
        Cells(1, i).EntireColumn.Insert
        Cells(1, i).Value = "dummy"
        Cells(2, i).Resize(FinalRow - 1, 1).FormulaR1C1 = MyFormula
    Next i

    ' Figure out the new Final Column
    FinalCol = Cells(1, Columns.Count).End(xlToLeft).Column

    ' Build the Chart
    ActiveSheet.Shapes.AddChart(xlAreaStacked).Select
    Set Cht = ActiveChart
    Cht.SetSourceData Source:=Range(Cells(1, NextCol), Cells(FinalRow, FinalCol))
    Cht.PlotBy = xlColumns

    ' Clear out the even number series from the Legend
    For i = FinalSeriesCount - 1 To 1 Step -2
        Cht.Legend.LegendEntries(i).Delete
    Next i

    ' Set the axis Maximum Scale & Gridlines
    TopScale = OrigSeriesCount * ChtHeight
    With Cht.Axes(xlValue)
        .MaximumScale = TopScale
```

```
         .MinorUnit = LabSize
         .MajorUnit = ChtHeight
    End With
    Cht.SetElement (msoElementPrimaryValueGridLinesMinorMajor)

    ' Fill the dummy series with no fill
    For i = FinalSeriesCount To 2 Step -2
        Cht.SeriesCollection(i).Interior.ColorIndex = xlNone
    Next i

    ' Hide the original axis labels
    Cht.Axes(xlValue).TickLabelPosition = xlNone

    ' Build a new range to hold a rogue XY series that will
    ' be used to create left axis labels
    AxisRow = FinalRow + 2
    Cells(AxisRow, 1).Resize(1, 3).Value = Array("Label", "X", "Y")
    TickMarkCount = OrigSeriesCount * (ChtHeight / LabSize) + 1
    ' Column B contains the X values. These are all zero
    Cells(AxisRow + 1, 2).Resize(TickMarkCount, 1).Value = 0
    ' Column C contains the Y values.
    Cells(AxisRow + 1, 3).Resize(TickMarkCount, 1).FormulaR1C1 = _
        "=R[-1]C+" & LabSize
    Cells(AxisRow + 1, 3).Value = 0
    ' Column A contains the labels to be used for each point
    Cells(AxisRow + 1, 1).Value = 0
    Cells(AxisRow + 2, 1).Resize(TickMarkCount - 1, 1).FormulaR1C1 = _
        "=IF(R[-1]C+" & LabSize & ">=" & ChtHeight & ",0,R[-1]C+" & LabSize & ")"
    NewFinal = Cells(Rows.Count, 1).End(xlUp).Row
    Cells(NewFinal, 1).Value = ChtHeight

    ' Add the new series to the chart
    Set Ser = Cht.SeriesCollection.NewSeries
    With Ser
        .Name = "Y"
        .Values = Range(Cells(AxisRow + 1, 3), Cells(NewFinal, 3))
        .XValues = Range(Cells(AxisRow + 1, 2), Cells(NewFinal, 2))
        .ChartType = xlXYScatter
        .MarkerStyle = xlMarkerStyleNone
    End With

    ' Label each point in the series
    ' This code actually adds fake labels along left axis
    For i = 1 To TickMarkCount
        Ser.Points(i).HasDataLabel = True
        Ser.Points(i).DataLabel.Text = Cells(AxisRow + i, 1).Value
    Next i

    ' Hide the Y label in the legend
    Cht.Legend.LegendEntries(Cht.Legend.LegendEntries.Count).Delete
End Sub
```

The websites of Andy Pope (www.andypope.info) and Jon Peltier (peltiertech.com/) are filled with examples of unusual charts that require extraordinary effort. If you find that you will regularly be creating stacked charts or any other chart like those on their websites, taking the time to write the VBA will ease the pain of creating the charts in the Excel user interface.

Exporting a Chart as a Graphic

You can export any chart to an image file on your hard drive. The `ExportChart` method requires you to specify a filename and a graphic type. The available graphic types depend on graphic file filters installed in your Registry. It is a safe bet that JPG, BMP, PNG, and GIF will work on most computers.

For example, the following code exports the active chart as a GIF file:

```
Sub ExportChart()
    Dim cht As Chart
    Set cht = ActiveChart
    cht.Export Filename:="C:\Chart.gif", Filtername:="GIF"
End Sub
```

> **CAUTION**
>
> Since Excel 2003, Microsoft has supported an `Interactive` argument in the `Export` method. Excel help indicates that if you set `Interactive` to TRUE, Excel asks for additional settings depending on the file type. However, the dialog to ask for additional settings never appears, at least not for the four standard types of JPG, GIF, BMP, or PNG.

Creating a Dynamic Chart in a Userform

With the ability to export a chart to a graphic file, you also have the ability to load a graphic file into an `Image` control in a userform. This means you can create a dialog box in which someone can dynamically control values used to plot a chart.

To create the dialog shown in Figure 11.17, follow these steps:

Figure 11.17
This dialog box is a VBA userform displaying a chart. The chart redraws based on changes to the dialog controls.

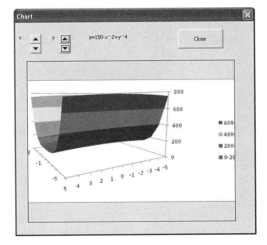

1. In the VBA window, choose Insert, UserForm. In the Properties window, rename the form **frmChart**.

2. Resize the userform.

3. Add a large `Image` control to the userform.

4. Add two spin buttons named **sbX** and **sbY**. Set them to have a minimum of 1 and a maximum of 5.

5. Add a `Label3` control to display the formula.

6. Add a command button labeled **Close**.

7. Enter this code in the code window behind the form:

```
Private Sub CommandButton1_Click()
    Unload Me
End Sub
Private Sub sbX_Change()
    Worksheets("Surface").Range("O2").Value = Me.sbX.Value
    Worksheets("Surface").Shapes(1).Chart.Export "C:\Chart.gif"
    Me.Label3.Caption = Worksheets("Surface").Range("O4").Value
    Me.Image1.Picture = LoadPicture("C:\Chart.gif")
End Sub
Private Sub sbY_Change()
    Worksheets("Surface").Range("O3").Value = Me.sbY.Value
    Worksheets("Surface").Shapes(1).Chart.Export "C:\Chart.gif"
    Me.Label3.Caption = Worksheets("Surface").Range("O4").Value
    Me.Image1.Picture = LoadPicture("C:\Chart.gif")
End Sub

Private Sub UserForm_Initialize()
    Me.sbX = Worksheets("Surface").Range("O2").Value
    Me.sbY = Worksheets("Surface").Range("O3").Value
    Me.Label3.Caption = Worksheets("Surface").Range("O4").Value
    Worksheets("Surface").Shapes(1).Chart.Export "C:\Chart.gif"
    Me.Image1.Picture = LoadPicture("C:\Chart.gif")
End Sub
```

8. Use Insert, Module to add a `Module1` component with this code:

```
Sub ShowForm()
    frmChart.Show
End Sub
```

As someone changes the spin buttons in the userform, Excel writes new values to the worksheet. This causes the chart to update. The userform code then exports the chart and displays it in the userform (refer to Figure 11.17).

Creating Pivot Charts

A pivot chart is a chart that uses a pivot table as the underlying data source. Unfortunately, pivot charts don't have the cool "show pages" functionality that regular pivot tables have. You can overcome this problem with a quick VBA macro that creates a pivot table and then a pivot chart based on the pivot table. The macro then adds the customer field to the report filter area of the pivot table. It then loops through each customer and exports the chart for each customer.

In Excel 2007, you first create a pivot cache by using the `PivotCache.Create` method. You can then define a pivot table based on the pivot cache. The usual procedure is to turn off pivot table updating while you add fields to the pivot table. Then you update the pivot table in order to have Excel perform the calculations.

It takes a bit of finesse to figure out the final range of the pivot table. If you have turned off the column and row totals, the chartable area of the pivot table starts one row below the `PivotTableRange1` area. You have to resize the area to include one fewer row to make your chart appear correctly.

After the pivot table is created, you can switch back to the `Charts.Add` code discussed earlier in this chapter. You can use any formatting code to get the chart formatted as you desire.

The following code creates a pivot table and a single pivot chart that summarize revenue by region and product:

```
Sub CreateSummaryReportUsingPivot()
    Dim WSD As Worksheet
    Dim PTCache As PivotCache
    Dim PT As PivotTable
    Dim PRange As Range
    Dim FinalRow As Long
    Dim ChartDataRange As Range
    Dim Cht As Chart
    Set WSD = Worksheets("Data")

    ' Delete any prior pivot tables
    For Each PT In WSD.PivotTables
        PT.TableRange2.Clear
    Next PT
    WSD.Range("I1:Z1").EntireColumn.Clear

    ' Define input area and set up a Pivot Cache
    FinalRow = WSD.Cells(Application.Rows.Count, 1).End(xlUp).Row
    FinalCol = WSD.Cells(1, Application.Columns.Count). _
        End(xlToLeft).Column
    Set PRange = WSD.Cells(1, 1).Resize(FinalRow, FinalCol)

    Set PTCache = ActiveWorkbook.PivotCaches.Create(SourceType:= _
        xlDatabase, SourceData:=PRange.Address)

    ' Create the Pivot Table from the Pivot Cache
    Set PT = PTCache.CreatePivotTable(TableDestination:=WSD. _
        Cells(2, FinalCol + 2), TableName:="PivotTable1")

    ' Turn off updating while building the table
    PT.ManualUpdate = True

    ' Set up the row fields
    PT.AddFields RowFields:="Region", ColumnFields:="Product", _
        PageFields:="Customer"
```

```
' Set up the data fields
With PT.PivotFields("Revenue")
    .Orientation = xlDataField
    .Function = xlSum
    .Position = 1
End With

With PT
    .ColumnGrand = False
    .RowGrand = False
    .NullString = "0"
End With

' Calc the pivot table
PT.ManualUpdate = False
PT.ManualUpdate = True

' Define the Chart Data Range
Set ChartDataRange = _
    PT.TableRange1.Offset(1, 0).Resize(PT.TableRange1.Rows.Count - 1)

' Add the Chart
WSD.Shapes.AddChart.Select
Set Cht = ActiveChart
Cht.SetSourceData Source:=ChartDataRange
' Format the Chart
Cht.ChartType = xlColumnClustered
Cht.SetElement (msoElementChartTitleAboveChart)
Cht.ChartTitle.Caption = "All Customers"
Cht.SetElement msoElementPrimaryValueAxisThousands
End Sub
```

Figure 11.18 shows the resulting chart and pivot table.

Figure 11.18
VBA creates a pivot table and then a chart from the pivot table. Excel automatically displays the PivotChart Filter window in response.

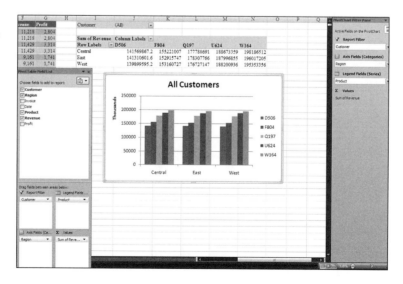

Next Steps

Charts provide a visual picture that can help to summarize data for a manager. In Chapter 12, "Data Mining with Advanced Filter," you will learn about using the Advanced Filter tools to quickly produce reports.

11

Data Mining with Advanced Filter

12

Advanced Filter Is Easier in VBA Than in Excel

Using the arcane Advanced Filter command is so hard in the Excel user interface that it is pretty rare to find someone who enjoys using it regularly. In versions of Excel prior to 2007, the AutoFilter command was probably used by most people rather than the Advanced Filter. In Excel 2007, Microsoft renamed the AutoFilter to Filter and made advances in the types of filters possible, making the Advanced Filter a less likely choice in the user interface.

However, in VBA, advanced filters are a joy to use. With a single line of code, you can rapidly extract a subset of records from a database or quickly get a unique list of values in any column. This is critical when you want to run reports for a specific region or customer.

Because not many people use the Advanced Filter feature, I walk you through examples, using the user interface to build an advanced filter, and then show you the analogous code. You will be amazed at how complex the user interface seems and yet how easy it is to program a powerful advanced filter to extract records.

One reason why Advanced Filter is hard to use is that you can use the filter in several different ways. You must make three basic choices in the Advanced Filter dialog box. Because each choice has two options, there are eight (2 x 2 x 2) possible combinations of these choices. The three choices are shown in Figure 12.1 and described here:

- **Action**—You can choose Filter the List, In-Place, or Copy to Another Location. If you choose to filter the records in place, the nonmatching rows are hidden. Choosing to copy to a new location copies the records that match the filter to a new range.

- **Criteria**—You can filter with or without criteria. Filtering with criteria is appropriate for getting a subset of rows. Filtering without criteria is still useful when you want a subset of columns or when you are using the Unique Records Only option.

- **Unique**—You can choose to request Unique Records Only or all matching records. The Unique option makes the Advanced Filter command one of the fastest ways to find a unique list of values in one field.

Figure 12.1
The Advanced Filter dialog is complicated to use in the Excel user interface. Luckily, it is far easier in VBA.

Using Advanced Filter to Extract a Unique List of Values

One of the simplest uses of Advanced Filter is to extract a unique list of a single field from a dataset. In this example, you want to get a unique list of customers from a sales report. You know that customer is in Column D of the dataset. You have an unknown number of records starting in cell A2. (Row 1 is the header row.) There is nothing located to the right of the dataset.

Extracting a Unique List of Values with the User Interface

To extract a unique list of values, follow these steps:

1. With the cursor anywhere in the data range, select Advanced from the Sort & Filter group on the Data ribbon. The first time that you use the Advanced Filter command on a worksheet, Excel automatically populates the List Range text box with the entire range of your dataset. On subsequent uses of the Advanced Filter command, this dialog box remembers the settings from the prior advanced filter.

2. Choose the Unique Records Only check box at the bottom of the dialog.

3. In the Action section, choose Copy to Another Location.

4. Type **J1** in the Copy To text box.

By default, Excel copies all the columns in the dataset. You can filter just the Customer column by either limiting the List Range to include only Column D, or by specifying one or more headings in the Copy To range. Either method has its own drawbacks.

Change the List Range to a Single Column

Edit the List Range to point to the Customer column. In this case, it means changing the default $A$1:$H$1127 to $D$1:$D$1127. The Advanced Filter dialog should appear.

> **CAUTION**
>
> When you initially edit any range in the dialog box, Excel might be in Point mode. In this mode, pressing a left- or right-arrow key will insert a cell reference in the text box. If you see the word *Point* in the lower-left corner of your Excel window, press the F2 key to change from Point mode to Edit mode.

The drawback of this method is that Excel remembers the list range on subsequent uses of the Advanced Filter command. If you later want to get a unique list of regions, you will be constantly specifying the list range.

Change the List Range to a Single Column

With a little forethought before invoking the Advanced Filter command, you can allow Excel to keep the default list range of $A$1:$H$1127. In cell J1, type the **Customer** heading. In Figure 12.2, you leave the List Range field pointing to Columns A through H. Because the Copy To range of J1 already contains a valid heading from the list range, Excel copies data only from the Customer column. I prefer this method, particularly if you will be doing multiple advanced filters. Because Excel remembers the prior settings from the last advanced filter, it is more convenient to always filter the entire columns of the list range and limit the columns by setting up headings in the Copy To range.

Figure 12.2
By setting up a heading in the Copy To range of J1, you can avoid having to respecify the list range for each advanced filter.

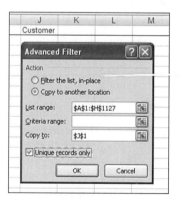

After using either of these methods to perform the Advanced Filter, a concise list of the unique customers appears in Column J (see Figure 12.3).

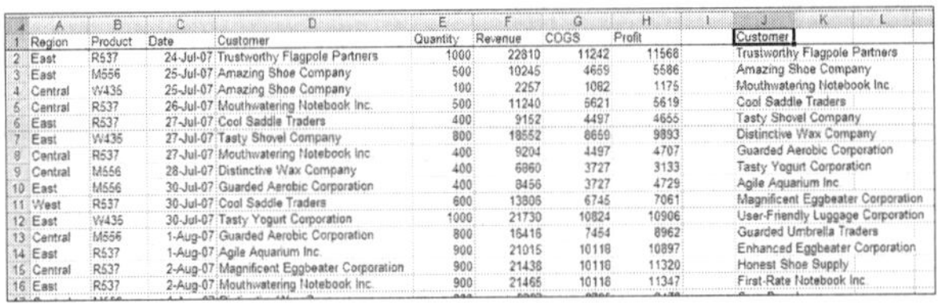

Figure 12.3
The Advanced Filter extracted a unique list of customers from the dataset and copied it to Column J.

Extracting a Unique List of Values with VBA Code

In VBA, you use the `AdvancedFilter` method to carry out the Advanced Filter command. Again, you have three choices to make:

- **Action**—Choose to either filter in place with the parameter `Action:=xlFilterInPlace` or to copy with `Action:=xlFilterCopy`. If you want to copy, you also have to specify the parameter `CopyToRange:=Range("J1")`.

- **Criteria**—To filter with criteria, include the parameter `CriteriaRange:=Range("L1:L2")`. To filter without criteria, omit this optional parameter.

- **Unique**—To return only unique records, specify the parameter `Unique:=True`.

The following code sets up a single column output range two columns to the right of the last-used column in the data range:

```
Sub GetUniqueCustomers()
    Dim IRange As Range
    Dim ORange As Range

    ' Find the size of today's dataset
    FinalRow = Cells(Rows.Count, 1).End(xlUp).Row
    NextCol = Cells(1, Columns.Count).End(xlToLeft).Column + 2

    ' Set up output range. Copy heading from D1 there
    Range("D1").Copy Destination:=Cells(1, NextCol)
    Set ORange = Cells(1, NextCol)

    ' Define the Input Range
    Set IRange = Range("A1").Resize(FinalRow, NextCol - 2)

    ' Do the Advanced Filter to get unique list of customers
    IRange.AdvancedFilter Action:=xlFilterCopy, CopyToRange:=ORange, Unique:=True

End Sub
```

By default, an advanced filter copies all columns. If you just want one particular column, use that column heading as the heading in the output range.

The first bit of code finds the final row and column in the dataset. Although it is not necessary to do so, I define an object variable for the output range (`ORange`) and for the input range (`IRange`).

This code is generic enough that it will not have to be rewritten if new columns are added to the dataset at a later time. Setting up the object variables for the input and output range is done for readability instead of out of necessity. The previous code could be written just as easily like this shortened version:

```
Sub UniqueCustomerRedux()
    ' Copy a heading to create an output range
    Range("J1").Value = Range("D1").Value
    ' Do the Advanced Filter
    Range("A1").CurrentRegion.AdvancedFilter xlFilterCopy, _
        CopyToRange:=Range("J1"), Unique:=True
End Sub
```

When you run either of the previous blocks of code on the sample dataset, you get a unique list of customers off to the right of the data. In Figure 12.3, you saw the original dataset in Columns A:H and the unique customers in Column J. The key to getting a unique list of customers is copying the header from the Customer field to a blank cell and specifying this cell as the output range.

After you have the unique list of customers, you can easily sort the list and add a SUMIF formula to get total revenue by customer. The following code gets the unique list of customers, sorts it, and then builds a formula to total revenue by customer. Figure 12.4 shows the results:

```
Sub RevenueByCustomers()
    Dim IRange As Range
    Dim ORange As Range

    ' Find the size of today's dataset
    FinalRow = Cells(Rows.Count, 1).End(xlUp).Row
    NextCol = Cells(1, Columns.Count).End(xlToLeft).Column + 2

    ' Set up output range. Copy heading from D1 there
    Range("D1").Copy Destination:=Cells(1, NextCol)
    Set ORange = Cells(1, NextCol)

    ' Define the Input Range
    Set IRange = Range("A1").Resize(FinalRow, NextCol - 2)

    ' Do the Advanced Filter to get unique list of customers
    IRange.AdvancedFilter Action:=xlFilterCopy, _
        CopyToRange:=ORange, Unique:=True

    ' Determine how many unique customers we have
    LastRow = Cells(Rows.Count, NextCol).End(xlUp).Row

    ' Sort the data
    Cells(1, NextCol).Resize(LastRow, 1).Sort Key1:=Cells(1, NextCol), _
        Order1:=xlAscending, Header:=xlYes

    ' Add a SUMIF formula to get totals
    Cells(1, NextCol + 1).Value = "Revenue"
    Cells(2, NextCol + 1).FormulaR1C1 = "=SUM(R2C4:R" & FinalRow & "C4,RC[-1], _
        R2C6:R" & FinalRow & "C6)"
    If LastRow > 2 Then
        Cells(2, NextCol + 1).Copy Cells(3, NextCol + 1).Resize(LastRow - 2, 1)
    End If

End Sub
```

12

Figure 12.4

This simple macro produced a summary report by customer from a lengthy dataset. Using AdvancedFilter is the key to powerful macros such as these.

f_x	=SUMIF($D$2:$D$1127,J2,$F$2:$F$1127)	
	J	K
	Customer	Revenue
	Agile Aquarium Inc.	97107
	Amazing Shoe Company	820384
	Appealing Eggbeater Corporation	92544
	Cool Saddle Traders	53170
	Distinctive Wax Company	947025
	Enhanced Eggbeater Corporation	1543677
	First-Rate Glass Corporation	106442
	First-Rate Notebook Inc.	104205
	Guarded Aerobic Corporation	1448081

Another use of a unique list of values is to quickly populate a list box or a combo box on a userform. Suppose, for instance, that you have a macro that can run a report for any one specific customer. To allow your clients to choose which customers to report, create a simple userform. Add a list box to the userform and set the list box's MultiSelect property to 1-fmMultiSelectMulti. I named my form frmReport. In addition to the list box, I have four command buttons: OK, Cancel, Mark All, Clear All. The code to run the form follows. Note the Userform_Initialize procedure includes an advanced filter to get the unique list of customers from the dataset:

```
Private Sub CancelButton_Click()
    Unload Me
End Sub

Private Sub cbSubAll_Click()
    For i = 0 To lbCust.ListCount - 1
        Me.lbCust.Selected(i) = True
    Next i
End Sub

Private Sub cbSubClear_Click()
    For i = 0 To lbCust.ListCount - 1
        Me.lbCust.Selected(i) = False
    Next i
End Sub

Private Sub OKButton_Click()
    For i = 0 To lbCust.ListCount - 1
        If Me.lbCust.Selected(i) = True Then
            ' Call a routine to produce this report
            RunCustReport WhichCust:=Me.lbCust.List(i)
        End If
    Next i
    Unload Me
End Sub

Private Sub UserForm_Initialize()
    Dim IRange As Range
    Dim ORange As Range

    ' Find the size of today's dataset
    FinalRow = Cells(Rows.Count, 1).End(xlUp).Row
    NextCol = Cells(1, Columns.Count).End(xlToLeft).Column + 2

    ' Set up output range. Copy heading from D1 there
    Range("D1").Copy Destination:=Cells(1, NextCol)
```

```
    Set ORange = Cells(1, NextCol)

    ' Define the Input Range
    Set IRange = Range("A1").Resize(FinalRow, NextCol - 2)

    ' Do the Advanced Filter to get unique list of customers
    IRange.AdvancedFilter Action:=xlFilterCopy, _
        CopyToRange:=ORange, Unique:=True

    ' Determine how many unique customers we have
    LastRow = Cells(Rows.Count, NextCol).End(xlUp).Row

    ' Sort the data
    Cells(1, NextCol).Resize(LastRow, 1).Sort Key1:=Cells(1, NextCol), _
        Order1:=xlAscending, Header:=xlYes

With Me.lbCust
    .RowSource = ""
    .List = Cells(2, NextCol).Resize(LastRow - 1, 1).Value
End With

    ' Erase the temporary list of customers
    Cells(1, NextCol).Resize(LastRow, 1).Clear
End Sub
```

Launch this form with a simple module such as this:

```
Sub ShowCustForm()
    frmReport.Show
End Sub
```

Your clients are presented with a list of all valid customers from the dataset. Because the list box's MultiSelect property is set to allow it, they can select any number of customers, as shown in Figure 12.5.

Getting Unique Combinations of Two or More Fields

To get all unique combinations of two (or more) fields, build the output range to include the additional fields. This code sample builds a list of unique combinations of two fields, Customer and Product:

```
Sub UniqueCustomerProduct()
    Dim IRange As Range
    Dim ORange As Range

    ' Find the size of today's dataset
    FinalRow = Cells(Rows.Count, 1).End(xlUp).Row
    NextCol = Cells(1, Columns.Count).End(xlToLeft).Column + 2

    ' Set up output range. Copy headings from D1 & B1
    Range("D1").Copy Destination:=Cells(1, NextCol)
    Range("B1").Copy Destination:=Cells(1, NextCol + 1)
    Set ORange = Cells(1, NextCol).Resize(1, 2)

    ' Define the Input Range
    Set IRange = Range("A1").Resize(FinalRow, NextCol - 2)

    ' Do the Advanced Filter to get unique list of customers & product
```

```
IRange.AdvancedFilter Action:=xlFilterCopy, _
    CopyToRange:=ORange, Unique:=True

' Determine how many unique rows we have
LastRow = Cells(Rows.Count, NextCol).End(xlUp).Row

' Sort the data
Cells(1, NextCol).Resize(LastRow, 2).Sort Key1:=Cells(1, NextCol), _
    Order1:=xlAscending, Key2:=Cells(1, NextCol + 1), _
    Order2:=xlAscending, Header:=xlYes
```

End Sub

In the result shown in Figure 12.6, you can see that Enhanced Eggbeater buys only one product, and Agile Aquarium buys three products. This might be useful to use as a guide in running reports on either customer by product or product by customer.

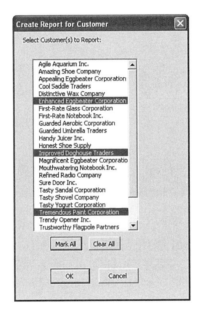

Figure 12.5
Your clients will have a list of customers from which to select quickly. Using an advanced filter on even a 1,000,000-row dataset is much faster than setting up a class to populate the list box.

Figure 12.6
By including two columns in the output range on a Unique Values query, we get every combination of Customer and Product.

J	K
Customer	Product
Agile Aquarium Inc.	M556
Agile Aquarium Inc.	R537
Agile Aquarium Inc.	W435
Amazing Shoe Company	M556
Amazing Shoe Company	R537
Amazing Shoe Company	W435
Appealing Eggbeater Corporation	M556
Appealing Eggbeater Corporation	R537
Appealing Eggbeater Corporation	W435
Cool Saddle Traders	M556
Cool Saddle Traders	R537
Cool Saddle Traders	W435
Distinctive Wax Company	M556
Distinctive Wax Company	R537
Distinctive Wax Company	W435
Enhanced Eggbeater Corporation	R537
First-Rate Glass Corporation	M556

Using Advanced Filter with Criteria Ranges

As the name implies, Advanced Filter is usually used to filter records—in other words, to get a subset of data. You specify the subset by setting up a criteria range. Even if you are familiar with criteria, be sure to check out using the powerful Boolean formula in criteria ranges later in this chapter, in the section "The Most Complex Criteria—Replacing the List of Values with a Condition Created as the Result of a Formula."

Set up a criteria range in a blank area of the worksheet. A criteria range always includes two or more rows. The first row of the criteria range contains one or more field header values to match the one(s) in the data range you want to filter. The second row contains a value showing what records to extract. In Figure 12.8, range J1:J2 is the criteria range, and range L1 is the output range.

In the Excel user interface, to extract a unique list of products that were purchased by a particular customer, select Advanced Filter and set up the Advanced Filter dialog as shown earlier in Figure 12.7. Figure 12.8 shows the results.

Figure 12.7

This is about the simplest criteria there is; to learn a unique list of products purchased by Cool Saddle Traders, set up the criteria range shown in J1:J2.

Figure 12.8

The results of the advanced filter that uses a criteria range and asks for a unique list of products. Of course, more complex and interesting criteria can be built.

J	K	L	M
Customer		Product	
Cool Saddle Traders		R537	
		M556	
		W435	

In VBA, you use the following code to perform an equivalent advanced filter:

```
Sub UniqueProductsOneCustomer()
    Dim IRange As Range
    Dim ORange As Range
```

```
Dim CRange As Range

' Find the size of today's dataset
FinalRow = Cells(Rows.Count, 1).End(xlUp).Row
NextCol = Cells(1, Columns.Count).End(xlToLeft).Column + 2

' Set up the Output Range with one customer
Cells(1, NextCol).Value = Range("D1").Value
' In reality, this value should be passed from the userform
Cells(2, NextCol).Value = Range("D2").Value
Set CRange = Cells(1, NextCol).Resize(2, 1)

' Set up output range. Copy heading from B1 there
Range("B1").Copy Destination:=Cells(1, NextCol + 2)
Set ORange = Cells(1, NextCol + 2)

' Define the Input Range
Set IRange = Range("A1").Resize(FinalRow, NextCol - 2)

' Do the Advanced Filter to get unique list of customers & product
IRange.AdvancedFilter Action:=xlFilterCopy, _
    CriteriaRange:=CRange, CopyToRange:=ORange, Unique:=True
' The above could also be written as:
'IRange.AdvancedFilter xlFilterCopy, CRange, ORange, True

' Determine how many unique rows we have
LastRow = Cells(Rows.Count, NextCol + 2).End(xlUp).Row

' Sort the data
Cells(1, NextCol + 2).Resize(LastRow, 1).Sort Key1:=Cells(1, NextCol + 2), _
    Order1:=xlAscending, Header:=xlYes

End Sub
```

Joining Multiple Criteria with a Logical OR

You may want to filter records that match one criteria or another (for example, extract customers who purchased either product M556 or product R537). This is called a logical OR criteria.

When your criteria should be joined by a logical OR, place the criteria on subsequent rows of the criteria range. For example, the criteria range shown in J1:J3 of Figure 12.9 tells you which customers order product M556 or product R537.

Figure 12.9

Place criteria on successive rows to join them with an OR. This criteria range gets customers who ordered either product M556 or R537.

Joining Two Criteria with a Logical AND

Other times, you will want to filter records that match one criteria and another criteria. For example, you might want to extract records where the product sold was W435 and the region was the West region. This is called a logical AND.

To join two criteria by AND, put both criteria on the same row of the criteria range. For example, the criteria range shown in J1:K2 of Figure 12.10 gets the customers who ordered product W435 in the West region.

Figure 12.10
Place criteria on the same row to join them with an AND. The criteria range in J1:K2 gets customers from the West region who ordered product W435.

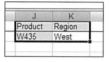

Other Slightly Complex Criteria Ranges

The criteria range shown in Figure 12.11 is based on two different fields. They are joined with an OR. The query finds all records from either the West region or records where the product is W435.

Figure 12.11
The criteria range in J1:K3 returns records where either the Region is West or the Product is W435.

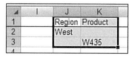

> **TIP**
> Joining two criteria with OR might be useful where new California legislation will impact shipments made to California or products sourced at the California plant.

The Most Complex Criteria—Replacing the List of Values with a Condition Created as the Result of a Formula

It is possible to have a criteria range with multiple logical AND and logical OR criteria joined together. Although this might work in some situations, in other scenarios it quickly gets out of hand. Luckily, Excel allows for criteria where the records are selected as the result of a formula to handle this situation.

CASE STUDY

Working with Very Complex Criteria

Your clients so loved the "Create a Customer" report, they hired you to write a new report. In this case, they could select any customer, any product, any region, or any combination of them. You can quickly adapt the frmReport userform to show three list boxes, as shown in Figure 12.12.

In your first test, imagine that you select two customers and two products. In this case, your program has to build a five-row criteria range, as shown in Figure 12.13. This isn't too bad.

This gets crazy if someone selects 10 products, all regions but the house region, and all customers except the internal customer. Your criteria range would need unique combinations of the selected fields. This could easily be 10 products times 9 regions times 499 customers, or more than 44,000 rows of criteria range. You can quickly end up with a criteria range that spans thousands of rows and three columns. I was once foolish enough to actually try running an advanced filter with such a criteria range. It would still be trying to compute if I hadn't rebooted the computer.

The solution for this report is to replace the lists of values with a formula-based condition.

Figure 12.12
This super-flexible form lets clients run any types of reports that they can imagine. It creates some nightmarish criteria ranges, unless you know the way out.

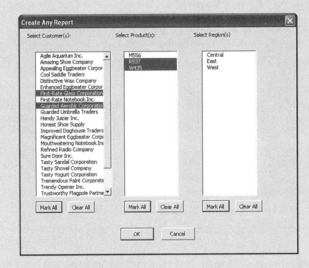

Figure 12.13
This criteria range returns any records where the two selected customers ordered any of the two selected products.

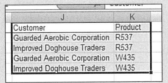

Setting Up a Condition as the Result of a Formula

Amazingly, there is an incredibly obscure version of Advanced Filter criteria that can replace the 44,000-row criteria range in the case study. In the alternative form of criteria range, the top row is left blank. There is no heading above the criteria. The criteria set up in Row 2 are a formula that results in True or False. If the formula contains any relative references to Row 2 of the input range, Excel compares that formula to every row of the input range, one by one.

For example, if we want all records where the Gross Profit Percentage is below 53%, the formula built in J2 would reference the Profit in H2 and the Revenue in F2. We would leave J1 blank to tell Excel that we are using a formula-based criterion. Cell J2 would contain the formula =(H2/F2)<0.53. The criteria range for the advanced filter would be specified as J1:J2.

As Excel performs the advanced filter, it logically copies the formula and applies it to all rows in the database. Anywhere that the formula evaluates to True, the record is included in the output range.

This is incredibly powerful and runs remarkably quickly. You can combine multiple formulas in adjacent columns or rows to join the formula criteria with AND or OR, just as you do with regular criteria.

CASE STUDY

Using Formula-Based Conditions in the Excel User Interface

You can use formula-based conditions to easily solve the report introduced in the prior case study.

To illustrate, off to the right of the criteria range set up a column of cells with the list of selected customers. Assign a name to the range, such as **MyCust**. In cell J2 of the criteria range, enter a formula such as =**Not(ISNA(Match(D2, MyCust,False)))**.

To the right of the MyCust range, set up a range with a list of selected products. Assign this range the name of **MyProd**. In the K2 of the criteria range, add a formula to check products, =**NOT(ISNA(Match(B2,MyProd,False)))**.

To the right of the MyProd range, set up a range with a list of selected regions. Assign this range the name of **MyRegion**. In L2 of the criteria range, add a formula to check for selected regions, =**NOT(ISNA(Match(A2,MyRegion,False)))**.

Now, with a criteria range of J1:L2, you can effectively retrieve the records matching any combination of selections from the userform.

Using Formula-Based Conditions with VBA

The following is the code for this new userform. Note the logic in OKButton_Click that builds the formula. Figure 12.14 shows the Excel sheet just before the Advanced Filter is run:

```
Private Sub CancelButton_Click()
    Unload Me
End Sub

Private Sub cbSubAll_Click()
    For i = 0 To lbCust.ListCount - 1
        Me.lbCust.Selected(i) = True
    Next i
```

```
End Sub

Private Sub cbSubClear_Click()
    For i = 0 To lbCust.ListCount - 1
        Me.lbCust.Selected(i) = False
    Next i
End Sub

Private Sub CommandButton1_Click()
    ' Clear all products
    For i = 0 To lbProduct.ListCount - 1
        Me.lbProduct.Selected(i) = False
    Next i
End Sub

Private Sub CommandButton2_Click()
    ' Mark all products
    For i = 0 To lbProduct.ListCount - 1
        Me.lbProduct.Selected(i) = True
    Next i
End Sub

Private Sub CommandButton3_Click()
    ' Clear all regions
    For i = 0 To lbRegion.ListCount - 1
        Me.lbRegion.Selected(i) = False
    Next i
End Sub

Private Sub CommandButton4_Click()
    ' Mark all regions
    For i = 0 To lbRegion.ListCount - 1
        Me.lbRegion.Selected(i) = True
    Next i
End Sub

Private Sub OKButton_Click()
    Dim CRange As Range, IRange As Range, ORange As Range
    ' Build a complex criteria that ANDS all choices together
    NextCCol = 10
    NextTCol = 15

    For j = 1 To 3
        Select Case j
            Case 1
                MyControl = "lbCust"
                MyColumn = 4
            Case 2
                MyControl = "lbProduct"
                MyColumn = 2
            Case 3
                MyControl = "lbRegion"
                MyColumn = 1
        End Select
        NextRow = 2
        ' Check to see what was selected.
        For i = 0 To Me.Controls(MyControl).ListCount - 1
            If Me.Controls(MyControl).Selected(i) = True Then
```

```
                    Cells(NextRow, NextTCol).Value = _
                        Me.Controls(MyControl).List(i)
                    NextRow = NextRow + 1
                End If
            Next i
            ' If anything was selected, build a new criteria formula
            If NextRow > 2 Then
                ' the reference to Row 2 must be relative in order to work
                MyFormula = "=NOT(ISNA(MATCH(RC" & MyColumn & ",R2C" & NextTCol & _
                    ":R" & NextRow - 1 & "C" & NextTCol & ",False)))"
                Cells(2, NextCCol).FormulaR1C1 = MyFormula
                NextTCol = NextTCol + 1
                NextCCol = NextCCol + 1
            End If
        Next j
        Unload Me

        ' Figure 12.14 shows the worksheet at this point
        ' if we built any criteria, define the criteria range
        If NextCCol > 10 Then
            Set CRange = Range(Cells(1, 10), Cells(2, NextCCol - 1))
            Set IRange = Range("A1").CurrentRegion
            Set ORange = Cells(1, 20)
            IRange.AdvancedFilter xlFilterCopy, CRange, ORange

            ' Clear out the criteria
            Cells(1, 10).Resize(1, 10).EntireColumn.Clear
        End If

        ' At this point, the matching records are in T1

End Sub

Private Sub UserForm_Initialize()
    Dim IRange As Range
    Dim ORange As Range

    ' Find the size of today's dataset
    FinalRow = Cells(Rows.Count, 1).End(xlUp).Row
    NextCol = Cells(1, Columns.Count).End(xlToLeft).Column + 2

    ' Define the input range
    Set IRange = Range("A1").Resize(FinalRow, NextCol - 2)

    ' Set up output range for Customer. Copy heading from D1 there
    Range("D1").Copy Destination:=Cells(1, NextCol)
    Set ORange = Cells(1, NextCol)

    ' Do the Advanced Filter to get unique list of customers
    IRange.AdvancedFilter Action:=xlFilterCopy, CriteriaRange:="", _
        CopyToRange:=ORange, Unique:=True

    ' Determine how many unique customers we have
    LastRow = Cells(Rows.Count, NextCol).End(xlUp).Row

    ' Sort the data
    Cells(1, NextCol).Resize(LastRow, 1).Sort Key1:=Cells(1, NextCol), _
        Order1:=xlAscending, Header:=xlYes
```

12

```
With Me.lbCust
    .RowSource = ""
    FinalRow = Cells(Rows.Count, 10).End(xlUp).Row
    For Each cell In Cells(2, NextCol).Resize(LastRow - 1, 1)
        .AddItem cell.Value
    Next cell
End With

' Erase the temporary list of customers
Cells(1, NextCol).Resize(LastRow, 1).Clear

' Set up output range for product. Copy heading from D1 there
Range("B1").Copy Destination:=Cells(1, NextCol)
Set ORange = Cells(1, NextCol)

' Do the Advanced Filter to get unique list of customers
IRange.AdvancedFilter Action:=xlFilterCopy, _
    CopyToRange:=ORange, Unique:=True

' Determine how many unique customers we have
LastRow = Cells(Rows.Count, NextCol).End(xlUp).Row

' Sort the data
Cells(1, NextCol).Resize(LastRow, 1).Sort Key1:=Cells(1, NextCol), _
    Order1:=xlAscending, Header:=xlYes

With Me.lbProduct
    .RowSource = ""
    FinalRow = Cells(Rows.Count, 10).End(xlUp).Row
    For Each cell In Cells(2, NextCol).Resize(LastRow - 1, 1)
        .AddItem cell.Value
    Next cell
End With

' Erase the temporary list of customers
Cells(1, NextCol).Resize(LastRow, 1).Clear

' Set up output range for Region. Copy heading from A1 there
Range("A1").Copy Destination:=Cells(1, NextCol)
Set ORange = Cells(1, NextCol)

' Do the Advanced Filter to get unique list of customers
' Figure 12.15 shows the worksheet state just before this line
IRange.AdvancedFilter Action:=xlFilterCopy, CopyToRange:=ORange, _
    Unique:=True

' Determine how many unique customers we have
LastRow = Cells(Rows.Count, NextCol).End(xlUp).Row

' Sort the data
Cells(1, NextCol).Resize(LastRow, 1).Sort Key1:=Cells(1, NextCol), _
    Order1:=xlAscending, Header:=xlYes

With Me.lbRegion
    .RowSource = ""
    FinalRow = Cells(Rows.Count, 10).End(xlUp).Row
    For Each cell In Cells(2, NextCol).Resize(LastRow - 1, 1)
        .AddItem cell.Value
```

```
    Next cell
End With

' Erase the temporary list of customers
Cells(1, NextCol).Resize(LastRow, 1).Clear

End Sub
```

Figure 12.14
The worksheet just before the macro runs the advanced filter.

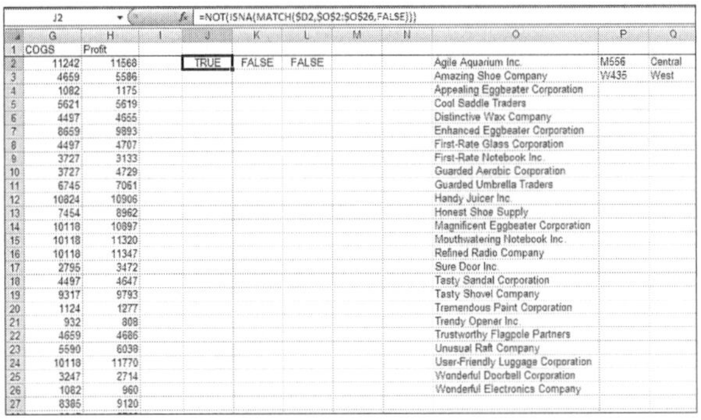

Figure 12.14 shows the worksheet just before the `AdvancedFilter` method is called. The user has selected customers, products, and regions. The macro has built temporary tables in Columns O, P, Q to show which values the user selected. The criteria range is J1:L2. That criteria formula in J2 looks to see whether the value in $D2 is in the list of selected customers in O. The formulas in K2 and L2 compare $B2 to Column P and $A2 to Column Q.

> **CAUTION**
>
> Excel VBA Help says that if you do not specify a criteria range, no criteria is used. This is not true in Excel 2007—if no criteria range is specified, the advanced filter inherits the criteria range from the prior advanced filter. You should include `CriteriaRange:=""` to clear the prior value.

Using Formula-Based Conditions to Return Above-Average Records

The formula-based conditions formula criteria are cool, but are a rarely used feature in a rarely used function. Some interesting business applications use this technique. For example, this criteria formula would find all the above-average rows in the dataset:

```
=$A2>Average($A$2:$A$60000)
```

Using Filter in Place in Advanced Filter

It is possible to filter a large dataset in place. In this case, you do not need an output range. You would normally specify criteria range—otherwise you return 100% of the records and there is no need to do the advanced filter!

12

In the user interface of Excel, running a Filter in Place makes sense: You can easily peruse the filtered list looking for something in particular.

Running a Filter in Place in VBA is a little less convenient. The only good way to programmatically peruse through the filtered records is to use the `xlCellTypeVisible` option of the `SpecialCells` method. In the Excel user interface, the equivalent action is to select Find & Select, Go to Special from the Home ribbon. In the Go to Special dialog, select Visible Cells Only, as shown in Figure 12.15.

Figure 12.15

The Filter in Place option hides rows that do not match the selected criteria, but the only way to programmatically see the matching records is to do the equivalent of selecting Visible Cells Only from the Go To Special dialog box.

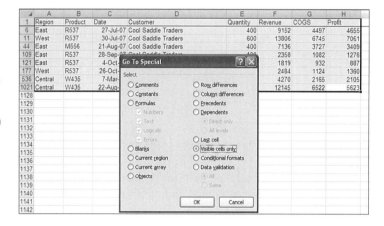

To run a Filter in Place, use the constant `XLFilterInPlace` as the Action parameter in the `AdvancedFilter` command and remove the `CopyToRange` from the command:

```
IRange.AdvancedFilter Action:=xlFilterInPlace, CriteriaRange:=CRange, _
    Unique:=False
```

Then, the programmatic equivalent to loop through Visible Cells Only is this code:

```
For Each cell In Range("A2:A" & FinalRow).SpecialCells(xlCellTypeVisible)
    Ctr = Ctr + 1
Next cell
MsgBox Ctr & " cells match the criteria"
```

Catching No Records When Using Filter in Place

Just as when using Copy, you have to watch out for the possibility of having no records match the criteria. In this case, however, it is more difficult to realize that nothing is returned. You generally find out when the `.SpecialCells` method returns a runtime error 1004—no cells were found.

To catch this condition, you have to set up an error trap to anticipate the 1004 error with the `SpecialCells` method. (See Chapter 25, "Handling Errors," for more information on catching errors.)

```
On Error GoTo NoRecs
For Each cell In Range("A2:A" & FinalRow).SpecialCells(xlCellTypeVisible)
```

```
        Ctr = Ctr + 1
    Next cell
    On Error GoTo 0
    MsgBox Ctr & " cells match the criteria"
    Exit Sub
NoRecs:
    MsgBox "No records match the criteria"
End Sub
```

This error trap works because I specifically exclude the header row from the SpecialCells range. The header row is always visible after an advanced filter. Including it in the range would prevent the 1004 error from being raised.

Showing All Records after Filter in Place

After doing a Filter in Place, you can get all records to show again by using the `ShowAllData` method:

```
ActiveSheet.ShowAllData
```

Using Filter in Place with Unique Records Only

It is possible to use Filter in Place and Unique Records Only. However, when you specified an output range of only Product and Customer, the advanced filter was able to give you only the unique combinations of Customer and Product. If you ask for unique records from a dataset with 10 fields, the only records that will not be shown are those records where all 10 fields are exact duplicates.

The Real Workhorse: `xlFilterCopy` with All Records Rather than Unique Records Only

12

The examples at the beginning of this chapter talked about using `xlFilterCopy` to get a unique list of values in a field. We used unique lists of customer, region, and product to populate the list boxes in our report-specific userforms.

A more common scenario, however, is to use an advanced filter to return all records that match the criteria. After the client selects which customer to report, an advanced filter can extract all records for that customer.

In all the examples in the following sections, you want to leave the Unique Records Only check box unselected. You do this in VBA by specifying `Unique:=False` as a parameter to the `AdvancedFilter` method.

This is easy to do, and you have some powerful options. If you need only a subset of fields for a report, copy only those field headings to the output range. If you want to resequence the fields to appear exactly as you need them in the report, you can do this by changing the sequence of the headings in the output range.

I walk you through three quick examples to show the options available.

Copying All Columns

To copy all columns, specify a single blank cell as the output range. You will get all columns for those records that match the criteria as shown in Figure 12.16:

```
Sub AllColumnsOneCustomer()
    Dim IRange As Range
    Dim ORange As Range
    Dim CRange As Range

    ' Find the size of today's dataset
    FinalRow = Cells(Rows.Count, 1).End(xlUp).Row
    NextCol = Cells(1, Columns.Count).End(xlToLeft).Column + 2

    ' Set up the criteria range with one customer
    Cells(1, NextCol).Value = Range("D1").Value
    ' In reality, this value should be passed from the userform
    Cells(2, NextCol).Value = Range("D2").Value
    Set CRange = Cells(1, NextCol).Resize(2, 1)

    ' Set up output range. It is a single blank cell
    Set ORange = Cells(1, NextCol + 2)

    ' Define the Input Range
    Set IRange = Range("A1").Resize(FinalRow, NextCol - 2)

    ' Do the Advanced Filter to get unique list of customers & product
    IRange.AdvancedFilter Action:=xlFilterCopy, _
        CriteriaRange:=CRange, CopyToRange:=ORange

End Sub
```

Figure 12.16
When using xlFilterCopy with a blank output range, you get all columns in the same order as they appear in the original list range.

Customer	Region	Product	Date	Customer	Quantity	Revenue	COGS	Profit
Trustworthy Flagpole	East	R537	24-Jul-07	Trustworth	1000	22810	11242	11568
	East	W435	8-Sep-07	Trustworth	200	4742	2165	2577
	West	M556	12-Sep-07	Trustworth	300	5700	2795	2905
	Central	W435	14-Sep-07	Trustworth	600	12282	6494	5788
	East	R537	17-Sep-07	Trustworth	100	2257	1082	1175
	Central	R537	18-Sep-07	Trustworth	1000	22680	11242	11438
	East	W435	18-Sep-07	Trustworth	600	13206	6494	6712
	Central	M556	19-Sep-07	Trustworth	900	16209	8385	7824
	Central	M556	26-Sep-07	Trustworth	200	4010	1863	2147
	East	W435	6-Oct-07	Trustworth	200	4526	2165	2361
	West	W435	10-Oct-07	Trustworth	100	2157	1082	1075

Copying a Subset of Columns and Reordering

If you are doing the advanced filter to send records to a report, it is likely that you might only need a subset of columns and you might need them in a different sequence.

Here is an example that will finish off the frmReport example from earlier in the chapter. As you remember, frmReport would allow the client to select a customer. The OK button would then call the RunCustReport routine, passing a parameter to identify for which customer to prepare a report.

Imagine this is a report being sent to the customer. The customer really doesn't care about the surrounding region, and we definitely do not want to reveal our cost of goods sold or profit. Assuming that we will put the customer in the title of the report, the fields that we really need to produce the report are Date, Quantity, Product, Revenue.

The following code copies those headings to the output range. The advanced filter produces data, as shown in Figure 12.17. The program then goes on to copy the matching records to a new workbook. A title and total row is added, and the report is saved with the customer's name. Figure 12.18 shows the final report.

```
Sub RunCustReport(WhichCust As Variant)
    Dim IRange As Range
    Dim ORange As Range
    Dim CRange As Range
    Dim WBN As Workbook
    Dim WSN As Worksheet
    Dim WSO As Worksheet

    Set WSO = ActiveSheet
    ' Find the size of today's dataset
    FinalRow = Cells(Rows.Count, 1).End(xlUp).Row
    NextCol = Cells(1, Columns.Count).End(xlToLeft).Column + 2

    ' Set up the criteria range with one customer
    Cells(1, NextCol).Value = Range("D1").Value
    Cells(2, NextCol).Value = WhichCust
    Set CRange = Cells(1, NextCol).Resize(2, 1)

    ' Set up output range. We want Date, Quantity, Product, Revenue
    ' These columns are in C, E, B, and F
    Cells(1, NextCol + 2).Resize(1, 4).Value = _
        Array(Cells(1, 3), Cells(1, 5), Cells(1, 2), Cells(1, 6))
    Set ORange = Cells(1, NextCol + 2).Resize(1, 4)

    ' Define the Input Range
    Set IRange = Range("A1").Resize(FinalRow, NextCol - 2)

    ' Do the Advanced Filter to get unique list of customers & products
    IRange.AdvancedFilter Action:=xlFilterCopy, _
        CriteriaRange:=CRange, CopyToRange:=ORange

    ' At this point, the data looks like Figure 12.18

    ' Create a new workbook with one blank sheet to hold the output
    Set WBN = Workbooks.Add(xlWBATWorksheet)
    Set WSN = WBN.Worksheets(1)

    ' Set up a title on WSN
    WSN.Cells(1, 1).Value = "Report of Sales to " & WhichCust

    ' Copy data from WSO to WSN
    WSO.Cells(1, NextCol + 2).CurrentRegion.Copy Destination:=WSN.Cells(3, 1)
    TotalRow = WSN.Cells(Rows.Count, 1).End(xlUp).Row + 1
    WSN.Cells(TotalRow, 1).Value = "Total"
    WSN.Cells(TotalRow, 2).FormulaR1C1 = "=SUM(R2C:R[-1]C)"
    WSN.Cells(TotalRow, 4).FormulaR1C1 = "=SUM(R2C:R[-1]C)"

    ' Format the new report with bold
    WSN.Cells(3, 1).Resize(1, 4).Font.Bold = True
```

```
WSN.Cells(TotalRow, 1).Resize(1, 4).Font.Bold = True
WSN.Cells(1, 1).Font.Size = 18

WBN.SaveAs "C:\" & WhichCust & ".xls"
WBN.Close SaveChanges:=False

WSO.Select

' clear the output range, etc.
Range("J1:Z1").EntireColumn.Clear

End Sub
```

Figure 12.17
Immediately after the advanced filter, we have just the columns and records needed for the report.

Customer	Date	Quantity	Product	Revenue
Cool Saddle Traders	27-Jul-07	400	R537	9152
	30-Jul-07	600	R537	13806
	21-Aug-07	400	M556	7136
	28-Sep-07	100	R537	2358
	4-Oct-07	100	R537	1819
	26-Oct-07	100	R537	2484
	7-Mar-08	200	W435	4270
	22-Aug-08	700	W435	12145

Figure 12.18
After copying the filtered data to a new sheet and applying some formatting, we have a good-looking report to send to each customer.

Report of Sales to Cool Saddle Traders

Date	Quantity	Product	Revenue
27-Jul-07	400	R537	9152
30-Jul-07	600	R537	13806
21-Aug-07	400	M556	7136
28-Sep-07	100	R537	2358
4-Oct-07	100	R537	1819
26-Oct-07	100	R537	2484
7-Mar-08	200	W435	4270
22-Aug-08	700	W435	12145
Total	2600		53170

CASE STUDY

Utilizing Two Kinds of Advanced Filters to Create a Report for Each Customer

The final advanced filter example for this chapter uses several advanced filter techniques. Let's say that after importing invoice records, you want to send a purchase summary to each customer. The process would be as follows:

1. Run an advanced filter requesting unique values to get a list of customers in J. This AdvancedFilter would specify the Unique:=True parameter and use a CopyToRange that includes a single heading for Customer:

```
' Set up output range. Copy heading from D1 there
Range("D1").Copy Destination:=Cells(1, NextCol)
Set ORange = Cells(1, NextCol)

' Define the Input Range
Set IRange = Range("A1").Resize(FinalRow, NextCol - 2)

' Do the Advanced Filter to get unique list of customers
IRange.AdvancedFilter Action:=xlFilterCopy, CriteriaRange:="", _
    CopyToRange:=ORange, Unique:=True
```

2. For each customer in the list of unique customers in Column J, perform steps 3 through 7. Find the number of customers in the output range from step 1. Then, use a `For Each Cell` loop to loop through the customers:

```
' Loop through each customer
FinalCust = Cells(Rows.Count, NextCol).End(xlUp).Row
For Each cell In Cells(2, NextCol).Resize(FinalCust - 1, 1)
    ThisCust = cell.Value
    ' … Steps 3 through 7 here
Next Cell
```

3. Build a criteria range in L1:L2 to be used in a new advanced filter. The criteria range would include a heading of Customer in L1 and the customer name from this iteration of the loop in cell L2:

```
' Set up the Criteria Range with one customer
Cells(1, NextCol + 2).Value = Range("D1").Value
Cells(2, NextCol + 2).Value = ThisCust
Set CRange = Cells(1, NextCol + 2).Resize(2, 1)
```

4. Do an advanced filter to copy matching records for this customer to Column N. This `Advanced Filter` statement would specify the `Unique:=False` parameter. Because we want only the columns for Date, Quantity, Product, and Revenue, the `CopyToRange` specifies a four-column range with those headings copied in the proper order:

```
' Set up output range. We want Date, Quantity, Product, Revenue
' These columns are in C, E, B, and F
Cells(1, NextCol + 4).Resize(1, 4).Value = _
    Array(Cells(1, 3), Cells(1, 5), Cells(1, 2), Cells(1, 6))
Set ORange = Cells(1, NextCol + 4).Resize(1, 4)

' Do the Advanced Filter to get unique list of customers & product
IRange.AdvancedFilter Action:=xlFilterCopy, CriteriaRange:=CRange, _
    CopyToRange:=Orange
```

5. Copy the customer records to a report sheet in a new workbook. The VBA code uses the `Workbooks.Add` method to create a new blank workbook. The extracted records from step 4 are copied to cell A3 of the new workbook:

```
' Create a new workbook with one blank sheet to hold the output
Set WBN = Workbooks.Add(xlWBATWorksheet)
Set WSN = WBN.Worksheets(1)

' Copy data from WSO to WSN
WSO.Cells(1, NextCol + 4).CurrentRegion.Copy _
    Destination:=WSN.Cells(3, 1)
```

6. Format the report with a title and totals. In VBA, add a title that reflects the customer's name in cell A1. Make the headings bold and add a total below the final row:

```
' Set up a title on WSN
WSN.Cells(1, 1).Value = "Report of Sales to " & ThisCust

TotalRow = WSN.Cells(Rows.Count, 1).End(xlUp).Row + 1
WSN.Cells(TotalRow, 1).Value = "Total"
WSN.Cells(TotalRow, 2).FormulaR1C1 = "=SUM(R2C:R[-1]C)"
WSN.Cells(TotalRow, 4).FormulaR1C1 = "=SUM(R2C:R[-1]C)"

' Format the new report with bold
WSN.Cells(3, 1).Resize(1, 4).Font.Bold = True
WSN.Cells(TotalRow, 1).Resize(1, 4).Font.Bold = True
WSN.Cells(1, 1).Font.Size = 18
```

12

7. Use `SaveAs` to save the workbook based on customer name. After the workbook is saved, close the new workbook. Return to the original workbook and clear the output range to prepare for the next pass through the loop:

```
WBN.SaveAs "C:\Reports\" & ThisCust & ".xls"
WBN.Close SaveChanges:=False

WSO.Select
Set WSN = Nothing
Set WBN = Nothing

' clear the output range, etc.
Cells(1, NextCol + 2).Resize(1, 10).EntireColumn.Clear
```

The complete code is as follows:

```
Sub RunReportForEachCustomer()
    Dim IRange As Range
    Dim ORange As Range
    Dim CRange As Range
    Dim WBN As Workbook
    Dim WSN As Worksheet
    Dim WSO As Worksheet

    Set WSO = ActiveSheet
    ' Find the size of today's dataset
    FinalRow = Cells(Rows.Count, 1).End(xlUp).Row
    NextCol = Cells(1, Columns.Count).End(xlToLeft).Column + 2

    ' First - get a unique list of customers in J
    ' Set up output range. Copy heading from D1 there
    Range("D1").Copy Destination:=Cells(1, NextCol)
    Set ORange = Cells(1, NextCol)

    ' Define the Input Range
    Set IRange = Range("A1").Resize(FinalRow, NextCol - 2)

    ' Do the Advanced Filter to get unique list of customers
    IRange.AdvancedFilter Action:=xlFilterCopy, CriteriaRange:="", _
        CopyToRange:=ORange, Unique:=True

    ' Loop through each customer
    FinalCust = Cells(Rows.Count, NextCol).End(xlUp).Row
    For Each cell In Cells(2, NextCol).Resize(FinalCust - 1, 1)
        ThisCust = cell.Value

        ' Set up the Criteria Range with one customer
        Cells(1, NextCol + 2).Value = Range("D1").Value
        Cells(2, NextCol + 2).Value = ThisCust
        Set CRange = Cells(1, NextCol + 2).Resize(2, 1)

        ' Set up output range. We want Date, Quantity, Product, Revenue
        ' These columns are in C, E, B, and F
        Cells(1, NextCol + 4).Resize(1, 4).Value = _
            Array(Cells(1, 3), Cells(1, 5), Cells(1, 2), Cells(1, 6))
        Set ORange = Cells(1, NextCol + 4).Resize(1, 4)

        ' Do the Advanced Filter to get unique list of customers & product
        IRange.AdvancedFilter Action:=xlFilterCopy, CriteriaRange:=CRange, _
            CopyToRange:=ORange
```

```
' Create a new workbook with one blank sheet to hold the output
Set WBN = Workbooks.Add(xlWBATWorksheet)
Set WSN = WBN.Worksheets(1)

' Copy data from WSO to WSN
WSO.Cells(1, NextCol + 4).CurrentRegion.Copy _
    Destination:=WSN.Cells(3, 1)

' Set up a title on WSN
WSN.Cells(1, 1).Value = "Report of Sales to " & ThisCust

TotalRow = WSN.Cells(Rows.Count, 1).End(xlUp).Row + 1
WSN.Cells(TotalRow, 1).Value = "Total"
WSN.Cells(TotalRow, 2).FormulaR1C1 = "=SUM(R2C:R[-1]C)"
WSN.Cells(TotalRow, 4).FormulaR1C1 = "=SUM(R2C:R[-1]C)"

' Format the new report with bold
WSN.Cells(3, 1).Resize(1, 4).Font.Bold = True
WSN.Cells(TotalRow, 1).Resize(1, 4).Font.Bold = True
WSN.Cells(1, 1).Font.Size = 18

WBN.SaveAs "C:\Reports\" & ThisCust & ".xlsx"
WBN.Close SaveChanges:=False

WSO.Select
Set WSN = Nothing
Set WBN = Nothing

' clear the output range, etc.
Cells(1, NextCol + 2).Resize(1, 10).EntireColumn.Clear
Next cell

Cells(1, NextCol).EntireColumn.Clear
MsgBox FinalCust - 1 & " Reports have been created!"
End Sub
```

This is a remarkable 75 lines of code. Incorporating a couple of advanced filters and not much else, we've managed to produce a tool that created 27 reports in less than 1 minute (see Figure 12.19). Even an Excel power user would normally take 2 to 3 minutes per report to create these manually. In less than 60 seconds, this code easily will save someone a few hours every time these reports need to be created. Imagine the real scenario where there are hundreds of customers. I guarantee that there are people in every city who are manually creating these reports in Excel because they simply don't realize the power of Excel VBA.

Figure 12.19
White-collar productivity would skyrocket if everyone knew how to create 27 reports in less than a minute.

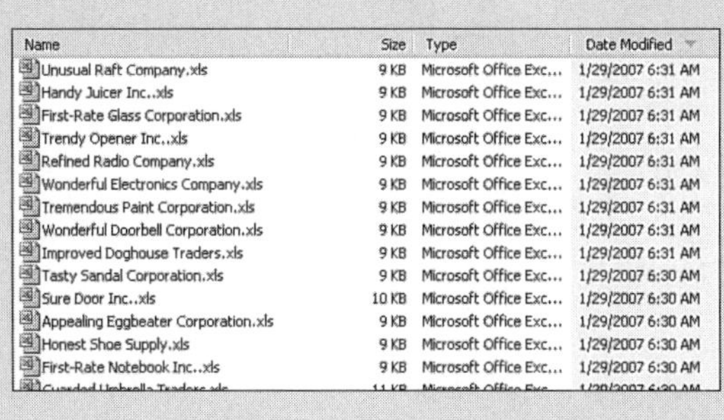

Using AutoFilter

The AutoFilter feature was added to Excel because people found advanced filters too hard. They are cool when used in the Excel user interface. I rarely had an occasion to use them in Excel VBA.

In Excel 2007, Microsoft renamed AutoFilter to Filter and added several dynamic new filters. These filters allow you to choose records with dates that fall in the last quarter, next week, or this year. Although the Excel user interface refers to them as filters, the VBA code still uses the term AutoFilter when referring to these filters.

The nature of the AutoFilter is that Excel will always filter in place. Thus, you have to use the `SpecialCells(xlCellTypeVisible)` method to access the rows returned from the filter.

Enabling AutoFilter with Code

There can be only one autofiltered dataset on each worksheet. To turn on the AutoFilter, you apply the `AutoFilter` method to any one cell in your dataset. For example, the following code turns on the AutoFilter drop-downs:

```
Range("A1").AutoFilter
```

The `AutoFilter` method is a toggle. If the AutoFilter drop-downs are already enabled, running the previous code will turn off the AutoFilter drop-downs. Excel 2007 adds a new `FilterMode` property, but it is only set to `True` if someone has selected a value from one of the AutoFilter drop-downs. Therefore, to figure out whether the AutoFilter is already enabled, you could the following macros to turn on/off the AutoFilter drop-downs:

```
Sub TurnOnAutoFilter()
    ' Turn on AutoFilters
    Worksheets("SalesReport").Select
    On Error Resume Next
    x = ActiveSheet.AutoFilter.Range.Areas.Count
    If Err.Number > 0 Then
        ActiveSheet.Range("A1").AutoFilter
    End If
    On Error Resume Next
End Sub
```

Use this code to turn off the AutoFilter drop-downs:

```
Sub TurnOffAutoFilter()
    ' Turn off AutoFilters
    Worksheets("SalesReport").Select
    On Error Resume Next
    x = ActiveSheet.AutoFilter.Range.Areas.Count
    If Err.Number = 0 Then
        ActiveSheet.Range("A1").AutoFilter
    End If
    On Error Resume Next
End Sub
```

12

Turning Off a Few Drop-Downs in the AutoFilter

One cool feature is available only in Excel VBA. When you AutoFilter a list in the Excel user interface, every column in the dataset gets a field drop-down in the heading row. Sometimes you have a field that doesn't make a lot of sense to AutoFilter. For example, in our current dataset, you might want to provide AutoFilter drop-downs for Region, Product, Customer, but not the numeric or date fields. After setting up the AutoFilter, you need one line of code to turn off each drop-down that you do not want to appear. The following code turns off the drop-downs for Columns C, E, F, G, and H:

```
Sub AutoFilterCustom()
    Range("A1").AutoFilter Field:=3, VisibleDropDown:=False
    Range("A1").AutoFilter Field:=5, VisibleDropDown:=False
    Range("A1").AutoFilter Field:=6, VisibleDropDown:=False
    Range("A1").AutoFilter Field:=7, VisibleDropDown:=False
    Range("A1").AutoFilter Field:=8, VisibleDropDown:=False
End Sub
```

I think using this tool is a fairly rare treat. Most of the time, Excel VBA lets us do things that are possible in the user interface (although it lets us do them very rapidly). The `VisibleDropDown` parameter actually allows us to do something in VBA that is generally not available in the Excel user interface. Your knowledgeable clients will be scratching their heads trying to figure out how you set up the cool AutoFilter with only a few filterable columns (see Figure 12.20).

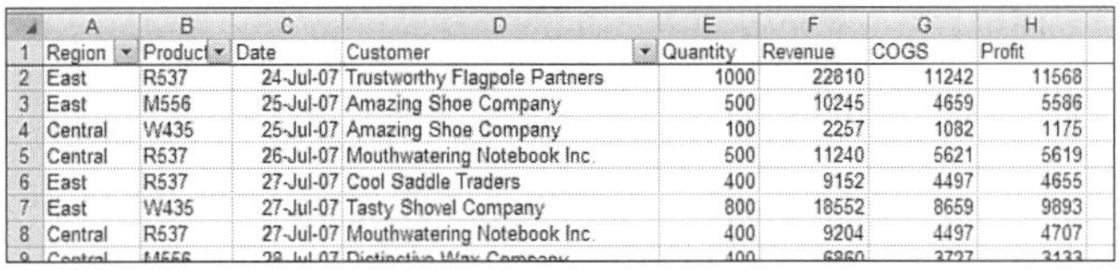

	A	B	C	D	E	F	G	H
1	Region	Product	Date	Customer	Quantity	Revenue	COGS	Profit
2	East	R537	24-Jul-07	Trustworthy Flagpole Partners	1000	22810	11242	11568
3	East	M556	25-Jul-07	Amazing Shoe Company	500	10245	4659	5586
4	Central	W435	25-Jul-07	Amazing Shoe Company	100	2257	1082	1175
5	Central	R537	26-Jul-07	Mouthwatering Notebook Inc.	500	11240	5621	5619
6	East	R537	27-Jul-07	Cool Saddle Traders	400	9152	4497	4655
7	East	W435	27-Jul-07	Tasty Shovel Company	800	18552	8659	9893
8	Central	R537	27-Jul-07	Mouthwatering Notebook Inc.	400	9204	4497	4707

Figure 12.20
Using VBA, you can set up an AutoFilter where only certain columns have the AutoFilter drop-down.

Filtering a Column Using AutoFilters

In the earliest incarnation of AutoFilters, you would specify a column number, a criteria, an operator, and a second criteria. Because AutoFilters were limited to two conditions, this handled any possible filtering scenario.

For example, the following code filters to show records for the Agile Aquarium customer. As Customer is the fourth column in the dataset, the Field number is 4:

```
Sub SimpleFilter()
    Worksheets("SalesReport").Select
    Range("A1").AutoFilter
    Range("A1").AutoFilter Field:=4, _
        Criteria1:="=Agile Aquarium Inc."
End Sub
```

To clear the filter from the customer column, you use this code:

```
Sub SimpleFilter()
    Worksheets("SalesReport").Select
    Range("A1").AutoFilter
    Range("A1").AutoFilter Field:=4
End Sub
```

In previous versions of Excel, you could join two criteria with OR or AND operators. The following code would filter the customer column to one of two customers, joined by the OR operator:

```
Sub SimpleOrFilter()
    Worksheets("SalesReport").Select
    Range("A1").AutoFilter
    Range("A1").AutoFilter Field:=4, _
        Criteria1:="=Agile Aquarium Inc.", _
        Operator:=xlOr, Criteria2:="=Amazing Shoe Company"
End Sub
```

The following code returns all customers that started with the letters *A* through *E*:

```
Sub SimpleAndFilter()
    Worksheets("SalesReport").Select
    Range("A1").AutoFilter
    Range("A1").AutoFilter Field:=4, _
        Criteria1:=">=A", _
        Operator:=xlAnd, Criteria2:="<=EZZ"
End Sub
```

As the AutoFilter command became more flexible, Microsoft continued to use the same three parameters, even if they didn't quite make sense. For example, Excel will let you filter a field by asking for the top five items or the bottom 8% of records. To use this type of filter, you specify either "5" or "8" as the Criteria1 argument, and then specify xlTop10Items, xlTop10Percent, xlBottom10Items, xlBottom10Percent as the operator. The following code produces the top 10 revenue records:

```
Sub Top10Filter()
    ' Top 12 Revenue Records
    Worksheets("SalesReport").Select
    Range("A1").AutoFilter
    Range("A1").AutoFilter Field:=6, _
        Criteria1:="12", _
        Operator:=xlTop10Items
End Sub
```

Excel 2007 offers several new filter options. Excel continues to force these filter options to fit in the old object model where the filter command must fit in an operator and up to two criteria fields.

Selecting Multiple Values from a Filter

If you specify three or more items from a filter drop-down, Excel VBA uses the xlFilterValues operator and specifies the complete list of selected items in an array passed to Criteria1. The following code selects five specific customers from the drop-down in D1:

```
Sub MultiSelectFilter()
    ' Select many customers
    Worksheets("SalesReport").Select
    Range("A1").AutoFilter
    Range("A1").AutoFilter Field:=4, _
        Criteria1:=Array( _
            "Amazing Shoe Company", "Cool Saddle Traders", _
            "Enhanced Eggbeater Corporation", _
            "First-Rate Notebook Inc.", "Handy Juicer Inc."), _
        Operator:=xlFilterValues
End Sub
```

Selecting a Dynamic Date Range Using AutoFilters

Perhaps the most powerful feature in Excel 2007 filters is the new dynamic filters. These filters enable you to choose records that are above average or with a date field to select virtual periods such as Next Week or Last Year.

To use a dynamic filter, specify xlFilterDynamic as the operator and then use one of 34 values as Criteria1.

The following code finds all dates that are in next year:

```
Sub DynamicAutoFilter()
    Worksheets("SalesReport").Select
    Range("A1").AutoFilter
    Range("A1").AutoFilter Field:=3, _
        Criteria1:=xlFilterNextYear, _
        Operator:=xlFilterDynamic
End Sub
```

The following lists all the dynamic filter criteria options. Specify these values as Criteria1 in the AutoFilter method:

- **Criteria for values**—Use xlFilterAboveAverage or xlFilterBelowAverage to find all the rows that are above or below average. Note that in Lake Wobegon, using xlFilterBelowAverage will likely return no records.

- **Criteria for future periods**—Use xlFilterTomorrow, xlFilterNextWeek, xlFilterNextMonth, xlFilterNextQuarter, or xlFilterNextYear to find rows that fall in a certain future period. Note that next week starts on Sunday and ends on Saturday.

- **Criteria for current periods**—Use xlFilterToday, xlFilterThisWeek, xlFilterThisMonth, xlFilterThisQuarter, or xlFilterThisYear to find rows that fall within the current period. Excel will use the system clock to find the current day.

- **Criteria for past periods**—Use xlFilterYesterday, xlFilterLastWeek, xlFilterLastMonth, xlFilterLastQuarter, xlFilterLastYear, or xlFilterYearToDate to find rows that fell within a previous period.

- **Criteria for specific quarters**—Use xlFilterDatesInPeriodQuarter1, xlFilterDatesInPeriodQuarter2, xlFilterDatesInPeriodQuarter3, or xlFilterDatesInPeriodQuarter4 to filter to rows that fall within a specific quarter. Note that these filters do not differentiate based on a year. If you ask for quarter 1, you might get records from this January, last February, and next March.

12

■ **Criteria for specific months**—Use xlFilterDatesInPeriodJanuary through xlFitlerDatesInPeriodDecember to filter to records that fall during a certain month. Like the quarters, the filter does not filter to any particular year.

Unfortunately, you cannot combine criteria. You might think that you could specify xlFilterDatesInPeriodJanuary as Criteria1 and xlFilterDatesNextYear as Criteria2. Although this is a brilliant thought, Microsoft doesn't support this syntax (yet).

Filtering Based on Color or Icon

Another new feature in Excel 2007 is the ability to filter based on font color, cell fill color, or conditional formatting icon.

If you are expecting the dataset to have an icon set applied, you can filter to show only records with one particular icon by using the xlFilterIcon operator.

For the criteria, you have to know which icon set has been applied and which icon within the set. The icon sets are identified using the names shown in Column A of Figure 12.21. The items range from 1 through 5. The following code filters the Revenue column to show the rows containing an upward-pointing arrow in the 5 Arrows Gray icon set:

```
Sub FilterByIcon()
    Worksheets("SalesReport").Select
    Range("A1").AutoFilter
    Range("A1").AutoFilter Field:=6, _
        Criteria1:=ActiveWorkbook.IconSets(xl5ArrowsGray).Item(5), _
        Operator:=xlFilterIcon
End Sub
```

Figure 12.21
To search for a particular icon, you need to know the icon set from Column A and the item number from Row 1.

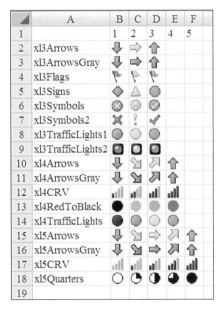

To find records that have no conditional formatting icon, use an operator of xlFilterNoIcon and do not specify any criteria.

To find records that have a particular fill color, use an operator of xlFilterCellColor and specify a particular RGB value as the criteria. This code finds all red cells in Column F:

```
Sub FilterByFillColor()
    Worksheets("SalesReport").Select
    Range("A1").AutoFilter
    Range("A1").AutoFilter Field:=6, _
        Criteria1:=RGB(255, 0, 0), Operator:=xlFilterCellColor
End Sub
```

To find records that have no fill color, use an operator of xlFilterNoFill and do not specify any criteria.

To find records that have a particular font color, use an operator of xlFilterFontColor and specify a particular RGB value as the criteria. This code finds all cells with a red font in Column F:

```
Sub FilterByFontColor()
    Worksheets("SalesReport").Select
    Range("A1").AutoFilter
    Range("A1").AutoFilter Field:=6, _
        Criteria1:=RGB(255, 0, 0), Operator:=xlFilterFontColor
End Sub
```

To find records that have no particular font color, use an operator of xlFilterAutomaticFillColor and do not specify any criteria.

CASE STUDY

Using AutoFilter to Copy All Records from Next Week

12

Suppose that you have a database showing maintenance tasks and the date that they need to be performed. Every Friday, you want to run a macro that generates a list of the items to be performed in the next week.

The new AutoFilter dynamic filter of Next Week is perfect for this task.

Because the AutoFilter can be applied to a single cell in the dataset, there is no need to figure out the number of rows or columns in the dataset. You can just apply the AutoFilter to Range("A1").

The dynamic filter constant for next week is xlFilterNextWeek. The following code sets up an AutoFilter on the WSO worksheet:

```
' Turn on the AutoFilter
WSO.Range("A1").AutoFilter
' Look for dates in column C
Range("A1").AutoFilter Field:=3, _
    Criteria1:=xlFilterNextWeek, _
    Operator:=xlFilterDynamic
```

After you have defined the AutoFilter, you need to copy the visible cells from the filtered range. New in Excel 2007, you can refer to the extent of the filtered data by using ActiveWorksheet.AutoFilter.Range. This property returns a range that includes the headings through the last row of the filtered data. Note that it includes the hidden rows, too. You can use the SpecialCells property to grab only the visible rows:

```
WSO.AutoFilter.Range.SpecialCells(xlCellTypeVisible).Copy _
    Destination:=WSN.Cells(3, 1)
```

Putting the steps in macros similar to the Advanced Filter macros yields a macro that is a few lines shorter than the Advanced Filter macro:

```
Sub AutoFilterNextWeekCopy()
    Dim WBN As Workbook
    Dim WSN As Worksheet
    Dim WSO As Worksheet

    Set WSO = ActiveSheet

    ' Turn on the AutoFilter
    WSO.Range("A1").AutoFilter
    ' Look for dates in column C

    Range("A1").AutoFilter Field:=3, _
        Criteria1:=xlFilterNextWeek, _
        Operator:=xlFilterDynamic

    ' Create a new workbook with one blank sheet to hold the output
    Set WBN = Workbooks.Add(xlWBATWorksheet)
    Set WSN = WBN.Worksheets(1)

    ' Set up a title on WSN
    WSN.Cells(1, 1).Value = "Projects Due Next Week"

    ' Copy data from WSO to WSN
    WSO.AutoFilter.Range.SpecialCells(xlCellTypeVisible).Copy _
        Destination:=WSN.Cells(3, 1)

    ' Format the new report with bold
    WSN.Cells(3, 1).Resize(1, FinalCol).Font.Bold = True
    WSN.Cells(1, 1).Font.Size = 18

    ' Save as a Macro-Enabled Workbook
    WBN.SaveAs "C:\NextWeek.xlsm", xlOpenXMLWorkbookMacroEnabled

    ' Turn off the AutoFilter
    WSO.Range("A1").AutoFilter
End Sub
```

The process of copying the visible cells adds some complexity to the AutoFilter process. However, if you need to use one of the new dynamic filters available in Excel 2007, this is clearly an easier way to grab a dynamic range of dates.

Next Steps

Using techniques from this chapter, you have many reporting techniques available to you by using the arcane Advanced Filter tool. Chapter 13, "Using VBA to Create Pivot Tables," introduces the most powerful feature in Excel: the pivot table. The combination of Advanced Filter and pivot tables creates reporting tools that enable amazing applications.

Using VBA to Create Pivot Tables

13

Introducing Pivot Tables

Pivot tables are the most powerful tools that Excel has to offer. The concept was first put into practice by Lotus with its Improv product.

I love pivot tables because they are a really fast way to summarize massive amounts of data. You can use the basic vanilla pivot table to produce a concise summary in seconds. However, pivot tables come in so many flavors that they can be the tools of choice for many different uses. You can build pivot tables to act as the calculation engine to produce reports by store, by style, or to quickly find the top 5 or bottom 10 of anything.

I am not suggesting you use VBA to build pivot tables to give to your user. I am suggesting you use pivot tables as a means to an end—use a pivot table to extract a summary of data, and then take this summary on to better uses.

Understanding Versions

Pivot tables have been evolving. They were introduced in Excel 5 and perfected in Excel 97. In Excel 2000, pivot table creation in VBA was dramatically altered. Some new parameters were added in Excel 2002. A few new properties such as `PivotFilters` and `TableStyle2` were added in Excel 2007. Therefore, you need to be extremely careful when writing code in Excel 2007 that might be run in Excel 2003 or Excel 2000 or Excel 97.

Just a few simple tweaks make 2003 code run in 2000, but a major overhaul is required to make any code run in Excel 97. Because it has been 10 years since the release of Excel 97 (and because Microsoft has not supported that product for 5+ years), this chapter focuses on using only the pivot cache method introduced in Excel 2000.

New in Excel 2007

Although the basic concept of pivot tables is the same in Excel 2007 as it was in Excel 2003, several new features are available in Excel 2007 pivot tables. The entire Design ribbon is new, including the concepts of subtotals at the top, the report layout options, blank rows, and the new PivotTable styles. Excel 2007 offers better filters than previous versions. It also makes the expand and collapse functionality more apparent by adding buttons to the pivot table grid. Every new feature adds one or more methods or properties to VBA.

If you are hoping to share your pivot table macro with people running earlier versions of Excel, you need to avoid these methods. Your best bet is to open an Excel 2003 workbook in Compatibility mode and record the macro while the workbook is in Compatibility mode. If you are using the macro only in Excel 2007 or later, you can use any of the new features.

Table 13.1 shows the methods that are new in Excel 2007. If you record a macro that uses these methods, you cannot share the macro with someone using Excel 2003 or earlier.

Table 13.1   Methods New in Excel 2007

Method	Description
ClearAllFilters	Clears all filters in the pivot table.
ClearTable	Removes all fields from the pivot table but keeps the pivot table intact.
ConvertToFormulas	Converts a pivot table to cube formulas. This method is valid only for pivot tables based on OLAP data sources.
DisplayAllMember PropertiesInTooltip	Equivalent to Options, Display, Show Properties in ToolTips.
RowAxisLayout	Changes the layout for all fields in the row area. Valid values are xlCompactRow, xlTabularRow, or xlOutlineRow.
SubtotalLocation	Controls whether subtotals appear at the top or bottom of each group. Valid arguments are xlAtTop or xlAtBottom.

Table 13.2 lists the properties that are new in Excel 2007. If you record a macro that refers to these properties, you cannot share the macro with someone using Excel 2003 or earlier.

Table 13.2   Properties New in Excel 2007

Property	Description
ActiveFilters	Indicates the active filters in the pivot table; this is a read-only property.
AllowMultipleFilters	Indicates whether a pivot field can have multiple filters applied to it at the same time.
CompactLayoutColumnHeader	Specifies the caption that is displayed in the column header of a pivot table when in compact row layout form.

Property	Description
CompactLayoutRowHeader	Specifies the caption that displays in the row header of a pivot table when in compact row layout form.
CompactRowIndent	Indicates the indent increment for pivot items when compact row layout form is turned on.
DisplayContextTooltips	Controls whether ToolTips display for pivot table cells.
DisplayFieldCaptions	Controls whether filter buttons and pivot field captions for rows and columns display in the grid.
DisplayMemberPropertyTooltips	Controls whether to display member properties in ToolTips.
FieldListSortAscending	Controls the sort order of fields in the PivotTable Field List. When this property is True, the fields are sorted in alphabetic order. When it is set to False, the fields are presented in the same sequence as the data source columns.
InGridDropZones	Controls whether you can drag and drop fields onto the grid. Changing the pivot table layout also changes this property. Changing this property forces the layout back to a table layout.
LayoutRowDefault	Specifies the layout settings for pivot fields when they are added to the pivot table for the first time. Valid values are xlCompactRow, xlTabularRow, or xlOutlineRow.
PivotColumnAxis	Returns a PivotAxis object representing the entire column axis.
PivotRowAxis	Returns a PivotAxis object representing the entire row axis.
PrintDrillIndicators	Specifies whether drill indicators are printed with the pivot table.
ShowDrillIndicators	Specifies whether drill indicators are shown in the pivot table.
ShowTableStyleColumnHeaders	Controls whether table style 2 should affect the column headers.
ShowTableStyleColumnStripes	Controls whether table style 2 should show banded columns.
ShowTableStyleLastColumn	Controls whether table style 2 should format the final column.
ShowTableStyleRowHeaders	Controls whether table style 2 should affect the row headers.
ShowTableStyleRowStripes	Controls whether table style 2 should show banded columns.
SortUsingCustomLists	Controls whether custom lists are used for sorting items of fields, both initially and later when applying a sort. Setting this property to False can optimize performance for fields with many items and allows you to avoid using custom-list-based sorting.
TableStyle2	Specifies the pivot table style currently applied to the pivot table. Note that previous versions of Excel offered a weak AutoFormat option. That feature's settings were held in the TableStyle property, so Microsoft had to use TableStyle2 as the property name for the new pivot table styles. The property might have a value such as PivotStyleLight17.

13

Creating a Vanilla Pivot Table in the Excel Interface

Although they are the most powerful feature in Excel, Microsoft estimates that pivot tables are used by only 7% of Excel users overall. Based on surveys at MrExcel.com, about 42% of advanced Excel users have used pivot tables. Because a significant portion of you have never used pivot tables, I walk through the steps of building a pivot table in the user interface. If you are already a pivot table pro, jump ahead to the next section.

Let's say you have 5,000 or 500,000 rows of data, as shown in Figure 13.1. You want a summary of revenue by region and product. Regions should go down the side, products across the top.

Figure 13.1
If you need to quickly summarize 500,000 rows of transactional data, a pivot table can do so in seconds. Your goal is to produce a summary of revenue by region and product.

	A	B	C	D	E	F	G	H
1	Region	Product	Date	Customer	Quantity	Revenue	COGS	Profit
2	West	D625	1/2/2007	Guarded Kettle Corporation	430	12019	6248	5771
3	Central	A292	1/2/2007	Mouthwatering Jewelry Company	400	8780	4564	4216
4	West	B722	1/2/2007	Agile Glass Supply	940	22513	11703	10810
5	Central	E438	1/2/2007	Persuasive Kettle Inc.	190	5691	2958	2733
6	East	E438	1/2/2007	Safe Saddle Corporation	130	3894	2024	1870
7	West	C409	1/2/2007	Agile Glass Supply	440	11418	5936	5482
8	West	C409	1/2/2007	Guarded Kettle Corporation	770	19982	10387	9595
9	Central	E438	1/2/2007	Matchless Yardstick Inc	570	17072	8875	8197
10	East	D625	1/2/2007	Unique Marble Company	380	10621	5521	5100
11	Central	D625	1/2/2007	Inventive Clipboard Corporation	690	19286	10026	9260
12	West	E438	1/2/2007	Agile Glass Supply	580	17371	9031	8340
13	West	A292	1/2/2007	Trouble-Free Eggbeater Inc.	550	12073	6276	5797
14	Central	C409	1/2/2007	Enhanced Toothpick Corporation	910	23615	12276	11339
15	West	D625	1/2/2007	Trouble-Free Eggbeater Inc.	160	4472	2325	2147
16	East	E438	1/3/2007	Unique Marble Company	400	11980	6228	5752

To build the pivot table to the right of the data, follow these steps:

1. Select a single cell in the transaction data. Choose the PivotTable icon from the Insert ribbon. Excel displays the Create PivotTable dialog.

2. Verify that Excel filled in the proper address for the table range. Provided that your data has no completely blank rows or blank columns, this address is usually correct.

3. Choose to create the pivot table on an existing worksheet. Click the Location reference box and choose cell J1, as shown in Figure 13.2.

Figure 13.2
Verify that Excel selected the correct data and specify a location for the pivot table.

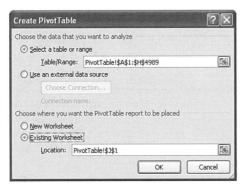

4. Click OK to create a blank pivot table. Instructions in the blank pivot table tell you to choose fields from the PivotTable Field List. The PivotTable Field List appears at the right side of your screen. A list of available fields is in the top of the task pane. Four drop zones, labeled Report Filter, Column Labels, Row Labels, and Σ Values appear at the bottom of the task pane (see Figure 13.3).

Figure 13.3
Excel presents you with a list of available fields and four drop zones in the PivotTable Field List.

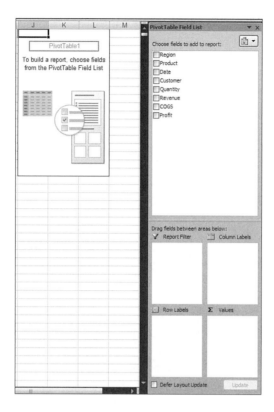

5. Click the Region and Revenue fields in the top section of the PivotTable Field List. Because the region field contains text data, it is automatically moved to the Row Labels drop zone. Because Revenue contains numeric data, it is automatically moved to the Σ Values drop zone.

6. Click the Product field in the top section of the PivotTable Field List and drag to the Column Labels drop zone in the bottom half of the PivotTable Field List. This adds a list of products stretching across the top row of your pivot table.

As shown in Figure 13.4, Excel has built a concise summary of your data in the pivot table.

After a pivot table has been created on your worksheet, you can easily change the data summarized in the report by dragging fields within the drop zones of the PivotTable Field List. In Figure 13.5, Customer was added to the Row Labels section of the existing pivot table.

Understanding New Features in Excel 2007 Pivot Tables

By default, all new pivot tables are created in a new layout called Compact Form. In this layout, multiple Row fields appear in a single column at the left of the pivot table. Excel also puts the subtotals above the detail rows.

13

Figure 13.4
Only six clicks were
required to create this
summary.

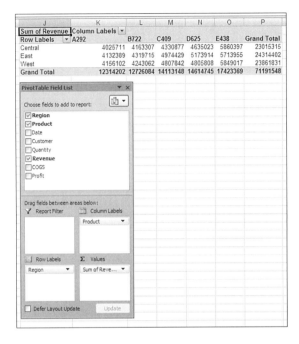

Figure 13.5
The name *pivot table*
comes from the ability
you have to drag fields in
the drop zones and have
them recalculate. In a
couple of clicks, you can
move Region across the
top, move Product down
the side, and add a sum-
mary by Customer.

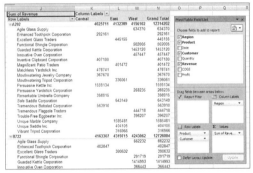

Although these changes might make for a better live pivot table, most of the pivot tables in
this chapter will be converted to values to produce a static summary of the data. In these
cases, you want to revert to the Outline layout that was the default in Excel 2003. The following steps in the user interface overcome these new default choices:

1. On the Design ribbon, choose Report Layout, Show in Outline Form, as shown in
   Figure 13.6.

2. On the Design ribbon, choose Subtotals, Show All Subtotals at the Bottom of Group.

3. On the Options ribbon, choose the Options icon on the left side of the ribbon. In the
   Layout & Format tab of the PivotTable Options dialog, type a zero next to For Empty
   Cells Show.

Figure 13.6
If you plan to reuse the output of the pivot table, you should change from Compact Form to Outline Form in order to give each Row field its own column.

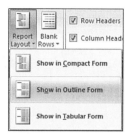

Building a Pivot Table in Excel VBA

In this chapter, I do not mean to imply that you use VBA to build pivot tables to give to your clients. Rather, the purpose of this chapter is to remind you that pivot tables can be used as a means to an end; you can use a pivot table to extract a summary of data and then use that summary elsewhere.

> **NOTE**
> The code listings from this chapter are available for download at www.MrExcel.com/getcode2007.html.

> **CAUTION**
> Although the Excel user interface has new names for the various sections of a pivot table, VBA code continues to refer to the old names. Microsoft had to use this choice; otherwise, millions of lines of code would stop working in Excel 2007 when they referred to a page field rather than a filter field. Although the four sections of a pivot table in the Excel user interface are Report Filter, Column Labels, Row Labels, and Values, VBA continues to use the old terms of Page fields, Column fields, Row fields, and Data fields.

Defining the Pivot Cache

In Excel 2000 and later, you first build a pivot cache object to describe the input area of the data:

```
Dim WSD As Worksheet
Dim PTCache As PivotCache
Dim PT As PivotTable
Dim PRange As Range
Dim FinalRow As Long
Dim FinalCol As Long
Set WSD = Worksheets("PivotTable")

' Delete any prior pivot tables
For Each PT In WSD.PivotTables
    PT.TableRange2.Clear
Next PT
```

13

```
' Define input area and set up a Pivot Cache
FinalRow = WSD.Cells(Rows.Count, 1).End(xlUp).Row
FinalCol = WSD.Cells(1, Columns.Count).End(xlToLeft).Column
Set PRange = WSD.Cells(1, 1).Resize(FinalRow, FinalCol)
Set PTCache = ActiveWorkbook.PivotCaches.Add(SourceType:=xlDatabase, _
    SourceData:=PRange)
```

Creating and Configuring the Pivot Table

After defining the pivot cache, use the `CreatePivotTable` method to create a blank pivot table based on the defined pivot cache:

```
Set PT = PTCache.CreatePivotTable(TableDestination:=WSD.Cells(2, FinalCol + 2), _
    TableName:="PivotTable1")
```

In the `CreatePivotTable` method, you specify the output location and optionally give the table a name. After running this line of code, you have a strange-looking blank pivot table, like the one shown in Figure 13.7. You now have to use code to drop fields onto the table.

Figure 13.7
When you use the `CreatePivotTable` method, Excel gives you a four-cell blank pivot table that is not very useful.

If you choose the Defer Layout Update setting in the user interface to build the pivot table, Excel does not recalculate the pivot table after you drop each field onto the table. By default in VBA, Excel calculates the pivot table as you execute each step of building the table. This could require the pivot table to be executed a half-dozen times before you get to the final result. To speed up your code execution, you can temporarily turn off calculation of the pivot table by using the `ManualUpdate` property:

```
PT.ManualUpdate = True
```

You can now run through the steps needed to lay out the pivot table. In the `.AddFields` method, you can specify one or more fields that should be in the row, column, or filter area of the pivot table.

The `RowFields` parameter enables you to define fields that appear in the Row Labels drop zone of the PivotTable Field List. The `ColumnFields` parameter corresponds to the Column Labels drop zone. The `PageFields` parameter corresponds to the Report Filter drop zone.

13

The following line of code populate a pivot table with two fields in the row area and one field in the column area:

```
' Set up the row & column fields
PT.AddFields RowFields:=Array("Region", "Customer"), _
    ColumnFields:="Product"
```

To add a field such as Revenue to the values area of the table, you change the Orientation property of the field to be xlDataField.

Getting a Sum Rather Than a Count

Excel is smart. When you build a report with revenue, it assumes you want to sum the revenue. But there is a problem. Suppose that one of the revenue cells is blank. When you build the pivot table, even though 99.9% of fields are numeric, Excel assumes you have alphanumeric data and offers to count this field. This is annoying. It seems to be an anomaly that, on one hand, you are expected to make sure that 100% of your cells have numeric data; on the other hand, however, the results of the pivot table are often filled with non-numeric blank cells.

When you build the pivot table in the Excel interface, you should take care in the Σ Values drop zone to notice that the field reads Count of Revenue rather than Sum of Revenue. At that point, the right course of action is to go back and fix the data, but what people usually do is double-click the Count of Revenue button and change it to Sum of Revenue.

In VBA, you should always explicitly define that you are creating a sum of revenue by explicitly setting the Function property to xlSum:

```
' Set up the data fields
With PT.PivotFields("Revenue")
    .Orientation = xlDataField
    .Function = xlSum
    .Position = 1
End With
```

At this point, you've given VBA all the settings required to correctly generate the pivot table. If you set ManualUpdate to False, Excel calculates and draws the pivot table. You can immediately thereafter set this back to True:

```
' Calc the pivot table
PT.ManualUpdate = False
PT.ManualUpdate = True
```

Your pivot table inherits the table style settings selected as the default on whatever computer happens to run the code. If you would like control over the final format, you can explicitly choose a table style. The following code applies banded rows and a medium table style:

```
' Format the pivot table
PT.ShowTableStyleRowStripes = True
PT.TableStyle2 = "PivotStyleMedium10"
```

At this point, you have a complete pivot table like the one shown in Figure 13.8.

13

Figure 13.8
Fewer than 50 lines of code create this pivot table in less than a second.

Sum of Revenue		Product
Region	Customer	A292
⊟Central	Enhanced Toothpick Corporation	292161
	Inventive Clipboard Corporation	407180
	Matchless Yardstick Inc.	478741
	Mouthwatering Jewelry Company	367670
	Persuasive Kettle Inc.	1559134
	Remarkable Umbrella Company	356915
	Tremendous Bobsled Corporation	563910
Central Total		4025711
⊟East	Excellent Glass Traders	445155

Listing 13.1 shows the complete code used to generate the pivot table.

Listing 13.1 Code to Generate a Pivot Table

```
Sub CreatePivot()
    Dim WSD As Worksheet
    Dim PTCache As PivotCache
    Dim PT As PivotTable
    Dim PRange As Range
    Dim FinalRow As Long
    Set WSD = Worksheets("PivotTable")

    ' Delete any prior pivot tables
    For Each PT In WSD.PivotTables
        PT.TableRange2.Clear
    Next PT

    ' Define input area and set up a Pivot Cache
    FinalRow = WSD.Cells(Application.Rows.Count, 1).End(xlUp).Row
    FinalCol = WSD.Cells(1, Application.Columns.Count). _
        End(xlToLeft).Column
    Set PRange = WSD.Cells(1, 1).Resize(FinalRow, FinalCol)
    Set PTCache = ActiveWorkbook.PivotCaches.Add(SourceType:= _
        xlDatabase, SourceData:=PRange.Address)

    ' Create the Pivot Table from the Pivot Cache
    Set PT = PTCache.CreatePivotTable(TableDestination:=WSD. _
        Cells(2, FinalCol + 2), TableName:="PivotTable1")

    ' Turn off updating while building the table
    PT.ManualUpdate = True

    ' Set up the row & column fields
    PT.AddFields RowFields:=Array("Region", "Customer"), _
        ColumnFields:="Product"

    ' Set up the data fields
    With PT.PivotFields("Revenue")
        .Orientation = xlDataField
        .Function = xlSum
        .Position = 1
    End With
```

```
        ' Calc the pivot table
        PT.ManualUpdate = False
        PT.ManualUpdate = True

        'Format the pivot table
        PT.ShowTableStyleRowStripes = True
        PT.TableStyle2 = "PivotStyleMedium10"

        WSD.Activate
        Range("J2").Select
End Sub
```

Learning Why You Cannot Move or Change Part of a Pivot Report

Although pivot tables are incredible, they have annoying limitations. You cannot move or change just part of a pivot table. For example, try to run a macro that would delete Column Q, which contains the Grand Total column of the pivot table. The macro comes to a screeching halt with an error 1004, as shown in Figure 13.9. To get around this limitation, you can change the summary from a pivot table to just values.

Figure 13.9
You cannot delete just part of a pivot table.

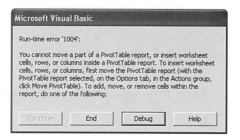

Determining Size of a Finished Pivot Table

Knowing the size of a pivot table in advance is difficult. If you run a report of transactional data on one day, you may or may not have sales from the West region, for example. This could cause your table to be either six or seven columns wide. Therefore, you should use the special property `TableRange2` to refer to the entire resultant pivot table.

Because of the limitations of pivot tables, you should generally copy the results of a pivot table to a new location on the worksheet and then delete the original pivot table. The code in `CreateSummaryReportUsingPivot()` creates a small pivot table. Note that you can set the `ColumnGrand` and `RowGrand` properties of the table to `False` to prevent the totals from being added to the table.

`PT.TableRange2` includes the entire pivot table. In Figure 13.10, TableRange2 includes the extra row at the top with the button Sum of Revenue. To eliminate that row, the code copies `PT.TableRange2` but offsets this selection by one row by using `.Offset(1, 0)`. Depending on the nature of your pivot table, you might need to use an offset of two or more rows to get rid of extraneous information at the top of the pivot table.

13

The code copies `PT.TableRange2` and uses `PasteSpecial` on a cell five rows below the current pivot table. At that point in the code, your worksheet appears as shown in Figure 13.10. The table in J2 is a live pivot table, and the table in J12 is just the copied results.

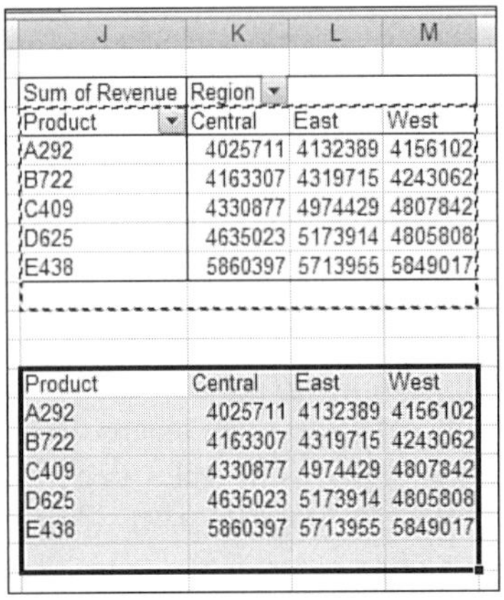

Figure 13.10
This figure shows an intermediate result of the macro. Only the summary in J12:M17 will remain after the macro finishes.

You can then totally eliminate the pivot table by applying the `Clear` method to the entire table. If your code is then going on to do additional formatting, you should remove the pivot cache from memory by setting `PTCache` equal to `Nothing`.

The code in Listing 13.2 uses a pivot table to produce a summary from the underlying data. At the end of the code, the pivot table will be copied to static values and the pivot table will be cleared.

Listing 13.2   Code to Produce a Static Summary from a Pivot Table

```
Sub CreateSummaryReportUsingPivot()
    ' Use a Pivot Table to create a static summary report
    ' with product going down the rows and regions across
    Dim WSD As Worksheet
    Dim PTCache As PivotCache
    Dim PT As PivotTable
    Dim PRange As Range
    Dim FinalRow As Long
    Set WSD = Worksheets("PivotTable")

    ' Delete any prior pivot tables
    For Each PT In WSD.PivotTables
        PT.TableRange2.Clear
    Next PT
    WSD.Range("J1:Z1").EntireColumn.Clear

    ' Define input area and set up a Pivot Cache
    FinalRow = WSD.Cells(Application.Rows.Count, 1).End(xlUp).Row
    FinalCol = WSD.Cells(1, Application.Columns.Count). _
        End(xlToLeft).Column
    Set PRange = WSD.Cells(1, 1).Resize(FinalRow, FinalCol)
    Set PTCache = ActiveWorkbook.PivotCaches.Add(SourceType:= _
```

```
        xlDatabase, SourceData:=PRange.Address)

    ' Create the Pivot Table from the Pivot Cache
    Set PT = PTCache.CreatePivotTable(TableDestination:=WSD. _
        Cells(2, FinalCol + 2), TableName:="PivotTable1")

    ' Turn off updating while building the table
    PT.ManualUpdate = True

    ' Set up the row fields
    PT.AddFields RowFields:="Product", ColumnFields:="Region"

    ' Set up the data fields
    With PT.PivotFields("Revenue")
        .Orientation = xlDataField
        .Function = xlSum
        .Position = 1
    End With

    With PT
        .ColumnGrand = False
        .RowGrand = False
        .NullString = "0"
    End With

    ' Calc the pivot table
    PT.ManualUpdate = False
    PT.ManualUpdate = True

    ' PT.TableRange2 contains the results. Move these to J12
    ' as just values and not a real pivot table.
    PT.TableRange2.Offset(1, 0).Copy
    WSD.Cells(5 + PT.TableRange2.Rows.Count, FinalCol + 2). _
        PasteSpecial xlPasteValues

    ' At this point, the worksheet looks like Figure 13.10
    ' Stop

    ' Delete the original Pivot Table & the Pivot Cache
    PT.TableRange2.Clear
    Set PTCache = Nothing

    WSD.Activate
    Range("J12").Select
End Sub
```

The code in Listing 13.2 creates the pivot table. It then copies the results as values and pastes them as values in J12:M13. Figure 13.10 (shown previously) shows an intermediate result just before the original pivot table is cleared.

So far, this chapter has walked you through building the simplest of pivot table reports. Pivot tables offer far more flexibility. The sections that follow present more complex reporting examples.

Creating a Report Showing Revenue by Product

A typical report might provide a list of regions by product with revenue by year. This report could be given to product line managers to show them which customers are buying their products. In this example, you want to show the customers in descending order by revenue with years going across the columns. Figure 13.11 shows a sample report.

Figure 13.11

A typical request is to take transactional data and produce a summary by product for product line managers. You can use a pivot table to get 90% of this report and then a little formatting to finish it.

	Product	Customer	2007	2008	Grand Total
1	Revenue by Customer and Year				
2					
3	Product	Customer	2007	2008	Grand Total
4	A292	Unique Marble Company	724K	862K	1,585K
5	A292	Persuasive Kettle Inc.	862K	698K	1,559K
6	A292	Guarded Kettle Corporation	715K	738K	1,453K
7	A292	Safe Saddle Corporation	182K	461K	643K
8	A292	Agile Glass Supply	358K	276K	634K
9	A292	Tremendous Bobsled Corporation	308K	256K	564K
10	A292	Functional Shingle Corporation	0K	502K	502K
11	A292	Matchless Yardstick Inc.	263K	216K	479K
12	A292	Innovative Oven Corporation	264K	193K	457K
13	A292	Excellent Glass Traders	173K	273K	445K
14	A292	Tremendous Flagpole Traders	169K	276K	445K
15	A292	Inventive Clipboard Corporation	205K	203K	407K
16	A292	Unique Saddle Inc.	251K	153K	404K
17	A292	Magnificent Patio Traders	249K	153K	401K
18	A292	Trouble-Free Eggbeater Inc.	163K	233K	396K
19	A292	Mouthwatering Jewelry Company	210K	158K	368K
20	A292	Remarkable Umbrella Company	199K	158K	357K
21	A292	Mouthwatering Tripod Corporation	134K	202K	336K
22	A292	Vibrant Tripod Corporation	122K	195K	317K
23	A292	Enhanced Toothpick Corporation	147K	145K	292K
24	A292	Persuasive Yardstick Corporation	93K	175K	268K
25	A292 Total		5,790K	6,525K	12,314K
26	B722	Unique Marble Company	760K	847K	1,607K
27	B722	Guarded Kettle Corporation	853K	562K	1,415K
28	B722	Persuasive Kettle Inc.	728K	661K	1,389K

The key to producing this data quickly is to use a pivot table. Although pivot tables are incredible for summarizing data, you will often have to do some additional steps to achieve the desired result.

To create this report, start with a pivot table that has Product and Customer as Row fields, Date grouped by year as a Column field, and Sum of Revenue as the Data field. Figure 13.12 shows the default pivot table created with these settings.

Here are just a few of the annoyances that most pivot tables present in their default state:

- The Outline view is horrible. In Figure 13.12, the value A292 appears in the Product column only once and is followed by 20 blank cells. This is the worst feature of pivot tables, and there is absolutely no way to correct it. Although humans can understand that this entire section is for A292 sales, it is radically confusing if your A292 section spills to a second or third page. Page 2 starts without any indication that the report is for A292 sales. If you intend to repurpose the data, you need the A292 sales value to be on every row.

Figure 13.12
Use the power of the pivot table to get the summarized data, but then use your own common sense in formatting the report.

Sum of Revenue		Date		
Product	Customer	2007	2008	Grand Total
⊟A292	Agile Glass Supply	353678	274526	628204
	Enhanced Toothpick Corporation	148419	144598	293017
	Excellent Glass Traders	176704	271067	447771
	Functional Shingle Corporation		504818	504818
	Guarded Kettle Corporation	710732	739378	1450110
	Innovative Oven Corporation	262822	189498	452320
	Inventive Clipboard Corporation	207939	203029	410968
	Magnificent Patio Traders	245236	149950	395186
	Matchless Yardstick Inc.	263819	212404	476223
	Mouthwatering Jewelry Company	211285	162715	374000
	Mouthwatering Tripod Corporation	138413	198687	337100
	Persuasive Kettle Inc.	868363	697005	1565368
	Persuasive Yardstick Corporation	92341	176053	268394
	Remarkable Umbrella Company	199373	163478	362851
	Safe Saddle Corporation	184144	462415	646559
	Tremendous Bobsled Corporation	304831	255928	560759
	Tremendous Flagpole Traders	169043	277756	446799
	Trouble-Free Eggbeater Inc.	162233	228684	390917
	Unique Marble Company	729836	870511	1600347
	Unique Saddle Inc.	258034	150080	408114
	Vibrant Tripod Corporation	124242	193711	317953
A292 Total		5811487	6526291	12337778
⊟B722	Agile Glass Supply	436866	215979	652845
	Enhanced Toothpick Corporation	189918	213846	403764

- The report contains blank cells rather than zeros. In Figure 13.12, the Functional Shingle had no sales in 2007. Excel produces a pivot table where cell L6 is blank rather than zero. This is simply bad form. Excel experts rely on being able to "ride the range," using the End and arrow keys. Blank cells ruin this ability.

- The title is boring. Most people would agree that Sum of Revenue is an annoying title.

- Some captions are extraneous. Date floating in cell L1 of Figure 13.12 really does not belong in a report.

- The default alphabetic sort order is rarely useful. Product line managers are going to want the top customers at the top of the list. It would be helpful to have the report sorted in descending order by revenue.

- Depending on your computer's default pivot table style, the borders could be ugly. Excel draws in a myriad of borders that really make the report look awful.

- The default number format is General. It would be better to set this up as data with commas to serve as thousands separators, or perhaps even data in thousands or millions.

- Pivot tables offer no obvious page-break logic. If you want to produce one report for each Line of Business manager, you would have to dig deep into the last setting of the back tab of the Field Settings dialog.

- Because of the page-break problem, you might find it is easier to do away with the pivot table's subtotal rows and have the Subtotal method add subtotal rows with page breaks. You need a way to turn off the pivot table subtotal rows offered for Product in Figure 13.12. These rows show up automatically whenever you have two or more Row fields. If you had four Row fields, you would want to turn off the automatic subtotals for the three outermost Row fields.

Even with all these problems in default pivot tables, they are still the way to go. You can overcome each complaint, either by using special settings within the pivot table or by entering a few lines of code after the pivot table is created and then copied to a regular dataset.

13

Eliminating Blank Cells in the Values Area

People started complaining about the blank cells immediately when pivot tables were first introduced. Anyone using Excel 97 or later can easily replace blank cells with zeros. In the user interface, you can find the setting on the Layout & Format tab of the PivotTable Options dialog box. Choose the For Empty Cells, Show option and type **0** in the box.

The equivalent operation in VBA is to set the `NullString` property for the pivot table to `"0"`.

> **NOTE** Although the proper code is to set this value to a text zero, Excel actually puts a real zero in the empty cells.

Ensuring Table Layout Is Utilized

In versions of Excel prior to 2007, multiple Row fields appeared in multiple columns. Three layouts are available in Excel 2007. The Compact layout squeezes all the Row fields into a single column.

To prevent this outcome and ensure that your pivot table is in the classic table layout, use this code:

```
PT.RowAxisLayout xlTabularRow
```

Controlling the Sort Order with AutoSort

The Excel user interface offers an AutoSort option that enables you to show markets in descending order based on revenue. The equivalent code in VBA to sort the product field by descending revenue uses the `AutoSort` method:

```
PT.PivotFields("Customer").AutoSort Order:=xlDescending, _
    Field:="Sum of Revenue"
```

Changing Default Number Format

To change the number format in the user interface, choose a revenue field, and from the Options ribbon, choose Active Field, Field Settings, Number Format. Then choose an appropriate number format.

When you have large numbers, displaying the thousands separator helps the person reading the report. To set up this format in VBA code, use the following:

```
PT.PivotFields("Sum of Revenue").NumberFormat = "#,##0"
```

Some companies have customers who typically buy thousands or millions of dollars' worth of goods. You can display numbers in thousands by using a single comma after the number format. Of course, you need to include a K abbreviation to indicate that the numbers are in thousands:

```
PT.PivotFields("Sum of Revenue").NumberFormat = "#,##0,K"
```

Local custom dictates the thousands abbreviation. If you are working for a relatively young computer company where everyone uses K for the thousands separator, you're in luck because Microsoft makes it easy to use this abbreviation. However, if you work at a 100+ year-old soap company where you use M for thousands and MM for millions, you have a few more hurdles to jump. You are required to prefix the M character with a backslash to have it work:

```
PT.PivotFields("Sum of Revenue").NumberFormat = "#,##0,\M"
```

Alternatively, you can surround the M character with double quotation marks. To put double quotation marks inside a quoted string in VBA, you must put two sequential quotation marks. To set up a format in tenths of millions that uses the #,##0.0,,"MM" format, you would use this line of code:

```
PT.PivotFields("Sum of Revenue").NumberFormat = "#,##0.0,,""M"""
```

In case it is difficult to read, the format for the code is quotation mark, pound, comma, pound, pound, zero, period, zero, comma, comma, quotation mark, quotation mark, M, quotation mark, quotation mark, quotation mark. The three quotation marks at the end are correct. You use two quotation marks to simulate typing one quotation mark in the custom number format box and a final quotation mark to close the string in VBA.

Suppressing Subtotals for Multiple Row Fields

As soon as you have more than one Row field, Excel automatically adds subtotals for all but the innermost Row field. However, you might want to suppress subtotals for any number of reasons. Although accomplishing this task manually may be relatively simple, the VBA code to suppress subtotals is surprisingly complex.

You must set the Subtotals property equal to an array of 12 False values. Read the VBA help for all the gory details, but it goes something like this: The first False turns off automatic subtotals, the second False turns off the Sum subtotal, the third False turns off the Count subtotal, and so on. It is interesting that you have to turn off all 12 possible subtotals, even though Excel displays only one subtotal. This line of code suppresses the Product subtotal:

```
PT.PivotFields("Product").Subtotals = Array(False, False, False, False, _
    False, False, False, False, False, False, False, False)
```

A different technique is to turn on the first subtotal. This method automatically turns off the other 11 subtotals. You can then turn off the first subtotal to make sure that all subtotals are suppressed:

```
PT.PivotFields("Product").Subtotals(1) = True
PT.PivotFields("Product").Subtotals(1) = False
```

Suppressing Grand Total for Rows

Because you are going to be using VBA code to add automatic subtotals, you can get rid of the Grand Total row. If you turn off Grand Total for Rows, you delete the column called Grand Total. Therefore, to get rid of the Grand Total row, you must uncheck Grand Total for Columns. This is handled in the code with the following line:

```
PT.ColumnGrand = False
```

Handling Additional Annoyances When Creating Your Final Report

You've reached the end of the adjustments that you can make to the pivot table. To achieve the final report, you have to make the remaining adjustments after converting the pivot table to regular data.

Figure 13.13 shows the pivot table with all the adjustments described in the preceding sections and with PT.TableRange2 selected.

Figure 13.13
Getting 90% of the way to the final report took less than a second and fewer than 30 lines of code. To solve the last five annoying problems, you have to change this data from a pivot table to regular data.

Sum of Revenue		Date ▼		
Product ▼	Customer ▼	2007	2008	Grand Total
⊟A292	Unique Marble Company	724K	862K	1,585K
	Persuasive Kettle Inc.	862K	698K	1,559K
	Guarded Kettle Corporation	715K	738K	1,453K
	Safe Saddle Corporation	182K	461K	643K
	Agile Glass Supply	358K	276K	634K
	Tremendous Bobsled Corporation	308K	256K	564K
	Functional Shingle Corporation	0K	502K	502K
	Matchless Yardstick Inc.	263K	216K	479K
	Innovative Oven Corporation	264K	193K	457K
	Excellent Glass Traders	173K	273K	445K
	Tremendous Flagpole Traders	169K	276K	445K
	Inventive Clipboard Corporation	205K	203K	407K
	Unique Saddle Inc.	251K	153K	404K
	Magnificent Patio Traders	249K	153K	401K
	Trouble-Free Eggbeater Inc.	163K	233K	396K
	Mouthwatering Jewelry Company	210K	158K	368K
	Remarkable Umbrella Company	199K	158K	357K
	Mouthwatering Tripod Corporation	134K	202K	336K
	Vibrant Tripod Corporation	122K	195K	317K
	Enhanced Toothpick Corporation	147K	145K	292K
	Persuasive Yardstick Corporation	93K	175K	268K
⊟B722	Unique Marble Company	760K	847K	1,607K
	Guarded Kettle Corporation	853K	562K	1,415K

Creating a New Workbook to Hold the Report

Say you want to build the report in a new workbook so that it can be easily mailed to the product managers. Doing this is fairly easy. To make the code more portable, assign object variables to the original workbook, new workbook, and first worksheet in the new workbook. At the top of the procedure, add these statements:

```
Dim WSR As Worksheet
Dim WBO As Workbook
Dim WBN As Workbook
Set WBO = ActiveWorkbook
Set WSD = Worksheets("Pivot Table")
```

After the pivot table has been successfully created, build a blank Report workbook with this code:

```
' Create a New Blank Workbook with one Worksheet
Set WBN = Workbooks.Add(xlWorksheet)
Set WSR = WBN.Worksheets(1)
WSR.Name = "Report"
' Set up Title for Report
With WSR.Range("A1")
    .Value = "Revenue by Customer and Year"
    .Font.Size = 14
End With
```

Creating a Summary on a Blank Report Worksheet

Imagine that you have submitted the pivot table in Figure 13.13, and your manager hates the borders, hates the title, and hates the word *Date* in cell L2. You can solve all three of these problems by excluding the first row(s) of PT.TableRange2 from the .Copy method and then using PasteSpecial(xlPasteValuesAndNumberFormats) to copy the data to the report sheet.

> **TIP**
> In Excel 2000 and earlier, xlPasteValuesAndNumberFormats was not available. You had to use Paste Special twice: once as xlPasteValues and once as xlPasteFormats.

In the current example, the .TableRange2 property includes only one row to eliminate, Row 2, as shown in Figure 13.13. If you had a more complex pivot table with several Column fields or one or more page fields, you would have to eliminate more than just the first row of the report. It helps to run your macro to this point, look at the result, and figure out how many rows you need to delete. You can effectively not copy these rows to the report by using the Offset property. Copy the TableRange2 property, offset by one row. Purists will note that this code copies one extra blank row from below the pivot table, but this really does not matter because the row is blank. After copying, you can erase the original pivot table and destroy the pivot cache:

```
' Copy the Pivot Table data to row 3 of the Report sheet
' Use Offset to eliminate the title row of the pivot table
PT.TableRange2.Offset(1, 0).Copy
WSR. Range("A3").PasteSpecial Paste:=xlPasteValuesAndNumberFormats
PT.TableRange2.Clear
Set PTCache = Nothing
```

Note that you use the Paste Special option to paste just values and number formats. This gets rid of both borders and the pivot nature of the table. You might be tempted to use the No Borders option under Paste, but this keeps the data in a pivot table, and you won't be able to insert new rows in the middle of the data.

Filling the Outline View

The report is almost complete. You are nearly a Data, Subtotals command away from having everything you need. Before you can use the Subtotals command, however, you need to fill in all the blank cells in the Outline view of Column A.

Fixing the Outline view requires just a few obscure steps. Here are the steps in the user interface:

1. Select all the cells in Column A that make up the report.
2. From the Home ribbon, select Editing, Find & Select, Go to Special to bring up the Go to Special dialog box. Select Blanks to select only the blank cells.
3. Enter an R1C1 style formula to fill the blank with the cell above it. This formula is =R[-1]C. In the user interface, you would type an equal sign, press the up-arrow key, and then press Ctrl+Enter.

13

4. Reselect all the cells in Column A that make up the report. This step is necessary because the Paste Special step cannot work with noncontiguous selections.

5. Copy the formulas in Column A and convert them to values by choosing Clipboard, Paste, Paste Values from the Home ribbon.

Fixing the Outline view in VBA requires fewer steps. The equivalent VBA logic is shown here:

1. Find the last row of the report.

2. Enter the formula `=R[-1]C` in the blank cells in A.

3. Change those formulas to values. The code to do this follows:

```
Dim FinalReportRow as Long
    ' Fill in the Outline view in column A
    ' Look for last row in column B since many rows
    ' in column A are blank
FinalReportRow = WSR.Cells(Rows.Count, 2).End(xlUp).Row
With Range("A3").Resize(FinalReportRow - 2, 1)
    With .SpecialCells(xlCellTypeBlanks)
        .FormulaR1C1 = "=R[-1]C"
    End With
    .Value = .Value
End With
```

Handling Final Formatting

The last steps for the report involve some basic formatting tasks and then adding the subtotals. You can bold and right-justify the headings in Row 3. Set up Rows 1 through 3 so that the top three rows print on each page:

```
' Do some basic formatting
' Autofit columns, bold the headings, right-align
Selection.Columns.AutoFit
Range("A3").EntireRow.Font.Bold = True
Range("A3").EntireRow.HorizontalAlignment = xlRight
Range("A3:B3").HorizontalAlignment = xlLeft

' Repeat rows 1-3 at the top of each page
WSR.PageSetup.PrintTitleRows = "$1:$3"
```

Adding Subtotals

Automatic subtotals are a powerful feature found on the Data ribbon. Figure 13.14 shows the Subtotal dialog box. Note the option Page Break Between Groups.

If you were sure that you would always have two years and a total, the code to add subtotals for each Line of Business group would be the following:

```
' Add Subtotals by Product.
' Be sure to add a page break at each change in product
Selection.Subtotal GroupBy:=1, Function:=xlSum, TotalList:=Array(3, 4, 5), _
    PageBreaks:=True
```

Figure 13.14
Use automatic subtotals because doing so enables you to add a page break after each product. Using this feature ensures that each product manager has a clean report with only her product on it.

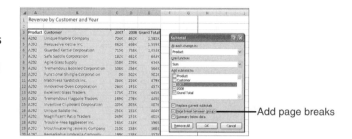

Add page breaks

However, this code fails if you have more or less than three years. The solution is to use the following convoluted code to dynamically build a list of the columns to total, based on the number of columns in the report:

```
Dim TotColumns()
Dim I as Integer
FinalCol = Cells(3, Columns.Count).End(xlToLeft).Column
ReDim Preserve TotColumns(1 To FinalCol - 2)
For i = 3 To FinalCol
    TotColumns(i - 2) = i
Next i
Selection.Subtotal GroupBy:=1, Function:=xlSum, TotalList:=TotColumns,_
    Replace:=True, PageBreaks:=True, SummaryBelowData:=True
```

Finally, with the new totals added to the report, you need to autofit the numeric columns again with this code:

```
Dim GrandRow as Long
' Make sure the columns are wide enough for totals
GrandRow = Cells(Rows.Count, 1).End(xlUp).Row
Cells(3, 3).Resize(GrandRow - 2, FinalCol - 2).Columns.AutoFit
Cells(GrandRow, 3).Resize(1, FinalCol - 2).NumberFormat = "#,##0,K"
' Add a page break before the Grand Total row, otherwise
' the product manager for the final Line will have two totals
WSR.HPageBreaks.Add Before:=Cells(GrandRow, 1)
```

Putting It All Together

Listing 13.3 produces the product line manager reports in a few seconds.

Listing 13.3   Code That Produces the Product Line Report in Figure 13.15

```
Sub ProductLineReport()
    ' Product and Customer as Row
    ' Years as Column
    Dim WSD As Worksheet
    Dim PTCache As PivotCache
    Dim PT As PivotTable
    Dim PRange As Range
    Dim FinalRow As Long
    Dim TotColumns()

    Set WSD = Worksheets("PivotTable")
```

13

continues

Listing 13.3   Continued

```
Dim WSR As Worksheet
Dim WBO As Workbook
Dim WBN As Workbook
Set WBO = ActiveWorkbook

' Delete any prior pivot tables
For Each PT In WSD.PivotTables
    PT.TableRange2.Clear
Next PT
WSD.Range("J1:Z1").EntireColumn.Clear

' Define input area and set up a Pivot Cache
FinalRow = WSD.Cells(Application.Rows.Count, 1).End(xlUp).Row
FinalCol = WSD.Cells(1, Application.Columns.Count). _
    End(xlToLeft).Column
Set PRange = WSD.Cells(1, 1).Resize(FinalRow, FinalCol)
Set PTCache = ActiveWorkbook.PivotCaches.Add(SourceType:= _
    xlDatabase, SourceData:=PRange.Address)

' Create the Pivot Table from the Pivot Cache
Set PT = PTCache.CreatePivotTable(TableDestination:=WSD. _
    Cells(2, FinalCol + 2), TableName:="PivotTable1")

' Turn off updating while building the table
PT.ManualUpdate = True

' Set up the row fields
PT.AddFields RowFields:=Array("Product", _
    "Customer"), ColumnFields:="Date"

' Set up the data fields
With PT.PivotFields("Revenue")
    .Orientation = xlDataField
    .Function = xlSum
    .Position = 1
End With

' Make sure to get tabular layout
' instead of the new compact layout
PT.RowAxisLayout xlTabularRow

' Calc the pivot table
PT.ManualUpdate = False
PT.ManualUpdate = True

' Group by Year
WSD.Activate
Cells(3, FinalCol + 4).Group Start:=True, End:=True, _
    Periods:=Array(False, False, False, False, False, False, True)

' Move Date to columns
PT.PivotFields("Date").Orientation = xlColumnField
PT.PivotFields("Customer").Orientation = xlRowField

' Format the Revenue fields
```

13

```
PT.PivotFields("Sum of Revenue").NumberFormat = "#,##0,K"

' Turn off the subtotals by product
PT.PivotFields("Product").Subtotals(1) = True
PT.PivotFields("Product").Subtotals(1) = False
PT.ColumnGrand = False

' Ensure that we get zeroes instead of blanks in the data area
PT.NullString = "0"

' Sort customers descending by sum of revenue
PT.PivotFields("Customer").AutoSort Order:=xlDescending, _
    Field:="Sum of Revenue"

' Calc the pivot table
PT.ManualUpdate = False
PT.ManualUpdate = True

' At this point, the data is like Figure 13.13
PT.TableRange2.Select
'   Stop

' Create a New Blank Workbook with one Worksheet
Set WBN = Workbooks.Add(xlWBATWorksheet)
Set WSR = WBN.Worksheets(1)
WSR.Name = "Report"
' Set up Title for Report
With WSR.[A1]
    .Value = "Revenue by Customer and Year"
    .Font.Size = 14
End With

' Copy the Pivot Table data to row 3 of the Report sheet
' Use Offset to eliminate the title row of the pivot table
PT.TableRange2.Offset(1, 0).Copy
WSR.[A3].PasteSpecial Paste:=xlPasteValuesAndNumberFormats
PT.TableRange2.Clear
Set PTCache = Nothing

' Fill in the Outline view in column A
' Look for last row in column B since many rows
' in column A are blank
FinalReportRow = WSR.Range("B65536").End(xlUp).Row
With Range("A3").Resize(FinalReportRow - 2, 1)
    With .SpecialCells(xlCellTypeBlanks)
        .FormulaR1C1 = "=R[-1]C"
    End With
    .Value = .Value
End With

' Do some basic formatting
' Autofit columns, bold the headings, right-align
Selection.Columns.AutoFit
Range("A3").EntireRow.Font.Bold = True
Range("A3").EntireRow.HorizontalAlignment = xlRight
Range("A3:B3").HorizontalAlignment = xlLeft
```

continues

Listing 13.3   Continued

```
' Repeat rows 1-3 at the top of each page
WSR.PageSetup.PrintTitleRows = "$1:$3"

' Add subtotals
FinalCol = Cells(3, 255).End(xlToLeft).Column
ReDim Preserve TotColumns(1 To FinalCol - 2)
For i = 3 To FinalCol
    TotColumns(i - 2) = i
Next i
Selection.Subtotal GroupBy:=1, Function:=xlSum, _
    TotalList:=TotColumns, Replace:=True, _
    PageBreaks:=True, SummaryBelowData:=True

' Make sure the columns are wide enough for totals
GrandRow = Cells(Rows.Count, 1).End(xlUp).Row
Cells(3, 3).Resize(GrandRow - 2, FinalCol - 2).Columns.AutoFit
Cells(GrandRow, 3).Resize(1, FinalCol - 2).NumberFormat = "#,##0,K"
' Add a page break before the Grand Total row, otherwise
' the product manager for the final Line will have two totals
WSR.HPageBreaks.Add Before:=Cells(GrandRow, 1)

End Sub
```

Figure 13.15 shows the report produced by this code.

Figure 13.15

Converting 50,000 rows of transactional data to this useful report takes less than a few seconds if you use the code that produced this example. Without pivot tables, the code would be much more complex.

Product	Customer	2007	2008	Grand Total
	Revenue by Customer and Year			
A292	Unique Marble Company	724K	862K	1,585K
A292	Persuasive Kettle Inc.	862K	698K	1,559K
A292	Guarded Kettle Corporation	715K	738K	1,453K
A292	Safe Saddle Corporation	182K	461K	643K
A292	Agile Glass Supply	358K	276K	634K
A292	Tremendous Bobsled Corporation	308K	256K	564K
A292	Functional Shingle Corporation	0K	502K	502K
A292	Matchless Yardstick Inc.	263K	216K	479K
A292	Innovative Oven Corporation	264K	193K	457K
A292	Excellent Glass Traders	173K	273K	445K
A292	Tremendous Flagpole Traders	169K	276K	445K
A292	Inventive Clipboard Corporation	205K	203K	407K
A292	Unique Saddle Inc.	251K	153K	404K
A292	Magnificent Patio Traders	249K	153K	401K
A292	Trouble-Free Eggbeater Inc.	163K	233K	396K
A292	Mouthwatering Jewelry Company	210K	158K	368K
A292	Remarkable Umbrella Company	199K	158K	357K
A292	Mouthwatering Tripod Corporation	134K	202K	336K
A292	Vibrant Tripod Corporation	122K	195K	317K
A292	Enhanced Toothpick Corporation	147K	145K	292K
A292	Persuasive Yardstick Corporation	93K	175K	268K
A292 Total		5,790K	6,525K	12,314K
B722	Unique Marble Company	760K	847K	1,607K
B722	Guarded Kettle Corporation	853K	562K	1,415K

Addressing Issues with Two or More Data Fields

So far, you have built some powerful summary reports, but you've touched only a portion of the powerful features available in pivot tables. The preceding example produced a report but had only one Data field. It is possible to have multiple fields in the Σ Values section of a pivot report. The data in this example includes not just revenue, but also a count of customers.

When you have two or more Data fields, you have a choice of placing the Data fields in one of four locations. By default, Excel builds the pivot report with the Data field as the innermost Column field. It is often preferable to have the Data field as the outermost Row field.

When a pivot table is going to have more than one Data field, you have a virtual field named Σ Values in the drop zones of the PivotTable Field List. In VBA, this equivalent virtual field is named Data.

To arrange the fields so that the data field is the innermost row, as shown in Figure 13.16, you would use this `AddFields` line:

```
PT.AddFields RowFields:=Array("Product", "Data")
```

Figure 13.16
Adding Data as the innermost Row field presents this view.

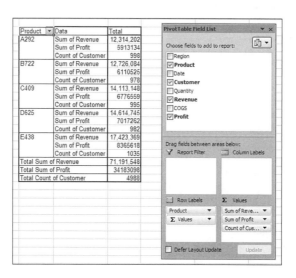

If you move the Data field as the first Row field, you will have the view shown in Figure 13.17. In this version, Total Sum of Revenue appears 10 rows away from all the other revenue fields. The view shown in Figure 13.17 would use this code:

```
PT.AddFields RowFields:=Array("Data", "Product")
```

One view that would make sense would have Data as the only Column field:

```
PT.AddFields RowFields:="Product", ColumnFields:="Data"
```

13

Figure 13.17
Move the Data field to before the Product field and you have this also bizarre view of the data. I really hate that the line with Total Sum of Revenue is located so far away from the individual Revenue subtotals.

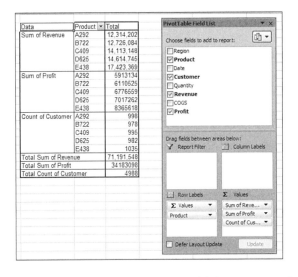

After adding a Column field called Data, you would then go on to define three Data fields:

```
' Set up the data fields
With PT.PivotFields("Revenue")
    .Orientation = xlDataField
    .Function = xlSum
    .Position = 1
    .NumberFormat = "#,##0,K"
End With

With PT.PivotFields("Profit")
    .Orientation = xlDataField
    .Function = xlSum
    .Position = 2
    .NumberFormat = "#,##0"
End With

With PT.PivotFields("Customer")
    .Orientation = xlDataField
    .Function = xlCount
    .Position = 3
    .NumberFormat = "#,##0"
End With
```

Figure 3.18 shows the report produced by the previous code.

Figure 13.18
By moving the Data field to the Column field, you have a report that appears fairly normal.

Calculated Data Fields

Pivot tables offer two types of formulas. The most useful type defines a formula for a calculated field. This adds a new field to the pivot table. Calculations for calculated fields are always done at the summary level. If you define a calculated field for average price as Revenue divided by Units Sold, Excel first adds the total revenue and total quantity, and then it does the division of these totals to get the result. In many cases, this is exactly what you need. If your calculation does not follow the associative law of mathematics, it might not work as you expect.

To set up a Calculated field, use the Add method with the CalculatedFields object. You have to specify a field name and a formula. Note that if you create a field called Profit Percent, the default pivot table produces a field called Sum of Profit Percent. This title is misleading and downright silly. The solution is to use the Name property when defining the Data field to replace Sum of Profit Percent with something such as GP Pct. Note that this name must differ from the name for the Calculated field.

Listing 13.4 produces the report shown in Figure 13.19.

Figure 13.19
The virtual Data dimension contains two fields from your dataset plus a calculation. It is shown along the column area of the report.

Product	Sum of Revenue	Sum of Profit	GP Pct
A292	12,337,778	5,936,710	48.1%
B722	12,683,061	6,067,502	47.8%
C409	14,101,763	6,765,174	48.0%
D625	14,569,960	6,972,477	47.9%
E438	17,411,966	8,354,215	48.0%
Grand Total	71,104,528	34,096,078	48.0%

Listing 13.4   Code That Calculates a Profit Percent as a Second Data Field

```
Sub CalculatedField()
    'Listing 13.4
    Dim WSD As Worksheet
    Dim PTCache As PivotCache
    Dim PT As PivotTable
    Dim PRange As Range
    Dim FinalRow As Long

    Set WSD = Worksheets("PivotTable")
    Dim WSR As Worksheet
    Dim WBO As Workbook
    Dim WBN As Workbook
    Set WBO = ActiveWorkbook

    ' Delete any prior pivot tables
    For Each PT In WSD.PivotTables
        PT.TableRange2.Clear
    Next PT
    WSD.Range("J1:Z1").EntireColumn.Clear

    ' Define input area and set up a Pivot Cache
    FinalRow = WSD.Cells(Application.Rows.Count, 1).End(xlUp).Row
    FinalCol = WSD.Cells(1, Application.Columns.Count). _
```

continues

Listing 13.4 Continued

```
        End(xlToLeft).Column
Set PRange = WSD.Cells(1, 1).Resize(FinalRow, FinalCol)
Set PTCache = ActiveWorkbook.PivotCaches.Add(SourceType:= _
    xlDatabase, SourceData:=PRange.Address)

' Create the Pivot Table from the Pivot Cache
Set PT = PTCache.CreatePivotTable(TableDestination:=WSD. _
    Cells(2, FinalCol + 2), TableName:="PivotTable1")

' Turn off updating while building the table
PT.ManualUpdate = True

' Set up the row fields
PT.AddFields RowFields:="Product", ColumnFields:="Data"

' Define Calculated Fields
PT.CalculatedFields.Add Name:="ProfitPercent", Formula:="=Profit/Revenue"

' Set up the data fields
With PT.PivotFields("Revenue")
    .Orientation = xlDataField
    .Function = xlSum
    .Position = 1
    .NumberFormat = "#,##0"
End With

With PT.PivotFields("Profit")
    .Orientation = xlDataField
    .Function = xlSum
    .Position = 2
    .NumberFormat = "#,##0"
End With

With PT.PivotFields("ProfitPercent")
    .Orientation = xlDataField
    .Function = xlSum
    .Position = 3
    .NumberFormat = "#0.0%"
    .Name = "GP Pct"
End With

' Ensure that we get zeros instead of blanks in the data area
PT.NullString = "0"

' Calc the pivot table
PT.ManualUpdate = False
PT.ManualUpdate = True

WSD.Activate
Range("J2").Select

End Sub
```

CASE STUDY

Calculated Items

Suppose that in your company one manager is responsible for the product lines A292 and C409. The idea behind a calculated item is that you can define a new item along the Product field to calculate the total of these two items. Listing 13.5 produces the report shown in Figure 13.20.

Figure 13.20

Unless you love restating numbers to the Securities and Exchange Commission, avoid using calculated items.

Sum of Revenue	
Product ▾	Total
A292	12,337,778
C409	14,101,763
MyDivision	26,439,541
B722	12,683,061
D625	14,569,960
E438	17,411,966
Grand Total	97,544,069

Listing 13.5   Code That Adds a New Item along the Product Dimension

```
Sub CalcItemsProblem()
    ' Listing 13.5
    Dim WSD As Worksheet
    Dim PTCache As PivotCache
    Dim PT As PivotTable
    Dim PRange As Range
    Dim FinalRow As Long

    Set WSD = Worksheets("PivotTable")
    Dim WSR As Worksheet

    ' Delete any prior pivot tables
    For Each PT In WSD.PivotTables
        PT.TableRange2.Clear
    Next PT
    WSD.Range("J1:Z1").EntireColumn.Clear

    ' Define input area and set up a Pivot Cache
    FinalRow = WSD.Cells(Application.Rows.Count, 1).End(xlUp).Row
    FinalCol = WSD.Cells(1, Application.Columns.Count). _
        End(xlToLeft).Column
    Set PRange = WSD.Cells(1, 1).Resize(FinalRow, FinalCol)
    Set PTCache = ActiveWorkbook.PivotCaches.Add(SourceType:= _
        xlDatabase, SourceData:=PRange.Address)

    ' Create the Pivot Table from the Pivot Cache
    Set PT = PTCache.CreatePivotTable(TableDestination:=WSD. _
        Cells(2, FinalCol + 2), TableName:="PivotTable1")

    ' Turn off updating while building the table
    PT.ManualUpdate = True

    ' Set up the row fields
    PT.AddFields RowFields:="Product"

    ' Define calculated item along the product dimension
```

13

continues

Listing 13.5 Continued

```
    PT.PivotFields("Product").CalculatedItems _
        .Add "MyDivision", "='A292'+'C409'"
    ' Resequence so that the report has A292 and C409 first
    PT.PivotFields("Product"). _
        PivotItems("A292").Position = 1
    PT.PivotFields("Product"). _
        PivotItems("C409").Position = 2
    PT.PivotFields("Product"). _
        PivotItems("MyDivision").Position = 3

    ' Set up the data fields
    With PT.PivotFields("Revenue")
        .Orientation = xlDataField
        .Function = xlSum
        .Position = 1
        .NumberFormat = "#,##0"
    End With

    ' Ensure that we get zeros instead of blanks in the data area
    PT.NullString = "0"

    ' Calc the pivot table
    PT.ManualUpdate = False
    PT.ManualUpdate = True
    WSD.Activate
    Range("J2").Select

End Sub
```

Look closely at the results shown in Figure 13.20. The calculation for MyDivision is correct. The approximate $26 million for the MyDivision is the sum of $12 million for A292 and $14 million of C409. However, the grand total should be about $71 million. Instead, Excel gives you a grand total of $97 million. The total revenue for the company just increased by $26 million. Excel gives the wrong grand total when a field contains both regular and calculated items. The only plausible method for dealing with this situation is to attempt to hide the products that make up MyDivision:

```
With PT.PivotFields("Product")
    .PivotItems("A292").Visible = False
    .PivotItems("C409").Visible = False
End With
```

Figure 13.21 shows the results.

Figure 13.21

After the components that make up the MyDivision item are hidden, the total revenue for the company is again correct. However, it would be easier to add a new field to the original data with a Division field.

Sum of Revenue	
Product	Total
MyDivision	26,439,541
B722	12,683,061
D625	14,569,960
E438	17,411,966
Grand Total	71,104,528

Summarizing Date Fields with Grouping

With transactional data, you often find your date-based summaries having one row per day. Although daily data might be useful to a plant manager, many people in the company want to see totals by month, or by quarter, and year.

The great news is that Excel handles the summarization of dates in a pivot table with ease. For anyone who has ever had to use the arcane formula =A2-DAY(A2)+1 to change daily dates into monthly dates, you will appreciate the ease with which you can group transactional data into months or quarters.

In Figure 13.22, select one cell that contains a date. From the Options ribbon, choose Group Field. In the Grouping dialog, choose to group by Months, Quarters, and Years.

Figure 13.22
Use the Grouping dialog to change a less-meaningful report of daily dates into a summary by month, quarter, and year.

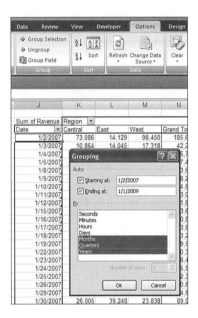

CAUTION

Never choose to group by only months without including years. If you do this, Excel combines January from this year and January from last year into a single item called January. Although this is great for seasonality analyses, it is rarely what you want in a summary. Always choose Years and Months in the Grouping dialog.

Understanding the Group Method in VBA

Creating a group with VBA is a bit quirky. The .Group method can be applied to only a single cell in the pivot table, and that cell must contain a date or the Date field label. This is the first example in this chapter where you must allow VBA to calculate an intermediate pivot table result.

You must define a pivot table with Invoice Date in the Row field. Turn off `ManualCalculation` to allow the Date field to be drawn. You can then use the `LabelRange` property to locate the date label and apply the `.Group` method.

```
PT.PivotFields("Date").LabelRange.Group
```

To specify how to group the Date field, you have to pass an array of seven `True`/`False` values. The first value corresponds to the Seconds selection in the Grouping dialog. The next value corresponds to Minutes, then Hours, Days, Months, Quarters, and Years. In this example, you want to group by months, quarters, and years, so the Periods argument is as follows:

```
Periods:=Array(False, False, False, False, True, True, True)
```

Figure 13.23 shows the result of Listing 13.6.

Figure 13.23
The Date field is now composed of three fields in the pivot table, representing year, quarter, and month.

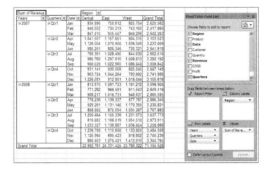

Listing 13.6   Code That Uses the Group Feature to Roll Daily Dates Up to Monthly Dates

```vba
Sub ReportByMonth()
    ' Listing 13.6
    Dim WSD As Worksheet
    Dim PTCache As PivotCache
    Dim PT As PivotTable
    Dim PRange As Range
    Dim FinalRow As Long

    Set WSD = Worksheets("PivotTable")
    Dim WSR As Worksheet

    ' Delete any prior pivot tables
    For Each PT In WSD.PivotTables
        PT.TableRange2.Clear
    Next PT
    WSD.Range("R1:AZ1").EntireColumn.Clear

    ' Define input area and set up a Pivot Cache
    FinalRow = WSD.Cells(Rows.Count, 1).End(xlUp).Row
    FinalCol = WSD.Cells(1, Columns.Count). _
        End(xlToLeft).Column
    Set PRange = WSD.Cells(1, 1).Resize(FinalRow, FinalCol)
    Set PTCache = ActiveWorkbook.PivotCaches.Add(SourceType:= _
        xlDatabase, SourceData:=PRange.Address)
```

```
' Create the Pivot Table from the Pivot Cache
Set PT = PTCache.CreatePivotTable(TableDestination:=WSD. _
    Cells(2, FinalCol + 2), TableName:="PivotTable1")

' Turn off updating while building the table
PT.ManualUpdate = True

' Set up the row fields
PT.AddFields RowFields:="Date", ColumnFields:="Region"

' Set up the data fields
With PT.PivotFields("Revenue")
    .Orientation = xlDataField
    .Function = xlSum
    .Position = 1
    .NumberFormat = "#,##0"
End With

' Ensure that we get zeros instead of blanks in the data area
PT.NullString = "0"

' Calc the pivot table to allow the date label to be drawn
PT.ManualUpdate = False
PT.ManualUpdate = True
WSD.Activate

' Group ShipDate by Month, Quarter, Year
PT.PivotFields("Date").LabelRange.Group _
    Start:=True, End:=True, _
    Periods:=Array(False, False, False, False, True, True, True)

' Calc the pivot table
PT.ManualUpdate = False
PT.ManualUpdate = True
WSD.Activate
Range("R1").Select

End Sub
```

Group by Week

You probably noticed that Excel enables you to group by day, month, quarter, and year. There is no standard grouping for week. You can, however, define a group that bunches groups of seven days.

By default, Excel starts the week based on the first date found in the data. This means that the default week would run from Tuesday, January 2, 2007, through Monday, January 8, 2007. You can override this by changing the Start parameter from True to an actual date.

Figuring out the correct first date requires some basic Excel functions. You can use the MIN function to find the earliest date in your pivot table with this code:

```
FirstDate = Application.WorksheetFunction.Min( _
    PT.PivotFields("Date").DataRange)
```

You can then use the WeekDay function to determine how many days to adjust the start date:

```
WhichDay = Application.WorksheetFunction.Weekday(FirstDate, 3)
StartDate = FirstDate - WhichDay
```

After you have determined the date that the first week should start on, use the following code to group the field by groups of seven days:

```
PT.PivotFields("Date").LabelRange.Group _
    Start:=StartDate, End:=True, By:=7, _
    Periods:=Array(False, False, False, True, False, False, False)
```

> **CAUTION**
>
> There is one limitation to grouping by week. When you group by week, you cannot also group by any other measure. For example, grouping by week and quarter is not valid.

Listing 13.7 creates the report shown in Figure 13.24.

Figure 13.24
Use the Number of Days setting to group by week.

Sum of Revenue	Region			
Date	Central	East	West	Grand Total
1/1/2007 - 1/7/2007	183,322	157,365	160,387	501,074
1/8/2007 - 1/14/2007	167,188	141,518	193,064	501,770
1/15/2007 - 1/21/2007	322,696	257,753	230,795	811,244
1/22/2007 - 1/28/2007	177,386	107,575	190,874	475,835
1/29/2007 - 2/4/2007	187,357	133,011	197,142	517,510
2/5/2007 - 2/11/2007	147,318	242,677	212,607	602,602
2/12/2007 - 2/18/2007	258,601	143,336	192,265	594,202
2/19/2007 - 2/25/2007	234,428	216,122	135,000	585,550
2/26/2007 - 3/4/2007	329,825	102,274	200,663	632,762
3/5/2007 - 3/11/2007	255,519	157,667	247,795	660,981
3/12/2007 - 3/18/2007	209,045	149,134	280,825	639,004
3/19/2007 - 3/25/2007	81,754	288,900	183,425	554,079
3/26/2007 - 4/1/2007	168,519	342,250	93,308	604,077
4/2/2007 - 4/8/2007	270,718	363,424	217,197	851,339

Listing 13.7   Code That Uses the Group Feature to Roll Daily Dates Up to Weekly Dates

```
Sub ReportByWeek()
    ' Listing 13.7
    Dim WSD As Worksheet
    Dim PTCache As PivotCache
    Dim PT As PivotTable
    Dim PRange As Range
    Dim FinalRow As Long

    Set WSD = Worksheets("PivotTable")
    Dim WSR As Worksheet

    ' Delete any prior pivot tables
    For Each PT In WSD.PivotTables
        PT.TableRange2.Clear
    Next PT
    WSD.Range("J1:Z1").EntireColumn.Clear

    ' Define input area and set up a Pivot Cache
    FinalRow = WSD.Cells(Application.Rows.Count, 1).End(xlUp).Row
    FinalCol = WSD.Cells(1, Application.Columns.Count). _
```

```
        End(xlToLeft).Column
Set PRange = WSD.Cells(1, 1).Resize(FinalRow, FinalCol)
Set PTCache = ActiveWorkbook.PivotCaches.Add(SourceType:= _
    xlDatabase, SourceData:=PRange.Address)

' Create the Pivot Table from the Pivot Cache
Set PT = PTCache.CreatePivotTable(TableDestination:=WSD. _
    Cells(2, FinalCol + 2), TableName:="PivotTable1")

' Turn off updating while building the table
PT.ManualUpdate = True

' Set up the row fields
PT.AddFields RowFields:="Date", ColumnFields:="Region"

' Set up the data fields
With PT.PivotFields("Revenue")
    .Orientation = xlDataField
    .Function = xlSum
    .Position = 1
    .NumberFormat = "#,##0"
End With

' Ensure that we get zeros instead of blanks in the data area
PT.NullString = "0"

' Calc the pivot table to allow the date label to be drawn
PT.ManualUpdate = False
PT.ManualUpdate = True
WSD.Activate

' Group Date by Week.
'Figure out the first Monday before the minimum date
FirstDate = Application.WorksheetFunction.Min( _
    PT.PivotFields("Date").DataRange)
WhichDay = Application.WorksheetFunction.Weekday(FirstDate, 3)
StartDate = FirstDate - WhichDay
PT.PivotFields("Date").LabelRange.Group _
    Start:=StartDate, End:=True, By:=7, _
    Periods:=Array(False, False, False, True, False, False, False)

' Calc the pivot table
PT.ManualUpdate = False
PT.ManualUpdate = True
WSD.Activate
Range("J2").Select

End Sub
```

Measuring Order Lead Time by Grouping Two Date Fields

Recall in the last section how Excel adds field names when you group by month and year. The less-aggregated measure (month) inherits the name of the original field. Any more-aggregated measures receive the name of the grouping—for example, Years.

Your manufacturing plant might be concerned with a measure of how far in advance the orders are received. If the plant has a 12-week lead time to procure components, they would love to have all orders placed 13 weeks in advance. When this doesn't happen, it is critical that you have an excellent forecasting system in place to accurately predict orders.

If you can add an OrderDate field to your transactional data, you could build a table to show how much revenue is received x months in advance of the ship date.

Follow these steps to set up an interesting potential anomaly:

1. Build a pivot table with **ShipDate** in the Column area, **OrderDate** in the Row area, and **Revenue** in the Data area.
2. Allow the pivot table to calculate.
3. Group ShipDate by month and year. This creates fields called ShipDate and Year.
4. Allow the pivot table to calculate. If you attempt to group the order Date field before calculating the results of step 3, you will get an error.
5. Group OrderDate by month and year. This creates a field called OrderDate with data by month. The grouping of OrderDate by year would tend to also be called Year, but Excel instead calls it Year2. Unless you know that the code grouped ShipDate before OrderDate, you would never know that Year2 referred to the order date and not the ship date.

Versions of Excel since 2000 correctly deal with the second set of grouped Date fields by changing the field name to Year2 rather than having a second Year.

Listing 13.8 creates the report shown in Figure 13.25.

Listing 13.8 Code Used to Create the Order Lead Time Report

```
Sub MeasureLeadtime2007()
    ' Listing 13.8
    Dim WSD As Worksheet
    Dim PTCache As PivotCache
    Dim PT As PivotTable
    Dim PRange As Range
    Dim FinalRow As Long

    Set WSD = Worksheets("LeadTime")
    Dim WSR As Worksheet

    ' Delete any prior pivot tables
    For Each PT In WSD.PivotTables
        PT.TableRange2.Clear
    Next PT

    ' Define input area and set up a Pivot Cache
    FinalRow = WSD.Cells(Application.Rows.Count, 1).End(xlUp).Row
```

```vba
   FinalCol = WSD.Cells(1, Application.Columns.Count). _
       End(xlToLeft).Column
   Set PRange = WSD.Cells(1, 1).Resize(FinalRow, FinalCol)
   Set PTCache = ActiveWorkbook.PivotCaches.Add(SourceType:= _
       xlDatabase, SourceData:=PRange.Address)

   ' Create the Pivot Table from the Pivot Cache
   Set PT = PTCache.CreatePivotTable(TableDestination:=WSD. _
       Cells(2, FinalCol + 2), TableName:="PivotTable1")

   ' Turn off updating while building the table
   PT.ManualUpdate = True

   ' Set up the row fields
   PT.AddFields RowFields:="OrderDate", ColumnFields:="ShipDate"

   ' Set up the data fields
   With PT.PivotFields("Revenue")
       .Orientation = xlDataField
       .Function = xlSum
       .Position = 1
       .NumberFormat = "#,##0"
   End With

   ' Ensure that we get zeros instead of blanks in the data area
   PT.NullString = "0"

   ' Calc the pivot table to allow the date label to be drawn
   PT.ManualUpdate = False
   PT.ManualUpdate = True
   WSD.Activate

   ' Group ShipDate by Month and Year
   PT.PivotFields("ShipDate").LabelRange.Group Start:=True, End:=True, _
       Periods:=Array(False, False, False, False, True, False, True)

   ' Calc the pivot table to allow the date label to be drawn
   PT.ManualUpdate = False
   PT.ManualUpdate = True

   ' Group OrderDate by Month and Year
   PT.PivotFields("OrderDate").LabelRange.Group Start:=True, End:=True, _
       Periods:=Array(False, False, False, False, True, False, True)

   ' Calc the pivot table
   PT.ManualUpdate = False
   PT.ManualUpdate = True
   WSD.Activate
   Range("K2").Select
End Sub
```

13

Figure 13.25
This order lead time report shows that you better have an excellent sales and operations planning system in place.

Sum of Revenue		Years ▾	ShipDate ▾			
		⊟2007				
Years2 ▾	OrderDate ▾	Jan	Feb	Mar	Apr	Ma
⊟2006	Aug	316,572	0	0	0	
	Sep	646,490	182,174	0	0	
	Oct	499,989	597,329	214,511	0	
	Nov	414,669	491,187	526,299	414,122	
	Dec	645,649	489,733	577,506	759,588	
⊟2007	Jan	97,193	532,951	553,808	634,511	
	Feb	0	124,491	648,716	541,929	
	Mar	0	0	121,423	613,597	
	Apr	0	0	0	139,776	
	May	0	0	0	0	

Using Advanced Pivot Table Techniques

You may be a pivot table pro and never have run into some of the really advanced techniques available with pivot tables. The following sections discuss such techniques.

Using AutoShow to Produce Executive Overviews

If you are designing an executive dashboard utility, you might want to spotlight the top five customers.

As with the AutoSort option, you could be a pivot table pro and never have stumbled across the AutoShow feature in Excel. This setting lets you select either the top or bottom *n* records based on any Data field in the report.

The code to use AutoShow in VBA uses the `.AutoShow` method:

```
' Show only the top 5 Customers
PT.PivotFields("Customer").AutoShow Top:=xlAutomatic, Range:=xlTop, _
    Count:=5, Field:= "Sum of Revenue"
```

When you create a report using the `.AutoShow` method, it is often helpful to copy the data and then go back to the original pivot report to get the totals for all markets. In the code shown in Listing 13.9, this is achieved by removing the Customer field from the pivot table and copying the grand total to the report. Listing 13.9 produces the report shown in Figure 13.26.

Figure 13.26
The Top 5 Customers report contains two pivot tables.

◢	A	B	C	D	E	F	G
1	Top 5 Customers						
2							
3	Customer	A292	B722	C409	D625	E438	Grand Total
4	Guarded Kettle Corporation	1,450,110	1,404,742	1,889,149	1,842,751	2,302,023	8,888,775
5	Unique Marble Company	1,600,347	1,581,665	1,765,305	1,707,140	2,179,242	8,883,699
6	Persuasive Kettle Inc.	1,565,368	1,385,296	1,443,434	1,584,759	2,030,578	8,009,435
7	Safe Saddle Corporation	646,559	857,573	730,463	1,038,371	1,053,369	4,326,335
8	Tremendous Bobsled Corporation	560,759	711,826	877,247	802,303	1,095,329	4,047,464
9	Top 5 Total	5,823,143	5,941,102	6,705,598	6,975,324	8,660,541	34,105,708
10							
11	Total Company	12,337,778	12,683,061	14,101,763	14,569,960	17,411,966	71,104,528
12							

13

Listing 13.9   Code Used to Create the Top 5 Customers Report

```
Sub Top5Customers()
    ' Listing 13.9
    ' Produce a report of the top 5 customers
    Dim WSD As Worksheet
    Dim WSR As Worksheet
    Dim WBN As Workbook
    Dim PTCache As PivotCache
    Dim PT As PivotTable
    Dim PRange As Range
    Dim FinalRow As Long
    Set WSD = Worksheets("PivotTable")

    ' Delete any prior pivot tables
    For Each PT In WSD.PivotTables
        PT.TableRange2.Clear
    Next PT
    WSD.Range("J1:Z1").EntireColumn.Clear

    ' Define input area and set up a Pivot Cache
    FinalRow = WSD.Cells(Application.Rows.Count, 1).End(xlUp).Row
    FinalCol = WSD.Cells(1, Application.Columns.Count). _
        End(xlToLeft).Column
    Set PRange = WSD.Cells(1, 1).Resize(FinalRow, FinalCol)
    Set PTCache = ActiveWorkbook.PivotCaches.Add(SourceType:= _
        xlDatabase, SourceData:=PRange.Address)

    ' Create the Pivot Table from the Pivot Cache
    Set PT = PTCache.CreatePivotTable(TableDestination:=WSD. _
        Cells(2, FinalCol + 2), TableName:="PivotTable1")

    ' Turn off updating while building the table
    PT.ManualUpdate = True

    ' Set up the row fields
    PT.AddFields RowFields:="Customer", ColumnFields:="Product"

    ' Set up the data fields
    With PT.PivotFields("Revenue")
        .Orientation = xlDataField
        .Function = xlSum
        .Position = 1
        .NumberFormat = "#,##0"
        .Name = "Total Revenue"
    End With

    ' Ensure that we get zeros instead of blanks in the data area
    PT.NullString = "0"

    ' Sort customers descending by sum of revenue
    PT.PivotFields("Customer").AutoSort Order:=xlDescending, _
        Field:="Total Revenue"

    ' Show only the top 5 customers
    PT.PivotFields("Customer").AutoShow Type:=xlAutomatic, Range:=xlTop, _
```

continues

Listing 13.9   Continued

```
        Count:=5, Field:="Total Revenue"

    ' Calc the pivot table to allow the date label to be drawn
    PT.ManualUpdate = False
    PT.ManualUpdate = True

    ' Create a new blank workbook with one worksheet
    Set WBN = Workbooks.Add(xlWBATWorksheet)
    Set WSR = WBN.Worksheets(1)
    WSR.Name = "Report"
    ' Set up ritle for report
    With WSR.[A1]
        .Value = "Top 5 Customers"
        .Font.Size = 14
    End With

    ' Copy the pivot table data to row 3 of the report sheet
    ' Use offset to eliminate the title row of the pivot table
    PT.TableRange2.Offset(1, 0).Copy
    WSR.[A3].PasteSpecial Paste:=xlPasteValuesAndNumberFormats
    LastRow = WSR.Cells(Rows.Count, 1).End(xlUp).Row
    WSR.Cells(LastRow, 1).Value = "Top 5 Total"

    ' Go back to the pivot table to get totals without the AutoShow
    PT.PivotFields("Customer").Orientation = xlHidden
    PT.ManualUpdate = False
    PT.ManualUpdate = True
    PT.TableRange2.Offset(2, 0).Copy
    WSR.Cells(LastRow + 2, 1).PasteSpecial Paste:=xlPasteValuesAndNumberFormats
    WSR.Cells(LastRow + 2, 1).Value = "Total Company"

    ' Clear the pivot table
    PT.TableRange2.Clear
    Set PTCache = Nothing

    ' Do some basic formatting
    ' Autofit columns, bold the headings, right-align
    WSR.Range(WSR.Range("A3"), WSR.Cells(LastRow + 2, 6)).Columns.AutoFit
    Range("A3").EntireRow.Font.Bold = True
    Range("A3").EntireRow.HorizontalAlignment = xlRight
    Range("A3").HorizontalAlignment = xlLeft

    Range("A2").Select
    MsgBox "CEO Report has been Created"
End Sub
```

The Top 5 Customers report actually contains two snapshots of a pivot table. After using the AutoShow feature to grab the top five markets with their totals, the macro went back to the pivot table, removed the AutoShow option, and grabbed the total of all customers to produce the Total Company row.

Using `ShowDetail` to Filter a Recordset

Take any pivot table in the Excel user interface. Double-click any number in the table. Excel inserts a new sheet in the workbook and copies all the source records that represent that number. In the Excel user interface, this is a great way to perform a drill-down query into a dataset.

The equivalent VBA property is `ShowDetail`. By setting this property to `True` for any cell in the pivot table, you generate a new worksheet with all the records that make up that cell:

```
PT.TableRange2.Offset(2, 1).Resize(1, 1).ShowDetail = True
```

Listing 13.10 produces a pivot table with the total revenue for the top three customers and `ShowDetail` for each of those stores. This is an alternative method to using the Advanced Filter report. The results of this macro are three new sheets. Figure 13.27 shows the first sheet created.

Figure 13.27

Pivot table applications are incredibly diverse. This macro created a pivot table of the top three stores and then used the `ShowDetail` property to retrieve the records for each of those stores.

	A	B	C	D	E	F	G	H
1	Detail for Guarded Kettle Corporation (Customer Rank: 1)							
2								
3	Region	Product	Date	Customer	Quantity	Revenue	COGS	Profit
4	West	D625	1/2/2007	Guarded Kettle Corporation	430	10937	6248	4689
5	West	A292	12/30/2008	Guarded Kettle Corporation	640	14891	7302	7589
6	West	B722	12/30/2008	Guarded Kettle Corporation	210	4980	2615	2365
7	West	E438	12/30/2008	Guarded Kettle Corporation	660	20360	10276	10084
8	West	E438	12/30/2008	Guarded Kettle Corporation	590	18024	9186	8838
9	West	D625	12/29/2008	Guarded Kettle Corporation	950	28677	13804	14873
10	West	C409	1/2/2007	Guarded Kettle Corporation	770	20382	10387	9995
11	West	E438	12/29/2008	Guarded Kettle Corporation	160	4552	2491	2061
12	West	A292	12/29/2008	Guarded Kettle Corporation	750	17451	8558	8893
13	West	A292	12/26/2008	Guarded Kettle Corporation	390	8561	4450	4111
14	West	A292	12/24/2008	Guarded Kettle Corporation	970	22570	11068	11502
15	West	C409	12/24/2008	Guarded Kettle Corporation	340	9529	4587	4942

Listing 13.10   Code Used to Create a Report for Each of the Top 3 Customers

```vba
Sub RetrieveTop3CustomerDetail()
    ' Listing 13.10
    ' Retrieve Details from Top 3 Stores
    Dim WSD As Worksheet
    Dim WSR As Worksheet
    Dim WBN As Workbook
    Dim PTCache As PivotCache
    Dim PT As PivotTable
    Dim PRange As Range
    Dim FinalRow As Long
    Set WSD = Worksheets("PivotTable")

    ' Delete any prior pivot tables
    For Each PT In WSD.PivotTables
        PT.TableRange2.Clear
    Next PT
    WSD.Range("J1:Z1").EntireColumn.Clear

    ' Define input area and set up a Pivot Cache
    FinalRow = WSD.Cells(Application.Rows.Count, 1).End(xlUp).Row
    FinalCol = WSD.Cells(1, Application.Columns.Count). _
        End(xlToLeft).Column
    Set PRange = WSD.Cells(1, 1).Resize(FinalRow, FinalCol)
    Set PTCache = ActiveWorkbook.PivotCaches.Add(SourceType:= _
        xlDatabase, SourceData:=PRange.Address)
```

13

continues

Listing 13.10 Continued

```vba
' Create the Pivot Table from the Pivot Cache
Set PT = PTCache.CreatePivotTable(TableDestination:=WSD. _
    Cells(2, FinalCol + 2), TableName:="PivotTable1")

' Turn off updating while building the table
PT.ManualUpdate = True

' Set up the row fields
PT.AddFields RowFields:="Customer", ColumnFields:="Data"

' Set up the data fields
With PT.PivotFields("Revenue")
    .Orientation = xlDataField
    .Function = xlSum
    .Position = 1
    .NumberFormat = "#,##0"
    .Name = "Total Revenue"
End With

' Sort Stores descending by sum of revenue
PT.PivotFields("Customer").AutoSort Order:=xlDescending, _
    Field:="Total Revenue"

' Show only the top 3 stores
PT.PivotFields("Customer").AutoShow Type:=xlAutomatic, Range:=xlTop, _
    Count:=3, Field:="Total Revenue"

' Ensure that we get zeros instead of blanks in the data area
PT.NullString = "0"

' Calc the pivot table to allow the date label to be drawn
PT.ManualUpdate = False
PT.ManualUpdate = True

' Produce summary reports for each customer
For i = 1 To 3
    PT.TableRange2.Offset(i + 1, 1).Resize(1, 1).ShowDetail = True
    ' The active sheet has changed to the new detail report
    ' Add a title
    Range("A1:A2").EntireRow.Insert
    Range("A1").Value = "Detail for " & _
        PT.TableRange2.Offset(i + 1, 0).Resize(1, 1).Value & _
        " (Customer Rank: " & i & ")"
Next i

MsgBox "Detail reports for top 3 customers have been created."
End Sub
```

Creating Reports for Each Region or Model

A pivot table can have one or more Report Filter fields. A Report Filter field goes in a separate set of rows above the pivot report. It can serve to filter the report to a certain region, certain model, or certain combination of region and model.

In VBA, Report Filter fields are called *page fields*.

To set up a page field in VBA, add the `PageFields` parameter to the `AddFields` method. The following line of code creates a pivot table with Region in the page field:

```
PT.AddFields RowFields:= "Product", ColumnFields:= "Data", PageFields:= "Region"
```

The preceding line of code sets up the Region page field with the value (All), which returns all regions. To limit the report to just the North region, use the `CurrentPage` property:

```
PT.PivotFields("Region").CurrentPage = "North"
```

One use of a page field is to build a user form in which someone can select a particular region or particular product. You then use this information to set the `CurrentPage` property and display the results of the user form.

Another interesting use is to loop through all `PivotItems` and display them one at a time in the page field. You can quickly produce top 10 reports for each region using this method.

To determine how many regions are available in the data, use `PT.PivotFields("Region").PivotItems.Count`. Either of these loops would work:

```
For i = 1 To PT.PivotFields("Region").PivotItems.Count
    PT.PivotFields("Region").CurrentPage = _
            PT.PivotFields("Region").PivotItems(i).Name
    PT.ManualUpdate = False
    PT.ManualUpdate = True
Next i

For Each PivItem In PT.PivotFields("Region").PivotItems
    PT.PivotFields("Region").CurrentPage = PivItem.Name
    PT.ManualUpdate = False
    PT.ManualUpdate = True
Next PivItem
```

Of course, in both of these loops, the three region reports fly by too quickly to see. In practice, you would want to save each report while it is displayed.

So far in this chapter, you have been using `PT.TableRange2` when copying the data from the pivot table. The `TableRange2` property includes all rows of the pivot table, including the page fields. There is also a `.TableRange1` property, which excludes the page fields. You can use either statement to get the detail rows:

```
PT.TableRange2.Offset(3, 0)
PT.TableRange1.Offset(1, 0)
```

Which you use is your preference; but if you use `TableRange2`, you won't have problems when you try to delete the pivot table with `PT.TableRange2.Clear`. If you were to accidentally attempt to clear `TableRange1` when there are page fields, you would end up with the dreaded "Cannot move or change part of a pivot table" error.

Listing 13.11 produces a new workbook for each region. The report for the final region is shown in Figure 13.28.

13

Figure 13.28

By looping through all items found in the Region page field, the macro produced one workbook for each regional manager.

▲	A	B	C
1	Top 5 Customers in the West Region		
2			
3	Customer	Revenue	
4	Guarded Kettle Corporation	8,889K	
5	Agile Glass Supply	3,877K	
6	Tremendous Flagpole Traders	2,361K	
7	Innovative Oven Corporation	2,359K	
8	Trouble-Free Eggbeater Inc.	2,303K	
9	Top 5 Total	19,789K	
10			

Listing 13.11 Code That Creates a New Workbook per Region

```
Sub Top5ByRegionReport()
    ' Listing 13.11
    ' Produce a report of top 5 Customers for each region
    Dim WSD As Worksheet
    Dim WSR As Worksheet
    Dim WBN As Workbook
    Dim PTCache As PivotCache
    Dim PT As PivotTable
    Dim PRange As Range
    Dim FinalRow As Long

    Set WSD = Worksheets("PivotTable")

    ' Delete any prior pivot tables
    For Each PT In WSD.PivotTables
        PT.TableRange2.Clear
    Next PT
    WSD.Range("J1:Z1").EntireColumn.Clear

    ' Define input area and set up a Pivot Cache
    FinalRow = WSD.Cells(Application.Rows.Count, 1).End(xlUp).Row
    FinalCol = WSD.Cells(1, Application.Columns.Count). _
        End(xlToLeft).Column
    Set PRange = WSD.Cells(1, 1).Resize(FinalRow, FinalCol)
    Set PTCache = ActiveWorkbook.PivotCaches.Add(SourceType:= _
        xlDatabase, SourceData:=PRange.Address)

    ' Create the Pivot Table from the Pivot Cache
    Set PT = PTCache.CreatePivotTable(TableDestination:=WSD. _
        Cells(2, FinalCol + 2), TableName:="PivotTable1")

    ' Turn off updating while building the table
    PT.ManualUpdate = True

    ' Set up the row fields
    PT.AddFields RowFields:="Customer", ColumnFields:="Data", _
        PageFields:="Region"

    ' Set up the data fields
    With PT.PivotFields("Revenue")
        .Orientation = xlDataField
        .Function = xlSum
        .Position = 1
        .NumberFormat = "#,##0,K"
        .Name = "Total Revenue"
    End With
```

```
    ' Sort customers descending by sum of revenue
    PT.PivotFields("Customer").AutoSort Order:=xlDescending, _
        Field:="Total Revenue"

    ' Show only the top 5 customers
    PT.PivotFields("Customer").AutoShow Type:=xlAutomatic, Range:=xlTop, _
        Count:=5, Field:="Total Revenue"

    ' Ensure that we get zeros instead of blanks in the data area
    PT.NullString = "0"

    ' Calc the pivot table
    PT.ManualUpdate = False
    PT.ManualUpdate = True
    Ctr = 0

    ' Loop through each region
    For Each PivItem In PT.PivotFields("Region").PivotItems
        Ctr = Ctr + 1
        PT.PivotFields("Region").CurrentPage = PivItem.Name
        PT.ManualUpdate = False
        PT.ManualUpdate = True

        ' Create a new blank workbook with one worksheet
        Set WBN = Workbooks.Add(xlWBATWorksheet)
        Set WSR = WBN.Worksheets(1)
        WSR.Name = PivItem.Name
        ' Set up Title for Report
        With WSR.[A1]
            .Value = "Top 5 Customers in the " & PivItem.Name & " Region"
            .Font.Size = 14
        End With

        ' Copy the pivot table data to row 3 of the report sheet
        ' Use offset to eliminate the page & title rows of the pivot table
        PT.TableRange2.Offset(3, 0).Copy
        WSR.[A3].PasteSpecial Paste:=xlPasteValuesAndNumberFormats
        LastRow = WSR.Cells(65536, 1).End(xlUp).Row
        WSR.Cells(LastRow, 1).Value = "Top 5 Total"

        ' Do some basic formatting
        ' Autofit columns, bold the headings, right-align
        WSR.Range(WSR.Range("A2"), WSR.Cells(LastRow, 3)).Columns.AutoFit
        Range("A3").EntireRow.Font.Bold = True
        Range("A3").EntireRow.HorizontalAlignment = xlRight
        Range("A3").HorizontalAlignment = xlLeft
        Range("B3").Value = "Revenue"

        Range("A2").Select

    Next PivItem

    ' Clear the pivot table
    PT.TableRange2.Clear
    Set PTCache = Nothing

    MsgBox Ctr & " Region reports have been created"

End Sub
```

Manually Filtering Two or More Items in a Pivot Field

In addition to setting up a calculated pivot item to display the total of a couple of products that make up a dimension, you can manually filter a particular pivot field.

For example, you have one client who sells shoes. In the report showing sales of sandals, he wants to see just the stores that are in warm-weather states. The code to hide a particular store is as follows:

```
PT.PivotFields("Store").PivotItems("Minneapolis").Visible = False
```

You need to be very careful never to set all items to False; otherwise, the macro ends with an error. This tends to happen more than you would expect. An application might first show products A and B and then on the next loop show products C and D. If you attempt to make A and B not visible before making C and D visible, no products will be visible along the PivotField, which causes an error. To correct this, always loop through all PivotItems, making sure to turn them back to visible before the second pass through the loop.

This process is easy in VBA. After building the table with Product in the page field, loop through to change the Visible property to show only the total of certain products:

```
' Make sure all PivotItems along line are visible
For Each PivItem In _
    PT.PivotFields("Product").PivotItems
    PivItem.Visible = True
Next PivItem

' Now - loop through and keep only certain items visible
For Each PivItem In _
    PT.PivotFields("Product").PivotItems
    Select Case PivItem.Name
        Case "Landscaping/Grounds Care", _
            "Green Plants and Foliage Care"
            PivItem.Visible = True
        Case Else
            PivItem.Visible = False
    End Select
Next PivItem
```

Controlling the Sort Order Manually

If your company has been reporting regions in the sequence East, Central, West forever, it is an uphill battle getting managers to accept seeing the report ordered Central, East, West just because this is the default alphabetic order offered by pivot tables.

Strangely enough, Microsoft offers a bizarre method for handling a custom sort order in a pivot table. It's called a *manual sort order*. To change the sort order in the user interface, you just go to a cell in the pivot table that contains Central, type the word **East**, and press Enter. As if by magic, Central and East switch places. Of course, all the numbers for East move to the appropriate column.

The VBA code to do a manual sort involves setting the `Position` property for a specific `PivotItem`. This is somewhat dangerous because you don't know whether the underlying fields will have data for East on any given day. Be sure to set error checking to resume in case East doesn't exist today:

```
On Error Resume Next
PT.PivotFields("Region").PivotItems("East").Position = 1
On Error GoTo 0
```

Using Sum, Average, Count, Min, Max, and More

So far, every example in this chapter has involved summing data. It is also possible to get an average, minimum, or maximum of data. In VBA, change the `Function` property of the Data field and give the Data field a unique name. For example, the following code fragment produces five different summaries of the Revenue field, each with a unique name:

```
' Set up the data fields
With PT.PivotFields("Revenue")
    .Orientation = xlDataField
    .Function = xlSum
    .Position = 1
    .NumberFormat = "#,##0,K"
    .Name = "Total Revenue"
End With

With PT.PivotFields("Revenue")
    .Orientation = xlDataField
    .Function = xlCount
    .Position = 2
    .NumberFormat = "#,##0"
    .Name = "Number Orders"
End With

With PT.PivotFields("Revenue")
    .Orientation = xlDataField
    .Function = xlAverage
    .Position = 3
    .NumberFormat = "#,##0"
    .Name = "Average Revenue"
End With

With PT.PivotFields("Revenue")
    .Orientation = xlDataField
    .Function = xlMin
    .Position = 4
    .NumberFormat = "#,##0"
    .Name = "Smallest Order"
End With

With PT.PivotFields("Revenue")
    .Orientation = xlDataField
    .Function = xlMax
    .Position = 5
    .NumberFormat = "#,##0"
    .Name = "Largest Order"
End With
```

13

The resultant pivot table provides a number of statistics about the average revenue, largest order, smallest order, and so on, as shown in Figure 13.29.

Figure 13.29
This pivot table presents four views of Sum of Revenue. Column K is the normal calculation. Column L is % of Total. Column M is % change from previous month. Column N is the running total.

	J	K	L	M	N	O
		Data				
	Region	Total Revenue	Number Orders	Average Revenue	Smallest Order	Largest Order
	East	24,331K	1,696	14,346	2K	32,023
	Central	22,993K	1,625	14,149	2K	31,993
	West	23,780K	1,667	14,265	2K	32,320
	Grand Total	71,105K	4,988	14,265	2K	32,320

Creating Report Percentages

In addition to the available choices, such as Sum, Min, Max, and Average, you can use another set of pivot table options called the *calculation options*. They allow you to show a particular field as a percentage of the total, a percentage of the row, a percentage of the column, or as the percent difference from the previous or next item. All these settings are controlled through the `.Calculation` property of the page field.

The valid properties for `.Calculation` are `xlPercentOf`, `xlPercentOfColumn`, `xlPercentOfRow`, `xlPercentOfTotal`, `xlRunningTotal`, `xlPercentDifferenceFrom`, `xlDifferenceFrom`, `xlIndex`, and `xlNoAdditionalCalculation`. Each has its own unique set of rules. Some require that you specify a `BaseField`, and others require that you specify both a `BaseField` and `BaseItem`. The following sections provide some specific examples.

Percentage of Total

To get the percentage of the total, specify `xlPercentOfTotal` as the `.Calculation` property for the page field:

```
' Set up a percentage of total
With PT.PivotFields("Revenue")
    .Orientation = xlDataField
    .Caption = "PctOfTotal"
    .Function = xlSum
    .Position = 2
    .NumberFormat = "#0.0%"
    .Calculation = xlPercentOfTotal
End With
```

Percentage Growth from Previous Month

With ship months going down the columns, you might want to see the percentage of revenue growth from month to month. You can set up this arrangement with the `xlPercentDifferenceFrom` setting. In this case, you must specify that the `BaseField` is `"Date"` and that the `BaseItem` is something called (previous):

```
' Set up % change from prior month
With PT.PivotFields("Revenue")
    .Orientation = xlDataField
    .Function = xlSum
    .Caption = "%Change"
    .Calculation = xlPercentDifferenceFrom
    .BaseField = "Date"
    .BaseItem = "(previous)"
    .Position = 3
    .NumberFormat = "#0.0%"
End With
```

Note that with positional calculations, you cannot use the AutoShow or AutoSort method. This is too bad; it would be interesting to sort the customers high to low and to see their sizes in relation to each other.

Percentage of a Specific Item

You can use the xlPercentDifferenceFrom setting to express revenues as a percentage of the West region sales:

```
' Show revenue as a percentage of California
With PT.PivotFields("Revenue")
    .Orientation = xlDataField
    .Function = xlSum
    .Caption = "% of West"
    .Calculation = xlPercentDifferenceFrom
    .BaseField = "Region"
    .BaseItem = "West"
    .Position = 3
    .NumberFormat = "#0.0%"
End With
```

Running Total

Setting up a running total is not intuitive; to do this, you must define a BaseField. In this example, Date runs down the column. To define a running total column for revenue, you must specify that BaseField is "Date":

```
' Set up Running Total
With PT.PivotFields("Revenue")
    .Orientation = xlDataField
    .Function = xlSum
    .Caption = "YTD Total"
    .Calculation = xlRunningTotal
    .Position = 4
    .NumberFormat = "#,##0,K"
    .BaseField = "Date"
End With
```

Figure 13.30 shows the results of a pivot table with three custom calculation settings, as discussed earlier.

13

Figure 13.30
This pivot table presents four views of Sum of Revenue. Column L is the normal calculation. Column M is % of Total. Column N is % change from previous month. Column O is the running total.

Years	Date	Sum of Revenue	PctOfTotal	%Change	YTD Total
⊟ 2007	Jan	2,621K	3.7%		2,621K
	Feb	2,418K	3.4%	-7.7%	5,038K
	Mar	2,642K	3.7%	9.3%	7,681K
	Apr	3,104K	4.4%	17.5%	10,784K
	May	3,233K	4.5%	4.2%	14,017K
	Jun	2,642K	3.7%	-18.3%	16,659K
	Jul	2,663K	3.7%	0.8%	19,322K
	Aug	3,292K	4.6%	23.6%	22,614K
	Sep	3,010K	4.2%	-8.6%	25,624K
	Oct	2,687K	3.8%	-10.7%	28,311K
	Nov	2,742K	3.9%	2.0%	31,053K
	Dec	3,156K	4.4%	15.1%	34,208K
⊟ 2008	Jan	3,097K	4.4%		3,097K
	Feb	2,649K	3.7%	-14.4%	5,746K
	Mar	2,866K	4.0%	8.2%	8,612K
	Apr	2,895K	4.1%	1.0%	11,507K
	May	3,231K	4.5%	11.6%	14,738K
	Jun	2,768K	3.9%	-14.3%	17,506K
	Jul	3,638K	5.1%	31.4%	21,144K
	Aug	2,974K	4.2%	-18.2%	24,118K
	Sep	3,209K	4.5%	7.9%	27,327K
	Oct	3,485K	4.9%	8.6%	30,811K
	Nov	2,740K	3.9%	-21.4%	33,551K
	Dec	3,345K	4.7%	22.1%	36,896K
Grand Total		71,105K	100.0%		

Using New Pivot Table Features in Excel 2007

Pivot tables offer a variety of new features in Excel 2007. The new label and value filters, conditional formatting, table formatting, and layout views are significant improvements to the pivot table environment.

If you want to use any of these features, the pivot table must exist in a file stored in Excel 2007 file format. If your file is in Compatibility mode, none of the new features are available in the user interface or in VBA.

Similarly, if you use any of these features, the code runs only in Excel 2007. There is no hope of going backward to share the code with someone using Excel 2003.

Using the New Filters

In previous versions of Excel, the filtering feature enabled you to choose one or more pivot items from a drop-down list. The only conceptual filter was the top 10 AutoShow filter.

Excel 2007 offers new conceptual filters that are easy to access. In the PivotTable Field List, hover the cursor over any active field in the field list portion of the dialog box. In the drop-down that appears, you can choose Label Filters, Date Filters, or Value Filters.

In Figure 13.31, the fly-out menu shows the list of Label filters available for the Customer field.

To apply a label filter in VBA, use the `PivotFilters.Add` method. The following code filters to the branches that start with 1:

```
PT.PivotFields("Customer").PivotFilters.Add _
    Type:=xlCaptionBeginsWith, Value1:="1"
```

13

Figure 13.31
You can easily choose all
the Customer items that
meet your criteria.

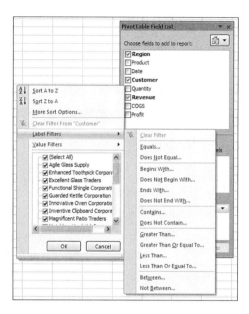

To clear the filter from the Branch field, use the `ClearAllFilters` method:

```
PT.PivotFields("Customer").ClearAllFilters
```

To apply a date filter to the Date field to find records from this week, use this code:

```
PT.PivotFields("Date").PivotFilters.Add Type:=xlThisWeek
```

The value filters enable you to filter one field based on the value of another field. For example, to find all the branches where the total revenue is more than $100,000, you would use this code:

```
PT.PivotFields("Customer").PivotFilters.Add _
    Type:=xlValueIsGreaterThan, _
    DataField:=PT.PivotFields("Sum of Revenue"), _
    Value1:=100000
```

Other value filters might allow you to specify that you want branches where the revenue is between $50,000 and $100,000. In this case, you specify one limit as `Value1` and the second limit as `Value2`:

```
PT.PivotFields("Branch").PivotFilters.Add _
    Type:=xlValueIsBetween, _
    DataField:=PT.PivotFields("Sum of Revenue"), _
    Value1:=50000, Value2:=100000
```

Table 13.3 provides a sampling of filter types.

13

Table 13.3   Sampling of Filter Types

Filter Type	Description
xlBefore	Filters for all dates before a specified date
xlAllDatesInPeriodJanuary	Filters for all dates in January
xlBottomCount	Filters for the specified number of values from the bottom of a list
xlBottomPercent	Filters for the specified percentage of values from the bottom of a list
xlBottomSum	Sums the values from the bottom of the list
xlCaptionBeginsWith	Filters for all captions beginning with the specified string
xlDateBetween	Filters for all dates that are between a specified range of dates
xlDateLastMonth	Filters for all dates that apply to the previous month
xlValueEquals	Filters for all values that match the specified value
xlYearToDate	Filters for all values that are within one year of a specified date

Applying a Table Style

The Design ribbon offers two groups dedicated to formatting the pivot table, as shown in Figure 13.32. The PivotTable Style Options group has four check boxes that modify the styles in the PivotTable Styles Gallery.

Figure 13.32
The four check boxes and gallery of styles offer many variations for formatting the pivot table.

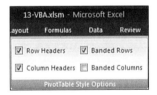

The following four lines of code are equivalent to turning on all four settings in the PivotTable Style Options group:

```
PT.ShowTableStyleRowHeaders = True
PT.ShowTableStyleColumnHeaders = True
PT.ShowTableStyleRowStripes = True
PT.ShowTableStyleColumnStripes = True
```

To apply a table style from the gallery, use the `TableStyle2` property. If you want to get the correct name, it might be best to record a macro:

```
' Format the pivot table
PT.ShowTableStyleRowStripes = True
PT.TableStyle2 = "PivotStyleMedium3"
```

If you hover over a style in the Style gallery, a ToolTip will show a style name such as Pivot Style Medium 3.

Changing the Layout From the Design Ribbon

The Layout group of the Design ribbon contains four drop-downs. These drop-downs control the location of subtotals (top or bottom), the presence of grand totals, the report layout, and the presence of blank rows.

Subtotals can appear either at the top or bottom of a group of pivot items. The `SubtotalLocation` property applies to the entire pivot table; valid values are `xlAtBottom` or `xlAtTop`:

```
PT.SubtotalLocation:=xlAtTop
```

Grand totals can be turned on or off for rows or columns. The following code turns them off for both:

```
PT.ColumnGrand = False
PT.RowGrand = False
```

There are three settings for the report layout. The Tabular layout is similar to the default layout in Excel 2003. The Outline layout was optionally available in Excel 2003. The Compact layout is new in Excel 2007.

Excel can remember the last layout used and apply it to additional pivot tables created in the same Excel session. For this reason, you should always explicitly choose the layout that you want. Use the `RowAxisLayout` method; valid values are `xlTabularRow`, `xlOutlineRow`, or `xlCompactRow`:

```
PT.RowAxisLayout xlTabularRow
PT.RowAxisLayout xlOutlineRow
PT.RowGrand = xlCompactRow
```

In Excel 2007, you can add a blank line to the layout after each group of pivot items. Although the Design ribbon offers a single setting to affect the entire pivot table, the setting is actually applied to each individual pivot field individually. The macro recorder responds by recording a dozen lines of code for a pivot table with 12 fields. You can intelligently add a single line of code for the outer Row field(s):

```
PT.PivotFields("Region").LayoutBlankLine = True
```

CASE STUDY

13

Applying a Data Visualization

Excel 2007 offers fantastic new data visualizations such as icon sets, color gradients, and in-cell data bars. When you apply a visualization to a pivot table, you should exclude the total rows from the visualization.

If you have 20 customers that average $3,000,000 in revenue each, the total for the 20 customers is $60 million. If you include the total in the data visualization, the total gets the largest bar, and all the customer records have tiny bars.

In the Excel user interface, you always want to use the Add Rule or Edit Rule choice to choose the option All Cells Showing "Sum of Revenue" for "Customer," as shown in Figure 13.33.

Figure 13.33
To create meaningful visualizations in your pivot table, exclude the totals by choosing the third option at the top of this dialog box.

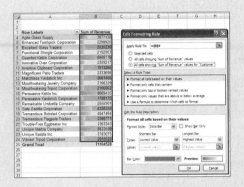

The code in Listing 13.12 adds a pivot table and applies a data bar to the revenue field.

Listing 13.12   Code That Creates a Pivot Table with Data Bars

```vba
Sub Sub CreatePivotDataBar()
    ' Listing 13.12
    Dim WSD As Worksheet
    Dim PTCache As PivotCache
    Dim PT As PivotTable
    Dim PRange As Range
    Dim FinalRow As Long
    Set WSD = Worksheets("PivotTable")

    ' Delete any prior pivot tables
    For Each PT In WSD.PivotTables
        PT.TableRange2.Clear
    Next PT
    WSD.Range("J1:Z1").EntireColumn.Clear

    ' Define input area and set up a Pivot Cache
    FinalRow = WSD.Cells(Rows.Count, 1).End(xlUp).Row
    FinalCol = WSD.Cells(1, Columns.Count). _
        End(xlToLeft).Column
    Set PRange = WSD.Cells(1, 1).Resize(FinalRow, FinalCol)
    Set PTCache = ActiveWorkbook.PivotCaches.Add(SourceType:= _
        xlDatabase, SourceData:=PRange.Address)

    ' Create the Pivot Table from the Pivot Cache
    Set PT = PTCache.CreatePivotTable(TableDestination:=WSD. _
        Cells(2, FinalCol + 2), TableName:="PivotTable1")

    ' Turn off updating while building the table
    PT.ManualUpdate = True

    ' Set up the row & column fields
    PT.AddFields RowFields:="Customer", _
        ColumnFields:="Data"
```

```vba
    ' Set up the data fields
    With PT.PivotFields("Revenue")
        .Orientation = xlDataField
        .Function = xlSum
        .Position = 1
    End With

    ' Calc the pivot table
    PT.ManualUpdate = False
    PT.ManualUpdate = True

    ' Apply a Databar
    PT.TableRange2.Cells(3, 2).Select
    Selection.FormatConditions.AddDatabar
    Selection.FormatConditions(1).ShowValue = True
    Selection.FormatConditions(1).SetFirstPriority
    With Selection.FormatConditions(1)
        .MinPoint.Modify newtype:=xlConditionValueLowestValue
        .MaxPoint.Modify newtype:=xlConditionValueHighestValue
    End With
    With Selection.FormatConditions(1).BarColor
        .ThemeColor = xlThemeColorAccent3
        .TintAndShade = -0.499984740745262
    End With
    Selection.FormatConditions(1).ScopeType = xlFieldsScope

    WSD.Activate
    Range("J2").Select

End Sub
```

Next Steps

If you couldn't already tell, pivot tables are my favorite feature in Excel. They are incredibly powerful and flexible. Combined with VBA, they provide an excellent calculation engine and power many of the reports that I build for clients. In Chapter 14, "Excel Power," you will learn multiple techniques for handling various tasks in VBA.

13

Excel Power

14

A major secret of successful programmers is to never waste time writing the same code twice. They all have little bits—or even big bits—of code that are used over and over again. Another big secret is to never take eight hours doing something that can be done in ten minutes—which is what this book is about!

This chapter contains programs donated by several Excel power programmers. These are programs they have found useful, and they hope these will help you, too. Not only can they save you time, but they may also teach you new ways of solving common problems.

Different programmers have different programming styles, and we did not rewrite the submissions. As you review the lines of code, you will notice different ways of doing the same task, such as referring to ranges.

File Operations

The following utilities deal with handling files in folders. Being able to loop through a list of files in a folder is a useful task.

List Files in a Directory

Submitted by Nathan P. Oliver of Minneapolis, Minnesota. Nathan is a financial consultant and application developer.

This program returns the filename, size, and date modified of all files in the selected directory and its subfolders:

```
Sub ExcelFileSearch()
Dim srchExt As Variant, srchDir As Variant, i As Long, j As Long
Dim strName As String, varArr(1 To 1048576, 1 To 3) As Variant
Dim strFileFullName As String
Dim ws As Worksheet
Dim fso As Object

Let srchExt = Application.InputBox("Please Enter File Extension", "Info Request")
If srchExt = False And Not TypeName(srchExt) = "String" Then
    Exit Sub
End If

Let srchDir = BrowseForFolderShell
If srchDir = False And Not TypeName(srchDir) = "String" Then
    Exit Sub
End If

Application.ScreenUpdating = False

Set ws = ThisWorkbook.Worksheets.Add(Sheets(1))
On Error Resume Next
Application.DisplayAlerts = False
ThisWorkbook.Worksheets("FileSearch Results").Delete
Application.DisplayAlerts = True
On Error GoTo 0
ws.Name = "FileSearch Results"

Let strName = Dir$(srchDir & "\*" & srchExt)
Do While strName <> vbNullString
    Let i = i + 1
    Let strFileFullName = srchDir & strName
    Let varArr(i, 1) = strFileFullName
    Let varArr(i, 2) = FileLen(strFileFullName) \ 1024
    Let varArr(i, 3) = FileDateTime(strFileFullName)
    Let strName = Dir$()
Loop

Set fso = CreateObject("Scripting.FileSystemObject")
Call recurseSubFolders(fso.GetFolder(srchDir), varArr(), i, CStr(srchExt))
Set fso = Nothing

ThisWorkbook.Windows(1).DisplayHeadings = False
With ws
    If i > 0 Then
        .Range("A2").Resize(i, UBound(varArr, 2)).Value = varArr
        For j = 1 To i
            .Hyperlinks.Add anchor:=.Cells(j + 1, 1), Address:=varArr(j, 1)
        Next
    End If
    .Range(.Cells(1, 4), .Cells(1, .Columns.Count)).EntireColumn.Hidden = True
    .Range(.Cells(.Rows.Count, 1).End(xlUp)(2), _
        .Cells(.Rows.Count, 1)).EntireRow.Hidden = True
    With .Range("A1:C1")
        .Value = Array("Full Name", "Kilobytes", "Last Modified")
        .Font.Underline = xlUnderlineStyleSingle
        .EntireColumn.AutoFit
        .HorizontalAlignment = xlCenter
    End With
```

```
    End With
    Application.ScreenUpdating = True
End Sub

Private Sub recurseSubFolders(ByRef Folder As Object, _
    ByRef varArr() As Variant, _
    ByRef i As Long, _
    ByRef srchExt As String)
Dim SubFolder As Object
Dim strName As String, strFileFullName As String
For Each SubFolder In Folder.SubFolders
    Let strName = Dir$(SubFolder.Path & "\*" & srchExt)
    Do While strName <> vbNullString
        Let i = i + 1
        Let strFileFullName = SubFolder.Path & "\" & strName
        Let varArr(i, 1) = strFileFullName
        Let varArr(i, 2) = FileLen(strFileFullName) \ 1024
        Let varArr(i, 3) = FileDateTime(strFileFullName)
        Let strName = Dir$()
    Loop
    If i > 1048576 Then Exit Sub
    Call recurseSubFolders(SubFolder, varArr(), i, srchExt)
Next
End Sub

Private Function BrowseForFolderShell() As Variant
Dim objShell As Object, objFolder As Object
Set objShell = CreateObject("Shell.Application")
Set objFolder = objShell.BrowseForFolder(0, "Please select a folder", 0, "C:\")
If Not objFolder Is Nothing Then
    On Error Resume Next
    If IsError(objFolder.Items.Item.Path) Then
        BrowseForFolderShell = CStr(objFolder)
    Else
        On Error GoTo 0
        If Len(objFolder.Items.Item.Path) > 3 Then
            BrowseForFolderShell = objFolder.Items.Item.Path & _
            Application.PathSeparator
        Else
            BrowseForFolderShell = objFolder.Items.Item.Path
        End If
    End If
Else
    BrowseForFolderShell = False
End If
Set objFolder = Nothing: Set objShell = Nothing
End Function
```

Import CSV

Submitted by Masaru Kaji of Kobe-City, Japan. Masaru provides Excel consultation through Colo's Excel Junk Room (www.puremis.net/excel/).

If you find yourself importing a lot of comma-separated variable (CSV) files and then having to go back and delete them, this program is for you. It quickly opens up a CSV in Excel and permanently deletes the original file:

```
Option Base 1

Sub OpenLargeCSVFast()
    Dim buf(1 To 16384) As Variant
    Dim i As Long
    'Change the file location and name here
    Const strFilePath As String = "C:\temp\Test.CSV"

    Dim strRenamedPath As String
    strRenamedPath = Split(strFilePath, ".")(0) & "txt"

    With Application
        .ScreenUpdating = False
        .DisplayAlerts = False
    End With
    'Setting an array for FieldInfo to open CSV
    For i = 1 To 16384
        buf(i) = Array(i, 2)
    Next
    Name strFilePath As strRenamedPath
    Workbooks.OpenText Filename:=strRenamedPath, DataType:=xlDelimited, _
                    Comma:=True, FieldInfo:=buf
    Erase buf
    ActiveSheet.UsedRange.Copy ThisWorkbook.Sheets(1).Range("A1")
    ActiveWorkbook.Close False
    Kill strRenamedPath
    With Application
        .ScreenUpdating = True
        .DisplayAlerts = True
    End With
End Sub
```

Read Entire CSV to Memory and Parse

Submitted by Suat Mehmet Ozgur of Istanbul, Turkey. Suat develops applications in Excel, Access, and Visual Basic for MrExcel.com and TheOfficeExperts.com.

This sample takes a different approach to reading a text file. Rather than read one record at a time, the macro loads the entire text file into memory in a single string variable. The macro then parses the string into individual records. The advantage of this method is that you access the file on disk only one time. All subsequent processing occurs in memory and is very fast:

```
Sub ReadTxtLines()
'No need to install Scripting Runtime library since we used late binding
Dim sht As Worksheet
Dim fso As Object
Dim fil As Object
Dim txt As Object
Dim strtxt As String
Dim tmpLoc As Long

    'Working on active sheet
    Set sht = ActiveSheet
```

```
    'Clear data in the sheet
    sht.UsedRange.ClearContents

    'File system object that we need to manage files
    Set fso = CreateObject("Scripting.FileSystemObject")

    'File that we like to open and read
    Set fil = fso.GetFile("c:\test.txt")

    'Opening file as a TextStream
    Set txt = fil.OpenAsTextStream(1)

    'Reading file include into a string variable at once
    strtxt = txt.ReadAll

    'Close textstream and free the file. We don't need it anymore.
    txt.Close

    'Find the first placement of new line char
    tmpLoc = InStr(1, strtxt, vbCrLf)

    'Loop until no more new line
    Do Until tmpLoc = 0
        'Use A column and next empty cell to write the text file line
        sht.Cells(sht.Rows.Count, 1).End(xlUp).Offset(1).Value = _
            Left(strtxt, tmpLoc - 1)

        'Remove the parsed line from the variable that we stored file include
        strtxt = Right(strtxt, Len(strtxt) - tmpLoc - 1)

        'Find the next placement of new line char
        tmpLoc = InStr(1, strtxt, vbCrLf)
    Loop

    'Last line that has data but no new line char
    sht.Cells(sht.Rows.Count, 1).End(xlUp).Offset(1).Value = strtxt

    'It will be already released by the ending of this procedure but
    ' as a good habit, set the object as nothing.
    Set fso = Nothing
End Sub
```

Combining and Separating Workbooks

The next four utilities demonstrate how to combine worksheets into single workbooks or separate a single workbook into individual worksheets or Word documents.

Separate Worksheets into Workbooks

Submitted by Tommy Miles of Houston, Texas.

This sample goes through the active workbook and saves each sheet as its own workbook in the same path as the original workbook. It names the new workbooks based on the sheet name. It will overwrite files without prompting. You'll also notice that you need to choose

14

whether you save the file as xlsm (macro-enabled) or xlsx (macros will be stripped). I've included both lines, xlsm or xlsx, in the following code but commented out the xlsx lines, making them inactive:

```
Sub SplitWorkbook()

Dim ws As Worksheet
Dim DisplayStatusBar As Boolean

DisplayStatusBar = Application.DisplayStatusBar
Application.DisplayStatusBar = True
Application.ScreenUpdating = False
Application.DisplayAlerts = False

For Each ws In ThisWorkbook.Sheets
    Dim NewFileName As String
    Application.StatusBar = ThisWorkbook.Sheets.Count & " Remaining Sheets"
    If ThisWorkbook.Sheets.Count <> 1 Then
        NewFileName = ThisWorkbook.Path & "\" & ws.Name & ".xlsm" 'Macro-Enabled
'        NewFileName = ThisWorkbook.Path & "\" & ws.Name & ".xlsx" _
    'Not Macro-Enabled
        ws.Copy
        ActiveWorkbook.Sheets(1).Name = "Sheet1"
        ActiveWorkbook.SaveAs Filename:=NewFileName, _
            FileFormat:=xlOpenXMLWorkbookMacroEnabled
'        ActiveWorkbook.SaveAs Filename:=NewFileName, _
            FileFormat:=xlOpenXMLWorkbook
        ActiveWorkbook.Close SaveChanges:=False
    Else
        NewFileName = ThisWorkbook.Path & "\" & ws.Name & ".xlsm"
'        NewFileName = ThisWorkbook.Path & "\" & ws.Name & ".xlsx"
        ws.Name = "Sheet1"
    End If
Next

Application.DisplayAlerts = True
Application.StatusBar = False
Application.DisplayStatusBar = DisplayStatusBar
Application.ScreenUpdating = True
End Sub
```

Combine Workbooks

Submitted by Tommy Miles.

This sample goes through all the Excel files in a specified directory and combines them into a single workbook. It renames the sheets based on the name of the original workbook:

```
Sub CombineWorkbooks()
    Dim CurFile As String, DirLoc As String
    Dim DestWB As Workbook
    Dim ws As Object 'allows for different sheet types
```

```
    DirLoc = ThisWorkbook.Path & "\tst\" 'location of files
    CurFile = Dir(DirLoc & "*.xls")

    Application.ScreenUpdating = False
    Application.EnableEvents = False

    Set DestWB = Workbooks.Add(xlWorksheet)

    Do While CurFile <> vbNullString
        Dim OrigWB As Workbook
        Set OrigWB = Workbooks.Open(Filename:=DirLoc & CurFile, ReadOnly:=True)

        ' Limit to valid sheet names and remove .xls*
        CurFile = Left(Left(CurFile, Len(CurFile) - 5), 29)

        For Each ws In OrigWB.Sheets
            ws.Copy After:=DestWB.Sheets(DestWB.Sheets.Count)

            If OrigWB.Sheets.Count > 1 Then
                DestWB.Sheets(DestWB.Sheets.Count).Name = CurFile & ws.Index
            Else
                DestWB.Sheets(DestWB.Sheets.Count).Name = CurFile
            End If
        Next

        OrigWB.Close SaveChanges:=False
        CurFile = Dir
    Loop

    Application.DisplayAlerts = False
        DestWB.Sheets(1).Delete
    Application.DisplayAlerts = True

    Application.ScreenUpdating = True
    Application.EnableEvents = True

    Set DestWB = Nothing
End Sub
```

Filter and Copy Data to Separate Worksheets

Submitted by Dennis Wallentin of Ostersund, Sweden. Dennis provides Excel tips and tricks at www.xldennis.com.

This sample uses a specified column to filter data and copies the results to new worksheets in the active workbook.

14

```
Sub Filter_NewSheet()
Dim wbBook As Workbook
Dim wsSheet As Worksheet
Dim rnStart As Range, rnData As Range
Dim i As Long

Set wbBook = ThisWorkbook
Set wsSheet = wbBook.Worksheets("Sheet1")

With wsSheet
    'Make sure that the first row contains headings.
    Set rnStart = .Range("A2")
    Set rnData = .Range(.Range("A2"), .Cells(.Rows.Count, 3).End(xlUp))
End With

Application.ScreenUpdating = True

For i = 1 To 5
    'Here we filter the data with the first criterion.
    rnStart.AutoFilter Field:=1, Criteria1:="AA" & i
    'Copy the filtered list
    rnData.SpecialCells(xlCellTypeVisible).Copy
    'Add a new worksheet to the active workbook.
    Worksheets.Add Before:=wsSheet
    'Name the added new worksheets.
    ActiveSheet.Name = "AA" & i
    'Paste the filtered list.
    Range("A2").PasteSpecial xlPasteValues
Next i

'Reset the list to its original status.
rnStart.AutoFilter Field:=1

With Application
    'Reset the clipboard.
    .CutCopyMode = False
    .ScreenUpdating = False
End With

End Sub
```

Export Data to Word

Submitted by Dennis Wallentin.

This program transfers data from Excel to the first table found in a Word document. It uses early binding, so a reference must be established in the VB Editor (using Tools, References) to the Microsoft Word Object Library:

```
Sub Export_Data_Word_Table()
Dim wdApp As Word.Application
Dim wdDoc As Word.Document
Dim wdCell As Word.Cell
Dim i As Long
Dim wbBook As Workbook
Dim wsSheet As Worksheet
```

```
Dim rnData As Range
Dim vaData As Variant

Set wbBook = ThisWorkbook
Set wsSheet = wbBook.Worksheets("Sheet1")

With wsSheet
    Set rnData = .Range("A1:A10")
End With

'Add the values in the range to a one-dimensional variant-array.
vaData = rnData.Value

'Here we instantiate the new object.
Set wdApp = New Word.Application
'Here the target document resides in the same folder as the workbook.
Set wdDoc = wdApp.Documents.Open(ThisWorkbook.Path & "\Test.docx")

'Import data to the first table and in the first column of a ten-row table.
For Each wdCell In wdDoc.Tables(1).Columns(1).Cells
    i = i + 1
    wdCell.Range.Text = vaData(i, 1)
Next wdCell

'Save and close the document.
With wdDoc
    .Save
    .Close
End With

'Close the hidden instance of Microsoft Word.
wdApp.Quit
'Release the external variables from the memory
Set wdDoc = Nothing
Set wdApp = Nothing

MsgBox "The data has been transfered to Test.docx.", vbInformation

End Sub
```

Working with Cell Comments

Cell comments are often underused features of Excel. The following four utilities help you to get the most out of cell comments.

List Comments

Submitted by Tommy Miles.

Excel allows the user to print the comments in a workbook, but it doesn't specify the workbook or worksheet on which the comments appear, only the cell, as shown in Figure 14.1. The following sample places comments, author, and location of each comment on a new sheet for easy viewing, saving, or printing. Figure 14.2 shows sample results.

Figure 14.1
Excel prints only the
origin cell address and
its comment.

```
        Cell: C5
Comment: Bill Jelen:
              Does not include the special sale.

        Cell: D14
Comment: Bill Jelen:
              Thanks for downloading our project files.

        Cell: A27
Comment: Bill Jelen:
              Visit MrExcel.com for over 70,000 articles on Microsoft Excel.
```

Figure 14.2
Easily list all the information pertaining to
comments.

	A	B	C	D	E	F	G	H	I	J
1	Author	Book	Sheet	Range	Comment					
2	Bill Jelen	ProjectFilesChapter14.xlsm	ListComments	$C$5	Does not include the special sale.					
3	Bill Jelen	ProjectFilesChapter14.xlsm	ListComments	$D$14	Thanks for downloading our project files.					
4	Bill Jelen	ProjectFilesChapter14.xlsm	ListComments	$A$27	Visit MrExcel.com for over 70,000 articles on Microsoft Excel.					

```
Sub ListComments()
    Dim wb As Workbook
    Dim ws As Worksheet

    Dim cmt As Comment

    Dim cmtCount As Long

    cmtCount = 2

    On Error Resume Next
        Set ws = ActiveSheet
            If ws Is Nothing Then Exit Sub
    On Error GoTo 0

    Application.ScreenUpdating = False

    Set wb = Workbooks.Add(xlWorksheet)

    With wb.Sheets(1)
        .Range("$A$1") = "Author"
        .Range("$B$1") = "Book"
        .Range("$C$1") = "Sheet"
        .Range("$D$1") = "Range"
        .Range("$E$1") = "Comment"
    End With

    For Each cmt In ws.Comments
        With wb.Sheets(1)
            .Cells(cmtCount, 1) = cmt.author
            .Cells(cmtCount, 2) = cmt.Parent.Parent.Parent.Name
            .Cells(cmtCount, 3) = cmt.Parent.Parent.Name
            .Cells(cmtCount, 4) = cmt.Parent.Address
            .Cells(cmtCount, 5) = CleanComment(cmt.author, cmt.Text)
        End With
```

```
            cmtCount = cmtCount + 1
        Next

        wb.Sheets(1).UsedRange.WrapText = False

        Application.ScreenUpdating = True

        Set ws = Nothing
        Set wb = Nothing
End Sub

Private Function CleanComment(author As String, cmt As String) As String
    Dim tmp As String

    tmp = Application.WorksheetFunction.Substitute(cmt, author & ":", "")
    tmp = Application.WorksheetFunction.Substitute(tmp, Chr(10), "")

    CleanComment = tmp
End Function
```

Resize Comments

Submitted by Tom Urtis of San Francisco, California. Tom is the principal owner of Atlas Programming Management, an Excel consulting firm in the Bay Area.

Excel doesn't automatically resize cell comments. And if you have several on a sheet, as shown in Figure 14.3, it can be a hassle to resize them one at a time. The following sample code resizes all the comment boxes on a sheet so that, when selected, the entire comment is easily viewable, as shown in Figure 14.4.

Figure 14.3
By default, Excel doesn't size the comment boxes to show all the entered text.

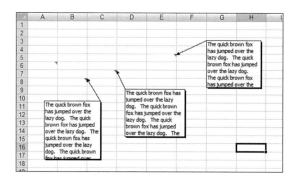

Figure 14.4
Resize the comment
boxes to fit all the text.

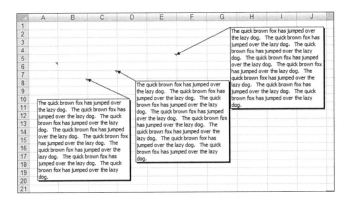

```
Sub CommentFitter1()
Application.ScreenUpdating = False
Dim x As Range, y As Long

For Each x In Cells.SpecialCells(xlCellTypeComments)
    Select Case True
        Case Len(x.NoteText) <> 0
            With x.Comment
                .Shape.TextFrame.AutoSize = True
                If .Shape.Width > 250 Then
                    y = .Shape.Width * .Shape.Height
                    .Shape.Width = 150
                    .Shape.Height = (y / 200) * 1.3
                End If
            End With
    End Select
Next x
Application.ScreenUpdating = True
End Sub
```

Resize Comments with Centering

Submitted by Tom Urtis.

This sample resizes all the comment boxes on a sheet by centering the comments (see
Figure 14.5).

The comment box, resized and centered

Figure 14.5
Center all the comments
on a sheet.

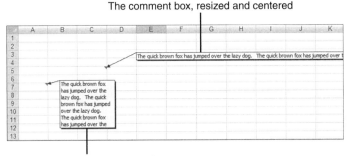

The default formatted comment box

```
Sub CommentFitter2()
Application.ScreenUpdating = False
Dim x As Range, y As Long

For Each x In Cells.SpecialCells(xlCellTypeComments)
    Select Case True
        Case Len(x.NoteText) <> 0
            With x.Comment
                .Shape.TextFrame.AutoSize = True
                If .Shape.Width > 250 Then
                    y = .Shape.Width * .Shape.Height
                    .Shape.ScaleHeight 0.9, msoFalse, msoScaleFromTopLeft
                    .Shape.ScaleWidth 1#, msoFalse, msoScaleFromTopLeft
                End If
            End With
    End Select
Next x
Application.ScreenUpdating = True
End Sub
```

Place a Chart in a Comment

Submitted by Tom Urtis.

A live chart cannot exist in a shape, but you can take a picture of the chart and load it into the comment shape, as shown in Figure 14.6.

Figure 14.6
Place a chart in a cell comment.

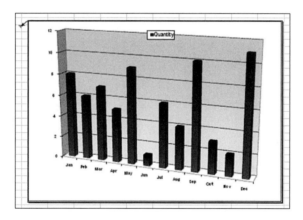

The steps to do this manually are as follows:

1. Create/save the picture image you want the comment to display.

2. Create the comment, if you have not already done so, and select the cell in which the comment is.

3. From the Review ribbon, choose Edit Comment, or right-click the cell and select Edit Comment.

4. Right-click the comment border and select Format Comment.

14

5. Select the Colors and Lines tab, and click the down arrow belonging to the Color field of the Fill section.

6. Select Fill Effects, select the Picture tab, and then click the Select Picture button.

7. Navigate to your desired image, select it, and click OK twice.

The effect of having a "live chart" in a comment can be achieved if, for example, the code is part of a SheetChange event when the chart's source data is being changed. Also, business charts are updated often, so you might want a macro to keep the comment updated and to avoid repeating the same steps. The following macro does just that: modifies the macro for file path name, chart name, destination sheet, and cell, and size of comment shape, depending on the size of the chart:

```
Sub PlaceGraph()
Dim x As String, z As Range

Application.ScreenUpdating = False

'assign a temporary location to hold the image
x = "C:\XWMJGraph.gif"

'assign the cell to hold the comment
Set z = Worksheets("ChartInComment").Range("A3")

'delete any existing comment in the cell
On Error Resume Next
z.Comment.Delete
On Error GoTo 0

'select and export the chart
ActiveSheet.ChartObjects("Chart 1").Activate
ActiveChart.Export x

'add a new comment to the cell, set the size and insert the chart
With z.AddComment
    With .Shape
        .Height = 322
        .Width = 465
        .Fill.UserPicture x
    End With
End With

'delete the temporary image
Kill x

Range("A1").Activate
Application.ScreenUpdating = True

Set z = Nothing
End Sub
```

14

Utilities to Wow Your Clients

The next four utilities will amaze and impress your clients.

Using Conditional Formatting to Highlight Selected Cell

Submitted by Ivan F. Moala of Auckland, New Zealand. Ivan is the site author of The XcelFiles (www.xcelfiles.com), where you will find out how to do things you thought you couldn't do in Excel.

Conditional formatting is used to highlight the row and column of the active cell to help you visually locate it, as shown in Figure 14.7. Important: Do *not* use this method if you already have conditional formats on the worksheet. Any existing conditional formats will be overwritten. Also, this program clears the clipboard, so it is not possible to use while doing copy, cut, or paste.

Figure 14.7
Use conditional formatting to highlight the selected cell in a table.

	A	B	C	D	
4	Tom	East	Q2	Jackets	Blac
5	Mike	West	Q2	Jackets	Yell
6	Jim	South	Q3	Hats	Yell
7	Nancy	North	Q3	Hats	Blac
8	Zelda	East	Q4	Hats	Blue
9	William	West	Q4	Shoes	Red
10	Mary	South	Q4	Shoes	Red
11	Bill	North	Q1	Shoes	Blue
12	Bob	East	Q1	Hats	Blac
13	Tom	West	Q2	Shoes	Yell
14	Mike	South	Q2	Shoes	Yell
15	Jim	North	Q3	Shoes	Blac
16	Nancy	East	Q3	Jackets	Blue
17	Zelda	West	Q4	Jackets	Red
18	William	South	Q4	Jackets	Red
19	Mary	North	Q4	Jackets	Blue
20	Bill	East	Q1	Hats	Blac
21	Bob	West	Q1	Hats	Yell
22	Tom	South	Q2	Hats	Yell
23	Mike	North	Q2	Shoes	Blac

```
Const iInternational As Integer = Not (0)

Private Sub Worksheet_SelectionChange(ByVal Target As Range)
Dim iColor As Integer
'// On error resume in case
'// user selects a range of cells
On Error Resume Next
iColor = Target.Interior.ColorIndex
'// Leave On Error ON for Row offset errors

If iColor < 0 Then
    iColor = 36
Else
    iColor = iColor + 1
End If

'// Need this test in case font color is the same
If iColor = Target.Font.ColorIndex Then iColor = iColor + 1
```

```
Cells.FormatConditions.Delete

'// Horizontal color banding
With Range("A" & Target.Row, Target.Address) 'Rows(Target.Row)
    .FormatConditions.Add Type:=2, Formula1:=iInternational 'Or just 1 '"TRUE"
    .FormatConditions(1).Interior.ColorIndex = iColor
End With

'// Vertical color banding
With Range(Target.Offset(1 - Target.Row, 0).Address & ":" & _
    Target.Offset(-1, 0).Address)
    .FormatConditions.Add Type:=2, Formula1:=iInternational 'Or just 1 '"TRUE"
    .FormatConditions(1).Interior.ColorIndex = iColor
End With

End Sub
```

Highlight Selected Cell Without Using Conditional Formatting

Submitted by Ivan F. Moala.

This example visually highlights the active cell without using conditional formatting when the keyboard arrow keys are used to move around the sheet.

Place the following in a standard module:

```
Dim strCol As String
Dim iCol As Integer
Dim dblRow As Double

Sub HighlightRight()
    HighLight 0, 1
End Sub

Sub HighlightLeft()
    HighLight 0, -1
End Sub

Sub HighlightUp()
    HighLight -1, 0, -1
End Sub

Sub HighlightDown()
    HighLight 1, 0, 1
End Sub

Sub HighLight(dblxRow As Double, iyCol As Integer, Optional dblZ As Double = 0)

On Error GoTo NoGo
strCol = Mid(ActiveCell.Offset(dblxRow, iyCol).Address, _
        InStr(ActiveCell.Offset(dblxRow, iyCol).Address, "$") + 1, _
        InStr(2, ActiveCell.Offset(dblxRow, iyCol).Address, "$") - 2)
iCol = ActiveCell.Column
dblRow = ActiveCell.Row

Application.ScreenUpdating = False

With Range(strCol & ":" & strCol & "," & dblRow + dblZ & ":" & dblRow + dblZ)
```

14

```
        .Select
        Application.ScreenUpdating = True
        .Item(dblRow + dblxRow).Activate
    End With

NoGo:
End Sub

Sub ReSet() 'manual reset
    Application.OnKey "{RIGHT}"
    Application.OnKey "{LEFT}"
    Application.OnKey "{UP}"
    Application.OnKey "{DOWN}"
End Sub
```

Place the following in the ThisWorkbook module:

```
Private Sub Workbook_Open()
    Application.OnKey "{RIGHT}", "HighlightRight"
    Application.OnKey "{LEFT}", "HighlightLeft"
    Application.OnKey "{UP}", "HighlightUp"
    Application.OnKey "{DOWN}", "HighlightDown"
    Application.OnKey "{DEL}", "DisableDelete"
End Sub

Private Sub Workbook_BeforeClose(Cancel As Boolean)
    Application.OnKey "{RIGHT}"
    Application.OnKey "{LEFT}"
    Application.OnKey "{UP}"
    Application.OnKey "{DOWN}"
    Application.OnKey "{DEL}"
End Sub
```

Custom Transpose Data

Submitted by Masaru Kaji.

You have a report where the data is set up in rows (see Figure 14.8), but you need the data formatted so each date and batch is in a single row, with the Value and Finish Position going across (Finish Position not shown in Figure 14.9). The following program does a customized data transposition based on the specified column, as shown in Figure 14.9.

Figure 14.8
The original data has similar records in separate rows.

	A	B	C	D	E
1	ItemName	ItemDate	Batch#	FinishPosition	Value
2	Thermal	10/23/2002	1	8	2.15
3	Thermal	10/23/2002	1	3	3.2
4	Thermal	10/23/2002	1	2	4.9
5	Thermal	10/23/2002	1	1	6.1
6	Thermal	10/23/2002	1	7	6.2
7	Thermal	10/23/2002	1	4	12.9
8	Thermal	10/23/2002	1	9	23
9	Thermal	10/23/2002	1	5	36
10	Thermal	10/23/2002	1	6	36.25
11	Thermal	10/23/2002	2	2	1.05
12	Thermal	10/23/2002	2	1	2.5
13	Thermal	10/23/2002	2	8	7.3
14	Thermal	10/23/2002	2	3	10.9
15	Thermal	10/23/2002	2	4	12.1
16	Thermal	10/23/2002	2	9	21.7
17	Thermal	10/23/2002	2	6	33.25

14

Figure 14.9
The formatted data transposes the data so identical dates and batches are merged into a single row.

	ItemName	ItemDate	Batch#	V1	V2	V3	V4	V5	V6	V7	V8	V9	V10	V11	V12	
1	ItemName	ItemDate	Batch#	V1	V2	V3	V4	V5	V6	V7	V8	V9	V10	V11	V12	
2	Thermal	10/23/2002	1	2.15	3.2	4.9	6.1	6.2	12.9	23	36	36.25				
3	Thermal	10/23/2002	2	1.05	2.5	7.3	10.9	12.1	21.7	33.25	43	43.25				
4	Thermal	10/23/2002	3	1.65	3.1	3.1	3.75	7.1	7.1	7.7	18.7	34	55.5			
5	Thermal	10/23/2002	4	1.1	2.75	4	9.5	14.3	25	37.75						
6	Thermal	10/23/2002	5	0.9	3.75	7.1	9	16	18.1	19.5	22.5	74.75				
7	Thermal	10/23/2002	6	1.6	3.4	5.2	7.8	8.2	9.4	11.5						
8	Thermal	10/23/2002	7	0.8	4.2	4.9	9.6	15	21.2	24.75	63.25					
9	Thermal	10/23/2002	8	0.7	6.2	8.4	10.3	10.6	12.3	28.75	31.75	52	76.75			
10	Thermal	10/23/2002	9	2.9	3.9	4.4	5.9	7	11.4	13.5	18.4	26.25	66.25			
11	Thermal	10/24/2002	1	1.4	3.85	6.2	8.1	10	12.3	17.2	27.5	37.5	55.5			
12	Thermal	10/24/2002	2	1.75	2.95	6	6.5	7.8	8.3	16.8						
13	Thermal	10/24/2002	3	1.15	5.4	8.7	9.9	10.9	11.8	13.3	17.1	24	37			
14	Thermal	10/24/2002	4	1.05	1.9	5.2	6.8	19.9								
15	Thermal	10/24/2002	5	2.5	3.15	3.15	4.2	6	12.2	12.3	19.9	23.2	25.25	42.25	150	
16	Thermal	10/24/2002	6	2.4	2.95	4.4	6.5	8.7	14.2	22.9	22.9	25.75	51	58.25	59.5	
17	Thermal	10/24/2002	7	1.2	3.35	6.3	9.5	11.3	12	14.4	36.25					
18	Thermal	10/24/2002	8	0.85	5	6.5	6.8	11.1	11.4	22.6						
19	Thermal	10/24/2002	9	2	3.3	4.5	6.8	8.6	9.7	20.5	30	58.5				
20	Thermal	10/25/2002	1	2.05	2.65	3.95	4.8	4.8	15.5	21	30	31.5	64.75	107.25		
21	Thermal	10/25/2002	2	1.25	2.25	7.5	9.1	9.1	12.3	27.25						
22	Thermal	10/25/2002	3	1	1	3.6	7.5	7.5	11.5	12.1	14.8	15.4	17.7			

```
Sub TransposeData()
Dim shOrg As Worksheet, shRes As Worksheet
Dim rngStart As Range, rngPaste As Range
Dim lngData As Long

Application.ScreenUpdating = False
On Error Resume Next
Application.DisplayAlerts = False
Sheets("TransposeResult").Delete
Application.DisplayAlerts = True
On Error GoTo 0

On Error GoTo terminate

Set shOrg = Sheets("TransposeData")
Set shRes = Sheets.Add(After:=shOrg)
shRes.Name = "TransposeResult"
With shOrg
    '--Sort
    .Cells.CurrentRegion.Sort Key1:=.[B2], Order1:=1, Key2:=.[C2], Order2:=1, _
        Key3:=.[E2], Order3:=1, Header:=xlYes
    '--Copy title
    .Rows(1).Copy shRes.Rows(1)
    '--Set start range
    Set rngStart = .[C2]
    Do Until IsEmpty(rngStart)
        Set rngPaste = shRes.Cells(shRes.Rows.Count, 1).End(xlUp).Offset(1)
        lngData = GetNextRange(rngStart)
        rngStart.Offset(, -2).Resize(, 5).Copy rngPaste

        'Copy to V1 toV14
        rngStart.Offset(, 2).Resize(lngData).Copy
        rngPaste.Offset(, 5).PasteSpecial Paste:=xlAll, Operation:=xlNone, _
         SkipBlanks:=False, Transpose:=True
        'Copy to V1FP to V14FP
        rngStart.Offset(, 1).Resize(lngData).Copy
        rngPaste.Offset(, 19).PasteSpecial Paste:=xlAll, Operation:=xlNone, _
         SkipBlanks:=False, Transpose:=True
        Set rngStart = rngStart.Offset(lngData)
```

```
      Loop
End With

Application.Goto shRes.[A1]
With shRes
    .Cells.Columns.AutoFit
    .Columns("D:E").Delete shift:=xlToLeft
End With

Application.ScreenUpdating = True
Application.CutCopyMode = False

If MsgBox("Do you want to delete the original worksheet?", 36) = 6 Then
    Application.DisplayAlerts = False
    Sheets("TransposeData").Delete
    Application.DisplayAlerts = True
End If

Set rngPaste = Nothing
Set rngStart = Nothing
Set shRes = Nothing

Exit Sub

terminate:
End Sub

Function GetNextRange(ByVal rngSt As Range) As Long
    Dim i As Long
    i = 0

    Do Until rngSt.Value <> rngSt.Offset(i).Value
        i = i + 1
    Loop

    GetNextRange = i
End Function
```

Select/Deselect Noncontiguous Cells

Submitted by Tom Urtis.

Ordinarily, to deselect a single cell or range on a sheet, you must click an unselected cell to deselect all cells and then start over by reselecting all the correct cells. This is inconvenient if you need to reselect a lot of noncontiguous cells.

This sample adds two new options to the contextual menu of a selection: Deselect ActiveCell and Deselect ActiveArea. With the noncontiguous cells selected, hold down the Ctrl key, click the cell you want to deselect to make it active, release the Ctrl key, and then right-click the cell you want to deselect. The contextual menu shown in Figure 14.10 appears. Click the menu item that deselects either that one active cell or the contiguously selected area of which it is a part of.

14

Figure 14.10
The
`ModifyRightClick`
procedure provides a
custom contextual menu
for deselecting non-
contiguous cells.

Enter the following procedures in a standard module:

```
Sub ModifyRightClick()
'add the new options to the right-click menu
Dim O1 As Object, O2 As Object

'delete the options if they exist already
On Error Resume Next
With CommandBars("Cell")
    .Controls("Deselect ActiveCell").Delete
    .Controls("Deselect ActiveArea").Delete
End With
On Error GoTo 0

'add the new options
Set O1 = CommandBars("Cell").Controls.Add

With O1
    .Caption = "Deselect ActiveCell"
    .OnAction = "DeselectActiveCell"
End With

Set O2 = CommandBars("Cell").Controls.Add

With O2
    .Caption = "Deselect ActiveArea"
    .OnAction = "DeselectActiveArea"
End With

End Sub

Sub DeselectActiveCell()
Dim x As Range, y As Range

If Selection.Cells.Count > 1 Then
    For Each y In Selection.Cells
        If y.Address <> ActiveCell.Address Then
```

```
            If x Is Nothing Then
                Set x = y
            Else
                Set x = Application.Union(x, y)
            End If
        End If
    Next y
    If x.Cells.Count > 0 Then
        x.Select
    End If
End If

End Sub

Sub DeselectActiveArea()
Dim x As Range, y As Range

If Selection.Areas.Count > 1 Then
    For Each y In Selection.Areas
        If Application.Intersect(ActiveCell, y) Is Nothing Then
            If x Is Nothing Then
                Set x = y
            Else
                Set x = Application.Union(x, y)
            End If
        End If
    Next y
    x.Select
End If
End Sub
```

Add the following procedures to the ThisWorkbook module:

```
Private Sub Workbook_Activate()
ModifyRightClick
End Sub

Private Sub Workbook_Deactivate()
Application.CommandBars("Cell").Reset
End Sub
```

Techniques for VBA Pros

The next ten utilities amaze me. In the various message board communities on the Internet, VBA programmers are constantly coming up with new ways to do something faster or better. When someone posts some new code that obviously runs circles around the prior generally accepted best code, everyone benefits.

Pivot Table Drill-Down

Submitted by Tom Urtis.

A pivot table's default behavior, when you're double-clicking the data section, is to insert a new worksheet and display that drill-down information on the new sheet. The following example serves as an option for convenience, to keep the drilled-down recordsets on the same sheet as the pivot table (see Figure 14.11), and letting you delete them as you want. To use this macro, double-click the data section or the Totals section to create stacked drill-down recordsets in the next available row of this sheet. To delete any drill-down recordsets you've created, double-click anywhere in their respective current region.

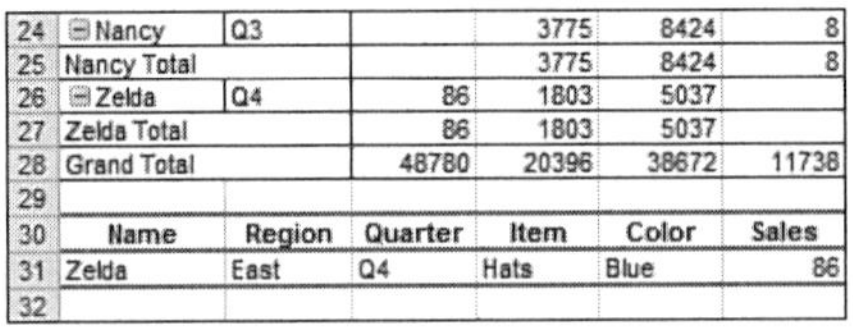

Figure 14.11
Show the drill-down recordset on the same sheet as the pivot table.

24	⊟ Nancy	Q3		3775	8424	8
25	Nancy Total			3775	8424	8
26	⊟ Zelda	Q4	86	1803	5037	
27	Zelda Total		86	1803	5037	
28	Grand Total		48780	20396	38672	11738
29						
30	**Name**	**Region**	**Quarter**	**Item**	**Color**	**Sales**
31	Zelda	East	Q4	Hats	Blue	86
32						

```
Private Sub Worksheet_BeforeDoubleClick(ByVal Target As Range, Cancel As Boolean)
Application.ScreenUpdating = False
Dim LPTR&

With ActiveSheet.PivotTables(1).DataBodyRange
    LPTR = .Rows.Count + .Row - 1
End With

Dim PTT As Integer
On Error Resume Next
PTT = Target.PivotCell.PivotCellType
If Err.Number = 1004 Then
    Err.Clear
    If Not IsEmpty(Target) Then
        If Target.Row > Range("A1").CurrentRegion.Rows.Count + 1 Then
            Cancel = True
            With Target.CurrentRegion
                .Resize(.Rows.Count + 1).EntireRow.Delete
            End With
        End If
    Else
        Cancel = True
    End If
Else
    CS = ActiveSheet.Name
End If
Application.ScreenUpdating = True
End Sub
```

Speedy Page Setup

Submitted by Juan Pablo González Ruiz of Bogotá, Colombia. Juan Pablo is the developer of the F&I Menu Wizard and handles all Spanish programming requests at MrExcel.com.

The following examples compare the runtimes of variations on changing the margins from the defaults to 1.5 inches and the footer/header to 1 inch in the Page Setup. The macro recorder was used to create Macro1. Macros 2, 3, and 4 show how the recorded code's runtime can be decreased. Figure 14.12 shows the results of the speed test running each variation.

Figure 14.12
Page setup speed tests.

	A	B	C	D
1	**Macro1**	**Macro2**	**Macro3**	**Macro4**
2	0.4305	0.1048	0.1045	0.0185
3	0.4044	0.1048	0.1057	0.0175
4	0.4017	0.1047	0.1047	0.0175
5	0.4012	0.1047	0.1045	0.0174
6	0.4012	0.1046	0.1047	0.0175
7	0.4026	0.1047	0.1046	0.0174
8	0.4021	0.1047	0.1045	0.0175
9	0.4017	0.1045	0.1050	0.0175
10	0.4007	0.1047	0.1044	0.0175
11	0.4007	0.1044	0.1044	0.0175
12	0.4009	0.1046	0.1046	0.0175
13	0.4009	0.1046	0.1044	0.0174
14	0.4019	0.1044	0.1046	0.0174
15	0.4013	0.1052	0.1048	0.0175
16	0.4009	0.1051	0.1044	0.0175
17	0.3992	0.1045	0.1045	0.0174
18	0.3791	0.1047	0.1046	0.0174
19	0.3845	0.1048	0.1044	0.0174
20	0.4011	0.1047	0.1046	0.0176
21	0.4018	0.1045	0.1044	0.0181
22	**40%**	**10%**	**10%**	**2%**
23	**4**	**3**	**2**	**1**

```
Sub Macro1()
'
' Macro1 Macro
' Macro recorded 3/28/2007
'
    With ActiveSheet.PageSetup
        .PrintTitleRows = ""
        .PrintTitleColumns = ""
    End With
    ActiveSheet.PageSetup.PrintArea = ""
    With ActiveSheet.PageSetup
        .LeftHeader = ""
        .CenterHeader = ""
        .RightHeader = ""
        .LeftFooter = ""
        .CenterFooter = ""
        .RightFooter = ""
        .LeftMargin = Application.InchesToPoints(1)
        .RightMargin = Application.InchesToPoints(1)
        .TopMargin = Application.InchesToPoints(1)
        .BottomMargin = Application.InchesToPoints(1)
        .HeaderMargin = Application.InchesToPoints(1)
        .FooterMargin = Application.InchesToPoints(1)
        .PrintHeadings = False
        .PrintGridlines = False
        .PrintComments = xlPrintNoComments
        .PrintQuality = -3
        .CenterHorizontally = False
        .CenterVertically = False
        .Orientation = xlPortrait
        .Draft = False
        .PaperSize = xlPaperLetter
        .FirstPageNumber = 1
        .Order = xlDownThenOver
        .BlackAndWhite = False
        .Zoom = False
        .FitToPagesWide = 1
```

14

```
            .FitToPagesTall = 1
            .PrintErrors = xlPrintErrorsDisplayed
            .OddAndEvenPagesHeaderFooter = False
            .DifferentFirstPageHeaderFooter = False
            .ScaleWithDocHeaderFooter = True
            .AlignMarginsHeaderFooter = False
            .EvenPage.LeftHeader.Text = ""
            .EvenPage.CenterHeader.Text = ""
            .EvenPage.RightHeader.Text = ""
            .EvenPage.LeftFooter.Text = ""
            .EvenPage.CenterFooter.Text = ""
            .EvenPage.RightFooter.Text = ""
            .FirstPage.LeftHeader.Text = ""
            .FirstPage.CenterHeader.Text = ""
            .FirstPage.RightHeader.Text = ""
            .FirstPage.LeftFooter.Text = ""
            .FirstPage.CenterFooter.Text = ""
            .FirstPage.RightFooter.Text = ""
        End With
End Sub
```

The macro recorder is doing a lot of extra work, which requires extra processing time. Considering that, plus the fact that the `PageSetup` object is one of the slowest objects to update, and you can have quite a mess. So, a cleaner version (that uses just the Delete key!) follows:

```
Sub Macro1_Version2()
    With ActiveSheet.PageSetup
        .LeftMargin = Application.InchesToPoints(1.5)
        .RightMargin = Application.InchesToPoints(1.5)
        .TopMargin = Application.InchesToPoints(1.5)
        .BottomMargin = Application.InchesToPoints(1.5)
        .HeaderMargin = Application.InchesToPoints(1)
        .FooterMargin = Application.InchesToPoints(1)
    End With
End Sub
```

Okay, this runs faster than Macro1 (the average reduction is around 70 percent on some simple tests!), but it can be improved even further. As noted earlier, the `PageSetup` object takes a long time to process, so if you reduce the number of operations that VBA has to make *and* include some `IF` functions to update only the properties that require changing, you can get much better results.

In the following case, the `Application.InchesToPoints` function was hard-coded to the `inches` value. The third version of Macro1 looks like this:

```
Sub Macro1_Version3()
    With ActiveSheet.PageSetup
        If .LeftMargin <> 108 Then .LeftMargin = 108
        If .RightMargin <> 108 Then .RightMargin = 108
        If .TopMargin <> 108 Then .TopMargin = 108
        If .BottomMargin <> 108 Then .BottomMargin = 108
        If .HeaderMargin <> 72 Then .HeaderMargin = 72
        If .FooterMargin <> 72 Then .FooterMargin = 72
    End With
End Sub
```

You should see the difference on this one when you're not changing all the default margins.

Another option can reduce the runtime by more than 95 percent! It uses the PAGE.SETUP XLM method. The necessary parameters are left, right, top, bot, head_margin, and foot_margin. They are measured in inches, not points. So, using the same margins that we have been changing already, a fourth version of Macro1 looks like this:

```
Sub Macro1_Version4()
    Dim St As String
    St = "PAGE.SETUP(, , " & _
                "1.5, 1.5, 1.5, 1.5" & _
                ", 0, False, False, False, 1, 1, True, 1, 1,False, , " & _
                "1, 1" & _
                ", False)"
    Application.ExecuteExcel4Macro St
End Sub
```

The second and fourth lines of St correspond to these parameters. However, you need to follow some simple precautions. First, this macro relies on XLM language, which is still included in Excel for backward compatibility, but we don't know when Microsoft will drop it. Second, be careful when setting the parameters of PAGE.SETUP because if one of them is wrong, the PAGE.SETUP is not executed and doesn't generate an error, which can possibly leave you with the wrong page setup.

Calculating Time to Execute Code

You may wonder how to calculate elapsed time down to the thousandth of a second, as shown earlier in Figure 14.12.

This is the code used to generate the time results for the macros in this section:

```
Public Declare Function QueryPerformanceFrequency _
    Lib "kernel32" (lpFrequency As Currency) As Long
Public Declare Function QueryPerformanceCounter _
    Lib "kernel32.dll" (lpPerformanceCount As Currency) As Long

Sub CalculateTime()
    Dim Ar(1 To 20, 1 To 4) As Currency, WS As Worksheet
    Dim n As Currency, str As Currency, fin As Currency
    Dim y As Currency

    Dim i As Long, j As Long

    Application.ScreenUpdating = False
    For i = 1 To 4
        For j = 1 To 20
            Set WS = ThisWorkbook.Sheets.Add
            WS.Range("A1").Value = 1
            QueryPerformanceFrequency y
            QueryPerformanceCounter str
            Select Case i
            Case 1: Macro1
            Case 2: Macro1_Version2
            Case 3: Macro1_Version3
            Case 4: Macro1_Version4
```

```
            End Select
            QueryPerformanceCounter fin
            Application.DisplayAlerts = False
            WS.Delete
            Application.DisplayAlerts = True
            n = (fin - str)
            Ar(j, i) = CCur(Format(n, "##########.############") / y)
        Next j
    Next i
    With Range("A1").Resize(1, 4)
        .Value = Array("Macro1", "Macro2", "Macro3", " Macro4")
        .Font.Bold = True
    End With
    Range("A2").Resize(20, 4).Value = Ar

    With Range("A22").Resize(1, 4)
        .FormulaR1C1 = "=AVERAGE(R2C:R21C)"
        .Offset(1).FormulaR1C1 = "=RANK(R22C,R22C1:R22C4,1)"
        .Resize(2).Font.Bold = True
    End With
    Application.ScreenUpdating = True
End Sub
```

Custom Sort Order

Submitted by Wei Jiang of Shiyan City, China. Jiang is a consultant for MrExcel.com.

By default, Excel enables you to sort lists numerically or alphabetically, but sometimes that is not what is needed. For example, a client might need each day's sales data sorted by the default division order of belts, handbags, watches, wallets, and everything else. This sample uses a custom sort order list to sort a range of data into default division order. Figure 14.13 shows the results.

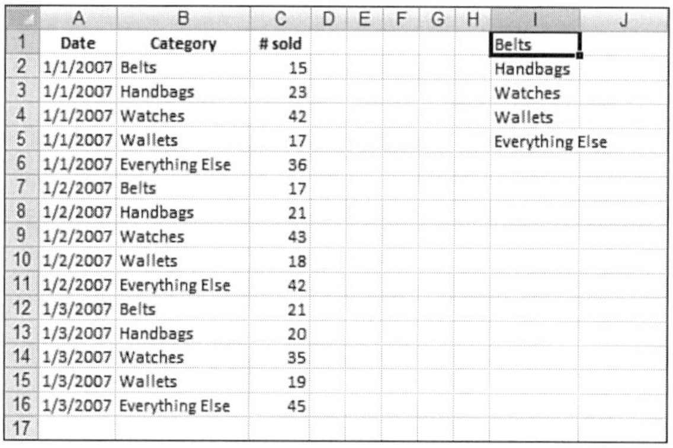

	A	B	C	D	E	F	G	H	I	J
1	Date	Category	# sold						Belts	
2	1/1/2007	Belts	15						Handbags	
3	1/1/2007	Handbags	23						Watches	
4	1/1/2007	Watches	42						Wallets	
5	1/1/2007	Wallets	17						Everything Else	
6	1/1/2007	Everything Else	36							
7	1/2/2007	Belts	17							
8	1/2/2007	Handbags	21							
9	1/2/2007	Watches	43							
10	1/2/2007	Wallets	18							
11	1/2/2007	Everything Else	42							
12	1/3/2007	Belts	21							
13	1/3/2007	Handbags	20							
14	1/3/2007	Watches	35							
15	1/3/2007	Wallets	19							
16	1/3/2007	Everything Else	45							
17										

Figure 14.13
When you use the macro, the list in A:C is sorted first by date, then by the custom sort list in Column I.

```
Sub CustomSort()

    ' add the custom list to Custom Lists
    Application.AddCustomList ListArray:=Range("I1:I5")
```

```
          ' get the list number
          nIndex = Application.GetCustomListNum(Range("I1:I5").Value)

          ' Now, we could sort a range with the custom list.
          ' Note, we should use nIndex + 1 as the custom list number here,
          ' for the first one is Normal order
          Range("A2:C16").Sort Key1:=Range("B2"), Order1:=xlAscending, _
                                Header:=xlNo, Orientation:=xlSortColumns, _
                                OrderCustom:=nIndex + 1
          Range("A2:C16").Sort Key1:=Range("A2"), Order1:=xlAscending, _
                                Header:=xlNo, Orientation:=xlSortColumns

          ' At the end, we should remove this custom list...
          Application.DeleteCustomList nIndex
      End Sub
```

Cell Progress Indicator

Submitted by Tom Urtis.

I have to admit, the new conditional formatting options in Excel, such as data bars, are fantastic. However, there still isn't an option for a visual like that shown in Figure 14.14. The following example builds a progress indicator in Column C based on entries in Columns A and B.

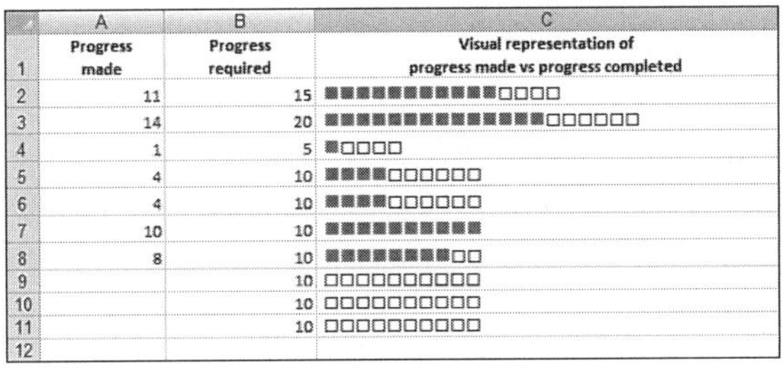

Figure 14.14
Use indicators in cells to show progress.

```
      Private Sub Worksheet_Change(ByVal Target As Range)
      If Target.Column > 2 Or Target.Cells.Count > 1 Then Exit Sub
      If Application.IsNumber(Target.Value) = False Then
          Application.EnableEvents = False
          Application.Undo
          Application.EnableEvents = True
          MsgBox "Numbers only please."
          Exit Sub
      End If
      Select Case Target.Column
          Case 1
              If Target.Value > Target.Offset(0, 1).Value Then
                  Application.EnableEvents = False
                  Application.Undo
                  Application.EnableEvents = True
                  MsgBox "Value in column A may not be larger than value in column B."
                  Exit Sub
```

```
            End If
        Case 2
            If Target.Value < Target.Offset(0, -1).Value Then
                Application.EnableEvents = False
                Application.Undo
                Application.EnableEvents = True
                MsgBox "Value in column B may not be smaller " & _
                    "than value in column A."
                Exit Sub
            End If
    End Select
    Dim x As Long
    x = Target.Row
    Dim z As String
    z = Range("B" & x).Value - Range("A" & x).Value
    With Range("C" & x)
        .Formula = "=IF(RC[-1]<=RC[-2],REPT(""n"",RC[-1]) _
            &REPT(""n"",RC[-2]-RC[-1]),REPT(""n"",RC[-2]) _
            &REPT(""o"",RC[-1]-RC[-2]))"
        .Value = .Value
        .Font.Name = "Wingdings"
        .Font.ColorIndex = 1
        .Font.Size = 10
        If Len(Range("A" & x)) <> 0 Then
            .Characters(1, (.Characters.Count - z)).Font.ColorIndex = 3
            .Characters(1, (.Characters.Count - z)).Font.Size = 12
        End If
    End With
End Sub
```

Protected Password Box

Submitted by Daniel Klann of Sydney, Australia. Daniel works mainly with VBA in Excel and Access, but dabbles in all sorts of languages. He maintains a website at www.danielklann.com.

Using an input box for password protection has a major security flaw: The characters being entered are easily viewable. This program changes the characters to asterisks as they are entered—just like a real password field (see Figure 14.15).

Figure 14.15
Use an input box as a
secure password field.

```
Private Declare Function CallNextHookEx Lib "user32" (ByVal hHook As Long, _
ByVal ncode As Long, ByVal wParam As Long, lParam As Any) As Long

Private Declare Function GetModuleHandle Lib "kernel32" _
    Alias "GetModuleHandleA" (ByVal lpModuleName As String) As Long
```

```
Private Declare Function SetWindowsHookEx Lib "user32" _
    Alias "SetWindowsHookExA" _
    (ByVal idHook As Long, ByVal lpfn As Long, _
    ByVal hmod As Long,ByVal dwThreadId As Long) As Long

Private Declare Function UnhookWindowsHookEx Lib "user32" _
    (ByVal hHook As Long) As Long

Private Declare Function SendDlgItemMessage Lib "user32" _
    Alias "SendDlgItemMessageA" _
    (ByVal hDlg As Long, _
    ByVal nIDDlgItem As Long, ByVal wMsg As Long, _
    ByVal wParam As Long, ByVal lParam As Long) As Long

Private Declare Function GetClassName Lib "user32" _
    Alias "GetClassNameA" (ByVal hwnd As Long, _
    ByVal lpClassName As String, _
    ByVal nMaxCount As Long) As Long

Private Declare Function GetCurrentThreadId _
    Lib "kernel32" () As Long

'Constants to be used in our API functions
Private Const EM_SETPASSWORDCHAR = &HCC
Private Const WH_CBT = 5
Private Const HCBT_ACTIVATE = 5
Private Const HC_ACTION = 0

Private hHook As Long

Public Function NewProc(ByVal lngCode As Long, _
    ByVal wParam As Long, ByVal lParam As Long) As Long
    Dim RetVal
    Dim strClassName As String, lngBuffer As Long

    If lngCode < HC_ACTION Then
        NewProc = CallNextHookEx(hHook, lngCode, wParam, lParam)
        Exit Function
    End If

    strClassName = String$(256, " ")
    lngBuffer = 255

    If lngCode = HCBT_ACTIVATE Then      'A window has been activated

        RetVal = GetClassName(wParam, strClassName, lngBuffer)

        'Check for class name of the Inputbox
        If Left$(strClassName, RetVal) = "#32770" Then
            'Change the edit control to display the password character *.
            'You can change the Asc("*") as you please.
            SendDlgItemMessage wParam, &H1324, EM_SETPASSWORDCHAR, Asc("*"), &H0
        End If

    End If
```

14

```
                    'This line will ensure that any other hooks that may be in place are
                    'called correctly.
                    CallNextHookEx hHook, lngCode, wParam, lParam

                End Function

                Public Function InputBoxDK(Prompt, Optional Title, _
                    Optional Default, Optional XPos, _
                Optional YPos, Optional HelpFile, Optional Context) As String
                    Dim lngModHwnd As Long, lngThreadID As Long

                    lngThreadID = GetCurrentThreadId
                    lngModHwnd = GetModuleHandle(vbNullString)

                    hHook = SetWindowsHookEx(WH_CBT, AddressOf NewProc, lngModHwnd, lngThreadID)
                    On Error Resume Next
                    InputBoxDK = InputBox(Prompt, Title, Default, XPos, YPos, HelpFile, Context)
                    UnhookWindowsHookEx hHook

                End Function

                Sub PasswordBox()
                If InputBoxDK("Please enter password", "Password Required") <> "password" Then
                        MsgBox "Sorry, that was not a correct password."
                    Else
                        MsgBox "Correct Password!  Come on in."
                    End If
                End Sub
```

Change Case

Submitted by Ivan F. Moala.

Word can change the case of selected text, but that capability is notably lacking in Excel. This program enables the Excel user to change the case of text in any selected range, as shown in Figure 14.16.

Figure 14.16
You can now change the case of words, just like in Word.

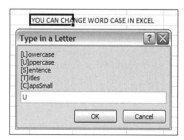

```
                Sub TextCaseChange()
                Dim RgText As Range
                Dim oCell As Range
                Dim Ans As String
                Dim strTest As String
```

```vba
Dim sCap As Integer, _
    lCap As Integer, _
    i As Integer

'// You need to select a range to alter first!

Again:
Ans = Application.InputBox("[L]owercase" & vbCr & "[U]ppercase" & vbCr & _
        "[S]entence" & vbCr & "[T]itles" & vbCr & "[C]apsSmall", _
        "Type in a Letter", Type:=2)

If Ans = "False" Then Exit Sub
If InStr(1, "LUSTC", UCase(Ans), vbTextCompare) = 0 _
    Or Len(Ans) > 1 Then GoTo Again

On Error GoTo NoText
If Selection.Count = 1 Then
    Set RgText = Selection
Else
    Set RgText = Selection.SpecialCells(xlCellTypeConstants, 2)
End If
On Error GoTo 0

For Each oCell In RgText
    Select Case UCase(Ans)
        Case "L": oCell = LCase(oCell.Text)
        Case "U": oCell = UCase(oCell.Text)
        Case "S": oCell = UCase(Left(oCell.Text, 1)) & _
            LCase(Right(oCell.Text, Len(oCell.Text) - 1))
        Case "T": oCell = Application.WorksheetFunction.Proper(oCell.Text)
        Case "C"
                lCap = oCell.Characters(1, 1).Font.Size
                sCap = Int(lCap * 0.85)
                'Small caps for everything.
                oCell.Font.Size = sCap
                oCell.Value = UCase(oCell.Text)
                strTest = oCell.Value
                'Large caps for 1st letter of words.
                strTest = Application.Proper(strTest)
                For i = 1 To Len(strTest)
                    If Mid(strTest, i, 1) = UCase(Mid(strTest, i, 1)) Then
                        oCell.Characters(i, 1).Font.Size = lCap
                    End If
                Next i
    End Select
Next

Exit Sub
NoText:
MsgBox "No text in your selection @ " & Selection.Address

End Sub
```

14

Selecting with SpecialCells

Submitted by Ivan F. Moala.

Typically, when you want to find certain values, text, or formulas in a range, the range is selected and each cell is tested. The following example shows how SpecialCells can be used to select only the desired cells. Having fewer cells to check will speed up your code:

```
Sub SpecialRange()
Dim TheRange As Range
Dim oCell As Range

    Set TheRange = Range("A1:Z200").SpecialCells(__
            xlCellTypeConstants, xlTextValues)

    For Each oCell In TheRange
        If oCell.Text = "Your Text" Then
            MsgBox oCell.Address
            MsgBox TheRange.Cells.Count
        End If
    Next oCell

End Sub
```

ActiveX Right-Click Menu

There is no built-in menu for the right-click event of ActiveX objects on a sheet. This is a utility for that, using a command button for the example in Figure 14.17. Set the Take Focus on Click property of the command button to False.

Figure 14.17
Customize the contextual (right-click) menu of an ActiveX control.

Place the following in the ThisWorkbook module:

```
Private Sub Workbook_Open()
With Application
    .CommandBars("Cell").Reset
    .WindowState = xlMaximized
    .Goto Sheet1.Range("A1"), True
End With
End Sub

Private Sub Workbook_Activate()
Application.CommandBars("Cell").Reset
End Sub

Private Sub Workbook_SheetBeforeRightClick(ByVal Sh As Object, _
    ByVal Target As Range, Cancel As Boolean)
Application.CommandBars("Cell").Reset
End Sub
```

```
Private Sub Workbook_Deactivate()
Application.CommandBars("Cell").Reset
End Sub

Private Sub Workbook_BeforeClose(Cancel As Boolean)
With Application
    .CommandBars("Cell").Reset
    .WindowState = xlMaximized
    .Goto Sheet1.Range("A1"), True
End With
ThisWorkbook.Save
End Sub
```

Place the following in a standard module:

```
Sub MyRightClickMenu()
Application.CommandBars("Cell").Reset
Dim cbc As CommandBarControl
  For Each cbc In Application.CommandBars("cell").Controls
      cbc.Visible = False
  Next cbc
With Application.CommandBars("Cell").Controls.Add(temporary:=True)
    .Caption = "My Macro 1"
    .OnAction = "Test1"
  End With
With Application.CommandBars("Cell").Controls.Add(temporary:=True)
    .Caption = "My Macro 2"
    .OnAction = "Test2"
  End With
With Application.CommandBars("Cell").Controls.Add(temporary:=True)
    .Caption = "My Macro 3"
    .OnAction = "Test3"
  End With
Application.CommandBars("Cell").ShowPopup
End Sub

Sub Test1()
MsgBox "This is the Test1 macro from the ActiveX object's custom " & _
    "right-click event menu.", , "''My Macro 1'' menu item."
End Sub

Sub Test2()
MsgBox "This is the Test2 macro from the ActiveX object's custom " & _
    "right-click event menu.", , "''My Macro 2'' menu item."
End Sub

Sub Test3()
MsgBox "This is the Test3 macro from the ActiveX object's custom " & _
    "right-click event menu.", , "''My Macro 3'' menu item."
End Sub
```

Cool Applications

These last samples are interesting applications that you might be able to incorporate into your own projects.

14

Historical Stock/Fund Quotes

Submitted by Nathan P. Oliver.

The following retrieves the average of a valid ticker or the close of a fund for the specified date (see Figure 14.18).

Figure 14.18
Retrieve stock information.

	A	B	C
1	Symbol	Date	Average/Close
2	Dell	1/12/1994	25.3125
3	MSFT	1/30/2003	49.18
4	VFINX	1/20/2000	
5	INNDX	1/6/2003	
6	INSTX	2/17/2004	

```
Private Sub GetQuote()
Dim ie As Object, lCharPos As Long, sHTML As String
Dim HistDate As Date, HighVal As String, LowVal As String
Dim cl As Range

Set cl = ActiveCell
HistDate = cl(, 0)

If Intersect(cl, Range("C2:C" & Cells.Rows.Count)) Is Nothing Then
    MsgBox "You must select a cell in column C."
    Exit Sub
End If

If Not CBool(Len(cl(, -1))) Or Not CBool(Len(cl(, 0))) Then
    MsgBox "You must enter a symbol and date."
    Exit Sub
End If

Set ie = CreateObject("InternetExplorer.Application")

With ie
    .Navigate _
        http://bigcharts.marketwatch.com/historical & _
        "/default.asp?detect=1&symbol=" _
        & cl(, -1) & "&close_date=" & Month(HistDate) & "%2F" & _
        Day(HistDate) & "%2F" & Year(HistDate) & "&x=31&y=26"
    Do While .Busy And .ReadyState <> 4
        DoEvents
    Loop
    sHTML = .Document.body.innertext
    .Quit
End With

Set ie = Nothing

lCharPos = InStr(1, sHTML, "High:", vbTextCompare)
If lCharPos Then HighVal = Mid$(sHTML, lCharPos + 5, 15)

If Not Left$(HighVal, 3) = "n/a" Then
```

```
    lCharPos = InStr(1, sHTML, "Low:", vbTextCompare)
    If lCharPos Then LowVal = Mid$(sHTML, lCharPos + 4, 15)
    cl.Value = (Val(LowVal) + Val(HighVal)) / 2
Else: lCharPos = InStr(1, sHTML, "Closing Price:", vbTextCompare)
    cl.Value = Val(Mid$(sHTML, lCharPos + 14, 15))
End If

Set cl = Nothing
End Sub
```

Using VBA Extensibility to Add Code to New Workbooks

You have a macro that moves data to a new workbook for the regional managers. What if you need to also copy macros to the new workbook? You can use Visual Basic for Application Extensibility to import modules to a workbook or to actually write lines of code to the workbook.

To use any of these examples, you must first open VB Editor, choose References from the Tools menu, and select the reference for Microsoft Visual Basic for Applications Extensibility 5.3. You must also trust access to VBA by going to the Developer ribbon, choosing Macro Security, and checking Trust Access to the VBA Project Object Model.

The easiest way to use VBA Extensibility is to export a complete module or userform from the current project and import it to the new workbook. Perhaps you have an application with thousands of lines of code. You want to create a new workbook with data for the regional manager and give her three macros to enable custom formatting and printing. Place all of these macros in a module called modToRegion. Macros in this module also call the frmRegion userform. The following code transfers this code from the current workbook to the new workbook:

```
Sub MoveDataAndMacro()
    Dim WSD as worksheet
    Set WSD = Worksheets("Report")
    ' Copy Report to a new workbook
    WSD.Copy
    ' The active workbook is now the new workbook
    ' Delete any old copy of the module from C
    On Error Resume Next
    ' Delete any stray copies from hard drive
    Kill ("C:\ModToRegion.bas")
    Kill ("C:\frmRegion.frm")
    On Error GoTo 0
    ' Export module & form from this workbook
    ThisWorkbook.VBProject.VBComponents("ModToRegion").Export _
        ("C:\ModToRegion.bas")
    ThisWorkbook.VBProject.VBComponents("frmRegion").Export ("C:\frmRegion.frm")
    ' Import to new workbook
    ActiveWorkbook.VBProject.VBComponents.Import ("C:\ModToRegion.bas")
    ActiveWorkbook.VBProject.VBComponents.Import ("C:\frmRegion.frm")
    On Error Resume Next
    Kill ("C:\ModToRegion.bas")
    Kill ("C:\frmRegion.bas")
    On Error GoTo 0
End Sub
```

14

The preceding method will work if you need to move modules or userforms to a new workbook. However, what if you need to write some code to the Workbook_Open macro in the ThisWorkbook module? There are two tools to use. The Lines method will allow you to return a particular set of code lines from a given module. The InsertLines method allows you to insert code lines to a new module.

> **CAUTION**
>
> With each call to InsertLines, you must insert a complete macro. Excel will attempt to compile the code after each call to InsertLines. If you insert lines that do not completely compile, Excel may crash with a general protection fault (GPF).

```
Sub MoveDataAndMacro()
    Dim WSD as worksheet
    Dim WBN as Workbook
    Dim WBCodeMod1 As Object, WBCodeMod2 As Object
    Set WSD = Worksheets("Report")
    ' Copy Report to a new workbook
    WSD.Copy
    ' The active workbook is now the new workbook
    Set WBN = ActiveWorkbook
    ' Copy the Workbook level Event handlers
    Set WBCodeMod1 = ThisWorkbook.VBProject.VBComponents("ThisWorkbook") _
        .CodeModule
    Set WBCodeMod2 = WBN.VBProject.VBComponents("ThisWorkbook").CodeModule
    WBCodeMod2.insertlines 1, WBCodeMod1.Lines(1, WBCodeMod1.countoflines)
End Sub
```

Next Steps

Excel 2007 offers fantastic new data-visualization tools, including data bars, color scales, icon sets, and improved conditional formatting rules. In Chapter 15, "Data Visualizations and Conditional Formatting," you will learn how to automate the new tools and use VBA to invoke choices not available in the Excel user interface.

14

✸NEW✸ Data Visualizations and Conditional Formatting

15

Introduction to Data Visualizations

The data visualization tools in Excel 2007 represent one of its best new features. Microsoft added a new drawing layer that can hold icon sets, data bars, and color scales. Unlike SmartArt graphics, Microsoft exposed the entire object model for the data visualization tools, so you can use VBA to add data visualizations to your reports.

Excel 2007 provides a variety of new data visualizations. A description of each appears below, with an example shown in Figure 15.1 on the next page.

- **Data bars**—The data bar adds an in-cell bar chart to each cell in a range. The largest numbers have the largest bars, and the smallest numbers have the smallest bars. You can control the bar color as well as the values that should receive the smallest and largest bar.

- **Color scales**—Excel applies a color to each cell from among a two- or three-color gradient. The two-color gradients are best for reports that will be presented in monochrome. The three-color gradients require a presentation in color, but can represent a report in a traditional traffic light color combination of red-yellow-green. You can control the points along the continuum where each color begins and you can control the two or three colors.

- **Icon sets**—Excel assigns an icon to each number. Icon sets can contain three icons (such as the red, yellow, green traffic lights), four icons, or five icons (such as the cell phone power bars). With icon sets, you can control the numeric limits for each icon, reverse the order of the icons, or choose to show only the icons.

■ **Above/below average**—Found under the top/bottom rules fly-out menu, these rules make it easy to highlight all of the cells that are above average. You can choose the formatting that should be applied to the cells. Note in column G of Figure 15.1 only 30 percent of the cells are above average. Contrast with the top 50 percent in column I.

■ **Top/bottom rules**—Excel highlights the top or bottom *n* percent of cells, or highlights the top or bottom *n* cells in a range.

■ **Duplicate values**—Excel highlights any values that are repeated within a dataset. Because the new Delete Duplicates command on the Data tab of the Ribbon is so destructive, you might prefer to highlight the duplicates and then intelligently decide which records to delete.

■ **Highlight cells**—The legacy conditional formatting rules, such as greater than, less than, between, and text that contains, are still available in Excel 2007. The powerful Formula conditions are also available, although you might have to use these less frequently with the addition of the average and top/bottom rules.

Figure 15.1
Visualizations such as data bars, color scales, icon sets, and top/bottom rules are controlled in the Excel user interface from the Conditional Formatting drop-down on the Home tab of the ribbon.

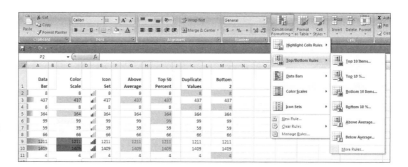

New VBA Methods and Properties for Data Visualizations

All the data visualization settings are managed in VBA with the FormatConditions collection. Excel 2007 adds seven new methods for adding conditions, such as the `AddDataBar`, `AddIconSet`, `AddTop10`, `AddUniqueValues`, and so on.

In Excel 2007, it is possible to apply several different conditional formatting conditions to the same range. For example, you can apply a two-color color scale, an icon set, and a data bar to the same range. Excel 2007 adds a `Priority` property to specify which conditions should be calculated first. Methods such as `SetFirstPriority` and `SetLastPriority` ensure that a new format condition is executed before or after all others.

The `StopIfTrue` property works in conjunction with the `Priority` property. In the "Using Visualization Tricks" section later in this chapter, you will see how to use the `StopIfTrue` property on a dummy condition to make other formatting apply only to certain subsets of a range.

The Type property has been dramatically expanded in Excel 2007. Whereas this property formerly was a toggle between CellValue and Expression, 13 new types were added in Excel 2007. Table 15.1 shows the valid values for the Type property. Items 3 through 18 are new in Excel 2007.

Table 15.1   Valid Types for a Format Condition

Value	Description	VBA Constant
1	Cell value	xlCellValue
2	Expression	xlExpression
3	Color scale	xlColorScale
4	Data bar	xlDatabar
5	Top 10 values	xlTop10
6	Icon set	XlIconSet
8	Unique values	xlUniqueValues
9	Text string	xlTextString
10	Blanks condition	xlBlanksCondition
11	Time period	xlTimePeriod
12	Above average condition	xlAboveAverageCondition
13	No blanks condition	xlNoBlanksCondition
16	Errors condition	xlErrorsCondition
17	No errors condition	xlNoErrorsCondition
18	Compare columns	xlCompareColumns

Adding Data Bars to a Range

The Data Bar command adds an in-cell bar chart to each cell in a range. Typically, the smallest values in the dataset receive a bar that is 4 pixels wide. The largest values in the dataset receive a bar that is 90 percent of the width of the cell.

In Figure 15.2, a value of -500 in cell A2 causes small values such as 0 and 10 in cells A3:A4 to have a relatively large data bar. By using the Edit Formatting Rule dialog, you can specify that any value of 0 or less should get the smallest data bar. In column C, the size of each data bar better represents the expected values of 0 to 500.

Figure 15.2
If your dataset might have outliers, you can tweak the data bar rules to specify a certain value that should get the largest or smallest data bar. Here, the Shortest Bar is changed from Lowest Value to a number of 0.

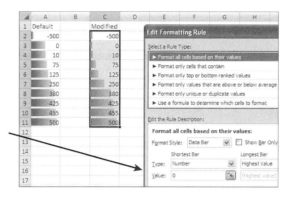

Use the `FormatConditions.AddDataBar` method to add a new `FormatCondition` member to the `FormatConditions` collection for a range:

```
Range("A1:A10").FormatConditions.AddDatabar
```

Because you can't be sure that you have only one condition applied to a range, you should refer to the new data bar condition by using the `Count` property:

```
ThisCond = Range("A1:A10").FormatConditions.Count
```

If you want to make sure that this is the only format condition applied to the range, use the `FormatConditions.Delete` method:

```
Rang Range("A1:A10").FormatConditions.Delete
```

Specify a color for the data bar using the `Color` and `TintAndShade` properties for the `BarColor`. The `Color` property can be any of 16 million colors. Define it using the `RGB` function. The `TintAndShade` property will modify the selected color. Specify a value from `-1` (darkest) to `1` (lightest). The following code changes the color of the data bar to red and makes it darker than usual:

```
With Range("A1:A10").FormatConditions(ThisCond).BarColor
    .Color = RGB(255, 0, 0) ' Red
    .TintAndShade = -0.5 ' Darker than normal
End With
```

By default, Excel assigns the shortest data bar to the minimum value and the longest data bar to the maximum value. If you want to override the defaults, use the `Modify` method for either the `MinPoint` or `MaxPoint` properties. Specify a type from those shown in Table 15.2. Types 0, 3, 4, and 5 require a value. Table 15.2 shows valid types.

Table 15.2   MinPoint and MaxPoint Types

Value	Description	VBA Constant
0	Number is used.	xlConditionNumber
1	Lowest value from the list of values.	xlConditionValueLowest Value
2	Highest value from the list of values.	xlConditionValueHighestValue
3	Percentage is used.	xlConditionValuePercent
4	Formula is used.	xlConditionValueFormula
5	Percentile is used.	xlConditionValuePercentile
-1	No conditional value.	xlConditionValueNone

To have the smallest bar assigned to values of 0 and below, use this code:

```
Range("A1:A10").FormatConditions(ThisCond).MinPoint.Modify _
    Newtype:=xlConditionValueNumber, NewValue:=0
```

To have the top 20 percent of the bars have the largest bar, use this code:

```
Range("A1:A10").FormatConditions(ThisCond).MaxPoint.Modify _
    Newtype:=xlConditionValuePercent, NewValue:=80
```

An interesting alternative is to only show the data bars and not the value. To do this, use this code:

```
Range("A1:A10").FormatConditions(ThisCond).ShowValue = False
```

To create the data bars shown in column C of Figure 15.2, use this code:

```
Sub AddDataBar()
' Add a Data bar
' Ensure any credits < 0 have a data bar like 0
'
    With Range("A1:A10")
        ' Add the data bars
        .FormatConditions.AddDataBar
        ' Set the lower limit
        ThisCond = .FormatConditions.Count
        .FormatConditions(ThisCond).MinPoint.Modify _
            newtype:=xlConditionValueNumber, newvalue:=0
        ' Use red, darker than usual
        With .FormatConditions(ThisCond).BarColor
            .Color = RGB(255, 0, 0)
            .TintAndShade = -0.5
        End With
    End With
End Sub
```

Adding Color Scales to a Range

Color scales can be added in either two-color or three-color scale varieties. Figure 15.3 shows the available settings in the Excel user interface for a color scale using three colors.

Figure 15.3
Color scales enable you
to show hot spots in your
dataset.

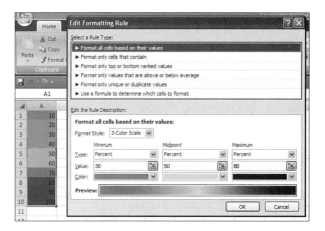

Like the data bar, a color scale is applied to a range object using the AddColorScale method. You should specify a ColorScaleType of either 2 or 3 as the only argument of the AddColorScale method.

You then indicate a color and tint for either both, or all three of the color scale criteria. You can also specify if the shade is applied to the lowest value, highest value, a particular value, a percentage, or at a percentile using the values shown previously in Table 15.2.

The following code generates a three-color color scale in range A1:A10:

```
Sub Add3ColorScale()
    With Range("A1:A10")
        .FormatConditions.Delete
        ' Add the Color Scale as a 3-color scale
        .FormatConditions.AddColorScale ColorScaleType:=3

        ' Format the first color as light red
        .FormatConditions(1).ColorScaleCriteria(1).Type = xlConditionValuePercent
        .FormatConditions(1).ColorScaleCriteria(1).Value = 30
        .FormatConditions(1).ColorScaleCriteria(1).FormatColor.Color = _
            RGB(255, 0, 0)
        .FormatConditions(1).ColorScaleCriteria(1).FormatColor.TintAndShade = 0.25

        ' Format the second color as green at 50%
        .FormatConditions(1).ColorScaleCriteria(2).Type = xlConditionValuePercent
        .FormatConditions(1).ColorScaleCriteria(2).Value = 50
        .FormatConditions(1).ColorScaleCriteria(2).FormatColor.Color = _
            RGB(0, 255, 0)
        .FormatConditions(1).ColorScaleCriteria(2).FormatColor.TintAndShade = 0

        ' Format the third color as dark blue
        .FormatConditions(1).ColorScaleCriteria(3).Type = xlConditionValuePercent
        .FormatConditions(1).ColorScaleCriteria(3).Value = 80
        .FormatConditions(1).ColorScaleCriteria(3).FormatColor.Color = _
            RGB(0, 0, 255)
```

```
        .FormatConditions(1).ColorScaleCriteria(3).FormatColor _
            .TintAndShade = -0.25
    End With

End Sub
```

Adding Icon Sets to a Range

Icon sets in Excel come with three, four, or five different icons in the set. Figure 15.4 shows the settings for an icon set with five different icons.

Figure 15.4
With additional icons, the complexity of the code increases.

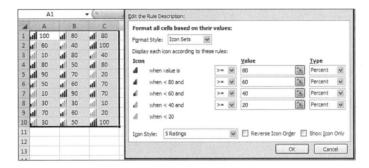

To add an icon set to a range, use the AddIconSet method. No arguments are required. You can then adjust three properties that apply to the icon set. You then use several additional lines of code to specify the icon set in use and the limits for each icon.

Specifying an Icon Set

After adding the icon set, you can control whether the icon order is reversed, whether Excel shows only the icons, and then specify 1 of the 16 built-in icon sets:

```
With Range("A1:C10")
    .FormatConditions.Delete
    .FormatConditions.AddIconSetCondition
    ' Global settings for the icon set
    With .FormatConditions(1)
        .ReverseOrder = False
        .ShowIconOnly = False
        .IconSet = ActiveWorkbook.IconSets(xl5CRV)
    End With
End With
```

> **NOTE**
> It is somewhat curious that the IconSets collection is a property of the active workbook. This seems to indicate that in future versions of Excel, new icon sets might be available.

Table 15.3 shows the complete list of icon sets.

Table 15.3   Available Icon Sets and Their VBA Constants

Icon	Value	Description	Constant
	1	3 arrows	xl3Arrows
	2	3 arrows gray	xl3ArrowsGray
	3	3 flags	xl3Flags
	4	3 traffic lights 1	xl3TrafficLights1
	5	3 traffic lights 2	xl3TrafficLights2
	6	3 signs	xl3Signs
	7	3 symbols	xl3Symbols
	8	3 symbols 2	xl3Symbols2
	9	4 arrows	xl4Arrows
	10	4 arrows gray	xl4ArrowsGray
	11	4 red to black	xl4RedToBlack
	12	4 power bars	xl4CRV
	13	4 traffic lights	xl4TrafficLights
	14	5 arrows	xl5Arrows
	15	5 arrows gray	xl5ArrowsGray
	16	5 power bars	xl5CRV
	17	5 quarters	xl5Quarters

Specifying Ranges for Each Icon

After specifying the type of icon set, you can then specify ranges for each icon within the set. By default, the first icon starts at the lowest value. You can adjust the settings for each of the additional icons in the set:

```
With Range("A1:C10")
        ' The first icon always starts at 0
        ' Settings for the second icon - start at 50%
        With .FormatConditions(1).IconCriteria(2)
            .Type = xlConditionValuePercent
            .Value = 50
            .Operator = xlGreaterEqual
        End With
        With .FormatConditions(1).IconCriteria(3)
            .Type = xlConditionValuePercent
            .Value = 60
            .Operator = xlGreaterEqual
        End With
        With .FormatConditions(1).IconCriteria(4)
            .Type = xlConditionValuePercent
            .Value = 80
            .Operator = xlGreaterEqual
        End With
        With .FormatConditions(1).IconCriteria(5)
            .Type = xlConditionValuePercent
            .Value = 90
            .Operator = xlGreaterEqual
        End With
    End With
```

Valid values for the Operator property are XlGreater or xlGreaterEqual.

> **CAUTION**
>
> It is very easy with VBA to create overlapping ranges (for example, icon 1 from 0 to 50, icon 2 from 30 to 90). Although the Edit Formatting Rule dialog box will prevent overlapping ranges, VBA allows them. Your icon set will display unpredictably if you create invalid ranges.

Using Visualization Tricks

If you use an icon set or a color scale, Excel applies a color to all cells in the dataset. Two tricks in this section enable you to apply an icon set to only a subset of the cells or to apply two different color data bars to the same range. The first trick is available in the user interface, but the second trick is only available in VBA.

Creating an Icon Set for a Subset of a Range

Sometimes, you might want to only apply a red X to the bad cells in a range. This is tricky to do in the user interface.

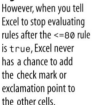

In the user interface, follow these steps to apply a red X to values greater than 80:

1. Add a three-symbols icon set to the range.
2. Specify that the symbols should be reversed.
3. Indicate that the third icon appears for values greater than 80. You now have a mix of all three icons, as shown in Figure 15.5.

Figure 15.5
First add a three-icon set, paying particular attention to the value for the red X.

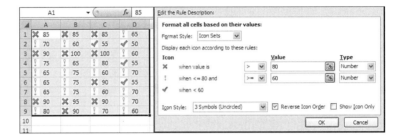

4. Add a new conditional format to highlight cells less than or equal to 80. Don't specify any special formatting for the cells that match this rule, as shown in Figure 15.6.

Figure 15.6
The new conditional formatting seems silly—when the value is less than or equal to 80, do nothing.

5. In the Conditional Formatting Rule Manager, indicate that Excel should stop evaluating conditions if the new condition is true. This will prevent Excel from getting to the icon set rule for any cell with a value of 80 or less. The result is that only cells greater than 80 will appear with a red X, as shown in Figure 15.7.

Figure 15.7
However, when you tell Excel to stop evaluating rules after the <=80 rule is true, Excel never has a chance to add the check mark or exclamation point to the other cells.

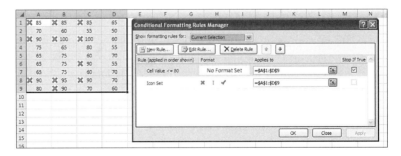

The code to create this effect in VBA is fairly straightforward. A great deal of the code is spent making sure that the icon set has the red X symbols on the cells greater than 80.

When you use the `FormatConditions.Add method` to add the second condition, Excel initially refers to that condition as `FormatConditions(2)`. However, you need to make sure this condition is executed first, so you use the `SetFirstPriority` method to move the new condition to the top of the list. The final step is to then turn on the `StopIfTrue` property; but you need to realize that the new condition is referred to as `FormatConditions(1)` after executing the `SetFirstPriority` method.

The code to highlight values greater than 80 with a red X is shown here:

```
Sub TrickyFormatting()
    With Range("A1:D9")
        .FormatConditions.Delete
        ' Add and format the 3 symbols icons
        .FormatConditions.AddIconSetCondition
        With .FormatConditions(1)
            .ReverseOrder = True
            .ShowIconOnly = False
            .IconSet = ActiveWorkbook.IconSets(xl3Symbols2)
        End With
        ' The threshhold for this icon doesn't really matter,
        ' but you have to make sure that it does not overlap the 3rd icon
        With .FormatConditions(1).IconCriteria(2)
            .Type = xlConditionValue
            .Value = 66
            .Operator = xlGreater
        End With
        ' Make sure the red X appears for cells above 80
        With .FormatConditions(1).IconCriteria(3)
            .Type = xlConditionValue
            .Value = 80
            .Operator = xlGreater
        End With

        ' Next, add a condition to catch items <=80
        .FormatConditions.Add Type:=xlCellValue, _
            Operator:=xlLessEqual, Formula1:="=80"
        ' Move this new condition from position 2 to position 1
        .FormatConditions(2).SetFirstPriority
        ' The new condition is now index #1. Add Stop if True.
        .FormatConditions(1).StopIfTrue = True
    End With
End Sub
```

Using Two Colors of Data Bars in a Range

This trick is particularly cool because it can only be achieved with VBA. Say that values above 90 are acceptable and below 90 indicate trouble. You would like acceptable values to have a green bar and others to have a red bar.

Using VBA, you first add the green data bars. Then, without deleting the format condition, you add red data bars.

In VBA, every format condition has a `Formula` property that defines whether the condition is displayed for a given cell. So, the trick is to write a formula that defines when the green bars are displayed. When the formula is not `True`, the red bars are allowed to show through.

In Figure 15.8, the effect is being applied to range A1:D10. You need to write the formula in A1 style, as if it applies to the top-left corner of the selection. The formula needs to evaluate to `True` or `False`. Excel automatically copies the formula to all the cells in the range. The formula for this condition is `=IF(A1>90,True,False)`.

> **TIP**
>
> The formula is evaluated relative to the current cell pointer location. Although it usually is not necessary to select cells before adding a `FormatCondition`, in this case, selecting the range ensures that the formula will work.

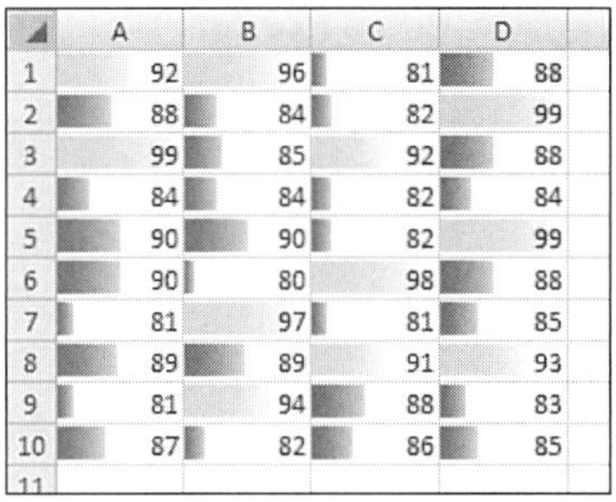

Figure 15.8
The dark bars are red, and the lighter bars are green. VBA was used to create two overlapping data bars, and then the `Formula` property hid the top bars for cells below 90.

The following code creates the two-color data bars:

```
Sub AddTwoDataBars()
    With Range("A1:D10")
        .Select ' The .Formula below requires .Select here
        .FormatConditions.Delete
        ' Add a Light Green Data Bar
        .FormatConditions.AddDataBar
        .FormatConditions(1).BarColor.Color = RGB(0, 255, 0)
        .FormatConditions(1).BarColor.TintAndShade = 0.25
        ' Add a Red Data Bar
        .FormatConditions.AddDataBar
        .FormatConditions(2).BarColor.Color = RGB(255, 0, 0)
        ' Make the green bars only
        .FormatConditions(1).Formula = "=IF(A1>90,True,False)"
    End With
End Sub
```

The `Formula` property works for all the conditional formats. This allows you to create some fairly obnoxious combinations of data visualizations. In Figure 15.9, five different icon sets are combined in a single range. Of course, no one would be able to figure out whether a red flag is worse than a gray down arrow, but this ability opens up interesting combinations for those with a little creativity.

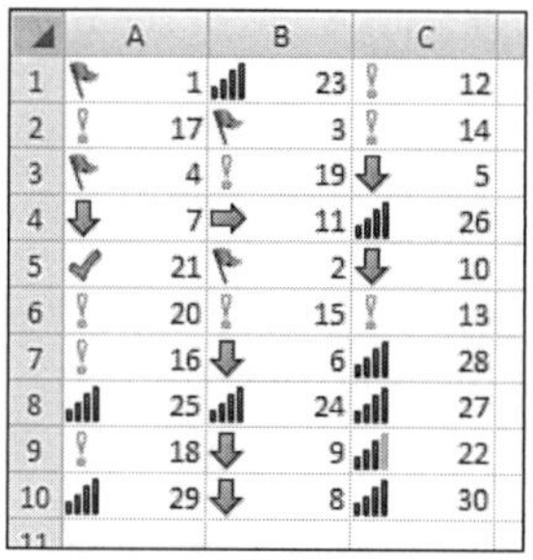

Figure 15.9
VBA created this mixture of five different icon sets in a single range. The `Formula` property in VBA is the key to combining icon sets.

```
Sub AddCrazyIcons()
    With Range("A1:C10")
        .Select ' The .Formula lines below require .Select here
        .FormatConditions.Delete

        ' First icon set
        .FormatConditions.AddIconSetCondition
        .FormatConditions(1).IconSet = ActiveWorkbook.IconSets(xl3Flags)
        .FormatConditions(1).Formula = "=IF(A1<5,TRUE,FALSE)"

        ' Next icon set
        .FormatConditions.AddIconSetCondition
        .FormatConditions(2).IconSet = ActiveWorkbook.IconSets(xl3ArrowsGray)
        .FormatConditions(2).Formula = "=IF(A1<12,TRUE,FALSE)"

        ' Next icon set
        .FormatConditions.AddIconSetCondition
        .FormatConditions(3).IconSet = ActiveWorkbook.IconSets(xl3Symbols2)
        .FormatConditions(3).Formula = "=IF(A1<22,TRUE,FALSE)"

        ' Next icon set
        .FormatConditions.AddIconSetCondition
        .FormatConditions(4).IconSet = ActiveWorkbook.IconSets(xl4CRV)
        .FormatConditions(4).Formula = "=IF(A1<27,TRUE,FALSE)"

        ' Next icon set
        .FormatConditions.AddIconSetCondition
        .FormatConditions(5).IconSet = ActiveWorkbook.IconSets(xl5CRV)
    End With
End Sub
```

15

Using Other Conditional Formatting Methods

Although the icon sets, data bars, and color scales get most of the attention, there are still plenty of other uses for conditional formatting.

The remaining examples in this chapter show off both some of the prior conditional formatting rules and some of the new methods available.

Formatting Cells That Are Above or Below Average

Use the `AddAboveAverage` method to format cells that are above or below average. After adding the conditional format, specify whether the `AboveBelow` property is `xlAboveAverage` or `xlBelowAverage`.

The following two macros highlight cells above and below average:

```
Sub FormatAboveAverage()
    With Selection
        .FormatConditions.Delete
        .FormatConditions.AddAboveAverage
        .FormatConditions(1).AboveBelow = xlAboveAverage
        .FormatConditions(1).Interior.Color = RGB(255, 0, 0)
    End With
End Sub

Sub FormatBelowAverage()
    With Selection
        .FormatConditions.Delete
        .FormatConditions.AddAboveAverage
        .FormatConditions(1).AboveBelow = xlBelowAverage
        .FormatConditions(1).Interior.Color = RGB(255, 0, 0)
    End With
End Sub
```

Formatting Cells in the Top 10 or Bottom 5

Four of the choices on the Top/Bottom Rules fly-out menu are controlled with the `AddTop10` method. After you add the format condition, you need to set three properties that control how the condition is calculated:

- **TopBottom**—Set this to either `xlTop10Top` or `xlTop10Bottom`.
- **Value**—Set this to 5 for the top 5, 6 for the top 6, and so on.
- **Percent**—Set this to `False` if you want the top 10 item. Set this to `True` if you want the top 10 percent of the items.

The following code highlights top or bottom cells:

```
Sub FormatTop10Items()
    With Selection
        .FormatConditions.Delete
        .FormatConditions.AddTop10
```

```
        .FormatConditions(1).TopBottom = xlTop10Top
        .FormatConditions(1).Value = 10
        .FormatConditions(1).Percent = False
        .FormatConditions(1).Interior.Color = RGB(255, 0, 0)
    End With
End Sub

Sub FormatBottom5Items()
    With Selection
        .FormatConditions.Delete
        .FormatConditions.AddTop10
        .FormatConditions(1).TopBottom = xlTop10Bottom
        .FormatConditions(1).Value = 5
        .FormatConditions(1).Percent = False
        .FormatConditions(1).Interior.Color = RGB(255, 0, 0)
    End With
End Sub

Sub FormatTop12Percent()
    With Selection
        .FormatConditions.Delete
        .FormatConditions.AddTop10
        .FormatConditions(1).TopBottom = xlTop10Top
        .FormatConditions(1).Value = 12
        .FormatConditions(1).Percent = True
        .FormatConditions(1).Interior.Color = RGB(255, 0, 0)
    End With
End Sub
```

Formatting Unique or Duplicate Cells

The Remove Duplicates command on the Data tab of the Ribbon is a destructive command. You might want to mark the duplicates without removing them. If so, the AddUniqueValues method marks the duplicate or unique cells.

After calling the method, set the DupeUnique property to either xlUnique or xlDuplicate.

As I have ranted about in *Special Edition Using Microsoft Office Excel 2007*, I don't quite like either option here. As you can see in Figure 15.10, choosing duplicate values, as in column A, marks both cells that contain the duplicate. For example, both A2 and A8 are marked, when really only A8 is the duplicate value.

Choosing unique values as in column B marks only the cells that don't have a duplicate. This leaves several cells unmarked. For example, none of the cells containing 17 is marked.

As any data analyst knows, the truly useful option would have been to mark the first unique value. In this wishful state, Excel would mark one instance of each unique value. In this case, the 17 in E2 would be marked, but any subsequent cells that contain 17, such as E8, would remain unmarked.

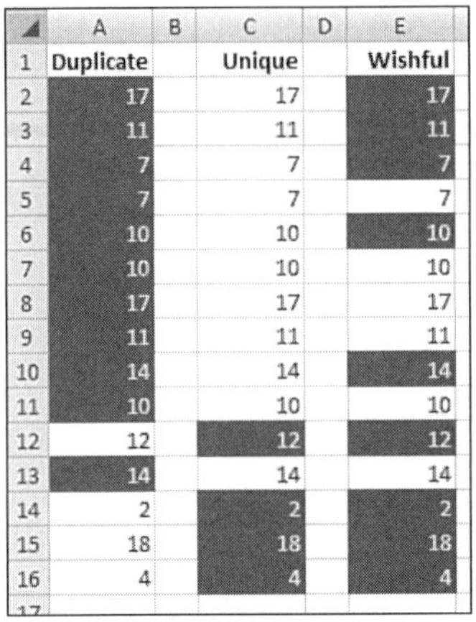

	A	B	C	D	E
1	Duplicate		Unique		Wishful
2	17		17		17
3	11		11		11
4	7		7		7
5	7		7		7
6	10		10		10
7	10		10		10
8	17		17		17
9	11		11		11
10	14		14		14
11	10		10		10
12	12		12		12
13	14		14		14
14	2		2		2
15	18		18		18
16	4		4		4

Figure 15.10
The `AddUniqueValues` method can mark cells as in column A or C. Unfortunately, it cannot mark the truly useful pattern in column E.

NOTE To achieve useful formatting in column E, see the `HighlightFirstUnique` code on page 391.

The code to mark duplicates or unique values is shown here:

```
Sub FormatDuplicate()
    With Selection
        .FormatConditions.Delete
        .FormatConditions.AddUniqueValues
        .FormatConditions(1).DupeUnique = xlDuplicate
        .FormatConditions(1).Interior.Color = RGB(255, 0, 0)
    End With
End Sub

Sub FormatUnique()
    With Selection
        .FormatConditions.Delete
        .FormatConditions.AddUniqueValues
        .FormatConditions(1).DupeUnique = xlUnique
        .FormatConditions(1).Interior.Color = RGB(255, 0, 0)
    End With
End Sub
```

Formatting Cells Based on Their Value

The value conditional formats have been around for several versions of Excel. Use the `Add` method with the following arguments:

- **`Type`**—In this section, the type will be `xlCellValue`.
- **`Operator`**—Can be `xlBetween`, `xlEqual`, `xlGreater`, `xlGreaterEqual`, `xlLess`, `xlLessEqual`, `xlNotBetween`, `xlNotEqual`.

- **Formula1**—Formula1 is used with each of the operators specified to provide a numeric value.

- **Formula2**—This is used for xlBetween and xlNotBetween.

The following code sample highlights cells based on their values:

```
Sub FormatBetween10And20()
    With Selection
        .FormatConditions.Delete
        .FormatConditions.Add Type:=xlCellValue, Operator:=xlBetween, _
            Formula1:="=10", Formula2:="=20"
        .FormatConditions(1).Interior.Color = RGB(255, 0, 0)
    End With
End Sub

Sub FormatLessThan15()
    With Selection
        .FormatConditions.Delete
        .FormatConditions.Add Type:=xlCellValue, Operator:=xlLess, _
            Formula1:="=15"
        .FormatConditions(1).Interior.Color = RGB(255, 0, 0)
    End With
End Sub
```

Formatting Cells That Contain Text

When you are trying to highlight cells that contain a certain bit of text, you will use the Add method, the xlTextString type, and an operator of xlBeginsWith, xlContains, xlDoesNotContain, or xlEndsWith.

The following code highlights all cells that contain a capital letter *A:*

```
Sub FormatContainsA()
    With Selection
        .FormatConditions.Delete
        .FormatConditions.Add Type:=xlTextString, String:="A", _
            TextOperator:=xlContains
        ' other choices: xlBeginsWith, xlDoesNotContain, xlEndsWith
        .FormatConditions(1).Interior.Color = RGB(255, 0, 0)
    End With
End Sub
```

Formatting Cells That Contain Dates

The date conditional formats are new in Excel 2007. The list of available date operators is a subset of the date operators available in the new pivot table filters. Use the Add method, the xlTimePeriod type, and one of these DateOperator values: xlYesterday, xlToday, xlTomorrow, xlLastWeek, xlLast7Days, xlThisWeek, xlNextWeek, xlLastMonth, xlThisMonth, xlNextMonth.

The following code highlights all dates in the past week:

```
Sub FormatDatesLastWeek()
    With Selection
        .FormatConditions.Delete
        ' DateOperator choices include xlYesterday, xlToday, xlTomorrow,
        ' xlLastWeek, xlThisWeek, xlNextWeek, xlLast7Days
        ' xlLastMonth, xlThisMonth, xlNextMonth,
        .FormatConditions.Add Type:=xlTimePeriod, DateOperator:=xlLastWeek
        .FormatConditions(1).Interior.Color = RGB(255, 0, 0)
    End With
End Sub
```

Formatting Cells That Contain Blanks or Errors

Buried deep within the Excel interface are options to format cells that contain blanks, contain errors, do not contain blanks, or do not contain errors. If you use the macro recorder, Excel uses the complicated xlExpression version of conditional formatting. For example, to look for a blank, Excel will test to see whether the =LEN(TRIM(A1))=0. Instead, you can use any of these four self-explanatory types. You are not required to use any other arguments with these new types.

```
.FormatConditions.Add Type:=xlBlanksCondition
.FormatConditions.Add Type:=xlErrorsCondition
.FormatConditions.Add Type:=xlNoBlanksCondition
.FormatConditions.Add Type:=xlNoErrorsCondition
```

Using a Formula to Determine Which Cells to Format

The most powerful conditional format is still the xlExpression type. In this type, you provide a formula for the active cell that evaluates to True or False. Make sure to write the formula with relative or absolute references so that the formula will be correct when Excel copies the formula to the remaining cells in the selection.

An infinite number of conditions can be identified with a formula. Two popular conditions are shown here.

Highlight the First Unique Occurrence of Each Value in a Range

In column A of Figure 15.11, you would like to highlight the first occurrence of each value in the column. The highlighted cells will then contain a complete list of the unique numbers found in the column.

The macro should select cells A1:A15. The formula should be written to return a True or False value for cell A1. Because Excel logically copies this formula to the entire range, a careful combination of relative and absolute references should be used.

The formula can use the COUNTIF function. Check to see how many times the range from A$1 to A1 contains the value A1. If the result is equal to 1, the condition is True, and the cell is highlighted. The first formula is =COUNTIF(A$1:A1,A1)=1. As the formula gets copied down to, say A12, the formula changes to =COUNTIF(A$1:A12,A12)=1.

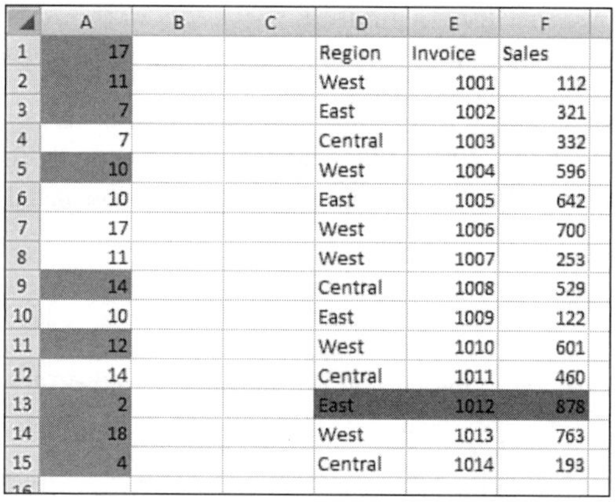

Figure 15.11
A formula-based condition can mark the first unique occurrence of each value, as shown in column A or the entire row with the largest sales, as shown in D:F.

⬛	A	B	C	D	E	F
1	17			Region	Invoice	Sales
2	11			West	1001	112
3	7			East	1002	321
4	7			Central	1003	332
5	10			West	1004	596
6	10			East	1005	642
7	17			West	1006	700
8	11			West	1007	253
9	14			Central	1008	529
10	10			East	1009	122
11	12			West	1010	601
12	14			Central	1011	460
13	2			East	1012	878
14	18			West	1013	763
15	4			Central	1014	193
16						

The following macro creates the formatting shown in column A of Figure 15.11:

```
Sub HighlightFirstUnique()
    With Range("A1:A15")
        .Select
        .FormatConditions.Delete
        .FormatConditions.Add Type:=xlExpression, _
            Formula1:="=COUNTIF(A$1:A1,A1)=1"
        .FormatConditions(1).Interior.Color = RGB(255, 0, 0)
    End With
End Sub
```

Highlight the Entire Row for the Largest Sales Value

Another example of a formula-based condition is when you want to highlight the entire row of a dataset in response to a value in one column. Consider the dataset in cells D2:F15 of Figure 15.11. If you want to highlight the entire row that contains the largest sale, you select cells D2:F15 and write a formula that works for cell D2: =$F2=MAX($F$2:$F$15). The code required to format the row with the largest sales value is as follows:

```
Sub HighlightWholeRow()
    With Range("D2:F15")
        .Select
        .FormatConditions.Delete
        .FormatConditions.Add Type:=xlExpression, _
            Formula1:="=$F2=MAX($F$2:$F$15)"
        .FormatConditions(1).Interior.Color = RGB(255, 0, 0)
    End With
End Sub
```

Using the New NumberFormat Property

In earlier versions of Excel, a cell that matched a conditional format could have a particular font, font color, border, or fill pattern. In Excel 2007, you can also specify a number format. This can prove useful for selectively changing the number format used to display the values.

For example, you might want to display numbers above 999 in thousands, numbers above 999,999 in hundred thousands, and numbers above 9 million in millions.

If you turn on the macro recorder and attempt to record setting the conditional format to a custom number format, the Excel 2007 VBA macro recorder actually records the action of executing an XL4 macro! Skip the recorded code and use the `NumberFormat` property as shown here:

```
Sub NumberFormat()
    With Range("E1:G26")
        .FormatConditions.Delete
        .FormatConditions.Add Type:=xlCellValue, Operator:=xlGreater, _
            Formula1:="=9999999"
        .FormatConditions(1).NumberFormat = "$#,##0,,""M"""
        .FormatConditions.Add Type:=xlCellValue, Operator:=xlGreater, _
            Formula1:="=999999"
        .FormatConditions(2).NumberFormat = "$#,##0.0,,""M"""
        .FormatConditions.Add Type:=xlCellValue, Operator:=xlGreater, _
            Formula1:="=999"
        .FormatConditions(3).NumberFormat = "$#,##0,K"
    End With
End Sub
```

Figure 15.12 shows the original numbers in columns A:C. The results of running the macro are shown in columns E:G. The dialog box shows the resulting conditional format rules.

Figure 15.12
New in Excel 2007, conditional formats can specify a specific number format.

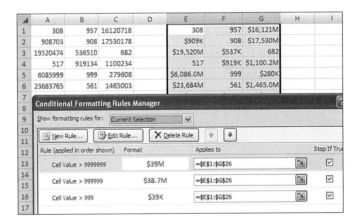

Next Steps

In Chapter 16, "Reading from and Writing to the Web," you will learn how to use Web queries to automatically import data from the Internet to your Excel applications.

Reading from and Writing to the Web

16

The Internet has become pervasive and has changed our lives. From your desktop, millions of answers are available at your fingertips. In addition, publishing a report on the web allows millions of others to instantly access your information.

This chapter discusses automated ways to pull data from the web into spreadsheets, using web queries. It also shows how to save data from your spreadsheet directly to the web.

Getting Data from the Web

Someone at a desk anywhere can get up-to-the-minute stock prices for a portfolio. Figure 16.1 shows a web page from Finance.Yahoo.com, which shows current stock quotes for a theoretical portfolio. Clearly, the people at Yahoo! understand how important spreadsheets are, because they offer a link to download the data to a spreadsheet.

Instead of manually downloading data from a website every day and then importing it into Excel, you can use the Web Query feature in Excel to allow it to automatically retrieve the data from a web page.

Web queries can be set up to refresh the data from the web every day or even every minute. While they were originally fairly hard to define, the Excel user interface now includes a web browser that you can use to build the web query.

Figure 16.1
A wealth of near-real-time data is available for free on websites everywhere. Finance.Yahoo.com even offers a link to download the portfolio to a spreadsheet. Web queries offer something so much more amazing than manually downloading the file each day.

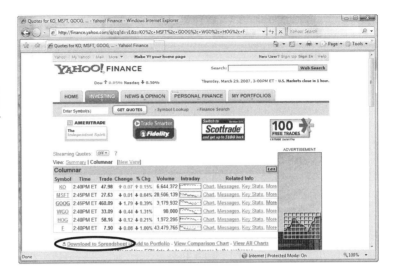

Manually Creating a Web Query and Refreshing with VBA

The easiest way to get started with web queries is to create your first one manually. Using any web browser, navigate to a website and enter the settings needed to display the information of interest to you. In the case of Figure 16.1, the URL to display that portfolio is as follows:

http://finance.yahoo.com/q/cq?d=v1&s=KO%2c+MSFT%2c+GOOG%2c+WGO%2c+HOG%2c+F

Open Excel. Find a blank area of the worksheet. From the Data tab of the Ribbon, choose Get External Data, from Web. Excel shows the New Web Query dialog with your Internet Explorer home page displayed. Copy the preceding URL to the Address text box and click Go. In a moment, the desired web page will display in the dialog box. Note that in addition to the web page, there are a number of yellow squares with a black arrow. These squares are in the upper-left corner of various tables on the web page. Click the square that contains the data that you want to import to Excel. In this case, you want the portfolio information. As shown in Figure 16.2, click the square by the table of quotes. While you are clicking, a blue border confirms the table that will be imported. After you click, the yellow arrow changes to a green check mark.

Click the Import button on the New Web Query dialog. Click OK on the Import Data dialog. In a few seconds, you will see the live data imported into a range on your spreadsheet, as shown in Figure 16.3.

Figure 16.2
Use the New Web Query dialog to browse to a web page. Highlight the table that you want to import to Excel by clicking on a yellow arrow adjacent to the table.

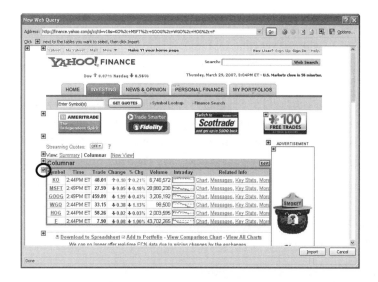

Figure 16.3
Data from the web page is automatically copied to your worksheet. You can now use VBA to automatically refresh this data at your command or periodically.

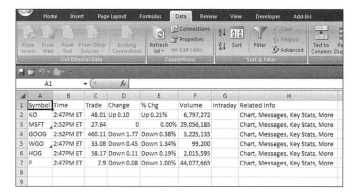

Using VBA to Update an Existing Web Query

To update all web queries on the current sheet, use this code:

```
Sub RefreshAllWebQueries()
    Dim QT As QueryTable
    For Each QT In ActiveSheet.QueryTables
        Application.StatusBar = "Refreshing " & QT.Connection
        QT.Refresh
    Next QT
    Application.StatusBar = False
End Sub
```

You could assign this macro to a hot key or to a macro button and refresh all queries on demand.

Building a New Web Query with VBA

The problem with the previous examples is that the web query URL is hard-coded into the VBA. Someone would be required to edit the VBA code every time that the portfolio changes.

It is fairly simple to build a web query on-the-fly. The key is to build a connect string. The connect string for the Yahoo! Finance stock quote is this:

```
URL: http://finance.yahoo.com/q/cq?d=v1&s=PSO,+SJM,+KO,+MSFT,+CSCO,+INTC
```

To build a flexible application, you need to use the concatenation character (&) to join the first part of the connect string with the various stock symbols.

Figure 16.4 shows a simple front end for a web query engine. Anyone can enter stock symbols of interest in the shaded area of Column A. The Get Quotes button is set up to call the CreateNewQuery macro.

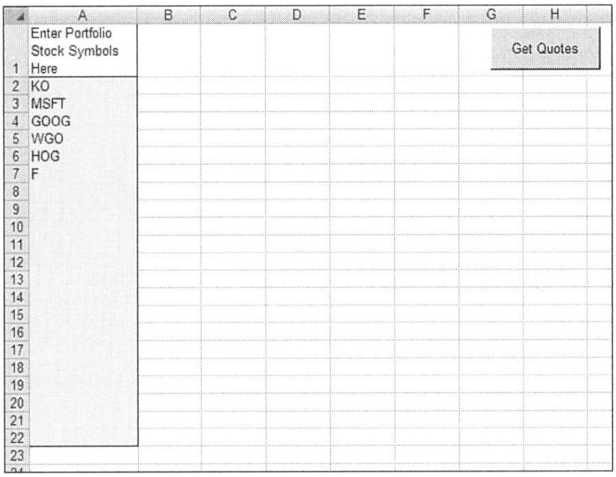

Figure 16.4

This worksheet serves as a front end to allow different stock symbols to be entered in Column A. Click the Get Quotes button to run a macro that builds a web query on-the-fly on a second worksheet and then copies the data to this sheet.

When the button is clicked, the macro builds a connect string by concatenating the first part of the URL with the first stock symbol from cell A2:

```
ConnectString = "URL;http://finance.Yahoo.com/q/cq?d=v1&s=" & _
    WSD.Cells(i, 1).Value
```

As the program loops through additional stock symbols, it takes the existing connect string and adds a comma and a plus sign, and then the next stock symbol:

```
ConnectString = ConnectString & ",+" & WSD.Cells(i, 1).Value
```

> **TIP**
>
> Another difficult task is determining the table number that you want to retrieve from the web page. The easiest solution is to record a macro while selecting the proper table. Then, look in the recorded macro for the `WebTables = "11"` property.

After the connect string has been built, the macro uses a worksheet called Workspace to build the web query. This hides the unformatted web query results from view. Because it is possible that the list of stock symbols has changed since the last web query, the program deletes any old query and then builds the new query.

It is important to set the query up with BackgroundRefresh set to False. This ensures that the macro pauses to give the query time to refresh before continuing.

After the results have been received, the program assigns a range name to the results and uses VLOOKUP formulas to retrieve the desired columns from the web query:

```
Sub CreateNewQuery()
    Dim WSD As Worksheet
    Dim WSW As Worksheet
    Dim QT As QueryTable
    Dim FinalRow As Long
    Dim i As Integer
    Dim ConnectString As String
    Dim FinalResultRow As Long
    Dim RowCount As Long

    Set WSD = Worksheets("Portfolio")
    Set WSW = Worksheets("Workspace")

    ' Read column A of Portfolio to find all stock symbols
    FinalRow = WSD.Cells(Rows.Count, 1).End(xlUp).Row
    For i = 2 To FinalRow
        Select Case i
            Case 2
                ConnectString = "URL;http://finance.Yahoo.com/q/cq?d=v1&s=" & _
                    WSD.Cells(i, 1).Value
            Case Else
                ConnectString = ConnectString & "%2c+" & WSD.Cells(i, 1).Value
        End Select
    Next i

    ' On the Workspace worksheet, clear all existing query tables
    For Each QT In WSW.QueryTables
        QT.Delete
    Next QT

    ' Define a new web Query
    Set QT = WSW.QueryTables.Add(Connection:=ConnectString, _
        Destination:=WSW.Range("A1"))
    With QT
        .Name = "portfolio"
        .FieldNames = True
        .RowNumbers = False
        .FillAdjacentFormulas = False
        .PreserveFormatting = True
        .RefreshOnFileOpen = False
        .BackgroundQuery = False
        .RefreshStyle = xlInsertDeleteCells
        .SavePassword = False
        .SaveData = True
        .AdjustColumnWidth = True
```

```
        .RefreshPeriod = 0
        .WebSelectionType = xlSpecifiedTables
        .WebFormatting = xlWebFormattingNone
        .WebTables = "11"
        .WebPreFormattedTextToColumns = True
        .WebConsecutiveDelimitersAsOne = True
        .WebSingleBlockTextImport = False
        .WebDisableDateRecognition = False
        .WebDisableRedirections = False
    End With

    ' Refresh the query
    QT.Refresh BackgroundQuery:=False

    ' Define a named range for the results
    FinalResultRow = WSW.Cells(Rows,Count, 1).End(xlUp).Row
    WSW.Cells(1, 1).Resize(FinalResultRow, 7).Name = "WebInfo"

    ' Build a VLOOKUP to get quotes from WSW to WSD
    RowCount = FinalRow - 1
    WSD.Cells(2, 2).Resize(RowCount, 1).FormulaR1C1 = _
        "=VLOOKUP(RC1,WebInfo,3,False)"
    WSD.Cells(2, 3).Resize(RowCount, 1).FormulaR1C1 = _
        "=VLOOKUP(RC1,WebInfo,4,False)"
    WSD.Cells(2, 4).Resize(RowCount, 1).FormulaR1C1 = _
        "=VLOOKUP(RC1,WebInfo,5,False)"
    WSD.Cells(2, 5).Resize(RowCount, 1).FormulaR1C1 = _
        "=VLOOKUP(RC1,WebInfo,6,False)"
    WSD.Cells(2, 6).Resize(RowCount, 1).FormulaR1C1 = _
        "=VLOOKUP(RC1,WebInfo,2,False)"

    MsgBox "Data Updated"
End Sub
```


When the program runs, you will get nicely formatted results, as shown in Figure 16.5.

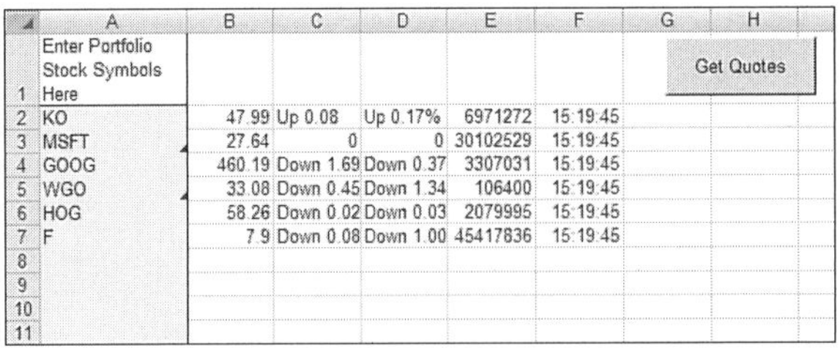

	A	B	C	D	E	F	G	H
1	Enter Portfolio Stock Symbols Here							Get Quotes
2	KO	47.99	Up 0.08	Up 0.17%	6971272	15:19:45		
3	MSFT	27.64	0	0	30102529	15:19:45		
4	GOOG	460.19	Down 1.69	Down 0.37	3307031	15:19:45		
5	WGO	33.08	Down 0.45	Down 1.34	106400	15:19:45		
6	HOG	58.26	Down 0.02	Down 0.03	2079995	15:19:45		
7	F	7.9	Down 0.08	Down 1.00	45417836	15:19:45		
8								
9								
10								
11								

Figure 16.5
After you run the macro, only the relevant columns are shown on the report. The back worksheet contains the unformatted web query from the website.

Using Streaming Data

A number of services offer live streaming data into your spreadsheet. These services use a technology such as dynamic data exchange (DDE) to automatically pipe information directly into cells in your worksheet. Although these services require a monthly subscription, it is pretty amazing to watch your spreadsheet automatically change every second with real-time stock prices.

These real-time DDE services typically use a formula that identifies the external EXE program, a pipe character (|), and data for the external program to use.

In Figure 16.6, the formula in cell A2 is calling the MktLink.exe program to return price data for stock symbol AA.

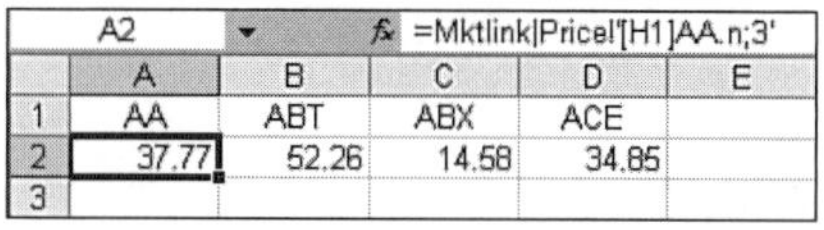

Figure 16.6
The MktLink.exe service allows live streaming data to be piped into cells on the spreadsheet.

	A	B	C	D	E
	A2		ƒx =Mktlink|Price!'[H1]AA.n;3'		
1	AA	ABT	ABX	ACE	
2	37.77	52.26	14.58	34.85	
3					

Although these services are amazing to watch, the data is fleeting. What do you do with information that flies by, updating every few seconds? The real power is using Excel to capture and save the data every so often to look for trends.

Using `Application.OnTime` to Periodically Analyze Data

VBA offers the `OnTime` method for running any VBA procedure at a specific time of day or after a specific amount of time has passed.

You could write a macro that would capture data every hour throughout the day. This macro would have times hard-coded. The following code will, theoretically, capture data from a website every hour throughout the day:

```
Sub ScheduleTheDay()
    Application.OnTime EarliestTime:=TimeValue("8:00 AM"), _
        Procedure:=CaptureData
    Application.OnTime EarliestTime:=TimeValue("9:00 AM"), _
        Procedure:=CaptureData
    Application.OnTime EarliestTime:=TimeValue("10:00 AM"), _
        Procedure:=CaptureData
    Application.OnTime EarliestTime:=TimeValue("11:00 AM"), _
        Procedure:=CaptureData
    Application.OnTime EarliestTime:=TimeValue("12:00 AM"), _
        Procedure:=CaptureData
    Application.OnTime EarliestTime:=TimeValue("1:00 PM"), _
        Procedure:=CaptureData
    Application.OnTime EarliestTime:=TimeValue("2:00 PM"), _
        Procedure:=CaptureData
    Application.OnTime EarliestTime:=TimeValue("3:00 PM"), _
        Procedure:=CaptureData
    Application.OnTime EarliestTime:=TimeValue("4:00 PM"), _
        Procedure:=CaptureData
    Application.OnTime EarliestTime:=TimeValue("5:00 PM"), _
        Procedure:=CaptureData
End Sub

Sub CaptureData()
    Dim WSQ As Worksheet
    Dim NextRow As Long
```

```
    Set WSQ = Worksheets("MyQuery")
    ' Refresh the web query
    WSQ.Range("A2").QueryTable.Refresh BackgroundQuery:=False
    ' Make sure the data is updated
    Application.Wait (Now + TimeValue("0:00:10"))
    ' Copy the web query results to a new row
    NextRow = WSQ.Cells(65536, 1).End(xlUp).Row + 1
    WSQ.Range("A2:B2").Copy WSQ.Cells(NextRow, 1)
End Sub
```

Scheduled Procedures Require Ready Mode

The OnTime method will run provided only that Excel is in Ready, Copy, Cut, or Find mode at the prescribed time. If you start to edit a cell at 7:59:55 a.m. and keep that cell in Edit mode, Excel cannot run the CaptureData macro at 8:00 a.m. as directed.

In the preceding code example, I specified only the start time for the procedure to run. Excel waits anxiously until the spreadsheet is returned to Ready mode and then runs the scheduled program as soon as it can.

The classic example is that you start to edit a cell at 7:59 a.m., and then your manager walks in and asks you to attend a surprise staff meeting down the hall. If you leave your spreadsheet in Edit mode and attend the staff meeting until 10:30 a.m., the program cannot run the first three scheduled hours of updates. As soon as you return to your desk and press Enter to exit Edit mode, the program runs all previously scheduled tasks. In the preceding code, you will find that the first three scheduled updates of the program all happen between 10:30 and 10:31 a.m.

Specifying a Window of Time for an Update

One alternative is to provide Excel with a window of time within which to make the update. The following code tells Excel to run the update at anytime between 8:00 a.m. and 8:05 a.m. If the Excel session remains in Edit mode for the entire five minutes, the scheduled task is skipped:

```
Application.OnTime EarliestTime:=TimeValue("8:00 AM"), Procedure:=CaptureData,
  LatestTime:=TimeValue("8:05 AM")
```

Canceling a Previously Scheduled Macro

It is fairly difficult to cancel a previously scheduled macro. You must know the exact time that the macro is scheduled to run. To cancel a pending operation, call the OnTime method again, using the Schedule:=False parameter to unschedule the event. The following code cancels the 11:00 a.m. run of CaptureData:

```
Sub CancelEleven()
Application.OnTime EarliestTime:=TimeValue("11:00 AM"), _
    Procedure:=CaptureData, Schedule:=False
End Sub
```

It is interesting to note that the `OnTime` schedules are remembered by a running instance of Excel. If you keep Excel open but close the workbook with the scheduled procedure, it still runs. Consider this hypothetical series of events:

1. Open Excel at 7:30 a.m.
2. Open `Schedule.XLS` and run a macro to schedule a procedure at 8:00 a.m.
3. Close Schedule.xls but keep Excel open.
4. Open a new workbook and begin entering data.

At 8:00 a.m., Excel reopens Schedule.xls and runs the scheduled macro. Excel doesn't close Schedule.xls. As you can imagine, this is fairly annoying and alarming if you are not expecting it. If you are going to make extensive use of `Application.Ontime`, you might want to have it running in one instance of Excel while you work in a second instance of Excel.

If you are using a macro to schedule a macro a certain amount of time in the future from the current time, you could remember the time in an out-of-the way cell to be able to cancel the update. See an example in the section "Scheduling a Macro to Run x Minutes in the Future."

Closing Excel Cancels All Pending Scheduled Macros

If you close Excel with File, Exit, all future scheduled macros are automatically canceled. When you have a macro that has scheduled a bunch of macros at indeterminate times, closing Excel is the only way to prevent the macros from running.

Scheduling a Macro to Run x Minutes in the Future

You can schedule a macro to run at a time at a certain point in the future. The macro uses the `TIME` function to return the current time and adds 2 minutes and 30 seconds to the time. The following macro runs something 2 minutes and 30 seconds from now:

```
Sub ScheduleAnything()
    ' This macro can be used to schedule anything
    WaitHours = 0
    WaitMin = 2
    WaitSec = 30
    NameOfScheduledProc = "CaptureData"
    ' --- End of Input Section -------

    ' Determine the next time this should run
    NextTime = Time + TimeSerial(WaitHours, WaitMin, WaitSec)

    ' Schedule ThisProcedure to run then
    Application.OnTime EarliestTime:=NextTime, Procedure:=NameOfScheduledProc

End Sub
```

If you need to later cancel this scheduled event, it would be nearly impossible. You won't know the exact time that the macro grabbed the `TIME` function. You might try to save this value in an out-of-the-way cell:

```
Sub ScheduleWithCancelOption
    NameOfScheduledProc = "CaptureData"

    ' Determine the next time this should run
    NextTime = Time + TimeSerial(0,2,30)
    Range("ZZ1").Value = NextTime

    ' Schedule ThisProcedure to run then
    Application.OnTime EarliestTime:=NextTime, Procedure:=NameOfScheduledProc

End Sub

Sub CancelLater()
        NextTime = Range("ZZ1").value
        Application.OnTime EarliestTime:=NextTime, _
    Procedure:=CaptureData, Schedule:=False
End Sub
```

Scheduling a Verbal Reminder

The text to speech tools in Excel can be fun. The following macro sets up a schedule that will remind you when it is time to go to the staff meeting:

```
Sub ScheduleSpeak()
    Application.OnTime EarliestTime:=TimeValue("9:14 AM"), _
        Procedure:="RemindMe"
End Sub

Sub RemindMe()
    Application.Speech.Speak Text:="Bill. It is time for the staff meeting."
End Sub
```

If you want to pull a prank on your manager, you can schedule Excel to automatically turn on the Speak on Enter feature. Follow this scenario:

1. Tell your manager that you are taking him out to lunch to celebrate April 1.
2. At some point in the morning, while your manager is getting coffee, run the ScheduleSpeech macro. Design the macro to run 15 minutes after your lunch starts.
3. Take your manager to lunch.
4. While the manager is away, the scheduled macro will run.
5. When the manager returns and starts typing data in Excel, the computer will repeat the cells as they are entered. This is slightly reminiscent of the computer on *Star Trek* that repeated everything that Lieutenant Uhura would say.

After this starts happening, you can pretend to be innocent; after all, you have a firm alibi for when the prank began to happen:

```
Sub ScheduleSpeech()
    Application.OnTime EarliestTime:=TimeValue("12:15 PM"), _
        Procedure:="SetUpSpeech"
End Sub
```

```
Sub SetupSpeech())
    Application.Speech.SpeakCellOnEnter = True
End Sub
```

NOTE To turn off Speak on Enter, you can either dig out the button from the QAT Customization panel (look in the category called Commands Not on the Ribbon). Or, if you can run some VBA, change the SetupSpeech macro to change the `True` to `False`.

16

Scheduling a Macro to Run Every Two Minutes

My favorite method is to ask Excel to run a certain macro every two minutes. However, I realize that if a macro gets delayed because I accidentally left the workbook in Edit mode while going to the staff meeting, I don't want dozens of updates to happen in a matter of seconds.

The easy solution is to have the `ScheduleAnything` procedure recursively schedule itself to run again in two minutes. The following code schedules a run in two minutes and then performs CaptureData:

```
Sub ScheduleAnything()
    ' This macro can be used to schedule anything
    ' Enter how often you want to run the macro in hours and minutes
    WaitHours = 0
    WaitMin = 2
    WaitSec = 0
    NameOfThisProcedure = "ScheduleAnything"
    NameOfScheduledProc = "CaptureData"
    ' --- End of Input Section -------

    ' Determine the next time this should run
    NextTime = Time + TimeSerial(WaitHours, WaitMin, WaitSec)

    ' Schedule ThisProcedure to run then
    Application.OnTime EarliestTime:=NextTime, Procedure:=NameOfThisProcedure

    ' Get the Data
    Application.Run NameOfScheduledProc

End Sub
```

This method has some advantages. I have not scheduled a million updates in the future. I have only one future update scheduled at any given time. Therefore, if I decide that I am tired of seeing the national debt every 15 seconds, I only need to comment out the `Application.OnTime` line of code and wait 15 seconds for the last update to happen.

Publishing Data to a Web Page

This chapter has highlighted many ways to capture data from the web. It is also useful for publishing Excel data back to the web.

In Chapter 14, "Excel Power," a macro was able to produce reports for each region in a company. Instead of printing and faxing the report, it would be cool to save the Excel file as HTML and post the results on a company intranet so that the regional manager could instantly access the latest version of the report.

Consider a report like the one shown in Figure 16.7. With the Excel user interface, it is easy to use save the report as a web page to create an HTML view of the data.

Figure 16.7

A macro from Chapter 13 was used to automatically generate this Excel workbook. Rather than email the report, we could save it as a web page and post it on the company intranet.

◢	A	B	C
1	Top 5 Customers in the West Region		
2			
3	Customer	Revenue	
4	Guarded Kettle Corporation	8,889K	
5	Agile Glass Supply	3,877K	
6	Tremendous Flagpole Traders	2,361K	
7	Innovative Oven Corporation	2,359K	
8	Trouble-Free Eggbeater Inc.	2,303K	
9	Top 5 Total	19,789K	
10			

In Excel 2007, use Save As, Other Formats on the Office Icon menu. Choose Web Page (*.htm, *html) in the Save as Type drop-down.

> **NOTE**
> The Excel 2003 option to add interactivity to a web page has been deprecated from Excel 2007 and is no longer available.

After Microsoft removed the interactivity option, you only have control over the title that appears in the top of the window. Click the Change Title button to change the `<Title>` tag for the web page. Type a name that ends in either .html or .html and click Publish....

The result is a file which can be viewed in any web browser. The web page accurately shows our number formats and font sizes (see Figure 16.9).

Several versions ago, Microsoft became enamored of saving a worksheet as HTML, then later opening the HTML file in Excel and having the original formulas intact. They called this feature "round tripping." This feature causes Excel to write out incredibly bloated HTML files. The data presented in Figure 16.9 is about 228 bytes of data, but Excel requires 5,662 bytes of data to store both the data for presentation and the data needed to load the file back into Excel.

Although the data is accurately presented in Figure 16.9, it is not extremely fancy. We don't have a company logo or navigation bar to examine other reports.

Figure 16.8
Use the Change Title button to add a new title to the blue title bar at the top of the web page.

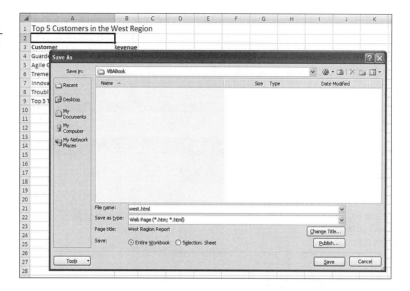

Figure 16.9
Excel does a nice job of rendering the worksheet as HTML.

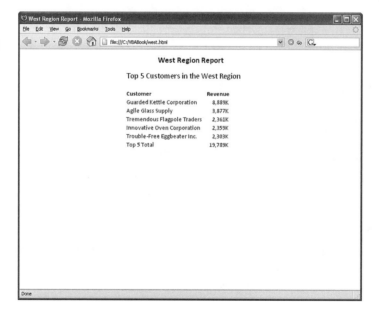

Using VBA to Create Custom Web Pages

Long before Microsoft introduced the Save as Web Page functionality, people had been using VBA to take Excel data and publish it as HTML. The advantage of this method is that you can write out specific HTML statements to display company logos and navigation bars.

Consider a typical web page template. There is code to display a logo and navigation bar at the top/side. There is data specific to the page, and then there is data to close the HTML file. Build an HTML template with the words **PUT DATA HERE** and examine the resulting HTML in Notepad, as shown in Figure 16.10.

Figure 16.10

Examining the `sample.html` file in Notepad and locating the words *PUT DATA HERE* allows you to separate the HTML file into three pieces: the top portion of the code used to write the navigation bar, the data, and the bottom portion used to close the HTML page.

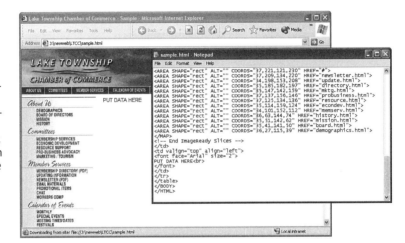

After you examine the code in Notepad, the task of creating a custom web page is fairly simple. First, write out the HTML needed to draw the navigation bars. Then, write the data from Excel. Then, write the few lines of HTML to close the table and finish the web page.

Using Excel as a Content Management System

Two hundred and fifty million people are proficient in Excel. Companies everywhere have data in Excel and many staffers who are comfortable in maintaining that data. Rather than force these people to learn how to create HTML pages, why not build a content management system to take their Excel data and write out custom web pages?

Figure 16.11 shows a typical membership database. We had a web designer offer to build an expensive PHP (Hypertext Preprocessor) database on the web to display the membership directory and allow maintenance of members.

The organization is already maintaining this data in Excel. Using the code from Figure 16.10, you pretty much know the top and bottom portions of the HTML needed to render the web page.

Building a content management system with these tools is simple. To the membership directory Excel file, I added two worksheets. In the worksheet called Top, I copied the HTML needed to generate the navigation bar of the website. To the worksheet called Bottom, I copied the HTML needed to generate the end of the HTML page. Figure 16.12 shows the simple Bottom worksheet.

Figure 16.11

Companies everywhere are maintaining all sorts of data in Excel and are comfortable updating the data in Excel. Why not marry Excel with a simple bit of VBA so that custom HTML can be produced from Excel?

	A	B	C	D	E	F	G	H
1	compan	address	city	state	zip	phone	formatted	
2	ACCom	2930 Edi	Uniontow	OH	44685	3305551212	(330) 555-1212	
3	ACTION	11806 Fe	Uniontow	OH	44685	3305551212	(330) 555-1212	
4	Allen K	2735 Gre	North Car	Oh	44720-142	3305551212	(330) 555-1212	
5	Allen M	3515 Ma	Uniontow	OH	44685	3305551212	(330) 555-1212	
6	Theresa	3500 Ma	Uniontow	OH	44685	3305551212	(330) 555-1212	
7	AlterCar	1420 Smi	Hartville	OH	44632	3305551212	(330) 555-1212	
8	America	317 Sout	Hartville	OH	44632	3305551212	(330) 555-1212	
9	America	2213 Cle	Canton	OH	44709	3305551212	(330) 555-1212	
10	Arnold F	504 Wes	Hartville	OH	44632	3305551212	(330) 555-1212	
11	ASAP, A	6551 Mi	Canton	OH	44721	3305551212	(330) 555-1212	
12	Aultman	2600 Sixt	Canton	OH	44710	3305551212	(330) 555-1212	
13	Baby Ty	878 Wes	Hartville	OH	44632	3305551212	(330) 555-1212	
14	Best Bib	311 S. Pr	Hartville	OH	44632	3305551212	(330) 555-1212	
15	Bicycle S	854-A W	Hartville	OH	44632	3305551212	(330) 555-1212	
16	Capital S	150 Gran	Hartville	OH	44632	3305551212	(330) 555-1212	
17	China V	808 Wes	Hartville	OH	44632	3305551212	(330) 555-1212	
18	ComDoc	3458 Ma	Uniontow	OH	44685	3305551212	(330) 555-1212	
19	CompuV	13163 M	Hartville	OH	44632	3305551212	(330) 555-1212	
20	Concord	850 Wes	Hartville	OH	44632	3305551212	(330) 555-1212	
21	Cooper I	300 N. C	Akron	OH	44333	3305551212	(330) 555-1212	
22	Country	10244 M	Hartville	OH	44632	3305551212	(330) 555-1212	
23	Cutty's S	8050 Edi	Louisville	OH	44641	3305551212	(330) 555-1212	
24	Doreen I	831 Sun	Hartville	OH	44632	3305551212	(330) 555-1212	

16

Figure 16.12

Two worksheets are added to the membership directory workbook. One lists the HTML code necessary to draw the navigation bar. The second lists the HTML code necessary to finish the web page after displaying the data.

A7		▼	*f* x 6
	A	B	C
1	Sequence	Content	
2	1	</font>	
3	2	</td>	
4	3	</tr>	
5	4	</table>	
6	5	</BODY>	
7	6	</HTML>	
8			

The macro code opens a text file called `directory.html` for output. First, all the HTML code from the Top worksheet is written to the file.

Then the macro loops through each row in the membership directory, writing data to the file.

After completing this loop, the macro writes out the HTML code from the Bottom worksheet to finish the file:

```
Sub WriteMembershipHTML()
    ' Write web Pages
    Dim WST As Worksheet
    Dim WSB As Worksheet
    Dim WSM As Worksheet
    Set WSB = Worksheets("Bottom")
    Set WST = Worksheets("Top")
    Set WSM = Worksheets("Membership")

    ' Figure out the path
    MyPath = ThisWorkbook.Path
```

```
    LineCtr = 0

    FinalT = WST.Cells(Rows.Count, 1).End(xlUp).Row
    FinalB = WSB.Cells(Rows.Count, 1).End(xlUp).Row
    FinalM = WSM.Cells(Rows.Count, 1).End(xlUp).Row

    MyFile = "sampledirectory.html"

    ThisFile = MyPath & Application.PathSeparator & MyFile
    ThisHostFile = MyFile

    ' Delete the old HTML page
    On Error Resume Next
    Kill (ThisFile)
    On Error GoTo 0

    ' Build the title
    ThisTitle = "<Title>LTCC Membership Directory</Title>"
    WST.Cells(3, 2).Value = ThisTitle

    ' Open the file for output
    Open ThisFile For Output As #1

    ' Write out the top part of the HTML
    For j = 2 To FinalT
        Print #1, WST.Cells(j, 2).Value
    Next j

    ' For each row in Membership, write out lines of data to HTML file
    For j = 2 To FinalM
        ' Surround Member name with bold tags
        Print #1, "<b>" & WSM.Cells(j, 1).Value & "</b><br>"
        ' Member Address
        Print #1, WSM.Cells(j, 2).Value & "<br>"
        ' City, State, Zip code
        Addr = WSM.Cells(j, 3) & " " & WSM.Cells(j, 4) & " " & WSM.Cells(j, 5)
        Print #1, Addr & "<br>"
        ' Telephone number with 2 line breaks after it
        Print #1, WSM.Cells(j, 6).Value & "<br><br>"
    Next j

    ' Close old file
    ' Write date updated, but make sure there are 20 rows first
    Print #1, "<br>"
    Print #1, "This page current as of " & Format(Date, "mmmm dd, yyyy") & _
        " " & Format(Time, "h:mm AM/PM")

    ' Write out HTML code from Bottom worksheet
    For j = 2 To FinalB
        Print #1, WSB.Cells(j, 2).Value
    Next j
    Close #1

    Application.StatusBar = False
    Application.CutCopyMode = False
    MsgBox "web pages updated"

End Sub
```

Figure 16.13 shows the finished web page. This web page looks a lot better than the generic page created by Excel's Save As Web Page option. It can maintain the look and feel of the rest of the site.

Figure 16.13
A simple content-management system in Excel was used to generate this web page. The look and feel matches the rest of the website. Excel achieved it without any expensive web database coding.

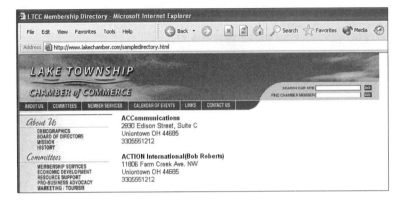

This system has many advantages. The person who maintains the membership directory is comfortable working in Excel. She has already been maintaining the data in Excel on a regular basis. Now, after updating some records, she presses a button to produce a new version of the web page.

Of course, the web designer is clueless about Excel. However, if he ever wants to change the web design, it is a simple matter to open his new `sample.html` file in Notepad and copy the new code to the Top and Bottom worksheet.

The resulting web page has a small file size—about one-sixth the size of the equivalent page created by Excel's Save As Web Page.

In real life, the content-management system in this example was extended to allow easy maintenance of the organization's calendar, board members, and so on. The resulting workbook made it possible to maintain 41 web pages at the click of a button.

Bonus: FTP from Excel

After you are able to update web pages from Excel, you still have the hassle of using an FTP program to upload the pages from your hard drive to the Internet. Again, we have lots of people proficient in Excel, but not so many comfortable with using an FTP client.

Ken Anderson has written a cool command-line FTP freeware utility. Download WCL_FTP from www.pacific.net/~ken/software/. Save WCL_FTP.exe to the root directory of your hard drive, and then use this code to automatically upload your recently created HTML files to your web server:

```
Sub DoFTP(fname, pathfname)
' To have this work, copy wcl_ftp.exe to the C:\ root directory
' Download from http://www.pacific.net/~ken/software/
```

```
' Build a string to FTP. The syntax is
' WCL_FTP.exe "Caption" hostname username password host-directory _
' host-filename local-filename get-or-put 0Ascii1Binanry 0NoLog _
' 0Background 1CloseWhenDone 1PassiveMode  1ErrorsText

If Not Worksheets("Menu").Range("I1").Value = True Then Exit Sub

s = """c:\wcl_ftp.exe "" " _
    & """Upload File to website"" " _
    & "ftp.MySite.com FTPUser FTPPassword www " _
    & fname & " " _
    & """" & pathfname & """ " _
    & "put " _
    & "0 0 0 1 1 1"

Shell s, vbMinimizedNoFocus
End Sub
```

Trusting Web Content

In Excel 2007, web queries are grouped into the untrusted content category. When you open a file that contains a web query, it is automatically disabled. A message appears in the information bar indicating that some active content has been disabled.

The person using the workbook could click the Options button to display the Multiple Issues in the workbook. The user must both enable any macros and enable the data connection, as shown in Figure 16.14. Enabling the data connection allows the web query to retrieve data.

Figure 16.14
When the Security Warning appears, click Options to enable the macros and the data connection.

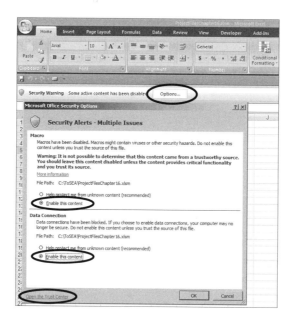

Dealing with the Security Warning is annoying. If you designate the folder that contains your file as trusted, you will not be warned about external data connections every time that you open the file. To set up a trusted location, follow these steps:

1. If you have the Security Warning displayed, click the Open the Trust Center link in the lower-left corner of the dialog and skip step 2.

2. Click the Office Icon button and choose Excel Options. In the left navigation bar of the Excel Options dialog, choose Trust Center. Click the Trust Center Settings button.

3. In the left navigation of the Trust Center, choose Trusted Locations. Excel shows a list of folders that are already trusted (see Figure 16.15).

Figure 16.15
Manage your trusted locations with this dialog.

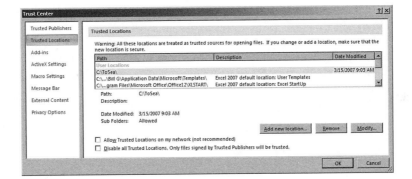

4. If your trusted location is on a network, you must choose the check box labeled Allow Trusted Locations on My Network. The dialog says that Microsoft does not recommend this. If you have control of your network, there is no problem with using a network location.

5. Click the Add New Location button. Excel displays the Microsoft Office Trusted Location dialog, as shown in Figure 16.16.

Figure 16.16
Add a trusted location to prevent Excel from disabling your content.

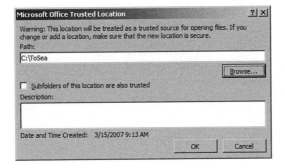

6. Click the Browse button. Navigate to your folder and click OK.

7. If you want all subfolders of the current folder to be trusted, click the Subfolders of This Location Are Also Trusted check box.

8. If you want to document why you are trusting this folder, type it in the Description text box.

9. Click OK to add the folder to the trusted locations list. Click OK two more times to return to Excel.

Any files stored in the trusted folder will have their web content and macros automatically enabled.

Next Steps

Chapter 17, "XML in Excel 2007," examines passing data between applications with XML. Some websites, such as Amazon, are offering data in XML today, which makes for a tool more powerful than web queries.

XML in Excel 2007

17

One of the features introduced in Office 2003 was the capability to better handle XML data. If you are working with a company that offers XML data and schemas, the opportunities are endless. Even if your company does not offer XML data, you can still test out these features using publicly available XML data. Later in this chapter, we look at using XML to retrieve data from Amazon.com.

Note that support for XML was only in certain editions of Excel 2003. You either needed the full boxed version of Excel 2003 or the Enterprise Edition of Excel 2003 to use the XML features. In Excel 2007, Microsoft has made the XML functionality available in every edition.

What Is XML?

If you have ever looked at the source code for a Web page, you are familiar with HTML tags. Near the top of a Web page's HTML source, you will see a tag that defines the Web page title to appear in the blue bar at the top of the browser window. The tag might look something like this:

```
<TITLE>Excel Tips from MrExcel</TITLE>
```

A Web page can contain tags to identify titles, paragraphs, tables, rows within tables, and so on. This is the language of HTML.

XML is like HTML on steroids. With XML, you can define absolutely any fields in XML. The following XML file contains information about today's orders received. There is no magic in creating an XML file; I actually typed this into Notepad:

```
<TodaysOrders>
    <SalesOrder>
        <Customer>BCA Co</Customer>
        <Address>123 North</Address>
        <City>Stow</City>
```

```
        <State>OH</State>
        <Zip>44224</Zip>
        <ItemSKU>23456</ItemSKU>
        <Quantity>500</Quantity>
        <UnitPrice>21.75</UnitPrice>
    </SalesOrder>
    <SalesOrder>
        <Customer>DEF Co</Customer>
        <Address>234 Carapace Lane</Address>
        <City>South Bend</City>
        <State>IN</State>
        <Zip>44685</Zip>
        <ItemSKU>34567</ItemSKU>
        <Quantity>20</Quantity>
        <UnitPrice>50.00</UnitPrice>
    </SalesOrder>
</TodaysOrders>
```

Simple XML Rules

If you are familiar with HTML, you need to aware of a few simple rules that differentiate XML from HTML:

- Every data element has to begin and end with an identical tag. Tag names are case sensitive. `<TagName>Data</Tagname>` is not valid. `<TagName>Data</TagName>` is valid.

- The XML file must begin and end with a root tag. There can be only one root tag in the file. In the example earlier, the root tag is `<TodaysOrders>`.

- It is valid to have an empty tag. Put a slash at the end of the tag. If there is no zip code for an international order, for example, use `<Zip/>` to indicate that there is no data for this field for this record.

- If you nest tags, the inner tag must be closed before you close the outer tag. This differs from HTML. In HTML, it is valid to code `<b>XML is very <i>cool</b></i>`. This is not valid in XML. `<Item><a>data</a></Item>` will work, but `<Item><a>data</Item></a>` will not.

For a more thorough discussion of XML, see Benoit Marchal's *XML by Example* (978-0-7897-2504-2).

Universal File Format

For many years, CSV was considered the universal file format. Just about any application could produce data in comma-separated values, and just about any spreadsheet could read in CSV data. XML promises to become the universal file format of the future, and it is much more powerful.

You may deal with CSV data every day. As developers, we need to talk to the other developer who is generating the CSV data, and we have to understand that the fifth column contains a zip code, and the sixth column contains a product SKU. If the source system ever leaves out a field, we are likely to end up with wrong results. For years, CSV has been the universal format to get data from another system into a spreadsheet. With CSV, both developers must understand that the fifth column contains a zip code, and the sixth column contains a product SKU (see Figure 17.1).

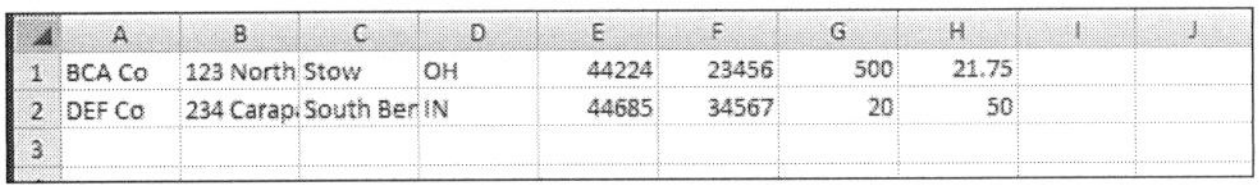

Figure 17.1
Open a CSV file and you may have this confusing view of the data.

XML as the New Universal File Format

XML is much more powerful. If you use Excel to open the simple XML file shown in Figure 17.1, Excel can offer headings and can even infer something called the *schema* of the data. A schema is a separate file that describes the columns and relationships inherent in the data. If the source system would happen to be missing a zip code for a record, we do not have to worry about the SKU moving over from Column F. Compare Figure 17.2 with the CSV example shown in Figure 17.1. Excel can present a much more meaningful view of the data.

Figure 17.2
Data can be written in XML format by any system and intelligently read into Excel. Unlike CSV data, the format of XML data is something Excel can understand.

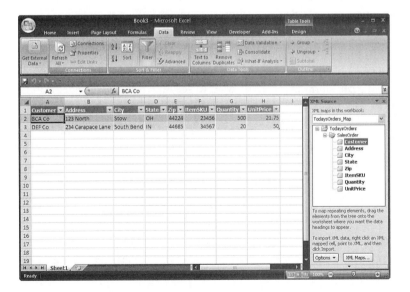

If you insert new records into the XML list in Excel, you can save the file back out as just the XML data. Use Office Icon, Save As, Other Formats. In the Save As Type drop-down, choose XML Data (*.xml). Excel can natively read from and write to XML files, allowing you to share data between applications.

After you save the document as an XML table, Excel nicely formats the XML with an appropriate structure and tab characters for subelements. This allows the data to be viewed in a simple text editor such as Notepad (see Figure 17.3).

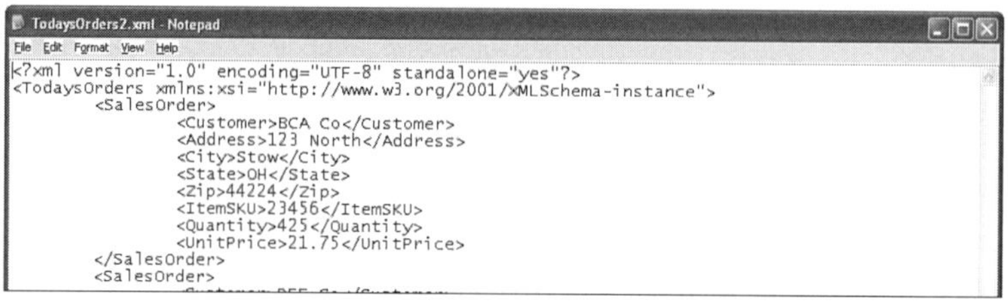

Figure 17.3
After you add records to the XML data in Excel and save, the resulting XML is neatly formatted.

```
TodaysOrders2.xml - Notepad
File  Edit  Format  View  Help
<?xml version="1.0" encoding="UTF-8" standalone="yes"?>
<TodaysOrders xmlns:xsi="http://www.w3.org/2001/XMLSchema-instance">
        <SalesOrder>
                <Customer>BCA Co</Customer>
                <Address>123 North</Address>
                <City>Stow</City>
                <State>OH</State>
                <Zip>44224</Zip>
                <ItemSKU>23456</ItemSKU>
                <Quantity>425</Quantity>
                <UnitPrice>21.75</UnitPrice>
        </SalesOrder>
        <SalesOrder>
```

The Alphabet Soup of XML

Note that in the preceding example we had only an XML file, and Excel was able to accurately read the data, allow editing, and write the data back out for use by another application.

Two additional file types—schemas and transforms—enhance XML files.

Although the XML file contains the data and field names, an XML schema file defines data relationships and data validation requirements. For example, a zip code field could require five numeric digits. XML schemas are typically stored in XSD files.

XSL files are called *transforms* or *solutions*. A transform describes how the fields in the XML file should be mapped to your document. If your data contains 20 elements, you can define in the transform file that you want to see only particular elements in this spreadsheet. You can have many XSL files for a particular schema to enable many views of the same data.

If you are reading someone else's XML data, XSD and XSL files have probably been provided for you. If you are reading your own XML data, Excel actually infers a data schema for you. After opening the XML file with TodaysOrders introduced at the start of this chapter, you can go to the immediate pane of the VB Editor and retrieve the XSD file. Type the following:

```
Print ActiveWorkbook.XmlMaps(1).Schemas(1).xml
```

Copy the result to a Notepad window and save as **TodaysOrders.xsd.** Figure 17.4 shows the inferred XSD file, although I have added line breaks and spacing to improve the readability.

The final step to fully use XML in Office 2007 is to create XSL transform files. There is no easy way to create this with the tools in Excel. For a discussion of the rather awkward process of manually creating an XSL file, see www.mrexcel.com/tip064.shtml.

Figure 17.4
Excel is able to infer a default schema for any XML file that it encounters. Having an XSD schema file is a requirement to use any higher-level XML features such as repurposing data.

```
TodaysOrders2.xsd - Notepad
File  Edit  Format  View  Help
<xsd:schema xmlns:xsd="http://www.w3.org/2001/XMLSchema"><xsd:element nillable="true"
name="TodaysOrders"><xsd:complexType><xsd:sequence minOccurs="0"><xsd:element minOccurs="0"
maxOccurs="unbounded" nillable="true" name="SalesOrder"
form="unqualified"><xsd:complexType><xsd:sequence minOccurs="0"><xsd:element minOccurs="0"
nillable="true" type="xsd:string" name="Customer"
form="unqualified"></xsd:element><xsd:element minOccurs="0" nillable="true" type="xsd:string"
name="Address" form="unqualified"></xsd:element><xsd:element minOccurs="0" nillable="true"
type="xsd:string" name="City" form="unqualified"></xsd:element><xsd:element minOccurs="0"
nillable="true" type="xsd:string" name="State" form="unqualified"></xsd:element><xsd:element
minOccurs="0" nillable="true" type="xsd:integer" name="Zip"
form="unqualified"></xsd:element><xsd:element minOccurs="0" nillable="true"
type="xsd:integer" name="ItemSKU" form="unqualified"></xsd:element><xsd:element minOccurs="0"
nillable="true" type="xsd:integer" name="Quantity"
form="unqualified"></xsd:element><xsd:element minOccurs="0" nillable="true"
type="xsd:double" name="UnitPrice"
form="unqualified"></xsd:element></xsd:sequence></xsd:complexType></xsd:element></xsd:sequenc
e></xsd:complexType></xsd:element></xsd:schema>
```

Microsoft's Use of XML as a File Type

Microsoft has been rapidly improving their support for XML:

- In Excel 2002, you were first able to read from an XML file.
- In Excel 2003, Excel could write XML files. This was also the first version in which you could opt to save Excel or Word files as XML rather than the usual binary XLS or DOC file type. In the previous edition of this book, we marveled at the ability for Excel to round-trip a file to XML and back to Excel without losing any formulas or formatting (see Figure 17.5). In Excel 2003, the XML file type would not support charts or VBA.

Figure 17.5
In Excel 2003, most spreadsheet elements, except charts and VBA, were supported by the XML file type.

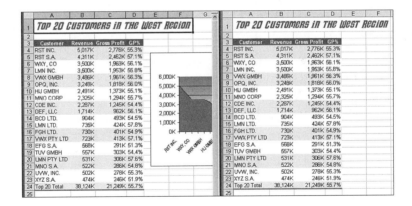

- In Excel 2007, the default file type for Excel files is a zipped XML file. The next section describes how Excel 2007 stores workbooks with XML.

How Excel 2007 Stores Workbooks with XML

Excel 2007 introduces new file formats such as XLSX, XLSM, and XLSB. The last file format is still a proprietary binary format. However, the XLSX and XLSM file formats are 100 percent XML formats. Excel saves the workbook, including charts, SmartArt graphics, formulas, formatting, and numbers in various XML files. All the XML formats are then zipped into a single file and the extension is changed from .zip to .xlsx.

In addition, the XLSM format includes support for macros, modules, and userforms.

You can easily explore the inner workings of an Excel 2007 file by following these steps.

1. Create an Excel file. Add formulas, formatting, a chart, and a bit of VBA macro code.

2. Save the file as an XLSM file.

3. Close the file.

4. Using Windows Explorer, browse to the folder that contains the file.

5. Rename the file to have a .zip extension. You may be warned that this might make the file unusable. This is okay.

6. Open the file with WinZip or your favorite unzipping utility. You will see that the file is composed of many XML parts. The chart and the VBA will each get its own XML part. You will have an XML part for each worksheet. The calculation tree is now fully exposed and explorable in CalcChain.xml.

Figure 17.6 shows the original workbook, the files in the zip file and one of the XML parts. Excel stores shared strings here in order to make the file size smaller.

Figure 17.6
In Excel 2007, Microsoft stores most spreadsheet parts in plain text XML files, and then zips them into a single file.

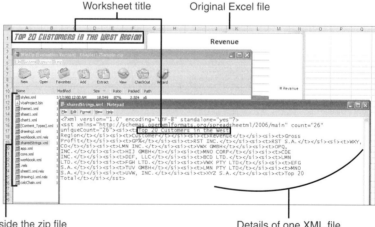

Worksheet title   Original Excel file

XML files inside the zip file   Details of one XML file

CASE STUDY

Using XML Data from Amazon.com

The promise is that all sorts of XML data will soon be available. One high-profile example available now is Amazon.com. They now offer a wide variety of queryable data that is returned in XML format.

It is possible to use VBA to query data from Amazon and have the results returned to Excel.

Amazon.com now offers more than 30 different XML streams that you can query as well as complete documentation of the information available at http://amazon.com/webservices.

Starting with a blank Excel workbook, first attach the schema to the workbook:

1. From the Developer tab of the ribbon, select Source from the XML group.
2. In the XML Source pane, click the XML Maps button.
3. In the XML Maps Dialog, click the Add button.
4. In the File Name box, type the URL for the Amazon heavy XSD file:
   `http://xml.amazon.com/schemas3/dev-heavy.xsd`. Select Open.
5. In the Multiple Roots dialog, select the ProductInfo as the root note of interest.
6. Click OK to close the XML Maps dialog.

All the fields available in the Amazon.com ProductInfo schema now appear in the XML Source pane. Drag any fields of interest to your spreadsheet, as shown in Figure 17.7.

Figure 17.7
After the XSD schema is attached to the workbook, you can drag fields of interest from the XML Source pane to the spreadsheet.

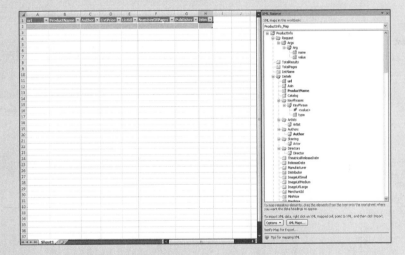

Now that the workbook is set up, you can switch to VBA to enter the code needed to retrieve data from Amazon.com.

The first step is to go to Tools, References and add a reference to Microsoft WinHTTP Services.

The Amazon Development Kit provides many sample URL strings to return various searches by author, publisher, ISBN, and so on.

After defining the proper URL string, the string is sent as a WinHttpRequest. The results are then mapped to the worksheet through the use of the .ImportXML method.

This sample code queries Amazon for all books written by Bill Jelen and published in 2006:

```
Sub QuerybyAuthor()
    ' Query all Bill Jelen books published in 2002
    Dim ws As Worksheet
    Dim whr As New WinHttpRequest
    Dim lobj As ListObject
```

```
Dim nCount As Integer
Dim objSelected As Object

Dim sURI As String

Set objSelected = Selection
Set ws = Worksheets("Sheet1")
Set lobj = ws.ListObjects(1)

Application.Cursor = xlWait

sURI = "http://xml.amazon.com/onca/xml2?t=webservices-20" _
    & "&dev-t=D3VCCO47XZEQFA" _
    & "&PowerSearch=author:Bill Jelen and pubdate:2006" _
    & "&mode=books&type=heavy&page=1&f=xml"

whr.Open "GET", sURI
whr.Send

ActiveWorkbook.XmlMaps(1).ImportXml whr.ResponseText

Application.Cursor = xlDefault

End Sub
```

After the query has run, the results are written to the List object on sheet1. Note that because I asked for an Author field and Author is a repeating element along the ProductInfo node, any titles with two authors appear twice, one with each author (see Figure 17.8).

Figure 17.8
The .ImportXML method returns the search results to the worksheet. Only the mapped fields that were dragged from the XML Source pane are displayed.

	B	C	D	E
1	ProductName	Author	ListPrice	ListId
2	Special Edition Using Microsoft(R) Office Excel 2007	Bill Jelen	$39.99	
3	Special Edition Using Microsoft(R) Office Excel 2007		$39.99	R1PT8TV1XR9EDD
4	Special Edition Using Microsoft(R) Office Excel 2007		$39.99	R3TRNUNDTLB0S5
5	Special Edition Using Microsoft(R) Office Excel 2007		$39.99	R2NQ78N8365PHX
6	Pivot Table Data Crunching for Microsoft(R) Office Excel(R) 2007 (Business Solutions)	Bill Jelen	$29.99	
7	Pivot Table Data Crunching for Microsoft(R) Office Excel(R) 2007 (Business Solutions)	Michael Alexander	$29.99	
8	Excel 2007 Miracles Made Easy: Mr. Excel Reveals 25 Amazing Things You Can Do with the	Bill Jelen	$24.95	
9	Excel 2007 Miracles Made Easy: Mr. Excel Reveals 25 Amazing Things You Can Do with the New Excel		$24.95	R1PT8TV1XR9EDD
10	Holy Macro! It's 2,500 Excel VBA Examples: Every Snippet of Excel VBA Code You'll Ever N	Hans Herber	$89.00	
11	Holy Macro! It's 2,500 Excel VBA Examples: Every Snippet of Excel VBA Code You'll Ever N	Bill Jelen	$89.00	
12	Holy Macro! It's 2,500 Excel VBA Examples: Every Snippet of Excel VBA Code You'll Ever N	Tom Urtis	$89.00	
13	Excel for Marketing Managers (Excel for Professionals series)	Ivana Taylor	$24.95	

It is interesting to note that the ProductInfo_Map offers six dozen fields and the results of the query are easily changed by dragging and dropping new data from the XML Source pane to the workbook. Without changing one line of VBA code, the query can easily focus on SalesRank or Lists or the number of Marketplace vendors offering the book for sale.

Next Steps

Although XML enables you to transfer data between unrelated applications, you already can transfer data programmatically between applications in the Microsoft Office suite. Chapter 18, "Automating Word," looks at using Excel VBA to automate and control Microsoft Word.

Automating Word

18

Word, Excel, PowerPoint, Outlook, and Access all use the same VBA language; the only difference between them is their object models (for example, Excel has a `Workbooks` object, Word has `Documents`). Any one of these applications can access another application's object model as long as the second application is installed.

To access Word's object library, Excel must establish a link to it. There are two ways of doing this: early binding or late binding. With early binding, the reference to the application object is created when the program is compiled; with late binding, it is created when the program is run.

This chapter is an introduction to accessing Word from Excel; we will not be reviewing Word's entire object model or the object models of other applications. Refer to the VBA Object Browser in the appropriate application to learn about other object models.

Early Binding

Code written with early binding executes faster than code with late binding. A reference is made to Word's object library before the code is written so that Word's objects, properties, and methods are available in the Object Browser. Tips also appear, as shown in Figure 18.1, such as a list of members of an object.

The disadvantage of early binding is that the referenced object library must exist on the system. For example, if you write a macro referencing Word 2007's object library and someone with Word 2003 attempts to run the code, the program fails because the program cannot find the 2007 object library.

Figure 18.1
Early binding allows easy access to the Word object's syntax.

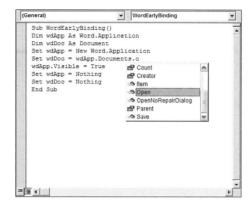

The object library is added through the VB Editor:

1. Select Tools, References.
2. Check Microsoft Word 12.0 Object Library in the Available References list (see Figure 18.2).
3. Click OK.

Figure 18.2
Select the object library from the References list.

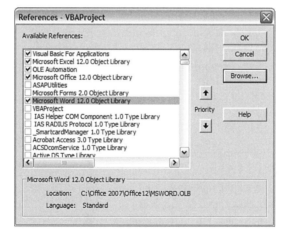

After the reference is set, Word variables can be declared with the correct (Word) variable type. However, if the object variable is declared As Object, this forces the program to use late binding:

```
Sub WordEarlyBinding()
Dim wdApp As Word.Application
Dim wdDoc As Document
Set wdApp = New Word.Application
Set wdDoc = wdApp.Documents.Open(ThisWorkbook.Path & _
    "\Chapter 18 - Automating Word.docx")
wdApp.Visible = True
Set wdApp = Nothing
Set wdDoc = Nothing
End Sub
```

> **TIP**
> Excel searches through the selected libraries to find the reference for the object type. If the type is found in more than one library, the first reference is selected. You can influence which library is chosen by changing the priority of the reference in the listing.

This example creates a new instance of Word and opens an existing Word document from Excel. The declared variables, wdApp and wdDoc, are of Word object types. wdApp is used to create a reference to the Word application in the same way the Application object is used in Excel. New Word.Application is used to create a new instance of Word.

> **TIP**
> If you are opening a document in a new instance of Word, Word is not visible. If the application needs to be shown, it must be unhidden (wdApp.Visible = True).

When finished, it's a good idea to set the object variables to Nothing and release the memory being used by the application, as shown here:

```
Set wdApp = Nothing
Set wdDoc = Nothing
```

Compile Error: Can't Find Object or Library

If the referenced version of Word does not exist on the system, an error message appears, as shown in Figure 18.3. View the References list; the missing object is highlighted with the word *MISSING* (see Figure 18.4).

Figure 18.3
Attempting to compile a program with a missing reference library will generate an error message.

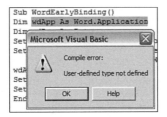

Figure 18.4
Excel will list the missing library for you.

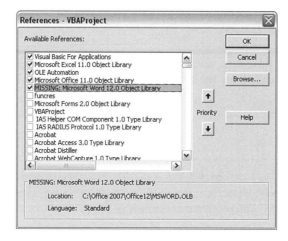

If a previous version of Word is available, you can try running the program with that version referenced. Many objects are the same between versions.

Late Binding

When using late binding, you are creating an object that refers to the Word application before linking to the Word library. Because you do not set up a reference beforehand, the only constraint on the Word version is that the objects, properties, and methods must exist. In the case where there are differences, the version can be verified and the correct object used accordingly.

The disadvantage of late binding is that Excel doesn't know what is going on—it doesn't understand that you are referring to Word. This prevents the tips from appearing when referencing Word objects. Also, built-in constants are not available and, when compiling, Excel cannot verify that the references to Word are correct. After the program is executed, the links to Word begin to build, and any coding errors are detected at that point.

The following example creates a new instance of Word and then opens and makes visible an existing Word document:

```
Sub WordLateBinding()
Dim wdApp As Object, wdDoc As Object
Set wdApp = CreateObject("Word.Application")
Set wdDoc = wdApp.Documents.Open(ThisWorkbook.Path & _
"\Chapter 18 - Automating Word.docx")
wdApp.Visible = True
Set wdApp = Nothing
Set wdDoc = Nothing
End Sub
```

An object variable (wdApp) is declared and set to reference the application (CreateObject("Word.Application")). Other required variables are then declared (wdDoc), and the application object is used to refer these variables to Word's object model.

> **CAUTION**
>
> Declaring wdApp and wdDoc as objects forces the use of late binding. The program cannot create the required links to the Word object model until it executes the CreateObject function.

Creating and Referencing Objects

The following sections describe how to create new objects as well as how to reference currently open objects.

Keyword New

In the early binding example, the keyword New was used to reference the Word application. The New keyword can be used only with early binding; it does not work with late binding. CreateObject or GetObject would also work, but New was best for that example. If an instance of the application is running and you want to use it, use the GetObject function instead.

> **CAUTION**
>
> If your code to open Word runs smoothly, but you don't see an instance of Word (and should), open your Task Manager and look for the process WinWord.exe. If it exists, from the Immediate window in Excel's VB Editor, type the following (early binding):
>
>   Word.Application.Visible = True
>
> If multiple instances of WinWord.exe are found, you must make each visible and close the extra instance(s) of WinWord.exe.

18

CreateObject **Function**

The CreateObject function was used in the late binding example, but can also be used in early binding. CreateObject has a class parameter consisting of the name and type of the object to be created (Name.Type). For example, in the examples I've shown you (Word.Application), Word is the Name, and Application is the Type.

It creates a new instance of the object; in this case, the Word application is created.

GetObject **Function**

The GetObject function can be used to reference an instance of Word that is already running. It creates an error if no instance can be found.

GetObject's two parameters are optional. The first parameter specifies the full path and filename to open, and the second parameter specifies the application program. In the following example, we leave off the application, allowing the default program (which is Word) to open the document:

```
Sub UseGetObject()
Dim wdDoc As Object
Set wdDoc = GetObject(ThisWorkbook.Path & "\Chapter 18 - Automating Word.docx")
wdDoc.Application.Visible = True
Set wdDoc = Nothing
End Sub
```

This example opens a document in an existing instance of Word and ensures the Word application's Visible property is set to True. Note that to make the document visible, you have to refer to the application object (wdDoc.Application.Visible) because wdDoc is referencing a document rather than the application.

> **NOTE** Although the Word application's Visible property is set to True, this code does not make the Word application the active application. In most cases, the Word application icon stays in the taskbar, and Excel remains the active application on the user's screen.

The following example uses errors to learn whether Word is already open before pasting a chart at the end of a document. If not, it opens Word and creates a new document:

```
Sub IsWordOpen()
Dim wdApp As Word.Application

ActiveChart.ChartArea.Copy

On Error Resume Next
Set wdApp = GetObject(, "Word.Application")
If wdApp Is Nothing Then
    Set wdApp = GetObject("", "Word.Application")
    With wdApp
        .Documents.Add
        .Visible = True
    End With
End If
On Error GoTo 0

With wdApp.Selection
    .EndKey Unit:=wdStory
    .TypeParagraph
    .PasteSpecial Link:=False, DataType:=wdPasteOLEObject, _
        Placement:=wdInLine, DisplayAsIcon:=False
End With

Set wdApp = Nothing
End Sub
```

Using On Error Resume Next forces the program to continue even if it runs into an error. In this case, an error occurs when we attempt to link wdApp to an object that does not exist. wdApp will have no value. The next line, If wdApp Is Nothing then, takes advantage of this and opens an instance of Word, adding an empty document and making the application visible. Note the use of empty quotes for the first parameter in `GetObject("", "Word.Application")`—this is how to use the `GetObject` function to open a new instance of Word. Use `On Error Goto 0` to return to normal VBA handling behavior.

Using Constant Values

In the previous example, we used constants that are specific to Word, such as `wdPasteOLEObject` and `wdInLine`. When you're programming using early binding, Excel helps you out by showing these constants in the tip window.

With late binding, these tips won't appear. So what can you do? You might write your program using early binding, then, after you've compiled and tested it, change it to late binding. The problem with this method is that it won't compile because Excel doesn't recognize the Word constants.

The words *wdPasteOLEObject* and *wdInLine* are for your convenience as a programmer. Behind each of these text constants is the real value that VBA understands. The solution to this is to retrieve and use these real values with your late binding program.

Using the Watch Window to Retrieve the Real Value of a Constant

One way to retrieve the value is to add a watch for the constants. Then, step through your code and check the value of the constant as it appears in the Watch window, as shown in Figure 18.5.

18

Figure 18.5
Use the Watch window to get the real value behind a Word constant.

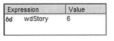

Expression	Value
66　wdStory	6

Using the Object Browser to Retrieve the Real Value of a Constant

A second method is to look up the constant in the Object Browser. You'll need the Word library set up as a reference. Right-click in the constant, select Definition, and the Object Browser opens to the constant, showing you the value in the bottom window, as shown in Figure 18.6.

> **NOTE**
> You can set up the Word reference library to access it from the Object Browser, but you don't have to set up your code with early binding. In this way, you can have the reference at your fingertips, but your code is still late binding. Turning off the reference library is just a few clicks away.

Figure 18.6
User the Object Browser
to get the real value
behind a Word constant.

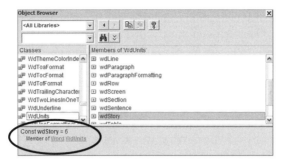

Replacing the constants in the earlier code example with their real values would look like this:

```
With wdApp.Selection
    .EndKey Unit:=6
    .TypeParagraph
    .PasteSpecial Link:=False, DataType:=0, _
        Placement:=0, DisplayAsIcon:=False
End With
```

But what happens a month from now when you return to the code and you're trying to remember what those numbers mean? The solution is up to you. Some programmers just add comments to the code referencing the Word constant. Other programmers create their own variables to hold the real value and use those variables in place of the constants, like this:

```
Const xwdStory As Long = 6
Const xwdPasteOLEObject As Long = 0
Const xwdInLine As Long = 0

With wdApp.Selection
    .EndKey Unit:=xwdStory
    .TypeParagraph
    .PasteSpecial Link:=False, DataType:=xwdPasteOLEObject, _
        Placement:=xwdInLine, DisplayAsIcon:=False
End With
```

Understanding Word's Objects

Word's macro recorder can be used to get a preliminary understanding of the Word object model. However, much like Excel's macro recorder, the results will be long-winded. Keep this in mind and use the recorder to lead you toward the objects, properties, and methods in Word.

> **CAUTION**
>
> The macro recorder is limited in what it will allow you to record. The mouse cannot be used to move the cursor or select objects, but there are no limits on doing so with the keyboard.

The following example is what the Word macro recorder produces when adding a new, blank document.

```
Documents.Add Template:="Normal", NewTemplate:=False, DocumentType:=0
```

Making this more efficient (still in Word) produces this:

```
Documents.Add
```

`Template`, `NewTemplate`, and `DocumentType` are all optional properties that the recorder includes but are not required unless you need to change a default property or ensure that a property is as you require.

To use the same line of code in Excel, a link to the Word object library is required, as you learned earlier. After that link is established, an understanding of Word's objects is all you need. Following is a review of *some* of Word's objects—enough to get you off the ground. For a more detailed listing, refer to the object model in Word's VB Editor.

Document **Object**

Word's `Document` object is equivalent to Excel's `Workbook` object. It consists of characters, words, sentences, paragraphs, sections, and headers/footers. It is through the `Document` object that methods and properties affecting the entire document, such as printing, closing, searching, and reviewing, are accomplished.

Create a New Blank Document

To create a blank document in an existing instance of Word, use the `Add` method (we already learned how to create a new document when Word is closed—refer to `GetObject` and `CreateObject`):

```
Sub NewDocument()
Dim wdApp As Word.Application

Set wdApp = GetObject(, "Word.Application")

wdApp.Documents.Add

Set wdApp = Nothing
End Sub
```

This example opens a new, blank document that uses the default template. To create a new document that uses a specific template, use this:

```
wdApp.Documents.Add Template:="Contemporary Memo.dot"
```

This creates a new document that uses the Contemporary Memo template. `Template` can be either just the name of a template from the default template location or the file path and name.

Open an Existing Document

To open an existing document, use the Open method. Several parameters are available, including Read Only and AddtoRecentFiles. The following example opens an existing document as Read Only, but prevents the file from being added to the Recent File List under the File menu:

```
wdApp.Documents.Open _
    Filename:="C:\Excel VBA 2007 by Jelen & Syrstad\Chapter 19 - Arrays.docx", _
    ReadOnly:=True, AddtoRecentFiles:=False
```

Save Changes to a Document

After changes have been made to a document, you most likely will want to save it. To save a document with its existing name, use this:

```
wdApp.Documents.Save
```

If the Save command is used with a new document without a name, the Save As dialog box appears. To save a document with a new name, you can use the SaveAs method instead:

```
wdApp.ActiveDocument.SaveAs "C:\Excel VBA 2007 by Jelen & Syrstad\MemoTest.docx"
```

SaveAs requires the use of members of the Document object, such as ActiveDocument.

Close an Open Document

Use the Close method to close a specified document or all open documents. By default, a Save dialog appears for any documents with unsaved changes. The SaveChanges argument can be used to change this. To close all open documents without saving changes, use this code:

```
wdApp.Documents.Close SaveChanges:=wdDoNotSaveChanges
```

To close a specific document, you can close the active document or you can specify a document name:

```
wdApp.ActiveDocument.Close
```

or

```
wdApp.Documents("Chapter 19 - Arrays.docx").Close
```

Print a Document

Use the PrintOut method to print part or all of a document. To print a document with all the default print settings, use this:

```
wdApp.ActiveDocument.PrintOut
```

By default, the print range is the entire document, but this can be changed by setting the Range and Pages arguments of the PrintOut method:

```
wdApp.ActiveDocument.PrintOut Range:=wdPrintRangeOfPages, Pages:="2"
```

Selection **Object**

The `Selection` object represents what is selected in the document—that is, a word, sentence, or the insertion point. It has a `Type` property that returns the type of what is selected (`wdSelectionIP`, `wdSelectionColumn`, `wdSelectionShape`, and so on).

HomeKey/EndKey

The `HomeKey` and `EndKey` methods are used to change the selection; they correspond to using the Home and End keys, respectively, on the keyboard. They have two parameters: `Unit` and `Extend`. `Unit` is the range of movement to make, either to the beginning (`Home`) or end (`End`) of a line (`wdLine`), document (`wdStory`), column (`wdColumn`), or row (`wdRow`). `Extend` is the type of movement: `wdMove` moves the selection, `wdExtend` extends the selection from the original insertion point to the new insertion point.

To move the cursor to the beginning of the document, use this code:

```
wdApp.Selection.HomeKey Unit:=wdStory, Extend:=wdMove
```

To select the document from the insertion point to the end of the document, use this code:

```
wdApp.Selection.EndKey Unit:=wdStory, Extend:=wdExtend
```

TypeText

The `TypeText` method is used to insert text into a Word document. User settings, such as the `Overtype` setting, can affect what will happen when text is inserted into the document:

```
Sub InsertText()
Dim wdApp As Word.Application
Dim wdDoc As Document
Dim wdSln As Selection

Set wdApp = GetObject(, "Word.Application")
Set wdDoc = wdApp.ActiveDocument
Set wdSln = wdApp.Selection

wdDoc.Application.Options.Overtype = False
With wdSln
    If .Type = wdSelectionIP Then
        .TypeText ("Inserting at insertion point. ")
    ElseIf .Type = wdSelectionNormal Then
            If wdApp.Options.ReplaceSelection Then
                .Collapse Direction:=wdCollapseStart
            End If
            .TypeText ("Inserting before a text block. ")
    End If
End With
Set wdApp = Nothing
Set wdDoc = Nothing
End Sub
```

18

Range **Object**

The Range object uses the following syntax:

```
Range(StartPosition, EndPosition)
```

The Range object represents a contiguous area, or areas, in the document. It has a starting character position and an ending character position. The object can be the insertion point, a range of text, or the entire document, including nonprinting characters (such as spaces or paragraph marks).

The Range object is similar to the Selection object but, in some ways, is better: It requires less code to accomplish the same tasks; it has more capabilities; and it saves time and memory because the Range object doesn't require Word to move the cursor or highlight objects in the document to manipulate them.

Define a Range

To define a range, enter a starting and ending position, as shown in this code segment:

```
Sub RangeText()
Dim wdApp As Word.Application
Dim wdDoc As Document
Dim wdRng As Word.Range

Set wdApp = GetObject(, "Word.Application")
Set wdDoc = wdApp.ActiveDocument

Set wdRng = wdDoc.Range(0, 22)
wdRng.Select

Set wdApp = Nothing
Set wdDoc = Nothing
Set wdRng = Nothing
End Sub
```

Figure 18.7 shows the results of running this code. The first 22 characters, including non-printing characters such as paragraph returns, are selected.

> **NOTE**
> The range was selected (wdRng.Select) for easier viewing. It is not required that the range be selected to be manipulated. For example, to delete the range, do this:
>
>   wdRng.Delete

The first character position in a document is always zero, and the last is equivalent to the number of characters in the document.

Figure 18.7
The Range object selects everything in its path.

```
16

Automating Word

Word, Excel, PowerPoint, Outlook and Access all use the same VBA
language; the only difference between them are their object
models (example: Excel has a Workbooks object, Word has
Documents). Any one of these applications can access another
application's object model as long as the second application is
installed.

To access Word's object library, Excel must establish a link to
it. There are two ways of doing this: early binding or late
binding. With early binding, the reference to the application
object is created when the program is compiled; with late
binding, it is created when the program is run.
```

The Range object also selects paragraphs. The following example copies the third paragraph in the active document and pastes it in Excel. Depending on how the paste is done, the text can be pasted into a text box (see Figure 18.8) or into a cell (see Figure 18.9):

```
Sub SelectSentence()
Dim wdApp As Word.Application
Dim wdRng As Word.Range

Set wdApp = GetObject(, "Word.Application")

With wdApp.ActiveDocument
    If .Paragraphs.Count >= 3 Then
        Set wdRng = .Paragraphs(3).Range
        wdRng.Copy
    End If
End With

'This line pastes the copied text into a text box
'because that's the default PasteSpecial method for Word text
Worksheets("Sheet2").PasteSpecial

'This line pastes the copied text in cell A1
Worksheets("Sheet2").Paste Destination:=Worksheets("Sheet2").Range("A1")

Set wdApp = Nothing
Set wdRng = Nothing
End Sub
```

18

Figure 18.8
Paste Word text into an Excel text box.

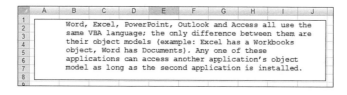

Figure 18.9
Paste Word text into an Excel cell.

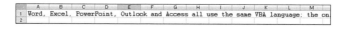

Format a Range

After a range is selected, formatting can be applied to it (see Figure 18.10). The following program loops through all the paragraphs of the active document and bolds the first word of each paragraph:

```
Sub ChangeFormat()
Dim wdApp As Word.Application
Dim wdRng As Word.Range
Dim count As Integer

Set wdApp = GetObject(, "Word.Application")

With wdApp.ActiveDocument
    For count = 1 To .Paragraphs.count
        Set wdRng = .Paragraphs(count).Range
        With wdRng
            .Words(1).Font.Bold = True
        End With
    Next count
End With

Set wdApp = Nothing
Set wdRng = Nothing
End Sub
```

Figure 18.10
Format the first word of each paragraph in a document.

Word, Excel, PowerPoint, Outlook and Access all use the same VBA language; the only difference between them are their object models (example: Excel has a Workbooks object, Word has Documents). Any one of these applications can access another application's object model as long as the second application is installed.

To access Word's object library, Excel must establish a link to it. There are two ways of doing this: early binding or late binding. With early binding, the reference to the application object is created when the program is compiled; with late binding, it is created when the program is run.

Note: This chapter is an introduction to accessing Word from Excel; we will not be reviewing Word's entire object model or the object models of other applications. Refer to the VBA Object Browser in the appropriate application to learn about other object models.

A quick way of changing the formatting of entire paragraphs is to change the style (see Figures 18.11 and 18.12). The following program finds the paragraph with the NO style and changes it to HA:

```
Sub ChangeStyle()
Dim wdApp As Word.Application
Dim wdRng As Word.Range
Dim count As Integer

Set wdApp = GetObject(, "Word.Application")

With wdApp.ActiveDocument
    For count = 1 To .Paragraphs.count
        Set wdRng = .Paragraphs(count).Range
```

```
        With wdRng
            If .Style = "NO" Then
                .Style = "HA"
            End If
        End With
    Next count
End With

Set wdApp = Nothing
Set wdRng = Nothing
End Sub
```

Figure 18.11
Before: A paragraph with the NO style needs to be changed to the HA style.

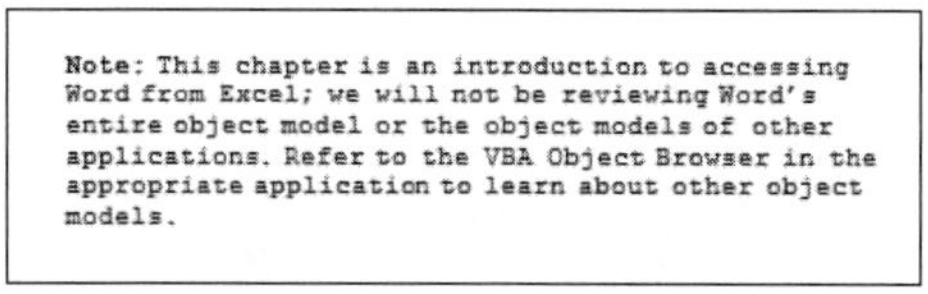

> Note: This chapter is an introduction to accessing Word from Excel; we will not be reviewing Word's entire object model or the object models of other applications. Refer to the VBA Object Browser in the appropriate application to learn about other object models.

Figure 18.12
After: Apply styles with code to quickly change paragraph formatting.

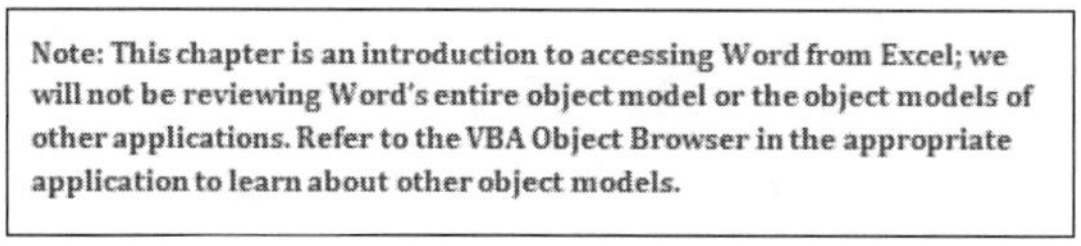

> Note: This chapter is an introduction to accessing Word from Excel; we will not be reviewing Word's entire object model or the object models of other applications. Refer to the VBA Object Browser in the appropriate application to learn about other object models.

Bookmarks

Bookmarks are members of the Document, Selection, and Range objects. They can help make it easier to navigate around Word. Instead of having to choose words, sentences, or paragraphs, use bookmarks to swiftly manipulate sections of a document.

> **NOTE** Bookmarks do not have to be existing; they can be created via code.

Bookmarks appear as gray I-bars in Word documents. In Word, click the Microsoft Office Button, go to Word Options, Advanced, Show Document Contents to turn on bookmarks (see Figure 18.13).

After you've set up bookmarks in a document, you can use the bookmarks to quickly move to a range. The following code automatically inserts text after four bookmarks that were previously set up in the document. Figure 18.14 shows the results.

```
Sub UseBookmarks()
Dim myArray()
Dim wdBkmk As String

Dim wdApp As Word.Application
Dim wdRng As Word.Range
```

```
myArray = Array("To", "CC", "From", "Subject")
Set wdApp = GetObject(, "Word.Application")

Set wdRng = wdApp.ActiveDocument.Bookmarks(myArray(0)).Range
wdRng.InsertBefore ("Bill Jelen")
Set wdRng = wdApp.ActiveDocument.Bookmarks(myArray(1)).Range
wdRng.InsertBefore ("Tracy Syrstad")
Set wdRng = wdApp.ActiveDocument.Bookmarks(myArray(2)).Range
wdRng.InsertBefore ("MrExcel")
Set wdRng = wdApp.ActiveDocument.Bookmarks(myArray(3)).Range
wdRng.InsertBefore ("Fruit Sales")

Set wdApp = Nothing
Set wdRng = Nothing
End Sub
```

Figure 18.13
Turn on bookmarks to find them in a document.

Figure 18.14
Use bookmarks to quickly enter text into a Word document.

Bookmarks can also be used as markers for bringing in charts created in Excel. The following code links an Excel chart (see Figure 18.15) to the memo:

```
Sub CreateMemo()
Dim myArray()
Dim wdBkmk As String

Dim wdApp As Word.Application
Dim wdRng As Word.Range
```

```
myArray = Array("To", "CC", "From", "Subject", "Chart")
Set wdApp = GetObject(, "Word.Application")

Set wdRng = wdApp.ActiveDocument.Bookmarks(myArray(0)).Range
wdRng.InsertBefore ("Bill Jelen")
Set wdRng = wdApp.ActiveDocument.Bookmarks(myArray(1)).Range
wdRng.InsertBefore ("Tracy Syrstad")
Set wdRng = wdApp.ActiveDocument.Bookmarks(myArray(2)).Range
wdRng.InsertBefore ("MrExcel")
Set wdRng = wdApp.ActiveDocument.Bookmarks(myArray(3)).Range
wdRng.InsertBefore ("Fruit & Vegetable Sales")

Set wdRng = wdApp.ActiveDocument.Bookmarks(myArray(4)).Range
ActiveSheet.ChartObjects("Chart 1").Copy
wdRng.PasteAndFormat Type:=wdPasteOLEObject

wdApp.Activate

Set wdApp = Nothing
Set wdRng = Nothing
End Sub
```

Figure 18.15
Use bookmarks to bring charts into Word documents.

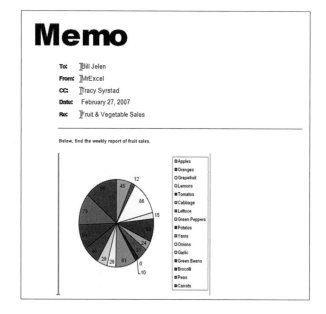

Controlling Word's Form Fields

You've seen how to modify a document by inserting charts and text, modifying formatting, and deleting text. However, a document may contain other items, such as controls, and you can modify those, too.

For the following example, I created a template consisting of text, bookmarks, and Form Field check boxes. (See the note following this paragraph for information on where the

Form Fields are hiding in Word.) The bookmarks are placed after the Name and Date fields. The check boxes have all been renamed (right-click the check box, select Properties, and type a new name in the Bookmark field) to make more sense to me, such as chk401k rather than Checkbox5. Save the template.

> **NOTE** The Word Form Fields are found on the Controls section of the Developer tab, under the Legacy Tools, as shown in Figure 18.16.

Figure 18.16
You can use the Form Fields found under the Legacy Tools to add check boxes to a document.

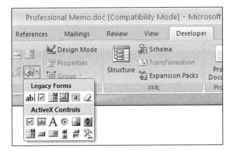

I set up the questionnaire in Excel, allowing the user to enter free text in B1 and B2, but setting up data validation in B3 and B5:B8, as shown in Figure 18.17.

Figure 18.17
Create an Excel sheet to collect your data.

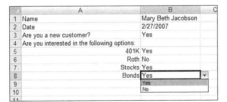

The code goes into a standard module. The name and date go straight into the document. The check boxes use logic to verify whether the user selected Yes or No to confirm whether the corresponding check box should be checked. Figure 18.18 shows a sample completed document.

```
Sub FillOutWordForm()

Dim TemplatePath As String
Dim wdApp As Object
Dim wdDoc As Object

'Open the template in a new instance of Word
TemplatePath = ThisWorkbook.Path & "\Word Example.dotx"
Set wdApp = CreateObject("Word.Application")
Set wdDoc = wdApp.documents.Add(Template:=TemplatePath)
```

```
'Place our text values in document
With wdApp.ActiveDocument
    .Bookmarks("Name").Range.InsertBefore Range("B1").Text
    .Bookmarks("Date").Range.InsertBefore Range("B2").Text
End With

'Using basic logic, select the correct form object
If Range("B3").Value = "Yes" Then
    wdDoc.formfields("chkCustYes").CheckBox.Value = True
Else
    wdDoc.formfields("chkCustNo").CheckBox.Value = True
End If

With wdDoc
    If Range("B5").Value = "Yes" Then .Formfields("chk401k").CheckBox.Value = True
    If Range("B6").Value = "Yes" Then .Formfields("chkRoth").CheckBox.Value = True
    If Range("B7").Value = "Yes" Then .Formfields("chkStocks"). _
        CheckBox.Value = True
    If Range("B7").Value = "Yes" Then .Formfields("chkBonds"). _
        CheckBox.Value = True
End With

wdApp.Visible = True

ExitSub:

    Set wdDoc = Nothing
    Set wdApp = Nothing

End Sub
```

Figure 18.18
Excel can control Word's
form fields.

Next Steps

In Chapter 19, "Arrays," you will learn how to use multidimensional arrays. Reading data into a multidimensional array, performing calculations on the array, and then writing the array back to a range can dramatically speed up your macros.

Arrays

19

An *array* is a type of variable that can be used to hold more than one piece of data. For example, if you have to work with the name and address of a client, your first thought might be to assign one variable for the name and another for the address of the client. Instead, consider using an array, **which** can hold both pieces of information—and not for just one client, but for hundreds.

Declare an Array

Declare an array by adding parentheses after the array name. The parentheses contain the number of elements in the array:

```
Dim myArray (2)
```

This creates an array, myArray, that contains three elements. Why three? Because, by default, the index count starts at zero:

```
myArray(0) = 10
myArray(1) = 20
myArray(2) = 30
```

If the index count needs to start on one, use `Option Base 1`. This forces the count to start at one. The `Option Base` statement is placed in the declarations section of the module:

```
Option Base 1
Dim myArray(2)
```

This now forces the array to have only two elements.

You can also create an array independent of the `Option Base` statement by declaring its lower bound:

```
Dim myArray (1 to 10)
Dim BigArray (100 to 200)
```

Every array has a lower bound (`Lbound`) and an upper bound (`Ubound`). When you declare `Dim myArray (2)`, you are declaring the upper bound and allowing the option base to declare the lower bound. By declaring `Dim myArray (1 to 10)`, you declare the lower bound, 1, and the upper bound, 10.

Multidimensional Arrays

The arrays just discussed are considered *one-dimensional arrays*—only one number designates the location of an element of the array. The array is like a single row of data, but because there can be only one row, you don't have to worry about the row number—only the column number. For example, to retrieve the second element (`Option Base 0`), use `myArray (1)`.

In some cases, a single dimension isn't enough. This is where multidimensional arrays come in. Where a one-dimensional array is a single row of data, a multidimensional array contains rows *and* columns.

> **NOTE** Another word for array is *matrix,* which is what a spreadsheet is. The `Cells` object refers to *elements* of a spreadsheet—and a cell consists of a row and a column. You've been using arrays all along!

To declare another dimension to an array, add another argument. The following creates an array of 10 rows and 20 columns:

```
Dim myArray (1 to 10, 1 to 20)
```

This places values in the first two columns of the first row, as shown in Figure 19.1:

```
myArray (1,1) = 10
myArray (1,2) = 20
```

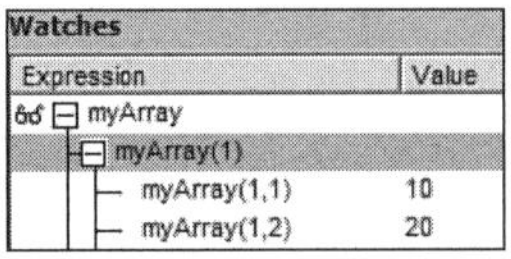

Figure 19.1
The VB Editor Watches window shows the first "row" of the array being filled from the previous lines of code.

This places values in first two columns of the second row:

```
myArray (2,1) = 20
myArray (2,2) = 40
```

And so on. Of course, this is very time-consuming and could take a lot of lines of code. There are other ways to fill an array, which are discussed in the next section.

Fill an Array

Now that you can declare an array, you need to fill it. One method was shown earlier—individually entering a value for each element of the array. There's a quicker way, as shown in the following sample code and Figure 19.2:

```
Option Base 1

Sub ColumnHeaders()
Dim myArray As Variant
Dim myCount As Integer

' Fill the array
myArray = Array("Name", "Address", "Phone", "Email")

' Empty the array
With Worksheets("Sheet2")
    For myCount = 1 To UBound(myArray)
        .Cells(1, myCount).Value = myArray(myCount)
    Next myCount
End With
End Sub
```

Figure 19.2

Use an array to quickly create column headers.

	A	B	C	D
1	Name	Address	Phone	Email
2				
3				
4				

Remember that Variant variables can hold any type of information. To quickstack the array, create a Variant-type variable that can be treated like an array. When the data is shoved into the variant, it is forced to take on the properties of an array.

But what if the information needed in the array is on the sheet already? Use the following to quickly fill an array.

```
Dim myArray As Variant

myArray = Worksheets("Sheet1").Range("B2:C17")
```

Although these two methods are quick and easy, they may not always suit the situation. What if you need every other row in the array? The code to do this follows (see Figure 19.3):

```
Sub EveryOtherRow()
Dim myArray(1 To 8, 1 To 2)
Dim i As Integer, j As Integer, myCount As Integer

'Fill the array with every other row
For i = 1 To 8
```

19

```
    For j = 1 To 2
        myArray(i, j) = Worksheets("Sheet1").Cells(i * 2, j + 1).Value
    Next j
Next i

'Empty the array
For myCount = LBound(myArray) To UBound(myArray)
    Worksheets("Sheet1").Cells(myCount * 2, 4) = _
    WorksheetFunction.Sum(myArray(myCount, 1), myArray(myCount, 2))
Next myCount
End Sub
```

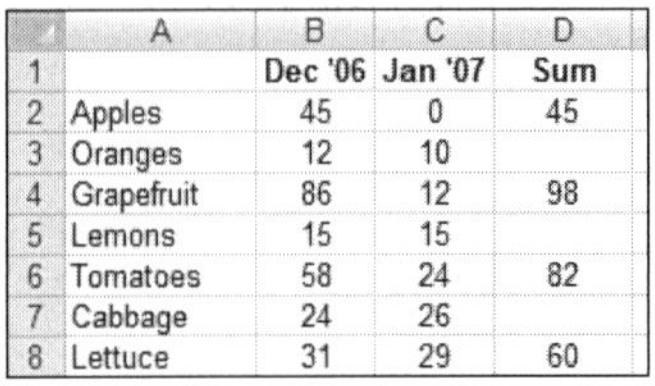

Figure 19.3
Fill the array with only the data needed.

	A	B	C	D
1		Dec '06	Jan '07	Sum
2	Apples	45	0	45
3	Oranges	12	10	
4	Grapefruit	86	12	98
5	Lemons	15	15	
6	Tomatoes	58	24	82
7	Cabbage	24	26	
8	Lettuce	31	29	60

Empty an Array

After an array is filled, the data needs to be retrieved. Before you do that, however, you can manipulate it or return information about it, such as the maximum integer, as shown in the following code (see Figure 19.4):

```
Sub QuickFillMax()
Dim myArray As Variant

myArray = Worksheets("Sheet1").Range("B2:C17")
MsgBox "Maximum Integer is: " & WorksheetFunction.Max(myArray)

End Sub
```

Figure 19.4
Return the Max variable in an array.

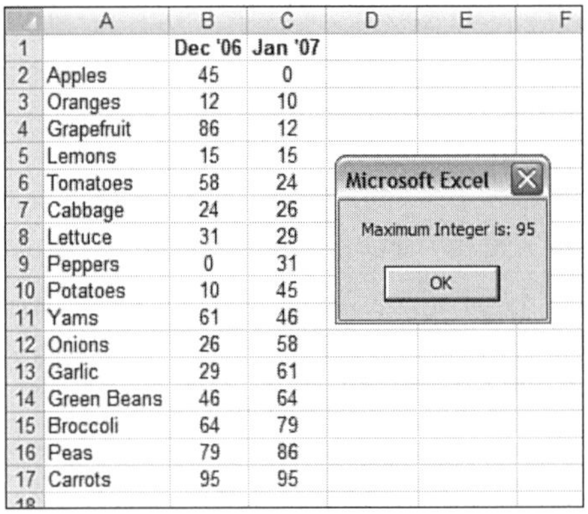

	A	B	C	D	E	F
1		Dec '06	Jan '07			
2	Apples	45	0			
3	Oranges	12	10			
4	Grapefruit	86	12			
5	Lemons	15	15			
6	Tomatoes	58	24			
7	Cabbage	24	26			
8	Lettuce	31	29			
9	Peppers	0	31			
10	Potatoes	10	45			
11	Yams	61	46			
12	Onions	26	58			
13	Garlic	29	61			
14	Green Beans	46	64			
15	Broccoli	64	79			
16	Peas	79	86			
17	Carrots	95	95			

Microsoft Excel

Maximum Integer is: 95

OK

Data can also be manipulated as it is returned to the sheet. In the following example, Lbound and Ubound are used with a For loop to loop through the elements of the array and average each set. The result is then placed on the sheet in a new column (see Figure 19.5).

NOTE MyCount + 1 is used to place the results back on the sheet because the Lbound is 1 and the data starts in row 2.

```
Sub QuickFillAverage()
Dim myArray As Variant
Dim myCount As Integer
'fill the array
myArray = Worksheets("Sheet1").Range("B2:C17")

'Average the data in the array just as it is placed on the sheet
For myCount = LBound(myArray) To UBound(myArray)
    Worksheets("Sheet1").Cells(myCount + 1, 5).Value = _
    WorksheetFunction.Average(myArray(myCount, 1), myArray(myCount, 2))
Next myCount

End Sub
```

Figure 19.5
Calculations can be done on the data as it is returned to the sheet.

	A	B	C	D	E
1		Dec '06	Jan '07	Sum	Average
2	Apples	45	0	45	22.5
3	Oranges	12	10		11
4	Grapefruit	86	12	98	49
5	Lemons	15	15		15
6	Tomatoes	58	24	82	41
7	Cabbage	24	26		25
8	Lettuce	31	29	60	30
9	Peppers	0	31		15.5
10	Potatoes	10	45	55	27.5
11	Yams	61	46		53.5
12	Onions	26	58	84	42
13	Garlic	29	61		45
14	Green Beans	46	64	110	55
15	Broccoli	64	79		71.5
16	Peas	79	86	165	82.5
17	Carrots	95	95		95

Arrays Can Make It Easier to Manipulate Data, But Is That All?

Okay, so arrays can make it easier to manipulate data and get information from it—but is that all they're good for? No, arrays are so powerful because they can actually make the code run *faster!*

Typically, if there are columns of data to average, as in the preceding example, your first thought might be for the following:

```
Sub SlowAverage()
Dim myCount As Integer, LastRow As Integer
```

19

```
LastRow = Worksheets("Sheet1").Cells(Worksheets("Sheet1").Rows.Count, 1). _
    End(xlUp).Row

For myCount = 2 To LastRow
    With Worksheets("Sheet1")
        .Cells(myCount, 6).Value = _
        WorksheetFunction.Average(Cells(myCount, 2), Cells(myCount, 3))
    End With
Next myCount

End Sub
```

Although this works fine, the program has to look at each row of the sheet individually, get the data, do the calculation, and place it in the correct column. Wouldn't it be easier to grab all the data at one time, and then do the calculations and place it back on the sheet? Also, with the slower version of the code, you need to know which columns on the sheet to manipulate (Columns 2 and 3 in our example). With an array, you need to know only what element of the array you want to manipulate.

To make this even more useful, rather than use an address range to fill the array, you could use a named range. With a named range in an array, it really doesn't matter where on the sheet the range is.

Instead of

```
myArray = Range("B2:C17")
```

use this:

```
myArray = Range("myData")
```

Whereas with the slow method you need to know where myData is so that you can return the correct columns, with an array all you need to know is that you want the first and second columns.

TIP

Make your array even faster! Technically, if you place a column of data into an array, it is a two-dimensional array. If you want to process it, you must process the row and column.

You can process the column more easily if it is just a single row, as long as it doesn't exceed 16,384 columns. Use the Transpose function to turn the one column into one row (see Figure 19.6).

```
Sub TransposeArray()
Dim myArray As Variant

    myArray = WorksheetFunction.Transpose(Range("myTran"))

    'return the 5th element of the array
    MsgBox "The 5th element of the Array is: " & myArray(5)
End Sub
```

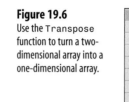

Figure 19.6
Use the `Transpose` function to turn a two-dimensional array into a one-dimensional array.

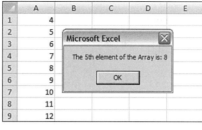

Dynamic Arrays

You can't always know how big of an array you will need. You could create an array based on how big it could ever need to be, but that's not only a waste of memory. What if it turns out it needs to be bigger? In this case, you can use a *dynamic array*.

A dynamic array is an array that does not have a set size. Declare the array, but leave the parentheses empty:

```
Dim myArray ()
```

Later, as the program needs to use the array, use `Redim` to set the size of the array. The following program, which returns the names of all the sheets in the workbook, creates a boundless array, but then sets the `upper bound` after it knows how many sheets are in the workbook:

```
Option Base 1
Sub MySheets()
Dim myArray() As String
Dim myCount As Integer, NumShts As Integer

NumShts = ActiveWorkbook.Worksheets.Count

' Size the array
ReDim myArray(1 To NumShts)

For myCount = 1 To NumShts
    myArray(myCount) = ActiveWorkbook.Sheets(myCount).Name
Next myCount

End Sub
```

Using `Redim` reinitializes the array; so if you were to use it many times, such as in a loop, you would lose all the data it holds. Use `Preserve` to prevent that from happening.

The following example looks for all the Excel files in a directory and puts the results in an array. Because we don't know how many files there will be until we look at them, we can't size the array before the program is run:

```
Sub XLFiles()
Dim FName As String
Dim arNames() As String
Dim myCount As Integer
```

```
FName = Dir("C:\Contracting Files\Excel VBA 2007 by Jelen & Syrstad\*.xls*")
Do Until FName = ""
    myCount = myCount + 1
    ReDim Preserve arNames(1 To myCount)
    arNames(myCount) = FName
    FName = Dir
Loop

End Sub
```

> **CAUTION**
>
> Using `Preserve` with large amounts of data in a loop can slow down the program. If possible, use code to figure out the maximum size of the array.

Passing an Array

Just like strings, integers, and other variables, arrays can be passed into other procedures. This makes for more efficient and easier-to-read code. The following sub, `PassAnArray`, passes the array, `myArray`, into the function `RegionSales`. The data in the array is summed for the specified region and the result returned to the sub.

```
Sub PassAnArray()
Dim myArray() As Variant
Dim myRegion As String

myArray = Range("mySalesData")
myRegion = InputBox("Enter Region - Central, East, West")
MsgBox myRegion & " Sales are: " & Format(RegionSales(myArray, _
    myRegion), "$#,#00.00")

End Sub

Function RegionSales(ByRef BigArray As Variant, sRegion As String) As Long
Dim myCount As Integer

RegionSales = 0
For myCount = LBound(BigArray) To UBound(BigArray)
    If BigArray(myCount, 1) = sRegion Then
        RegionSales = BigArray(myCount, 6) + RegionSales
    End If
Next myCount

End Function
```

Next Steps

Arrays are a type of variable used for holding more than one piece of data. Chapter 20, "Text File Processing," covers importing from a text file and writing to a text file. Being able to write to a text file is useful when you need to write out data for another system to read, or even when you need to produce HTML files.

Text File Processing

Despite the promise in Chapter 17, "XML in Excel 2007," that XML will be the next great file format of the future, we still have a lot of files in CSV or TXT file format today.

VBA makes it easy to both read and write from text files. This chapter covers importing from a text file and writing to a text file. Being able to write to a text file proves useful when you need to write out data for another system to read, or even when you need to produce HTML files.

Importing from Text Files

There are two basic scenarios when reading from text files. If the file contains fewer than 1,048,576 records, it is easy to import the file using the `Workbooks.OpenText` method. If the file contains more than 1,048,576 records, you have to read the file one record at a time.

Importing Text Files with Fewer Than 1,084,576 Rows

Text files typically come in one of two formats. In one format, the fields in each record are separated by some delimiter, such as a comma, pipe, or tab. In the second format, each field takes a particular number of character positions. This is called a fixed-width file and was very popular in the days of COBOL.

Excel can import either type of file easily. You can open both types using the `OpenText` method. In both cases, it is best to record the process of opening the file and use the recorded snippet of code.

Opening a Fixed-Width File

Figure 20.1 shows a text file where each field takes up a certain amount of space in the record. Writing the code to open this type of file is slightly arduous because you need to specify the length of each field. In my collection of antiques, I still have the metal ruler used by COBOL programmers to measure the number of characters in a field printed on a green-bar printer. You could, in theory, change the font of your file to a monospace font and use this same method. However, using the macro recorder is a slightly more up-to-date method.

Figure 20.1

This file is space delimited or fixed width. Because you must specify the exact length of each field in the file, opening this file is fairly involved.

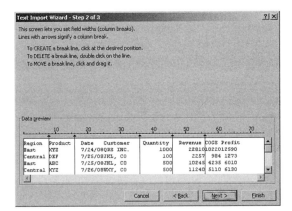

```
sales.prn - Notepad
File  Edit  Format  View  Help
Region  Product  Date    Customer      Quantity    Revenue COGS Profit
East    XYZ      7/24/08QRS INC.           1000   22810102012590
Central DEF      7/25/08JKL, CO             100    2257  984 1273
East    ABC      7/25/08JKL, CO             500   10245 4235 6010
Central XYZ      7/26/08WXY, CO             500   11240 5110 6130
East    XYZ      7/27/08FGH, CO             400    9152 4088 5064
Central XYZ      7/27/08WXY, CO             400    9204 4088 5116
East    DEF      7/27/08RST INC.            800   18552 787210680
Central ABC      7/28/08EFG S.A.            400    6860 3388 3472
East    DEF      7/30/08UVW, INC.          1000   21730 984011890
West    XYZ      7/30/08FGH, CO             600   13806 6132 7674
East    ABC      7/30/08FGH LTD.            400    8456 3388 5068
East    XYZ      8/1/08MNO S.A.             900   21015 919811817
Central ABC      8/1/08FGH LTD.             800   16416 6776 9640
Central XYZ      8/2/08OPQ, INC.            900   21438 919812240
East    XYZ      8/2/08WXY, CO              900   21465 919812267
West    XYZ      8/4/08WXY, CO              400    9144 4088 5056
Central ABC      8/4/08EFG S.A.             300    6267 2541 3726
Central ABC      8/6/08TUV GMBH             100    1740  847  893
West    ABC      8/6/08OPQ, INC.           1000   19110 847010640
East    XYZ      8/6/08TUV GMBH             100    2401 1022 1379
East    ABC      8/7/08JKL, CO              500    9345 4235 5110
East    ABC      8/8/08LMN PTY LTD          600   11628 5082 6546
Central XYZ      8/8/08OPQ, INC.            900   21888 919812690
East    XYZ      8/9/08DEF, LLC             300    5961 2952 3009
West    DEF      8/11/08JKL, CO             100    2042  984 1058
Central ABC      8/12/08LMN PTY LTD         900   17505 7623 9882
West    ABC      8/13/08RST INC.            200    3552 1694 1858
East    ABC      8/13/08LMN LTD.            800   14440 6776 7664
West    XYZ      8/13/08DEF, LLC            300    7032 2952 4080
```

Turn on the macro recorder by selecting Record Macro from the Developer ribbon. From the File menu, select Open. Change the Files of Type to All Files and find your text file.

In the Text Import Wizard's Step 1, specify that the data is Fixed Width and click Next.

Excel then looks at your data and attempts to figure out where each field begins and ends. Figure 20.2 shows Excel's guess on this particular file. Because the Date field is too close to the Customer field, Excel missed drawing that line.

Figure 20.2

Excel guesses at where each field starts. In this case, it missed two fields and probably did not leave enough room for a longer product name.

To add a new field indicator in Step 2 of the wizard, just click in the appropriate place in the Data Preview window. If you click in the wrong column, click the line and drag it to the right place. If Excel inadvertently put in an extra field line, double-click the line to remove it. Figure 20.3 shows the data preview after the appropriate changes have been made. Note the little ruler above the data. When you click to add a field marker, Excel is actually handling the tedious work of figuring out that the Customer field starts in position 25 for a length of 11.

Figure 20.3

After you add two new field markers and move the marker between Product and Date to the right place, Excel can build the code that gives us an idea of start position and length of each field.

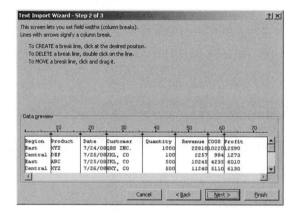

In Step 3 of the wizard, Excel always assumes that every field is in General format.

Change the format of any fields that require special handling. Click the column and choose the appropriate format from the Column Data Format section of the dialog box. Figure 20.4 shows the selections for this file.

Figure 20.4

Here, I've indicated that the third column is a date and that I do not want to import the Cost and Profit columns. If you ever receive files from Italy, for example, where they use periods as a thousands separator, you will need to click the Advanced button to set the options to handle this.

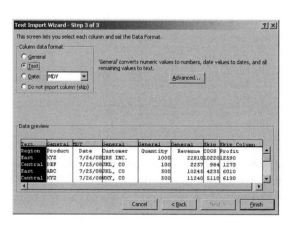

20

If you have date fields, click the heading above that column, and change the column data format choice to a date. If you have a file with dates in year-month-day format or day-month-year format, select the drop-down next to date and choose the appropriate date sequence.

If you would prefer to skip some fields, click that column and select Do Not Import Column (Skip) from the Column Data Format selection. There are a couple of times when this is useful. If the file includes sensitive data that you do not want to show to the client, you can leave it out of the import. For example, perhaps this report is for a customer and I don't want to show our cost of goods sold or profit. I can choose to skip these fields in the import. Also, you will occasionally run into a text file that is both fixed width and delimited by a character such as the pipe character. Setting the 1-wide pipe columns as "do not import" is a great way to get rid of the pipe characters, as shown in Figure 20.5.

Figure 20.5
This file is both fixed width and pipe delimited. Liberal use of the Do Not Import Column setting for each pipe column eliminates the pipe characters from the file.

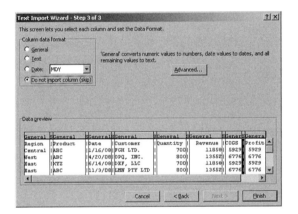

If you have text fields that contain alphabetic characters, you can choose the General format. The only time you should choose the Text format is if you have a numeric field that you explicitly need imported as text. One example of this is an account number with leading zeros or a column of zip codes. To ensure that zip code 01234 does not lose the leading zero, change the field to Text format.

___ CAUTION ___

After you import a text file and specify that one field is text, that field will exhibit seemingly bizarre behavior. Try inserting a new row and entering a formula in the middle of a column imported as text. Instead of getting the results of the formula, Excel enters the formula as text. The solution is to delete the formula, format the entire column as General, and then enter the formula again.

After opening the file, turn off the macro recorder and examine the recorded code:

```
Workbooks.OpenText Filename:="C:\sales.prn", Origin:=437, StartRow:=1, _
DataType:=xlFixedWidth, FieldInfo:=Array(Array(0, 1), Array(8, 1), _
Array(17, 3), Array(25, 1), Array(36, 1), Array(46, 1), Array(56, 9), _
Array(61, 9)), TrailingMinusNumbers:=True
```

The most confusing part of this code is the `FieldInfo` parameter. You are supposed to code an array of two-element arrays. Each field in the file gets a two-element array to identify where the field starts and the field type.

The field start position is zero based; because the Region field is in the first character position, its start position is listed as 0.

The field type is a numeric code. If you were coding this by hand, you would use the `xlColumnDataType` constant names; but for some reason, the macro recorder uses the harder-to-understand numeric equivalents.

With Table 20.1, you can decode the meaning of the individual arrays in the `FieldInfo` array. `Array(0, 1)` means that this field starts zero characters from the left edge of the file and is a general format. `Array(8, 1)` indicates that the next field starts eight characters from the left edge of the file and is also General format. `Array(17, 3)` indicates that the next field starts 17 characters from the left edge of the file and is a date format in month-day-year sequence.

Table 20.1 `xlColumnDataType` **Values**

Value	Constant	Used For
1	xlGeneralFormat	General
2	xlTextFormat	Text
3	xlMDYFormat	MDY date
4	xlDMYFormat	DMY date
5	xlYMDFormat	YMD date
6	xlMYDFormat	MYD date
7	xlDYMFormat	DYM date
8	xlYDMFormat	YDM date
9	xlSkipColumn	Skip Column
10	xlEMDFormat	EMD date

As you can see, the `FieldInfo` parameter for fixed-width files is arduous to code and confusing to look at. It is really one situation where it is easier to record the macro and copy the code snippet.

20

> ┌─ C A U T I O N ──────────────────────────────
> │
> │ The `xlTrailingMinusNumbers` parameter was new in Excel 2002. If you have any clients who
> │ might be using Excel 97 or Excel 2000, take the recorded parameter out. The code runs fine without
> │ the parameter in newer versions, but if left in, it leads to a compile error on older versions. In my
> │ experience, this is the number one cause for code to crash on earlier versions of Excel.

Opening a Delimited File

Figure 20.6 shows a text file where each field is comma separated. The main task in opening such a file is to tell Excel that the delimiter in the file is a comma and then identify any
special processing for each field. In this case, we definitely want to identify the third column as being a date in mm/dd/yyyy format.

> ┌─ C A U T I O N ──────────────────────────────
> │
> │ If you try to record the process of opening a comma-delimited file where the filename ends in .csv,
> │ Excel records the `Workbooks.Open` method rather than `Workbooks.OpenText`. If you need
> │ to control the formatting of certain columns, rename the file to have a .txt extension before record-
> │ ing the macro.

Figure 20.6

This file is comma delim-
ited. Opening this file
involves telling Excel to
look for a comma as the
delimiter and then iden-
tifying any special han-
dling, such as treating
the third column as a
date. This is far easier
than handling fixed-
width files.

```
sales.csv - Notepad
File  Edit  Format  View  Help
Region,Product,Date,Customer,Quantity,Revenue,COGS,Profit
East,XYZ,7/24/2008,QRS INC.,1000,22810,10220,12590
Central,DEF,7/25/2008,"JKL, CO",100,2257,984,1273
East,ABC,7/25/2008,"JKL, CO",500,10245,4235,6010
Central,XYZ,7/26/2008,"WXY, CO",500,11240,5110,6130
East,XYZ,7/27/2008,"FGH, CO",400,9152,4088,5064
Central,XYZ,7/27/2008,"WXY, CO",400,9204,4088,5116
East,DEF,7/27/2008,RST INC.,800,18552,7872,10680
Central,ABC,7/28/2008,EFG S.A.,400,6860,3388,3472
East,DEF,7/30/2008,"UVW, INC.",1000,21730,9840,11890
West,XYZ,7/30/2008,"FGH, CO",600,13806,6132,7674
East,ABC,7/30/2008,FGH LTD.,400,8456,3388,5068
East,XYZ,8/1/2008,MNO S.A.,900,21015,9198,11817
Central,ABC,8/1/2008,FGH LTD.,800,16416,6776,9640
Central,XYZ,8/2/2008,"OPQ, INC.",900,21438,9198,12240
East,XYZ,8/2/2008,"WXY, CO",900,21465,9198,12267
West,XYZ,8/4/2008,"WXY, CO",400,9144,4088,5056
```

Turn on the macro recorder and record the process of opening the text file. In Step 1 of
the wizard, specify that the file is delimited.

In the Text Import Wizard—Step 2 of 3, the data preview may initially look horrible. This
is because Excel defaults to assuming that each field is separated by a tab character (see
Figure 20.7).

After unchecking the Tab box and checking the proper delimiter choice (in this case, a
comma), the data preview in Step 2 looks perfect, as shown in Figure 20.8.

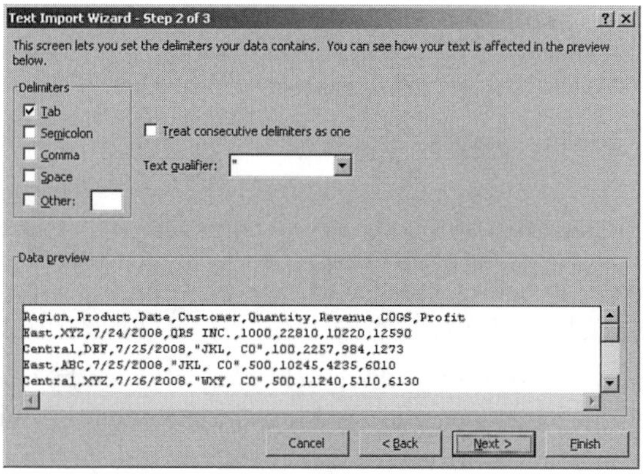

Figure 20.7
Before you import a delimited text file, the initial data preview looks like a confusing mess of data because Excel is looking for tab characters between each field when a comma is actually the delimiter in this file.

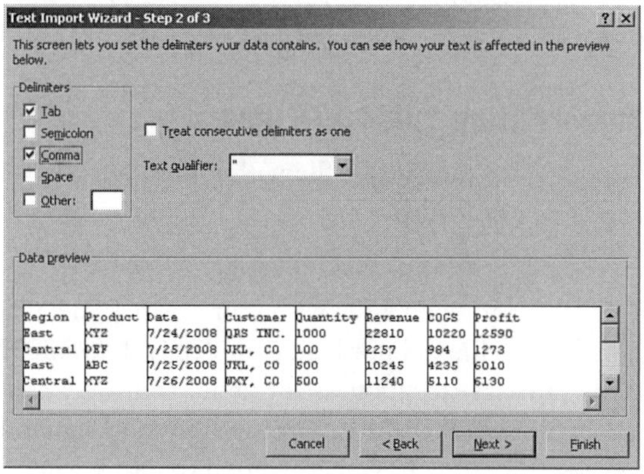

Figure 20.8
After changing the delimiter field from a tab to a comma, the data preview looks perfect. This is certainly easier than the cumbersome process in Step 2 for a fixed-width file.

Step 3 of the wizard is identical to Step 3 for a fixed-width file. In this case, specify that the third column has a date format. Click Finish, and you will have this code in the macro recorder:

```
Workbooks.OpenText Filename:="C:\sales.txt", Origin:=437, _
    StartRow:=1, DataType:=xlDelimited, TextQualifier:=xlDoubleQuote, _
    ConsecutiveDelimiter:=False, Tab:=False, Semicolon:=False, Comma:=True _
    , Space:=False, Other:=False, FieldInfo:=Array(Array(1, 1), Array(2, 1), _
    Array(3, 3), Array(4, 1), Array(5, 1), Array(6, 1), Array(7, 1), _
    Array(8, 1)), TrailingMinusNumbers:=True
```

Although this code appears longer, it is actually far simpler. In the FieldInfo parameter, the two element arrays consist of a sequence number (starting at 1 for the first field) and then an xlColumnDataType from Table 20.1. In this example, Array(2, 1) is simply saying "the second field is of general type." Array(3, 3) is saying, "the third field is a date in M-D-Y format." The code is longer because they explicitly specify each possible delimiter is set to False. Because False is the default for all delimiters, you really need only the one that you will use. The following code is equivalent:

```
Workbooks.OpenText Filename:= "C:\sales.txt", DataType:=xlDelimited, Comma:=True, _
    FieldInfo:=Array(Array(1, 1), Array(2, 1), Array(3, 3), Array(4, 1), _
    Array(5, 1), Array(6, 1), Array(7, 1), Array(8, 1))
```

Finally, to make the code more readable, you can use the constant names rather than the code numbers:

```
Workbooks.OpenText Filename:="C:\sales.txt", DataType:=xlDelimited, Comma:=True, _
FieldInfo:=Array(Array(1, xlGeneralFormat), Array(2, xlGeneralFormat), _
Array(3, xlMDYFormat), Array(4, xlGeneralFormat), Array(5, xlGeneralFormat), _
Array(6, xlGeneralFormat), Array(7, xlGeneralFormat), Array(8, xlGeneralFormat))
```

Excel has built-in options to read files where fields are delimited by tabs, semicolons, commas, or spaces. Excel can actually handle anything as a delimiter. If someone sends pipe-delimited text, you would set the `Other` parameter to `True` and specify an `OtherChar` parameter:

```
Workbooks.OpenText Filename:= "C:\sales.txt", Origin:=437, _
    DataType:=xlDelimited, Other:=True, OtherChar:= "¦", FieldInfo:=...
```

Reading Text Files with More Than 1,084,576 Rows

If you use the Text Import Wizard to read a file with more than 1,084,576 rows of data, you will get an error saying "File not loaded completely". The first 1,084,576 rows of the file will load correctly.

If you use `Workbooks.OpenText` to open a file with more than 1,084,576 rows of data, you are given no indication that the file did not load completely. Excel 2007 loads the first 1,084,576 rows and allows macro execution to continue. Your only real indication that there is a problem is if someone notices that the reports aren't reporting all the sales. If you think that your files will ever get this large, it would be good to check whether cell A1084576 is nonblank after an import. If it is, the odds are that the entire file was not loaded.

Reading Text Files One Row at a Time

You might run into a text file with more than 1,084,576 rows. When this happens, the alternative is to read the text file one row at a time. The code for doing this is the same code you might remember in your first high school BASIC class.

You need to open the file for `INPUT` as `#1`. You can then use the `Line Input #1` statement to read a line of the file into a variable. The following code opens sales.txt, reads ten lines of the file into the first ten cells of the worksheet, and closes the file:

```
Sub Import10()
    ThisFile = "C\sales.txt"
    Open ThisFile For Input As #1
    For i = 1 To 10
        Line Input #1, Data
```

```
            Cells(i, 1).Value = Data
        Next i
        Close #1
End Sub
```

Rather than read only ten records, you will want to read until you get to the end of the file. A variable called EOF is automatically updated by Excel. If you open a file for input as #1, checking EOF(1) will tell you whether you've read the last record or not.

Use a Do...While loop to keep reading records until you've reached the end of the file:

```
Sub ImportAll()
    ThisFile = "C:\sales.txt"
    Open ThisFile For Input As #1
    Ctr = 0
    Do
        Line Input #1, Data
        Ctr = Ctr + 1
        Cells(Ctr, 1).Value = Data
    Loop While EOF(1) = False
    Close #1
End Sub
```

After reading records with code such as this, you will note in Figure 20.9 that the data is not parsed into columns. All the fields are in Column A of the file.

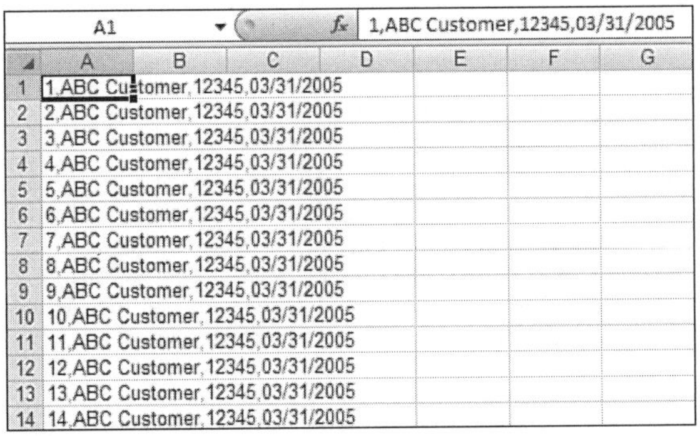

Figure 20.9
When you are reading a text file one row at a time, all the data fields end up in one long entry in Column A.

Use the TextToColumns method to parse the records into columns. The parameters for TextToColumns are nearly identical to the OpenText method:

```
Cells(1, 1).Resize(Ctr, 1).TextToColumns Destination:=Range("A1"), _
DataType:=xlDelimited, Comma:=True, FieldInfo:=Array(Array(1, _
xlGeneralFormat), Array(2, xlMDYFormat), Array(3, xlGeneralFormat), _
Array(4, xlGeneralFormat), Array(5, xlGeneralFormat), Array(6, _
xlGeneralFormat), Array(7,xlGeneralFormat), Array(8, xlGeneralFormat), _
Array(9, xlGeneralFormat), Array(10,xlGeneralFormat), Array(11, _
xlGeneralFormat))
```

20

CAUTION

For the remainder of your Excel session, Excel will remember the delimiter settings. There is an annoying bug (feature?) in Excel. After Excel remembers that you are using a comma or a tab as a delimiter, any time that you attempt to paste data from the clipboard to Excel, the data is parsed automatically by the delimiters specified in the OpenText method. Therefore, if you attempted to paste some text that includes the customer ABC, Inc., the text will be parsed automatically into two columns, with text up to ABC in one column and Inc. in the next column.

Rather than hard-code that you are using the #1 designator to open the text file, it is safer to use the FreeFile function. This returns an integer representing the next file number available for use by the Open statement. The complete code to read a text file smaller than 1,084,576 rows is as follows:

```
Sub ImportAll()
    ThisFile = "C:\sales.txt"
    FileNumber = FreeFile
    Open ThisFile For Input As #FileNumber
    Ctr = 0
    Do
        Line Input #FileNumber, Data
        Ctr = Ctr + 1
        Cells(Ctr, 1).Value = Data
    Loop While EOF(FileNumber) = False
    Close #FileNumber
    Cells(1, 1).Resize(Ctr, 1).TextToColumns Destination:=Range("A1"), _
        DataType:=xlDelimited, Comma:=True, _
        FieldInfo:=Array(Array(1, xlGeneralFormat), _
        Array(2, xlMDYFormat), Array(3, xlGeneralFormat), _
        Array(4, xlGeneralFormat), Array(5, xlGeneralFormat), _
        Array(5, xlGeneralFormat), Array(6, xlGeneralFormat), _
        Array(7, xlGeneralFormat), Array(8, xlGeneralFormat), _
        Array(9, xlGeneralFormat), Array(10, xlGeneralFormat), _
        Array(10, xlGeneralFormat), Array(11, xlGeneralFormat))
End Sub
```

Reading Text Files with More Than 1,084,576 Rows

You can use the Line Input method for reading a large text file. My strategy is to read rows into cells A1:A1084575, and then begin reading additional rows into cell AA2. I start in Row 2 on the second set so that the headings can be copied from Row 1 of the first dataset. If the file is large enough that it fills up Column AA, move to BA2, CA2, and so on. Also, I stop writing columns when I get to Row 1084574, leaving two blank rows at the bottom. This ensures that the code Cells(Rows.Count, 1)"""".End(xlup).Row finds the final row. The following code reads a large text file into several sets of columns:

```
Sub ReadLargeFile()
    ThisFile = "C:\sales.txt"
    FileNumber = FreeFile
    Open ThisFile For Input As #FileNumber
```

```
NextRow = 1
NextCol = 1
Do While Not EOF(1)
    Line Input #FileNumber, Data
    Cells(NextRow, NextCol).Value = Data
    NextRow = NextRow + 1
    If NextRow = (Rows.Count -2)  Then
        ' Parse these records
        Range(Cells(1, NextCol), Cells(Rows.Count, NextCol)).TextToColumns _
            Destination:=Cells(1, NextCol), DataType:=xlDelimited, _
            Comma:=True, FieldInfo:=Array(Array(1, xlGeneralFormat), _
            Array(2, xlMDYFormat), Array(3, xlGeneralFormat), _
            Array(4, xlGeneralFormat), Array(5, xlGeneralFormat), _
            Array(6, xlGeneralFormat), Array(7, xlGeneralFormat), _
            Array(8, xlGeneralFormat), Array(9, xlGeneralFormat), _
            Array(10, xlGeneralFormat), Array(11, xlGeneralFormat))
        ' Copy the headings from section 1
        If NextCol > 1 Then
            Range("A1:K1").Copy Destination:=Cells(1, NextCol)
        End If
        ' Set up the next section
        NextCol = NextCol + 26
        NextRow = 2
    End If
Loop
Close #FileNumber
' Parse the final Section of records
FinalRow = NextRow - 1
If FinalRow = 1 Then
    ' Handle if the file coincidentally had 1084574 rows exactly
    NextCol = NextCol - 26
Else
    Range(Cells(2, NextCol), Cells(FinalRow, NextCol)).TextToColumns _
            Destination:=Cells(1, NextCol), DataType:=xlDelimited, _
            Comma:=True, FieldInfo:=Array(Array(1, xlGeneralFormat), _
            Array(2, xlMDYFormat), Array(3, xlGeneralFormat), _
            Array(4, xlGeneralFormat), Array(5, xlGeneralFormat), _
            Array(6, xlGeneralFormat), Array(7, xlGeneralFormat), _
            Array(8, xlGeneralFormat), Array(9, xlGeneralFormat), _
            Array(10, xlGeneralFormat), Array(11, xlGeneralFormat))
    If NextCol > 1 Then
            Range("A1:K1").Copy Destination:=Cells(1, NextCol)
    End If
End If

DataSets = (NextCol - 1) / 26 + 1

End Sub
```

I usually write the DataSets variable to a named cell somewhere in the workbook so that I know how many datasets I have in the worksheet later.

As you can imagine, it is possible, using this method, to read 683,281,620 rows of data into a single worksheet. The code that you formerly used to filter and report the data now becomes more complex. You might find yourself creating pivot tables from each set of columns to create a dataset summary, and then finally summarizing all the summary tables

20

with a final pivot table. At some point, you need to consider whether the application really belongs in Access, or whether the data should be stored in Access with an Excel front end, as discussed in Chapter 21, "Using Access as a Back End to Enhance Multi-User Access to Data."

Writing Text Files

The code for writing text files is similar to reading text files. You need to open a specific file for output as #1. Then, as you loop through various records, you write them to the file using the Print #1 statement.

Before you open a file for output, make sure that any prior examples of the file have been deleted. You can use the Kill statement to delete a file. Kill returns an error if the file wasn't there in the first place, so you will want to use On Error Resume Next to prevent an error.

The following code writes out a text file for use by another application:

```
Sub WriteFile()
    ThisFile = "C:\Results.txt"

    ' Delete yesterday's copy of the file
    On Error Resume Next
    Kill (ThisFile)
    On Error GoTo 0

    ' Open the file
    Open ThisFile For Output As #1
    FinalRow = Range("A65536").End(xlUp).Row
    ' Write out the file
    For j = 1 To FinalRow
        Print #1, Cells(j, 1).Value
    Next j
End Sub
```

This is a fairly trivial example. You can use this method to write out any type of text-based file. The code at the end of Chapter 16, "Reading from and Writing to the Web," uses the same concept to write out HTML files.

Next Steps

You will sometimes find yourself writing to text files out of necessity—either to import data from another system or to produce data compatible with another system. Using text files is a slow method for reading and writing data. In Chapter 21 you will learn about writing to Access Multidimensional Database (MDB) files. These files are faster, indexable, and allow multi-user access to data.

Using Access as a Back End to Enhance Multi-User Access to Data

21

The example near the end of Chapter 20, "Text File Processing," proposed a method for storing 683 million records in an Excel worksheet. At some point, you need to admit that even though Excel is the greatest product in the world, there is a time to move to Access and take advantage of the Access Multidimensional Database (MDB) files.

Even before you have more than one million rows, another compelling reason to use MDB data files is to allow multi-user access to data without the headaches associated with shared workbooks.

Microsoft Excel offers an option to share a workbook, but you automatically lose a number of important Excel features when you share a workbook. After you share a workbook, you cannot use automatic subtotals, pivot tables, Group and Outline mode, scenarios, protection, Autoformat, Styles, Pictures, Add Charts, or Insert worksheets.

By using an Excel VBA front end and storing data in an MDB database, you have the best of both worlds. You have the power and flexibility of Excel and the multi-user access capability available in Access.

> **NOTE**
>
> MDB is the official file format of both Microsoft Access and Microsoft Visual Basic. This means that you can deploy an Excel solution that reads and writes from an MDB to customers who do not have Microsoft Access. Of course, it helps if you as the developer have a copy of Access because you can use the Access front end to set up tables and queries.

ADO Versus DAO

For several years, Microsoft recommended DAO (data access objects) for accessing data in external database. DAO became very popular and a great deal of code was written for DAO. When Microsoft released Excel 2000, they started pushing ADO (ActiveX data objects). The concepts are similar, and the syntax differs only slightly. I use the newer ADO in this chapter. Realize that if you start going through code written a while ago, you might run into DAO code. Other than a few syntax changes, the code for both ADO and DAO looks similar. If you discover that you have to debug some old code using DAO, check out the Microsoft Knowledge Base articles that you can find at the following address, which discuss the differences:

http://support.microsoft.com/default.aspx?scid=KB;EN-US;q225048&

The following two articles provide the Rosetta Stone between DAO and ADO. The ADO code is shown at the following site:

http://support.microsoft.com/default.aspx?scid=KB;EN-US;q146607&

The equivalent DAO code is shown here:

http://support.microsoft.com/default.aspx?scid=KB;EN-US;q142938&

To use any code in this chapter, open the VB Editor. Select Tools, References from the main menu, and then select Microsoft ActiveX Data Objects 2.8 Library (or higher) from the Available References list, as shown in Figure 21.1.

Figure 21.1
To read or write from an Access MDB file, add the reference for Microsoft ActiveX Data Objects 2.8 Library or higher.

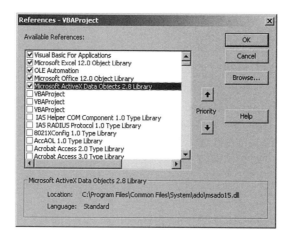

CASE STUDY

Linda and Janine are two buyers for a retail chain of stores. Each morning, they import data from the cash registers to get current information on sales and inventory for 2,000 styles. Throughout the day, either buyer may enter transfers of inventory from one store to another. It would be ideal if Linda could see the pending transfers entered by Janine and vice versa.

Each buyer has an Excel application with VBA running on her desktop. They each import the cash register data and have VBA routines that facilitate the creation of pivot table reports to help them make buying decisions.

Attempting to store the transfer data in a common Excel file causes problems. When either buyer attempts to write to the Excel file, the entire file becomes read-only for the other buyer. With a shared workbook, Excel turns off the capability to create pivot tables, and this is required in their application.

Neither Linda nor Janine have the professional version of Office, so they do not have Access running on their desktop PCs.

The solution is to produce an Access database on a network drive that both Linda and Janine can see:

1. Using Access on another PC, produce a new database called **transfers.mdb** and add a table called **tblTransfer**, as shown in Figure 21.2.

Figure 21.2
Multiple people using their own Excel workbooks will read and write to this table inside an MDB file on a network drive.

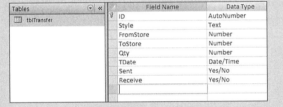

2. Move the Transfers.mdb file to a network drive. You might find that this common folder uses different drive letter mappings on each machine. It might be H:\Common\ on Linda's machine and I:\Common\ on Janine's machine.

3. On both machines, go to the VB Editor and under Tools, References, add a reference to ActiveX Data Objects 2.8 Library (or higher).

4. In both of their applications, find an out-of-the-way cell to store the path to transfers.mdb. Name this cell **TPath**.

The remainder of this chapter gives you the code necessary to allow the application to read or write data from the tblTransfer table.

The application provides nearly seamless multi-user access to both buyers. Both Linda and Janine can read or write to the table at the same time. The only time a conflict would occur is if they both happened to try to update the same record at the same time.

Other than the out-of-the-way cell reference to the path to transfers.mdb, neither buyer is aware that her data is being stored in a shared Access table and neither computer needs to have Access installed.

21

The Tools of ADO

You encounter several terms when using ADO to connect to an external data source.

- **Recordset**—When connecting to an Access database, the recordset will either be a table in the database or a query in the database. Most of the ADO methods will reference the recordset. You might also want to create your own query on the fly. In this case, you would write a SQL statement to extract only a subset of records from a table.

- **Connection**—Defines the path to the database and the type of database. In the case of Access databases, you specify that the connection is using the Microsoft Jet Engine.

- **Cursor**—Think of the cursor as a pointer that keeps track of which record you are using in the database. There are several types of cursor and two places for the cursor to be located (described in the following bullets).

- **Cursor type**—A dynamic cursor is the most flexible cursor. If you define a recordset and someone else updates a row in the table while a dynamic cursor is active, the dynamic cursor will know about the updated record. While this is the most flexible, it requires the most overhead. If your database doesn't have a lot of transactions, you might specify a static cursor—this type of cursor returns a snapshot of the data at the time the cursor is established.

- **Cursor location**—The cursor can be located either on the client or on the server. For an Access database residing on your hard drive, a server location for the cursor means that the Access Jet Engine on your computer is controlling the cursor. When you specify a client location for the cursor, your Excel session is controlling the cursor. On a very large external dataset, it would be better to allow the server to control the cursor. For small datasets, a client cursor is faster.

- **Lock type**—The point of this entire chapter is to allow multiple people to access a dataset at the same time. The lock type defines how ADO will prevent crashes when two people try to update the record at the same time. With an optimistic lock type, an individual record is locked only when you attempt to update the record. If your application will be doing 90% reads and only occasionally updating, then an optimistic lock is perfect. However, if you know that every time you read a record you will soon update the record, then you would use a pessimistic lock type. With pessimistic locks, the record is locked as soon as you read it. If you know that you will never write back to the database, you can use a read-only lock. This allows you to read the records without preventing others from writing to the records.

The primary objects needed to access data in an MDB file are an ADO connection and an ADO recordset.

The ADO connection defines the path to the database and specifies that the connection is based on the Microsoft Jet Engine.

After you have established the connection to the database, you usually will use that connection to define a recordset. A recordset can be a table or a subset of records in the table or a predefined query in the Access database. To open a recordset, you have to specify the connection and the values for the `CursorType`, `CursorLocation`, `LockType`, and `Options` parameters. Assuming that you have only two users trying to access the table at a time, I generally use a dynamic cursor and an optimistic lock type. For large datasets, the `adUseServer` value of the `CursorLocation` property allows the database server to process records without using up RAM on the client machine. If you have a small dataset, it might be faster to use `adUseClient` for the `CursorLocation`. When the recordset is opened, all the records are transferred to memory of the client machine. This allows faster navigation from record to record.

Reading data from the Access database is easy. You can use the `CopyFromRecordset` method to copy all selected records from the recordset to a blank area of the worksheet.

To add a record to the Access table, use the `AddNew` method for the recordset. You then specify the value for each field in the table and use the `Update` method to commit the changes to the database.

To delete a record from the table, you can use a pass-through query to delete records that match a certain criteria.

> **NOTE**
> If you ever find yourself frustrated with ADO and think,"If I could just open Access, I could knock out a quick SQL statement that will do exactly what I need," then the pass-through query is for you. Rather than use ADO to read through the records, the pass-through query sends a request to the database to run the SQL statement that your program builds. This effectively enables you to handle any tasks that your database might support but that are not handled by ADO. The types of SQL statements handled by the pass-through query are dependent on which database type you are connecting to.

Other tools are available that let you make sure a table exists or that a particular field exists in a table. You can also use VBA to add new fields to a table definition on the fly.

Adding a Record to the Database

Going back to our case study earlier in the chapter, the application we are creating has a userform where buyers can enter transfers. To make the calls to the Access database as simple as possible, a series of utility modules handle the ADO connection to the database. This way, the userform code can simply call `AddTransfer(Style, FromStore, ToStore, Qty)`.

The technique for adding records, after the connection is defined, is as follows:

1. Open a recordset that points to the table. In the code that follows, see the sections commented `Open the Connection`, `Define the Recordset`, and `Open the Table`.

2. Use `AddNew` to add a new record.

3. Update each field in the new record.

21

4. Use Update to update the recordset.

5. Close the recordset, and then close the connection.

The following code adds a new record to the tblTransfer table:

```
Sub AddTransfer(Style As Variant, FromStore As Variant, _
    ToStore As Variant, Qty As Integer)
    Dim cnn As ADODB.Connection
    Dim rst As ADODB.Recordset

    MyConn = "J:\transfers.mdb"

    ' open the connection
    Set cnn = New ADODB.Connection
    With cnn
        .Provider = "Microsoft.Jet.OLEDB.4.0"
        .Open MyConn
    End With

    ' Define the Recordset
    Set rst = New ADODB.Recordset
    rst.CursorLocation = adUseServer

    ' open the table
    rst.Open Source:="tblTransfer", _
        ActiveConnection:=cnn, _
        CursorType:=adOpenDynamic, _
        LockType:=adLockOptimistic, _
        Options:=adCmdTable

    ' Add a record
    rst.AddNew

    ' Set up the values for the fields. The first four fields
    ' are passed from the calling userform. The date field
    ' is filled with the current date.
    rst("Style") = Style
    rst("FromStore") = FromStore
    rst("ToStore") = ToStore
    rst("Qty") = Qty
    rst("tDate") = Date
    rst("Sent") = False
    rst("Receive") = False

    ' Write the values to this record
    rst.Update

    ' Close
    rst.Close
    cnn.Close

End Sub
```

Retrieving Records from the Database

Reading records from the Access database is very easy. As you define the recordset, you pass a SQL string to return the records in which you are interested.

A great way to generate the SQL is to design a query in Access that retrieves the records. While viewing the query in Access, choose SQL View from the View dropdown on the Query Tools Design tab of the Ribbon. Access shows you the proper SQL statement required to execute that query. You can use this SQL statement as a model for building the SQL string in your VBA code.

After the recordset is defined, use the `CopyFromRecordSet` method to copy all the matching records from Access to a specific area of the worksheet.

The following routine queries the Transfer table to find all records where the `Sent` flag is not yet set to `True`. The results are placed on a blank worksheet. The final few lines display the results in a userform to illustrate how to update a record in the next section:

```
Sub GetUnsentTransfers()
    Dim cnn As ADODB.Connection
    Dim rst As ADODB.Recordset
    Dim WSOrig As Worksheet
    Dim WSTemp As Worksheet
    Dim sSQL as String
    Dim FinalRow as Long

    Set WSOrig = ActiveSheet

    'Build a SQL String to get all fields for unsent transfers
    sSQL = "SELECT ID, Style, FromStore, ToStore, Qty, tDate FROM tblTransfer"
    sSQL = sSQL & " WHERE Sent=FALSE"

    ' Path to Transfers.mdb
    MyConn = "J:\transfers.mdb"

    Set cnn = New ADODB.Connection
    With cnn
        .Provider = "Microsoft.Jet.OLEDB.4.0"
        .Open MyConn
    End With

    Set rst = New ADODB.Recordset
    rst.CursorLocation = adUseServer
    rst.Open Source:=sSQL, ActiveConnection:=cnn, _
        CursorType:=AdForwardOnly, LockType:=adLockOptimistic, _
            Options:=adCmdText

    ' Create the report in a new worksheet
    Set WSTemp = Worksheets.Add

    ' Add Headings
    Range("A1:F1").Value = Array("ID", "Style", "From", "To", "Qty", "Date")

    ' Copy from the recordset to row 2
    Range("A2").CopyFromRecordset rst

    ' Close the connection
    rst.Close
    cnn.Close
```

```
' Format the report
FinalRow = Range("A65536").End(xlUp).Row

' If there were no records, then stop
If FinalRow = 1 Then
    Application.DisplayAlerts = False
    WSTemp.Delete
    Application.DisplayAlerts = True
    WSOrig.Activate
    MsgBox "There are no transfers to confirm"
    Exit Sub
End If

' Format column F as a date
Range("F2:F" & FinalRow).NumberFormat = "m/d/y"

' Show the userform - used in next section
frmTransConf.Show

' Delete the temporary sheet
Application.DisplayAlerts = False
WSTemp.Delete
Application.DisplayAlerts = True

End Sub
```

The CopyFromRecordSet method copies records that match the SQL query to a range on the worksheet. Note that you receive only the data rows. The headings do not come along automatically. You must use code to write the headings to Row 1. Figure 21.3 shows the results.

Figure 21.3

Range("A2").Copy FromRecordSet brought matching records from the Access database to the worksheet.

▲	A	B	C	D	E	F
1	ID	Style	From	To	Qty	Date
2	1935	B11275	340000	340000	8	6/4/08
3	1936	B10133	340000	340000	4	6/4/08
4	1937	B15422	340000	340000	5	6/4/08
5	1938	B10894	340000	340000	9	6/4/08
6	1939	B10049	340000	340000	3	6/4/08
7	1941	B18722	340000	340000	10	6/4/08
8	1944	B12886	340000	340000	10	6/4/08
9	1947	B17947	340000	340000	7	6/4/08
10	1950	B16431	340000	340000	9	6/4/08
11	1953	B19857	340000	340000	7	6/4/08
12	1954	B11562	340000	340000	1	6/4/08
13	1955	B19413	340000	340000	2	6/4/08
14	1957	B17370	340000	340000	1	6/4/08
15	1958	B14304	340000	340000	5	6/4/08
16	1959	B19881	340000	340000	5	6/4/08
17	1960	B13722	340000	340000	1	6/4/08
18	1961	B16873	340000	340000	6	6/4/08
19	1962	B14620	340000	340000	7	6/4/08
20	1963	B12306	340000	340000	1	6/4/08
21	1964	B18110	340000	340000	9	6/4/08
22	1965	B15963	340000	340000	4	6/4/08
23	1966	B12256	340000	340000	6	6/4/08
24	1967	B15878	340000	340000	10	6/4/08

Updating an Existing Record

To update an existing record, you need to build a recordset with exactly one record. This requires that the user select some sort of unique key when identifying the records. After you have opened the recordset, use the `Fields` property to change the field in question and then the Update method to commit the changes to the database.

The earlier example returned a recordset to a blank worksheet and then called a userform frmTransConf. This form uses a simple `Userform_Initialize` to display the range in a large list box. The list box's properties have the `MultiSelect` property set to `True`:

```
Private Sub UserForm_Initialize()

    ' Determine how Records we have
    FinalRow = Cells(Rows.Count, 1).End(xlUp).Row
    If FinalRow > 1 Then
        Me.lbXlt.RowSource = "A2:F" & FinalRow
    End If

End Sub
```

After the initialize procedure is run, the unconfirmed records are displayed in a list box. The logistics planner can mark all the records that have actually been sent, as shown in Figure 21.4.

Figure 21.4
This userform displays particular records from the Access recordset. When the buyer selects certain records and then chooses the Confirm button, you'll have to use ADO's Update method to update the Sent field on the selected records.

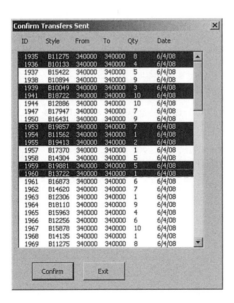

The code attached to the Confirm button follows. Including the ID field in the fields returned in the prior example is important if you want to narrow the information down to a single record:

21

```
Private Sub cbConfirm_Click()
    Dim cnn As ADODB.Connection
    Dim rst As ADODB.Recordset

    ' If nothing is selected, warn them
    CountSelect = 0
    For x = 0 To Me.lbXlt.ListCount - 1
        If Me.lbXlt.Selected(x) Then
            CountSelect = CountSelect + 1
        End If
    Next x

    If CountSelect = 0 Then
        MsgBox "There were no transfers selected. " & _
            "To exit without confirming any tranfers, use Cancel."
        Exit Sub
    End If

    ' Establish a connection transfers.mdb
    ' Path to Transfers.mdb is on Menu
    MyConn = "J:\transfers.mdb"

    Set cnn = New ADODB.Connection

    With cnn
        .Provider = "Microsoft.Jet.OLEDB.4.0"
        .Open MyConn
    End With

    ' Mark as complete
    For x = 0 To Me.lbXlt.ListCount - 1
        If Me.lbXlt.Selected(x) Then
            ThisID = Cells(2 + x, 1).Value
            ' Mark ThisID as complete
            'Build SQL String
            sSQL = "SELECT * FROM tblTransfer Where ID=" & ThisID
            Set rst = New ADODB.Recordset
            With rst
                .Open Source:=sSQL, ActiveConnection:=cnn, _
                    CursorType:=adOpenKeyset, LockType:=adLockOptimistic
                ' Update the field
                .Fields("Sent").Value = True
                .Update
                .Close
            End With
        End If
    Next x

    ' Close the connection
    cnn.Close
    Set rst = Nothing
    Set cnn = Nothing

    ' Close the userform
    Unload Me

End Sub
```

21

Deleting Records via ADO

Like updating a record, the key to deleting record(s) is being able to write a bit of SQL to uniquely identify the record(s) to be deleted. The following code uses the Execute method to pass the Delete command through to Access:

```
Public Sub ADOWipeOutAttribute(RecID)
    ' Establish a connection transfers.mdb
    MyConn = "J:\transfers.mdb"

    With New ADODB.Connection
        .Provider = "Microsoft.Jet.OLEDB.4.0"
        .Open MyConn
        .Execute "Delete From tblTransfer Where ID = " & RecID
        .Close
    End With
End Sub
```

Summarizing Records via ADO

One of Access's strengths is running summary queries that group by a particular field. If you build a summary query in Access and examine the SQL view, you will see that complex queries can be written. Similar SQL can be built in Excel VBA and passed to Access via ADO.

The following code uses a fairly complex query to get a net total by store:

```
Sub NetTransfers(Style As Variant)
    ' This builds a table of net open transfers
    ' on Styles AI1
    Dim cnn As ADODB.Connection
    Dim rst As ADODB.Recordset

    ' Build the large SQL query
    ' Basic Logic:  Get all open Incoming Transfers by store,
    ' union with -1* outgoing transfers by store
    ' Sum that union by store, and give us min date as well
    ' A single call to this macro will replace 60 _
    ' calls to GetTransferIn, GetTransferOut, TransferAge
    sSQL = "Select Store, Sum(Quantity), Min(mDate) From _
        (SELECT ToStore AS Store, Sum(Qty) AS Quantity, _
        Min(TDate) AS mDate FROM tblTransfer where Style='" & Style _
        & "' AND Receive=FALSE GROUP BY ToStore "
    sSQL = sSQL & " Union All SELECT FromStore AS Store, _
        Sum(-1*Qty) AS Quantity, Min(TDate) AS mDate _
        FROM tblTransfer where Style='" & Style & "' AND _
        Sent=FALSE GROUP BY FromStore)"
    sSQL = sSQL & " Group by Store"

    MyConn = "J:\transfers.mdb"

    ' open the connection.
    Set cnn = New ADODB.Connection
    With cnn
        .Provider = "Microsoft.Jet.OLEDB.4.0"
```

21

```
            .Open MyConn
        End With

        Set rst = New ADODB.Recordset

        rst.CursorLocation = adUseServer

        ' open the first query
        rst.Open Source:=sSQL, _
            ActiveConnection:=cnn, _
            CursorType:=AdForwardOnly, _
            LockType:=adLockOptimistic, _
            Options:=adCmdText

        Range("A1:C1").Value = Array("Store", "Qty", "Date")
        ' Return Query Results
        Range("A2").CopyFromRecordset rst
        rst.Close
        cnn.Close

    End Sub
```

Other Utilities via ADO

Consider the application we created for our case study; the buyers now have an Access database located on their network, but possibly no copy of Access. It would be ideal if you could deliver changes to the Access database on the fly as their application opens up.

> **TIP**
>
> If you are wondering how you would ever coax the person using the application to run these queries, consider using an Update macro hidden in the Workbook_Open routine of the client application. Such a routine might first check to see if a field does not exist and then add the field. For details on the mechanics of hiding the update query in the Workbook_Open routine, see the case study, "Using a Hidden Code Workbook to Hold All Macros and Forms," in Chapter 27, "Add-Ins."

Checking for Existence of Tables

If the application needs a new table in the database, you can use the code in the next section. However, because we have a multi-user application, only the first person who opens the application has to add the table on the fly. When the next buyer shows up, the table may have already been added by the first buyer's application.

This code uses the OpenSchema method to actually query the database schema:

```
Function TableExists(WhichTable)
    Dim cnn As ADODB.Connection
    Dim rst As ADODB.Recordset
    Dim fld As ADODB.Field
    TableExists = False
```

```
    ' Path to Transfers.mdb is on Menu
    MyConn = "J:\transfers.mdb"

    Set cnn = New ADODB.Connection

    With cnn
        .Provider = "Microsoft.Jet.OLEDB.4.0"
        .Open MyConn
    End With

    Set rst = cnn.OpenSchema(adSchemaTables)

    Do Until rst.EOF
        If LCase(rst!Table_Name) = LCase(WhichTable) Then
            TableExists = True
            GoTo ExitMe
        End If
        rst.MoveNext
    Loop

ExitMe:
    rst.Close
    Set rst = Nothing
    ' Close the connection
    cnn.Close

End Function
```

Checking for Existence of a Field

Sometimes, you will want to add a new field to an existing table. Again, this code uses the OpenSchema method, but this time looks at the columns in the tables:

```
Function ColumnExists(WhichColumn, WhichTable)
    Dim cnn As ADODB.Connection
    Dim rst As ADODB.Recordset
    Dim WSOrig As Worksheet
    Dim WSTemp As Worksheet
    Dim fld As ADODB.Field
    ColumnExists = False

    ' Path to Transfers.mdb is on menu
    MyConn = ActiveWorkbook.Worksheets("Menu").Range("TPath").Value
    If Right(MyConn, 1) = "\" Then
        MyConn = MyConn & "transfers.mdb"
    Else
        MyConn = MyConn & "\transfers.mdb"
    End If

    Set cnn = New ADODB.Connection

    With cnn
        .Provider = "Microsoft.Jet.OLEDB.4.0"
        .Open MyConn
    End With

    Set rst = cnn.OpenSchema(adSchemaColumns)
```

```
        Do Until rst.EOF
            If LCase(rst!Column_Name) = LCase(WhichColumn) And _
                LCase(rst!Table_Name) = LCase(WhichTable) Then
                ColumnExists = True
                GoTo ExitMe
            End If
            rst.MoveNext
        Loop

ExitMe:
    rst.Close
    Set rst = Nothing
    ' Close the connection
    cnn.Close

End Function
```

Adding a Table On the Fly

This code uses a pass-through query to tell Access to run a `Create Table` command:

```
Sub ADOCreateReplenish()
    ' This creates tblReplenish
    ' There are five fields:
    ' Style
    ' A = Auto replenishment for A
    ' B = Auto replenishment level for B stores
    ' C = Auto replenishment level for C stores
    ' RecActive = Yes/No field
    Dim cnn As ADODB.Connection
    Dim cmd As ADODB.Command

    ' Define the connection
    MyConn = "J:\transfers.mdb"

    ' open the connection
    Set cnn = New ADODB.Connection
    With cnn
        .Provider = "Microsoft.Jet.OLEDB.4.0"
        .Open MyConn
    End With

    Set cmd = New ADODB.Command
    Set cmd.ActiveConnection = cnn
    'create table
    cmd.CommandText = "CREATE TABLE tblReplenish (Style Char(10) Primary Key, _
        A int, B  int, C Int, RecActive YesNo)"
    cmd.Execute , , adCmdText
    Set cmd = Nothing
    Set cnn = Nothing
    Exit Sub
End Sub
```

Adding a Field On the Fly

If you determine that a field does not exist, you can use a pass-through query to add a field to the table:

```
Sub ADOAddField()
    ' This adds a grp field to tblReplenish
    Dim cnn As ADODB.Connection
    Dim cmd As ADODB.Command

    ' Define the connection
    MyConn = "J:\transfers.mdb"
    End If

    ' open the connection
    Set cnn = New ADODB.Connection
    With cnn
        .Provider = "Microsoft.Jet.OLEDB.4.0"
        .Open MyConn
    End With


    Set cmd = New ADODB.Command
    Set cmd.ActiveConnection = cnn
    'create table
    cmd.CommandText = "ALTER TABLE tblReplenish Add Column Grp Char(25)"
    cmd.Execute , , adCmdText
    Set cmd = Nothing
    Set cnn = Nothing

End Sub
```

Next Steps

In Chapter 22, "Creating Classes, Records, and Collections," you will learn about the powerful technique of setting up your own Class module. With this technique, you can set up your own object with its own methods and properties.

21

Creating Classes, Records, and Collections

22

Excel already has many objects available, but there are times when a custom object would be better suited for the job at hand. You can create custom objects that you use in the same way as Excel's built-in objects. These special objects are created in *class modules*.

Class modules are used to create custom objects with custom properties and methods. They can trap application events, embedded chart events, ActiveX control events, and more.

Inserting a Class Module

From the VB Editor, select Insert, Class Module. A new module, Class1, is added to the VBAProject workbook and can be seen in the Project Explorer window (see Figure 22.1). Two things to keep in mind concerning class modules:

- Each custom object must have its own module. (Event trapping can share a module.)
- The class module should be renamed to reflect the custom object.

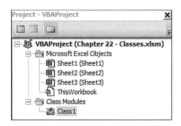

Figure 22.1
Custom objects are created in class modules.

Trapping Application and Embedded Chart Events

Chapter 9, "Event Programming," showed you how certain actions in workbooks, worksheets, and nonembedded charts could be trapped and used to activate code. Briefly, it reviewed how to set up a class module to trap application and chart events. The following goes into more detail about what was shown in that chapter.

Application Events

The `Workbook_BeforePrint` event is triggered when the workbook in which it resides is printed. If you want to run the same code in every workbook available, you have to copy the code to each workbook. Or, you could use an application event, `Workbook_BeforePrint`, which is triggered when any workbook is printed.

The application events already exist, but a class module must be set up first so that they can be seen. To create a class module, follow these steps:

1. Insert a class module into the project. Rename it to something that will make sense to you, such as `clsAppEvents`. Choose View, Properties Window to rename a module.

2. Enter the following into the class module:

   ```
   Public WithEvents xlApp As Application
   ```

   The name of the variable, `xlApp`, can be any variable name. The `WithEvents` keyword exposes the events associated with the Application object.

3. `xlApp` is now available from that class module's Object drop-down list. Select it from the drop-down, and then click the Procedure drop-down menu to the right of it to view the list of events that is available for the `xlApp`'s object type (Application), as shown in Figure 22.2.

→ For a review of the various Application Events, **see** "Application-Level Events," **p. 171**, in Chapter 9, "Event Programming."

Any of the events listed can by captured, just as workbook and worksheet events were captured in an earlier chapter. The following example uses the `NewWorkbook` event to automatically set up footer information. This code is placed in the class module, below the `xlApp` declaration line you just added:

Figure 22.2
Events are made available after the object is created.

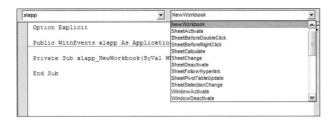

```
Private Sub xlApp_NewWorkbook(ByVal Wb As Workbook)
Dim wks As Worksheet

With Wb
```

```
      For Each wks In .Worksheets
          wks.PageSetup.LeftFooter = "Created by: " & .Application.UserName
          wks.PageSetup.RightFooter = Now
      Next wks
End With

End Sub
```

The procedure placed in a class module does not run automatically as events in workbook or worksheet modules would. An instance of the class module must be created and the Application object assigned to the xlApp property. After that is complete, the TrapAppEvent procedure needs to run. As long as the procedure is running, the footer will be created on each sheet every time a new workbook is added. Place the following in a standard module:

```
Public myAppEvent As New clsAppEvents

Sub TrapAppEvent()

Set myAppEvent.xlApp = Application

End Sub
```

> **CAUTION**
>
> The application event trapping can be terminated by any action that resets the module level or public variables. This includes editing code in the VB Editor. To restart, run the procedure that creates the object (TrapAppEvent).

In this example, the public myAppEvent declaration was placed in a standard module with the TrapAppEvent procedure. To automate the running of the entire event trapping, all the modules could be transferred to the Personal.xlsb and the procedure transferred to a Workbook_Open event. In any case, the Public declaration of myAppEvent *must* remain in a standard module so that it can be shared between modules.

Embedded Chart Events

Preparing to trap embedded chart events is the same as preparing for trapping application events. Create a class module, insert the public declaration for a chart type, create a procedure for the desired event, and then add a standard module procedure to initiate the trapping. The same class module used for the application event can be used for the embedded chart event.

Place the following line in the declaration section of the class module. The available chart events are now viewable (see Figure 22.3):

```
Public WithEvents xlChart As Chart
```

→ For a review of the various charts events, **see** "Chart Sheet Events," **p. 167**, in Chapter 9, "Event Programming."

Figure 22.3
The chart events are available after the chart type variable has been declared.

Three events are set up. The primary event, MouseDown, changes the chart scale with a right-click or double-click. Because these actions also have actions associated with them, you need two more events, BeforeRightClick and BeforeDoubleClick, to prevent the usual action from taking place:

This BeforeDoubleClick event prevents the normal result of a double-click from taking place:

```
Private Sub xlChart_BeforeDoubleClick(ByVal ElementID As Long, _
    ByVal Arg1 As Long, ByVal Arg2 As Long, Cancel As Boolean)
Cancel = True
End Sub
```

This BeforeRightClick event prevents the normal result of a right-click from taking place:

```
Private Sub xlChart_BeforeRightClick(Cancel As Boolean)
Cancel = True
End Sub
```

Now that the normal actions of the double-click and right-click have been controlled, ChartMouseDown rewrites what actions are initiated by a right-click and double-click:

```
Private Sub xlChart_MouseDown(ByVal Button As Long, ByVal Shift As Long, _
    ByVal x As Long, ByVal y As Long)
    If Button = 1 Then
       xlChart.Axes(xlValue).MaximumScale = _
    xlChart.Axes(xlValue).MaximumScale - 50
    End If

    If Button = 2 Then
       xlChart.Axes(xlValue).MaximumScale = _
    xlChart.Axes(xlValue).MaximumScale + 50
    End If

End Sub
```

After the events are set in the class module, all that's left to do is declare the variable in a standard module, as follows:

```
Public myChartEvent As New clsEvents
```

Then, create a procedure that will capture the events on the embedded chart:

```
Sub TrapChartEvent()

Set myChartEvent.xlChart = Worksheets("EmbedChart"). _
    ChartObjects("Chart 2").Chart

End Sub
```

> **NOTE**
> The `BeforeDoubleClick` and `BeforeRightClick` events are only triggered when the user clicks the plot area itself. The area around the plot area does not trigger the events. However, the `MouseDown` event is triggered from anywhere on the chart.

Creating a Custom Object

Class modules are useful for trapping events, but they are also valuable because they can be used to create custom objects. When you are creating a custom object, the class module becomes a template of the object's properties and methods. To better understand this, we are going to create an employee object to track employee name, ID, hourly wage rate, and hours worked.

Insert a class module and rename it to **clsEmployee.** The clsEmployee object has four properties:

- **EmpName**—Employee name
- **EmpID**—Employee ID
- **EmpRate**—Hourly wage rate
- **EmpWeeklyHrs**—Hours worked

Properties are variables that can be declared `Private` or `Public`. These properties need to be accessible to the standard module, so they will be declared `Public`. Place the following lines at the top of the class module:

```
Public EmpName As String
Public EmpID As String
Public EmpRate As Double
Public EmpWeeklyHrs As Double
```

Methods are actions that the object can take. In the class module, these actions take shape as procedures and functions. The following code creates a method, `EmpWeeklyPay()`, for the object that calculates weekly pay:

```
Public Function EmpWeeklyPay() As Double
EmpWeeklyPay = EmpRate * EmpWeeklyHrs
End Function
```

The object is now complete. It has four properties and one method. The next step is using the object in an actual program.

Using a Custom Object

After a custom object is properly configured in a class module, it can be referenced from another module. Declare a variable as the custom object type in the declarations section:

```
Dim Employee As clsEmployee
```

In the procedure, Set the variable to be a New object:

```
Set Employee = New clsEmployee
```

Continue entering the rest of the procedure. As you refer to the properties and method of the custom object, a screen tip appears, just as with Excel's standard objects (see Figure 22.4).

Figure 22.4
The properties and method of the custom object are just as easily accessible as they are for standard objects.

```
(General)                                  ▼   EmpPay

    Option Explicit

    Dim Employee As clsEmployee
    Sub EmpPay()
    Set Employee = New clsEmployee

    With Employee
        .EmpName = "Tracy Syrstad"
        .EmpID = "1651"
        .EmpRate = 25
        .
   ⌐⊞ EmpID          & " earns $" & .EmpWeeklyPay & " per week."
 En⌐⊞ EmpName
   ⌐⊞ EmpRate
 En⌐⊞ EmpWeeklyHrs
      ◈ EmpWeeklyPay
```

```
Option Explicit

Dim Employee As clsEmployee

Sub EmpPay()

Set Employee = New clsEmployee

With Employee
    .EmpName = "Tracy Syrstad"
    .EmpID = "1651"
    .EmpRate = 25
    .EmpWeeklyHrs = 40
    MsgBox .EmpName & " earns $" & .EmpWeeklyPay & " per week."
End With

End Sub
```

The subprocedure declares an object Employee as a new instance of clsEmployee. It then assigns values to the four properties of the object and generates a message box displaying the employee name and weekly pay (see Figure 22.5). The object's method, EmpWeeklyPay, is used to generate the displayed pay.

Figure 22.5
Create custom objects to make code more efficient.

Microsoft Excel

Tracy Syrstad earns $1000 per week.

OK

Using Property Let and Property Get to Control How Users Utilize Custom Objects

Public variables, as declared in the earlier example, have read/write properties. When they are used in a program, the values of the variables can be retrieved or changed. To assign read/write limitations, use Property Let and Property Get procedures.

Property Let procedures give you control of how properties can be assigned values. Property Get procedures give you control of how the properties are accessed. In the custom object example, there is a public variable for weekly hours. This variable is used in a method for calculating pay for the week, but doesn't take overtime pay into consideration. Variables for normal hours and overtime hours are needed, but the variables must be read-only.

To accomplish this, the class module must be reconstructed. It needs two new properties, EmpNormalHrs and EmpOverTimeHrs. Because these two properties are to be confined to read-only, however, they are not declared as variables. Property Get procedures are used to create them.

If EmpNormalHrs and EmpOverTimeHrs are going to be read-only, they must have values assigned somehow. Their values are a calculation of the EmpWeeklyHrs. Because EmpWeeklyHrs is going to be used to set the property values of these two object properties, it can no longer be a public variable. There are two private variables. These private variables, NormalHrs and OverHrs, are used within the confines of the class module:

```
Public EmpName As String
Public EmpID As String
Public EmpRate As Double

Private NormalHrs As Double
Private OverHrs As Double
```

A Property Let procedure is created for EmpWeeklyHrs to break the hours down into normal and overtime hours:

```
Property Let EmpWeeklyHrs(Hrs As Double)

NormalHrs = WorksheetFunction.Min(40, Hrs)
OverHrs = WorksheetFunction.Max(0, Hrs - 40)

End Property
```

The Property Get EmpWeeklyHrs totals these hours and returns a value to this property. Without it, a value cannot be retrieved from EmpWeeklyHrs:

```
Property Get EmpWeeklyHrs() As Double

EmpWeeklyHrs = NormalHrs + OverHrs

End Property
```

Property Get procedures are created for `EmpNormalHrs` and `EmpOverTimeHrs` to set their values. If you use Property Get procedures only, the values of these two properties are read-only. They can be assigned values only through the `EmpWeeklyHrs` property:

```
Property Get EmpNormalHrs() As Double

EmpNormalHrs = NormalHrs

End Property


Property Get EmpOverTimeHrs() As Double

EmpOverTimeHrs = OverHrs

End Property
```

Finally, the method `EmpWeeklyPay` is updated to reflect the changes in the properties and goal:

```
Public Function EmpWeeklyPay() As Double

EmpWeeklyPay = (EmpNormalHrs * EmpRate) + (EmpOverTimeHrs * EmpRate * 1.5)

End Function
```

Update the procedure in the standard module to take advantage of the changes in the class module. Figure 22.6 shows the new message box resulting from this updated procedure:

```
Sub EmpPayOverTime()
Dim Employee As New clsEmployee

With Employee
    .EmpName = "Tracy Syrstad"
    .EmpID = "1651"
    .EmpRate = 25
    .EmpWeeklyHrs = 45
    MsgBox .EmpName & Chr(10) & Chr(9) & _
    "Normal Hours: " & .EmpNormalHrs & Chr(10) & Chr(9) & _
    "OverTime Hours: " & .EmpOverTimeHrs & Chr(10) & Chr(9) & _
    "Weekly Pay : $" & .EmpWeeklyPay
End With

End Sub
```

Figure 22.6

Use Property Let and Property Get procedures for more control over custom object properties.

Collections

Up to now, you've been able to have only one record at a time of the custom object. To create more, a *collection* is needed. A collection allows more than a single record to exist at a time. For example, Worksheet is a member of the Worksheets collection. You can add, remove, count, and refer to each worksheet in a workbook by item. This functionality is also available to your custom object.

Creating a Collection in a Standard Module

The quickest way to create a collection is to use the built-in `Collection` method. By setting up a collection in a standard module, you can access the four default collection methods: `Add`, `Remove`, `Count`, and `Item`.

The following example reads a list of employees off a sheet and into an array. It then processes the array, supplying each property of the object with a value, and places each record in the collection:

```
Sub EmpPayCollection()
Dim colEmployees As New Collection
Dim recEmployee As New clsEmployee
Dim LastRow As Integer, myCount As Integer
Dim EmpArray As Variant

LastRow = ActiveSheet. Cells(ActiveSheet.Rows.Count, 1).End(xlUp).Row
EmpArray = ActiveSheet.Range(Cells(1, 1), Cells(LastRow, 4))

For myCount = 1 To UBound(EmpArray)
    Set recEmployee = New clsEmployee
    With recEmployee
        .EmpName = EmpArray(myCount, 1)
        .EmpID = EmpArray(myCount, 2)
        .EmpRate = EmpArray(myCount, 3)
        .EmpWeeklyHrs = EmpArray(myCount, 4)
        colEmployees.Add recEmployee, .EmpID
    End With
Next myCount

MsgBox "Number of Employees: " & colEmployees.Count & Chr(10) & _
    "Employee(2) Name: " & colEmployees(2).EmpName
MsgBox "Tracy's Weekly Pay: $" & colEmployees("1651").EmpWeeklyPay

Set recEmployee = Nothing

End Sub
```

The collection, colEmployees, is declared as a new collection and the record, recEmployee, as a new variable of the custom object type.

After the object's properties are given values, the record, recEmployee, is added to the collection. The second parameter of the Add method applies a unique key to the record—in this case, the employee ID number. This allows a specific record to be quickly accessed, as shown by the second message box (colEmployees("1651").EmpWeeklyPay) (see Figure 22.7).

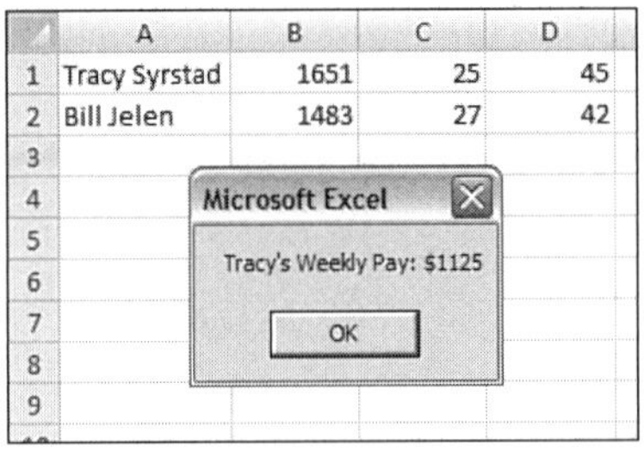

Figure 22.7
Individual records in a collection can be easily accessed.

> **NOTE**
> The unique key is an optional parameter. An error message appears if a duplicate key is entered.

Creating a Collection in a Class Module

Collections can be created in a class module but, in this case, the innate methods of the collection (Add, Remove, Count, Item) are not available; they have to be created in the class module. The advantages of creating a collection in a class module are that the entire code is in one module, you have more control over what is done with the collection, and you can prevent access to the collection.

Insert a new class module for the collection and rename it **clsEmployees.** Declare a private collection to be used within the class module:

```
Option Explicit
Private AllEmployees As New Collection
```

Add the new properties and methods required to make the collection work. The innate methods of the collection are available within the class module and can be used to create the custom methods and properties:

Insert an Add method for adding new items to the collection:

```
Public Sub Add(recEmployee As clsEmployee)

AllEmployees.Add recEmployee, recEmployee.EmpID

End Sub
```

Insert a Count property to return the number of items in the collection:

```
Public Property Get Count() As Long

Count = AllEmployees.Count

End Property
```

Insert an Items property to return the entire collection:

```
Public Property Get Items() As Collection
```

```
Set Items = AllEmployees

End Property
```

Insert an `Item` property to return a specific item from the collection:

```
Public Property Get Item(myItem As Variant) As clsEmployee

Set Item = AllEmployees(myItem)

End Property
```

Insert a `Remove` property to remove a specific item from the collection:

```
Public Sub Remove(myItem As Variant)

AllEmployees.Remove (myItem)

End Sub
```

`Property Get` is used with `Count`, `Item`, and `Items` because these are read-only properties. `Item` returns a reference to a single member of the collection, whereas `Items` returns the entire collection (so that it can be used in `For Each Next` loops).

After the collection is configured in the class module, a procedure can be written in a standard module to use it:

```
Sub EmpAddCollection()
Dim colEmployees As New clsEmployees
Dim recEmployee As New clsEmployee
Dim LastRow As Integer, myCount As Integer
Dim EmpArray As Variant

LastRow = ActiveSheet.Cells(ActiveSheet.Rows.Count, 1).End(xlUp).Row
EmpArray = ActiveSheet.Range(Cells(1, 1), Cells(LastRow, 4))

For myCount = 1 To UBound(EmpArray)
    Set recEmployee = New clsEmployee
    With recEmployee
        .EmpName = EmpArray(myCount, 1)
        .EmpID = EmpArray(myCount, 2)
        .EmpRate = EmpArray(myCount, 3)
        .EmpWeeklyHrs = EmpArray(myCount, 4)
        colEmployees.Add recEmployee
    End With
Next myCount

MsgBox "Number of Employees: " & colEmployees.Count & Chr(10) & _
    "Employee(2) Name: " & colEmployees.Item(2).EmpName
MsgBox "Tracy's Weekly Pay: $" & colEmployees.Item("1651").EmpWeeklyPay

For Each recEmployee In colEmployees.Items
    recEmployee.EmpRate = recEmployee.EmpRate * 1.5
Next recEmployee

MsgBox "Tracy's Weekly Pay (after Bonus): $" & colEmployees.Item("1651"). _
    EmpWeeklyPay
```

22

```
Set recEmployee = Nothing

End Sub
```

This program isn't that different from the one used with the standard collection, but there are a few key differences. `colEmployees` is declared as type `clsEmployees`, the new class module collection, instead of as `Collection`. The array and collection are filled the same way, but the way the records in the collection are referenced has changed. When referencing a member of the collection, such as employee record 2, the `Item` property must be used. Compare the syntax of the message boxes in this program to the previous program.

The `For Each Next` loop goes through each record in the collection and multiplies the `EmpRate` by 1.5, changing its value. The result of this "bonus" is shown in a message box similar to the one shown previously in Figure 22.7.

CASE STUDY

Help Buttons

You have a complex sheet that requires a way for the user to get help. You could place the information in comment boxes, but they aren't very obvious, especially to the novice Excel user. Another option is to create help buttons.

On the worksheet, create small labels with a question mark in each one. To get the buttonlike appearance shown in Figure 22.8, set the `SpecialEffect` property of the labels to `Raised` and darken the `BackColor`. Place one label per row. Two columns over from the button, enter the help text you want to appear when the label is clicked. Hide this help text column.

Figure 22.8
Attach help buttons to the sheet and enter help text.

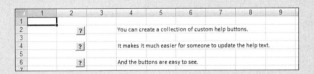

Create a simple userform with a label and a Close button. Rename the form to **HelpForm,** the button to **CloseHelp,** and the label to **HelpText.** Size the label large enough to hold the help text. Add a macro behind the form to hide the form when the button is clicked:

```
Private Sub CloseHelp_Click()
Unload Me
End Sub
```

Insert a class module named **clsLabel.** You'll need a variable, Lbl, to capture the control events:

```
Public WithEvents Lbl As MSForms.Label
```

Also, you need a method of finding and displaying the corresponding help text:

```
Private Sub Lbl_Click()
Dim Rng As Range
```

```
Set Rng = Lbl.TopLeftCell

If Lbl.Caption = "?" Then
    HelpForm.Caption = "Label in cell " & Rng.Address(0, 0)
    HelpForm.HelpText.Caption = Rng.Offset(, 2).Value
    HelpForm.Show
End If

End Sub
```

In the ThisWorkbook module, create a `Workbook_Open` procedure to create a collection of the labels in the workbook:

```
Option Explicit
Option Base 1
Dim col As Collection

Sub Workbook_Open()
Dim WS As Worksheet
Dim cLbl As clsLabel
Dim OleObj As OLEObject

Set col = New Collection

For Each WS In ThisWorkbook.Worksheets
    For Each OleObj In WS.OLEObjects
        If OleObj.OLEType = xlOLEControl Then
            If TypeName(OleObj.Object) = "Label" Then
                Set cLbl = New clsLabel
                Set cLbl.Lbl = OleObj.Object
                col.Add cLbl
            End If
        End If
    Next OleObj
Next WS

End Sub
```

Run `Workbook_Open` to create the collection. Click a label on the worksheet. The corresponding help text appears in the help form, as shown in Figure 22.9.

Figure 22.9
Help text is only a click away.

User-Defined Types (UDTs)

User-defined types provide some of the power of a custom object but without the need of a class module. A class module allows the creation of custom properties and methods, whereas a UDT allows only custom properties. But sometimes, that's all you need.

A UDT is declared with a `Type..End Type` statement. It can be `Public` or `Private`. A name that is treated like an object is given to the UDT. Within the `Type`, individual variables are declared that become the properties of the UDT.

Within an actual procedure, a variable is defined of the custom type. When that variable is used, the properties are available, just as they are in a custom object (see Figure 22.10).

Figure 22.10
The properties of a UDT are available as they are in a custom object.

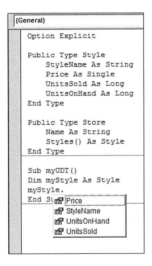

The following example uses two UDTs to summarize a report of product styles in various stores.

The first UDT consists of properties for each product style:

```
Option Explicit
Public Type Style
    StyleName As String
    Price As Single
    UnitsSold As Long
    UnitsOnHand As Long
End Type
```

The second UDT consists of the store name and an array whose type is the first UDT:

```
Public Type Store
    Name As String
    Styles() As Style
End Type
```

After the UDTs are established, the main program is written. Only a variable of the second UDT type, Store, is needed because that type contains the first type, Style (see Figure 22.11). But all the properties of the UDTs are easily available. And with the use of the UDT, the various variables are easy to remember—they're only a dot (.) away:

```
Sub Main()
Dim FinalRow As Integer, ThisRow As Integer, ThisStore As Integer
Dim CurrRow As Integer, TotalDollarsSold As Integer, TotalUnitsSold As Integer
Dim TotalDollarsOnHand As Integer, TotalUnitsOnHand As Integer
Dim ThisStyle As Integer
Dim StoreName As String

ReDim Stores(0 To 0) As Store ' The UDT is declared

FinalRow = Cells(Rows.Count, 1).End(xlUp).Row


' The following For loop fills both arrays. The outer array is filled with the
' store name and an array consisting of product details.
' To accomplish this, the store name is tracked and when it changes,
'the outer array is expanded.
'The inner array for each outer array expands with each new product
For ThisRow = 2 To FinalRow
    StoreName = Range("A" & ThisRow).Value
' Checks whether this is the first entry in the outer array
    If LBound(Stores) = 0 Then
        ThisStore = 1
        ReDim Stores(1 To 1) As Store
        Stores(1).Name = StoreName
        ReDim Stores(1).Styles(0 To 0) As Style
    Else
        For ThisStore = LBound(Stores) To UBound(Stores)
            If Stores(ThisStore).Name = StoreName Then Exit For
        Next ThisStore
        If ThisStore > UBound(Stores) Then
            ReDim Preserve Stores(LBound(Stores) To UBound(Stores) + 1) As Store
            Stores(ThisStore).Name = StoreName
            ReDim Stores(ThisStore).Styles(0 To 0) As Style
        End If
    End If
    With Stores(ThisStore)
        If LBound(.Styles) = 0 Then
            ReDim .Styles(1 To 1) As Style
        Else
            ReDim Preserve .Styles(LBound(.Styles) To _
        UBound(.Styles) + 1) As Style
        End If
        With .Styles(UBound(.Styles))
            .StyleName = Range("B" & ThisRow).Value
            .Price = Range("C" & ThisRow).Value
            .UnitsSold = Range("D" & ThisRow).Value
            .UnitsOnHand = Range("E" & ThisRow).Value
        End With
    End With
Next ThisRow


' Create a report on a new sheet
Sheets.Add
```

```
Range("A1:E1").Value = Array("Store Name", "Units Sold", _
    "Dollars Sold", "Units On Hand", "Dollars On Hand")
CurrRow = 2

For ThisStore = LBound(Stores) To UBound(Stores)
    With Stores(ThisStore)
        TotalDollarsSold = 0
        TotalUnitsSold = 0
        TotalDollarsOnHand = 0
        TotalUnitsOnHand = 0
' Go through the array of product styles within the array
' of stores to summarize information
        For ThisStyle = LBound(.Styles) To UBound(.Styles)
            With .Styles(ThisStyle)
                TotalDollarsSold = TotalDollarsSold + .UnitsSold * .Price
                TotalUnitsSold = TotalUnitsSold + .UnitsSold
                TotalDollarsOnHand = TotalDollarsOnHand + .UnitsOnHand * .Price
                TotalUnitsOnHand = TotalUnitsOnHand + .UnitsOnHand
            End With
        Next ThisStyle
        Range("A" & CurrRow & ":E" & CurrRow).Value = _
        Array(.Name, TotalUnitsSold, TotalDollarsSold, _
        TotalUnitsOnHand, TotalDollarsOnHand)
    End With
    CurrRow = CurrRow + 1
Next ThisStore

End Sub
```

Figure 22.11
UDTs can make a potentially confusing multi-variable program easier to write. (Note: The results of the program have been combined with the raw data for convenience.)

	1	2	3	4	5
1	Store	Style	Price	Units Sold	Units On Hand
2	Store A	Style C	96.87	16	45
3	Store A	Style A	38.43	7	94
4	Store A	Style B	91.24	5	18
5	Store A	Style E	19.89	0	96
6	Store A	Style D	2.45	20	66
7	Store B	Style B	92.59	4	83
8	Store B	Style A	15.75	9	66
9	Store B	Style F	13.12	2	35
10	Store B	Style G	30.86	22	37
11	Store B	Style H	37.38	21	77
12					
13					
14					
15					
16					
17	Store Name	Units Sold	Dollars Sold	Units On Hand	Dollars On Hand
18	Store A	48	$ 2,324	319	$ 11,684
19	Store B	58	$ 2,002	298	$ 13,203
20					

Next Steps

In Chapter 23, "Advanced Userform Techniques," you'll learn about more controls and techniques you can use in building userforms.

Advanced Userform Techniques

23

Chapter 10, "Userforms—An Introduction," covered the basics of adding controls to userforms. This chapter continues on this topic by looking at more advanced controls and methods for making the most out of userforms.

Using the UserForm Toolbar in the Design of Controls on Userforms

In the VB Editor, hidden under the View menu in the Toolbars command are a few toolbars that don't appear unless the user intervenes. One of these is the UserForm toolbar, shown in Figure 23.1.

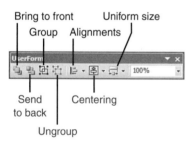

Figure 23.1
The UserForm toolbar has tools to organize the controls on a userform.

More Userform Controls

Chapter 10 began a review of some of the controls available on userforms. The review is continued here. At the end of each control review is a table listing that control's events.

Check Boxes

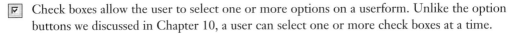 Check boxes allow the user to select one or more options on a userform. Unlike the option buttons we discussed in Chapter 10, a user can select one or more check boxes at a time.

The value of a checked box is True; the value of an unchecked box is False. If you clear the value of a check box (Checkbox1.value = ""), when the userform runs, the check box will have a faded check in it, as shown in Figure 23.2. This could be useful to verify that users have viewed all options and made a selection.

Figure 23.2
Use the null value of the check box to verify that users have viewed and answered all options.

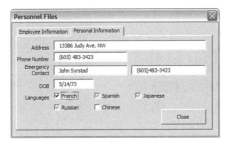

The following code reviews all the check boxes in the language group and, if a value is null, prompts the user to review the selections:

```
Private Sub btnClose_Click()

Dim Msg As String
Dim Chk As Control

Set Chk = Nothing

'narrow down the search to just the 2nd page's controls
For Each Chk In frm_Multipage.MultiPage1.Pages(1).Controls
    'only need to verify checkbox controls
    If TypeName(Chk) = "CheckBox" Then
        'and just in case we add more check box controls,
    'just check the ones in the group
        If Chk.Object.GroupName = "Languages" Then
            'if the value is null (the property value is empty)
            If IsNull(Chk.Object.Value) Then
                'add the caption to a string
                Msg = Msg & vbNewLine & Chk.Caption
            End If
        End If
    End If
Next Chk

If Msg <> "" Then
    Msg = "The following check boxes were not verified:" & vbNewLine & Msg
    MsgBox Msg, vbInformation, "Additional Information Required"
End If

End Sub
```

Table 23.1 lists the events for CheckBox controls.

Table 23.1   Events for CheckBox Controls

Event	Description
AfterUpdate	Occurs after a check box has been checked/unchecked.
BeforeDragOver	Occurs while the user drags and drops data onto the check box.
BeforeDropOrPaste	Occurs right before the user is about to drop or paste data onto the check box.
BeforeUpdate	Occurs before the check box is checked/unchecked.
Change	Occurs when the value of the check box is changed.
Click	Occurs when the user clicks the control with the mouse.
DblClick	Occurs when the user double-clicks the check box with the mouse.
Enter	Occurs right before the check box receives the focus from another control on the same userform.
Error	Occurs when the check box runs into an error and can't return the error information.
Exit	Occurs right after the check box loses focus to another control on the same userform.
KeyDown	Occurs when the user presses a key on the keyboard.
KeyPress	Occurs when the user presses an ANSI key. An ANSI key is a typeable character, such as the letter *A*.
KeyUp	Occurs when the user releases a key on the keyboard.
MouseDown	Occurs when the user presses the mouse button within the borders of the check box.
MouseMove	Occurs when the user moves the mouse within the borders of the check box.
MouseUp	Occurs when the user releases the mouse button within the borders of the check box.

23

Tab Strips

The MultiPage control allows a userform to have several pages. Each page of the form can have its own set of controls, unrelated to any other control on the form. A TabStrip control also allows a userform to have many pages, but the controls on a tab strip are identical; they are drawn only once. Yet, when the form is run, the information changes according to the tab strip that is active (see Figure 23.3).

Figure 23.3
A tab strip allows a userform with multiple
pages to share controls,
but not information.

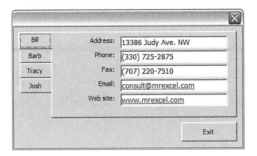

→ To learn more about MultiPage controls, **see** "Using the MultiPage Control to Combine Forms," **p. 191**, in Chapter 10.

By default, a tab strip is thin, with two tabs at the top. Right-clicking a tab enables you to add, remove, rename, or move a tab. The tab strip should also be sized to hold all the controls. A button for closing the form should be drawn outside the tab strip area.

The tabs can also be moved around the strip. This is done by changing the TabOrientation property. The tabs can be at the top, bottom, left, or right side of the userform.

The following lines of code were used to create the tab strip form shown in Figure 23.3. The Initialize sub calls the sub SetValuestoTabStrip, which sets the value for the first tab:

```
Private Sub UserForm_Initialize()
SetValuesToTabStrip 1 'As default
End Sub
```

These lines of code handle what happens when a new tab is selected.

```
Private Sub TabStrip1_Change()
Dim lngRow As Long

lngRow = TabStrip1.Value + 1
SetValuesToTabStrip lngRow

End Sub
```

This sub provides the data shown on each tab. A sheet was set up, with each row corresponding to a tab.

```
Private Sub SetValuesToTabStrip(ByVal lngRow As Long)
With frm_Staff
    .lbl_Name.Caption = Cells(lngRow, 2).Value
    .lbl_Phone.Caption = Cells(lngRow, 3).Value
    .lbl_Fax.Caption = Cells(lngRow, 4).Value
    .lbl_Email.Caption = Cells(lngRow, 5).Value
    .lbl_Website.Caption = Cells(lngRow, 6).Value
    .Show
End With
End Sub
```

The tab strip's values are automatically filled in. They correspond to the tab's position in the strip; moving a tab changes its value.

Table 23.2 lists the events for the TabStrip control.

Table 23.2 Events for TabStrip Controls

Event	Description
BeforeDragOver	Occurs while the user drags and drops data onto the control.
BeforeDropOrPaste	Occurs right before the user drops or pastes data into the control.
Change	Occurs when the value of the control is changed.
Click	Occurs when the user clicks the control with the mouse.
DblClick	Occurs when the user double-clicks the control with the mouse.
Enter	Occurs right before the control receives the focus from another control on the same userform.
Error	Occurs when the control runs into an error and can't return the error information.
Exit	Occurs right after the control loses focus to another control on the same userform.
KeyDown	Occurs when the user presses a key on the keyboard.
KeyPress	Occurs when the user presses an ANSI key. An ANSI key is a typeable character, such as the letter *A*.
KeyUp	Occurs when the user releases a key on the keyboard.
MouseDown	Occurs when the user presses the mouse button within the borders of the control.
MouseMove	Occurs when the user moves the mouse within the borders of the control.
MouseUp	Occurs when the user releases the mouse button within the borders of the control.

RefEdit

The RefEdit control allows the user to select a range on a sheet; the range is returned as the value of the control. It can be added to any form. Once activated by a click of the button on the right side of the field, the userform disappears and is replaced with the range selection form, used when selecting ranges with Excel's many wizard tools. Click the button on the right to show the userform once again.

The form in Figure 23.4 and the following code allow the user to select a range, which is then made bold.

Figure 23.4
Use RefEdit to enable
the user to select a range
on a sheet.

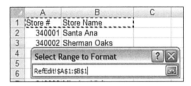

```
Private Sub cb1_Click()
Range(RefEdit1.Value).Font.Bold = True
End Sub
```

Table 23.3 lists the events for RefEdit controls.

Table 23.3   Events for RefEdit Controls

Event	Description
AfterUpdate	Occurs after the control's data has been changed by the user.
BeforeDragOver	Occurs while the user drags and drops data onto the control.
BeforeDropOrPaste	Occurs right before the user drops or pastes data into the control.
BeforeUpdate	Occurs before the data in the control is changed.
Change	Occurs when the value of the control is changed.
Click	Occurs when the user clicks the control with the mouse.
DblClick	Occurs when the user double-clicks the control with the mouse.
DropButtonClick	Occurs when the drop-down list appears by pressing on the drop-down arrow of the combo box or press F4 on the keyboard.
Enter	Occurs right before the control receives the focus from another control on the same userform.
Error	Occurs when the control runs into an error and can't return the error information.
Exit	Occurs right after the control loses focus to another control on the same userform.
KeyDown	Occurs when the user presses a key on the keyboard.
KeyPress	Occurs when the user presses an ANSI key. An ANSI key is a typeable character, such as the letter *A*.
KeyUp	Occurs when the user releases a key on the keyboard.
MouseDown	Occurs when the user presses the mouse button within the borders of the control.
MouseMove	Occurs when the user moves the mouse within the borders of the control.
MouseUp	Occurs when the user releases the mouse button within the borders of the control.

Toggle Buttons

 A toggle button looks like a normal command button, but when the user presses it, it stays pressed until it's selected again. This allows a True or False value to be returned based on the status of the button. Table 23.4 lists the events for the ToggleButton controls.

Table 23.4   Events for ToggleButton **Controls**

Event	Description
AfterUpdate	Occurs after the control's data has been changed by the user.
BeforeDragOver	Occurs while the user drags and drops data onto the control.
BeforeDropOrPaste	Occurs right before the user drops or pastes data into the control.
BeforeUpdate	Occurs before the data in the control is changed.
Change	Occurs when the value of the control is changed.
Click	Occurs when the user clicks the control with the mouse.
DblClick	Occurs when the user double-clicks the control with the mouse.
Enter	Occurs right before the control receives the focus from another control on the same userform.
Error	Occurs when the control runs into an error and can't return the error information.
Exit	Occurs right after the control loses focus to another control on the same userform.
KeyDown	Occurs when the user presses a key on the keyboard.
KeyPress	Occurs when the user presses an ANSI key. An ANSI key is a typeable character, such as the letter A.
KeyUp	Occurs when the user releases a key on the keyboard.
MouseDown	Occurs when the user presses the mouse button within the borders of the control.
MouseMove	Occurs when the user moves the mouse within the borders of the control.
MouseUp	Occurs when the user releases the mouse button within the borders of the control.

Using a Scrollbar as a Slider to Select Values

 Chapter 10 discussed using a SpinButton control to allow someone to choose a date. The spin button is good, but it allows clients to adjust up or down by only one unit at a time. An alternative method is to draw a horizontal scrollbar in the middle of the userform and use it as a slider. Clients can use arrows on the ends of the scrollbar like the spin button arrows, but they can also grab the scrollbar and instantly drag it to a certain value.

The userform shown in Figure 23.5 includes a label named Label1 and a scrollbar called ScrollBar1.

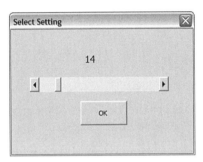

Figure 23.5
Using a scrollbar control allows the user to quickly drag to a particular numeric or data value.

The userform's `Initialize` code sets up the `Min` and `Max` values for the scrollbar. It initializes the scrollbar to a value from cell A1 and updates the `Label1.Caption`:

```
Private Sub UserForm_Initialize()
    Me.ScrollBar1.Min = 0
    Me.ScrollBar1.Max = 100
    Me.ScrollBar1.Value = Range("A1").Value
    Me.Label1.Caption = Me.ScrollBar1.Value
End Sub
```

Two event handlers are needed for the scrollbar. The `Change` event handles if users click the arrows at the ends of the scrollbar. The `Scroll` event handles if they drag the slider to a new value:

```
Private Sub ScrollBar1_Change()
    ' This event handles if they touch
    ' the arrows on the end of the scrollbar
    Me.Label1.Caption = Me.ScrollBar1.Value
End Sub

Private Sub ScrollBar1_Scroll()
    ' This event handles if they drag the slider
    Me.Label1.Caption = Me.ScrollBar1.Value
End Sub
```

Finally, the event attached to the button writes the scrollbar value out to the worksheet:

```
Private Sub CommandButton1_Click()
    Range("A1").Value = Me.ScrollBar1.Value
    Unload Me
End Sub
```

Table 23.5 lists the events for `Scrollbar` controls.

Table 23.5   Events for `Scrollbar` **Controls**

Event	Description
`AfterUpdate`	Occurs after the control's data has been changed by the user.
`BeforeDragOver`	Occurs while the user drags and drops data onto the control.
`BeforeDropOrPaste`	Occurs right before the user drops or pastes data into the control.
`BeforeUpdate`	Occurs before the data in the control is changed.
`Change`	Occurs when the value of the control is changed.
`Click`	Occurs when the user clicks the control with the mouse.
`DblClick`	Occurs when the user double-clicks the control with the mouse.
`DropButtonClick`	Occurs when the drop-down list appears by pressing on the drop-down arrow of the combo box or pressing F4 on the keyboard.
`Enter`	Occurs right before the control receives the focus from another control on the same userform.
`Error`	Occurs when the control runs into an error and can't return the error information.
`Exit`	Occurs right after the control loses focus to another control on the same userform.
`KeyDown`	Occurs when the user presses a key on the keyboard.
`KeyPress`	Occurs when the user presses an ANSI key. An ANSI key is a typeable character, such as the letter *A*.
`KeyUp`	Occurs when the user releases a key on the keyboard.
`MouseDown`	Occurs when the user presses the mouse button within the borders of the control.
`MouseMove`	Occurs when the user moves the mouse within the borders of the control.
`MouseUp`	Occurs when the user releases the mouse button within the borders of the control.

Controls and Collections

In Chapter 22, "Creating Classes, Records, and Collections," several labels on a sheet were grouped together into a collection. With a little more code, these labels were turned into help screens for the users. Userform controls can be grouped into collections, too, and take advantage of class modules.

The following example checks or unchecks all the check boxes on the userform, depending on which label the user chooses.

Place the following code in the class module, `clsFormEvents`. It consists of one property, `chb`, and two methods, `SelectAll` and `UnselectAll`.

The SelectAll method places a check in a check box by setting its value to True:

```
Option Explicit
Public WithEvents chb As MSForms.CheckBox

Public Sub SelectAll()
chb.Value = True
End Sub
```

The UnselectAll method removes the check from the check box:

```
Public Sub UnselectAll()
chb.Value = False
End Sub
```

That sets up the class module. Next, the controls need to be placed in a collection. The following code, placed behind the form, frm_Movies, places the check boxes into a collection. The check boxes are part of a frame, f_Selection, which makes it easier to create the collection because it narrows down the number of controls that need to be checked from the entire userform to just those controls within the frame:

```
Option Explicit
Dim col_Selection As New Collection

Private Sub UserForm_Initialize()
Dim ctl As MSForms.CheckBox
Dim chb_ctl As clsFormEvents

' Go thru the members of the frame and add them to the collection
For Each ctl In f_Selection.Controls
    Set chb_ctl = New clsFormEvents
    Set chb_ctl.chb = ctl
    col_Selection.Add chb_ctl
Next ctl

End Sub
```

When the form is opened, the controls are placed into the collection. All that's left now is to add the code for labels to select and unselect the check boxes:

```
Private Sub lbl_SelectAll_Click()
Dim ctl As clsFormEvents

For Each ctl In col_Selection
    ctl.SelectAll
Next ctl

End Sub
```

The following code unselects the check boxes in the collection:

```
Private Sub lbl_unSelectAll_Click()
Dim ctl As clsFormEvents

For Each ctl In col_Selection
    ctl.Unselectall
Next ctl

End Sub
```

All the check boxes can be checked and unchecked with a single click of the mouse, as shown in Figure 23.6.

Figure 23.6
Use frames, collections, and class modules together to create quick and efficient userforms.

23

> **TIP**
> If your controls can't be placed in a frame, you can use a `tag` to create an improvised grouping. A `tag` is a property that holds more information about a control. Its value is of type `string`, so it can hold any type of information. For example, it can be used to create an informal group of controls from different groupings.

Modeless Userforms

Ever had a userform active but needed to look at something on a sheet? There was a time when the form had to be shut down before anything else in Excel could be done. No longer! Forms can now be *modeless*, which means they don't have to interfere with the functionality of Excel. The user can type in a cell, switch to another sheet, copy/paste data, and use toolbars and menus—it is as if the userform were not there.

By default, a userform is modal, which means that there is no interaction with Excel other than the form. To make the form modeless, change the `ShowModal` property to `False`. After it is modeless, the user can select a cell on the sheet while the form is active, as shown in Figure 23.7.

Figure 23.7
A modeless form enables the user to enter a cell while the form is still active.

	A	B	C	D	E	F
1	Store #	Store Name				
2	340001	Santa Ana				
3	340002	Sherman Oaks				
4	340003	Brea				
5	340004	Tucson				
6	340005	Roseville				
7	340006	Mission Viejo				
8	340007	Corona del Mar				
9	340008	San Francisco				
10	340009	Keirland				
11	340010	Scottsdale F.S.				
12	340011	Valley Fair				
13	340012	Seattle - Bellevue				
14	340013	Atlanta - Perimeter				
15	340014	Santa Barbara				
16	340015	Topanga				
17	340016	Walnut Creek				
18	340017	Westlake Village				
19	340018	Indianapolis				
20	340019	Chicago - Woodfield				

Exit

Color Invoices

Errors

Corrections

Changes

Using Hyperlinks in Userforms

In the userform example shown in Figure 23.3, there is a field for email and a website address. Wouldn't it be nice to be able to click these and have a blank email message or web page automatically appear? You can! The following program creates a new message or opens a web browser when the corresponding label is clicked.

The application programming interface (API) declaration, and any other constants, go at the very top of the code.

```
Private Declare Function ShellExecute Lib "shell32.dll" Alias _
    "ShellExecuteA"(ByVal hWnd As Long, ByVal lpOperation As String, _
    ByVal lpFile As String, ByVal lpParameters As String, _
    ByVal lpDirectory As String, ByVal nShowCmd As Long) As Long

Const SWNormal = 1
```

This sub controls what happens when the email label is clicked, as shown in Figure 23.8:

```
Private Sub lbl_Email_Click()
Dim lngRow As Long

lngRow = TabStrip1.Value + 1
ShellExecute 0&, "open", "mailto:" & Cells(lngRow, 5).Value, _
    vbNullString, vbNullString, SWNormal

End Sub
```

This sub controls what happens when the website label is clicked:

```
Private Sub lbl_Website_Click()
Dim lngRow As Long

lngRow = TabStrip1.Value + 1
ShellExecute 0&, "open", Cells(lngRow, 6).Value, vbNullString, _
    vbNullString, SWNormal

End Sub
```

Figure 23.8
Turn email addresses and websites into clickable links.

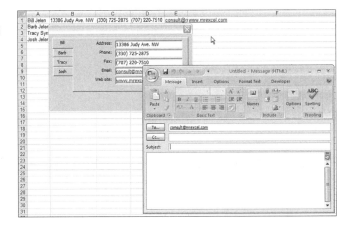

Adding Controls at Runtime

It is possible to add controls to a userform at runtime. This is convenient if you are not sure how many items you will be adding to the form.

Figure 23.9 shows a plain form. It has only one button. This plain form is used to display any number of pictures from a product catalog. The pictures and accompanying labels appear at runtime, as the form is being displayed.

Figure 23.9
Flexible forms can be created if you add most controls at runtime.

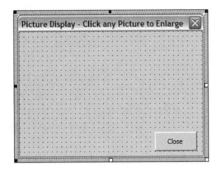

A sales rep making a sales presentation uses this form to display a product catalog. He can select any number of SKUs from an Excel worksheet and press a hot key to display the form. If he selects 20 items on the worksheet, the form displays with each picture fairly small, as shown in Figure 23.10.

If the sales rep selects fewer items, the images are displayed larger, as shown in Figure 23.11.

A number of techniques are used to create this userform on-the-fly. The initial form contains only one button, called `cbClose`. Everything else is added on-the-fly.

Figure 23.10
Here, the sales rep has asked to see photos of 20 SKUs. The `UserForm_Initialize` procedure adds each picture and label on-the-fly.

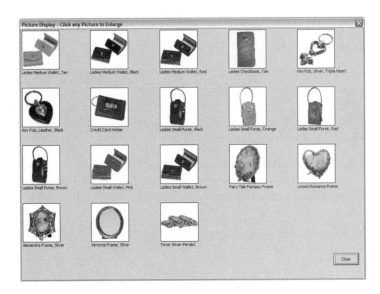

Figure 23.11
The logic in `Userform_Initialize` decides how many pictures are being displayed and adds the appropriate size controls.

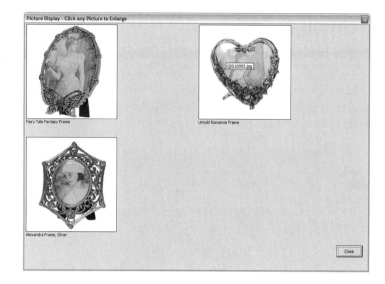

Resizing the Userform On-the-Fly

One goal is to give the best view of the images in the product catalog. This means having the form appear as large as possible. The following code uses the form's `Height` and `Width` properties to make sure the form fills almost the entire screen:

```
' resize the form
Me.Height = Int(0.98 * ActiveWindow.Height)
Me.Width = Int(0.98 * ActiveWindow.Width)
```

Adding a Control On-the-Fly

For a normal control added at design time, it is easy to refer to the control by using its name:

```
Me.cbSave.Left = 100
```

But, for a control that is added at runtime, you have to use the `Controls` collection to set any properties for the control. Therefore, it is important to set up a variable to hold the name of the control. Controls are added with the `.Add` method. The important parameter is the `bstrProgId`. This code name dictates whether the added control is a label, text box, command button, or something else.

The following code adds a new label to the form. `PicCount` is a counter variable used to ensure that each label has a new name. After the form is added, specify a position for the control by setting the `Top` and `Left` properties. You should also set a `Height` and `Width` for the control:

```
LC = "LabelA" & PicCount
Me.Controls.Add bstrProgId:="forms.label.1", Name:=LC, Visible:=True
Me.Controls(LC).Top = 25
Me.Controls(LC).Left = 50
```

```
Me.Controls(LC).Height = 18
Me.Controls(LC).Width = 60
Me.Controls(LC).Caption = cell.value
```

> **CAUTION**
>
> You lose some of the AutoComplete options with this method. Normally, if you would start to type **Me.cbClose.**, the AutoComplete options would present the valid choices for a command button. However, when you use the Me.Controls(LC) collection to add controls on-the-fly, VBA doesn't know what type of control is referenced. In this case, it is helpful to know you need to set the Caption property rather than the Value property for a label.

23

Sizing On-the-Fly

In reality, you need to be able to calculate values for Top, Left, Height, and Width on the fly. You would do this based on the actual height and width of the form and on how many controls are needed.

Adding Other Controls

To add other types of controls, change the ProgId used with the Add method. Table 23.6 shows the ProgIds for various types of controls.

Table 23.6   Userform Controls and Corresponding ProgIds

Control	ProgId
CheckBox	Forms.CheckBox.1
ComboBox	Forms.ComboBox.1
CommandButton	Forms.CommandButton.1
Frame	Forms.Frame.1
Image	Forms.Image.1
Label	Forms.Label.1
ListBox	Forms.ListBox.1
MultiPage	Forms.MultiPage.1
OptionButton	Forms.OptionButton.1
ScrollBar	Forms.ScrollBar.1
SpinButton	Forms.SpinButton.1
TabStrip	Forms.TabStrip.1
TextBox	Forms.TextBox.1
ToggleButton	Forms.ToggleButton.1

Adding an Image On-the-Fly

There is some unpredictability in adding images. Any given image might be shaped either landscape or portrait. The image might be small or huge. The strategy you might want to use is to let the image load full size by setting the `.AutoSize` parameter to `True` before loading the image:

```
TC = "Image" & PicCount
Me.Controls.Add bstrProgId:="forms.image.1", Name:=TC, Visible:=True
Me.Controls(TC).Top = LastTop
Me.Controls(TC).Left = LastLeft
Me.Controls(TC).AutoSize = True
On Error Resume Next
Me.Controls(TC).Picture = LoadPicture(fname)
On Error GoTo 0
```

Then, after the image has loaded, you can read the control's `Height` and `Width` properties to determine whether the image is landscape or portrait and whether the image is constrained by available width or available height:

```
' The picture resized the control to full size
' determine the size of the picture
Wid = Me.Controls(TC).Width
Ht = Me.Controls(TC).Height
WidRedux = CellWid / Wid
HtRedux = CellHt / Ht
If WidRedux < HtRedux Then
    Redux = WidRedux
Else
    Redux = HtRedux
End If
NewHt = Int(Ht * Redux)
NewWid = Int(Wid * Redux)
```

After you find the proper size for the image to have it draw without distortion, you can set the `AutoSize` property to `False` and use the correct height and width to have the image not appear distorted:

```
' Now resize the control
Me.Controls(TC).AutoSize = False
Me.Controls(TC).Height = NewHt
Me.Controls(TC).Width = NewWid
Me.Controls(TC).PictureSizeMode = fmPictureSizeModeStretch
```

Putting It All Together

This is the complete code for the Picture Catalog userform:

```
Private Sub UserForm_Initialize()
    ' Display pictures of each SKU selected on the worksheet
    ' This may be anywhere from 1 to 36 pictures
    PicPath = "C:\qimage\qi"
    Dim Pics ()

    ' resize the form
    Me.Height = Int(0.98 * ActiveWindow.Height)
    Me.Width = Int(0.98 * ActiveWindow.Width)
```

```
' determine how many cells are selected
' We need one picture and label for each cell
CellCount = Selection.Cells.Count
ReDim Preserve Pics(1 To CellCount)

' Figure out the size of the resized form
TempHt = Me.Height
TempWid = Me.Width

' The number of columns is a roundup of SQRT(CellCount)
' This will ensure 4 rows of 5 pictures for 20, etc.
NumCol = Int(0.99 + Sqr(CellCount))
NumRow = Int(0.99 + CellCount / NumCol)

' Figure out the ht and wid of each square
' Each column will have 2 pts to left & right of pics
CellWid = Application.WorksheetFunction.Max(Int(TempWid / NumCol) - 4, 1)
' each row needs to have 33 points below it for the label
CellHt = Application.WorksheetFunction.Max(Int(TempHt / NumRow) - 33, 1)

PicCount = 0 ' Counter variable
LastTop = 2
MaxBottom = 1
' Build each row on the form
For x = 1 To NumRow
    LastLeft = 3
    ' Build each column in this row
    For Y = 1 To NumCol
        PicCount = PicCount + 1
        If PicCount > CellCount Then
            ' There are not an even number of pictures to fill
            ' out the last row
            Me.Height = MaxBottom + 100
            Me.cbClose.Top = MaxBottom + 25
            Me.cbClose.Left = Me.Width - 70
            Repaint
            Exit Sub
        End If
        ThisStyle = Selection.Cells(PicCount).Value
        ThisDesc = Selection.Cells(PicCount).Offset(0, 1).Value
        fname = PicPath & ThisStyle & ".jpg"
        TC = "Image" & PicCount
        Me.Controls.Add bstrProgId:="forms.image.1", Name:=TC, Visible:=True
        Me.Controls(TC).Top = LastTop
        Me.Controls(TC).Left = LastLeft
        Me.Controls(TC).AutoSize = True
        On Error Resume Next
        Me.Controls(TC).Picture = LoadPicture(fname)
        On Error GoTo 0

        ' The picture resized the control to full size
        ' determine the size of the picture
        Wid = Me.Controls(TC).Width
        Ht = Me.Controls(TC).Height
        WidRedux = CellWid / Wid
        HtRedux = CellHt / Ht
        If WidRedux < HtRedux Then
            Redux = WidRedux
```

```
              Else
                   Redux = HtRedux
              End If
              NewHt = Int(Ht * Redux)
              NewWid = Int(Wid * Redux)

              ' Now resize the control
              Me.Controls(TC).AutoSize = False
              Me.Controls(TC).Height = NewHt
              Me.Controls(TC).Width = NewWid
              Me.Controls(TC).PictureSizeMode = fmPictureSizeModeStretch
              Me.Controls(TC).ControlTipText = "Style " & _
          ThisStyle & " " & ThisDesc

              ' Keep track of the bottom-most & right-most picture
              ThisRight = Me.Controls(TC).Left + Me.Controls(TC).Width
              ThisBottom = Me.Controls(TC).Top + Me.Controls(TC).Height
              If ThisBottom > MaxBottom Then MaxBottom = ThisBottom

              ' Add a label below the picture
              LC = "LabelA" & PicCount
              Me.Controls.Add bstrProgId:="forms.label.1", Name:=LC, Visible:=True
              Me.Controls(LC).Top = ThisBottom + 1
              Me.Controls(LC).Left = LastLeft
              Me.Controls(LC).Height = 18
              Me.Controls(LC).Width = CellWid
              Me.Controls(LC).Caption = "Style " & ThisStyle & " " & ThisDesc

              ' Keep track of where the next picture should display
              LastLeft = LastLeft + CellWid + 4
          Next Y ' end of this row
          LastTop = MaxBottom + 21 + 16
      Next x

      Me.Height = MaxBottom + 100
      Me.cbClose.Top = MaxBottom + 25
      Me.cbClose.Left = Me.Width - 70
      Repaint
End Sub
```

Adding Help to the Userform

You've designed a great userform, but now there's just one thing missing—guidance for the users. The following sections show you four ways you can help users fill out the form properly.

Showing Accelerator Keys

Built-in forms often have keyboard shortcuts that allow actions to be triggered or fields selected with a few keystrokes. These shortcuts are identified by an underlined letter on a button or label.

You can add this same capability to custom userforms by entering a value in the Accelerator property of the control. Alt + the accelerator key selects the control. For example, in Figure 23.12, Alt+H checks the VHS check box. Repeating the combination unchecks the box.

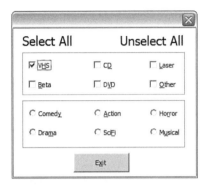

Figure 23.12
Use accelerator key combinations to give userforms the power of keyboard shortcuts.

Adding Control Tip Text

When a cursor is waved over a toolbar, tip text appears, hinting at what the control does. You can also add tip text to userforms by entering a value in the `ControlTipText` property of a control. In Figure 23.13, tip text has been added to the frame surrounding the various categories.

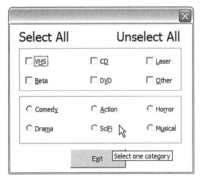

Figure 23.13
Add tips to controls to provide help to users.

Creating the Tab Order

Users can also tab from one field to another. This is an automatic feature in a form. To control which field the next tab brings a user to, you can set the `TapStop` property value for each control.

The first tab stop is zero, and the last tab stop is equal to the number of controls in a group. Remember, a group can be created with a frame. Excel does not allow multiple controls to have the same tab stop. After tab stops are set, the user can use the Tab key and spacebar to select/deselect various options, as shown in Figure 23.14.

Figure 23.14
The options in this form were selected with the Tab key and spacebar.

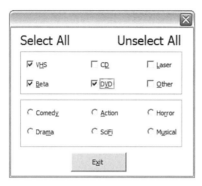

Coloring the Active Control

Another method for helping a user fill out a form is to color the active field. The following example changes the color of a text box or combo box when it is active.

Place the following in a class module called `clsCtlColor`:

```
Public Event GetFocus()
Public Event LostFocus(ByVal strCtrl As String)
Private strPreCtr As String

Public Sub CheckActiveCtrl(objForm As MSForms.UserForm)

With objForm
    If TypeName(.ActiveControl) = "ComboBox" Or _
        TypeName(.ActiveControl) = "TextBox" Then
        strPreCtr = .ActiveControl.Name
        On Error GoTo Terminate
        Do
            DoEvents
            If .ActiveControl.Name <> strPreCtr Then
                If TypeName(.ActiveControl) = "ComboBox" Or _
                    TypeName(.ActiveControl) = "TextBox" Then
                    RaiseEvent LostFocus(strPreCtr)
                    strPreCtr = .ActiveControl.Name
                    RaiseEvent GetFocus
                End If
            End If
        Loop
    End If
End With

Terminate:
    Exit Sub

End Sub
```

Place the following behind the userform:

```
Private WithEvents objForm As clsCtlColor
```

```
Private Sub UserForm_Initialize()
Set objForm = New clsCtlColor
End Sub
```

This sub changes the BackColor of the active control when the form is activated:

```
Private Sub UserForm_Activate()
If TypeName(ActiveControl) = "ComboBox" Or _
   TypeName(ActiveControl) = "TextBox" Then
   ActiveControl.BackColor = &HC0E0FF
End If
objForm.CheckActiveCtrl Me
End Sub
```

This sub changes the BackColor of the active control when it gets the focus:

```
Private Sub objForm_GetFocus()
ActiveControl.BackColor = &HC0E0FF
End Sub
```

This sub changes the BackColor back to white when the control loses the focus:

```
Private Sub objForm_LostFocus(ByVal strCtrl As String)
Me.Controls(strCtrl).BackColor = &HFFFFFF
End Sub
```

This sub clears the objForm when the form is closed:

```
Private Sub UserForm_QueryClose(Cancel As Integer, CloseMode As Integer)
Set objForm = Nothing
End Sub
```

23

CASE STUDY

Multicolumn List Boxes

You've created several spreadsheets containing store data. The primary key of each set is the store number. The workbook is used by several people, but not everyone memorizes stores by his or her store numbers. You need some way of letting a user select a store by its name, but at the same time, return the store number to be used in the code. You could use VLOOKUP or MATCH, but there's another way.

A list box can have more than one column, but not all the columns need to be visible to the user. Also, the user can select an item from the visible list, but the list box returns the corresponding value from another column.

Draw a list box and set the ColumnCount property to 2. Set the RowSource to a two-column range called Stores. The first column of the range is the store number; the second column is the store name. At this point, the list box is displaying both columns of data. To change this, set the column width to 0, 20—the text automatically updates to 0 pt;20 pt. The first column is now hidden. Figure 23.15 shows the list box properties as they need to be.

Figure 23.15
Setting the list box properties creates a two-column list box that appears to be a single column of data.

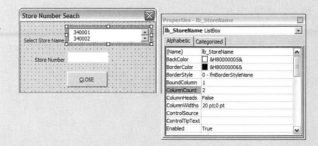

The appearance of the list box has now been set. When the user activates the list box, she will see only the store names. To return the value of the first column, set the BoundColumn property to 1. This can be done through the Properties window or through code. This example uses code to maintain the flexibility of returning the store number (see Figure 23.16):

```
Private Sub UserForm_Initialize()
    lb_StoreName.BoundColumn = 1
End Sub

Private Sub lb_StoreName_Click()
lbl_StoreNum.Caption = lb_StoreName.Value
End Sub
```

Figure 23.16
Use a two-column list box to allow the user to select a store name, but return the store number.

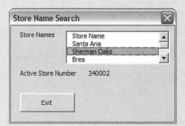

Transparent Forms

Ever had a form that you had to keep moving out of the way so you could see the data behind it? The following code sets the userform at a 50 percent transparency (see Figure 23.17) so that you can see the data behind without moving the form somewhere else on the screen (and blocking more data).

Figure 23.17
Create a 50 percent transparent form to view the data on the sheet behind it.

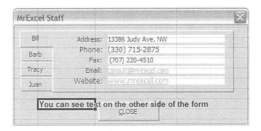

Place the following in the declarations section of the userform:

```
Private Declare Function GetActiveWindow Lib "USER32" () As Long
Private Declare Function SetWindowLong Lib "USER32" Alias _
    "SetWindowLongA" (ByVal hWnd As Long, ByVal nIndex As Long, _
    ByVal dwNewLong As Long) As Long
Private Declare Function GetWindowLong Lib "USER32" Alias _
    "GetWindowLongA" (ByVal hWnd As Long, ByVal nIndex As Long) As Long
Private Declare Function SetLayeredWindowAttributes Lib "USER32" _
    (ByVal hWnd As Long, ByVal crKey As Integer, _
    ByVal bAlpha As Integer, ByVal dwFlags As Long) As Long
Private Const WS_EX_LAYERED = &H80000
Private Const LWA_COLORKEY = &H1
Private Const LWA_ALPHA = &H2
Private Const GWL_EXSTYLE = &HFFEC
Dim hWnd As Long
```

Place the following behind a userform. When the form is activated, the transparency will be set:

```
Private Sub UserForm_Activate()
Dim nIndex As Long

hWnd = GetActiveWindow
nIndex = GetWindowLong(hWnd, GWL_EXSTYLE)
SetWindowLong hWnd, GWL_EXSTYLE, nIndex Or WS_EX_LAYERED
'50% semitransparent
SetLayeredWindowAttributes hWnd, 0, (255 * 50) / 100, LWA_ALPHA

End Sub
```

Next Steps

In Chapter 24, "Windows Application Programming Interface (API)," you will learn how to access functions and procedures hidden in files on your computer.

Windows Application Programming Interface (API)

24

What Is the Windows API?

With all the wonderful things you can do in Excel VBA, there are some things that are out of its reach or just difficult to do—such as finding out what the user's screen resolution setting is. This is where the Windows application programming interface, or API, can help.

If you look in the folder \Winnt\System32 (Windows NT systems), you'll see a lot of files with the extension .dll. These files are dynamic link libraries; they contain various functions and procedures that other programs, including VBA, can access. They give the user access to functionality used by the Windows operating system and many other programs. Keep in mind that Windows API declarations are accessible only on computers running the Microsoft Windows operating system.

This chapter doesn't teach you how to write API declarations, but it does teach you the basics of interpreting and using them. Several useful examples have also been included and you will be shown how to find more.

Understanding an API Declaration

The following line is an example of an API function:

```
Private Declare Function GetUserName _
  Lib "advapi32.dll" Alias "GetUserNameA" _
  (ByVal lpBuffer As String, nSize As Long) _
  As Long
```

There are two types of API declarations: functions, which return information, and procedures, which do something to the system. The declarations are structured similarly.

Basically, what this declaration is saying is

- It's `Private`, meaning it can only be used in the module in which it is declared. Declare it `Public` in a standard module if you want to share it among several modules.

> **CAUTION**
>
> API declarations in standard modules can be public or private. API declarations in class modules must be private.

- It will be referred to as `GetUserName` in your program. This is the variable name assigned by you.
- The function being used is found in advapi32.dll.
- The alias, `GetUserNameA`, is what the function is referred to in the DLL. This name is case sensitive and cannot be changed; it is specific to the DLL. There are often two versions of each API function. One version uses the ANSI character set and has aliases that end with the letter *A*. The other version uses the Unicode character set and has aliases that end with the letter *W*. When specifying the alias, you are telling VBA which version of the function to use.
- There are two parameters: `lpBuffer` and `nSize`. These are two arguments that the DLL function accepts.

The downside of using APIs is that there may be no errors when your code compiles or runs, and then an incorrectly configured API call can cause your computer to crash or lock up. So, it's a good idea to save often.

Using an API Declaration

Using an API is no different from calling a function or procedure you created in VBA. The following example uses the `GetUserName` declaration in a function to return the `UserName` in Excel:

```
Public Function UserName() As String
Dim sName As String * 256
Dim cChars As Long

cChars = 256
If GetUserName(sName, cChars) Then
    UserName = Left$(sName, cChars - 1)
End If
End Function
Sub ProgramRights()
Dim NameofUser As String
```

```
NameofUser = UserName

Select Case NameofUser
    Case Is = "Administrator"
        MsgBox "You have full rights to this computer"
    Case Else
        MsgBox "You have limited rights to this computer"
End Select

End Sub
```

Run the ProgramRights macro and you will learn whether you are currently signed on as the administrator. The result shown in Figure 24.1 indicates an administrator sign-on.

Figure 24.1
The `GetUserName` API function can be used to get a user's Windows login name—which is more difficult to edit than the Excel username.

API Examples

The following sections provide more examples of useful API declarations you can use in your Excel programs. Each example starts with a short description of what the example can do, followed by the actual declaration(s), and an example of its use.

Retrieve the Computer Name

This API function returns the computer name. This is the name of the computer found under MyComputer, Network Identification:

```
Private Declare Function GetComputerName Lib "kernel32" Alias _
    "GetComputerNameA" (ByVal lpBuffer As String, ByRef nSize As Long) As Long

Private Function ComputerName() As String

Dim stBuff As String * 255, lAPIResult As Long
Dim lBuffLen As Long

lBuffLen = 255
lAPIResult = GetComputerName(stBuff, lBuffLen)
If lBuffLen > 0 Then ComputerName = Left(stBuff, lBuffLen)

End Function

Sub ComputerCheck()
Dim CompName As String

CompName = ComputerName

If CompName <> "BillJelenPC" Then
    MsgBox _
```

```
        "This application does not have the right to run on this computer."
            ActiveWorkbook.Close SaveChanges:=False
    End If

    End Sub
```

The ComputerCheck macro uses an API call to get the name of the computer. In Figure 24.2, the program refuses to run for any computer except the hard-coded computer name of the owner.

Figure 24.2
Use the computer name to verify that an application has the rights to run on the installed computer.

Check Whether an Excel File Is Open on a Network

You can check whether you have a file open in Excel by trying to set the workbook to an object. If the object is Nothing (empty), you know the file isn't opened. But what if you want to see whether someone else on a network has the file open? The following API function returns that information:

```
Private Declare Function lOpen Lib "kernel32" Alias "_lopen" _
    (ByVal lpPathName As String, ByVal iReadWrite As Long) As Long

Private Declare Function lClose Lib "kernel32" _
    Alias "_lclose" (ByVal hFile As Long) As Long

Private Const OF_SHARE_EXCLUSIVE = &H10
Private Function FileIsOpen(strFullPath_FileName As String) As Boolean
Dim hdlFile As Long
Dim lastErr As Long

hdlFile = -1

hdlFile = lOpen(strFullPath_FileName, OF_SHARE_EXCLUSIVE)

If hdlFile = -1 Then
    lastErr = Err.LastDllError
Else
    lClose (hdlFile)
End If

FileIsOpen = (hdlFile = -1) And (lastErr = 32)

End Function
Sub CheckFileOpen()

If FileIsOpen("C:\XYZ Corp.xlsx") Then
    MsgBox "File is open"
```

```
Else
    MsgBox "File is not open"
End If

End Sub
```

Calling the FileIsOpen function with a particular path and filename as the parameter will tell you whether someone has the file open.

Retrieve Display-Resolution Information

The following API function retrieves the computer's display size:

```
Declare Function DisplaySize Lib "user32" Alias _
    "GetSystemMetrics" (ByVal nIndex As Long) As Long

Public Const SM_CXSCREEN = 0
Public Const SM_CYSCREEN = 1

Function VideoRes() As String
Dim vidWidth
Dim vidHeight

vidWidth = DisplaySize(SM_CXSCREEN)
vidHeight = DisplaySize(SM_CYSCREEN)

Select Case (vidWidth * vidHeight)
    Case 307200
        VideoRes = "640 x 480"
    Case 480000
        VideoRes = "800 x 600"
    Case 786432
        VideoRes = "1024 x 768"
    Case Else
        VideoRes = "Something else"
End Select

End Function

Sub CheckDisplayRes()
Dim VideoInfo As String
Dim Msg1 As String, Msg2 As String, Msg3 As String

VideoInfo = VideoRes

Msg1 = "Current resolution is set at " & VideoInfo & Chr(10)
Msg2 = "Optimal resolution for this application is 1024 x 768" & Chr(10)
Msg3 = "Please adjust resolution"

Select Case VideoInfo
    Case Is = "640 x 480"
        MsgBox Msg1 & Msg2 & Msg3
    Case Is = "800 x 600"
        MsgBox Msg1 & Msg2
    Case Is = "1024 x 768"
        MsgBox Msg1
    Case Else
        MsgBox Msg2 & Msg3
```

24

```
End Select

End Sub
```

The CheckDisplayRes macro warns the client that the display setting is not optimal for the application.

Custom About Dialog

If you go to Help, About Windows in Windows Explorer, you get a nice little About dialog with information about the Windows Explorer and a few system details. With the following code, you can pop up that window in your own program and customize a few items, as shown in Figure 24.3.

Figure 24.3
You can customize the About dialog used by Windows for your own program.

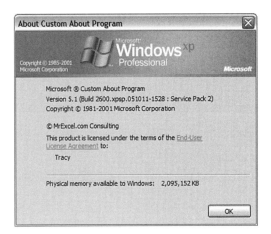

```
Declare Function ShellAbout Lib "shell32.dll" Alias "ShellAboutA" _
    (ByVal hwnd As Long, ByVal szApp As String, ByVal szOtherStuff As String, _
    ByVal hIcon As Long) As Long
Declare Function GetActiveWindow Lib "user32" () As Long

Sub AboutMrExcel()
    Dim hwnd As Integer
    On Error Resume Next
    hwnd = GetActiveWindow()
    ShellAbout hwnd, Nm, vbCrLf + Chr(169) + "" & " MrExcel.com Consulting" _
        + vbCrLf, 0
    On Error GoTo 0
End Sub
```

Disable the X for Closing a Userform

In the upper-right corner of a userform, there is an X button that can be used to shut down the application. The following API declarations work together to disable that X, forcing the user to use the Close button. When the form is initialized, the button is disabled. After the form is closed, the X button is reset to normal:

```
Private Declare Function FindWindow Lib "user32" Alias "FindWindowA" _
    (ByVal lpClassName As String, ByVal lpWindowName As String) As Long
Private Declare Function GetSystemMenu Lib "user32" (ByVal hWnd As Long, _
    ByVal bRevert As Long) As Long
Private Declare Function DeleteMenu Lib "user32" _
    (ByVal hMenu As Long, ByVal nPosition As Long, _
    ByVal wFlags As Long) As Long
Private Const SC_CLOSE As Long = &HF060

Private Sub UserForm_Initialize()
Dim hWndForm As Long
Dim hMenu As Long

hWndForm = FindWindow("ThunderDFrame", Me.Caption)  'XL2000
hMenu = GetSystemMenu(hWndForm, 0)
DeleteMenu hMenu, SC_CLOSE, 0&

End Sub
```

The DeleteMenu macro in the `UserForm_Initialize` procedure causes the X in the corner of the userform to be grayed out, as shown in Figure 24.4. This forces the client to use your programmed Close button.

Figure 24.4
Disable the X button on a userform, forcing users to use the Close button to shut down the form properly and rendering them unable to bypass any code attached to the Close button.

Running Timer

You can use the NOW function to get the time, but what if you needed a running timer? A timer displaying the exact time as the seconds tick by? The following API declarations work together to provide that functionality. The timer is placed in cell A1 of Sheet1:

```
Public Declare Function SetTimer Lib "user32" _
    (ByVal hWnd As Long, ByVal nIDEvent As Long, _
    ByVal uElapse As Long, ByVal lpTimerFunc As Long) As Long
Public Declare Function KillTimer Lib "user32" _
    (ByVal hWnd As Long, ByVal nIDEvent As Long) As Long
Public Declare Function FindWindow Lib "user32" _
    Alias "FindWindowA" (ByVal lpClassName As String, _
    ByVal lpWindowName As String) As Long

Private lngTimerID As Long
Public datStartingTime As Date

Public Sub StartTimer()
lngTimerID = SetTimer(0, 1, 10, AddressOf RunTimer)
End Sub
```

```
Public Sub StopTimer()
Dim lRet As Long
lRet = KillTimer(0, lngTimerID)
End Sub

Private Sub RunTimer(ByVal hWnd As Long, _
    ByVal uint1 As Long, ByVal nEventId As Long, _
    ByVal dwParam As Long)
On Error Resume Next
Sheet1.Range("A1").Value = Now - datStartingTime
End Sub
```

Run the StartTimer macro to have the current date and time constantly updated in cell A1.

Playing Sounds

Ever wanted to play a sound to warn users or congratulate them? You could add a sound object to a sheet and call that, but it would be much easier just to use the following API declaration and specify the proper path to a sound file:

```
Public Declare Function PlayWavSound Lib "winmm.dll" _
    Alias "sndPlaySoundA" (ByVal LpszSoundName As String, _
    ByVal uFlags As Long) As Long

Public Sub PlaySound()
Dim SoundName As String

SoundName = "C:\WinNT\Media\Chimes.wav"
PlayWavSound SoundName, 0

End Sub
```

Retrieving a File Path

The following API enables you to create a custom file browser. The program example using the API customizes the function call to create a browser for a specific need—in this case, returning the file path of a user-selected file:

```
Type tagOPENFILENAME
    lStructSize As Long
    hwndOwner As Long
    hInstance As Long
    strFilter As String
    strCustomFilter As String
    nMaxCustFilter As Long
    nFilterIndex As Long
    strFile As String
    nMaxFile As Long
    strFileTitle As String
    nMaxFileTitle As Long
    strInitialDir As String
    strTitle As String
    Flags As Long
    nFileOffset As Integer
    nFileExtension As Integer
    strDefExt As String
    lCustData As Long
```

```
        lpfnHook As Long
        lpTemplateName As String
    End Type

    Declare Function aht_apiGetOpenFileName Lib "comdlg32.dll" _
        Alias "GetOpenFileNameA" (OFN As tagOPENFILENAME) As Boolean
    Declare Function aht_apiGetSaveFileName Lib "comdlg32.dll" _
        Alias "GetSaveFileNameA" (OFN As tagOPENFILENAME) As Boolean
    Declare Function CommDlgExtendedError Lib "comdlg32.dll" () As Long

    Global Const ahtOFN_READONLY = &H1
    Global Const ahtOFN_OVERWRITEPROMPT = &H2
    Global Const ahtOFN_HIDEREADONLY = &H4
    Global Const ahtOFN_NOCHANGEDIR = &H8
    Global Const ahtOFN_SHOWHELP = &H10
    Global Const ahtOFN_NOVALIDATE = &H100
    Global Const ahtOFN_ALLOWMULTISELECT = &H200
    Global Const ahtOFN_EXTENSIONDIFFERENT = &H400
    Global Const ahtOFN_PATHMUSTEXIST = &H800
    Global Const ahtOFN_FILEMUSTEXIST = &H1000
    Global Const ahtOFN_CREATEPROMPT = &H2000
    Global Const ahtOFN_SHAREAWARE = &H4000
    Global Const ahtOFN_NOREADONLYRETURN = &H8000
    Global Const ahtOFN_NOTESTFILECREATE = &H10000
    Global Const ahtOFN_NONETWORKBUTTON = &H20000
    Global Const ahtOFN_NOLONGNAMES = &H40000
    Global Const ahtOFN_EXPLORER = &H80000
    Global Const ahtOFN_NODEREFERENCELINKS = &H100000
    Global Const ahtOFN_LONGNAMES = &H200000

    Function ahtCommonFileOpenSave( _
                Optional ByRef Flags As Variant, _
                Optional ByVal InitialDir As Variant, _
                Optional ByVal Filter As Variant, _
                Optional ByVal FilterIndex As Variant, _
                Optional ByVal DefaultExt As Variant, _
                Optional ByVal FileName As Variant, _
                Optional ByVal DialogTitle As Variant, _
                Optional ByVal hwnd As Variant, _
                Optional ByVal OpenFile As Variant) As Variant

    ' This is the entry point you'll use to call the common
    ' file Open/Save As dialog. The parameters are listed
    ' below, and all are optional.
    '
    ' In:
    ' Flags: one or more of the ahtOFN_* constants, OR'd together.
    ' InitialDir: the directory in which to first look
    ' Filter: a set of file filters
    '    (Use AddFilterItem to set up Filters)
    ' FilterIndex: 1-based integer indicating which filter
    ' set to use, by default (1 if unspecified)
    ' DefaultExt: Extension to use if the user doesn't enter one.
    ' Only useful on file saves.
    ' FileName: Default value for the filename text box.
    ' DialogTitle: Title for the dialog.
    ' hWnd: parent window handle
    ' OpenFile: Boolean(True=Open File/False=Save As)
```

24

```
' Out:
' Return Value: Either Null or the selected filename

Dim OFN As tagOPENFILENAME
Dim strFileName As String
Dim strFileTitle As String
Dim fResult As Boolean

' Give the dialog a caption title.
If IsMissing(InitialDir) Then InitialDir = CurDir
If IsMissing(Filter) Then Filter = ""
If IsMissing(FilterIndex) Then FilterIndex = 1
If IsMissing(Flags) Then Flags = 0&
If IsMissing(DefaultExt) Then DefaultExt = ""
If IsMissing(FileName) Then FileName = ""
If IsMissing(DialogTitle) Then DialogTitle = ""
If IsMissing(OpenFile) Then OpenFile = True

' Allocate string space for the returned strings.
strFileName = Left(FileName & String(256, 0), 256)
strFileTitle = String(256, 0)

' Set up the data structure before you call the function
With OFN
    .lStructSize = Len(OFN)
    .strFilter = Filter
    .nFilterIndex = FilterIndex
    .strFile = strFileName
    .nMaxFile = Len(strFileName)
    .strFileTitle = strFileTitle
    .nMaxFileTitle = Len(strFileTitle)
    .strTitle = DialogTitle
    .Flags = Flags
    .strDefExt = DefaultExt
    .strInitialDir = InitialDir
    .hInstance = 0
    .lpfnHook = 0
    .strCustomFilter = String(255, 0)
    .nMaxCustFilter = 255
End With

' This passes the desired data structure to the
' Windows API, which will in turn display
' the Open/Save As dialog.
If OpenFile Then
    fResult = aht_apiGetOpenFileName(OFN)
Else
    fResult = aht_apiGetSaveFileName(OFN)
End If

' The function call filled in the strFileTitle member
' of the structure. You have to write special code
' to retrieve that if you're interested.
If fResult Then
' You might care to check the Flags member of the
' structure to get information about the chosen file.
' In this example, if you bothered to pass a
```

```
' value for Flags, we'll fill it in with the outgoing
' Flags value.
    If Not IsMissing(Flags) Then Flags = OFN.Flags
        ahtCommonFileOpenSave = TrimNull(OFN.strFile)
    Else
        ahtCommonFileOpenSave = vbNullString
    End If

End Function

Function ahtAddFilterItem(strFilter As String, _
    strDescription As String, Optional varItem As Variant) As String
' Tack a new chunk onto the file filter.
' That is, take the old value, stick onto it the description,
' (like "Databases"), a null character, the skeleton
' (like "*.mdb;*.mda"), and a final null character.

If IsMissing(varItem) Then varItem = "*.*"
ahtAddFilterItem = strFilter & strDescription & _
    vbNullChar & varItem & vbNullChar

End Function

Private Function TrimNull(ByVal strItem As String) As String
Dim intPos As Integer

intPos = InStr(strItem, vbNullChar)

If intPos > 0 Then
    TrimNull = Left(strItem, intPos - 1)
Else
    TrimNull = strItem
End If

End Function
```

This is the actual program created to use this information:

```
Function GetFileName(strPath As String)
Dim strFilter As String
Dim lngFlags As Long

strFilter = ahtAddFilterItem(strFilter, "Excel Files (*.xls)")
GetFileName = ahtCommonFileOpenSave(InitialDir:=strPath, _
    Filter:=strFilter, FilterIndex:=3, Flags:=lngFlags, _
    DialogTitle:="Please select file to import")

End Function
```

Then create the userform. The following code is attached to the Browse button, as shown in Figure 24.5. Note that the function specifies the starting directory:

```
Private Sub cmdBrowse_Click()

txtFile = GetFileName("c:\")

End Sub
```

Figure 24.5
Create a custom browse window to return the file path of a user-selected file. This can be used to ensure the user doesn't select the wrong file for import.

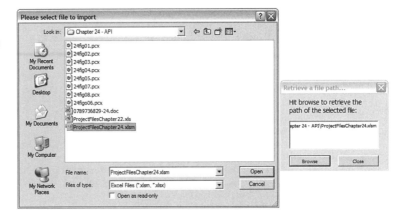

Finding More API Declarations

There are many more API declarations out there than the ones we have shown—we've barely scratched the surface of the wealth of procedures and functions available. Microsoft has many tools available to help you create your own APIs (search Platform SDK), but there are also many programmers who have developed declarations to share, such as Ivan F. Moala at http://xcelfiles.homestead.com/APIIndex.html. He has created a site full of not only examples, but instruction, too.

Next Steps

In Chapter 25, "Handling Errors," you will learn about error handling. In a perfect world, you want to be able to hand your applications off to a co-worker, leave for vacation, and not have to worry about an unhandled error appearing while you are on the beach. Chapter 25 discusses how to handle obvious and not-so-obvious errors.

Handling Errors

Errors are bound to happen. You can test and retest your code, but after a report is put into daily production and used for hundreds of days, something unexpected will eventually happen. Your goal should be to try to head off obscure errors as you code. Always be thinking of what unexpected things could someday happen that would make your code not work.

What Happens When an Error Occurs

If VBA encounters an error and you have no error-checking code in place, the program stops and you (or your client) will be presented with the "Continue, End, Debug, Help" error message, as shown in Figure 25.1.

Figure 25.1
An unhandled error in an unprotected module presents you with a choice to End or Debug.

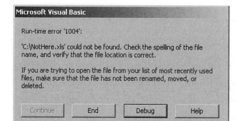

When presented with the choice to End or Debug, you should click Debug. The VB Editor highlights the line that caused the error in yellow. You can hover your cursor over any variable to see the current value of the variable. This provides a lot of information about what could have caused the error (see Figure 25.2).

Figure 25.2
After clicking Debug, the macro is in break mode. You can hover the cursor over a variable; after a few seconds, the current value of the variable is shown.

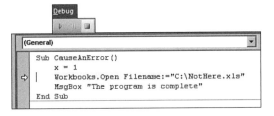

```
(General)
    Sub CauseAnError()
        x = 1
   ⇨  [x=1]kbooks.Open Filename:="C:\NotHere.xls"
        MsgBox "The program is complete"
    End Sub
```

Excel is notorious for returning errors that are not very meaningful. For example, dozens of situations can cause a 1004 error. Being able to see the offending line highlighted in yellow, plus being able to examine the current value of any variables, will help you to discover the real cause of an error.

After examining the line in error, click the Reset button to stop execution of the macro. The Reset button is the square button under the Run item in the main menu, as shown in Figure 25.3.

Figure 25.3
The Reset button looks like the Stop button in the set of three buttons that resemble a VCR control panel.

```
Debug
  ▶  ❙❙  ■

(General)
    Sub CauseAnError()
        x = 1
   ⇨  ❘  Workbooks.Open Filename:="C:\NotHere.xls"
            MsgBox "The program is complete"
    End Sub
```

CAUTION

If you fail to click Reset to end the macro, and then attempt to run another macro, you are presented with the annoying error message shown in Figure 25.4. The message is annoying because you start in Excel, but when this message window is displayed, the screen automatically switches to display the VB Editor. However, immediately after you click OK, you are returned to the Excel user interface instead of being left in the VB Editor. For as often as this message happens, it would be much more convenient if you could be returned to the VB Editor after clicking OK.

Figure 25.4
This message appears if you forget to click Reset to end a debug session and then attempt to run another macro.

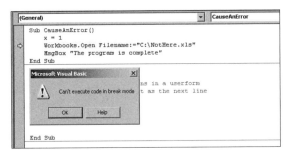

```
(General)                                    ▼   CauseAnError
    Sub CauseAnError()
        x = 1
   ⇨  Workbooks.Open Filename:="C:\NotHere.xls"
        MsgBox "The program is complete"
    End Sub

    ┌─ Microsoft Visual Basic ──────── X ┐
    │                         ns in a userform
    │  ⚠  Can't execute code in break mode  t as the next line
    │
    │     ┌────────┐  ┌──────┐
    │     │   OK   │  │ Help │
    │     └────────┘  └──────┘
    └──────────────────────────────────┘

    End Sub
```

Debug Error Inside Userform Code Is Misleading

The line highlighted as the error after you click Debug can be misleading in one situation. Suppose that you call a macro. This macro then displays a userform. Somewhere in the userform code, an error occurs. When you click Debug, instead of showing the problem inside the userform code, Excel highlights the line in the original macro that displayed the userform. Follow these steps to find the real error.

1. After an error message box is shown as in Figure 25.5, click the Debug button.

Figure 25.5
Choose Debug in response to this error 13.

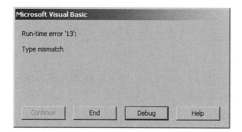

You will see that the error allegedly occurred on a line that shows a userform, as shown in Figure 25.6. Because you've read this chapter, you will know that this is not the line in error.

Figure 25.6
frmChoose.Show is indicated as the line in error.

```
(General)                                              PrepareAndDisplay
      Sub PrepareAndDisplay()
        ' sometimes an error happens in a userform
        ' yet the editor reports it as the next line
        Dim WS As Worksheet
        Set WS = Worksheets("Sheet1")

        FinalRow = WS.Cells(Rows.Count, 1).End(xlUp).Row
        WS.Cells(1, 1).Sort _
            Key1:=WS.Cells(1, 1), Order1:=xlAscending, Header:=xlYes

        frmChoose.Show

        MsgBox "Macro complete"

      End Sub
```

2. Press F8 to execute the Show method. Instead of getting an error, you are taken into the Userform_Initialize procedure.

3. Keep pressing F8 until you get the error message again. You must stay alert. As soon as you encounter the error, the error message box is displayed. Click Debug and you are returned to the userform.Show line. It is particularly difficult to follow the code when the error occurs on the other side of a long loop, as shown in Figure 25.7.

Imagine trying to step through the code in Figure 25.7. You carefully press F8 five times with no problems through the first pass of the loop. Because the problem could be in future iterations through the loop, you continue to press F8. If there are 25 items to add to the list box, 48 more presses of F8 are required to get through the loop safely. Each time before pressing F8, you should mentally note that you are about to run some specific line.

Figure 25.7
With 25 items to add to the list box, you must press F8 51 times to get through this three-line loop.

```
Private Sub UserForm_Initialize()
    Dim WS As Worksheet
    Set WS = Worksheets("Sheet1")

    FinalRow = WS.Cells(Rows.Count, 1).End(xlUp).Row
    For i = 2 To FinalRow
        Me.ListBox1.AddItem WS.Cells(i, 1)
    Next i

    ' The next line is actually the line that causes an error
    Me.ListBox1(0).Selected = True


End Sub
```

At the point shown in Figure 25.7, the next press of the F8 key displays the error and returns you to the `frmChoose.Show` line back in Module1.

This is an annoying situation. When you click Debug and see that the line in error is a line that displays a userform, you need to start pressing the F8 key to step into the userform code until you get the error. Invariably, I get incredibly bored pressing F8 a million times and forget to pay attention to which line caused the error. As soon as the error happens, I am thrown back to the Debug message, which returns me to the `frmChoose.Show` line of code. At that point, you need to start pressing F8 again. If you can recall the general area where the debug error occurred, click the mouse cursor in a line right before that section and use Ctrl+F8 to run the macro up to the cursor.

Basic Error Handling with the On Error GoTo Syntax

The basic error-handling option is to tell VBA that in the case of an error you want to have code branch to a specific area of the macro. In this area, you might have special code that alerts users of the problem and enables them to react.

A typical scenario is to add the error-handling routine at the end of the macro. To set up an error handler, follow these steps:

1. After the last code line of the macro, insert the code line **Exit Sub**. This makes sure that the execution of the macro does not continue into the error handler.

2. After the **Exit Sub** line, add a label. A label is a name followed by a colon. For example, you might create a label called MyErrorHandler:.

3. Write the code to handle the error. If you want to return control of the macro to the line after the one that caused the error, use the statement `Resume Next`.

In your macro, just before the line that may likely cause the error, add a line reading **On Error GoTo MyErrorHandler**. Note that in this line, you do not include the colon after the label name.

Immediately after the line of code that you suspect will cause the error, add code to turn off the special error handler. This is very nonintuitive and tends to confuse people. The code to cancel any special error handling is On Error Goto 0. There is no label named 0. This line is a fictitious line that instructs Excel to go back to the normal state of displaying the End/Debug error message when an error is encountered. Do you see why it is important to cancel the error handling? In the following code, we've written a special error handler to handle the necessary action if the file has been moved or is missing. We definitely do not want this error handler invoked for another error later in the macro, such as a division by zero:

```
Sub HandleAnError()
    Dim MyFile as Variant
    ' Set up a special error handler
    On Error GoTo FileNotThere
    Workbooks.Open Filename:="C:\NotHere.xls"
    ' If we get here, cancel the special error handler
    On Error GoTo 0
    MsgBox "The program is complete"

    ' The macro is done. Use Exit sub, otherwise the macro
    ' execution WILL continue into the error handler
    Exit Sub

    ' Set up a name for the Error handler
FileNotThere:
    MyPrompt = "There was an error opening the file. It is possible the "
    MyPrompt = MyPrompt & " file has been moved. Click OK to browse for the "
    MyPrompt = MyPrompt & "file, or click Cancel to end the program"
    Ans = MsgBox(Prompt:=MyPrompt, VbMsgBoxStyle:=vbOKCancel)
    If Ans = vbCancel Then Exit Sub

    ' The client clicked OK. Let him browse for the file
    MyFile = Application.GetOpenFilename
    If MyFile = False Then Exit Sub

    ' What if the 2nd file is corrupt? We don't want to recursively throw
    ' the client back into this error handler. Just stop the program
    On Error GoTo 0
    Workbooks.Open MyFile
    ' If we get here, then return the macro execution back to the original
    ' section of the macro, to the line after the one that caused the error.
    Resume Next


End Sub
```

> **TIP**
>
> It is possible to have more than one error handler at the end of a macro. Make sure that each error handler ends with either Resume Next or Exit Sub so that macro execution does not accidentally move into the next error handler.

25

Generic Error Handlers

Some developers like to direct any error to a generic error handler. They make use of the `Err` object. This object has properties for error number and description. You can offer this information to the client and prevent them from getting a debug message:

```
    On Error GoTo HandleAny
    Sheets(9).Select

    Exit Sub

HandleAny:
    Msg = "We encountered " & Err.Number & " - " & Err.Description
    MsgBox Msg
    Exit Sub
```

Handling Errors by Choosing to Ignore Them

Some errors can simply be ignored. Suppose, for instance, that you are going to use the HTML Creator macro from Chapter 16, "Reading from and Writing to the Web." Your code erases any existing index.html file from a folder before writing out the next file.

The `Kill (FileName)` statement returns an error if `FileName` does not exist. Is this something you need to worry about? You are trying to delete the file. Who cares if someone already deleted it before running the macro? In this case, you should tell Excel to simply skip over the offending line and resume macro execution with the next line. The code to do this is `On Error Resume Next`:

```
Sub WriteHTML()
    MyFile = "C:\Index.html"
    On Error Resume Next
    Kill (MyFile)
    On Error Goto 0
    Open MyFile for Output as #1
    ' etc…
End Sub
```

You need to be careful with `On Error Resume Next`. It can be used selectively in situations where you know that the error can be ignored. You should immediately return error checking to normal after the line that might cause an error with `On Error GoTo 0`.

If you attempt to have `On Error Resume Next` skip an error that cannot be skipped, the macro immediately steps out of the current macro. If you have a situation where MacroA calls MacroB and MacroB encounters a nonskippable error, the program jumps out of MacroB and continues with the next line in MacroA. This is rarely a good thing.

25

Page Setup Problems Can Often Be Ignored

Record a macro and perform a page setup. Even if you change only one item in the Page Setup dialog, the macro recorder records two dozen settings for you. These settings notoriously differ from printer to printer. For example, if you record the PageSetup on a system with a color printer, it might record a setting for `.BlackAndWhite = True`. This setting will fail on another system where the printer doesn't offer the choice. Your printer may offer a `.PrintQuality = 600` setting. If the client's printer offers only 300 resolution, this code will fail. Surround the entire PageSetup with `On Error Resume Next` to ensure that most settings happen but the trivial ones that fail will not cause a runtime error:

```
On Error Resume Next
With ActiveSheet.PageSetup
    .PrintTitleRows = ""
    .PrintTitleColumns = ""
End With
ActiveSheet.PageSetup.PrintArea = "$A$1:$L$27"
With ActiveSheet.PageSetup
    .LeftHeader = ""
    .CenterHeader = ""
    .RightHeader = ""
    .LeftFooter = ""
    .CenterFooter = ""
    .RightFooter = ""
    .LeftMargin = Application.InchesToPoints(0.25)
    .RightMargin = Application.InchesToPoints(0.25)
    .TopMargin = Application.InchesToPoints(0.75)
    .BottomMargin = Application.InchesToPoints(0.5)
    .HeaderMargin = Application.InchesToPoints(0.5)
    .FooterMargin = Application.InchesToPoints(0.5)
    .PrintHeadings = False
    .PrintGridlines = False
    .PrintComments = xlPrintNoComments
    .PrintQuality = 300
    .CenterHorizontally = False
    .CenterVertically = False
    .Orientation = xlLandscape
    .Draft = False
    .PaperSize = xlPaperLetter
    .FirstPageNumber = xlAutomatic
    .Order = xlDownThenOver
    .BlackAndWhite = False
    .Zoom = False
    .FitToPagesWide = 1
    .FitToPagesTall = False
    .PrintErrors = xlPrintErrorsDisplayed
End With
On Error GoTo 0
```

25

Suppressing Excel Warnings

Some messages appear even if you have set Excel to ignore errors. Try to delete a work-sheet using code and you will still get the message "Data may exist in the sheet(s) selected for deletion." To permanently delete the data, click Delete. This is annoying. We don't want our clients to have to answer this warning. It turns out that this is not an error, but an alert. To suppress all alerts and force Excel to take the default action, use `Application.DisplayAlerts = False`:

```
Sub DeleteSheet()
    Application.DisplayAlerts = False
    Worksheets("Sheet2").Delete
    Application.DisplayAlerts = True
End Sub
```

Encountering Errors on Purpose

Because programmers hate errors, this concept might seem counterintuitive, but errors are not always bad. Sometimes it is faster to simply encounter an error.

Let's say you want to find out whether the active workbook contains a worksheet named Data. To find this out without causing an error, you could code this:

```
DataFound = False
For each ws in ActiveWorkbook.Worksheets
    If ws.Name = "Data" then
        DataFound = True
        Exit For
    End if
Next ws
If not DataFound then Sheets.Add.Name = "Data"
```

This takes eight lines of code. If your workbook has 128 worksheets, the program would loop through 128 times before deciding that the data worksheet is missing.

The alternative is to simply try to reference the data worksheet. If you have error checking set to resume next, the code runs, and the Err object is assigned a number other than zero:

```
On Error Resume Next
X = Worksheets("Data").Name
If not Err.Number = 0 then Sheets.Add.Name = "Data"
On Error GoTo 0
```

This code runs much faster. Errors usually make me cringe; in this case, however, and in many other cases, they are perfectly acceptable.

Train Your Clients

You might be developing code for a client across the globe or for the administrative assistant so that he can run the code while you are on vacation. In either instance, you might find yourself remotely trying to debug code while you are on the telephone with the client.

It is important to train clients about the difference between an error and a simple MsgBox. A MsgBox is a planned message. It still appears out of the blue with a beep. Teach your users that error messages are bad but not everything that pops up is an error message. I had a client keep reporting to her boss that she was getting an error from my program. In reality, she was getting an informational MsgBox. Both Debug errors and Msgbox messages beep at the user.

When clients get Debug errors, train them to call you while the Debug message is still on the screen. You can then get the error number and the description, and ask them to click Debug and tell you the module name, the procedure name, and the line in yellow. Armed with this information, you can usually figure out what is going on. Without this information, it is unlikely that you'll be able to figure out the problem. Getting a call from a client saying that there was a 1004 error is of little help—1004 is a catchall error that can mean any number of things.

Errors While Developing Versus Errors Months Later

When you have just written code and are running it for the first time, you expect errors. In fact, you may decide to step through code line by line to watch the progress of the code the first time through.

It is another thing to have a program that has been running daily in production suddenly stop working with an error. This seems perplexing; the code has been working for months. Why did it suddenly stop working today?

It is easy to blame this on the client; but when you get right down to it, it is really the fault of developers for not considering the possibilities.

The following sections describe a couple of common problems that can strike an application months later.

Runtime Error 9: Subscript Out of Range

You've set up an application for the client. You have provided a Menu worksheet where you store some settings. One day, the client reports the error message shown in Figure 25.8.

Your code expected there to be a worksheet named Menu. For some reason, the client either accidentally deleted the worksheet or renamed it. As soon as you tried to select the sheet, you received an error:

```
Sub GetSettings()
    ThisWorkbook.Worksheets("Menu").Select
    x = Range("A1").Value
End Sub
```

25

Figure 25.8
The Runtime Error 9 is often caused when you expect a worksheet to be there and it has been deleted or renamed by the client.

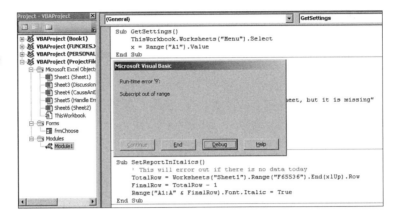

This is a classic situation where you can't believe the client would do something so crazy. After you've been burned by this one a few times, you might go to these lengths to prevent an unhandled Debug error:

```
Sub GetSettings()
    On Error Resume Next
    x = ThisWorkbook.Worksheets("Menu").Name
    If Not Err.Number = 0 Then
        MsgBox "Expected to find a Menu worksheet, but it is missing"
        Exit Sub
    End If
    On Error GoTo 0

    ThisWorkbook.Worksheets("Menu").Select
    x = Range("A1").Value
End Sub
```

RunTime Error 1004: Method Range of Object Global Failed

You have code that imports a text file each day. You expect the text file to end with a Total row. After importing the text, you want to convert all the detail rows to italics.

The following code works fine for months:

```
Sub SetReportInItalics()
    TotalRow = Cells(Rows.Count,1).End(xlUp).Row
    FinalRow = TotalRow - 1
    Range("A1:A" & FinalRow).Font.Italic = True
End Sub
```

Then one day, the client calls with the error message shown in Figure 25.9.

Upon examination of the code, you discover that something bizarre went wrong when the text file was FTP'ed to the client that day. The text file ended up as an empty file. Because the worksheet was empty, TotalRow was determined to be Row 1. When we assumed the last detail row was TotalRow - 1, this set our code up to attempt to format Row 0, which clearly does not exist.

Figure 25.9
The Runtime Error 1004 can be caused by a number of things.

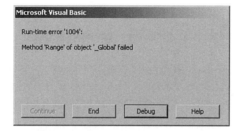

After this episode, you will find yourself writing code that preemptively looks for this situation:

```
Sub SetReportInItalics()
    TotalRow = Cells(Rows.Count,1).End(xlUp).Row
    FinalRow = TotalRow - 1
    If FinalRow > 0 Then
        Range("A1:A" & FinalRow).Font.Italic = True
    Else
        MsgBox "It appears the file is empty today. Check the FTP process"
    End If
End Sub
```

The Ills of Protecting Code

It is possible to lock a VBA project so that it cannot be viewed. I do not recommend this at all. When code is protected and an error is encountered, your user is presented with an error message, but no opportunity to debug. The Debug button is there, but it is grayed out. This is useless in helping you discover the problem.

Further, the Excel VBA protection scheme is horribly easy to break. Programmers in Estonia offer $40 software that lets you unlock any project. So, understand that office VBA code is not secure and get over it.

CASE STUDY

Password Cracking

The password-hacking schemes were very easy in Excel 97 and Excel 2000. The password cracking software could immediately locate the actual password in the VBA project and report it to the software user.

Then, in Excel 2002, Microsoft offered a brilliant protection scheme that temporarily appeared to foil the password-cracking utilities. The password was tightly encrypted. For several months after the release of Excel 2002, password-cracking programs had to try brute-force combinations. The software could crack a password like *blue* in 10 minutes. But given a 24-character password, like *A6%kJJ542(9$GgU44#2drt8, the program would take 20 hours to find the password. This was a fun annoyance to foist upon other VBA programmers who would potentially break into your code.

25

However, the next version of the password-cracking software was able to break a 24-character password in Excel 2002 in about 2 seconds. When I tested my 24-character password-protected project, the password utility quickly told me that my password was XVII. I thought this was certainly wrong, but after testing, I found the project had a new password of XVII. Yes, this latest version of the software resorted to another approach. Instead of using brute force to crack the password, it simply wrote a new random four-character password to the project and saved the file.

Now, this causes an embarrassing problem for whoever cracked the password. The developer has a sign on his wall reminding him the password is *A6%kJJ542(9$GgU44#2drt8. But, in the cracked version of the file, the password is now XVII. If there is a problem with the cracked file and it is sent back to the developer, the developer can't open the file anymore. The only person getting anything from this is the programmer in Estonia who wrote the cracking software.

There are not enough Excel VBA developers in the world. There are more projects than programmers right now. In my circle of developer friends, we all acknowledge that business prospects slip through the cracks because we are too busy with other customers.

So, the situation of a newbie developer is not uncommon. He does an adequate job of writing code for a customer and then locks the VBA project.

The customer needs some changes. The original developer does the work. A few weeks later, some more changes, and the developer delivers. A month later, the customer needs more work. Either the developer is busy with other projects or he has underpriced these maintenance jobs and has more lucrative work. The client tries to contact the programmer a few times, then, realizing he needs to get the project fixed, calls another developer—you!

You get the code. It is protected. You break the password and see who wrote the code. This is a tough call. You have no interest in stealing the guy's customer. You would prefer to do this one job and then have the customer return to the original developer. However, because of the password hacking, you've now created a situation where the two developers have a different password. Your only choice is to remove the password entirely.

More Problems with Passwords

The password scheme for any version of Excel from 2002 forward is incompatible with Excel 97. If you protected code in Excel 2002, you cannot unlock the project in Excel 97. A lot of people are still using Excel 97. As your application is given to more employees in a company, you invariably find one employee with Excel 97. Of course, that user comes up with some runtime error. However, if you've locked the project in Excel 2002 or newer, you cannot unlock the project in Excel 97, and therefore cannot debug in Excel 97.

Bottom line: Locking code causes more trouble than it is worth.

> **NOTE**
> If you are using a combination of Excel 2003 and Excel 2007, the passwords transfer easily back and forth. This holds true even if the file is saved as an XLSM file and opened in Excel 2003 using the file converter. You can change code in Excel 2003, save the file, and successfully round-trip back to Excel 2007.

Errors Caused by Different Versions

Microsoft does improve VBA in every version of Excel. Pivot table creation was drastically improved between Excel 97 and Excel 2000 and new features were added in Excel 2007. Certain chart features were improved between Excel 97 and Excel 2000 and charting was completely rewritten in Excel 2007. Excel started supporting XML in Excel 2003 and stopped supporting interactivity in saved Web pages in Excel 2007.

The `TrailingMinusNumbers` parameter was new in Excel 2002. If you write code in Excel 2007 and then send the code to a client with Excel 2000, that user gets a compile error as soon as she tries to run any code in the same module as the offending code. Consider this application with two modules.

Module1 has macros ProcA, ProcB, and ProcC. Module2 has macros ProcD and ProcE. It happens that ProcE has an `ImportText` method with the `TrailingMinusNumbers` parameter.

The client can run ProcA and ProcB on the Excel 2000 machine without problem. As soon as she tries to run ProcD, she will get a compile error reported in ProcD because Excel tries to compile all of Module2 as soon as she tries to run code in that module. This can be incredibly misleading: An error being reported when the client runs ProcD is actually caused by an error in ProcE.

One solution is to have access to every supported version of Excel, plus Excel 97, and test the code in all versions. Note that Excel 97 SR-2 was far more stable than the initial releases of Excel 97. A lot of clients are hanging on to Excel 97, but it is frustrating when you find someone who doesn't have the stable service release.

Macintosh users will believe that their version of Excel is the same as the Excel for Windows. Microsoft promised compatibility of files, but that promise ends in the Excel user interface. VBA code is *not* compatible between Windows and the Mac. It is close, but annoyingly different. Certainly, anything that you do with the Windows API is not going to work on a Mac.

Next Steps

This chapter discussed how to make your code more bullet-proof for your clients. In Chapter 26, "Customizing the Ribbon to Run Macros," you will learn how to customize the Ribbon to allow your clients to enjoy a professional user interface.

25

Customizing the Ribbon to Run Macros

26

Out with the Old, In with the New

One of the first changes you notice when you open Excel 2007 is the new ribbon toolbar. Gone are the menus and toolbars of old. And this change isn't just visual—the method of modifying custom menu controls has changed just as radically. One of the biggest bonuses of this new method—you no longer have to worry about your custom toolbar sticking around after the workbook is closed because the custom toolbar is now part of the inner workings of the workbook.

The original Command Bars object still works, but the customized menus and toolbars are all placed on the Add-ins ribbon. If you had custom menu commands, they will appear on the Menu Commands group, as shown in Figure 26.1. In Figure 26.2, the custom toolbars from two different workbooks appear together on the Custom Toolbars group.

If you want to modify the Ribbon and add your own tab, you need to modify the Excel file itself, which isn't as impossible as it sounds. The new Excel file is actually a zipped file, containing various files and folders. All you need to do is unzip it, make your changes, and you're done. Okay, it's not *that* simple—a few more steps are involved—but it's not impossible.

Before we begin, go to the Office menu and select Excel Options, Advanced, General, and select Show Add-In User Interface Errors. This will allow error messages to appear so that you can troubleshoot errors in your custom toolbar. See the "Troubleshooting Error Messages" section later in this chapter for more details.

Figure 26.1

Previous version custom menus will be grouped together under the Menu Commands group.

Figure 26.2

Custom toolbars from previous versions of Excel appear in the Custom Toolbars group.

CAUTION _____

Unlike programming in the VB Editor, you won't have any assistance with automatic correction of letter case, and the XML code is very particular. Note the case of the XML-specific words, such as `id`; using `ID` will generate an error.

Where to Add Your Code: customui Folder and File

Create a folder called **customui.** This folder will contain the elements of your custom Ribbon tab. Within the folder, create a text file and call it **customui.xml,** as shown in Figure 26.3. Open the XML file in a text editor; either Notepad or WordPad will work.

Figure 26.3

Create a customui.xml file within a customui folder.

Insert the basic structure for the XML code, shown here, into your XML file. For every opening tag grouping, such as `<ribbon>`, there must be a closing tag, `</ribbon>`:

```
<customUI xmlns="http://schemas.microsoft.com/office/2006/01/customui">
  <ribbon startFromScratch="false">
    <tabs>
```

```
        <!-- your ribbon controls here -->

    </tabs>
  </ribbon>
</customUI>
```

startFromScratch is optional with a default value of false. It's how you tell the code the other tabs in Excel will not be shown, only yours. True means to show only your tab; false means to show your tab and all the other tabs.

⎡ **C A U T I O N**

Note the case of the letters in startFromScratch—the small *s* at the beginning followed by the capital *F* in From and capital *S* in Scratch. It is crucial you do not deviate from this.

The <!-- your ribbon controls here --> you see in the previous code is commented text. Just enter your comments between <!-- and -->, and the program will ignore the line when it runs.

Creating the Tab and Group

Before you can add a control to a tab, you need to identify the tab and group. A tab can hold many different controls on it, which you can group together, like the Font group on the Home ribbon, as shown in Figure 26.4.

Figure 26.4
Individual controls are placed in groups on a tab. A tab may contain several such groups.

We'll name our tab MrExcel Add-ins and add a group called Reports to it, as shown in Figure 26.5:

```
<customUI xmlns="http://schemas.microsoft.com/office/2006/01/customui">
  <ribbon startFromScratch="false">
    <tabs>
      <tab id="CustomTab" label="MrExcel Add-ins">
        <group id="CustomGroup" label="Reports">

          <!-- your ribbon controls here -->

        </group>
      </tab>
    </tabs>
  </ribbon>
</customUI>
```

Figure 26.5
Add Tab and Group tags to your code to create a custom tab and group.

The `id` is a unique identifier for the control (in this case, the tab and group). The `label` is the text you want to appear on your ribbon for the specified control.

Adding a Control to Your Ribbon

After you've set up the ribbon and group, you can add controls. Depending on the type of control, there are different attributes you can include in your XML code. (Refer to Table 26.1 for more information on various controls and their attributes.)

The following code adds a normal-sized button to the Reports group, set to run the sub called HelloWorld when the button is clicked (see Figure 26.6):

```xml
<customUI xmlns="http://schemas.microsoft.com/office/2006/01/customui">
  <ribbon startFromScratch="false">
    <tabs>
      <tab id="CustomTab" label="MrExcel Add-ins">
        <group id="CustomGroup" label="Reports">

          <button id="button1" label="Click to run"
              onAction="Module1.HelloWorld" size="normal"  />

        </group>
      </tab>
    </tabs>
  </ribbon>
</customUI>
```

The `id` is a unique identifier for the control button. The `label` is the text you want to appear on your button. `Size` is the size of the button. `Normal` is the default value, and the other option is `Large`. `onAction` is the sub, HelloWorld, to call when the button is clicked. The sub, shown here, goes in a standard module, Module1, in the workbook:

```vba
Sub HelloWorld(control As IRibbonControl)
MsgBox "Hello World"
End Sub
```

Notice the argument `control As IRibbonControl`. This is the standard argument for a sub called by a button control using the `onAction` attribute. Refer to Table 26.2 for the required arguments for other attributes and controls.

Figure 26.6
Run a program with a click of a button on your custom ribbon.

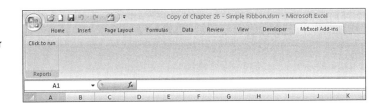

Table 26.1 Ribbon Control Attributes

Attribute	Type or Value	Description
description	String	Specifies description text displayed in menus when the itemSize attribute is set to Large
enabled	true, false	Specifies whether the control is enabled
getContent	Callback	Retrieves XML content that describes a dynamic menu
getDescription	Callback	Gets the description of a control
getEnabled	Callback	Gets the enabled state of a control
getImage	Callback	Gets the image for a control
getImageMso	Callback	Gets a built-in control's icon by using the control ID
getItemCount	Callback	Gets the number of items to be displayed in a combo box, drop-down list, or gallery
getItemID	Callback	Gets the ID for a specific item in a combo box, drop-down list, or gallery
getItemImage	Callback	Gets the image of a combo box, drop-down list, or gallery
getItemLabel	Callback	Gets the label of a combo box, drop-down list, or gallery
getItemScreentip	Callback	Gets the ScreenTip for a a combo box, drop-down list, or gallery
getItemSupertip	Callback	Gets the Enhanced ScreenTip for a combo box, drop-down list, or gallery
getKeytip	Callback	Gets the KeyTip for a control
getLabel	Callback	Gets the label for a control
getPressed	Callback	Gets a value that indicates whether a toggle button is pressed or not pressed Gets a value that indicates whether a check box is selected or cleared
getScreentip	Callback	Gets the ScreenTip for a control
getSelectedItemID	Callback	Gets the ID of the selected item in a drop-down list or gallery
getSelectedItemIndex	Callback	Gets the index of the selected item in a drop-down list or gallery
getShowImage	Callback	Gets a value specifying whether to display the control image

26

continues

Table 26.1   Continued

Attribute	Type or Value	Description
getShowLabel	Callback	Gets a value specifying whether to display the control label
getSize	Callback	Gets a value specifying the size of a control (normal or large)
getSupertip	Callback	Gets a value specifying the Enhanced ScreenTip for a control
getText	Callback	Gets the text to be displayed in the edit portion of a text box or edit box
getTitle	Callback	Gets the text to be displayed (rather than a horizontal line) for a menu separator
getVisible	Callback	Gets a value that specifies whether the control is visible
id	String	A user-defined unique identifier for the control (mutually exclusive with idMso and idQ—specify only one of these values)
idMso	Control id	Built-in control ID (mutually exclusive with id and idQ—specify only one of these values)
idQ	Qualified id	Qualified control ID, prefixed with a namespace identifier (mutually exclusive with id and idMso—specify only one of these values)
image	String	Specifies an image for the control
imageMso	Control id	Specifies an identifier for a built-in image
insertAfterMso	Control id	Specifies the identifier for the built-in control after which to position this control
insertAfterQ	Qualified id	Specifies the identifier of a a control whose idQ property was specified after which to position this control
insertBeforeMso	Control id	Specifies the identifier for the built-in control before which to position this control
insertBeforeQ	Qualified id	Specifies the identifier of a control whose idQ property was specified before which to position this control
itemSize	large, normal	Specifies the size for the items in a menu
keytip	String	Specifies the KeyTip for the control
label	String	Specifies the label for the control
onAction	Callback	Called when the user clicks the control
onChange	Callback	Called when the user enters or selects text in an edit box or combo box

Attribute	Type or Value	Description
screentip	String	Specifies the control's ScreenTip
showImage	true, false	Specifies whether the control's image is shown
showItemImage	true, false	Specifies whether to show the image in a combo box, drop-down list, or gallery
showItemLabel	true, false	Specifies whether to show the label in a combo box, drop-down list, or gallery
showLabel	true, false	Specifies whether the control's label is shown
size	large, normal	Specifies the size for the control
sizeString	String	Indicates the width for the control by specifying a string, such as "xxxxxx"
supertip	String	Specifies the Enhanced ScreenTip for the control
tag	String	Specifies user-defined text
title	String	Specifies the text to be displayed, rather than a horizontal line, for a menu separator
visible	true, false	Specifies whether the control is visible

Table 26.2 Control Arguments

Control	Callback Name	Signature
Various controls	getDescription	Sub GetDescription(control as IRibbonControl, ByRef description)
	getEnabled	Sub GetEnabled(control As IRibbonControl, ByRef enabled)
	getImage	Sub GetImage(control As IRibbonControl, ByRef image)
	getImageMso	Sub GetImageMso(control As IRibbonControl, ByRef imageMso)
	getLabel	Sub GetLabel(control As IRibbonControl, ByRef label)
	getKeytip	Sub GetKeytip (control As IRibbonControl, ByRef label)
	getSize	sub GetSize(control As IRibbonControl, ByRef size)
	getScreentip	Sub GetScreentip(control As IRibbonControl, ByRef screentip)
	getSupertip	Sub GetSupertip(control As IRibbonControl, ByRef screentip)
	getVisible	Sub GetVisible(control As IRibbonControl, ByRef visible)

26

continues

Table 26.2 Continued

Control	Callback Name	Signature
button	getShowImage	Sub GetShowImage (control As IRibbonControl, ByRef showImage)
	getShowLabel	Sub GetShowLabel (control As IRibbonControl, ByRef showLabel)
	onAction	Sub OnAction(control As IRibbonControl)
checkBox	getPressed	Sub GetPressed(control As IRibbonControl, ByRef returnValue)
	onAction	Sub OnAction(control As IRibbonControl, pressed As Boolean)
comboBox	getItemCount	Sub GetItemCount(control As IRibbonControl, ByRef count)
	getItemID	Sub GetItemID(control As IRibbonControl, index As Integer, ByRef id)
	getItemImage	Sub GetItemImage(control As IRibbonControl, index As Integer, ByRef image)
	getItemLabel	Sub GetItemLabel(control As IRibbonControl, index As Integer, ByRef label)
	getItemScreenTip	Sub GetItemScreenTip(control As IRibbonControl, index As Integer, ByRef screentip)
	getItemSuperTip	Sub GetItemSuperTip (control As IRibbonControl, index As Integer, ByRef supertip)
	getText	Sub GetText(control As IRibbonControl, ByRef text)
	onChange	Sub OnChange(control As IRibbonControl, text As String)
customUI	loadImage	Sub LoadImage(imageId As string, ByRef image)
	onLoad	Sub OnLoad(ribbon As IRibbonUI)
dropDown	getItemCount	Sub GetItemCount(control As IRibbonControl, ByRef count)
	getItemID	Sub GetItemID(control As IRibbonControl, index As Integer, ByRef id)
	getItemImage	Sub GetItemImage(control As IRibbonControl, index As Integer, ByRef image)

Control	Callback Name	Signature
dropDown	getItemLabel	Sub GetItemLabel(control As IRibbonControl, index As Integer, ByRef label)
	getItemScreenTip	Sub GetItemScreenTip(control As IRibbonControl, index As Integer, ByRef screenTip)
	getItemSuperTip	Sub GetItemSuperTip (control As IRibbonControl, index As Integer, ByRef superTip)
	getSelectedItemID	Sub GetSelectedItemID(control As IRibbonControl, ByRef index)
	getSelectedItemIndex	Sub GetSelectedItemIndex(control As IRibbonControl, ByRef index)
	onAction	Sub OnAction(control As IRibbonControl, selectedId As String, selectedIndex As Integer)
dynamicMen	getContent	Sub GetContent(control As IRibbonControl, ByRef content)
editBox	getText	Sub GetText(control As IRibbonControl, ByRef text)
	onChange	Sub OnChange(control As IRibbonControl, text As String)
gallery	getItemCount	Sub GetItemCount(control As IRibbonControl, ByRef count)
	getItemHeight	Sub getItemHeight(control As IRibbonControl, ByRef height)
	getItemID	Sub GetItemID(control As IRibbonControl, index As Integer, ByRef id)
	getItemImage	Sub GetItemImage(control As IRibbonControl, index As Integer, ByRef image)
	getItemLabel	Sub GetItemLabel(control As IRibbonControl, index As Integer, ByRef label)
	getItemScreenTip	Sub GetItemScreenTip(control As IRibbonControl, index as Integer, ByRef screen)

continues

Table 26.2   Continued

Control	Callback Name	Signature
gallery	getItemSuperTip	Sub GetItemSuperTip (control As IRibbonControl, index as Integer, ByRef screen)
	getItemWidth	Sub getItemWidth(control As IRibbonControl, ByRef width)
	getSelectedItemID	Sub GetSelectedItemID(control As IRibbonControl, ByRef index)
	getSelectedItemIndex	Sub GetSelectedItemIndex(control As IRibbonControl, ByRef index)
	onAction	Sub OnAction(control As IRibbonControl, selectedId As String, selectedIndex As Integer)
menuSeparator	getTitle	Sub GetTitle (control As IRibbonControl, ByRef title)
toggleButton	getPressed	Sub GetPressed(control As IRibbonControl, ByRef returnValue)
	onAction	Sub OnAction(control As IRibbonControl, pressed As Boolean)

Accessing the File Structure

The new Excel file types are actually zipped files containing various files and folders to create the workbook and worksheets you see when you open the workbook. To view this structure, rename the file, adding a .zip extension to the end of the filename. For example, if your filename is Chapter 26 – Simple Ribbon.xlsm, rename it to **Chapter 26 - Simple Ribbon.xlsm.zip.** You can then use your zip utility to access the folders and files within.

Copy into the zip file your customui folder and file, as shown in Figure 26.7. After placing them in the XLSM file, we need to let the rest of the Excel file know that they are there and what their purpose is. To do that, we modify the RELS file.

Figure 26.7
Using a zip utility, open the XLSM file and copy over the customui folder and file.

Understanding the RELS File

The RELS file, found in the _rels folder, contains the various relationships of the Excel file. Extract this file from the zip and open it using a text editor.

The file already contains existing relationships that we do not want to change. Instead, we need to add one for the customui folder. Scroll all the way to the right of the `<Relationships` line and place your cursor before the `</Relationships>` tag, as shown in Figure 26.8. Insert the following syntax:

```
<Relationship Id="rAB67989"
➥Type="http://schemas.microsoft.com/office/2006/relationships/ui/extensibility"
➥Target="customui/customui.xml"
```

Figure 26.8
Place your cursor in the correct spot for entering your custom ribbon relationship.

```
.rels - Notepad
File  Edit  Format  View  Help
lationships/officeDocument" Target="xl/workbook.xml"/></Relationships>
```

CAUTION

Even though the previous code appears as three lines in this book, it should appear as a single line in the RELS file. If you want to enter it as three separate lines, do not separate the lines within the quoted strings. The preceding examples are correct breaks. An incorrect break of the third line, for example, would be this:

```
Target = "customui/
customui.xml"
```

Note that Excel will merge the three separate lines above into one, when the workbook is opened.

`Id` is any unique string to identify the relationship. If Excel has a problem with the string you enter, it may change it when you open the file. (See the troubleshooting section "Excel Found Unreadable Content" later in this chapter for more information.) `Target` is the customui folder and file.

Save your changes and add the RELS file back into the zip file.

Renaming the Excel File and Opening the Workbook

Rename the Excel file back to its original name by removing the .zip extension. Open your workbook. Refer to the "Troubleshooting Error Messages" section in this chapter if any error messages appear.

RibbonCustomizer

It can be a little time-consuming to perform all the steps involved in adding a custom ribbon, especially if you make little mistakes and have to keep renaming your workbook, opening the zip file, extracting your file, modifying, adding it back to the zip, renaming, and testing. To aid in this, Patrick Schmid of pschmid.net has created the RibbonCustomizer, which does most of these actions for you within its interface. Go to http://pschmid.net/office2007/ribboncustomizer/index.php for more information about this tool.

Using Images on Buttons

The image that appears on a button can be either an image from the Microsoft Office icon library or a custom image you create and include within the workbook's customui folder. With a good icon image, you can hide the button label, but still have a friendly ribbon with images that are self-explanatory.

Microsoft Office icons

Remember in earlier versions of Excel if you wanted to reuse an icon from an Excel button, you had to identify the `faceid`? It was a nightmare to do manually, though thankfully there were many tools out there to help you retrieve the information. Well, Microsoft must have heard the screams of agony because they've made it so much easier to reuse their icons. Not only that, instead of some meaningless number, they've provided easy-to-understand text!

Choose Office menu, Excel Options, Customize. Place your cursor over any menu command in the list and a ScreenTip will appear, providing more information about the command. Included at the very end in parentheses is the image name, as shown in Figure 26.9.

26

Figure 26.9
Placing your cursor over a command, such as Insert Hyperlink, brings up the icon name, HyperlinkInsert.

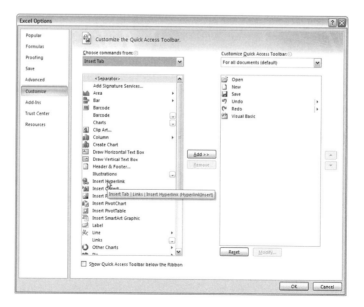

To place an image on our button, we need to go back into the customui file and advise Excel of what we want. The following code uses the HyperlinkInsert icon for the HelloWorld button and also hides the label, as shown in Figure 26.10. Note that the icon name is case sensitive:

```
<customUI xmlns="http://schemas.microsoft.com/office/2006/01/customui">
  <ribbon startFromScratch="false">
    <tabs>
      <tab id="CustomTab" label="MrExcel Add-ins">
        <group id="CustomGroup" label="Reports">

          <button id="button1" label="Click to run"
            onAction="Module1.HelloWorld" imageMso="HyperlinkInsert"
            showLabel = "false" />

        </group>
      </tab>
    </tabs>
  </ribbon>
</customUI>
```

Figure 26.10
You can apply the image from any Microsoft Office icon to your custom button.

> **TIP**
> You aren't limited to just the icons available in Excel. You can use the icon for any installed Microsoft Office application. You can download a workbook from Microsoft with several galleries showing the icons available (and their names) from here: www.microsoft.com/downloads/details.aspx?familyid=12b99325-93e8-4ed4-8385-74d0f7661318.

Custom Icon Images

What if the icon library just doesn't have the icon you're looking for? You can create your own image file and modify the ribbon to use it:

1. Create a folder called **images** in the customui folder. Place your image in this folder.

2. Create a folder called **_rels** in the customui folder. Create a text file called **customui.xml.rels** in this new folder, as shown in Figure 26.11. Place the following code in the file. Note the Id for the image relationship is the name of the image file, mrexcellogo:

```
<?xml version="1.0" encoding="UTF-8" standalone="yes"?>
<Relationships xmlns="http://schemas.openxmlformats.org/package/2006/
➥relationships"><Relationship Id="mrexcellogo"
➥Type=http://schemas.openxmlformats.org/officeDocument/2006/relationships/image
➥Target="images/mrexcellogo.jpg"/></Relationships>
```

Figure 26.11
Create a _rels and an images folder within the customui folder to hold files relevant to your custom image.

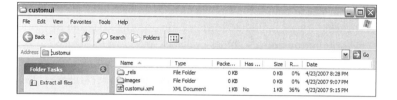

3. Open the customui.xml file and add the image attribute to the control, as shown here. Save and close the file:

```
<customUI xmlns="http://schemas.microsoft.com/office/2006/01/customui">
  <ribbon startFromScratch="false">
    <tabs>
      <tab id="CustomTab" label="MrExcel Add-ins">
        <group id="CustomGroup" label="Reports">

          <button id="button1" label="Click to run"
            onAction="Module1.HelloWorld" image="mrexcellogo"
            size="large" />

        </group>
      </tab>
    </tabs>
  </ribbon>
</customUI>
```

4. Open the [Content_Types].xml file and add the following at the very end of the file but before the </Types>:

```
<Default Extension="jpg" ContentType="application/octet-stream"/>
```

5. Save your changes, rename your folder, and open your workbook. The custom image appears on the button, as shown in Figure 26.12.

Figure 26.12
With a few more changes to your customui, you can add a custom image to a button.

CASE STUDY

Converting an Excel 2003 Custom Toolbar to Excel 2007

You have a workbook and custom toolbar designed in Excel 2003 with several buttons. You're now ready to transfer over to Excel 2007. When you open the workbook in 2007, the toolbar doesn't appear on the Add-ins ribbon because the toolbar wasn't designed with VBA; it is a manually created custom toolbar.

After saving the workbook as an XLSM file, create the customui file, as shown here. The tab is called My Quick Macros, and it has two groups: Viewing Options and Shortcuts:

```
<customUI xmlns="http://schemas.microsoft.com/office/2006/01/customui">
  <ribbon startFromScratch="false">
    <tabs>
        <tab id="customMacros" label="My Quick Macros">
            <group id="customview" label="Viewing Options">

                <button id="btn_r1c1" label="Toggle R1c1"
                  onAction="mod_2007.myButtons" />

                <button id="btn_Headings" label="Show Headings."
                  onAction="mod_2007.myButtons" imageMso = "TableStyleClear"/>

                <button id="btn_gridlines" label="Show Gridlines"
                  onAction="mod_2007.myButtons" imageMso = "BordersAll"/>

                <button id="btn_tabs" label="Show Tabs"
                  onAction="mod_2007.myButtons" imageMso = "Connections"/>
            </group>

            <group id="customshortcuts" label="Shortcuts">

                <button id="btn_formulas" label="Highlight Formulas"
                  onAction="mod_2007.myButtons" imageMso = "FunctionWizard"/>
            </group>
        </tab>
    </tabs>
  </ribbon>
```

After updating the RELS file (see the section "Understanding the RELS File" earlier in this chapter for more details), open the workbook to see the new tab, as shown in Figure 26.13.

Figure 26.13
Re-create your Excel 2003 toolbar in Excel 2007 as its own ribbon.

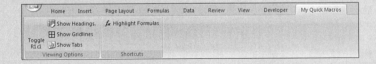

Now it's time to update the code in the workbook. You'll notice the onAction in the customui folder all pointed to the same sub, mod_2007.myButtons, instead of each having a custom call. Because all the controls are of the same type, buttons, and have the same argument type, iRibbonControl, we can take advantage of these facts. Create a single sub, myButtons, in a module called mod_2007 to handle all the button calls using Select Case to manage the IDs of each button:

```
Sub myButtons(control As IRibbonControl)
Select Case control.ID
    Case Is = "btn_r1c1"
        SwitchR1C1
```

```
        Case Is = "btn_Headings"
            ShowHeaders
        Case Is = "btn_gridlines"
            ShowGridlines
        Case Is = "btn_tabs"
            ShowTabs
        Case Is = "btn_formulas"
            GoToFormulas
        End Select
    End Sub
```

The `control.IDs` are the ids assigned each button in the customui.xml file. The action within each `Case` statement is a call to the desired sub. Here is a sample of one of the subs being called, `ShowHeaders`. It is the same sub that was in the original 2003 workbook:

```
Sub ShowHeaders()
If ActiveWindow.DisplayHeadings = False Then
    ActiveWindow.DisplayHeadings = True
Else
    ActiveWindow.DisplayHeadings = False
End If
End Sub
```

Troubleshooting Error Messages

To be able to see the error messages generated by a custom ribbon, go to the Office menu and select Excel Options, Advanced, General, and check Show Add-in User Interface Errors, as shown in Figure 26.14.

26

Figure 26.14
Check the Show Add-in User Interface Errors option to allow custom ribbon error messages to appear and aid you in troubleshooting.

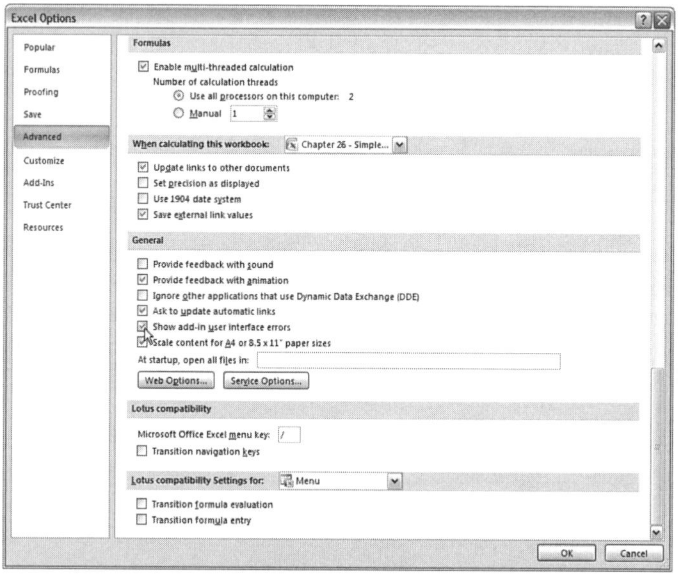

The Attribute *"Attribute Name"* on the Element *"customui Ribbon"* Is Not Defined in the DTD/Schema

As noted in the section "Where to Add Your Code: customui Folder and File" of this chapter, the case of the attributes is very particular. If an attribute is "mis-cased," the error shown in Figure 26.15 may occur. The code in the customui.xml that generated the error had the following line:

```
<ribbon startfromscratch="false">
```

Instead of `startFromScratch`, the code contained `startfromscratch` (all lowercase letters). The error message even helps you narrow down the problem by naming the attribute it's having a problem with.

Figure 26.15
Mis-cased attributes can generate errors. Read the error message carefully; it might help you trace the problem.

Illegal Qualified Name Character

For every opening <, you need a closing >. If you forget a closing >, the error shown in Figure 26.16 may appear. The error message is not specific at all, but it does provide a line and column number where it's having a problem. Still, it's not the actual spot where the missing > would go. Instead, it's the beginning of the next line. You'll have to review your code to find the error, but you have an idea of where to start. The following code in the customui.xml generated the error:

```
<tab id="CustomTab" label="MrExcel Add-ins">
  <group id="CustomGroup" label="Reports"
    <button id="button1" label="Click to run"
      onAction="Module1.HelloWorld" image="mrexcellogo"
      size="large" />
```

Note the missing > for the group line (second line of code). The line should have been this:

```
<group id="CustomGroup" label="Reports">
```

Figure 26.16
For every opening <, you need a closing >.

26

Element "customui Tag Name" Is Unexpected According to Content Model of Parent Element "customui Tag Name"

If your structure is in the wrong order, such as the group tag placed before the tab tag, as shown here, a chain of errors will appear, beginning with the one shown in Figure 26.17:

```
<group id="CustomGroup" label="Reports">
  <tab id="CustomTab" label="MrExcel Add-ins">
```

Figure 26.17
An error in one line can lead to string of error messages because the other lines are now considered out of order.

Excel Found Unreadable Content

Figure 26.18 shows a generic catchall message for different types of problems Excel can find. If you click Yes, you then receive the message shown in Figure 26.19. If you click No, the workbook doesn't open. While creating ribbons, though, I found it appearing most often when Excel didn't like the relationship id I had assigned the customui relationship in the .RELS file. What's nice is that if you click Yes, Excel will assign a new id file, and the next time you open the file, the error should not appear.

Original relationship:

```
<Relationship Id="rId3"
➥Type=http://schemas.microsoft.com/office/2006/relationships/ui/extensibility
➥Target="customui/customui.xml"/>
```

Excel modified relationship:

```
<Relationship Id="rE1FA1CF0-6CA9-499E-9217-90BF2D86492F"
➥Type="http://schemas.microsoft.com/office/2006/relationships/ui/extensibility"
➥Target="customui/customui.xml"/>
```

The error also appears if, in the RELS file, you split the relationship line within a quoted string, as cautioned against in the section "Understanding the RELS File" earlier in this chapter. In this case, Excel will not fix the file, and you must make the correction yourself.

Figure 26.18
This rather generic message could appear for many reasons. Click Yes to try to repair the file.

Figure 26.19
Excel will let you know if it has succeeded in repairing the file.

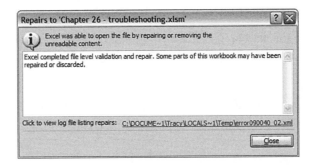

Wrong Number of Arguments or Invalid Property Assignment

If there is a problem with the sub being called by your control, you might see the error in Figure 26.20 when you go to your ribbon. For example, the onAction of a button requires a single IRibbonControl argument, such as the following:

```
Sub HelloWorld(control As IRibbonControl)
```

It would be incorrect to leave off the argument, as shown here:

```
Sub HelloWorld()
```

Figure 26.20
It's important the subs being called by your controls have the proper arguments. Refer to Table 26.2 for the various control arguments.

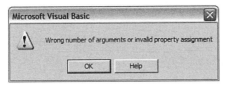

Nothing Happens

If you open your modified workbook, your ribbon doesn't appear, but you don't get any error messages, double-check your RELS file. It's possible you forgot to update it with the required relationship to your custumui.xml.

Other Ways to Run a Macro

Custom ribbons are the best ways to run a macro; however, if you have only a couple of macros to run, it can be a bit of work to modify the file. In Excel 2003, it wasn't a big deal to have a client invoke a macro by going to Tools, Macro, Macros, selecting the macro from the Macro dialog, and clicking the Run button (although it was a bit unprofessional). However, that option is far from convenient now.

26

Keyboard Shortcut

The easiest way to run a macro is to assign a keyboard shortcut to a macro. From the Macro dialog box (Developer ribbon, click Macros, or press Alt+F8), select the macro and click Options. Assign a shortcut key to the macro. Figure 26.21 shows the shortcut Ctrl+Shift+C being assigned to the Clean1stCol macro. You can now conspicuously post a note on the worksheet reminding the client to press Ctrl+Shift+C to clean the first column.

Figure 26.21
The simplest way to enable a client to run a macro is to assign a shortcut key to the macro. Ctrl+Shift+C now runs the Clean1stCol macro.

CAUTION

Be careful when assigning keyboard shortcuts. Many of the keys are already mapped to important Windows shortcuts. If you would happen to assign a macro to Ctrl+C, anyone who uses this short-cut to copy the selection to the clipboard will be frustrated when your application does something else in response to this common shortcut. Letters E, J, M, Q, and T are usually good choices because as of Excel 2007, they have not yet been assigned to Excel's menu of "Ctrl+" shortcut combinations. Ctrl+L used to be available, but this is now used to create a table in Excel 2007.

Attach a Macro to a Command Button

Two types of buttons can be embedded in your sheet: the traditional button shape that can be found on the Forms control or an ActiveX command button (both can be accessed on the Developer ribbon, under the Insert option).

To add a Forms control button with a macro to your sheet, follow these steps:

1. On the Developer tab, click the Insert button, and select the button control from the Forms section of the drop-down, as shown in Figure 26.22.

Figure 26.22
The Forms controls are found under the Insert icon on the Developers ribbon.

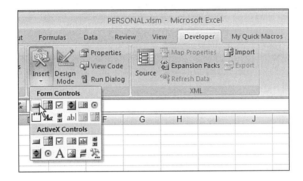

2. Place your cursor in the worksheet where you want to insert the button, and then click and drag to create the shape of your new button.

3. When you release the mouse button, the Assign Macro dialog displays. Select a macro to assign to the button and choose OK.

4. Highlight the text on the button and type new meaningful text.

5. To change the color, font, and other aspects of the button's appearance, right-click the button and choose Format Control from the pop-up menu.

> **CAUTION**
>
> There are two versions of the Format Control dialog box. One version offers seven tabs with settings for Font, Alignment, Size, Protection, Properties, Margins, and Web. The second version offers only one tab with settings for Font.
>
> Which version you see is based on something very subtle. When you right-click the control, the look of the selection border can be either diagonal lines, as shown in Figure 26.23, or dots, as shown in Figure 26.24. The diagonal lines selection border tends to appear immediately after editing the text on the button and leads to the Font-only Format Control dialog. The dots selection border leads to the full-featured Format Control dialog.

26

continues

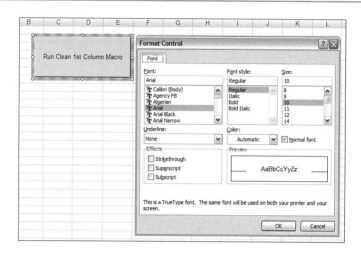

Figure 26.23
The diagonal lines selection border leads to a lesser Format Control dialog.

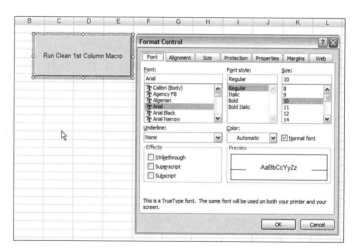

Figure 26.24
The dots selection border leads to the full version of the Format Control dialog.

If you right-click and diagonal lines appear as the selection border, you should first left-click the diagonal line selection border to change it to dots. You can then right-click again and choose Format Control.

6. To reassign a new macro to the button, right-click the button and choose Assign Macro from the pop-up menu.

This method assigned a macro to an object that looks like a button. You can also assign a macro to any drawing object on the worksheet. To assign a macro to an Autoshape, right-click the shape and select Assign Macro, as shown in Figure 26.25.

Figure 26.25
Macros can be assigned to any drawing object on the worksheet.

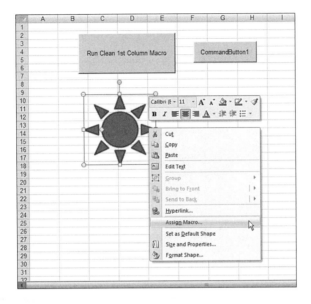

I prefer this method because I can easily add a drawing object with macro code and use the OnAction property to assign a macro to the object. There is one big drawback to this method: If you assign a macro that exists in another workbook, and the other workbook is saved and closed, Excel changes the OnAction for the object to be hard-coded to a specific folder.

Attach a Macro to an ActiveX Control

ActiveX controls are newer than Form controls and slightly more complicated to set up. Instead of simply assigning a macro to the button, you will have a button_click procedure where you can either call another macro or have the macro code actually embedded in the button_click procedure. Follow these steps:

1. On the Developer tab, click the Insert button, and select the Command Button icon from the ActiveX Controls section of the drop-down Control toolbox.
2. Draw a button shape on the worksheet as described in step 2 for the Forms button.
3. To format the button, right-click the button and select Properties or select Properties from the Developer ribbon. You can now adjust the button's caption and color in the

26

Properties window, as shown in Figure 26.26. If nothing happens when you right-click the button, enter Design mode by clicking the Design Mode button on the Developer ribbon.

Figure 26.26
Clicking the Properties icon brings up the Properties window, where you can adjust many aspects of the ActiveX button.

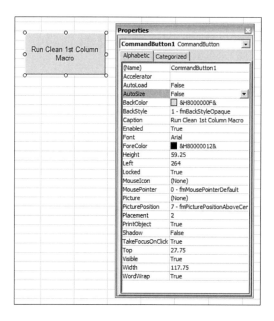

> **NOTE**
>
> There is one annoying aspect of this Properties window: It is huge and covers a large portion of your worksheet. Eventually, if you want to use the worksheet, you are going to have to close this Properties window. When you close the Properties window, it also hides the Properties window in the VB Editor. You can see that this is missing in Figure 26.27. I would prefer that I could close this Properties window without affecting my VB Editor environment.

4. To assign a macro to the button, click the View Code button on the Controls group of the Developer ribbon. This creates a new procedure on the code pane for the current worksheet. Type the code that you want to have run, or the name of the macro you want to run in this procedure. Figure 26.27 shows the code for the button. This code appears on the code pane for the worksheet.

Figure 26.27
Click the View Code button in the Control Toolbox toolbar to open the macro for this button.

```
CommandButton1                              ▼    Click                              ▼
    Private Sub CommandButton1_Click()
    'You can specify any code in here that you want
    'Run Clean1stCol Macro
    Clean1stCol
    End Sub
```

Running a Macro from a Hyperlink

Using a trick, it is possible to run a macro from a hyperlink. Because many clients are used to clicking a hyperlink to perform an action, this method might be more intuitive for your clients.

The trick is to set up placeholder hyperlinks that simply link back to themselves. Select a cell and from the Insert ribbon, select Hyperlink, and press Ctrl+K. In the Insert Hyperlink dialog, click Place in This Document. Figure 26.28 shows a worksheet with four hyperlinks. Each hyperlink points back to its own cell.

When a client clicks a hyperlink, you can intercept this action and run any macro by using the FollowHyperlink event. Enter the following code on the code module for the worksheet:

```
Private Sub Worksheet_FollowHyperlink(ByVal Target As Hyperlink)
Select Case Target.TextToDisplay
    Case "Widgets"
        RunWidgetReport
    Case "Gadgets"
        RunGadgetReport
    Case "Gizmos"
        RunGizmoReport
    Case "Doodads"
        RunDooDadReport
End Select
End Sub
```

Figure 26.28
To run a macro from a hyperlink, you have to create placeholder hyperlinks that link back to their cells. Then, using an event handler macro on the worksheet's code pane, you can intercept the hyperlink and run any macro.

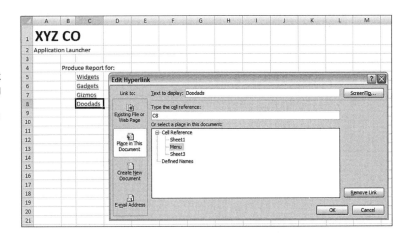

26

Next Steps

From custom ribbons to simple buttons or hyperlinks, there are plenty of ways to ensure your clients never need to see the Macro dialog box. In Chapter 27, "Creating Add-Ins," you will learn how to package your macros into add-ins that can be easily distributed to others.

26

Creating Add-Ins

27

Using VBA, you can create standard add-in files for your clients to use. After the client installs the add-in on his PC, the program will be available to Excel and loads automatically every time he opens Excel.

This chapter discusses standard add-ins. Be aware that there are two other kinds of add-ins: COM add-ins and DLL add-ins. Neither of these can be created with VBA. To create these types of add-ins, you need either Visual Basic.NET or Visual C++.

Characteristics of Standard Add-Ins

If you are going to distribute your applications, you might want to package the application as an add-in. Typically saved with an .xlam extension for Excel 2007 or an .xla extension for Excel 97-2003, the add-in offers several advantages:

- Usually, clients can bypass your Workbook_Open code by holding down the Shift key while opening the workbook. With an add-in, they cannot bypass the Workbook_Open code in this manner.

- After the Add-Ins dialog is used to install an add-in (select Office Icon, Excel Options, Add-Ins, Manage Excel Add-Ins, Go), the add-in will always be loaded and available.

- Even if the macro security level is set to disallow macros, programs in an installed add-in can still run.

- Generally, custom functions work only in the workbook in which they are defined. A custom function added to an add-in is available to all open workbooks.

- The add-in does not show up in the list of open files in the Window menu item. The client cannot unhide the workbook by choosing Window, Unhide.

There is one strange rule you need to plan for. The add-in is a hidden workbook. Because the add-in can never be displayed, your code cannot select or activate any cells in the add-in workbook. You are allowed to save data in your add-in file, but you cannot select the file. Also, if you do write data to your add-in file that you want to be available in the future, your add-in codes need to handle saving the file. Because your clients will not realize that the add-in is there, they will never be reminded or asked to save an unsaved add-in. You might add `ThisWorkbook.Save` to the add-in's `Workbook_BeforeClose` event.

Converting an Excel Workbook to an Add-In

Add-ins are typically managed by through the Add-Ins dialog. This dialog presents an add-in name and description. You can control these by entering two specific properties for the file before you convert it to an add-in.

To change the title and description shown in the Add-Ins dialog, follow these steps:

1. From the Office icon, choose Prepare, Properties. Excel displays the Document Properties pane at the top of the worksheet.
2. Enter the name for the add-in in the Title field.
3. Enter a short description of the add-in in the Comments field (see Figure 27.1).
4. Click the X in the upper-right corner of the Document Properties to close the pane.

Figure 27.1
Fill in the Title and Comments fields before converting a workbook to an add-in.

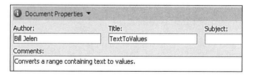

There are two ways to convert the file to an add-in. The first method, using Save As, is easier, but has an annoying by-product. The second method uses the VB Editor and requires two steps, but gives you some extra control. The sections that follow describe the steps for using these methods.

Using Save As to Convert a File to an Add-In

From the Office icon, select Save As, Other Formats. In the Save as Type field, scroll through the list and select Excel Add-In (*.xlam).

> **NOTE**
> If your add-in might be used in Excel 97 through Excel 2007, choose Excel 97-2003 Add-In (*.xla).

As shown in Figure 27.2, the filename changes from Something.xlsm to Something.xlam. Also note that the save location automatically changes to an AddIns folder. This folder location varies by operating system, but it will be something along the lines of C:\Documents and Settings\Customer\Application Data\Microsoft\AddIns. It is also confusing that, after saving the XLSM file as an XLAM type, the unsaved XLSM file remains open. It is not necessary to keep an XLSM version of the file, because it is easy to change an XLAM back to an XLSM for editing.

Figure 27.2
If you are creating an add-in for your own use, the Save As method changes the `IsAddIn` property, changes the name, and automatically saves the file in your AddIns folder.

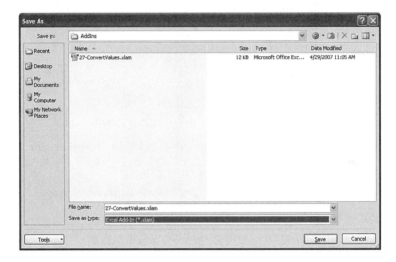

CAUTION _____

When using the Save As method to create an add-in, a worksheet must be the active sheet. The Add-In file type is not available if a Chart sheet is the active sheet.

Using the VB Editor to Convert a File to an Add-In

The Save As method is great if you are creating an add-in for your own use. However, if you are creating an add-in for a client, you probably want to keep the add-in stored in a folder with all the client's application files. It is fairly easy to bypass the Save As method and create an add-in using the VB Editor:

1. Open the workbook that you want to convert to an add-in.

2. Switch to the VB Editor.

3. In the Project Explorer, double-click ThisWorkbook.

4. In the Properties window, find the property called `IsAddIn` and change its value to `True`, as shown in Figure 27.3.

27

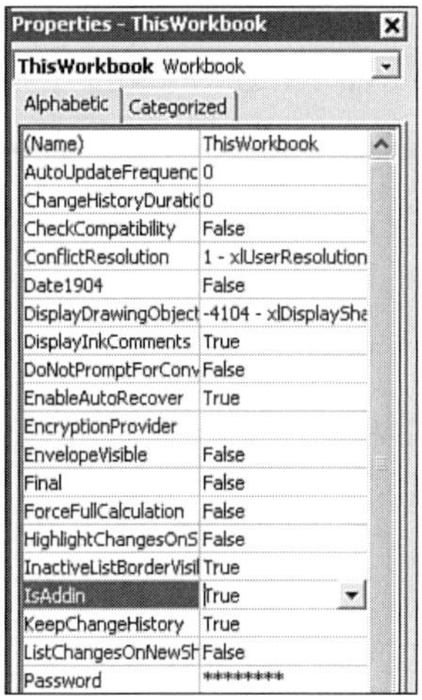

Figure 27.3
Creating an add-in is as simple as changing the `IsAddIn` property of ThisWorkbook.

5. Press Ctrl+G to display the Immediate window. In the Immediate window, save the file, using an .xlam extension:

```
ThisWorkbook.SaveAs FileName:="C:\ClientFiles\Chap27.xlam", FileFormat:=xlAddIn8
```

> **NOTE**
> If your add-in might be used in Excel 97 through Excel 2003, change the final parameter from xlAddIn8 to xlAddIn.

You've now successfully created an add-in in the client folder that you can easily find and email to your client.

Having Your Client Install the Add-In

After you email the add-in to your client, have her save it on her desktop or in another easy-to-find folder. She should then follow these steps:

1. Open Excel 2007. From the Office icon menu, select Excel Options.
2. Along the left navigation, select Add-Ins.
3. At the bottom of the window, choose Excel Add-Ins from the Manage drop-down (see Figure 27.4).
4. Click Go. Excel displays the familiar Add-Ins dialog.
5. In the Add-Ins dialog, click the Browse button (see Figure 27.5).
6. In the Browse dialog, select Desktop. Highlight your add-in and choose OK.

The add-in is now installed. Excel actually copies the file from the desktop to the proper location of the AddIns folder. In the Add-Ins dialog, the title of the add-in and comments as specified in the File Properties dialog are displayed (see Figure 27.6).

Figure 27.4
The Excel 2007 Add-Ins tab in Excel Options is significantly more complex than in Excel 2003. Choose Excel Add-Ins from the bottom and click Go.

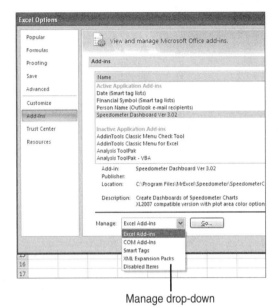

Manage drop-down

Figure 27.5
Your client selects Browse from the Add-Ins dialog.

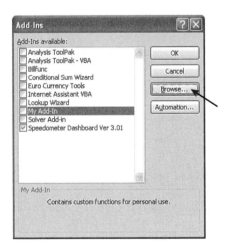

Figure 27.6
The add-in is now
available for use.

Standard Add-Ins Are Not Secure

Remember that anyone can go to the VB Editor, select your add-in, and change the
`IsAddin` property to `False` to unhide the workbook. You can discourage this process by
locking the XLAM project for viewing and protecting it in the VB Editor, but be aware that
plenty of vendors sell a password-hacking utility for less than $40. To add a password to
your add-in, follow these steps:

1. Go to the VB Editor.
2. From the Tools menu, select VBAProject Properties.
3. Select the Protection tab.
4. Check the Lock Project For Viewing box.
5. Enter the password twice for verification.

Closing Add-Ins

Add-ins can be closed in three ways:

1. Uncheck the add-in from the Add-Ins dialog. This closes the add-in for this session
   and ensures that it does not open during future sessions.
2. Use VB Editor to close the add-in. In the VB Editor's Immediate pane, type this code
   to close the add-in:
   ```
   Workbooks("YourAddinName.xlam").Close
   ```
3. Close Excel. All add-ins are closed when Excel is closed.

Removing Add-Ins

You might want to remove an add-in from the list of available add-ins in the Add-In dialog
box. There is no effective way to do this within Excel. Follow these steps:

1. Close all running instances of Excel.

2. Use Windows Explorer to locate the file. The file might be located in %AppData%\ Microsoft\AddIns\.

3. In Windows Explorer, rename the file or move it to a different folder.

4. Open Excel. You get a note warning you that the add-in could not be found. Click OK to dismiss this box.

5. Use the Office icon, Add-Ins, Manage Excel Add-Ins, Go. In the Add-Ins dialog box, uncheck the name of the add-in you want to remove. Excel notifies you that the file cannot be found and asks whether you want to remove it from the list. Choose Yes.

Using a Hidden Workbook as an Alternative to an Add-In

One cool feature of an add-in is that the workbook is hidden. This keeps most novice users from poking around and changing formulas. However, it is possible to hide a workbook without creating an add-in.

It is easy enough to hide a workbook by selecting Hide from the Window menu in Excel. The trick is to then save the workbook as Hidden. Because the file is hidden, the normal Office icon, Save choice does not work. This can be done from the VB Editor window. In the VB Editor, make sure that the workbook is selected in the Project Explorer. Then, in the Immediate window, type the following:

```
ThisWorkbook.Save
```

CASE STUDY

Using a Hidden Code Workbook to Hold All Macros and Forms

Access developers routinely use a second database to hold macros and forms. They place all forms and programs in one database and all data in a separate database. These database files are linked through the Link Tables function in Access.

For large projects in Excel, I recommend the same method. You use a little bit of VBA code in the Data workbook to open the Code workbook.

The advantage to this method is that when it is time to enhance the application, you can mail a new code file without affecting the client's data file.

I once encountered a single-file application rolled out by another developer that the client had sent out to 50 sales reps. The reps replicated the application for each of their 10 largest customers. Within a week, there were 500 copies of this file floating around the country. When they discovered a critical flaw in the program, patching 500 files was a nightmare.

We designed a replacement application that used two workbooks. The data workbook ended up with about 20 lines of code. This code was responsible for opening the code workbook and passing control to the code workbook. As the files were being closed, the data workbook would close the code workbook.

27

There were many advantages to this method. First, the customer data files were kept to a very small size. Each sales rep now has one workbook with program code and ten or more data files for each customer. As enhancements are completed, we distribute new program code workbooks. The sales rep opens his or her existing customer data workbook, which automatically grabs the new code workbook.

Because the previous developer had been stuck with the job of trying to patch 500 workbooks, we were extremely careful to have as few lines of code in the customer workbook as possible. There are maybe ten lines of code, and they were tested extremely thoroughly before being sent out. By contrast, the code workbook contains 3,000+ lines of code. So, if something goes wrong, I have a 99 percent chance that the bad code will be in the easy-to-replace code workbook.

In the customer data workbook, the `Workbook_Open` procedure has this code:

```
Private Sub Workbook_Open()
    On Error Resume Next
    X = Workbooks("Code.xls").Name
    If Not Err = 0 then
        On Error Goto 0
        Workbooks.Open Filename:= _
            ThisWorkbook.Path & Application.PathSeparator & "Code.xlsm"
    End If
    On Error Goto 0
    Application.Run "Code.xls!CustFileOpen"
End Sub
```

The `CustFileOpen` procedure in the code workbook handles adding a custom menu for the application. It also calls a macro named DeliverUpdates. If we ever have to change the 500 customer data files, the DeliverUpdates macro will handle this via code.

This dual-workbook solution works well and allows updates to be seamlessly delivered to the client without touching any of the 500 customer files.

Next Steps

If as authors we've done our job correctly, you now have the tools you need to design your own VBA applications in Excel. You understand the shortcomings of the macro recorder, yet know how to use it as an aid in learning how to do something. You know how to use Excel's power tools in VBA to produce workhorse routines that can save you hours of time per week. You've also learned how to have your application interact with others so that you can create applications to be used by others in your organization or other organizations.

If you have found any sections of the book that you thought were confusing or could have been spelled out better, we welcome your comments, and they will be given consideration as we prepare the next edition of this book. Write to us: Bill@MrExcel.com and Tracy@MrExcel.com.

Whether your goal was to automate some of your own tasks or to become a paid Excel consultant, we hope that we've helped you on your way. Both are rewarding goals. With 500 million potential customers, we find that being Excel consultants is a friendly business. If you are interested in joining our ranks, this book is your training manual. Master the topics, and you will be qualified to join the team of Excel consultants.

INDEX

W

How can we make this index more useful? Email us at indexes@quepublishing.com

THIS BOOK IS SAFARI ENABLED

INCLUDES FREE 45-DAY ACCESS TO THE ONLINE EDITION

The Safari® Enabled icon on the cover of your favorite technology book means the book is available through Safari Bookshelf. When you buy this book, you get free access to the online edition for 45 days.

Safari Bookshelf is an electronic reference library that lets you easily search thousands of technical books, find code samples, download chapters, and access technical information whenever and wherever you need it.

TO GAIN 45-DAY SAFARI ENABLED ACCESS TO THIS BOOK:

- Go to **http://www.quepublishing.com/safarienabled**
- Complete the brief registration form
- Enter the coupon code found in the front of this book on the "Copyright" page

If you have difficulty registering on Safari Bookshelf or accessing the online edition, please e-mail customer-service@safaribooksonline.com.

GET TO WORK WITH BUSINESS SOLUTIONS

Let's face it, when it comes to working with software in your job, you only have time to learn enough to get things going. The time may come, however, when you have to push the limits of Microsoft Excel, Access, and other Office applications to complete more sophisticated tasks. You probably have even less time to learn new software skills now than you did before, and you certainly don't want to read multiple books just to learn how to complete a specific task. Sound familiar? We have a solution.

The **Business Solutions** series was created to provide professionals like you books focused on a specific use or application of a software program. You won't find general software information here, only details on specific software features and functions that help you perform complex tasks related to your particular productivity use. You don't need to be a programmer or a power user to become more proficient with your software. You just need some motivation and a **Business Solutions** book, written by authors who are experienced practitioners of the specific solution presented.

LOOK FOR THESE BOOKS AT YOUR FAVORITE BOOKSTORE
OR VISIT www.quepublishing.com

0789736675

VBA for the 2007 Microsoft® Office System

0789736012

Pivot Table Data Crunching for Microsoft® Office Excel® 2007

0789736829

VBA and Macros for Microsoft® Office Excel® 2007

0789736683

Formulas and Functions with Microsoft® Office Excel® 2007

0789737310

Microsoft® Office Access 2007 VBA

0789736101

Charts and Graphs for Microsoft® Office Excel® 2007

0789736667

Tricks of the Microsoft® Office 2007 Gurus

0789736691

Microsoft® Office Access 2007 Forms, Reports, and Queries

Don't wait any longer. Stop solving software problems and start focusing on business.
Get a book in the **Business Solutions** series today!